# Dogmatic theology

William Greenough Thayer Shedd

# DOGMATIC THEOLOGY

BY

WILLIAM G. T. SHEDD, D.D.
ROOSEVELT PROFESSOR OF SYSTEMATIC THEOLOGY IN UNION THEOLOGICAL SEMINARY
NEW YORK

*VOLUME II.*

NEW YORK
CHARLES SCRIBNER'S SONS
1888

TROW'S
PRINTING AND BOOKBINDING COMPANY,
NEW YORK.

# CONTENTS OF VOLUME II.

## ANTHROPOLOGY.



## CHRISTOLOGY.

## SOTERIOLOGY.



## ESCHATOLOGY.

# ANTHROPOLOGY.

---

## CHAPTER I.

### MAN'S CREATION.

Augustine. City of God, XII.; On the Soul and its Origin. Odo Tornacensis: De Peccato Originali. Biblioth. Max., XXI. 229 sq. Aquinas. Summa, II. cxviii cxix. xci. xcii. Turrettin: Institutio, V. xiii Maresius: Theologia Elenchtica. Controversia X. Howe: Oracles, [illegible] II. Lecture xxxvii. Edwards. Against Watts (Works, III. 533) [illegible] Hopkins: Works, II. 289. Delitzsch: Biblical Psychology, 128–144 Nitzsch: Christian Doctrine, § 107. Evelyn: History of Religion, I. 164. Muller: Sin, IV. iii. iv. Philippi: Glaubenslehre, III. 96. Dorner: Christian Doctrine, § 83 Gangauf Psychologie des Augustinus, III. § 1–4 Hagenbach: History of Doctrine, § 55, 106, 173, 248. Ulrici: Leib and Seele. Hodge: Theology, II. 65 sq Smith: Christian Theology, 166 sq Shedd: History of Doctrine, II 10–25; 114–127; 152–163 Strong. Theology, 328 sq. Baird: Elohim Revealed, XI Landis: Original Sin, and Gratuitous Imputation Martensen Dogmatics, § 74.

Anthropology (ἀνθρώπου λόγος) includes the topics that relate to man as created and holy, and as apostate and sinful. It excludes those relating to man as regenerate and sanctified, because these belong to redemption, which is a special provision not contained in creation. Man's endowment by creation provided for his actual holiness, and his possible apostasy, but not for his recovery from apostasy. Anthropology comprises only what man is and becomes under the ordinary arrangements of the Creator: what he is by creation, and what he makes himself by self-determination. Man's creation, primitive state, probation, apostasy, original sin and its transmission, are anthropological topics. Anthropology is principally concerned with the doctrine of sin, not because man is ideally and originally a sinner, but because he remained holy but a short time, and consequently his history, apart from redemption, is that of moral evil and its development.

Respecting man's creation, the Westminster Confession, IV. ii., teaches that "God created man male and female, with reasonable and immortal souls." The first part of this statement is supported by Gen. 1:27, "Male and female created he them" The second part is supported by Gen. 1:26, "God said, Let us make man in our image, after our likeness;" by Gen. 2:7, "God breathed into man's nostrils the breath of life, and man became a living soul;" by Eccl. 12:7, "Then shall the dust return to the earth as it was, and the spirit shall return to God who gave it;" and by Matt. 10:28, "Fear not them which kill the body, but are not able to kill the soul: but rather fear him which is able to destroy both soul and body in hell."

In this statement, two particulars are to be marked: 1. That man is bisexual. "God created man male and female." This implies that the idea of man is incomplete, if either the male or the female be considered by itself, in isolation from the other. The two together constitute the human species. A solitary male or female individual would not be the species man, nor include it, nor propagate it. In Milton's phrase, "Two great sexes animate the world."

The angels are sexless. Like man, they were created "with reasonable and immortal souls," but unlike him, they were not "created male and female." Matt. 22:30, "They neither marry nor are given in marriage, but are as the angels of God." Angels being sexless are not a race or species of creatures. They were created one by one, as distinct and separate individuals. This is proved by the fact that they do not have a common character and history; some remain holy, and some lapse into sin.

2. That the body is of a different nature and substance from the soul. Gen. 2:7, "God formed man of the dust of the ground, and breathed into his nostrils the breath of life, and man became a living soul" (נֶפֶשׁ חַיָּה), a breath, or soul of life. According to this statement, man is composed of a material part, resulting from the vivification of the dust of the ground by creative energy, and of an immaterial part resulting from the spiration or imbreathing of God. The Creator first enlivens inorganic matter into a body, and then creates a rational spirit which he infuses into it. The same difference between body and soul is taught in Eccl. 12:7. The "dust" returns to the earth, and the "spirit" returns to God. Christ "commends his spirit into God's hands," and "and gave up the spirit," Luke 23:46. Stephen said, "Lord Jesus receive my spirit," Acts 7:59. "Jacob gathered up his feet into the bed, and yielded up the ghost," Gen. 49:33. Job exclaims, "O that I had given up the ghost," Job 10:18. "The hope of the wicked shall be as the giving up of the ghost," Job 11:20. "She hath given up the ghost," Jer. 15:9.

In Gen. 1:20, God says, "Let the waters bring forth abundantly the moving creature that hath life;" literally, "Let the waters swarm a swarm of the soul of life" (נֶפֶשׁ חַיָּה). And in Gen. 1:21 it is said, that "God created every living creature that moveth;" literally, "God created every living soul of life that creepeth." See also Gen 1:24. The irrational animal is here denominated a "soul of life" as man is; but it is not added, as in the case of man, that God "breathed" the "soul of life" into him. On the contrary, the origin of animals is associated with the material world alone. When God creates man, he addresses himself. "Let us make man in our image," Gen. 1.26. But when he creates animals, he addresses the inanimate world: "Let the waters bring forth the moving creature," Gen. 1:20; "Let the earth bring forth the living creature," Gen. 1:24. The "soul of life" in the instance of the animal is only the animal soul, which is physical and material in its nature, and perishes with the body of which it is the vital principle. The "soul of life" in the instance of the man is a higher principle, the rational soul, which was imbreathed by the Creator, and made in his image Hence it is said, in Eccl. 3:21, that "the spirit (רוּחַ) of man goeth upward," and "the spirit (רוּחַ) of the beast goeth downward to the earth"

Three theories have been formed of the mode of man's creation: 1. Pre-existence. 2 Traducianism. 3. Creationism.

Pre-existence teaches that all human souls were created in the beginning of creation, and before the creation of Adam. Each individual human soul existed in an antemundane state, and is united with a human body by ordinary generation. This theory found some support in Plato's speculations respecting intuitive knowledge as the relics of a pre-existent state of the soul. Some of the Jewish Rabbinical schools adopted it, and Origen endeavored, unsuccessfully, to give it currency in the Christian church. Muller, in his work on Sin, has revived it in a modified form. He assumes, not an ante-temporal but a supra-temporal state, in which the soul existed and the origin of sin occurred. The fall of man was not in a time before time, but is timeless. This is virtually the same as Kant's conception of sin as a noumenon, or thing in itself, which is always timeless and spaceless, in distinction from a phenomenon, which always occurs in space and time. Philippi (Glaubenslehre, III. 96) contends that Muller's view is virtually that of pre-existence. The propagation of the body still leaves the ego pre-existent.

Pre-existence confines the idea of species to the body. As this is propagated, it is derived out of a common physical nature. The body, consequently, cannot be older than that physical human nature which was created on the sixth day. The spirit, on the other hand, was created prior to the sixth day. The human spirit is purely individual, like that of an angel.

Traducianism applies the idea of species to both body and soul. Upon the sixth day, God created two human individuals, one male and one female, and in them also created the specific psychico-physical nature from which all the subsequent individuals of the human family are procreated both psychically and physically. Hase (Hutterus Redivivus, § 79) represents this theory as having been adopted by Tertullian, Augustine, and the elder Protestant divines, in the interest of the stricter theory of original sin. Hagenbach (§ 55, 106) says that Tertullian was an earnest advocate of traducianism; that Augustine and Gregory the Great express themselves doubtfully and "with reserve respecting creationism;" and that "traducianism was professed not only by heterodox writers like Apollinaris, but by some orthodox theologians like Gregory of Nyssa." The writer in the Middle ages who maintains traducianism with most decision is Odo, bishop of Cambray. His treatise upon Original Sin has received little attention even from the historians of doctrine, though it is marked by great profundity and acumen.

Neander (I. 615) describes the traducianism of Tertullian in the following terms: "It was his opinion, that our first parent bore within him the undeveloped germ of all mankind; that the soul of the first man was the fountain head of all human souls, and that all varieties of individual human nature are but different modifications of that one spiritual substance. Hence the whole nature became corrupted in the original father of the race, and sinfulness is propagated at the same time with souls. Although this mode of apprehending the matter, in Tertullian, is connected with his sensuous habits of conception, yet this is by no means a *necessary* connection." This last remark of Neander is important. Bellarmine claims Augustine as a creationist. Melanchthon and Klee reckon him among traducianists. Gangauf says that he was undecided. Delitzsch (Biblical Psychology, § vii.) asserts that he was wrestling with the subject all his life. Luther, according to Delitzsch, was at first inclined to traducianism, being urged by Bugenhagen, but afterwards distinguished the creation and infusion of the soul into the body as the second conception, from the first bodily conception Smith (Theology, 168) asserts that "traducianism, on the whole, has been the most widely spread theory."

Turrettin (Institutio, IX. xii. 6) remarks as follows respecting the traducian view. "Some are of opinion that the difficulties pertaining to the propagation of original sin are best resolved by the doctrine of the propagation of the soul (animae traducem); a view held by not a few of the Fathers, and to which Augustine frequently seems to incline. And there is no doubt that by this theory all the difficulty seems to be removed; but since it does not accord with scripture or with sound reason, and is exposed to great difficulties, we do not think that recourse should be had to it."

Maresius (De Marets), a Calvinistic theologian whose opinions had great weight, speaks as follows respecting traducianism. "Although Augustine seems sometimes to have been undecided (fluctuasse aliquando) respecting the origin of the soul; whether it is by immediate creation or by propagation; he is fixed in the opinion that original sin cannot be transmitted otherwise than by propagation. And he is far more inclined (longe pronior) to the last mentioned doctrine, nay, to speak truly, he constantly held it (constanter retinuit), in order to save the justice of God; because it is difficult to show the justice of infusing a soul newly created, and destitute of sin, and having no guilt of its own, into a vitiated body, by whose concupiscence and lust it is stained and burdened, is exposed to many and great evils in this life, and condemned to everlasting punishment hereafter. Augustine, Epist. 28, 137; De anima; and Jansenius, De statu naturae, I. 15. This was the opinion of Apollinaris, and of nearly all the western divines in Jerome's day; and is defended by Marnixius, Sohnius, and Combachius, truly great divines of our communion; to which, if this were the place to lay down the statements, I should not be much disinclined (valde alienus)." Maresius: Theologia Elenchtica, Controversia XI.

Charnocke (Discourse I), after remarking that wisdom and folly, virtue and vice, and other accidents of the soul, are not propagated, adds: "I do not dispute whether the soul were generated or not. Suppose the substance of it was generated by the parents, yet those more excellent qualities were not the result of them," i.e., of the parents. Hooker (Eccl. Pol., II. vii.), also, speaks doubtfully. "Of some things, we may very well retain an opinion that they are probable, and not unlikely to be true, as when we hold that men have their souls rather by creation, than propagation."

Creationism confines the idea of species to the body. In this respect, it agrees with the theory of pre-existence; the difference relating only to the time when the soul is created. Creationism and pre-existence both alike maintain that the human soul is individual only, and never had a race-existence in Adam. The creationist holds that God on the sixth day created two human individuals, one male and one female, and in them also created the specific physical nature from which the bodies of all the subsequent individuals were procreated; the soul in each instance being a new creation ex nihilo, and infused into the propagated body.

Hase (Hutterus Redivivus, 79) represents this view as having been favored by Aristotle, and adopted by Ambrose, Jerome, Pelagius, Bellarmine, and Calixtus. Hagenbach (§ 106) mentions as advocates of creationism, Lactantius,

Hilary, and Jerome, and remarks (§ 173) that this theory gained gradually upon traducianism in the middle ages. John of Damascus, Anselm, and Aquinas were creationists. Heppe (Reformirter Dogmatik, XII.) says that the Lutheran theologians almost without exception adopted traducianism, while the Reformed divines with very few exceptions maintained creationism. Creationism has been the most common view during the last two centuries.

The choice must be made between traducianism and creationism, since the opinion that man as to his soul existed before Adam has no support from revelation. The Bible plainly teaches that Adam was the first man; and that all finite spirits existing before him were angels.

The question between the traducianist and the creationist is this: When God created the first two human individuals, Adam and Eve, did he create in and with them the invisible substance of all the succeeding generations of men, both as to the soul and body, or only as to the body? Was the human nature that was created in Adam and Eve simple, or complex? Was it physical solely, or was it psychico-physical? Had the human nature in the first pair two sides, or only one? Was provision made for propagating out of the specific nature deposited in Adam, individuals who would be a union of body and soul, or only a mere body without a soul? [1]

The question, consequently, between the parties involves the *quantity* of being that was created on the sixth day, when God is said to have created "man" The traducianist asserts that the entire invisible substance of all the generations of mankind was originated ex nihilo, by that single act of God mentioned in Gen. 1:27, by which he created

[1] Augustine describes man as the union of spiritual and corporeal substance. "Persona hominis mixtura est animae et corporis, duarum rerum commixtio: unius incorporeae, et alterius corporeae; nam si anima in sua natura non fallatur, incorpoream se esse comprehendit" Ep 137, Ad Volusianum. "Quicquid enim corpus non est, et tamen aliquid est, jam recte spiritus dicitur" De Genesi ad literam, XII vii. 16. Compare Gangauf Aug. Psychologie, 101

"man male and female." The creationist asserts that only a part of the invisible substance of all the generations of mankind was created by that act: namely, that of their bodies; the invisible substance which constitutes their souls being created subsequently, by as many distinct and separate creative acts as there are individual souls.

Traducianism and creationism agree with each other in respect to the most difficult point in the problem: namely, a kind of existence that is prior to the individual existence. The creationist concedes that human history does not start with the birth of the individual man. He does not attempt to explain original sin with no reference to Adam. He maintains that the body and physical life of the individual is not a creation ex nihilo in each instance, but is derived from a common physical nature that was originated on the sixth day. In so doing, the creationist concedes existence in Adam, quoad hoc. But this race-mode of human existence, which is prior to the individual mode, is the principal difficulty in the problem, and in conceding its reality as to the body, the creationist carries a common burden with the traducianist. For it is as difficult to think of an invisible existence of the human body in Adam, as to think of an invisible existence of the human soul in him. In reality, it is even more difficult; because the body of an individual man, as we now know it, is visible and tangible, while his soul is not. And an invisible and intangible existence in Adam is more conceivable than a visible and tangible

In discussing either traducianism or creationism, it is important to define the idea of "substance." The term, in this connection, does not imply either extension or figure It is taken in its etymological and metaphysical sense, to denote that entity which *stands under* phenomena, and is the base for them. As in theology, the Divine "substance" or nature is unextended and formless, yet a real entity, so in anthropology, the human "substance" or nature is without extension and figure, yet is a certain amount of real being with definite and distinguishable properties. Shedd: Theological Essays, 135–137.

So far as the mental or psychical side of the human nature is concerned, when it is said that the "substance" of all individual souls was created in Adam, of course nothing extended and visible is implied. The substance in this case is a spiritual, rational, and immortal essence, similar to the unextended essence of God, in whose image it was made ex nihilo. And so far as the physical and corporeal side of man is concerned, the notion of "substance" must be determined in the same manner. That which stands under, that which is the *substans* of the corporeal form and phenomena, is an invisible principle that has no one of the geometrical dimensions. Physical life, or the animal soul, though not spiritual and immortal like the rational soul, is nevertheless beyond the reach of the five senses. It occupies no space; it is not divisible by any material instruments; it cannot be examined by the microscope. In speaking therefore of the primary created "substance" of the human body, we must abstract from the notion everything that implies figure and extension of parts. "The things which are seen were not made of things which do appear," Heb. 11:3. The visible body is constituted, and built up by an invisible vitality. Neither the cell, nor protoplasm, nor the "aether" of Carus (Physiologie, I. 13), nor any *visible* whatever, can be regarded as the *substans* of the body; as the vital principle in its primordial mode. These are all of them extended, and objects of sensuous perception. They are the first form, in which the primarily formless physical life embodies itself. They each presuppose life as an *invisible*. In thinking, therefore, of the "substance" of all individual bodies as having been created in Adam, we must not with Tertullian and others think of microscopic atoms, corpuscles, or protoplasm: but only of the unseen principle of life itself, of which these are the first visible organization. Modern physiology (Haeckel: Creation, I. 297) describes the human egg as $\frac{1}{120}$ part of an inch in diameter, so that in a strong light it can just be perceived as a small speck, by the naked eye. This egg is a small globular bladder which contains all the constituent parts of a simple organic cell. These parts are: (*a*) The mucous cell-substance or protoplasm, called the "yolk;" (*b*) The nucleus or cell-kernel, called the "germinal vesicle," which is surrounded by the yolk. This nucleus is a clear glassy globule of albumen about $\frac{1}{600}$ part of an inch in diameter; (*c*) The nucleolus, the kernel speck or "germinal spot" This is enclosed and surrounded by the nucleus, and is the last phase of *visible* life under the present microscope. But this nucleolus is not the invisible life itself in its first phase, as immediately created ex nihilo. This "germinal spot" is only the first hardening, as it were, of the invisible into visibility. It is life in this *form;* whereas, in the beginning, as created in Adam, physical life was formless and invisible.

Before entering upon the discussion of the two theories of traducianism and creationism, we observe that there are several ways of handling the doctrine of original sin, or sin as related to Adam.

1. It may be held simply as a revealed fact, without any attempt at explanation. The theologian contents himself with affirming that Scripture teaches that all men were created holy in Adam, had an advantageous probation in Adam, sinned freely in Adam, and are justly exposed to physical and spiritual death upon these three grounds, and declines to construct any explanatory theory. In this case, he treats the doctrine of original sin as he does that of the creation of the universe. "Through faith he understands that the worlds were framed by the word of God, so that the things which are seen were not made of things which do appear," Heb 11:3. Similarly, through faith he understands that "death passed upon all men because all sinned," Rom. 5:12; that "by one offence, judgment came upon all men to condemna-

tion," Rom. 5–18; and that "in Adam all die," 1 Cor. 15:22; and formulates this in the statement that "all mankind descending from Adam by ordinary generation sinned in him, and fell with him, in the first transgression," L C. 22. But as he does not undertake to explain creation ex nihilo, neither does he undertake to explain the fall in Adam. He accepts the fact of revelation, in each case. He has reason to believe that the doctrine of the fall in Adam is truth, not error: first, because God would not reveal error; secondly, because God has made an infinite self-sacrifice in order to deliver man from the guilt and pollution of original sin: a thing he would not have done, if he knows that it is not really and truly sin.

2. The doctrine may be held as a revealed fact, and an explanation attempted by the theory of *natural* or *substantial* union with Adam. In this case, Adam and his posterity existed together, and sinned together, as a unity. The posterity were not vicariously represented in the first sin, because representation implies the absence of the party represented; but they sinned the first sin being seminally existent and present; and this first sin is deservedly imputed to them, because in this generic manner it was committed by them The guilt of the first sin, both as culpability (culpa) and obligation to the penalty of eternal death (reatus poenae), is chargeable upon Adam and his posterity upon the common principle that sin is chargeable upon the actor and author of it. The imputation of Adam's sin, upon this theory, differs from the imputation of Christ's righteousness, in being deserved, not undeserved or gratuitous.

3. The doctrine may be held as a fact of revelation, and an explanation of it attempted by the theory of *representative* or *forensic* union with Adam. In this case, Adam as an individual, distinct from Eve, and distinct from his posterity whom in respect to the soul he did not seminally include, sinned representatively and vicariously for his non-existent and absent posterity. As their vicar and representative, he

disobeyed the Eden statute in their room and place, precisely as Christ obeyed the moral law, in respect to both precept and penalty, as the vicar and representative of his people. The sin of Adam, consequently, is imputed to his posterity in the very same way that the righteousness of Christ is imputed to the believer—namely, undeservedly or gratuitously. The posterity are not guilty in the sense of being inherently and personally ill deserving on account of Adam's sin, just as the believer is not righteous in the sense of being inherently and personally deserving on account of Christ's obedience. As in the latter instance, only the consequences without the inherent merit of Christ's obedience: namely, freedom from the obligation to suffer the penalty of eternal death, and a title to eternal life, inure to the believer, so in the former instance, only the consequences of Adam's disobedience without the inherent demerit: namely, the obligation to suffer the penalty of eternal death, and forfeiture of a title to eternal life, inure to his posterity. On this theory, Adam's sin *itself*, as a disobedient and rebellious *act* causative of the penalty of eternal death, is not imputed to the posterity, because it was not committed by them. Only its penal consequences are imputed. Adam's act is separated from its effect, namely, the penalty: the former not being chargeable to the posterity; the latter being imputed to and inflicted upon them. The posterity suffer the punitive evil produced by Adam's sin, but are not inherently and personally guilty of this sin itself.

4 The doctrine may be held as a fact of revelation, and an explanation of it attempted by a *combination* of natural with representative union. This is a middle theory between traducianism and creationism, combining elements of both. But like middle theories generally, it contains contradictory elements. If the posterity were present, as natural union implies, they could not be represented; for this supposes absence. If they were absent, as representative union implies, they could not be present, as natural union supposes.

A consistent scheme can be constructed upon either view of the Adamic union by itself, but not upon both in combination.[1] This is evinced by the fact that the tendency on the part of the advocates of representation has been to minimize natural union, in the combination. The latest and one of the ablest of its defenders, the elder Hodge, founds imputation solely on representation. See p. 45. It is important to observe that the earlier advocates of the combination, such as Turrettin for example, asserted that Adam's sin is imputed both as culpa and reatus poenae. Some of the later advocates assert that it is imputed only as reatus poenae; only as obligation to suffer the penalty of eternal death.

These four ways of handling the doctrine of Adam's sin fall, generally, into the Augustino-Calvinistic anthropology, though some of them have a closer and more self-consistent conformity to it than others. All four assert that *penal* evil befalls the posterity on account of Adam's transgression, and that this penal evil is *physical* and *spiritual death*. This differentiates them from all theories which deny these two points. "Any man who holds that there is such an ascription of the sin of Adam to his posterity, as to be the ground of their bearing the punishment of that sin, holds the doctrine of imputation; whether he undertakes to justify this imputation merely on the ground that we are the children of Adam, or on the principle of representation, or of scientia media; or whether he chooses to philosophize

[1] Hodge notices the contrariety of the two views. "If we reconcile the condemnation of men on account of the sin of Adam, on the ground that he was our representative, or that he sustained the relation which all parents bear to their children we renounce the ground of a realistic union. If the latter theory be true, then Adam's sin was our act as truly as it was his If we adopt the representative theory, his act was not our act in any other sense than that in which a representative acts for his constituents." Theology, II 164. "A union of representation is not a union of identity. If Adam and his race were one and the same, he was not their representative, for a thing cannot represent itself. The two ideas are inconsistent. Where the one is asserted, the other is denied" Princeton Essays, I. 138

on the nature of unity until he confounds all notions of personal identity, as President Edwards appears to have done" Princeton Essays, I. 139.

5. A fifth method is that of the ancient Semi-Pelagian, and the modern Arminian. The doctrine of original sin is received as a truth of revelation, and an explanation is attempted by the theory of *representative* union. Adam acted as an individual for the individuals of his posterity. The latter are not guilty of his first sin, either in the sense of culpability or of obligation to punishment, but are exposed on account of it to certain *non-penal* evils; principally physical suffering and death. They do not either deserve or incur spiritual and eternal death on account of it. This results only from actual transgression, not from Adam's sin.

The doctrine of the unity of Adam and his posterity, in the commission of the first sin and the fall from God, is of the utmost importance in anthropology. Without it, it is impossible to maintain the justice of God in the punishment of *inherited* sin For it is evident, that an individual person cannot be morally different from the species to which he belongs. He cannot be holy, if his race is sinful. No individual can rise above his species, and exhibit a character and conduct radically different from theirs. Consequently, in order to establish the responsibility and guilt of the individual in respect to the origin of sin, a foothold must be found for him in the being and agency of the race to which he belongs. He must exist in, and act with his species This foothold is furnished in the Biblical doctrine of a primary existence, and a primary act of the common human nature in Adam, of which the secondary individual existence, and the secondary individual character and acts are the manifestation. Accordingly, all schools of evangelical anthropology have held on upon St. Paul's representation of the Adamic connection, however differently they may have explained it. No one of them has adopted the Pelagian dogma of pure individualism, and absolute isolation from Adam. In contending that the human species was a complete whole, and an objective reality, in the first parents, traducianism obtains a foundation for that community of action whereby a common sinful character was originated by a single voluntary act of apostasy, the consequences of which appear in the historical series of individuals who are propagated parts of the species. The sinful disposition of an individual is the evil inclination of his will; this evil inclination comes along in and with his will; and his will comes from Adam by ordinary descent.

The perplexity into which a devout and thoughtful mind is thrown, which resolutely holds on upon the Augustinian position that inherited sin is damning and brings eternal death, while not holding on upon the co-ordinate Augustinian position of a primary existence and act of the species in Adam, is seen in the following extract from Pascal. "How astonishing is the fact, that the mystery, the most profound of all in the whole circle of our experience, namely, the transmission of original sin, is that of which from ourselves we can gain no knowledge. It is not to be doubted that there is nothing more revolting to our reason, than to maintain that the first man's sin has entailed guilt upon those whose remoteness from the original source seems to render them incapable of its participation. Such transmission appears to us not only impossible, but even unjust. For what can be more opposed to the laws of man's poor justice, than eternally to condemn an infant incapable of free will, for a sin in which he had so little share that it was committed six thousand years before he came into existence. Nothing, assuredly, is more repugnant to us than this doctrine: yet, without this mystery, of all the most incomprehensible, we are incomprehensible to ourselves. Through this abyss it is, that the whole tangled thread of our moral condition takes its mazy and devious way; and man is actually more inconceivable apart from this mystery, than the mystery itself is inconceivable by man." Thoughts: Greatness and Misery of Man.

There are difficulties attending either theory of the origin of man, but fewer connected with traducianism than with creationism. If the mystery of a *complete* existence in Adam on both the psychical and physical side is accepted, the difficulties connected with the imputation of the first sin and the propagation of corruption are relieved. As Turrettin says, "there is no doubt that by this theory all the difficulty seems to be removed." It is only the first step that costs. Adopting a revealed mystery in the start, the mystery in this instance, as in all the other instances of revealed mysteries, throws a flood of light, and makes all things plain.

There are three principal supports of Traducianism. 1. Scripture. 2. Systematic Theology. 3. Physiology.

1. The preponderance of the Biblical representations favors it. The Bible teaches that man is a species, and the idea of a species implies the propagation of the *entire* individual out of it. Individuals, generally, are not propagated in parts, but as wholes. In Gen. 1 : 26, 27, the man and the woman together are denominated "man." In these two verses, as in the remainder of the first chapter, the Hebrew אָדָם is not a proper name It does not denote the masculine individual Adam alone, but the two individuals, Adam and Eve, together. Adam, here, is the name of the human *pair*, or *species*. It is not until the second chapter of Genesis, that the word is used as a proper name, to denote the masculine, and to exclude the feminine. "God said, Let us make man (אָדָם) in our image, and let *them* have dominion. So God created man (אֶת־הָאָדָם) in his own image; in the image of God created he *him*; male and female created he *them*," Gen. 1 : 26, 27 Compare Gen. 5 : 2, where the same usage occurs. In employing the singular pronoun "him," the writer still has both individuals in his mind, as is evinced by the change of "him" to "them." Eve is in-

cluded, when it is said that God created "man" in his own image. In such connections Adam = Adam and Eve. The term is specific, not individual. Augustine (City of God, XV. xvii.) thus notices the specific use of the word "man." "Enos (אנוש) signifies 'man' not as Adam does, which also signifies man, but is used in Hebrew indifferently for man and woman; as it is written, 'male and female created he them, and blessed them, and called their name Adam,' (Gen. 5 : 2), leaving no room to doubt that though the woman was distinctively called Eve, yet the name Adam, meaning man, was common to both. But Enos means man in so restricted a sense, that Hebrew linguists tell us it cannot be applied to woman"[1]

The same usage is found in the New Testament In Rom. 7 : 1, St. Paul asks, "Know ye not, brethren, how that the law hath dominion over the man (*τοῦ ἀνθρώπου*) as long as he liveth?" The law spoken of is that of marriage, to which the wife equally with the husband is subject, both of whom are here denominated "the man." When, in verse 2, the apostle wishes to individualize, and distinguish the husband from the wife, he designates him not by *ἄνθρώπος*, but by *ἀνήρ*. When St. Paul asserts (1 Cor. 15 : 21) that "by man came death," he means both Adam and Eve, whom in the next clause he denominates *τὸ 'Αδὰμ*. Again, our Lord is denominated the Son of man (*ἀνθρώπου*), although only the woman was concerned in his human origin, showing that woman is "man." When Christ (Matt. 12 : 5) asks: "How much then is a man better than a sheep?" he includes both sexes When St Paul addresses a letter to the "saints and faithful brethren which are at Colosse," Coloss. 1 1; and St. John (1 John 3 : 15) asserts that "whosoever hateth his brother is a murderer;" they

---

[1] With this statement, Gesenius does not agree He says (sub voce) that "אֱנוֹשׁ is rarely put for the singular, is more commonly collective for the whole race Job 7.17, 15 14, Ps 8 5 It is the same as אָדָם, but only in poetic style."

mean both male and female alike and equally. And this original unity of species is referred to in St. Paul's statement respecting the marriage relation: "They two shall be one flesh," Eph. 5:31 In accordance with this, Augustine denominates Adam and Eve, "primos illos homines in paradiso." De Civitate, XI. xii. The elder Protestant divines call them "protoplasti."

That man was created a species in two individuals appears, also, from the account of the creation of Eve. According to Gen. 2:21–23, the female body was not made, as was the male, out of the dust of the ground, but out of a bone of the male. A fractional part of the male man was formed by creative power into the female man. Eve was derived out of Adam. "The man," says St. Paul (1 Cor 11:8), "is not made out of (ἐκ) the woman, but the woman out of (ἐξ) the man" And the *entire* woman, soul and body, was produced in this way. For Moses does not say that the body of Eve was first made out of Adam's rib, and then that her soul was separately created and breathed into it—as was the method, when Adam's body was made out of the dust of the ground—but represents the *total* Eve, soul and body, as formed out of a part of Adam. "The rib which the Lord God had taken from man made he a woman, and brought her unto the man. And Adam said, This is now bone of my bones, and flesh of my flesh: she shall be called woman, because she was taken out of man," Gen. 2:22, 23. The fact that the total female was supernaturally produced from the male, favors the traducian position that the total man is propagated; that the soul like the body may be derived. The same creative act which produced the body of Eve out of a rib of Adam, produced her soul also. By a single Divine energy, Eve was derived from Adam, psychically as well as physically This goes to show that when a child of Adam is propagated, the propagation includes the whole person, and is both psychical and physical. For the connection between a child and its parents is nearer and closer than was the connection between Adam and Eve at creation. See Augustine: On the Soul, I. 29, where this argument is employed.

These two individuals, created ex nihilo in the manner thus described, are in Scripture sometimes both together called "man;" and sometimes separately are called "male-man," and "female-man" (אִישׁ and אִשָּׁה), man and wo-man. Gen. 1:27; 2:23. In and with them, was also created the entire human species: namely, the invisible substance, both psychical and physical, of all their posterity. This one substance, or "human nature," was to be transformed into millions of individuals by sexual propagation. The creation proper of "man" was finished and complete on the sixth day. After this, there is only the generation of "man." The Biblical phraseology now changes. Eve is "the mother of all living," Gen. 3:20. Adam "begat a son after his own image," Gen 5:3. There is no longer any creation of man ex nihilo by supernatural power; but only the derivation of individual men out of an existing human substance or nature, by means of natural law, under Divine providence and supervision.

The question now arises: Why is not this propagation only physical, as the creationist asserts? Why should not propagation be confined to the body?

1. The first reply is, because it is contrary to Scripture. Certain texts forbid it. In John 3:6, Christ affirms that "that which is born (begotten) of the flesh is flesh, and that which is born of the spirit is spirit." The term "flesh," here, denotes man in his entirety of soul and body. The spiritual birth certainly includes both; and the connection implies that the natural birth is equally comprehensive. Men, says our Lord, are born naturally of their parents, and spiritually of God; and it is the same whole man in both instances. Now to the term "flesh" employed in this signification of the total person, Christ applies the participle *γεγεννημένον*. The "flesh," or man, consisting of soul and

body together, is "begotten" and "born." That σάρξ often comprehends the soul as well as the body, is clear from many passages. Compare Matt. 24 : 22. Luke 3 : 6. John 1 : 14; 17 : 2. Acts 2 : 17. Rom. 3 . 20 Rom. 8 : 4, 5, 8. Gal. 5 : 16, 19. In all these places "flesh" comprises both the psychical and physical nature of man. Christ employs it in the same signification in John 3 : 6, and teaches that it is a generation and birth.

Traducianism is taught in John 1 : 13. Here, the regenerate are said to be "begotten (ἐγεννήθησαν) not of blood (human seed), nor of the will of the flesh (sexual appetite), nor of the will of man (human decision)." This implies that the unregenerate *are* "begotten of blood, and of the will of the flesh, and of the will of man" But an unregenerate man is an entire man, consisting of soul and body. His soul and body, therefore, were "begotten and born of blood, and of the will of the flesh, and of the will of man." In this passage, the soul sustains the same relation to generation and birth that the body does; both come under one and the same category. It

In Rom. 1 : 3, it is said that Christ "according to the flesh (κατὰ σάρκα) was made of the seed of David" The term "flesh" here denotes the entire humanity of our Lord, antithetic to his divinity, denominated, πνεῦμα ἁγιωσύνης. Christ's soul and body together constituted his σάρξ; and this is represented as being "made of the seed of David." St. Paul employs the verb γίνομαι, to denote that there was a generation, in distinction from a creation, in the origin of Christ's humanity. The connection forbids the confinement of this generation to the physical side of his human nature, so that his human body only, not his human soul, sprang from David. Shedd: On Romans 1 : 3.

In Heb. 12 : 9, it is said that "we have had fathers of our flesh (τῆς σαρκὸς ἡμῶν), and we gave them reverence: shall we not much rather be in subjection to the Father of Spirits (τῶν πνευμάτων) and live?" This text is quoted by the creationist, to prove that man is the father of the body only, God being the father of the soul. There are two objections to this explanation. 1. God is not called the "Father of *our* spirits," which would be the required antithesis to "fathers of *our* flesh." He is denominated "the Father of spirits" generally, not of human spirits in particular. The omission of ἡμῶν with πνευμάτων shows that the fatherhood is universal—relating to men and angels. God is the heavenly Father, in distinction from an earthly father. 2. Had the writer intended to set the human spirit in contrast with the human body, as the creationist interpretation supposes, he would have said: "the Father of our *spirit*" (τοῦ πνεύματος ἡμῶν), instead of "the Father of spirits" (τῶν πνευμάτων). In this text, therefore, as in John 3 : 6, σάρξ comprehends the whole man, soul and body. Chrysostom and Theophylact refer "spirits," in this text, to angels exclusively. Calvin and Bengel find creationism in it. Moll (Lange) and Ebrard find traducianism. "Σάρξ bezeichnet hier so wenig als irgendwo, den Leib (daher der Creationismus sich fur die Lehre, dasz der Leib allein von den Aeltern gezeugt werde, die Seele aber von Gott geschaffen werde, mit Unrecht auf diese Stelle beruft) ; sondern σάρξ bezeichnet hier, wie immer, das naturliche durch creaturliche Krafte zu Stande kommende Leben." Ebrard in loco.

Traducianism is taught in Acts 17 : 26 God "hath made of one blood all nations." The natural interpretation of this text is, that men of all nationalities are made of one common human nature as to their whole constitution, mental and physical There is nothing to require the creationist qualification : "Every man, as to his body," but everything to exclude it. For the apostle was speaking particularly of man as rational, immortal, and having the image of God ; and therefore in saying that "man is made of one blood," he certainly could not have intended to exclude his rational soul in this connection.

In Heb. 7:10, it is said that "Levi," that is, the whole tribe of Levi (verse 9), "was yet in the loins of father, when Melchisedec met" Abraham Here Abraham is called the father of Levi, though he was Levi's great-grandfather. Levi and his descendants are said to have had an existence that was real, not fictitious, in Abraham. But it contradicts the context, to confine this statement to the physical and irrational side of Levi and his descendants. The "paying of tithes" which led to the statement is a rational and moral act, and implies a rational and moral nature as the basis of it.

In Psalm 139:15, 16, there is a description of the mysterious generation of man. "My substance was not hid from thee when I was made in secret." Though the reference is to the embryonic and foetal life, yet it includes the mental and moral part of man with the physical. The clauses, "*I* was made," and "*my* substance," certainly denote the speaker as an entire whole. The same is true of the passage Job 10:10, "Hast thou not poured me out as milk, and curdled me like cheese?" The "me" here, is the whole person. The total ego is described as begotten, in Jer. 1:5: "Before I formed *thee* in the belly, I knew *thee*." In Ps. 22:9, 10, David says, "Thou art he that took me from the womb. I was cast upon thee from the womb; thou art my God from my mother's belly."

Gen. 2:1–3 teaches that the work of creation was complete on the sixth day. "God blessed the seventh day and sanctified it; because that in it he had rested from all his work which God had created and made." If the human soul has been a creation ex nihilo, daily and hourly, ever since Adam and Eve were created on the sixth day, it could not be said that "on the seventh day God *ended* his work which he had made" Compare Ex. 20:11, "In six days God made heaven and earth, the sea, and all that in them is, and rested on the seventh day;" and Heb. 4:4, God "rested from *all* his works."

1 Cor. 15 : 22 supports traducianism. "In Adam (τῷ Ἀδὰμ) all die." The article shows that Adam here, as in Gen. 1 : 17, denotes Adam and Eve inclusive of the species. To "die in Adam" implies existence in Adam. The non-existent cannot die. Merely metaphorical existence in Adam is non-existence. Merely physical existence in Adam without psychical, would allow of physical death in Adam, but not of spiritual. To die in Adam, both spiritually and physically, supposes existence in Adam both as to soul and body.

The same remark is true respecting Eph. 2 : 3 : "We were by nature (φύσει) children of wrath." Here the term φύσις denotes a real nature derived from foregoing ancestors; as in Gal. 2 : 15. ἡμεῖς φύσει Ἰουδαῖοι. And this nature is the whole nature of man, not a part of it. The apostle does not mean to teach that men are exposed to the divine displeasure, because of a sensuous and physical corruption which belongs to the body in distinction from the soul; but because of a corruption that is mental as well as physical.

The word ἥμαρτον in Rom. 5 : 12 strongly supports the traducian view. The invariable usage in both the Old and New Testaments makes it an active verb. There is not a single instance of the alleged passive signification. Had the apostle meant to teach that all men were "regarded" as having sinned, he would not have said πάντες ἥμαρτον, but πάντες ἡμαρτηκότες ἦσαν, as in Gen. 44 : 32; 43 : 9. But if all "sinned" in Adam in the active sense of ἥμαρτον, all must have existed in him. Nonentity cannot sin; and merely physical substance cannot sin. Shedd: On Romans 5 : 12.

These Scripture texts support the traducian position, that the individual man is propagated as an entire whole consisting of soul and body, and contradict that of the creationist, that a part of him is propagated and a part is created. These Biblical data countenance the view, however difficult it may be to explain it, that man being a *unity* of body and soul is *begotten* and *born* as such a unity. "To be the son of a woman," says Edwards (Against Watts's notion of the Pre-existence of Christ's Human Soul), "is to receive being in both soul and body, in consequence of a conception in her womb. The soul is the principal part of the man; and sonship implies derivation of the soul as well as the body, by conception. Not that the soul is a [material] part of the mother as the body is. Though the soul is no [material] part of the mother, and be immediately given by God, yet that hinders not its being derived by conception; it being consequent on it according to a law of nature. It is agreeable to a law of nature, that when a perfect human body is conceived in the womb of a woman, and properly nourished and increased, a human soul should come into being: and conception may as properly be the cause whence it is derived, as any other natural effects are derived from natural causes and antecedents. For it is the power of God which produces these effects, though it be according to an *established law*.[1] The soul being so much the principal part of man, a derivation of the soul by conception is the chief thing implied in a man's being the son of a woman." In saying that the soul is "no part of the mother as the body is;" that it is "immediately given by God;" and yet that this "does not hinder its derivation by conception," Edwards evidently means that the soul is not physical substance like the body, and has a psychical in distinction from physical derivation or generation that is peculiar to itself.

Samuel Hopkins (Works, I. 289) follows Edwards, in saying that "the mother, according to a law of nature, conceives both the soul and body of her son; she does as much towards the one as towards the other, and is equally the instrumental cause of both." Says Nitzsch: "That the individual dispositions of the soul are propagated by generation, will scarcely be disputed.[1] Why not their generic

[1] Compare, As you Like It, I. i. 'I know you are my elder brother; the courtesy of nations allows you my better, in that you are the first born; but the

dispositions also? Hence, we cannot but maintain the doctrine of derivation, together with creation." Christian Doctrine, § 107. Weiss (Theology of the New Testament, § 67) explains St. Paul as teaching that "the soul is begotten."

The few texts that are quoted in favor of creationism are as easily applicable to traducianism. Isa. 57:16, "The souls which I have made." The context does not imply a distinction of the soul from the body. On the contrary, "soul" here is put for the whole person. Traducianism equally with creationism holds that God is the maker of the soul. The body, certainly, is propagated, yet God is its maker. Augustine (On the Soul, xvii.) remarks that God may as properly be said to "make" or "create" in the instance of the propagation of the soul, as in that of its individual creation. "Victor wishes the passage, 'Who giveth breath to the people,' to be taken to mean that God creates souls not by propagation, but by insufflation of new souls in every case. Let him, then, boldly maintain, on this principle, that God is not the creator of our body, on the ground that it is derived from our parents; and that because corn springs from corn, and grass from grass, therefore God is not the maker of each, and does not 'give each a body as it hath pleased him.'"

Zechariah 12:1, God "formeth the spirit of man in him." The verb (יָצַר) in this place favors the traduction of the soul. See Lewis's Note, in Lange's Genesis, p. 164. Job 33:4, "The spirit of God hath made me, and the breath of the Almighty hath given me life." This is true also from the traducian position. Numbers 16:22, "The God of the spirits of all flesh." The context shows that "spirit," here, is put for the whole man: "Shall one man sin, and thou be wroth with the whole congregation." Heb. 12:9, "Father of spirits." The antithesis is not between the body and soul of man, but between man and

---

same tradition takes not away my blood, were there twenty brothers betwixt us I have as much of my father in me as you."

spirits generally. If we are subject to our earthly fathers, ought we not to be subject to the universal Father? See page 24. John 5:17, "My father worketh hitherto" God works perpetually in preservation and providence. Another explanation, favored by the context, refers the statement to the exertion of miraculous power. Christ asserts that he works miracles, like his Father.

2. Secondly, the theological argument strongly favors traducianism. (*a*) The imputation of the first sin of Adam to all his posterity as a culpable act, is best explained and defended upon the traducian basis. The Augustinian and Calvinistic anthropologies affirm that the act by which sin came into the world of mankind was a self-determined and guilty act, and that it is justly chargeable upon every individual man equally and alike. But this requires that the posterity of Adam and Eve should, in some way or other, participate in it. Participation is the ground of *merited* imputation; though not of unmerited or gratuitous imputation. Shedd: On Romans 4:3, 8. The posterity could not participate in the first sin in the form of individuals, and hence they must have participated in it in the form of a race. This supposes that the race-form is prior to the individual form; that man first exists as a race or species, and in this mode of existence commits a single and common sin. The individual, now a separate and distinct unit, was once a part of a greater whole. The Westminster Shorter Catechism, 16, asserts the commission of a common sin, in the following terms: "All mankind, descending from Adam by ordinary generation, sinned in him and fell with him in his first transgression." The term "mankind" denotes here the human nature before it was individualized by propagation. This nature sinned. Human nature existing primarily as a unity in Adam and Eve, and this same human nature as subsequently distributed and metamorphosed into the millions of individual men, are two modes of the same thing.

Again, that a participation of some kind or other in the first sin is postulated in the Westminster formula, is proved by the fact that the first sin is called "a transgression." "Every sin, both *original* and actual, being a transgression of the righteous law of God, doth bring guilt upon the sinner." Confession, VI. vi. This agrees with Rom. 5 : 15; where the first sin of Adam is denominated *παράπτωμα*. But a transgression supposes a transgressor; and the transgressor in this instance must be the "all" who "sinned," spoken of in Rom. 5 : 12; and who are the "man*kind* descending by ordinary generation"—that is to say, the human nature existing in Adam and subsequently individualized by propagation. Anselm (De conceptu virginali, X.) reasons as follows: "Each and every child of Adam is man by propagation, and a person by that individuation whereby he is distinguished from others. He is not responsible for original sin because he is man, or because he is a person. For if this were so, it would follow that Adam would have been responsible for original sin before he sinned, because he was both man and a person prior to sin. It remains, therefore, that each and every child of Adam is responsible for original sin because he is Adam. Yet not merely and simply because he is Adam, but because he is *fallen* Adam." Anselm, here, uses "Adam" to designate the "human nature" created in Adam and Eve.

The doctrine of the specific unity of Adam and his posterity removes the great difficulties connected with the imputation of Adam's sin to his posterity, that arise from the injustice of punishing a person for a sin in which he had no kind of participation. This is the Gordian knot in the dogma. Here the standing objections cluster. But if whatever is predicable of Adam as an individual is also predicable of his posterity, and in precisely the same way that it is of Adam, the knot is not cut but untied. No one denies: 1. That the *individual* Adam committed the first sin prior to its imputation to him, and that it was righteously imputed to him as a culpable and damning act of disobedience. 2. That his first sin corrupted his nature simultaneously with its commission, and that this corruption, like its cause the first sin, was prior to its imputation as culpable and damning corruption. There is certainly nothing unjust, in imputing the first sin, and the ensuing corruption, to the individual Adam, on the ground that he was the author of both.

Now if the traducian postulate be true, namely, that Adam and his posterity were specifically one in the apostasy, all that is said of the individual Adam can be said of his posterity. The posterity committed the first sin prior to its imputation to them, and it was imputed to them as a culpable and damning act of disobedience. And the first sin corrupted the nature of the posterity simultaneously with its commission, and this corruption, like its cause the first sin, was prior to its imputation to them as culpable and damning corruption. There is certainly nothing unjust in imputing the first sin, and the ensuing corruption, to the posterity, on the ground that they were the author of both. There is indeed something inscrutably mysterious in the postulate of specific unity, but not more than there is in the postulate that God creates individual souls each by itself, and brings about corruption of nature in them negatively, by the withdrawment of grace, instead of positively by the first sin of Adam.

Edwards argues that a *coexistence* of the posterity with the first parents, if conceded, would relieve the difficulties connected with the imputation of their sin. For this implies coagency, and this implies common responsibility. "I appeal," he says (Original Sin, Works, I. 491), "to such as are habituated to examine things strictly and closely, whether, on supposition that all mankind had *coexisted* in the manner mentioned before, any good reason can be given why their Creator might not, if he had pleased, have established such a union between Adam and the rest of mankind as was in the case supposed. Particularly, if it had been the case that Adam's posterity had, actually, according to a law of nature, somehow *grown out of him*, and yet remained *contiguous* and literally *united* to him, as the branches to a tree, or the members of the body to the head; and had all, before the fall, existed together at the same *time* though in different *places*, as the head and members are in different places: in this case, who can determine that the Author of nature might not have established such a union between the root and branches of this complex being, as that all should constitute one moral whole; so that there should be a communion in each *moral alteration*, and that the heart of every *branch* should at the same moment participate with the heart of the *root*, be conformed to it, and concurring with it in all its affections and acts, and so jointly partaking in its state, as a *part* of the *same thing*." This is defective, in that Edwards supposes a unity composed of *individual* persons aggregated together, instead of a single specific nature not yet individualized by propagation, as in Augustinianism. But it shows that in his opinion, if a unity of action in the first sin can be obtained for all mankind, then the imputation of the first sin to them is just

The following from Coleridge (Aids to Reflection, Harper's Ed., I. 289) also implies, that if oneness of nature and substance between Adam and his posterity could be proved, the justice of imputing the first sin would follow "Should a professed believer ask you, whether that which is the ground of responsible action in your will could in any way be *responsibly present* in the will of Adam—answer him in these words: 'You, sir, can no more demonstrate the negative, than I can conceive the affirmative.'"

(*b*) The transmission of a sinful inclination is best explained by the traducian theory. "Original sin," says the Westminster Larger Catechism, 26, "is conveyed from our first parents unto their posterity by *natural generation*, so that all that proceed from them in that way are conceived and born in sin." Job 14:4; Ps. 51:5; 58:3; John 3:6; Eph. 2:3. This moral corruption, resulting from the first transgression, could not be transmitted and inherited unless there were a vehicle for its transmission; unless there were a common human nature, both as to *soul* and body, to convey it. Tertullian's maxim is logical: "Tradux peccati, tradux animae." The transmission of sin requires the transmission of the sinning soul. Sin cannot be propagated, unless that psychical substance in which sin inheres is also propagated. Sin cannot be transmitted along absolute non-entity. Neither can it be transmitted by a merely physical substance If each individual soul never had any other than an individual existence, and were created ex nihilo in every instance, nothing mental could pass from Adam to his posterity. There could be the transmission of only bodily and physical traits. There would be a chasm of six thousand years between an individual soul of this generation and the individual soul of Adam, across which "original sin" or moral corruption could not go "by natural generation."

The difficulty of accounting for the transmission of sin upon the creationist theory, has led some creationists to assert the creation of all individual human souls simultaneously with the creation of Adam, and their quiescent state until each is united with its body. Ashbel Green adopts this view, in his Lectures on the Catechism. Presbyterian Board's Ed. But this does not relieve the difficulty; because, as distinct and separate individuals, the souls of the posterity could not commit the *one single* sin, the "one offence" of Adam. They could only sin "after the similitude of Adam's transgression," Rom. 5:14; that is, imitate and repeat Adam's sin; and there would be as many sins to be the cause of death as there were souls. These souls must therefore primarily have been a single specific psychical nature, in order to "sin in Adam, and fall with him in his first transgression."

These difficulties in respect to participation in the sin that is imputed, and its transmission, are felt by those who hold to the imputation of original sin, and yet reject traducianism. Hence, the creationist partially adopts traducianism. The theory of representative union is compelled to fall back upon the natural union of Adam and his posterity for support. Turrettin does this. "There can be," he says (IX. ix. 11, 12), "no imputation of another's sin (peccati alieni) unless some *conjunction* with him is supposed. This union (communio) may be three-fold. 1. Natural, like that between parent and child; 2. Moral and political, like that between king and subject; 3. Voluntary, like that between friends, and between a debtor and his surety. This latter kind of union we do not include here, since we acknowledge that it implies a previous consent of the parties; but only the first two kinds, in which it is not necessary that there should be an actual consent in order that the sin of one should be imputed to another. Adam was conjoined with us by this double bond: *natural*, so far as he is our father and we are his children; *political* and also *forensic*, as far as he was the head (princeps), and representativè head (caput representativum) of the whole human race. The foundation therefore of imputation is not only the natural union, but especially (praecipue) the moral and federal union, by means of which God made a covenant with Adam as our head." Turrettin mentions the "natural" union first in the order, but describes it as second in importance. In explaining what he means by denominating Adam a public and representative person, he quotes the statement of Augustine, that "all those were one man, who by *derivation* from that one man were to be so many distinct and separate individuals." But he then qualifies Augustine's phraseology, by adding, that "they were not one man by a specific or numerical unity, but partly by a unity of origin, since all are of one blood, and partly by a unity of representation, since one represented all by the ordinance of God." This qualification shows that Turrettin was not willing to adopt Augustine's statement in full, and that he departed in some degree from the Augustinian anthropology. He denies what Augustine affirms, namely, that all men were in Adam by both a *specific* and a *numerical* unity, and introduces an idea foreign to Augustine, namely, that of unity by representation. Furthermore, he implies that there is a difference between "specific unity" and "unity of origin." But they are the same thing. Specific unity is of course the unity of a species; and this means that all the individuals are propagated from a common nature or substance. This, certainly, is unity of origin. Secondly, he implies that numerical unity is identical with specific unity. But the two are distinct from each other. A numerical unity may, or may not be a specific unity. In the instance of the persons of the Trinity, there is a numerical unity of nature or substance, but not a specific unity. A specific unity implies the possibility of the *division* of the same numerical substance among the propagated individuals of the species. But there is no possibility of a division of the Divine essence among the trinitarian persons. Consequently, they constitute a numerical but not a specific unity. But in the instance of man, the unity is both numerical and specific. The human nature while in Adam, is both numerically and specifically one. But when it is subdivided and individualized by propagation, it is no longer numerically one. The numerically one human nature becomes a multitude of individual persons, who are no longer the single numerical unity which they were at first. But they are still specifically one.

It is evident that while this eminent theologian lays more stress upon representative union than upon natural, he does not think that it can stand alone. He supports the representation by the unity of nature. He does not venture to rest the imputation of an act of Adam that brought eternal death upon all his posterity as a penal consequence, solely upon a representation by Adam of an absent and non-existent posterity. A mere and simple representative acts *vicariously* for those whom he represents; and to make the eternal damnation of a human soul depend upon vicarious *sin* contradicts the profound convictions of the human conscience. To impute Adam's first sin to his posterity merely, and only, because Adam sinned as a representative in their room and place, makes the imputation an arbitrary act of sovereignty, not a righteous judicial act which carries in it an intrinsic morality and justice. This, Turrettin seems to have been unwilling to maintain; and therefore, in connection with representative union, he also asserted to some extent the old Augustinian doctrine of a union of nature and substance. Yet, adopting creationism as he did, this substantial union, in his system, could be only physical (sensu physico et ratione seminali, IX. ix. 23), not psychical.

Turrettin marks the transition from the elder to the later Calvinism; from the theory of the Adamic *union* to that of the Adamic *representation*. Both theories are found in his system, and are found in conflict. He vibrates from one to the other, in his discussion of the subject of imputation. Sometimes he represents the union of Adam with his posterity as precisely like that of Christ with his people; namely, that of vicarious representation alone, without natural and seminal union. Adam's posterity, he says, "nondum erant in rerum natura," when Adam's sin was committed, and consequently "eadem ratione constituimur peccatores in Adamo, qua justi constituimur in Christo. At in Christo justi constituimur per justitiae imputationem; ergo et peccatores in Adamo per peccati ipsius imputationem." IX. ix. 16 Sometimes, on the other hand, he teaches that Adam's posterity *were* "in rerum natura," having seminal existence in Adam, and for *this reason* the exaction of penalty from them is a matter of justice The following is an example of this style of reasoning. "In the imputation of

Adam's sin, the justice of God does not exact punishment from the undeserving, but the ill-deserving—ill-deserving, if not by proper and personal ill-desert, yet by a *participated* and common ill-desert founded in the *natural* and federal union between Adam and us. As Levi was tithed by Melchisedec in the person of Abraham, so far as he was potentially in his loins, so that he was regarded as justly tithed in and with Abraham, who then bore the person of his whole family (qui [illegible] principio [illegible] personam [illegible]) [illegible], much more can the posterity of Adam be regarded as having sinned in him, seeing that they were in him as the branches in the *root*, the *mass* in the first fruits, and the members in the head (ut rami in radice, massa in primitiis, et membra in capite)." IX. ix. 15. This phraseology denotes more than vicarious representation. A representative, pure and simple, does not contain his constituents as the root contains the branches, the first fruits contain the mass or species, as the head contains the members. Turrettin defines Adam as the "stem, root, and head of the human race" (stirps, radix et caput generis humani. IX. ix. 15), but qualifies it by saying that he was so "not only physically and seminally, but morally and *representatively*." But a representative could not be denominated the stem, root, and [illegible] of his constituents.

Comparing this latter passage with the first cited, [illegible] that Turrettin [illegible] between natural and [illegible]

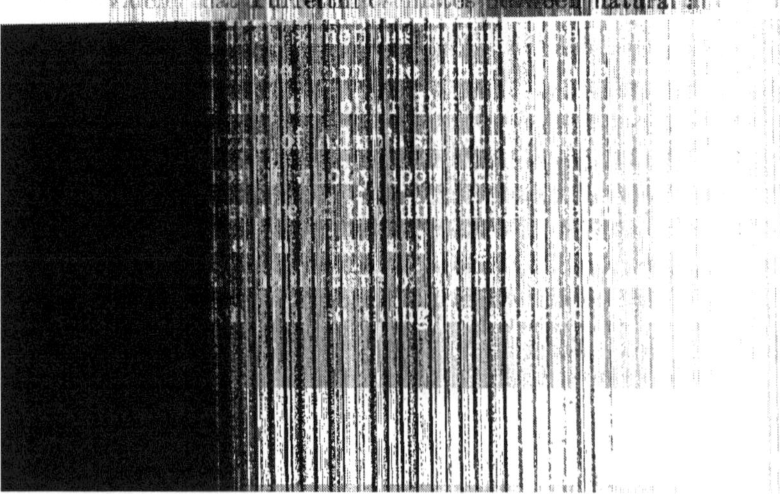

with clay. For the two ideas of natural union and representation are incongruous, and exclude each other. The natural or substantial union of two things implies the presence of both. But vicarious representation implies the absence of one of them. Says Heidegger (Heppe: Reformirter Dogmatik, 228), "representare est vi quadam juris exhibere praesentiam ejus, quod praesens non est." The natural union of the posterity with Adam implies their existence in him Two things cannot be naturally or substantially united, one of which is not present; and still less if one is non-existent. A soul created ex nihilo in A.D. 1880 could not have been naturally or substantially united with the soul of Adam in B.C. 4004. And, on the other hand, the vicarious representation of the posterity by Adam implies their absence from him, and is consistent with even their non-existence.

If, therefore, the posterity were existent and present in the progenitors by natural or substantial union, they did not need to be represented, and could not be, since representation supposes absence of substance. If, on the other hand, the posterity were absent as to substance when the representative acted, then it is contradictory to endeavor to have them present by means of a natural or substantial union. In other words, natural union logically excludes representation, and representation logically excludes natural union. Either theory by itself is consistent; but the two in combination are incongruous.[1] Nevertheless, the two ideas since the time of Turrettin have been combined very extensively in Calvinistic schools; the combination being favored by the rise and progress of representative, in the place of monarchical government. De Moor-Marck (XV. xxxi) employs both. Witsius (Covenants, I. i. 1, 3) unites the two. "Adam sustained a two-fold relation: 1. As man.

[1] There is a similar incongruity in the combination of creationism with traducianism, attempted by Martensen (Dogmatics, § 74), and Dorner (Doctrine, II 353)

2. As head, and *root* or *representative* of mankind." Here, the root is regarded as a representative of the tree, when in fact it *is* the tree itself in a certain mode or form of its existence.

It may be said that political representation requires that the parties should be of the same nation, and that this implies a natural union as the foundation of the political. But in this case reference is had to *expediency*, or the fitness of the representative to conduct the business of his constituent, not to the *justice* of the proceeding. So far as justice is concerned, a constituent may be represented by anyone whom he pleases to select, and who pleases to act in the capacity of a representative. An American might be represented by an Englishman, provided all the parties concerned are willing Representative union requires and supposes the consent of the individuals who are to be represented, and properly falls under Turrettin's third division of "voluntary union," which he excludes in the explanation of imputation. But natural union does not require the consent of the individuals. The posterity, prior to their individual existence, are created a specific unity in Adam by the will of God, and while in this status they participate in the first sin. The human species created in this manner acted in and with Adam, and the act had all the characteristics for the species that it had for Adam. It was a moral, a self-determined, and a guilty act, for the progenitors and the posterity alike, because it was such for the one human nature itself, which was the first mode in which the posterity were created and existed.

Since the idea of representation by Adam is incompatible with that of specific existence in Adam, the choice must be made between representative union and natural union. A combination of the two views is illogical. But the doctrine of the *covenant of works* is consistent with either theory of the Adamic connection. The covenant of works was "made *with* Adam as a public person," L. C. 22. If a "public person" means the individual Adam solely, acting representatively and vicariously for his posterity, both in obeying and sinning, then the covenant of works was made between God and the individual Adam acting as a representative. If a "public person" means Adam and his posterity as a specific unity, acting directly and not by representation, both in obeying and sinning, then the covenant of works was made between God and the specific Adam. But in either case, it must be observed, that it was not the covenant of works that *made* the union of Adam and his posterity. The union of Adam and his posterity, be it representative or natural, was prior to the covenant, and is supposed in order to it. If Adam was a mere individual, and represented his non-existent and absent posterity, this was provided for before the covenant of works was made *with* him. If Adam was specific, and included his existent and present posterity, this also was provided for before the covenant of works was made *with* him. Hence, the so-called "foederal union" does not mean a union constituted *by* the foedus or covenant of works. It is rather a *status*, or *relation*, than a union proper. There is a covenant relation resting either upon a representative or a natural union. The union itself of Adam and his posterity, in either case, was not made by the covenant of works, but by a prior act of God—by a sovereign declarative act, if the union is representative; by a creative act, if the union is natural, and substantial.

According to the traducianist, the facts are as follows: Adam and his posterity were made a unity by the creative act of God. The human species was created in and with Adam and Eve, both psychically and physically. This is natural or substantial union. With this unity, namely, Adam and the human species in him, God then made the covenant of works; according to which, this unity was freely to stand or fall together. "Est unitas naturae, cui unitas foederalis erat innixa." Leydecker, in Heppe: Reformirter Dogmatik, Loc. XV. Having reference to this covenant, Adam and his posterity were "federally one:" that is, one *in*, not *by* a foedus, league, or covenant. They were not constituted a unity by the covenant; for they were already and previously a unity by creation. And because they were so, God established the covenant with them. When therefore a "federal union" is spoken of, it must be remembered that it is a secondary union resting upon a primary union: namely, upon natural union, according to the traducianist; or upon representative union, according to the creationist.[1]

In the symbols and theological treatises, both Lutheran and Calvinistic, of the Reformation period, the unity of Adam and his posterity is described as natural, substantial, and specific. It is denoted by such terms as "massa," "natura," "essentia." And Adam means Adam and Eve inclusive of their posterity, as in the first chapter of Genesis. "Etsi enim in Adamo et Heva, natura initio pura, bona, et sancta creata [illegible] tamen per lapsum, peccatum ipsorum naturam invasi[illegible] Formula Concordiae, Solida Declaratio. Hase, 643. "Lapsus Adae vi pessima, humana tota massa, natura, et ipsa essentia corrupta est." Formula Concordiae, Epitome. Hase, 574. Witsius (Covenants, II. iv. 11) quotes Cloppenberg as saying that "the apostle in Rom. 5, did not so understand one man Adam as to exclude Eve: which is here the leading error of some" De Moor-Marck (XV. x) remarks respecting Paul's statement in Tim. 2:14: "Nec negat ab altera parte apostolus mulieris peccatum, cum *unum hominem*, quem ceu τυπον τοῦ μέλλοντος Christo opponit, peccati propagati auctorem, in quo peccavimus et morimur omnes, esse docet, quem expresse quoque *Adamum* vocat. Coll. Rom. 5:12–19 cum 1 Cor. 15:21, 22." De Moor (V. x.) cites Paraeus as making Adam to include Eve: (*a*) By a common nature. (*b*) By husband and wife

[1] Turrettin denominates the federal union the principal union (praecipue) But if it be true that Adam and his posterity were not constituted a unity by the covenant (foedus) of works, it cannot be the primary and principal one

being one flesh. Gen. 2:24. Augustine (City of God, XI. xii) denominates Adam and Eve "primos illos homines in paradiso." Odo (Bib. Patrum, XXI. 230) remarks: "Quaeritur quomodo peccatum habeamus ab origine nostra quae est Adam et Eva." All this agrees with St. Paul, who asserts that "the woman being deceived was in the [first] transgression," 2 Tim. 2:14 And the narrative in Genesis (3:16–19) shows that the punishment for the first sin fell upon Eve as well as upon Adam.

The elder Calvinistic theologians say nothing respecting representation. The term is foreign to their thought. The order with them is: 1. Specific existence in Adam; 2. Specific participation in the first sin; 3. Imputation of the first sin; 4. Inherence and propagation of original sin. Paraeus, on Romans 5:12, explains πάντες ἥμαρτον by "omnes peccaverunt, hoc est, *culpa* et *reatu* tenentur." All men are both culpable and punishable. He proves that they are so, by three particulars: 1. By participation in the first act of sin, "participatione culpae;" because the posterity existed seminally in Adam. "All men committed the first sin when Adam committed it, as Levi paid tithes in the loins of Abraham, when Abraham paid them." 2. By the imputation of the liability to punishment resulting from participation in the first sin, "imputatione reatus;" because "the first man so stood in grace, that if he should sin, not he alone but all his posterity should fall from grace and become liable with him to eternal death, according to the threatening, 'In the day thou eatest thereof thou shalt surely die.'" 3. By the propagation of the inherent corruption of nature which results from the participation in, and imputation of the first sin.

According to the elder Calvinism, as represented by Paraeus and those of his class, original sin *propagated* in every individual rests upon original sin *inherent* in every individual; original sin inherent in every individual rests upon original sin *imputed* to every individual; and original sin imputed to every individual rests upon original sin *committed* by all men as a common nature in Adam. On this scheme, the justice and propriety of each particular, and of the whole are apparent. The first sin, which it must be remembered consisted of both an internal lust and an external act, of both an inclination and a volition, is justly imputed to the common nature because it was voluntarily committed by it; is justly inherent in the common nature, because justly imputed; and is justly propagated with the common nature because justly inherent. This scheme if taken entire is ethically consistent. But if mutilated by the omission of one or more particulars, its ethical consistency is gone. To impute the first sin without prior participation in it, is unjust. To make it inherent without prior imputation, is unjust. To propagate it without prior inherence is unjust. The derangement of the scheme by omission has occurred in the later Calvinism. The advocate of mediate imputation deranges it, by imputing original sin as inherent, but not as committed either substantially or representatively. The advocate of representative imputation deranges it, by imputing original sin as inherent, but not as committed, except in the deluding sense of nominal and putative commission.

The elder Calvinism, like Augustinianism, starts with a unity, namely, Adam and his posterity in him as a common unindividualized nature. This unity commits the first sin: "all sinned," Rom. 5:12. This sin is imputed to the unity that committed it, inheres in the unity, and is propagated out of the unity. Consequently, all the particulars regarding sin that apply to the unity or common nature apply equally and strictly to each individualized portion of it. The individual Socrates was a fractional part of the human nature that "sinned in, and fell with Adam in his first transgression," L. C. 22. Consequently, the commission, imputation, inherence, and propagation of original sin cleave indissolubly to the individualized part of the common nature, as they did to the unindividualized whole of it. The distribution and propagation of the nature make no alteration in it, except in respect to *form*. Its natural properties and characteristics by creation, and its acquired properties and characteristics by apostasy, remain unchanged.

Calvin relies upon the natural union between Adam and his posterity, for the explanation of the imputation of original sin. "Two things," he says (Inst., II. i. 8), "should be distinctly noticed; first, that our nature being so totally vitiated and depraved, we are on account of this very corruption considered as deservedly condemned in the sight of God. And this liability (obligatio) arises not from the fault of another (alieni delicti). For when it is said that the sin of Adam renders us obnoxious to the Divine judgment, it is not to be understood as if we being innocent were undeservedly loaded with the guilt (culpam) of his sin. We derive from him not only the punishment, but also the pollution to which the punishment is justly due. Wherefore Augustine, though he frequently calls it the sin of another, in order to indicate its transmission to us by propagation, yet at the same time also asserts it to belong properly to every individual. Therefore infants themselves, as they bring their condemnation into the world with them, are rendered obnoxious to punishment by their own sinfulness, not by the sinfulness of another For though they have not yet produced the fruits of their iniquity, yet they have the seed of it within them, nay, their whole nature is as it were a seed of sin, and therefore odious and abominable to God. Whence it follows, that it is properly accounted sin in the sight of God, because there could not be liability to punishment without guilt (quia non esset reatus absque culpa)."[1]

---

[1] The proof that participation in the first sin is an essential point in the early Calvinism has been carefully collected by Landis, in a volume entitled, "Original Sin, and Gratuitous Imputation" The author, however, while asserting participation, and combating the later doctrine of mere representation by Adam,

The later Calvinism, in some of its representatives, takes the extreme ground of rejecting natural union altogether, as a support of the doctrine of imputation, and resting it wholly upon representation. The elder Hodge is one of the most positive and ablest of this class.[1] "Adam," he says (Princeton Essays, I. 187), "was our representative; as a public person, we sinned in him in virtue of a union *resulting from a covenant or contract.* Let it be noted, that this is the *only* union here [Larger Catechism, 22] mentioned. The bond arising from our natural relation to him as our parent is not even referred to." The objections to this statement are the following: 1. The Catechism in this place denominates Adam a "public person," but does not denominate him a "representative." The term "representative" is not once employed in the Westminster standards. It has been introduced from the outside, to define a "public person." 2. The Catechism, in this place, gives its own definition, and defines a "public person" as one "from whom all mankind *descend by ordinary generation.*" Here, only our natural relation to Adam is mentioned; as it is also in Confession, VI. iii., where "our first parents," as public persons, are denominated "the *root* of all mankind." Natural, not representative union is the "only" union referred to, in this definition of a public person by the terms "root," "descent," and "ordinary generation." A representative is not the root of his constituents, nor do they

with particular reference to the views of Hodge, yet rejects the realistic doctrine of race-existence as the true explanation (pp 13, 20, 31) In so doing, he departs from both Augustine and the elder Calvinists, as much as do the advocates of the representative theory. For it is clear that there can be no participation in the first sin, unless the posterity are in existence to participate in it And the only way in which they could exist and act in Adam, is as a single specific nature They could not exist in Adam as an aggregate of millions of individuals

[1] Breckenridge (Theology, 499), on the contrary, contends that "we must not attempt to separate Adam's federal from his natural headship, by which he is the *root* of the human race, since we have not a particle of reason to believe that the former would ever have existed without the latter"

descend from him by ordinary generation. 3. The Catechism, in this place, states that the covenant was made "*with* Adam as a public person." Consequently, Adam could not have been made a public person *by* the covenant; nor could the union between him and his posterity "*result from* the covenant or contract," as Hodge asserts. Adam and his posterity, *prior* to the covenant of works, had been made a natural unity by the creative act of God, as the traducianist contends, or else a representative unity by the sovereign act of God, as Hodge contends; and with this unity, God established the covenant of works. The covenant presupposes the unity, in both cases.

Natural union is excluded, and representative union made the sole ground of the imputation of Adam's sin, in the following statement of Hodge. "In the imputation of Adam's sin to us, and of our sins to Christ, and of Christ's righteousness to believers, *the nature of the imputation is the same*, so that the one case illustrates the others. By virtue of the union between Adam and his descendants, his sin is the judicial ground of the condemnation of his race, *precisely as* the righteousness of Christ is the judicial ground of the justification of his people." Theology, II. 194, 195. There is confessedly no natural union between Christ and his people, therefore, argues Hodge, there is none between Adam and his posterity. Christ did not include his people by race-union with them, therefore Adam did not include his posterity by race-union with them. Christ's people did not participate in his obedience, therefore Adam's posterity did not participate in his disobedience. Natural union being thus excluded, nothing but representative union remains. Hence it follows, that as Christ vicariously represented his absent people when he obeyed, Adam also vicariously represented his absent posterity when he disobeyed, and "his sin is the judicial ground of the condemnation of his race, *precisely as* the righteousness of Christ is the judicial ground of the justification of his people." The correctness of this reasoning depends upon that of the assumption, that there is an exact similarity between union in Adam and union in Christ. For proof that this is an erroneous assumption, see p 57 sq.

An examination of the Westminster standards evinces, that in the judgment of their authors natural or substantial union is the true ground of the imputation of Adam's sin, and that vicarious representation is inadequate. They never once use the verb "represent," or the noun "representative," in their Confession of Faith and Catechisms—a fact utterly inconsistent with the assertion that "representative union was the only one they maintained." The avoidance and total omission of these terms, when they were making careful definitions of Adam's sin, shows that they regarded them as unsuitable in this connection. The terms "represent" and "representative," it is true, occur in the theological treatises of this period, even in those of the Westminster divines themselves; but they are excluded from their dogmatic formulas, because while in a loose popular sense Adam may be called a representative of the posterity whom he seminally included, in the strict scientific sense he cannot be. A thing existing in one mode is sometimes said to represent itself as existing in another mode; as when the root is said to represent the tree. But the two are one and the same thing, in two forms.

The Westminster Assembly explained original sin and its imputation by "natural generation," "ordinary generation," the figure of a "root," and the phrase "public person." All the passages in the Westminster documents relating to Adam's sin are the following: Confession, VI. iii., "They being the *root* of all mankind, the guilt of this sin was imputed, and death in sin and corrupted nature conveyed to all their posterity descending from them by *ordinary generation.*" Confession, VII. ii , iii., "The first covenant made with man was a covenant of works, wherein life was promised to Adam, and *in him* to his *posterity.*" Confession,

XIX. i., "God gave to Adam a law, by which he bound *him* and all his *posterity* to obedience." Larger Catechism, 26, "Original sin is conveyed from our first parents unto their posterity, by *natural generation?*" L. C. 22, "The covenant being made with Adam as a public person, not for *himself* only but for his *posterity*, all mankind descending from him by *ordinary generation* sinned *in him* and fell *with him*, in that first transgression." L. C. 92, "The rule of obedience revealed to *Adam*, and to *all mankind in him*, beside a special command not to eat of the fruit of the tree of knowledge, was the moral law"

In the first of these statements, it is said that "the guilt of the first sin was imputed, and death and corruption of nature is conveyed," because "our first parents were the *root* of all mankind." This teaches natural, not representative union. For the root does not vicariously *represent* the tree, as something other than and different from itself, and absent and apart from it, but it *is* the tree itself in the first mode of its existence. A root buried in the ground does not stand for an absent tree, and still less for a non-existent one. When a potato is planted, all the subsequent individuals are seminally present. The vital principle and substance that will produce them is all in the root. And the same is true, when the figure of "seed" is taken instead of that of a "root," as is so often the case in Scripture.

Again, when it is said that "original sin is conveyed from our first parents unto their posterity by *natural generation*," unity of substance and nature is taught. Whatever descends by natural generation must be seminally and substantially present in the progenitors. And the same is taught in the explanation of the phrase "public person." A public person is described as one "from whom all mankind *descend by ordinary generation*, in whom *all mankind* sinned, and with whom *all mankind* fell in the first transgression."

In all these Westminster statements, there is not a syllable that teaches that Adam was a non-specific individual who vicariously represented a non-existent and absent posterity. And even if it be conceded that the posterity were existent and present *physically*, their merely physical existence and presence would not justify the assertion that they "sinned with and fell in him." The verbs "sinned" and "fell," and the prepositions "with" and "in," are too strong to be applied to the theory of vicarious representation. Men say that a constituent acts "by" his representative, not "in" and "with" him.

(*c*) The temptation by Satan is best explained by traducianism. Upon the theory of creationism, it is impossible to account for the fall of the individual soul by means of a temptation of the devil. The individual soul viewed as newly created ex nihilo is holy. The Calvinistic creationist denies equally with the Calvinistic traducianist, that God creates a soul without character. This is the Pelagian view. God's creative work is always "good," and is so pronounced by him. The soul as a new creation must therefore first be positively holy, and then freely fall from this created holiness into sin. And it must be tempted to fall. But on the creationist theory, there is no possibility of a temptation by Satan, or from any other quarter. And no attempt is made by the representationist to explain the fall of the posterity by temptation. The only reason which he assigns is, that God withdraws grace from the posterity. It is not so, in the traducian theory. In the instance of the fall of the entire species in the first human pair, the species was tempted to fall in and with Adam. Adam and Eve were mature and perfect in all their powers, physical, intellectual, and moral. The human nature acted in and with the two sinless individuals, in and with whom it was created. In them, it was tempted by Satan, and yielded to the temptation.

(*d*) The universality of sin is best accounted for by traducianism. The fall being that of the species in the first pair, is of course coextensive with the species. But upon the creationist theory, the fall is that of the individual only. Each soul apostatizes from God by itself. Why should every soul without exception fall? Why not a fall of only a part, as in the case of the angels, who fell as individuals, not as a species? A soul as created and holy "has the law written upon the heart, and power to fulfil it." (L. C. 17.) Why should it *invariably* apostatize?

If it be replied that God withdraws common supporting grace in the instant when he creates each individual soul, and therefore every soul apostatizes, this is of the nature of punishment, and punishment according to Scripture and reason supposes previous fault (culpa) God did not withdraw the common supporting grace of his Spirit from Adam, until after transgression. But here, by the supposition of the creationist, is a pure and holy soul fresh from the hand of God, from whom previous to its apostasy God totally withdraws one of his own gifts by creation, in order to bring about apostasy. The withdrawing of grace occurs not because of apostasy, but in order to produce it.

If it be said that this is done because of the transgression of Adam, this is a good reason from the position of traducianism, because the withdrawal, in this case, is after the fall of the *posterity* in and with Adam. An act has now been performed by Adam and his posterity *together*, which makes the withdrawal of created gifts from the whole unity righteous and just. But from the creationist position, a newly created and innocent soul that never was substantially one with Adam, and did not participate with him in the first transgression, is deprived of certain created gifts by an act of sovereignty. There is no reason, upon this theory, why by the same sovereignty men might not be deprived of Divine gifts on account of the transgression of Lucifer. Upon the theory of creationism, the withdrawal of the Holy Spirit from the newly created soul is an arbitrary, not a judicial act. The so-called "guilt" of obligation to penalty (reatus poenae), on the ground of which the withdrawment of grace rests, is putative and fictitious, not real. It is constructive guilt—the product of an act of sovereign will which decides that an innocent person shall be liable to penal suffering because of another's sin. As in the gospel scheme there is a "righteousness of God," that is, a constructive and unmerited righteousness, when the obedience of Christ is gratuitously imputed, so in this scheme there is an "*un*righteousness of God," that is, a constructive and unmerited unrighteousness, when the disobedience of Adam is gratuitously imputed. But this confounds all moral distinctions and destroys all ethics, by annulling the difference between righteousness and unrighteousness, and putting each in precisely the same relation to the Divine sovereignty.

If it be replied, as it is by those who combine representative with natural union, that between Adam and his posterity there is a natural union such as does not obtain between man and Lucifer, and that this relieves the imputation of the first sin and withdrawal of grace from the charge of arbitrariness, this is creationism betaking itself to traducianism for support. Because, natural union when examined will be found to be race-union; and race-union must be total not partial, psychical as well as physical, in order to be of any use in justifying the imputation of Adam's sin. Sin is mental, and a merely bodily connection with Adam is not a sufficient ground for imputing his transgression.

The representative theory of imputation endeavors to parry the objection to an arbitrary punishment for another's culpability, by separating punishment (poena) from culpability (culpa) and asserting that Adam's posterity are punishable for his sin, but are not culpable for it. They are compelled to endure penal suffering on Adam's account, though they are not chargeable with his fault or crime. To this separation between the punishment and the culpability of Adam's first sin, so frequently employed in the later Calvinism, but never in the earlier, there are the following objections:

1. It conflicts with the intuitive conviction of the human mind that culpability and punishment stand in the relation of *cause* and *effect*, and hence, like these, are inseparable. A free agent is punished because he is culpable. No culpability, then no punishment. No cause, then no effect. That there can be an *involuntary* obligation to endure the punishment of culpability, when there is no culpability, contravenes the common-sense and judgment of mankind. "There could be no punishment without culpability; non esset reatus absque culpa," says Calvin (Inst., II. i 8). The position that there can be involuntary punishment without culpability nullifies ethics, as completely as the position that there can be an effect without a cause nullifies physics. No more demoralizing postulate could be introduced into the province of law and penalty. When the instance of Christ's suffering punishment without culpability is cited to justify this in the instance of Adam's posterity, it is forgotten that Christ *consented* and *agreed* to this uncommon arrangement, while Adam's posterity have no option in the matter. If an innocent person, having the proper qualifications and the right to do so, agrees to suffer judicial infliction for another's culpability, of course no injustice is done to him by the infliction; but if he is compelled to do so, it is the height of injustice.

2. The separation of punishment from culpability is a characteristic of the Semi-Pelagian and Arminian anthropology, and when adopted introduces a Semi-Pelagian and Arminian tendency into Augustinianism and Calvinism. Chrysostom, and the Greek fathers generally, make this separation. They explain *ἥμαρτον*, in Rom. 12 : 5, to mean, not "sinned," but "regarded as a sinner;" not culpability (culpa), but liability to suffer what is due to culpability (poena). They denied that the posterity of Adam participated by natural union in the first sin, and are culpable and damnable for it. Adam, they contended, only represented his posterity in their non-existence and absence, and conse-

quently the statement of the Apostle that "death passed upon all men for that all have sinned" means, that all men are liable by the sovereign appointment of God to suffer certain evils on account of Adam's sin, but are not really guilty of it in his sight. This same interpretation reappears in the modern Arminianism. Grotius, Limborch, Locke, Whitby, John Taylor, Wahl, and Bretschneider explain ἥμαρτον, in Rom. 12:5, to mean: "To be exposed to suffering and death;" "to be regarded as sinners;" "peccati poenam subire" (Grotius); "pro peccati culpam sustines," Wahl: Clavis, in voce. And the reason for giving such an uncommon signification to an active verb which nowhere else in Scripture has such a sense, was the opinion that "all men sinned" representatively, not really.

This is wholly foreign to Augustine. In his theory of imputation, "death passed upon all men because all men sinned," not because "all men were reckoned to have sinned." He explained ἥμαρτον, in Rom. 5:12, in its active sense, and as denoting the act of the species in Adam. According to him, Adam's sin is both culpable and punishable, in the posterity. The culpability (reatus culpae), as well as the obligation to suffer penalty (reatus poenae), passes by participation, not by representation—an idea unknown to Augustine. Julian, for example, crowds him with the common objection, that the posterity could not voluntarily sin in Adam "before they themselves were born, and before even their parents or grandparents were begotten." Augustine replies, first citing the high authority of Ambrose to the same effect, by saying: "Per unius illius voluntatem malam omnes in eo peccaverunt, quando omnes ille unus fuerunt." Opus Imperfectum, IV 104. The same reply is made in a multitude of instances. Compare, De Meritis, I. 9; III. 7; De Nuptiis, II. 5; Opus Imperfectum, II. 179; City of God, XXI. xii.

This Augustinian method of defending the imputation

of Adam's sin passed, as we have observed (p. 41 sq ), to the Lutheran and Calvinistic creeds of the Reformation, and to the Calvinistic theologians generally, down to the 17th century. Turrettin, we have seen (p. 34 sq.), while laying the first stress upon representation, yet retains the doctrine of natural union in connection with it, though adopting creationism With Augustine and the elder Reformed theologians, he regards culpability and punishability as inseparable; and the imputation of Adam's sin, with him as with them, meant the imputation of *both* reatus culpae and reatus poenae. While holding, of course, to the separation of punishment from culpability in the instance of Christ's *vicarious atonement* for sin, he denies that such separation is possible when the *personal punishment* of Adam's posterity for original sin is the instance. The Tridentine theologians had misemployed this valid separation of the two obligations in the case of Christ's suffering, by transferring it to the ordinary ethical relations of man to the moral law, in order to establish their doctrine of ecclesiastical penance They contended that although the sacrifice of Christ had freed the believer from the culpability of original sin, it had not freed him altogether from its punishment, and therefore he was still bound, more or less, by the reatus poenae; and must therefore do penance. From the Tridentine divines, this separation passed subsequently, for a different dogmatic reason, to the Arminians, and to some of the later Calvinists. Turrettin combats this Papistic distinction. He argues as follows to prove that when original sin is in question, there is no possible separation between culpability and punishability, and that if the sacrifice of Christ frees a believer from the culpability of original sin, it frees him from all obligation to suffer the punishment of it. "The Papists erroneously distinguish judicial obligation (reatus), into obligation of culpability (reatus culpae), and obligation to punishment (reatus poenae). Obligation of culpability, they say, is that whereby the sinner is undeserving of the favor of God but *deserving* of his wrath and condemnation; but obligation to punishment is that whereby he is *liable* to condemnation and is bound to it. The former obligation, they say, was taken away by Christ; but the latter can remain, at least in respect to the obligation to temporal punishment. But the falsity (vanitas) of this distinction is evident from the nature of each. For since culpability (culpa) and punishment (poena) are correlated, and judicial obligation (reatus) is nothing else than obligation to a punishment that springs from *culpability* (reatus nihil aliud est quam obligatio ad poenam quam nascitur ex *culpa*), they mutually establish or abolish each other (se mutuo ponunt et tollunt); so that if culpability and its obligation is taken away, punishment, which *cannot be inflicted except on account of culpability*, ought necessarily to be taken away. Otherwise it cannot be said that culpability is remitted and its obligation taken away, if anything still remains to be expiated by the suffering of the sinner."

De Moor on Marck (XV. viii.) repudiates this separation of punishment from culpability, in similar terms. "Repudianda prorsus est Papistica distinctio inter reatum culpae et poenae." Heppe (Reformirter Dogmatik, Locus XV.), by quotations, shows that this was the common view among the elder Calvinists. Amesius (XII 2) founds the obligation to suffer punishment on culpability. "Reatus est obligatio peccatoris ad poenam justam sustinendam propter culpam" Rissen (IX 57) distinguishes between reatus potentialis and actualis, but rejects the distinction between reatus culpae and poenae "Reatus est *potentialis*, qui notat meritum intrinsicum poenae, quod a peccato inseparabile est; vel *actualis*, qui per dei misericordiam ab eo separari potest, per remissionem scilicet, quae proprie est reatus actualis ablatio. *Ille* pertinet ad peccati *demeritum*, et τὸ κατακριτικὸν seu *condemnabilitatem*, quae semper, peccato adhaeret. *Iste* vero ad demeriti judicium, seu κατάκριμα, condemnationem, quae tollitur in iis quibus venia peccati facta est" (IX 59.) "Perperam vero a Pontificiis distinguitur *reatus* in lapsum *culpae* et *poenae:* reatus culpae illis dicitur, quo peccator ex se indignus est dei gratia, dignus autem est ipsius ira et damnatione; poenae vero, quo obnoxius est damnationi, et ad eam obligatur." Braun (I. iii. 3, 14) also distinguishes between potential and actual obligation, but denies that punishment can be separated from culpability. "Inepte distinguunt Pontificii inter reatum poenae et reatum culpae, quasi a nobis possit tolli reatus culpae manente tamen reatu poenae: quasi Christus nos liberasset a *culpa*, sed ita ut nos ipsi luamus *poenam*, vel in purgatorio, vel alibi. quod est falsissimum. Ubi enim nulla est *culpa*, ibi nullus prorsus *reatus*, nullaque *poena* concipi potest."

As late as the middle of the 18th century, we find the elder Edwards objecting to the separation of punishment from culpability, which is implied in the passive signification given to ἥμαρτον by Taylor and the Arminian writers of that day. "No instance is produced wherein the verb 'sin' which is used by the apostle, when he says 'all have sinned,' is anywhere used in our author's sense for 'being brought into a state of suffering,' and that not as a punishment for sin. St. Paul very often speaks of 'condemnation,' but where does he express it 'by being made sinners?' Especially how far is he from using such a phrase to signify being condemned *without guilt*, or any imputation or supposition of guilt. Vastly more still, is it remote from his language so to use the word 'sin,' and to say man 'sinneth' or 'has sinned,' though hereby meaning nothing more nor less than that he by a judicial act is condemned. He has much occasion to speak of 'death,' temporal and eternal; he has much occasion to speak of 'suffering' of all kinds, in this world and the world to come; but where does he call these things 'sin,' and denominate innocent men 'sinners,' or say that they 'have sinned,' meaning thereby that they are brought into a state of suffering?" Original Sin, II. iv. i.

The position that there may be punishment without culpability, in the instance of Adam's posterity, is sought to be supported, as we have before noticed, by the parallel between Adam and Christ. It is said that Christ confessedly suffered punishment "for the sins of the whole world" (1 John 2 : 2) without being culpable for them, and therefore Adam's posterity may suffer punishment for Adam's first sin without being culpable for it. If Christ may endure penal suffering for a sin in which he did not participate, then Adam's posterity may also. This is the standing argument of the representationist, and is often accompanied with the assertion that the two unities are so exactly alike, that it is impossible for the traducianist to hold that Adam's posterity are inherently and personally culpable through their union with Adam, and not also hold that believers are inherently and personally meritorious through their union with Christ; that participation in Adam's disobedience carries with it participation in Christ's obedience. But an examination will show that the two unities, though alike in some particulars, are wholly unlike in others; so that certain characteristics, particularly those of vicariousness and gratuitousness, that are connected with one cannot be with the other. St. Paul himself directs attention to some points of difference in the parallel. See Rom. 5 : 15, 16.

1. In the first place, Christ suffered *freely* and *voluntarily* for the sin of man, but Adam's posterity suffer necessarily and involuntarily for the sin of Adam. Christ was under no obligation to suffer penalty for man's sin, and had he so pleased need not have suffered for it. "No man taketh my life from me, but I lay it down of myself," John 10 : 17, 18. Phil. 2 : 6, 7. But Adam's posterity *owe* penal suffering on account of Adam's sin, and have no option in regard to its endurance. They do not, like Christ, volun-

teer and agree to suffer, but are compelled to suffer; and their suffering, unlike that of Christ, is accompanied with the sense of ill-desert. Original sin as imputed, inherent, and propagated, is felt to be guilt, is confessed as such, and is forgiven as such. This implies that, unlike Christ, they must in some way have committed the sin for which they feel personally guilty, and for which they are liable to suffer eternal death.

2. Secondly, Christ was *undeservedly* punished when he suffered for the sin of man; but Adam's posterity are not undeservedly punished when they suffer for the sin of Adam. Christ "suffered the just for the unjust;" but Adam's posterity do not suffer the just for the unjust. Christ was innocent of the sin for which he suffered; but Adam's posterity are not innocent of the sin for which they suffer. Consequently inherent and personal guilt is separable from punishment in the instance of Christ's suffering, but not in that of Adam's posterity.

3. Thirdly, Christ was a *substitute* when he suffered, but Adam's posterity are the principals. They do not suffer in the place of sinners when they suffer for Adam's sin, but they suffer as sinners They are not vicarious sufferers, as Christ was. They suffer for themselves, not for others. Consequently, the imputation of sin to Christ was constructive and putative; but the imputation of sin to Adam's posterity is real, like that in the case of an actual criminal.

4. Fourthly, the purpose of Christ's suffering is *expiatory;* that of the suffering of Adam's posterity is *retributive.* Christ endured penalty in order to the remission and removal of sin, but Adam's posterity endure penalty solely for the satisfaction of justice. Their suffering obtains neither the remission nor the removal of sin.

5. Fifthly, the guilt of Adam's sin did not rest upon Christ as it does upon Adam's posterity, and hence he could voluntarily consent and agree to endure its penalty, without being under obligation to do so. Christ was free from the

guilt of Adam's sin, both in the sense of culpa and poena. But the posterity are obligated by both. Christ therefore suffers as an innocent person to expiate a sin in which he did not participate; but Adam's posterity suffer as guilty persons to satisfy the law for a sin in which they did participate.[1]

This comparison of the union of Christ and his people with that of Adam and his posterity shows clearly, that Christ's relation to the penal suffering which he voluntarily endured was radically different in several particulars from that which Adam's posterity sustain to the penal suffering which they involuntarily endure, and that it is a great error to argue from one union to the other, so far as *these particulars* are concerned; and especially in regard to the particulars of vicariousness and gratuitousness.[2]

The obvious fallacy in this argument from the parallel between Christ and Adam lies in the assumption, that because there may be vicarious *penal suffering* there may be vicarious *sinning;* and that because there may be gratui-

---

[1] It may be objected, that on the traducian theory the human nature of Christ did participate in Adam's sin, because it was a fractional part of the original human nature which committed this sin This is true, and if Christ had been born by ordinary generation, and his human nature had not been supernaturally prepared for a union with the Divine, he would have shared the common guilt of Adam's sin But the effect of the miraculous conception and incarnation upon Christ's humanity was, to abolish both the guilt and the pollution derived through the Virgin mother from Adam. Christ's human nature was both justified and sanctified, before it was assumed into union with the Logos, justified proleptically, as were the Old Testament saints, on the ground of an atonement yet to be made, and sanctified completely by the power of the Holy Spirit This justification and sanctification of Christ's human nature was tantamount to non-participation in Adam's sin For it placed Christ's human nature in the same *innocent* and *perfect* state that the common human nature was in by creation, and before apostasy See p 39 For Owen's statement on this point, see Communion with the Trinity, I

[2] While dissenting from the views of Hodge upon the nature of the union between Adam and his posterity, and of the imputation of the first sin, the writer has the most profound respect for the opinions of this learned and logical theologian With the exception of the elder Edwards, to no divine is American theology more indebted

tous *justification* without any merit on the part of the justified, there may be gratuitous *condemnation* without any ill-desert on the part of the condemned. The former is conceivable, but the latter is not. One person may obey in the place of others in order to save them; but one person may not disobey in the place of others in order to ruin them. Christ could suffer by mere representation for his absent people, for the purpose of their justification; but Adam could not sin by mere representation for his absent posterity, for the purpose of their condemnation.

Those who force the parallel between Adam and Christ so far as to make the imputation of Adam's sin precisely like that of Christ's righteousness, commit the great error of supposing that sin, like righteousness, may be imputed to man in *two* ways: namely, meritoriously, and unmeritoriously or gratuitously. This is contrary both to Scripture and reason. St Paul teaches that *righteousness* may be imputed either κατὰ ὀφείλημα, or κατὰ χάριν = δωρεάν = χωρὶς ἔργων. Rom. 3:21, 24, 28; 4:3–6. He asserts that righteousness may be placed to a man's account either deservedly or undeservedly; either when he has obeyed or when he has not obeyed. "To him that worketh, is the reward not reckoned of grace, but of debt. But to him that worketh not, but believeth on him that justifieth the ungodly, his faith is counted for righteousness," Rom. 4:4, 5. But St. Paul nowhere teaches the same thing respecting *sin*. He never says that sin may be put to a man's account either deservedly or undeservedly; either when he has sinned or when he has not sinned. His doctrine is that of Scripture uniformly, that sin is always imputed to man and angel κατὰ ὀφείλημα; never δωρεὰν, never χωρὶς ἔργων, never undeservedly and gratuitously. The punishment of man's disobedience he denominates "wages," but the reward of his obedience he denominates a "gift." Rom. 6:23. Christ's obedience, which is the same thing as "the righteousness of God" (Rom. 1:17; 9:3), can be a gift to his people; but Adam's disobedience cannot be a gift to his posterity. Heaven can be bestowed upon the sinner for nothing that he has done; but hell cannot be. The characteristic of gratuitousness, or absence of inherent desert, can be associated with righteousness, but not with unrighteousness. Shedd: On Romans 4:3.

Turrettin directs attention to this radical difference between the imputation of Christ's righteousness, and that of Adam's sin He shows that the nature of the imputation is not identical in both cases, but differs in respect to the *ground* and *reason* of the imputation. The ground and reason is *judicial* and *forensic*, when Christ's obedience is imputed, but *inherent* and *personal* when Adam's disobedience is imputed. His language is as follows: "Christ by his obedience is rightly said to constitute us righteous not by inherent righteousness, but by imputed: as Rom. 4:6 teaches, and verse 19 implies, where the contrast with the antecedent condemnation is mentioned. For those are constituted righteous before God who are absolved from merited punishment on account of the obedience of Christ imputed to them, not less than Adam's posterity are constituted unrighteous, that is liable to death and condemnation, on account of the disobedience of Adam. Nor does it follow, that because Adam constituted us unrighteous *efficiently, through the propagation of inherent depravity* (effectivé, per propagationem vitiositatis inhaerentis), on account of *which* we are liable to death before God, Christ in like manner constituted us forensically and judicially righteous before God by an inherent righteousness given to us by himself. Because the scope of the apostle, which alone is to be considered, does not tend to this, but only exhibits the ground of the condemnation on the one side, and of the justification on the other, in our union with the first and second Adam respectively, as to the *fact* (rem), though the *mode* of the union is different, owing to the diversity of the subject.[1] Institutio, XVI. ii. 19. It is plain that Turrettin here founds the imputation of Adam's sin, upon some kind of participation in it. Adam, he says, constituted his posterity unrighteous "effectivé, per propagationem vitiositatis inhaerentis." The propagation of inherent holiness is not the way in which Christ makes his people righteous. The ground of the imputation of Adam's disobedience, according to this statement of Turrettin, is different from that of the imputation of Christ's obedience, because "the mode of the union is different, owing to the diversity of the subject," or agent. The former imputation rests upon something propagated, inherent, and subjective in the posterity; the latter rests upon something wholly objective—namely, the sovereign decision and judicial declaration of God.

The common distinction between legal and evangelical righteousness also shows that righteousness may be imputed in two ways, but sin in only one. "The foundation," says Turrettin (XVI. iii. 7), "of imputation, is either in the merit and worth of the person to whom something is imputed, or else it is outside of the person, in the mere grace and compassion of him who imputes The first mode is legal im-

[1] "Nec si Adamus nos injustos constituit effective per propagationem vitiositatis inhaerentis, propter quam etiam rei sumus mortis coram deo; sequitur pariter Christum nos justos constituere per justificationem forensem judicii dei per justitiam inhaerentem nobis ab ipso datam Quia scopus Apostoli, qui unice respiciendus, non eo tendet, sed tantum vult aperire fundamentum communionis reatus ad mortem, et juris ad vitam, ex unione nostra cum Adamo primo et secundo, quoad rem, licet modus sit diversus propter diversitatem subjecti" This phraseology of Turrettin, taken by itself, would teach the mediate imputation of Adam's sin; which Turrettin combated If Adam's posterity are constituted unrighteous *merely* and *only* "by the propagation of inherent depravity" (and this is all he says here), this was the view of Placaeus But in other places, Turrettin abundantly teaches that there is a *reason* for this propagation of depravity—namely, the immediate imputation of the first sin. The propagation of inherent depravity requires an explanatory and justifying reason, but the advocate of mediate imputation in denying the imputation of the first sin itself, gives none So far as Turrettin held to natural union, the logical reason for the propagation of depravity would be the imputation of the first sin to the posterity because of their participation in it, so far as he held to representative union, the logical reason would be the imputation of the first sin to the posterity constructively, and without participation.

putation, and the last evangelical imputation." It is clear that while both of these imputations apply to righteousness, only one of them is applicable to sin. Obedience may be imputed to man both legally and evangelically, but disobedience may be imputed to him only legally.

The inference that because God gratuitously imputes Christ's righteousness to Christ's people, he also gratuitously imputes Adam's sin to Adam's posterity, is the same kind of fallacy that lies in the inference that because God works in the human will "to will and to do" when it wills rightly, he also works in it "to will and to do" when it wills wrongly. And to argue that if gratuitous imputation is not true in the case of Adam's sin, it is not true in the case of Christ's righteousness, is like arguing that if God is not the author of sin by direct efficiency, he is not the author of holiness by direct efficiency Both errors proceed upon the false assumption, that God sustains precisely the same relation to holiness and sin. But holiness and sin are absolute and irreconcilable contraries; so that some things that are true of the former are untrue of the latter. God may be the author of holiness, but not of sin. He can "give," that is gratuitously and undeservedly impute, righteousness, but not unrighteousness. He can pronounce a man innocent when he is guilty, because Christ has obeyed for him; but he cannot pronounce a man guilty when he is innocent, because Adam disobeyed for him. These are self-evident propositions, and intuitive convictions; and they agree with the Scripture representations respecting the difference between the imputation of righteousness, and the imputation of sin.

3. Thirdly, the physiological argument favors traducianism. Sex in man implies a species, and a species implies that the entire invisible rudimental substance of the posterity is created in the first pair of the species. In nature universally, the Creator does not create a species piecemeal. The term "species" has a two-fold definition, according to the point of view taken. A species may be defined at its

beginning, prior to its generation and propagation; or at its close, subsequent to its generation and propagation. In the first case, the species is a unity; in the second case, it is an aggregate, or multitude.

Defining in the first manner: (*a*) A species is a single invisible nature created in a primitive pair of individuals, which nature, by division of substance through generation and propagation, becomes a multitude of individuals. This defines the human species at the beginning of its history, or at the moment of its creation on the sixth day. He who saw Adam and Eve prior to the conception of Cain, saw the human species in its first mode. The species then was one and undistributed, in the first pair of individuals.

Defining in the second manner: (*b*) A species is a multitude of individuals, who are procreated portions of a single invisible nature that was created in a primitive pair, and have descended from them in a natural succession of families. This defines the human species at the close of its history, or at the end of the world. He who shall see all the individuals of the human species in the day of judgment, will see the human species in its second mode. The species then will be a multitude, not a unity.

Naturalists generally define in the second manner: that is, as an aggregate of individuals. De Candolle defines a botanical species as "a collection of all the individuals which resemble each other more than they resemble anything else; which can by mutual fecundation produce fertile individuals; and which reproduce themselve by generation, in such a manner that we may from analogy suppose them to have sprung from a single individual." Penny Cyclopaedia: Article, Species. Quatrefages defines an animal species as "a collection of individuals more or less resembling each other, which may be regarded as having descended from a single primitive pair, by an uninterrupted and natural succession of families." Human Species, I. iii.

A species, or a specific nature, is that primitive invisible substance, or plastic principle, which God created from non-entity, as the rudimental matter of which all the individuals of the species are to be composed. The first oak tree, for example, contained the seminal substance of all oak trees. The Creator has exerted no strictly creative power in the line of the oak, since he originated that vegetable species. He has exerted only a sustaining and providential agency, in the propagation of individual oak after individual oak, as this agency is seen in the law of vegetable growth. This doctrine of the creation of a species is taught in Gen. 2 : 5. God "made every plant of the field, *before it was in the earth*, and every herb of the field, *before it grew*"[1] This describes the origination ex nihilo of a species in the vegetable kingdom. A plant made by God "before it was in the earth, and before it grew," could not have been an evolution out of the earth. It is true that into the composition of the first oak there entered various material elements that were already in existence, the earths and gases, but these did not constitute the oak proper. The oak itself, considered as a new and previously non-existent species, was that *invisible principle* of vegetable life which the creator originated ex nihilo, in this particular instance, by which these earths and gases were built up into the visible oak. It belongs among those "things invisible" of which the eternal Son of God is said to be the creator, in Col. 1 : 16. It is one of those "things not seen" (*μὴ φαινομένα*) of which the "things seen" (*τὰ βλεπόμενα*) are made. Heb. 11 : 1, 3. Hodge (Theology, II. 80–82) explains the original invisibility of a species by the following quotations. "The immaterial [invisible][2] principle," says Agassiz, "determines

[1] This is the rendering of the Septuagint and Vulgate The Targums and Syriac render "Now no plant of the field was yet in the earth, and no herb of the field had yet sprouted forth." Speaker's Commentary, in loco

[2] "Invisible" is preferable to "immaterial" in this connection, because the "immaterial" strictly speaking is the *mental* and *spiritual* Physical life is neither. It belongs to the material world It is matter, not mind, but in an invisible state or mode.

the constancy of the species from generation to generation, and is the source of all the varied exhibitions of instinct and intelligence which we see displayed. The constancy of species is a phenomenon dependent upon the immaterial [invisible] nature. All animals may be traced back in the embryo to a mere point upon the yolk of an egg, bearing no resemblance whatever to the future animal. But even here, an immaterial [invisible] principle which no external influence can prevent or modify is present, and determines its future form; so that the egg of a hen can produce only a chicken, and the egg of a codfish only a cod." Similarly Dana says, that "the true notion of the species is not in the resulting group, but in the *idea* or *potential element* which is at the basis of every individual of the group." "Here," says Hodge, "we reach solid ground. Unity of species does not consist in unity or sameness of organic structure, in sameness as to size, color, or anything merely external; but in the sameness of the immaterial [invisible] principle or 'potential idea' which constitutes and determines the sameness of nature."

This view of life as an *invisible* formative principle lies under all the historical physics, and has been adopted by the leading scientific minds. None but the materialists have rejected it, and their speculations have been destructive of scientific progress whenever they have prevailed. Agassiz' "invisible principle," and Dana's "idea" or "potential element" is the same thing as the "vis vitae" of Haller, the "nisus formativus" of Blumenbach, the "vis medicatrix naturae" of Stahl, the "living principle" of Hunter, the "individuating principle" of Coleridge, the "animating form" of Saumerez. "The animating form," says Saumerez (Physiology, I. 16, 17), "of a physical body, is neither its external organization nor its figure, nor any of those inferior forms which make up the system of its visible qualities; but it is the power, which not being that organization nor those visible qualities, is yet able to produce, to preserve, and to employ them. It is the presiding principle which constitutes the power of the system; the bond of its elementary part; the cement that connects them in one whole; the efficient cause whence the individuality of every system arises, and in which the form it assumes resides. It is the power by which the human species differs from the brute, the brute from the vegetable, the vegetable from inanimate matter; it is the cause that inanimate matter is converted into organs living and active; that the acorn is evolved into an oak; that the brute embryo is evolved into an animal, and the human embryo into a man." Compare Heinroth: Anthropologie, 54.

The generation and propagation of individuals succeeds the creation of a species, in the Biblical account. God having originated an invisible specific nature or substance, then provides for its division and propagation into a multitude of distinct and separate individuals This is taught in Gen. 1:12. "The earth brought forth grass and herb *yielding seed* after his kind, and the tree *yielding fruit*, whose seed is in itself, after his kind." This is vegetable propagation. The generation of the animal is taught in Gen. 1.22. "Be fruitful and multiply" In the Mosaic cosmogony, the creation of a species is the base, and its evolution into individuals is the superstructure. Every true and real species begins by a creative fiat, back of which there is no species of this kind in existence. A true and real species cannot be accounted for by evolution, because this implies existing substance to be evolved. But when the invisible specific substance has been originated from non-entity, it then develops When God has made a vegetable species "before it was in the earth," it then "yields seed after its kind."

That the species contains all the individuals, is proved: (*a*) By non-sexual propagation. In the lowest range of vegetable and animal life, propagation is without sex. The moner (cell) simply divides itself into two (fission); and these divide again, and so on indefinitely. Here the child is as old as the parent. Roget: Physiology, II. 583. Again in the instance of propagation by buds (gemmation), the cell protrudes a part of itself. It buds. And this protruded part may exist either partially or entirely separate from the stock. In both fission and gemmation, there is no impregnation of egg by sperm, of female by male.

Now in both of these instances, the creative act that originated ex nihilo the species or primitive type, inlaid in it all that evolves from it either by fission or by gemmation. The species is capable of producing all this series by innumerable splittings or dividings, without the intervention of a second creative act of God. This is all prepared and provided for, in the one act that originated the species from non-entity.

(*b*) Sexual propagation, which is the usual method in the higher plants and animals, also proves that the species contains all the individuals The two sexes may exist in one individual, who is hermaphrodite, or double-sexed. In most of the higher plants, every blossom contains both the male organs (the stamen and anther), and the female organs (the pistil and germ). The garden snail produces eggs in one part of the sexual gland, and in another part sperm, but the conjunction of the two individuals is requisite to impregnation

The majority of plants are hermaphrodites. Only a few, like the willow and poplar, and some aquatic plants, propagate themselves by sex in two individuals. But in the animal world, the rule is the reverse. Propagation of a species, here, is by male and female individuals; and each successive pair is the offspring of a preceding pair, and so backward, until the very first primitive pair is reached. This primitive pair was a creation ex nihilo; and the creator of the first pair created in and with them the invisible but real substance of all their posterity.

A species, or specific nature, then, though an invisible

principle, is a real entity, not a mere idea. When God creates a primordial substance which is to be individualized by propagation, that which is created is not a mental abstraction, or general term having no objective correspondent. A specific nature has a real existence, not a nominal.

The dispute between the realist and nominalist is easily settled, if the parties distinguish carefully between specific and non-specific substance; or, in other words, between organic and inorganic substance When specific or vital substance is in view, then realism is the truth; the species is a reality equally with the individuals that are produced out of it. Both species and individuals are entities. But when there is no species; when there is no vital specific substance out of which the individual is produced; then the only reality is the individual. "Species," in this case, is employed in a nominal and improper sense. It is only an abstract term, denoting a collection of individuals who are the only reality in the case.

Accordingly, the answer to the question between realism and nominalism: namely, whether a general conception has objective reality or not, depends upon the *nature of the thing* referred to. The dispute between the parties has overlooked this. In respect to certain things, the assertion of the nominalist is correct; in respect to certain others, the realist is correct. For example, the general conception of an ink-stand has no objective correspondent, because ink-stands are not propagated from a specific substance or nature. They are inorganic, non-vital substance They are not a species. They are only individuals. The only reality is the particular single ink-stand. "Ink-stand," as a general term, is merely a name, not a thing. The assertion of the nominalist is correct here. The same is true of the crystal. There is no propagation of crystals from a common specific substance. The only reality here is the individual crystal. Again, there is no objective correspondent to such general terms as biped, quadruped, animal, vegetable, etc., because these denote classes or orders, not species; neither is there an objective correspondent to the general term "state" or "nation." "Although we speak of communities as sentient beings; although we ascribe to them happiness and misery, desires, interests, and passions; nothing really exists or feels but *individuals*." Paley: Moral Philosophy, VI. xi. The individuals of a nation are not propagated out of the nation, but out of the race. There is no English or French propagation. Propagation is human, not national. Englishmen and Frenchmen are primarily the sons of Adam, and only secondarily the sons of Alfred and Clovis.

But the general conception of an oak, an eagle, a lion, or a man, has objective reality, because each of these is a species. All of them belong to the organic world. The individual oak is a portion of a primitive invisible substance, which substance really exists, because God created it from nothing "in the day that he made every plant of the field before it was in the earth," Gen. 2 : 5. The oak has two modes of existence, while the crystal has only one. The oak first exists as a single specific nature, and then afterwards as a multitude of individuals. The crystal has no existence but that of the single particular crystal. And the same is true of the eagle, the lion, and the man. In reference to these propagated things, realism is correct in asserting that the general conception has objective reality, and nominalism is incorrect in denying it.

Realism, then, is true within the sphere of *specific, organic*, and *propagated* being; and nominalism is true within that of *non-specific, inorganic*, and *unpropagated* being. "Crystal," as a general conception, denotes only the collective aggregate of all the individual crystals that ever exist. The individual, here, is the only actual and objective reality. But "man," as a general conception, denotes not only the collective aggregate of all the individual men that ever exist, but *also* that primitive human nature of which they are fractional parts, and out of which they have been derived. The individual, in this instance, is not the only actual and objective reality. The species is real also. The one human nature in Adam was an entity, as truly as the multitude of individuals produced out of it. The primitive unity "man" was as objective and real, as the final aggregate "men."

There is a spurious realism arising from a wrong definition of the term "human nature" Human nature is sometimes explained to be merely a common *property* of a substance, like "rationality" or "immortality." As all individual men have rationality and immortality as a characteristic quality, so all men have "humanity," or "human nature" as a characteristic quality. Human nature, as thus defined, is only an attribute, or adjunct of each individual; and the *whole* of "human nature," in this case, belongs equally and alike to each individual, as does the whole of the property or quality of rationality or immortality. Dr. Hodge, in his explanation of realism, and objections to it, so understands and defines "human nature." He regards it as an adjunct of the individual; as something united with it. He explains it as "the manifestation of the general principle of humanity *in union with* a given corporeal organization." Theology, II 51. "An individual man is a given corporeal organization, *in which* humanity as a general life or force is *present.*" Theology, II. 52. "That which constitutes the species, or genus, is a real objective existence, one and the same numerically as well as specifically This one general substance *exists in* every individual belonging to the species, and constitutes its essence." Theology, II 53. "Individual men are the manifestations of this substance, numerically and specifically one and the same, *in connection with* their several corporeal organizations." Theology, II. 54. He illustrates his view, by magnetism, electricity, etc. "As magnetism is a force in nature existing antecedently, independently, and outside of any and all individual magnets; and as electricity exists independently of the Leyden jars in which it may be collected, or through which it is manifested as present; so humanity exists antecedently to individual men, and independently of them" Theology, II. 52.

This is an erroneous definition. Human nature is a *substance*, not the property or quality of a substance. It is not the property or quality of an individual substance, but is itself a specific or general substance. Nor is it a specific or general substance *added* to, or *united* with an individual; because the latter is only an individualized *part* of the former. Nor is it a "general principle manifesting itself in a given corporeal organization." All of these definitions are incorrect.[1] Human nature is a specific or general substance created in and with the first individuals of a human species, which is not yet individualized, but which by ordinary generation is subdivided into parts, and these parts are formed into distinct and separate individuals of the species. The one specific substance, by propagation, is metamorphosed into millions of individual substances, or persons. An individual man is a fractional part of human nature separated from the common mass, and constituted a particular person having all the essential properties of human nature. The individual Socrates, for example, is not a previously existing "corporeal organization," to which "human nature," either in the sense of a property like rationality, or in the sense of a "general substance," or "general principle," is *added*, but he is a distinct *part* of the human nature created in Adam, which part has been separated from the common mass and individualized by ordinary genera-

[1] Anselm complained of this same misapprehension of the notion of a species, on the part of Roscellin and the Nominalists He contended that general conceptions were not mere flatus vocis, but denoted *substances* "Nondum intellegit," he says of Roscellin "quomodo plures hommes in specie sint unus homo; non potest intelligere aliquid esse hominem, nisi individuum" Baur · Dreieinigkeitslehre, II 411 sq.

tion, and which individualized part has the very same properties that the common mass has, but a different *form.* Suppose that a bit of clay is broken off from a larger mass, and then moulded into a cup. This cup now has an individual *form* that is peculiar to itself, such as it did not have before it was broken off and moulded. This cup still has all the specific properties of clay; such as extension, color, mineral and earthy elements, etc. But the clay that is in this individual cup, is not the clay that is left in the lump from which it was broken off. Nor is it the clay that is in other individual cups, that have been formed from other pieces broken off from the lump. Neither is this cup a piece of clay without properties, to which a certain set of properties belonging to the lump are *added;* but it is simply a piece of the lump itself, having all the essential properties of the clay, but with an individual shape peculiar to itself. Take another illustration of individuality. There is a definite and fixed amount of carbon in the universe. A certain part of it is individualized under the providential law of crystallization, and becomes a black diamond; and a certain other part of it is individualized by the same method, and becomes the Kohinoor. The substance of each of these individual diamonds is a fraction of carbon, taken from the original sum total of carbon in the universe. But the form, or *individuality*, of the one is quite different from that of the other. And no atom of the carbon that enters into the black diamond enters into the Kohinoor. Similarly, no integrant of that portion of "human nature" which constitutes the individual Peter, is an integrant of the individual John. But John is as truly human as Peter. The common properties of human nature belong to each alike.[1]

[1] The inquiry may arise whether carbon, here, is not a species, and the crystal an individual under it—contrary to what was said on p. 69, respecting the inorganic sphere. The reply is, that the crystal though having an individuality has not a *specific* individuality. This requires that the individual be produced by propagation, and have no other properties than those which are in the specific substance. But a crystal is not produced by propagation, and even in the in-

Another illustration of individuality is furnished by the magnetic stone. If it be broken into small fragments, each piece will be a complete magnet by itself, having all the qualities of the original unity. Each fragment will have its magnetic poles, and its point of indifference, like the undivided mass. The only difference will be in the quantity and the form; that is, in the individuality of the piece.

The question respecting the priority of the universal (the species) and the individual (res) arises here. Whether the universal is prior to the individuals, depends upon *what* individuals are meant. If the first two individuals of a species are in mind, then the universal, i.e. the species, is not prior, but simultaneous (universale in re). The instant God created the first pair of human individuals, he created the human nature or species in and with them. But if the individuals subsequent to the first pair are in mind, then the universal, i.e. the species, is prior to the individuals (universale ante rem). God created the human nature in Adam and Eve before their posterity were produced out of it.

Accordingly, the doctrine of "universale ante rem" is the true realism, in case "res" denotes the individuals of the *posterity*. The species as a single nature is created and exists prior to its distribution by propagation. The universal as a species exists before the individuals (res) formed out of it. And the doctrine of "universale in re" is the true realism, in case "res" denotes only the *first pair* of individuals. The specific nature as created and existing in these two primitive individuals (res) is not prior to them, but simultaneous with them.[1]

stance of the diamond, which is the purest form of carbon, it is not absolutely, free from other properties than those of carbon, while anthracite, charcoal, and graphite, and other individual forms of carbon are highly impure Carbon, however, is one of those general terms which denote an objective reality within the sphere of inorganic being, and so far goes to prove the truth of realism The original sum total of carbon is as objectively real, as any one of its individualized parts.

[1] On realism and nominalism, see Hasse: Anselm, II. 77; Neander History, IV. 356; Dorner. Person of Christ, II. 377, Ueberweg. History of Philoso-

Traducianism, or propagation, on the side of the body presents less difficulty, and is adopted by creationism. It should not be confined to the body but extended to the soul, for the following physiological reasons:

1. Man at every point in his history, embryonic as well as foetal, is a *union* of soul and body, of mind and matter He is both psychical and physical. There is no instant, when he is a mere brute. An embryo without a rational principle in it would be brutal, not human. The human embryo is only *potentially* a human body; and it is also potentially a human soul. The development of the psychical part keeps pace with that of the physical. The body of a new-born infant is as distant from the body of manhood, as the mind of a new-born infant is from the mind of manhood. That the human egg-cell under the microscope cannot be distinguished from the canine egg-cell, does not prove that the two are identical in species. If they were, the evolution of one into a man and the other into a dog is unaccountable. There must be a psychical principle in one that is not in the other, which makes the difference in the growth and development of each. The fact that there is no manifestation of mind, does not prove that there is no mental principle in the human embryo. The new-born child reveals moral and mental traits as little as does the unborn child. Foeticide is murder in the eye of God, and of a pure human conscience; but it could not be, unless there is rational as well as animal life in that which is killed. Were there merely and only a physical entity without a psychical, the extinguishment of this life would no more be criminal than the crushing of a caterpillar. Creationists themselves suppose a very early creation of the individual soul, and its infusion into the body. Some make the date, the fortieth day after conception.

In the foetal state, the soul sleeps as it does in the in-

---

phy, I 365 sq, Baur Dreieinigkeit, II. 406 sq, Baumgarten-Crusius. De vero scholasticorum realium et nominalium discrimine.

fant, or the adult; only it is a continual sleep. But the soul is as really existent in its sleeping state, as in its waking state. "Sleep," says Saumerez (Physiology, I. 231), "is that condition of the system when the sentient and rational principles have a total suspension of action, when external impressions are of none effect, and the mind itself is in a dormant state. Such is the natural condition of the foetal state, that the various substances are absent upon which the organs of sense and of sensation are destined to act; and the organs themselves are not properly evolved. Sleep, therefore, must be its natural condition."

2. The creation of the soul subsequently to the conception of the body, and its infusion into it, is contrary to all the analogies in nature. Under the common providence of God, as seen in nature, one portion of a living organism is not first propagated, and then a second part created and *added* to it. Composition and juxtaposition of parts is not the method in propagation; but generation and growth of the *whole* individual creature at once, and altogether. "Nature," says Bolingbroke, borrowing from Bacon, "does not proceed as a statuary proceeds in forming a statue, who works, sometimes on the face, sometimes on one part, and sometimes on another; but 'rudimenta partium omnium simul parit et producit:' she throws out altogether, and at once, the whole system of every being, and the rudiments of all the parts. The vegetable or the animal grows in bulk, and increases in strength; but it is the same from the first." Patriot King. So, too, the soul and the body have a parallel, and equal growth.

> "Nature, crescent, does not grow alone
> In thews and bulk; but as this temple waxes,
> The inward service of the mind and soul
> Grows wide withal."—HAMLET, I. III.

3. If the body is propagated and the soul created, the body is six thousand years older than the soul, in the in-

stance of an individual of this generation. Personal identity is jeoparded by such an hypothesis.

The doctrine of the creation of a specific nature that is psychical as well as physical, and its individualization by propagation, is a mystery like that of all creation ex nihilo, and is a matter of faith. The creation of all mankind in Adam cannot be explained. All that can be done, is to keep the doctrine clear of self-contradiction. "By faith we rationally understand (*νοοῦμεν*) that the worlds were framed by the word of God," Heb. 11:3. By the exercise of the same kind of reasonable faith, we understand that all men existed and apostatized in the first human pair. The fall in Adam is a doctrine of revealed religion, not of natural religion. Human consciousness and observation teach the doctrine of sin, but not of the sin in Adam. If the Scriptures teach this, and the symmetry of doctrine requires it, and all the analogies of nature favor it, and it explains other doctrines that are inexplicable without it, then it is rational to hold it as a constituent part of the Christian system. And in some form or other, the sin in Adam is affirmed in all evangelical anthropologies.

But like all the mysteries of the Christian religion, there is an element of reason and intelligence in this mystery, and it is possible to say something in its defence. The following particulars are to be noted, in this reference:

1. The distinction between "nature" and "person" required in Traducianism, is acknowledged to be valid in both Trinitarianism and Christology. God is one nature in three persons. Christ is one person in two natures. In these spheres, the general term "nature" denotes an objective entity or substance, as much as the general term "person" Realism, not nominalism, is the philosophy adopted by the church, when constructing the doctrines of the Trinity and the God-man Traducianism carries this same distinction into anthropology. Man was originally one single human nature, which by propagation became millions of persons.

This human nature was as much an objective reality as the Divine nature. And a human person is of course a reality.

2. The individualization, or personalizing, of a common nature in and by its issuing persons, is wholly different in anthropology from what it is in theology. Human generation is infinitely diverse from eternal generation and procession. Each trinitarian person is the *whole* Divine nature in a particular mode or "form of God," Phil. 2:6; but each human person is only a *portion* of the human nature in a particular mode or form of man. In trinitarianism, there is no division and distribution of essence; but in anthropology there is. The persons of the trinity are, each one of them, the same numerical essence, identical, and *entire.* When it is said, that the Son is "of" the essence of the Father, the preposition ἐκ is not used partitively, as it is when it is said that an individual man is "of" the substance of mankind. The trinitarian persons are also said to be "in" the essence—a preposition never used respecting a human person. God the Father is not a portion of the Divine essence, but is the whole essence in that hypostasis. The same is true of the Son, and the Spirit. But a human person is only a part of the specific human nature. If we should suppose God to create a human species that was intended to be propagated into a million of human persons or individuals, and that the distribution of substance was to be mathematically equal in every instance, then each individual of such a species would be one-millionth part of it.

Adam and Eve were two human persons created by God, on the sixth day. In and with them, God also created the entire invisible nature of the human species; the masculine side of it in Adam, the feminine in Eve. This nature was complex: being both psychical and physical, spiritual and material.[1] Adam and Eve procreated Cain "in their own image and likeness," Gen. 5:3. As they were each of

[1] Creationism asserts that it was incomplex and simple. It was only physical and material.

them a synthesis and union of body and soul, so was their son. This son was an individualized part of the psychico-physical nature that was created and included in the parents. Abel was another individualized part. Four individuals now constituted, and also included the human species, instead of two as at first. "Human nature" was now comprised in four persons, instead of two. By ordinary generation, the specific nature was still further subdivided and individualized into millions of persons. There is no creation ex nihilo in this process, but procreation out of an existing substance. He who looked upon Adam and Eve in Eden, the moment after their creation, saw the whole human race in its first form And he who shall look on the millions of individuals in the day of judgment, will see the same human race in its last form. The difference between the two visions is formal, not material.

3. The conception of a "nature" or "specific substance" must be kept metaphysical in Anthropology, as it is in Theology and Christology. All visible and ponderable elements must be banished, and we must think of a substance that is unextended, invisible, and formless. It was at this point, that Tertullian and other traducianists erred. They attempted to explain the mystery by "atoms," "corpuscles," and "animalcules."

In conceiving of the one human nature of which all individual men are portions, we are to think of an invisible, in accordance with Heb. 11 : 3. "The things which are seen were not made of things that do appear." Visibilities were made out of invisibilities. This way of conceiving is possible, so far as the psychical or mental side of the human nature is concerned. The mind of man is substance; yet spiritual substance, occupying no space and having no form. It is also possible, so far as the physical or bodily side of the human nature is concerned. For scientific physiology cannot stop with the microscopic cell. It goes back of this, to the invisible life which no microscope can exhibit, as the ultimate or metaphysical mode of the human body. The vital principle is as invisible as the human spirit itself, though it is animal, not rational entity or substance. We can think of the invisible substance or formative principle of a human body as still in existence, although the body as a visible organization and an extended form has been dissolved to dust for centuries. The body of Alexander the Great, as an invisible, is still a part of the physical universe. It has not been annihilated. And yet it is as difficult to explain its present existence, as to explain its existence in Adam. "The life," says our Lord, "is more than the meat." The invisible principle that animates the body is "more," that is, more *real* and *permanent*, than the food that nourishes it, or even the material elements which it builds up into a visible form.

The elder Edwards was unquestionably tending towards the Augustinian doctrine of a specific human nature, in his scheme of a unity of Adam and his posterity constituted by Divine omnipotence working after the manner of a continual creation, in unifying the *acts* and *affections* of the posterity. The defect in this, is the absence of an underlying *substance*, to be the ground and support of the phenomenal acts and exercises. Adam's posterity lack substantial being in him, on this theory. Had Edwards definitely employed the old category of "substance," instead of "a communion and coexistence in acts and affections" (Original Sin, Works, II. 483), he would have simply reaffirmed the doctrine of Augustine, of the more orthodox of the schoolmen, and of the theologians of the Reformation—namely, that the posterity were one in Adam as "natura," "massa," "substantia." A mere "unity of acts and affections" brought about by a Divine constitution, would not be a unity of nature and substantial being. Neither is this conceivable. For acts and affections require a subject; and this subject must be either an individual substance, or a specific substance; either an individual soul, as the creationist postulates, or a specific one, as the traducianist contends.

In some places Edwards, however, suggests that there may be unity of *substance* between Adam and his posterity "From these things," he says (Original Sin, Works, II. 487), "it will clearly follow that identity of consciousness depends wholly on a law of nature, and so on the sovereign will and agency of God; and therefore, that personal identity, and so the derivation of the pollution and guilt of past sins in the same person, depends on an arbitrary divine *constitution;* and this, even though we should allow the same consciousness not to be the only thing which constitutes oneness of person, but should, beside that, suppose *sameness of substance* requisite. For even this oneness of created substance, existing at different times, is merely *dependent* identity—dependent on the pleasure and sovereign constitution of him who worketh all in all"

The following are the principal objections urged against the theory of Traducianism:

1. It is said that it conflicts with the doctrine of Christ's sinlessness. It does not, if the doctrine of the miraculous conception is held. The Scriptures teach that the human nature of our Lord was perfectly sanctified, in and by his conception by the Holy Ghost Sanctification implies that the nature needed sanctification. Had Christ been born of Mary's substance in the ordinary manner, he would have been a sinful man. His humanity prior to conception was an undividualized part of the common human nature. He was the "seed of the woman," the "seed of David." As such simply, his human nature was like that of Mary and of David, fallen and sinful. It is denominated "sinful flesh," in Rom. 8: 3. It required perfect sanctification before it could be assumed into union with the second trinitarian person, and it obtained it through the miraculous conception. Says Pearson (Creed, Art. III.), "the original and total sanctification of the human nature was first

necessary, to fit it for the personal union with the Word, who out of his infinite love humbled himself to become flesh, and at the same time out of his infinite purity could not defile himself by becoming sinful flesh. The human nature was formed by the Spirit, and in its formation sanctified, and in its sanctification united to the Word." See Christology, pp. 29–35; Shedd. Romans, 8:3.

Theologians have confined their attention mainly to the sanctification of Christ's human nature, saying little about its *justification*. But a complete Christology must include the latter as well as the former. Any nature that requires *sanctification* requires *justification;* because sin is guilt as well as pollution. The Logos could not unite with a human nature taken from the Virgin Mary, and transmitted from Adam, unless it had previously been delivered from both the condemnation and the corruption of sin. The idea of *redemption*, also, includes both justification and sanctification; and it is conceded that that portion of human nature which the Logos assumed into union with himself was redeemed. His own humanity was the "first fruits" of his redemptive work. "Christ the first fruits, afterwards they that are Christ's," 1 Cor. 15:23. Consequently, the doctrine is not fully constructed, unless this side of it is presented.

So far, then, as the guilt of Adam's sin rested upon that unindividualized portion of the common fallen nature of Adam assumed by the Logos, it was expiated by the one sacrifice on Calvary. The human nature of Christ was prepared for the personal union with the Logos, by being justified, as well as sanctified "God was manifested in the flesh, was justified (ἐδικαιώθη) by (ἐν) the Spirit," 1 Tim. 3:16. Here, the "flesh" denotes the entire humanity, psychical and physical, and it was "justified." The justification in this instance, like that of the Old Testament believers, was proleptical, in view of the future atoning death of Christ.[1]

[1] That the antithesis, here, between σάρξ and πνεῦμα, is the same as in 1 Pet. 3.18, and Rom. 1 3, 4. namely, between the humanity and the divinity in

The gracious redemption of the humanity which the Logos assumed into union with himself, is a familiar point in the patristic Christology. Augustine (Enchiridion, xxxvi.) teaches it as follows: "Wherefore was this unheard-of glory of being united with deity conferred on human nature—a glory which, as there was no antecedent merit, was of course wholly of grace—except that here those who have looked at the matter soberly and honestly might behold a clear manifestation of the power of God's free grace, and might understand that they are justified from their sins *by the same grace* which made the man Christ Jesus free from the possibility of sin?" To the same effect, Athanasius (Contra Arianos, II. lxi.) says that Christ's human nature was "first saved and redeemed (ἐσώθη καὶ ἠλευθερώθη), and so became the means of our salvation and redemption."

2. It is objected that traducianism implies division of substance, and that all division implies extended material substance. Not necessarily. When it is said that that which is divisible is material, divisibility by *man* is meant. It is the separation of something that is visible, extended, and ponderable, by means of material instruments. But there is another kind of divisibility that is effected by the Creator, by means of a law of propagation established for this purpose. God can divide and distribute a primary substance that is not visible, extended, and ponderable, and yet is real, by a method wholly different from that by which a man divides a piece of clay into two portions. There is an example of this even in the propagation of the body. Here, individual physical life is derived from specific physical life. But this is division of life. Imponderable physi-

Christ's person, is plain from the context If this be so, the dative is instrumental in both instances; denoting the agency by which the action of the verb is brought about. "God was manifested by the humanity, and justified by the Divinity" The "justification" of the human nature was through the atonement made by the Divine nature incarnate. This view of the antithesis between σάρξ and πνεῦμα was taken generally by the older commentators. Of modern exegetes, it is adopted by Wiesinger.

cal substance is separated from imponderable physical substance. An individual body is not animated by the total physical life of the species, but by a derived part of it. That invisible principle which constitutes the reality and identity of the individual human body (p. 65 sq.) is abscided, invisibly, and mysteriously, from the specific physical nature of man.[1] But this process is wholly different from the division of extended and visible substance by human modes. Animal life in its last analysis is as invisible as psychical life, and is as little capable of human divisibility.

Accordingly, the advocates of traducianism distinguish between physical and psychical propagation. Maresius, a Reformed theologian of high authority, refers to this distinction in the following terms: "Whatever be the origin of the soul, these three things are to be held as fixed and certain: First, that the soul is immortal; second, that God is not the author of sin; third, that we are born from Adam corrupt and depraved. It would not be more difficult to harmonize the propagation of the soul with its immateriality and immortality, than to harmonize the creation of each individual soul with the propagation of original sin. Only it must be remembered that the propagation in this instance is not a coarse (crassam) material propagation from animal substance, but a subtile spiritual derivation from a mental essence similar to that of the light of one candle propagating itself to another." Theologia Elenchtica, Controversia XI. Heppe (Reformirter Dogmatik, XI.) quotes the testimony of Riissen: "Communior est sententia eorum, qui volunt animam esse ex traduce; i.e., animam traduci ex anima, non per decisionem aut partitionem animae paternae, sed modo quodem spirituali, ut lumen accenditur de lumine Nos autem statuimus, animas omnes immediate a deo creari, et creando infundi."

But if there may be division and derivation of invisible

[1] A species or specific nature is divisible, but an individual is not—as the etymology (in-dividuus) implies.

substance, in the case of the body, there may be in the case of the soul. It is the invisibility and imponderability that constitutes the difficulty, and if this is no bar to propagation in respect to the physical part of man, it is not in respect to the psychical part. When God by means of his own law of propagation derives an individual soul from a specific psychical nature, he does not sever and separate substance in any material manner. The words of our Lord may be used by way of accommodation here: "That which is born of the spirit is spirit." Psychical propagation yields a psychical product. When God causes an individual soul to be conceived and born simultaneously with the conception and birth of an individual body, that entity which he thus derives out of the psychical side of the specific human nature is really and truly mind, not matter. "Deus est qui nos personat," says Augustine. God is the author of our personality. If he can *create* an entity which at the very first instant of its existence is a spiritual and self-determined substance, then certainly he can *propagate* an entity that is a spiritual and self-determined substance. The propagation of the soul involves no greater difficulty than its creation. If creation may be associated with both spirit and matter, without materializing the former, so may propagation. We do not argue that if spirit is created, it must be material because matter is created. And neither should we argue that if spirit is propagated, it must be material because matter is propagated. God creates matter as matter, and mind as mind. And he propagates matter as matter, and mind as mind. We continually speak of the "growth of the soul," "the development of the mind." These are primarily physical terms, but we apply them literally to a spiritual substance, not supposing that we thereby materialize it. Why may we not, then, speak of the "propagation" or "derivation" of a soul without thereby materializing it?

If the distinction between creation and propagation is

carefully observed, there is no danger of materialism in the doctrine of the soul's propagation. For propagation cannot *change the qualities* of that which is being propagated. Propagation is only *transmission* of something that has already been created, and which is already in existence The quality is *fixed* by the original creative act. Propagation consequently can only yield what is given in creation. If we grant, therefore, that God did create the human species in its *totality*, as a complex of matter and mind, body and soul, physical substance and mental substance, it is plain that the mere individualizing of this species by propagation must leave matter and mind, body and soul, just as it finds them. Matter cannot be converted into mind by being conceived and born, and neither can mind be converted into matter by propagation Propagation makes no alteration of qualities, because propagation is transmission only. Both sides of man, the physical and the psychical, will therefore retain their original created qualities and characteristics in this process of procreation, which, it must be remembered, is the Creator's work, carried on by means of laws which he has established for this very purpose of propagating a species, and which is conducted under his immediate and continual providence. That which is body, or physical, will be propagated as body; and that which is soul, or psychical, will be propagated as soul; and this because propagation is merely transmission, and makes no changes in the created qualities of that which is propagated or transmitted.[1]

Propagation implies continuity of substance, and immutability of properties In the propagation of the body, there is continuity of substance and sameness of properties, between the producing and the produced individuals; between the parents and the child. There is no creation ex nihilo, of new substance and properties. In every instance

[1] Shedd Theological Essays, 252. Delitzsch. Biblical Psychology, VII. p. 137

of bodily conception, a certain amount of cellular substance which has been secreted and prepared by the invisible physical life issues, and is transformed into a child's embryo. The child, physically considered, is a part of the specific human nature transmitted through the parents, and by their instrumentality formed into a separate individual body. It is an *off*spring from them. Now suppose this continuity of substance and unchangeableness of properties in the instance of psychical or spiritual substance, and we have the propagation of the soul. Spiritual substance is transmitted under the same providential law by which physical substance is. The soul of the child, simultaneously with his body, is derived psychically out of the common human nature, which is both psychical and physical, upon the traducian theory.

Traducianism would be liable to the charge of materialism, if it maintained either of the two following positions: 1. That the soul is *originated* by propagation. 2. That the soul is propagated by *physical* propagation. Neither of these positions belong to the theory. In the first place, traducianism contends as strenuously as creationism that the human soul is the product of creative power, only, this power was exerted once on the sixth day, not millions of times subsequently. The origin of the soul is supernatural, on this theory as well as on the other. The human soul as specific was not an evolution from physical substance, but a creation ex nihilo of spiritual substance. Propagation merely transmits and individualizes what was given in creation In the second place, the transmission is not by a physical but a psychical propagation. There is nothing in the term "propagate" that necessarily implies materialism Before this can be charged, it must be asked: What *kind* of substance is it that is propagated; and by what *kind* of propagation? To assert that there is only one kind and mode of propagation, and that propagation can only mean the propagation of matter, is to beg the question.

3. It is objected, that upon the traducian theory all the sinful acts of Adam and Eve ought to be imputed to their posterity, as well as the first sin. The reply is, that the sinful acts of Adam and Eve after the fall differed from the act of eating of the forbidden fruit in two respects: 1. They were transgressions of the moral law, not of the probationary statute. 2. They were not committed by the entire race in and with Adam.

In the first place, by the Divine arrangement in the covenant of works, it was only that particular act of disobedience that related to the positive statute given in Eden that was to be probationary. This statute and this transgression alone were to test the obedience of the race. God never gave this commandment a second time. The command not to eat of the tree of knowledge of good and evil would be superfluous after the fall. Fallen man had got the knowledge. Consequently, all sins subsequent to this one peculiar transgression of a peculiar statute belonged to a different class from the first sin, because they were transgressions of the moral law, and the moral law was not the statute chosen by God to decide man's probation. According to Rom. 5 : 15–19, Adam and his posterity were to stand or fall according as they did not, or did commit this *one* sin, and this only. Postlapsarian sins were violations of the moral law, not of the probationary law. Rom. 5 : 13, 14 teaches that infants sinned in Adam against the probationary statute only. They did not sin "after the *similitude* of Adam's transgression," but sinned Adam's transgression itself. They did not commit individual transgressions *like* Adam's first transgression, by sinning against either the law of conscience or the written law, but they sinned Adam's identical transgression. The fact that "death passes" upon them, as upon all of Adam's posterity, proves this.

Secondly, only the first act of sin is imputed, because the entire posterity were in Adam and Eve when it was committed, but ceased to be in them afterwards. Unity of nature and participation are the ground of the imputation of the first sin. When this unity is broken even in the least, the ground is taken from under imputation, and imputation ceases. The conception of the first individual of the species destroys the original unity. When Cain was begotten, his separate individual existence began. He was no longer "in Adam;" and no longer an unindividualized part of the species. He was now the *off*spring of Adam and Eve; an individualized part of the human nature that was created on the sixth day. He received and inherited the corruption that was now in human nature, and subsequently acted it out in individual transgressions. His natural and substantial union with his progenitors being at an end, whatever transgressions they might commit were no sins of his, and whatever sins he might commit were no sins of theirs. With reference to the first sin committed by Adam and Eve before the conception of any individual man, St Paul (Rom. 5 : 18, 19) says: "By one offence, judgment came upon all men to condemnation; by one man's disobedience many were made sinners." With reference to the subsequent individual sins committed after the conception of the first individual man, Ezekiel (18 : 20) says · "The soul that sinneth, it shall die The son shall not bear the iniquity of the father, neither shall the father bear the iniquity of the son."

When the advocate of representative union is asked why the sins of Adam after the first sin are not imputed to the posterity, his answer is, that Adam ceased to represent; ceased to be a public person. In like manner, the advocate of natural union replies to the same inquiry, that Adam ceased to be the race-unity postulated in order to the imputation of the first sin. The moment the individualization of the nature begins by propagation, the unity is at an end. If it be objected, that at least the individual transgressions of Adam and Eve during the interval between the first sin and the conception of Cain must be imputed to the posterity, because the entire posterity are still in Adam and Eve during this interval, the reply is, that the imputation, even in this case, would not lie upon any *individual persons* of the posterity, for there are none, but only upon the non-individualized nature. These personal transgressions of Adam, if charged at all, could be charged only upon the species. But the fact, already mentioned, namely, that it was the transgression of the Eden statute, and not of the moral law, that was made the probationary sin by the Divine arrangement, shows that the personal transgressions of Adam after his first sin would not be imputable even to the non-individualized nature in him.

The first two individuals *included* the species, but considered simply as individuals were not the species. Adam and Eve viewed as individuals were not the entire human race, but contained it. So Milton, Paradise Lost, IX. 414:

> "Where likeliest he might find
> The only two of mankind, *but in them*
> *The whole included race*, his destined prey."

"In Adam, as a common receptacle, the whole nature of man was reposited, from him to flow down in a channel to his posterity; for all mankind 'is made of one blood,' Acts 17:26, so that according as this nature proves through his standing or falling, before he puts it out of his hands, accordingly it is propagated from him. Adam, therefore, falling and sinning, the nature became guilty and corrupted, and is so derived. Thus in him 'all have sinned.'" Matthew Henry: On Rom. 5:12. The specific nature was a deposited invisible substance in the first human pair. The prepositions "in" and "with," in the clause, "sinned in and fell with," imply this. As thus deposited by creation in Adam and Eve, it was to be transmitted. In like manner, every individual man along with his individuality receives, not as Adam did, the *whole* human nature but a fraction of it, to transmit and individualize. Every individual is to assist in perpetuating his species. Gen. 1 : 28.[1] Every man, consequently, includes a portion of non-individualized human nature transmitted to him from his ancestors immediately, and from Adam primarily. When, and so long as, Adam and Eve were the only two individuals, the entire species was in two individuals. When, and so long as, Adam, Eve, and Cain were the only three individuals, the whole species was in three. At this present moment of time, the whole species consists of millions of individuals ; namely, of the millions now living in this world together with the non-individualized human nature in them, and the disembodied millions in the other world who include no non-individualized substance, because they " are as the angels of God," Matt. 22 : 30. Thus it appears that the human nature was *single*, *entire*, and *undivided*, only in those first two individuals in whom it was created. All individuals excepting the first two include each but a fractional part of human nature. A sin committed by a fraction is not a sin committed by the whole unity. Individual transgression is not the original transgression, or Adam's first sin.

Hence it follows, that what is strictly and purely individual in a human person must not be confounded with what is specific in him. As an individual, he sins individually ; but what he does in this individual manner does not affect that portion of fallen human nature which he receives to transmit. This fractional part of the nature does not " sin in and with " the individual containing and transmitting it. He may be regenerated as an individual, but this does not regenerate that part of the human species which he includes, and which he is to individualize by generation. His children are born unregenerate. Regeneration is individual

[1] It is certainly an error, when Baird (Elohim, p 356), asserts that "the blood of Cain and Abel does not now flow in any human veins, that human nature is not any longer transmitted from them, but that Seth is the father of the present population of the earth." The line of Seth was that of the church, and that of Cain, of the world as the opposite of the church. Both individuals were concerned in the propagation of the species.

only, not specific. It is founded upon an election out of an aggregate of separate individuals. Consequently, it does not sanctify that fraction of human nature which is deposited in each individual to be propagated. Neither do the individual transgressions of a natural man make the corrupt nature of his children any more corrupt. The non-individualized nature in his person remains just as it came from Adam. Nor are his individual transgressions imputable to his children; because the portion of human nature which he has received, and which he transmits, does not act with him and sin with him in his individual transgressions. It is a latent nature or principle which remains in a quiescent state, in reference to his individuality. It is inactive, as existing in him. It does not add to, or subtract from his individual power. It constitutes no part of his individuality. Not until it is individualized, and being separated from the progenitor becomes a distinct person by itself, does it begin to act out the sinful disposition originated in it when Adam fell.

It is no valid objection to the doctrine of existence in Adam, and in foregoing ancestors, that it is impossible to explain the mode The question: "How can these things be?" as in the instance of Nicodemus, must be answered by the affirmation that it is a fact, and a mystery. It is no refutation of the doctrine, to ask how the nature exists before it is individualized or procreated, any more than it is a refutation of the doctrine of the resurrection, to ask how the invisible substance of a human body still continues to exist after death. We know the fact from Scripture; and science also confirms it by its maxim that there is no annihilation of rudimental substance in the created universe. The body of Julius Caesar is still in being, as to its fundamental invisible substance, whatever that substance may be. Resurrection, though miraculous, is not the creation of a body ex nihilo. In like manner, the elementary invisible substance of the individual Julius Caesar, both as to soul and body, was in existence between the time of the creation of the whole human species on the sixth day, and the time of the conception of Julius Caesar. The Westminster Shorter Catechism (Q. 37) states that the bodies of believers, "being still united to Christ, do rest in their graves till the resurrection." This implies that the believer's body, as to its invisible substance, continues to exist for hundreds or thousands of years between its death and its resurrection. But this kind of existence is no more mysterious than the existence of the human nature in Adam, and its continued existence between Adam and the year 1875. In one sense, the posterity of Adam are as old as Adam; the children as old as the parents. The human nature out of which all individuals are derived was created on the sixth day, and all sustain the same relation to it so far as the time of its creation is concerned The Seyn of all was then, though the Daseyn was not; the noumenon, though not the phenomenon, was in existence.

It is important to distinguish traits that are derived and inherited from secondary ancestors, either immediate or remote, and traits that are derived and inherited from the first ancestors. To inherit the gout from one's father, is very different from inheriting the carnal mind from Adam. Such inherited idiosyncrasies are not sinful, though they tempt to sin A hankering for alcohol or opium may be inherited from a grandfather or father, without culpability for it; but pride, and enmity towards God are inherited from Adam, and are accompanied with a sense of guilt. To inherit a temperament, is to inherit a secondary trait. A choleric temper is not guilt. But envy and hatred are. The testimony of conscience in each case is different. These qualities inherited from secondary ancestors may run themselves out in a few generations. But original sin never runs itself out. The former are conquerable without grace; some persons overcome their hankering for alcohol and opium without regeneration. But original sin is unconquerable without regeneration.

Derivation and inheritance of sinful character is compatible with responsibility for sinful character, provided that while it is derived and inherited at a *secondary* point, it is *self-originated* at a *primary* one. If sinful character be derived at both the primary and the secondary points, then responsibility is impossible. The individual man derives and inherits his sinful disposition from his immediate ancestors, but originated it in his first ancestors. He is born sinful from his father and mother, but was created holy in Adam and Eve. But if he had derived his sinfulness at *both* points; if sin in Adam had been derived from God; then its transmission from Adam to the posterity would not have involved any responsibility or fault. In Ps. 50:5, David mentions the fact that he was born sinful, as an *aggravation* of his particular act of adultery, not as an excuse for it. It evinced the depth and intensity of his wickedness. This could not be, if to be born sinful is the same thing as to be *created* sinful.

The difficulty in regard to existence in Adam, the first ancestor, is really no greater than the difficulty in regard to existence in the immediate ancestors. The mystery is only farther off.

## CHAPTER II.

### MAN'S PRIMITIVE STATE.

Augustine: City of God, XII. i.–ix. xxiii. Anselm: De Casu Diaboli, XII. Aquinas: Summa, II. xciii.–xcvii. Calvin: Institutes, I. xv. Ursinus: Christian Religion, Qu. 6. Turrettin: Institutio, V. ix–xii Howe: Oracles, Lectures XVI–XX. Muller: Sin, IV. iv. Edwards: Original Sin, II i; Efficacious Grace, § 43–51. Hodge: Theology, II 92–15. Strong: Theology, 262–268. Shedd: History of Doctrine, II. 54–65. Smith: Theology, 252–259.

Holiness, in the order, is prior to sin. Man must be holy, before he can be sinful. "The good," says Plato (Protagoras, 344), "may become bad; but the bad does not become bad; he is always bad." Similarly, Aristotle (Categories, IX. v.) remarks that *τὸ βέλτιον καὶ τό τιμιώτερον πρότερον εἶναι τῇ φύσει δοκεῖ.* The golden age of the poets is the echo and corruption of the Biblical account of man's original state. Tacitus describes the earliest generation of men as follows: "Vetustissimi mortalium, nulla adhuc mala libidine, sine probro, scelere, eoque sine poena aut coercitationibus, agebant: neque praemiis opus erat, cum honesta suopte ingenio peterentur: et ubi nihil contra morem cuperent, nihil per metum vetabantur" Annalium, III. 26.

The Westminster statement is the common one in the Augustino-Calvinistic creeds: "God created man after his own image, in knowledge, righteousness, and holiness," S. C, 10. "God said, Let us make man in our own image. So God created man in his own image," Gen. 1:26, 27. "God hath made man upright; but they have sought out many inventions," Eccl. 7:29. "The new man is renewed in knowledge after the image of him that created him," Coloss. 3:10.

Holiness is more than innocence. It is not sufficient to say that man was created in a state of innocence. This would be true, if he had been destitute of a moral disposition either right or wrong. Man was made not only negatively innocent, but positively holy. Man's regenerate condition is a restoration of his primitive state; and his righteousness as regenerate is described as κατὰ ϑεόν, Eph. 4:21; and as "true holiness," Eph. 4:24. This is positive character, not mere innocency.

Con-created holiness is one of the distinguishing tenets of Augustinianism. Pelagianism denies that holiness is con-created. It asserts that the will of man by creation, and in its first condition, is characterless. Its first act is to originate either holiness or sin. "Non pleni nascimur;" we are not born full of character. Adam's posterity are born, as he was created, without holiness and without sin. Pelagius, quoted by Augustine: De peccato originis, XIII. Semi-Pelagianism holds the same opinion; excepting that it concedes a transmission of a vitiated physical nature, which Pelagianism denies. So far as the rational and voluntary nature of man is concerned, the Semi-Pelagian asserts that holiness like sin must be self-originated by each individual. The Tridentine anthropology is a mixture of Pelagianism and Augustinianism. God created man "in puris naturalibus," without either holiness or sin. This creative act, which left man characterless, God followed with another act by which he endowed man with holiness. Holiness was something supernatural, and not contained in the first creative act. Creation is, thus, imperfect, and is improved by an after-thought. In the Modern church, the Calvinists and early Lutherans adopted the Augustinian view. The Arminians and some of the later Lutherans reject the doctrine of con-created holiness.

Holiness has two sides or phases: 1. It is *perception* and *knowledge*. As such, it relates to the understanding. God and divine things must be apprehended, in order to holiness. 2. It is *inclination* and *feeling*. As such, it relates to the will and affections. God and divine things must be desired and delighted in, in order to holiness.

1. The *knowledge* in which man was created, was the knowledge of God. It was conscious and spiritual, in distinction from speculative. It was that immediate and practical apprehension spoken of in 1 Cor 2:14, "The things of the Spirit are spiritually discerned." This is proved: (*a*) By the fact that regeneration "is a renewal in knowledge," after the Divine image, Coloss. 3:10; but regeneration restores what man had by creation. (*b*) By the fact that being associated with love and reverence, it must have been experimental.

The knowledge possessed by Adam and Eve before the fall was different from what it was after. This is proved by Gen. 2:25, "They were naked and were not ashamed." They were conscious of holiness, and had no consciousness of sin. But apostasy brought with it the conscious knowledge of evil. Gen. 3:7, "The eyes of both of them were opened, and they knew that they were naked." Gen. 3:22, "God said, Behold the man is become as one of us, to know good and evil." God knows good consciously, and evil, not consciously but, intuitively by his omniscience. Thus his knowledge of both good and evil is perfect; although his knowledge of the former is by a different method from that by which he knows the latter.[1] Unfallen man knew good consciously, and evil only speculatively and

---

[1] The narrative in Genesis speaks of a knowledge like that of "God" (Gen 3:22), and like that of "the gods," or Satan and his angels (Gen 3:5). The knowledge is described from two points of view. Adam, by apostasy, came to have a knowledge of evil *similar* to that of God, in that it was a thorough knowledge, and a knowledge *identical* with that of Satan, because it was a conscious knowledge. Respecting the knowledge of unfallen Adam, see Augustine: City of God, XXII. xxx., Stillingfleet: Origines Sacrae, I. ii. iii.

theoretically. Hence his knowledge of sin was imperfect. On the other hand, fallen man knew evil consciously, and good only speculatively and theoretically. "The eyes of both of them were opened, and Adam and his wife hid themselves from the presence of the Lord, amongst the trees of the garden," Gen. 3:7, 8. "The natural man receiveth not the things of the Spirit of God; for they are foolishness unto him," 1 Cor. 2:14.

There are two ways of knowing sin: (*a*) As the sinner knows it; and, (*b*) As the saint knows it. A sinful man knows vice by the immediate consciousness of it; a holy angel perceives it as the contrast of his own virtue and purity. The latter knowledge of sin is far inferior in thoroughness to the former. Thus it appears, that in Adam the conscious experimental knowledge of holiness implied only a speculative and inadequate knowledge of sin; and the conscious experimental knowledge of sin implied only a speculative and inadequate knowledge of holiness. Holy man was ignorant of sin; and sinful man was ignorant of holiness. Consciously to know good, is a good; consciously to know evil, is an evil.

2. The *inclination* and *moral disposition* with which man was created, consisted in the perfect harmony of his will with the Divine law The agreement was so perfect and entire, that there was no distinction between the two in holy Adam's consciousness Inclination was duty, and duty was inclination. Unfallen Adam, like the holy angels, did not feel the law to be over him as a taskmaster, but in him like a living actuating principle. In a perfect moral condition, law and will are one; as in the sphere of physical nature, the laws of nature and the forces of nature are identical. It is in this reference that St. Paul (1 Tim. 1:9) affirms that "the law is not made for a righteous man, but for the lawless and disobedient, for the ungodly and for sinners" Law coupled with the threat of punishment, is law in a form suited only to a will at enmity with it. Law when

proclaimed at Sinai to rebellious man is accompanied with thunders and lightnings; but not when proclaimed in heaven to the holy and obedient. Shedd: Sermons to the Spiritual Man, 212–224.

The positive holiness, then, with which man was endowed by creation, consisted in an understanding enlightened in the spiritual knowledge of God and divine things, and a will wholly inclined to them. The following are some of the rational proofs that man was so created.

1. The maturity and perfection of man suppose it. Adam was not created an infant, but an adult. To suppose him to be vacant of the knowledge of God, and of moral character, in this advanced stage of existence, contradicts the idea of complete and mature manhood. A perfect man who has neither the knowledge nor the love of God, is a contradiction.

2. The idea of the will, as a mental faculty, implies a con-created holiness. Inclination enters into the definition of the will, as necessarily as triangularity does into that of a triangle; as intelligence does into that of an understanding; as properties do into that of a substance. To create a will, therefore, is to create an inclination also. If we should suppose God to create a certain faculty which at the instant of its creation was uninclined, and undetermined either to good or evil, it would not be a voluntary faculty. For a voluntary faculty is one that is marked by voluntariness. It is determined and inclined, and evinces thereby that it is a will. If it is destitute of inclination, it is involuntary; and an involuntary will is a solecism To say that it will become voluntary by becoming inclined, does not relieve the difficulty. This is to concede that at present it is not voluntary.

The human will is by creation voluntary, as the human understanding is by creation cognitive. When God creates the understanding, he endows it with innate ideas, and laws of thought, by virtue of which it is an intelligent faculty.

These are the content of the understanding. And when he creates the human will, he endows it with an inclination, or a disposition, or a self-determination, whatever be the term employed, by virtue of which it is a voluntary faculty. This is the content of the will. As the understanding without this created intelligence in its constitution would not be an understanding at all, so the will without this created voluntariness in its constitution would not be a will at all.

3. The creation of a finite mind or spirit implies the creation of holiness. Spiritual substance is distinguished from matter, by the characteristic of self-motion, or motion ab intra. Matter must be moved from without, by another material substance impinging upon it But mind moves from within Its motion is not from external impact, but is self-motion. Adam was created a *spirit.* The instant, therefore, that he was created, he had all the characteristics that distinguish spirit from matter. One of these, and one of the most important, is self-motion. But self-motion is self-determination, and self-determination is inclination.[1] The Scripture asserts that Adam was created a "living soul" Life implies motion; and the motion in this case was not mechanical or material, but the motion of mind. Thus in creating a rational spirit, God creates a self-moving essence, and this is a self-determining will

4. If holiness is not created, the creature improves the Creator's work. Augustine (City of God, XII. ix) thus argues: "Was the good inclination of the good angels created along with them, or did they exist for a time without it? If along with themselves, then doubtless it was created by him who created them; and as soon as ever they were created, they attached themselves to him who created them with that love which he created in them But if the

[1] Throughout this discussion, self-determination is synonymous with spontaneity or inclination.

good angels existed for a time without a good inclination, and produced it in themselves without God's interference, then it follows that they made themselves better than he made them We must therefore acknowledge that not only of holy men, but also of the holy angels, it can be said, that 'the love of God is shed abroad in their hearts, by the Holy Ghost which is given unto them.'"

5. The dependent nature of finite holiness implies that it is created. Uncreated, independent holiness is possible only in a self-existent and self-sustaining Being. Holiness in the creature is ultimately suspended upon the action of the Creator. It is derived from him. In its first beginning, it must be given both to angels and men. "The nature of virtue," says Edwards (Efficacious Grace, §§ 43–51), "being a positive thing, can proceed from nothing but God's immediate influence, and must take its rise from creation, or infusion from God. There can be no one virtuous choice unless God immediately gives it. Reason shows that the *first* existence of a principle of virtue cannot be given from man himself, nor in any created being whatsoever; but must be immediately given from God. God is said, in Scripture, to give true virtue and purity to the heart of man; to work it in him, to create it, to form it; and with regard to it, we are said to be his workmanship. Lev. 20:8, 'I am the Lord which sanctify you;' Rom. 11:26, 27, 'There shall come out of Zion the deliverer, and shall turn away ungodliness from Jacob.'"

Anselm (De casu diaboli, xii.) argues similarly for the derivation of holiness in the finite will. He contends that if the will of man or angel be supposed to be created in a state of indifference, without any inclination whatever, it could not begin any self-motion at all. It would remain indifferent forever, and never have any inclination. A creature with no character will never originate a character. Consequently, the first inclination of the will must be given to the will when the will is made ex nihilo; and since the holy Creator cannot give to his own work a bad inclination, he must give a good one.

6. That holiness is creatable in man, is proved by the facts of regeneration and sanctification. The regeneration of the soul is the origination of holiness a second time, within it. This is described, in Scripture, as "giving a heart of flesh," "renewing a right spirit within," "working in you to will." This phraseology teaches that God produces a holy inclination. Again, such terms as "creating anew," "begetting," "quickening" imply the creation of holiness.

Sanctification likewise proves that holiness is creatable. Sanctification is the increase of holiness; and the increase is by derivation, not by original production. No Christian augments his own holiness by his own isolated decision. The law of sanctification is stated in John 15:4. "Abide in me and I in you: as the branch cannot bear fruit of itself except it abide in the vine, no more can ye except ye abide in me." The vine branch bears fruit spontaneously (*ἀφ' ἑαυτοῦ*). The grape is a vital, not a mechanical product. But this spontaneity is possible to the branch, only in case it is in the vine. Similarly, sanctification is spontaneous and free, yet only as it is derived from Christ the source of holiness. Another passage in point is 2 Cor. 9:8, "God is able to make all grace abound toward you, so that having all sufficiency (*ἀυταρκεῖαν*) in all things, ye may abound to every good work" This "sufficiency" is that genuine and spontaneous inclination to holiness which impels to good acts; but this inclination is "made to abound" in the Christian by the grace of God. These facts prove that the spontaneous motion of the will may be a product of God, as well as a characteristic of man; in other words, that a good inclination, while it is the personal quality of a man, may be likewise a created quality in him.

The arguments that have been presented for the creatability of holiness assume the correctness of the Augustinian definition of voluntariness, or free agency: namely, that it is the spontaneous self-determination of the will. This can be created along with the will, if the will itself can be created. Consequently, it is necessary to establish the correctness of this definition. The freedom of the will is its *self*-motion. That which is self-moved is not forced to move; and that which is not forced to move is free. Simple self-motion or self-determination, therefore, is the freedom of the will. "God hath indued the will of man with that natural liberty that it is neither forced, nor by any absolute necessity of nature determined, to good or evil." Westminster Confession, IX. i. "Voluntarie moveri est ex se moveri, et non ab alio." Aquinas: Summa, I. cv. 4.

It is indispensable to voluntary freedom, that the motion shall proceed from an *ego*, or true *self*. The falling of water, and the rising of sap, is only seeming self-motion. One globule pushes another by mechanical law, or by vital force. No globule is self-moved. Could a man demonstrate that his action, either internal or external, is not the energy of his own personal essence, but that of another personal essence, or is caused by some physical law or force, he would demonstrate that his action is neither voluntary nor free. But if this indispensable characteristic exists, the substance of moral freedom is secured Many things may still be out of the power of the will, for omnipotence is not necessary in order to freedom, yet if the will be really *self*-inclined and *self*-determined in its activity, internal and external, it is a free will. It is important, here, to notice that the *central* as well as the superficial activity of the will must be self-activity, in order to freedom and responsibility. The central action of the will is its steady inclination; and the superficial action is its momentary volition in a particular instance. The murderer's hate is the central activity of his will; the murderer's act is the superficial. Both must be self-moved, in order to responsibility and guilt. And both are self-moved. The murderer is not forced to hate

He is willing in his hatred, and in all his moral desires and feelings; willing in anger, envy, malice, pride, and all forms of sinful inclination. While, however, the central and the superficial activity of the will are alike in regard to free self-motion, they differ in regard to the power to the contrary. The superficial activity, or the volition, is accompanied with this power; the central, or the inclination, is not. The murderer can refrain from the outward act of murder, by a volition; but he cannot refrain from his inward hatred, by a volition. A volition can stop another volition; but a volition cannot stop an inclination. A man can reverse his sinful volition, but not his sinful inclination. This is an indisputable fact of consciousness.

1. It follows from this, that the *power to the contrary*, or of antagonistic action, is not necessary in order to the freedom of the will. Simple self-determination, without the additional power to antagonize the existing self-determination, is enough to constitute voluntariness. If the will move in the direction of holiness by its own self-motion, this fact alone demonstrates the freeness of its action. It is not necessary to add a power to act in opposition to the existing self-motion, in order that the existing self-motion may be *self*-motion; any more than it is necessary to add the power to fly, in order that the power to walk may be a power to walk.[1] When holy Adam was self-determining in holiness, it was not necessary to give him the power to self-determine to sin, in order that he might be self-determining in holiness. The possibilitas peccandi was associated with Adam's primitive state, not in order to his freedom, but in order to his *probation*. If God, by the operation of his Spirit, had preserved Adam from the exercise of an antagonistic and contrary self-determination, Adam would still have been self-determined and spontaneously inclined to

[1] "Fons erroris est, libertatis naturam metiri ex *ἰσοῤῥοπίᾳ*, et ei *τὸ ἀμφιῤῥεπὲς* essentiale facere, cum per lubentiam et spontaneitatem definienda sit." Turrettin Institutio, VI. v. 11.

holiness. And the same is true upon the side of sin. If the will of Satan, or of fallen Adam, is spontaneously self-inclined to sin, this fact alone demonstrates the unforced nature of its sinful action. It is not necessary to add the power to the contrary, i.e., the power to self-incline to holiness, in order that the existing sinful self-inclination may be *self*-inclination. It is not necessary in order to responsibility for a sinful inclination, that the sinner be able to reverse his sinful inclination. It is only necessary, that he was able to *originate* it, and that he did originate it.

That self-determining or inclining is compatible with inability to the contrary, is proved by the following examples. A man wills to be happy. He is free in thus willing, because the action of his will is self-action. It is his own spontaneous inclination. Yet he cannot will the contrary. No man is able to will to be miserable. If the power to the contrary necessarily enters into the definition of freedom along with the power of inclining or self-determining, then this man who wills to be happy is not free in so willing. But if self-determination alone, and simply, is the proper definition of freedom, then this man is free in his will or inclination to be happy, because it is his real and genuine spontaneity.

Another instance of moral freedom with inability to the contrary, is that of the unregenerate sinner. His sin is voluntary self-determination. It issues out of the self, and it is the working of the self. It is not another man who sins, but this very man and no other. This fact establishes his free agency in this sin. He is inclined to sin, and inclination is free agency. Yet he is unable to overcome and eradicate this sinful inclination. This is a well-established fact of consciousness. It is also the teaching of revelation. "No man can come unto me except the Father which hath sent me draw him," John 6:44. "Whosoever committeth sin is the slave of sin," John 8:34. "Without me ye can do nothing," John 15:5. Here are two facts: (*a*) That the will wills its own sin; this is self-determination; (*b*) That having so willed, it cannot unwill its own sin; this is inability.

It is false to infer that the will does not will its own sin, if it cannot unwill it; that a person does not act freely, if he cannot recall his act. If the fact of *self*-determination has been established by conclusive proofs, the fact must stand. A man throws himself off a precipice. This is an act of the self. He was not flung off by another self, or by a physical force in nature. It was his own spontaneous act. This makes it a free act. Yet he cannot undo his act. He has no power to the contrary, at any point of his fall. Nevertheless, his fall from top to bottom is chargeable to him as his own responsible act. At no point in his fall, is he *innocent* of suicide. He is guilty of self-murder, at every inch in the descent. An inability that results from an act of the self, is as absolute as that which results from the act of another. A man who kills himself is as dead as a man killed by another. In like manner, an inclination to sin that is originated by the self is as insuperable by the self that originated it, and which now has it, as it would be if it were originated by a third party and forced upon him. Moral inability is as real inability as natural inability; but the former is guilty inability, because it is the product of the will itself, while the latter is innocent inability, because it is the product of God in creation and providence In every act of transgressing the law of God, there is a reflex action of the will upon itself, whereby it becomes unable perfectly to keep that law A man is not forced to sin, but if he does, he cannot of himself get back where he was before sinning. He cannot get back to innocency, nor can he get back to holiness of heart.

Another instance of self-determination without power to the contrary, is that of God The Supreme Being is self-moved. But he is unable to sin. This is taught in James 1:13: "God cannot be tempted." A being who is intemptable is impeccable. Yet in the Supreme Being is to be found the highest form of moral freedom. The more intense the self-determination in any being, the more intense the freedom. Consequently, a will self-determined to holiness in an infinite degree is marked by a higher grade of freedom, than one self-determined in only a finite degree. But in proportion as self-determination increases, the power to the contrary diminishes. In God, the infinitude of self-determination excludes the possibility of a change in the self-determination; that is, excludes a power to the contrary Freedom and moral necessity are one and the same thing, in the Supreme Being.

Freedom in the Infinite Being is *immutable* self-determination; in a finite being, it is *mutable* self-determination. God is free in his holiness, because he is self-moved in the righteous action of his will. That this motion is eternal and unchangeable in one and the same direction, does not destroy the self-motivity, and convert it into compulsion. Man also was free in his holiness, yet could sin. He was free, because self-moved in the right action of his will. That this self-motion was mutable, and could take another direction, did not destroy the self-motivity, and convert it into compulsion. Thus it appears, that the power to the contrary, or the power to reverse the existing self-determination of the will, is not the substance of freedom, but only the accident. The freedom of both the Infinite and the finite will is in the self-motion of mind or spirit, as diverse from matter. That God cannot alter his self-determination to good, does not diminish his self-determination. That man could alter his self-determination to good, did not increase his self-determination. The freedom, in both instances, is in the *existing* action of the will, not in a conceivable or possible action. The present inclining is willing unforced agency.

2. Inclination, or self-determination, excludes *indifference.* A will that is determined or inclined towards God,

is not indifferent towards God. Indifference is the exact contrary of inclination or self-determination.

It is here that the two principal theories of moral freedom find their starting-point The Augustinian asserts, that the essence of voluntariness is self-determination *merely* and *only*. The Pelagian asserts that indetermination, or indifference, with power to will in either direction, is the essence of voluntariness. Unless this power of alternative choice continually exist, there is no freedom. Hence it perpetually accompanies the will, both here and hereafter. The Augustinian affirms that if a will be really *self*-moved in a particular activity, such as hatred of a fellow-man for example, it is free, even though it be not able to start another activity of a contrary nature, such as love of that fellow-man. A man who is walking is really and truly walking, though he is not able to fly. His inability to fly does not affect the nature of the act of walking. And similarly man's inability to love, does not destroy the spontaneity and self-motion of his hate.

The Pelagian contends that such self-motion is insufficient. There must be an indefectible, inalienable power of alternative choice, in order to freedom of the will. But in order that there may be this constant power, the will must have no inclination in either direction. Consequently indifference or indetermination, not positive self-determination, is the sine qua non of moral freedom for the Pelagian. The text Deut. 30 : 19, is quoted to prove indifference, and the power of alternative choice. "I have set before you life and death : therefore choose life." But no alternative between these two final ends, and no indifference, is allowed. Only one final end is permitted. Men are not bidden to choose *either* life or death, but to choose life. Death is set before them that it may be rejected, not that it may be elected. Life is set before them that it may be elected, not that it may be rejected. Simple self-determination to good is required. Indifference is forbidden. "Choose *life.*" The election of good is ipso facto the *rejection* of evil, and vice versa. The holiness of Immanuel is described in a similar manner, in Isa. 7:16: "Before the child shall know to refuse the evil, and choose the good," etc. He is not indifferent, choosing *either* evil or good, but positively inclined to good, and ipso facto disinclined to evil. In brief, the difference between the Augustinian and the Pelagian doctrine of freedom is this: The Pelagian asserts that the will as uninclined and indifferent chooses. He postulates a volition antecedent to any inclination. The Augustinian asserts that the will is never uninclined or indifferent. There is no volition prior to inclination. The former places freedom in an act of the will prior to inclining; the latter places it in the very act itself of inclining.

The objections to the theory that freedom is indetermination, or indifference, are the following:

1. The free will, in this case, has no contents. The power of choosing either one of two contrary ways implies that as yet there is no action of the will at all. The will is undetermined. But we have seen that an undetermined will is a contradiction in terms. "Libertas indifferentiae est impossibilis," says Leibnitz. De Libertate. Ed. Erdmann, 669.[1]

---

[1] Sometimes "indifference" is employed to denote the possibilitas peccandi connected with Adam's mutable holiness Maresius (Systema, VI 23) so uses it. "Libertatem tribuimus homini primo, non solum *spontaneitatis*, quod nempe ultro et absque coactione ruerit in peccatum, sed etiam *indifferentiae*, juxta quam potuisset abstinere a peccato, et in illo statu permanere" But this is not the ordinary use of the term Nor is it a proper use of it. Holy Adam, while "able to abstain from sin and to continue holy," was not *indifferent* to holiness

Howe also asserts that the human will "was created without any determination to good, it was made in such a state of liberty as to be in a certain sort of equipoise, according as things should be truly or falsely represented by the leading faculty, the mind or understanding" Oracles, II xxii Howe supposes this, in order to explain the possibility of the fall. The understanding of Adam was capable of being deceived, because it was finite. And the will was capable of yielding to the deception This capability he calls an "equipoise"

2. The freedom of indifference is never found in actual existence. There is no example of it. The so-called "formal freedom" is indifference. It is defined by Muller (Sin, II. 28) as "the ability, from an undetermined state, to self-determine." This supposes the faculty to be in equilibrio It is uncommitted either to right or wrong. From this position of equilibrium and indifference, it starts a decision in one direction, or the other. Such a condition, and such an act of the human will, never occurred within the domain of human consciousness. Consciousness always reports an inclined will, never an indifferent one. Hence Muller places the first act of self-determination to evil from an undetermined state of the will, back of consciousness and beyond time. Muller, however, differs from the Pelagian, in holding that formal freedom is confined to a particular instant. It is not a perpetual accompaniment of the will Having out of the indifferent state of formal freedom taken a determination, the will afterwards is inclined and the indifference ceases Starting with the Pelagian view of freedom, Muller ends with the Augustinian view of sin.

The freedom of the will is primarily a self-determination to a single end, not a choice between two yet unchosen contrary ends. The central and deepest activity of the will is to incline or tend, not to select or choose It moves forward by self-motion, and self-decision, to one point. Two contrary objects or ends are not requisite in order to self-determination. It is not necessary that there should be a

---

of the will But a will not in equipoise, but inclined to holiness, is capable of yielding to deception, or any other temptation, provided it be a finite and mutable will. It is not necessary to assume absolute indifference to holiness and sin, in order to account for the apostasy of Adam's will While, however, asserting this indifference, Howe does not regard it as a necessary element in freedom. It was necessary only in order to probation It is "not a perfection belonging immutably to the nature of man," he says After the fall, it disappears The sinful will is not in equipoise Nor is the holy will, in its perfect state in heaven

comparison of one object with a contrary one, and a choice of the one rather than of the other, in order to the self-determination of the will. If the will should know of but one object, say, its Creator, it might tend or incline to that object, and the tendency or inclination would be the free voluntariness of the will. It is true that the will, in this case, would not be *forced* to incline to the one object before it. It would have an option to incline, or to disincline, to the one object. But this is already said, in saying that the inclining is *self-motion*. This liberty to incline or to disincline to *one* object is very different, however, from the liberty to choose either of two *contrary* objects. In the latter case, there is a comparison of one object with another; in the former, there is no such comparison But what is far more important, in the latter case there is *indifference* towards *both* objects; but in the former, there is no indifference towards the single object. For if there is not inclination to it, there is aversion to it; if there is not desire for it, there is hatred of it; if the will does not incline to God, it disinclines and is at enmity with him; if there is not the spiritual mind, there is the carnal mind; if there is not holy self-determination, there is sinful self-determination The will, in this instance, is not indifferent, as in the other, but is committed to an ultimate end; if not to its Creator, then to itself.

That self-determining, or inclining is the ultimate fact in the freedom of the will, is evident from considering the relation of motives to the will. The will, it is said, is determined by motives. This is often understood to mean, that the will is *efficiently* and *ultimately* determined by a motive out of itself, and other than itself. This is an error The will is only proximately and occasionally determined by external motives. Take a case. A man's will is determined by wealth, as a motive. But only because his will is already so *self*-determined or inclined, that wealth is a motive for him; that is, is *desirable* to him. Were his will self-determined or inclined to ambition instead of avarice, wealth would not be a motive for him, but power would be. Again, were his will inclined or self-determined to sensual pleasure, this would be the motive that would move or determine it, and neither wealth nor power would be. Thus it is evident that the motivity of a motive, that is, its power to move or influence the will, depends primarily and ultimately upon the will's prior inclination, or self-determination. The inclination makes the motive, instead of the motive making the inclination. But the inclination itself is *self*-made, in the sense of being self-motion. If the will is inclined to the Creator as an ultimate end, then the only motives that influence and move it are spiritual and heavenly. If the will is inclined to the creature as an ultimate end, then the only motives that influence and move it are carnal and earthly. The motives in each instance are determinants, only because of the prior bias or self-determination of the will; they influence the person, only because of his existing inclination. They are only the proximate and occasional, not the ultimate and efficient cause of the will's action.

The first activity, therefore, of the will, considered as a faculty, is inclination, not volition. Man is always disposed or biassed in his will, before he exerts choices. The will does not incline, because it first chooses from out of a state of indifference; but it chooses, because it has already inclined. Inclining or self-determining is the primary and central action of the will, and volition or choice is the secondary and superficial. The will, therefore, in its idea and nature, is *causative* and *originative*, rather than *elective*. Hence guilt is denoted in Greek by *ἀιτία*. It implies causation. "The notion of pure will," says Kant (Practical Reason, 205, Abbott's Tr.), "contains that of a causality accompanied with freedom, that is, one which is not determinable by physical laws."

The truth of this view of voluntary freedom is evident

from considering the case of Adam, first as holy, and secondly as sinful. 1. First, the will of holy Adam was by the *creative* act inclined to God as the chief good, before it exerted any volitions and made any choices. Adam as a created spirit was self-determined to God and goodness the instant he was created, and in consequence of this internal bias and disposition chose the various means of gratifying it. Holy Adam at the instant of his creation did not find himself set to choose either the Creator or the creature as an ultimate end, being indifferent to both, but he found himself inclined to the Creator, and choosing means accordingly. He was committed to one and only one supreme end of existence, God and goodness, and selected means corresponding. That Adam's self-determination to God was created with his will itself, is not inconsistent with its being *self*-determination. His will if created at all must have been created as voluntary; since it could not be created as involuntary or uninclined. This inclination was *self-motion*. It was the spontaneity of a spiritual essence, not an activity forced ab extra God necessarily creates a self-determining, self-moving faculty, in creating a will Consequently, holy inclination is both a creation and a self-determination, according as it is viewed Viewed with reference to God, it is created: inclinatio *originata*. Viewed with reference to the voluntary faculty, it is spontaneous and self-moving. inclinatio *originans*. Holy inclination is at once the Creator's product, and the creature's activity.

2. Secondly, the will of sinful Adam by *his own* act had been inclined to the creature as the chief good, before it exerted sinful volitions and made sinful choices. Adam as fallen was *self*-determined to evil, and in consequence of this inward bias of his will chose the various means of gratifying it. The first of these choices was plucking and eating of the tree of knowledge. But there is this important difference; namely, that the evil inclination was not created by God, but was originated by Adam. Sinful inclina-

tion is both the creature's product, and the creature's activity. It is referable to the creature, both as inclinatio originans, and originata.

Thus the term "self-determination" has two significations. It may mean that the self-motion is *in* the self, but not *from* the self as the ultimate author. This is created self-determination, which is always holy. Or it may mean that the self-motion is both *in* the self, and *from* the self as the ultimate author. This is sinful self-determination Holiness is self-determined, but not self-originated. Sin is both self-determined and self-originated.

Created self-determination, or holy inclination, is only relatively meritorious or deserving, because man is not the efficient in its origination. Being either con-created in creation, or re-created in regeneration, the reward due to a holy inclination of the will is gracious. "Eternal life is the *gift* of God," Rom. 6 : 23. Self-originated self-determination, or sinful inclination, on the contrary, is absolutely demeritorious or ill-deserving. Man is the sole efficient in its origination, and therefore the retribution due to it is a strict debt. "Eternal death is the *wages* of sin" Justice owes retribution to the sinner. Man is absolutely rewardable for trangression, but only relatively rewardable for obedience.

## CHAPTER III.

### THE HUMAN WILL.

Augustine: City of God, XIV vi. Gangauf: Psychologie des Augustinus, VI. i.-v. Anselm: De Libertate Arbitrii Aquinas: Summa, I. cv. 4. Calvin: Institutes, II. ii. 4-12; iii. 5-11. Witsius: Covenants, III. vii. 4-5. Howe: Oracles, I. xxiv.; II. xxv. Des Cartes: Passions, Pt. I. Art. 17-19. Turrettin: Institutio, VI. v. Owen Indwelling Sin, III. Hooker: Polity, I. xi. Burgess: Original Sin, III. iv J. Taylor: Efficient Causes of Human Actions. Edwards: Religious Affections (in initio); Will, III. iv., Reality of Spiritual Light. Hopkins: Works, I 83 Locke. Understanding, II. xxi. Butler: Nature of Virtue (in initio). Reid. On the Intellectual and Active Powers. Shedd. Theological Essays, 230-243; Literary Essays, 324-328. Kant: Practical Reason (Abbott's tr.) 94, 197, 205-212, 269-289. Coleridge: Aids, Harper's Ed, I 154, 263, 271-274. Marsh: Remains, 368-390. Delitzsch: Biblical Psychology, IV. v. xii. Beck: Biblical Psychology Muller Sin, III. i. 1-3. Baur: Gegensatz, 118-173. Smith: Theology, 236-252 Green: Prolegomena to Ethics. Hamilton On the Conative Power. Hopkins: Outline Study of Man, 225-257. Hickok. Empirical Psychology, 382-292

In discussing the subject of original sin, much depends upon the definition of the Will; whether it be taken in a wide, or in a narrow sense. The elder psychology divides the powers of the soul into Understanding and Will; the later psychology divides them into Intellect, Sensibility, and Will. The former includes the moral affections and desires in the Will; the latter excludes them from it. For the former, inclination is the principal characteristic of voluntariness; for the latter, volition is the principal characteristic. In classifying the powers of the soul under two modes, it is not meant that there is a division of the soul into two parts. The whole soul as cognizing, is the understanding; and the whole soul as inclining, is the will.

Locke laid the foundation for the later view of the will, by excluding moral desire and affection from the faculty. "I find," he says (Essay II. xxi.), "the will often confounded with several of the affections, especially *desire*, and one put for the other. This, I imagine, has been no small occasion of obscurity and mistake in this matter, and therefore is, as much as may be, to be avoided. For he that shall turn his thoughts inwards upon what passes in his mind when he wills, shall see that the *will*, or power of *volition*, is conversant about nothing but that *particular* determination of the mind whereby, barely by a thought, the mind endeavors to give rise, continuation, or stop to any action which it takes to be in its power. This, well considered, plainly shows that the *will* is perfectly distinguished from *desire*, which may have quite a contrary tendency from that which our will sets us upon. A man whom I cannot deny may oblige me to use persuasions to another, which, at the same time I am speaking, I may wish may not prevail with him. In this case, it is plain the will and desire run counter. I will the action that tends one way, whilst my desire tends another, and that the direct contrary." Here, "will" denotes a *particular* act of the faculty, namely, a volition, and excludes a general act of it, namely, desire or inclination A man's desire, according to Locke's use of terms, is involuntary. If "will" means only volition, then a man's inclination is not "will," because inclination is the same as desire.

Edwards (Will, I. i) combats Locke, and contends that "a man never wills anything contrary to his desires, or desires anything contrary to his will. In the instance cited, it is not carefully observed what is the thing willed, and what is the thing desired: if it were, it would be found that will and desire do not clash in the least. The thing willed, on some consideration, is to utter such words; and certainly, the same consideration so influences him that he does not desire the contrary: all things considered, he *chooses* to utter such words, and does not *desire* not to utter them. And so, as to the thing which Mr. Locke speaks of as desired; namely, that the words, though they tend to persuade, should not be effectual to that end; his will is not contrary to this; he does not will that they should be effectual, but rather wills that they should not, as he desires. In order to prove that will and desire never run counter, it should be shown that they may be contrary one to the other in the *same* thing; but here the objects are two; and in each, taken by themselves, the will and desire agree"[1]

Kant, on the other hand, defines the will as the faculty of desire: Begehrungsvermogen. "The notion of the chief good determines the faculty of desire." "The will may be defined as the faculty of ultimate ends (das Vermogen der Zwecke), since these are always determinants of the desires." Kant also denominates the will the practical reason, "because the objects of the practical reason are good and evil. By good, is meant an object necessarily *desired* according to a principle of reason; by evil, one necessarily shunned according to a principle of reason." Practical Reason, 210. Abbott's Translation. Green (Prolegomena to Ethics, 152) contends that will is desire towards a moral end. "The man as desiring, or putting himself forth in desire for the realization of some object present to him in idea, is the same thing as willing. Will is desire having

[1] In this reasoning, however, Edwards, as is frequently the case, does not mark off choice, or volition, from desire He calls a volition, a desire "All things considered," he says, "the man *chooses* to utter such words, and does not *desire* not to utter them" Here, the volition by which the words are spoken is called a "desire" But this is not desire as spoken of by Locke, when he says that the man does not desire that the words shall be effectual to persuade. The desire and the volition, in Locke's use of the terms, which is also the correct use, are two different acts of the will, and one may not agree with the other But the desire and the volition, in Edwards's use, in this place, are one and the same act, and of course cannot disagree with each other

the action of a self-determining self upon and within it."

We regard the elder psychology as correct, in including the moral desires and affections in the total action of the will, and in making two faculties of the soul: namely, understanding and will.[1]

The Understanding is the cognitive faculty or mode of the soul. It comprises the intellect and the conscience. These are percipient and preceptive powers. They are destitute of desire and inclination; and they are not self-determining and executive powers. The intellect perceives what ought to be done, and the conscience commands what ought to be done, but they never do anything themselves. They do not incline to an end. They have no love and desire for what is commanded; and no hatred and aversion towards what is forbidden. The intellect neither loves nor hates; neither desires nor is averse. The conscience approves and disapproves; but approbation is not love and desire, nor is disapprobation hatred and abhorrence. Shedd: Sermons to the Natural Man (XV.).

The understanding is the fixed and stationary faculty or mode of the soul. It can be vitiated and injured, but not radically changed. The operation of the human intellect cannot be totally reversed and revolutionized, as that of the human will may be. After the apostasy, the understanding of man obeys the same rules of logic as before, and possesses the same mathematical and ethical ideas and intuitions. And the same is true of the human conscience, as involving the perception of right and wrong. Its structure and laws are unaltered by apostasy. After the fall, man does not have moral perceptions that are exactly contrary to those he had before it. He does not perceive that the

[1] A full classification on this basis would be, understanding, will, and instinct: using the latter term in a wide sense. The old psychology, however, did not formally appropriate the term instinct, to designate the involuntary side of man's nature, but left it undesignated.

love of God is evil, and the love of sin is good. He does not approve of disobedience of law, and disapprove of obedience. The energy with which both intellect and conscience operate after apostasy is, indeed, greatly diminished; but the same general mode of operation continues. The effect of sin upon the cognitive side of the human soul is to darken, dim, and stupefy, but not radically to change. This fixedness of the understanding is in striking contrast, as we shall see, with the mobility and mutability of the will.

The Will is that faculty or mode of the soul which self-determines, inclines, desires, and chooses in reference to moral and religious objects and ends. These objects and ends are all centred and summed up in God. We say moral and religious objects and ends, because there is a class of propensities and desires that refer to non-moral and non-religious objects. They are the *natural* or *instinctive* desires, which are involuntary. Speaking generally, the voluntary and moral desires relate to God. They are either inclined or averse to him; they are either love or hatred The natural and instinctive desires, on the other hand, relate to the creature. Of these latter, there are four kinds. (*a*) Physical appetites (*b*) Family affections. (*c*) Social affections. (*d*) Æsthetic feeling These all relate to some form or phase of the Finite, and therefore are not in themselves of the nature of virtue or religion, because religion relates to the Infinite. They may be sanctified by the moral and religious desires, and are so sanctified when the religious desires coexist with them; but they are in themselves neither sinful nor holy. They are constitutional, non-moral propensities, flowing necessarily from man's physical and mental structure. Unregenerate men have them, as well as regenerate. They are none of them the object of a divine command or prohibition, like the moral and religious desires. When husbands are commanded to "love their wives" (Col. 3:19), and wives to "love their husbands and children" (Titus 2 : 4), they are commanded to love "*in the Lord*." The mere *instinctive* love itself is not commanded. This is provided for in the created relation of husband and wife; of parent and child. The instinctive affection as *sanctified* by a connection and union with the religious affection of supreme love of God, is what is enjoined. The same is true of the love and obedience of children towards their parents (Col. 3 : 20), of the love and care of parents towards their children (Col. 3 : 21), of the relation of the citizen to the state (Rom. 13 : 5 ; 1 Pet. 2 : 13, 14), of the relation between master and servant (Col. 3 : 22 ; 1 Tim. 6 : 1, 2), and of the physical appetites (Rom. 14 : 6 ; 1 Cor. 10 : 31). None of these are commanded merely as *natural* instinctive desires and affections, but as *sanctified* instinctive desires and affections.

The instinctive or natural desires and affections are transient. They relate to the temporal, not the eternal. The family, and the state, are institutions that are confined to earth and time. This fact shows that they are non-moral in their nature. The moral and religious is eternal. None of the natural and instinctive desires were lost by the fall, though all of them were vitiated and corrupted by it. None of them were converted into their contraries, by the apostasy of Adam. Compare Edwards : Nature of Virtue, V.–VIII. Calvin : Inst. II. ii. 13.[1]

The elder theologians include the moral and religious desires and affections in the Will. Edwards (Affections, in initio) states the view in the following terms. "The will and the affections of the soul are not two faculties; the affections are not essentially distinct from the will, nor do they differ from the mere actings of the will and inclination

[1] The classification of the instinctive desires is various. Hopkins (Outlines, Lect IX ), besides the physical appetites, enumerates the desire of existence, of good (happiness), of power, of knowledge, of property, of esteem, of liberty, of society, of beauty. These can all be brought under the category of the Finite No one of them is desire for God, and spiritual good

of the soul, but only in the liveliness and sensibleness of exercise." Again he says (Will, III. iv.), "The affections are only certain modes of the exercise of the will." "The inclination of the will is a *leading* act of the will." In this sense of the term "will," the religious affections are voluntary affections. Edwards identifies the will with the heart, and contradistinguishes it from the understanding. "In the former case, is exercised merely the speculative faculty, or the understanding strictly so called, in distinction from the will or disposition of the soul. In the latter, the will, or inclination, or heart, is mainly concerned." Spiritual Light. Works, IV 442. Augustine's psychology is the same: "Amor seu dilectio valentior est voluntas." Trinity, XV. xxi 41. "What are desire and joy, but a will inclined towards the things we desire and rejoice in And what are fear and hatred, but a will disinclined towards the things we fear and hate?" City of God, XIV. vi. Clement of Alexandria (Miscellanies, II. xv ) says that "what is voluntary is either what is by desire, or what is by choice." It is the common view among the elder theologians. "Affectus in deo nihil aliena sunt quam actus voluntatis divinae." Van Mastricht, II. xv. 19. "The will of God, according to its divers objects, hath different names, to wit: of holiness, goodness, love, mercy, and such like." Ross's Wollebius, p. 17. The elder Calvinists often defined the will as rational appetency: "Voluntas, quae est appetitus rationalis, semper est conjuncta cum appetitu sensitivo, ita quidem, ut ipse appetitus sensitivus in homine proportionaliter respondeat voluntati." Keckermann: in Heppe's Reformirter Dogmatik, Locus XV. Consequently, they regarded the inward motions of this rational appetency as sinful and punishable, and refused to call them involuntary. "Non omnino involuntarii sunt isti motus, quia nostra voluntate eos attraximus. Nihil obstat, quominus ad peccatum actuale eos etiam motus referamus: quia nimirum *concupiscentia actuale peccatum* est: motus autem isti aut partes, aut prima puncta, concupiscentiae." Keckerman: in Heppe, ut supra. "As the will doth now work upon that object [viz, God] by desire, which is as it were a motion towards the end as yet unobtained, so likewise upon the same hereafter received, it shall work also by love." Hooker: Polity, I. xi. "The knowledge of man is of two kinds: the one respecting his understanding and reason, and the other respecting his will, appetite, and affections; whereof the former produceth position or decree, the latter action or execution." Bacon: Advancement of Learning, II. "The difference of men is very great; you would scarce think them to be of the same species; and yet it consists more in affection than in intellect." Selden: Table Talk, p. 71, Ed. Auber.

The terms inclination, desire, and affection, are interchangeable. The "desire" of the Psalmist's heart is one and the same thing with the "inclination" of his will. He often asks God to "incline" his heart. The inclination of the will is its constant self-determination. The affections or desires are the various phases or aspects of the inclination. Love of God is an affection of the heart; but it is also one variety of the disposition or inclination of the Christian. Hatred of sin is the aversion of a good man's will, its disinclination to evil. "Velle, nihil aliud est quam inclinatio quaedam in objectum voluntatis, quod est bonum universale." Aquinas: Summa, I. cv. 4.

In the Authorized version, "willing" sometimes means "desiring," and sometimes "purposing," according as it translates θέλω or βουλεύω. Rom. 9:22, "What if God [though] willing (inclined, θέλων) to show his wrath [yet] endured," etc. 2 Pet. 3:5, "Willingly (θέλοντας) ignorant" = desiring to be ignorant. Compare 1 Tim. 2:4. Acts 27:43, "The centurion willing (βουλόμενος, purposing) to save Paul." Compare 1 Tim. 2:8; 5:14; 2 Pet. 3:9. In Eph. 2:3, the "lusts" (ἐπιθυμίαι) are called "inclinations" (θελήματα). St. James (4:2) represents sinful desire to be the same as sinful inclination, when he says, "Ye lust (ἐπιθυμεῖτε) and have not, ye desire to have (ζηλοῦτε) and cannot obtain" When Christ (John, 5 : 6) asks, "Wilt thou be made whole?" "will" means desire.

The will, unlike the understanding, is mutable. It is capable of a radical and total change, or revolution. It has met with such a change in the apostasy of Adam. Man now is inclined exactly contrary to what he was by creation. In respect to moral and religious ends and objects, he inclines, desires, loves, and acts directly contrary to what he did when he came from the Creator's hand. This great change is denominated a "fall." It is an overthrow, a catastrophe. It is not a mere difference in the degree or intensity with which the will operates, but it is an entire alteration of the direction of its activity. The fall of the will was a revolution, not an evolution.

The elder psychology, by regarding the moral desires and affections as modes of the inclination of the will brings them within the sphere of responsibility; and distinguishes in kind between the moral or voluntary, and the natural or involuntary desires. In this way, it precludes necessitating theories of human nature and agency. Spinoza, for example, breaks down the distinction between the natural and the moral, the instinctive and the voluntary, by rejecting Des Cartes' view of the moral affections as voluntary inclination, and contending that "the affections of hatred, anger, envy, etc, considered in themselves, follow from the same necessity and force (virtus) of nature as other things." Ethics, III., Preface. The physical appetites, together with the family, social, and aesthetic desires and affections, are clearly different from such affections as envy, pride, hatred, and malice, in their origin and nature The report and verdict of conscience concerning them is wholly different. They are instinct, not will. That a man craves food is neither praiseworthy nor blameworthy. That he feels love and desire towards his kindred, his country, and artistic beauty, is neither praiseworthy nor blameworthy. But to feel love and desire when God is presented as the supreme object and end, is holiness; and to feel hatred and aversion, is sin. These latter are not instinctive and constitutional affections, but modes of the man's moral inclination, for which he is approved or condemned.

Moral desires and affections are the self-activity of the will; its inclination and tendency showing itself in the phases of love or hatred of God; of desire or aversion towards goodness. They are commanded or prohibited by the moral law; which proves that they are voluntary. The feelings of supreme love towards God, and of equal love towards a fellow-creature, are not instinctive, but voluntary. Such love and inclination is not, like the storgé of the parental relation, or the involuntary affection of the citizen for his country, a merely natural and necessary efflux from the human constitution, deserving neither praise nor blame; but it is the free determination of the human will. To have it, is meritorious. Not to have it, or to have its contrary, is guilt requiring atonement and remission. Again, the feeling of aversion towards God, or of hatred towards a fellow-man, is not like the shrinking of animal life from death, say, the recoil of a child from a viper, an involuntary activity of the soul which stands in no relation to law and justice, and is deserving of no punishment. This aversion towards God is called "enmity" (Rom 8:7), the positive hostility of the inclination, the disinclination of the will in its deepest recesses. This hatred of a fellow-creature is the repugnance of the will, and is murderous in its quality; for "he that hateth his brother is a murderer," 1 John 3:15. Accordingly, in Scripture, holy desire is holy inclination. Ps. 63:1, "My soul thirsteth for thee, my flesh longeth for thee." Ps. 42:1, "So panteth my soul after thee." Such desire is the object of command. Ps. 37:4, "Delight thyself in the Lord." The sum of the moral law is a command to love. "Thou shalt love the Lord thy God with all thy heart." And evil desire is evil inclination. Ps. 112 : 20, "The desire of the wicked shall perish." Ps. 140 : 8, "Grant not, O Lord, the desires of the wicked." Prov. 10 : 28, "The expectation of the wicked shall perish." Job 21 : 14, "Depart from us; for we desire not the knowledge of thy ways."

The recent psychology distributes the faculties of the soul into three divisions: Intellect, Sensibility, and Will. The objections to this classification are the following:

1. The moral desires and religious affections must, if anywhere, be included under the Sensibility, by this arrangement. But this is too narrow and shallow a term, to denote those profound feelings, desires, and inclinations that relate to religion. "Sensibility," by its etymology, refers us to the five senses. Properly speaking, it comprises only sensuous feelings and desires. Hence it is wholly inadequate to denote feelings and desires that have no connection at all with the five senses: such as the holy affections of reverence, faith, hope, humility, joy, peace, love; or the sinful affections of pride, envy, malice, hatred, and the like. Both holy and sinful affections, in their deeper forms, are mental, and disconnected with a physical organism They have no connection with the sensuous sensibility. The seraph who adores and burns does not inherit flesh and blood. His religious desires and feelings are purely mental. The fiend, also, is intellectual in his depravity. Lucifer, the ethereal son of the morning, was not tempted to apostasy by any sensuous appetite; and his existing moral condition is mainly intellectual. The wickedness of the fallen angels is denominated by St. Paul, "spiritual wickedness," Eph 6 : 12 "Sensibility," therefore, is an inadequate term to cover that wide domain which includes the moral desires of the heart, and the inclination of the will, and which is entirely distinct from the physical and fleshly side of man.

2. The explanation of the moral desires, and religious affections, is inadequate, by this classification. According to

this division, the will excludes inclination and desire, and is only the power of exerting volitions; and the sensibility includes only the physical appetites, together with certain instinctive, involuntary, and innocent desires. The love of approbation, and the love of happiness, are mentioned as the principal of these latter. When these physical appetites and involuntary desires are "adopted" and "strengthened" by a volition, or are weakened and rejected by it, then sinful or holy affections arise. Virtue and vice thus differ only in degree, not in kind The love of approbation intensified by volition, becomes pride; diminished by volition, becomes humility. The love of happiness strengthened by volition, becomes selfishness; weakened by volition, becomes benevolence. The rudimental base of virtue and vice is neither virtuous nor vicious. Thus there is no positive intrinsic morality upon this theory. Those sinful affections mentioned in Gal. 5:19, 20, "hatred, variance, emulations wrath, strife, seditions, heresies, envyings, murders," instead of being regarded as the simple and immediate inclination of the will, and therefore culpable in their own intrinsic nature, are regarded as complex and compounded. They are made out of innocent and involuntary material derived from the "sensibility," which when intensified by volitions or particular choices becomes guilt.

Furthermore, when a list of involuntary and innocent sensibilities sufficiently large to account for all the virtuous and vicious moral affections is asked for, it is not forthcoming. It is impossible to find innocent bases for "malice, envy, wrath, strife, seditions, heresies, murders, and such like." Neither can "the fruits of the Spirit, love, joy, peace, long-suffering gentleness, goodness, meekness, temperance" (Gal 5:22), be explained out of involuntary and characterless materials.

The theory, moreover, breaks down when the so-called innocent sensibility, the "love of approbation," is examined. This is really nothing but the love of human applause; the sinful desire mentioned by St. John (5:44; 12:43), when he speaks of those who "receive honor one of another, and seek not the honor that cometh from God only," and who "love the praise of men more than the praise of God;" and by St. Paul, in 1 Cor. 4:3, affirming that "it is a very small thing to be judged of man's judgment." This desire for popular approbation is not the same thing as the desire for *self*-approbation, or the approval of conscience. The latter is virtuous and proper; but the former is the base of all egotism, pride, and ambition. It is exactly contrary to the meekness and lowliness of Christ, and utterly opposed to that poverty of spirit, and humbleness of mind which every sinful man ought to have, and upon which Christ pronounces a blessing. Such a "sensibility" as this cannot be the elementary base of holy affections. And the other "sensibility," also, the "love of happiness," is essentially selfish. It underlies the selfish theory of morals, which is ethically unsound. No mere modification of the love of happiness can possibly produce the love of God, or the love of holiness, or the love of man. This scheme, in reality, derives and explains virtue out of vice. Pope describes the method, with his usual condensation and brilliancy.

"As fruits ungrateful to the planter's care,
On savage stocks inserted, learn to bear;
The surest virtues thus from passions shoot,
Wild nature's vigor working at the root.
What crops of wit and honesty appear
From spleen, from obstinacy, hate, or fear!
See anger, zeal and fortitude supply;
E'en avarice, prudence, sloth, philosophy;
Lust, through certain strainers well refined,
Is gentle love, and charms all womankind;
Envy, to which th' ignoble mind 's a slave,
Is emulation in the learn'd or brave;
Nor virtue male or female can we name,
But what will grow on pride, or grow on shame"

ESSAY ON MAN, II.

Spinoza represents all affections, good and bad, as alike springing out of "the endeavor of a thing to persevere in its being." From this one source, he derives the affections of anger, revenge, jealousy, ambition, sensuality, covetousness, love, benevolence, humility, compassion, hatred, joy, grief, envy, contempt, hope, fear, self-distress, pride, repentance, etc. Ethics, Part III.

The elder psychology agrees with Scripture, in its definition of the will. In the Biblical psychology, the will includes the moral desires, and is antithetic to the understanding. In the New Testament, *καρδία, θέλημα,* and *βουλή* are terms for the voluntary side of the soul; and in the Old Testament, לב denotes the same. The cognitive side of the soul is designated in the New Testament by *πνεῦμα, νοῦς,* and *φρὴν*; and in the Old Testament, by נפש and רוח. Girdlestone: Synonyms of the Old Testament.

The primary and dominant meaning of *καρδία* is will, as antithetic to understanding It includes the inclination, together with the moral desires, and affections. Rom. 1:24, "Lusts of the heart" Rom. 2:5, "Impenitent heart." 2 Cor. 9:7, "Purposed in the heart." Rom. 10:9, 10, "With the heart man believeth." Luke 1:17, "Turn the hearts" Deut. 4:29, "If thou seek with all thy heart." Deut. 6:5, "Love with all thy heart." Ps. 119:112, "I have inclined my heart." Prov. 31:11, "The heart of her husband doth trust her." Lament. 3:33, "Doth not afflict willingly" (Heb., "from the heart").

These passages evince that in the Biblical psychology, the will comprehends the heart. It comprises all that moral activity of the soul which is manifested in loving, hating, inclining, desiring, purposing, seeking, repenting, turning, delighting, trusting, hoping, believing. Each and all of these affections are phases of the will. They are modes of a man's inclination and self-determination. If they are conformed to the moral law, they are right affections, and the will is a holy will. If they are contrary to the moral law, they are evil affections, and the will is a sinful will. This species of psychical activity is not intellectual and percipient, but affectionate and executive. "The *καρδία*, or heart," says Owen (On the Spirit, III. iii.), "in Scripture, is *τὸ πράκτικον* in the soul, the practical principle of operation, and so includes the will also. It is the actual compliance of the will and affections with the mind and understanding, with respect to the objects proposed by them."

*Θέλημα* denotes inclination and desire, in distinction from volition. Matt. 6 : 10, "Thy will be done." Matt. 7 : 21, "Do the will of my Father." Matt. 18 : 14, "It is not the will of your Father." John 4 : 34, "The will of him that sent me." Rom. 2 : 18, "Knowest his will." Eph. 1 : 15, "Good pleasure of his will." Eph. 2 : 3, "The desires (*θελήματα*) of the flesh, and of the mind." In these passages, the "will" is the will of desire and delight. See Bruder, in voce.

*Βουλή* and *βούλημα* denote volition, in distinction from inclination and desire Luke 23 : 51, "The same had not consented to the counsel [decision] of them." Acts 18 : 15, "I will be [decide to be] no judge of such matters." Acts 19 : 30, "When Paul would have [purposed to] entered." Acts 25 : 22, "I would [decide] also hear the man, myself" 2 Cor. 1 : 15, "I was minded [purposed] to come unto you" Acts 2 : 23, "The determinate counsel [purpose] of God." Heb. 2 : 17, "God willing [purposing] to show more abundantly unto the heirs of promise the immutability of his council." See Bruder, in vocibus. In these passages, *βουλή* denotes, not a continuous and steady inclination of the will, but its single decision or volition in a particular instance. This decision may agree, or disagree with the inclination. When Christ was crucified by God's will of purpose (Acts 2 : 23), it was contrary to his will of desire and delight.

The primary and dominant meaning of *πνεῦμα*, and its cognates *νοῦς* and *φρήν*, is understanding, as antithetic to will. It comprises all the perceptive agencies of the soul. Mark 2 : 8, "Knowing in his spirit" 1 Cor. 2 : 11, "What man knoweth the things of a man, save the spirit of man that is in him?" 1 Cor. 14 : 20, "Be not children in understanding" (*φρεσίν*) Luke 24 : 45, "Opened their understanding" (*νοῦν*). 1 Cor. 14 : 15, "Sing with the understanding" (*νοΐ*). Ps 139 : 14, "My soul (נֶפֶשׁ) knoweth right well." Prov. 19 : 2, "That the soul be without knowledge is not good." Deut. 4 : 9, "Keep thy soul diligently, lest thou forget." Job 20 : 3, "The spirit (רוּחַ) of my understanding." Isa. 29 : 24, "They that erred in spirit shall come to understanding." Ex. 28 : 3, "The spirit of wisdom."

As the understanding and will are one soul or person, the terms for each are frequently interchanged. *Καρδία* is put for *πνεῦμα*, in Mark 2 : 6, "Reasoning in their hearts." Rom 2 : 15, "The law [of conscience] written in their hearts." 2 Cor. 4 : 6, "Shined in the heart, to give the light of the knowledge of God." 1 John 3 : 20, "God is greater than our heart [conscience] and knoweth all things." Job 9 : 4, "Wise in heart" (לֵב). Prov. 7 : 7, "Void of understanding" (לֵב). Job 12 : 3, "I have understanding (לב) as well as you." 1 Kings 10 : 2, "She spake with him all that was in her heart," i e all she knew. Gesenius in loco. Hodge on Eph. p. 249

Similarly, *πνεῦμα* is put for *καρδία*, in Matt 5 : 3, "Poor in spirit." 1 Cor 4 : 21, "Spirit of meekness." Rom. 7 : 6, "Newness of spirit." Rom. 8 : 6, "Mind (*φρόνημα*) of the spirit." Rom. 8 : 27, "He who searcheth the heart (*καρδία*) knoweth what is the mind (*φρόνημα*) of the spirit (*πνεύματος*)." Luke 10 : 21, "Rejoiced in spirit" Isa. 42 : 1, "In whom my soul (נֶפֶשׁ) delighteth." Ps. 42 : 2, "My soul thirsteth for God." Gen. 23 : 8, "If it be your mind (נֶפֶשׁ)." 2 Kings 9 : 15. 1 Chron. 28 : 9, "With a willing mind (נפש)." In the Old Testament, נֶפֶשׁ is very often used to denote the heart and will.

The distinction between the will's *inclination*, and its *volition*, is of the highest importance in both psychology and theology. The key to the distinction is found in the following discrimination by Descartes (Les Passions, Partie I Article xviii.). "Our acts of will are of two kinds. One are the actions of the soul which terminate on the soul itself; as when we will to love God. The other kind are the actions of the soul that terminate on the body; as when from the mere will to take a walk, there follows the movement of our limbs, and we go forward" The first of these acts of will is inclining; the last is the exertion of a volition. The same distinction is referred to by Constant: "Je puis faire de bonnes et fortes actions; je ne puis avoir de bons procédés."

When I say, "I will pick up that stone," this is volition The action of the will terminates on the body. I am conscious of ability to do it, or not. In this instance, there is a power of alternative choice. I can do one as easily as the other But when I say, "I will love God supremely," this is inclination. The action of the will terminates on the will. I am not conscious of ability to do it, or not. In this instance, there is not a power of alternative choice. I cannot do one as easily as the other. And the reason is, that I am already loving myself supremely. I am already *inclined* or self-determined. I am already doing the contrary of loving God supremely. And the existing inclination precludes the other. I can do the one which I am doing, but not the other which I am not doing. But when I said, "I will pick up that stone," I was not already inclined to the contrary act—namely, not to pick it up In this instance, I was *indifferent* and undetermined in regard to the act of picking up the stone. Consequently, I could do one thing as easily as the other. In the instance of a proposed change of self-determination or inclination, there is a contrary self determination or inclination already existing and *opposing*. In the instance of a change of volition, there is indifference, or the absence of inclination or self-determination.

The difference between inclination and volition is seen by considering the moral desires and affections. The desire of human applause, or ambition, does not rise by a volition. In this sense, it is involuntary, and those who resolve all the action of the will into volition so denominate it Yet it is free and unforced activity. It rises by spontaneous inclination. In this sense, it is voluntary. The man is *willingly* proud and ambitious, and is punishable for it. His desire for fame is the determination of the self. If it is not *self*-determination, it must be determination by some cause other than self. But in this case, the sense of guilt which accompanies it is inexplicable. The same reasoning applies to envy, hatred, malice, and all other sinful desires. They are not volitionary, but they are voluntary; they are the inclination of the will, not its volition.

The following particulars mark the difference between inclination and volition:

1. Inclination is the central action of the will; volition is the superficial action The inclination is the source of volitions. "It is," says Edwards (Original Sin, II. i. 1), "the general notion, not that principles derive their goodness from actions, but that actions derive their goodness from the principles whence they proceed." By "principles" Edwards means, as he teaches in the context, the disposition or inclination; and by "actions" he means particular choices or volitions. That the inclination is more profound action than a volition, is proved by the fact that a man cannot incline himself by a volition, or resolution. When he is already inclined, no exertion of that volitionary power by which he lifts a hand, or applies his mind to a given subject, like geometry for example, can originate a contrary inclination. He may, by volitionary effort, fix his

thoughts upon God as the Being towards whom he ought to incline, but this is as far as he can go, if he is not already inclined. No conceivable amount of resolution, even though it rise to spasm, can start that profound and central action of the will which is its inclination, and is identical with its moral affection and disposition. The central action of the will in inclining is better denominated "voluntary," and the superficial action in choosing, "volitionary." The voluntary is the spontaneous. Milton speaks of "thoughts that voluntary (i.e. spontaneously) move harmonious numbers" If the term "voluntary" is made to do double duty, and designate both the central and the superficial action of the will, both inclination and volition, it leads to confusion. Some things are predicable of a volition that are not of an inclination. Volitions can be originated at any instant, and in any number; an inclination cannot be. If, however, the term "choice" be used to denote the inclination, it should be qualified as the choice of an ultimate *end*, in distinction from the means to it; and also, as not proceeding from an indifferent state of the will.[1]

2. The volition has the same moral quality with the inclination. This is taught by Christ, in Matt. 7.17: "Every good tree bringeth forth good fruit; but a corrupt tree bringeth forth evil fruit." Hence the volition has been denominated "executive volition," and the inclination "immanent volition," by those who do not discriminate technically between inclination and volition.

All the volitionary acts of particular choice are performed in order to gratify the prevailing inclination, or determination of the will. A man is inclined to ambition; and he endeavors to attain the ambitious end to which he is self-determined, by thousands and tens of thousands of voli-

[1] Preference is inclination, not choice, though Locke (Understanding, IV xxi ) considers them to be identical Preference is bias A man can choose what he does not prefer. He can choose pain in a particular instance, though he prefers pleasure He can control his choice by a volition, but not his preference.

tions. These are all of them of the same moral quality with the inclination. They are vicious, not virtuous. Self-seeking or selfishness is the generic character of human inclination; pride, envy, malice, covetousness, etc, are varieties of this. These are modes of man's inclination, all of which have the creature not the Creator for the ultimate end. Volitions are exercised in choosing and using means, in order to gratify these varieties of inclination. In their moral quality, they are the same as the inclination. A volition exerted to attain an ambitious end, and gratify an ambitious inclination, is ambitious. A volition exerted to attain a malignant end, is malignant. And so through the entire list. Volitions cannot be morally different from the inclination which prompts them. This also is taught by our Lord, in Matt. 7:18. "A good tree cannot bring forth evil fruit, neither can a corrupt tree bring forth good fruit."

The volition sometimes seems to run counter to the inclination, but really it does not. A drunkard, from fear or shame, may by a volition reject the cup that is offered to him. He acts contrary, in this particular instance, to his physical appetite for alcohol, but not contrary to the central inclination of his will to self. By the supposition, he is still determined to the creature as the ultimate end, not to the Creator He still loves himself supremely. The motive, consequently, from which he rejects the intoxicant in the instance supposed, is a selfish one: shame, pride, fear of man, or some other merely prudential consideration. He is still controlled by his inclination to self. The volition by which he rejected the cup agrees in its moral quality with the state of his heart. It is not holy, because not prompted by the desire and determination to please and obey God. Had he rejected the intoxicant from regard to the Divine command against drunkenness, this would prove him to have obtained a new inclination of the will. But in the case supposed, his volition, though counter to his physical appetite, yet agrees with his moral character and disposition of will. He has carried out his selfish inclination by his volition; only in a different manner from common. His volition in this instance ministered to his pride, instead of to his physical appetite.[1]

3. The inclination of the will is the result of self-determination, not of a volition, because the inclination *is* the self-determination viewed objectively. Consider the facts. Adam as created was inclined to holiness. This inclination, although created with his will, was at the same time the self-motion of his will. Viewed with reference to its first author and origin, it was the product of his Maker; but viewed with reference to his own will, it was the activity of his will, and in this secondary sense the product of his will. This holy inclination was both con-created, and self-determined; the former, because it was a created voluntariness; the latter, because of the intrinsic nature of voluntariness.

Now it is evident that this holy inclination was not the product of a volition exerted prior to the inclination, and when there was no inclination, but it was the simple self-motion of the will. The will of Adam moved spontaneously to God as a supreme end, and this spontaneity of the will was identical with the will's inclination. The will as uninclined did not choose to incline, and by this choice *made* an inclination, but it simply inclined, and this inclining was its inclination.

And the same is true of Adam's evil inclination. This, also, was the result of self-determination, not of a volition. Adam, in the act of apostasy, did not make a choice between two contraries, God and the creature, to neither of which was he yet inclined; but he passed or "lapsed" from

[1] Sometimes a volition may be exerted without any inclination prompting it. Out of thirty silver dollars, all newly minted and all alike, a man may take one arbitrarily He has no motive or inclination to take the one he does take, rather than another Stat pro ratione voluntas. This is *caprice* Such a volition is uncommon, and has no morality. It is only a sporadic spasmodic act of the will that moves the muscles convulsively.

one inclination to another; from one self-determination to another. This instant, he is wholly inclined to good; the next instant, he is wholly inclined to evil Such a *fall* of the will, cannot be accounted for by an antecedent choice from an indifferent state of the will. It is explained by the possibilitas peccandi. This is the power of self-determining to evil, implied in the *mutable* holiness of a creature who is not self-sustaining and omnipotent. When God created Adam's will with a holy inclination, this inclination, because *finite*, was not immutable. Mutable Adam, unlike his immutable Maker, could lose holiness. He was able to persevere in his holy self-determination, and he was able to start a sinful self-determination. God left it to Adam himself to decide whether he would continue in his first created inclination, or would begin a second evil inclination. This was his probation. The first sin was the self-determining of the will to evil, which expelled the existing self-determination to good, and not a volition in a state of indifference. It was self-determination to an ultimate end, not a choice of means to an ultimate end. Sinful inclination began in Adam immediately by self-determination, and not mediately by a foregoing volition. He did not choose to incline to evil, but he inclined.

In the instance of regeneration, also, a new inclination is begun immediately by the Holy Spirit, not mediately by the exertion of a human volition. The Holy Spirit regenerates the fallen will instantaneously, and the effect is a new inclining or self-determining of the faculty. The will is "powerfully determined," as the Westminster Confession phrases it. The sinner does not choose or resolve to incline to God, but God the Spirit immediately inclines him. The inclination or self-determination of regeneration differs from that of apostasy, in that it is the effect of God "working in the will to *will*." God, in this instance, determines the will by renewing it; while in the instance of the apostasy, Adam determined himself to evil without any immediate operation of God. Yet there is no compulsion of the will in regeneration, because the Holy Spirit operates as spirit upon spirit; that is, in accordance with the nature of a mental and self-moving substance, and not as matter operates upon matter. The new inclination of the will is real and true spontaneity, or self-determination. But, there are two beings concerned in it: namely, the Holy Spirit the efficient, and the human spirit the recipient. In the case of the sinful self-determination in the apostasy, there was only a single being concerned, namely, man.

Consequently, inclination or self-determination may be viewed either subjectively or objectively; either as an activity, or as a result; as an act, or as a fact. Holy inclination, viewed subjectively, is the activity of the will, its voluntary spontaneity: justitia *originans*. Viewed objectively, it is this spontaneity as originally created, or subsequently re-created by God: justitia *originata*. Sinful inclination, viewed subjectively, is the activity of the will, its voluntary spontaneity: peccatum *originans*. Viewed objectively, it is this spontaneity considered as an abiding state of the will originated by the will itself, in Adam's fall: peccatum *originatum*.[1]

4. Inclination differs from volition, as the end differs from

---

[1] This designation of the subjective and objective aspect of an active principle by the active and passive participle, is employed by the philosopher as well as the theologian. A force of nature contemplated subjectively, as energizing and producing effects, is called natura *naturans*, contemplated objectively, as having energized and produced an effect, it is called natura *naturata*. Gravitation viewed subjectively, as cause, is the invisible force. This is natura *naturans*. Gravitation viewed objectively, as effect, is the visible phenomenon or fact: e.g., the falling apple. This is natura *naturata*. The old English poet Hawes (Pastime of Pleasure, Capit. 25, 39) employs the terms:

> "The right hye power Nature, *naturyng*
> *Naturate* made the bodyes above,
> In sundry wise, to take their workyng
> That aboute the worlde naturallye do move."

> "Till that dame Nature *naturyng* had made
> All thinges to growe."

the means. Inclination is self-determination to an ultimate end, God or the world. When Adam apostatized, his will inclined to self and the creature, as the supreme end. This was a self-originated self-determination. When this new inclination to self and sin had begun, then began a series of choices or volitions by means of which he might attain the new end of existence which he had set up. And the first of these choices, the first volition that succeeded the origination of the inclination, was the reaching forth of the hand and taking the forbidden fruit. This volitionary act was the means of attaining the selfish end he had now assumed. He gratified his new inclination by a choice. For Adam had fallen in his heart and will, before he ate the fruit of the tree of knowledge He was already inclined to self, prior to this outward act; and the volition by which he reached forth the hand and took the fruit was executive of his new inclination. It did not originate his inclination, but expressed and exhibited it.

The term "choice," as has been observed, is applied indiscriminately to the election of the end as well as of the means, by those who do not distinguish between voluntary and volitionary action Adam, they say, chose self as the ultimate end, instead of choosing God. But this indiscriminate use of the term is confusing. It is preferable to appropriate each term to its proper act. The will "inclines" to an end, and "chooses" a means. Edwards sometimes appropriates the term "choice" to volitions, and uses the term "disposition," or "affection," to denote inclination. "It is agreeable," he says (Original Sin, II. i 1), "to the sense of the minds of men in all nations and ages, not only that the fruit or effect of a good choice is virtuous, but the good choice itself from which that effect proceeds; yea, and not only so, but also the antecedent good disposition, temper, or affection of mind, from whence proceeds that good choice is virtuous." In this passage, three elements are mentioned: (*a*) The outward act: "the fruit or effect of a good choice." (*b*) The choice, or volition that caused the outward act. (*c*) The "disposition, temper, or affection" which produced the volition. Edwards's position in regard to each of them is: (*a*) That the outward act is preceded and produced by the volition. (*b*) That the volition is preceded and produced by the disposition, or inclination. (*c*) That the disposition or inclination, if holy, is either con-created with the will, or else re-originated in regeneration; if sinful, is originated in Adam's apostasy. But inasmuch as Edwards does not formally and technically appropriate the term "choice" to volitions, but employs it oftentimes to designate the inclination; and still more, because he uses the term "voluntary," as his Arminian opponents did, to denote alike what is volitionary or "caused by antecedent choice" (Works, II. 122), and what is bias or inclination, he has exposed himself to the misinterpretation which his views have sometimes met with.[1]

Julius Muller (Sin, I. 31) remarks that "the true conception of the will does not lie in the element of self-determination alone. This we must attribute in a certain sense to creatures without rational intelligence. Self-determination becomes will, only when it is conscious of itself." But it is incorrect to call the volitions of animals, "self-determination;" and to make the only difference between human and animal will, to lie in an act of *knowledge*. There is a difference in the *kind* of activity. Will in man is rational, unnecessitated self-activity towards a moral end.

---

[1] The following are examples of the indiscriminate use of inclination and choice, by Edwards "If the will, all things now considered, *inclines* or *chooses* to go that way, then it cannot choose, all things now considered, to go the other way, and so cannot choose to be made to go the other way" Will, III. iv Edwards, here, is speaking of inclination, not of volition Again, he says, "The thing which has led men into this inconsistent notion of action when applied to *volition*, as though it were essential to this *internal action*," etc Will, IV. ii. Here, Edwards designates the internal action, or inclination of the will, by the term volition.

Will in animals is irrational, necessitated activity in choosing means to a physical end necessitated by physical instinct. The former is real self-determination; the latter is not. The animal is *forced* by the law of his physical nature to the end aimed at in his volitions; the man is not. The brute *must* attain the end of his creation; the man may or may not. Instinct in the animal is involuntary; inclination in man is voluntary.[1]

5. Volition is common to man and the animal creation; inclination or self-determination belongs only to man, and other rational beings. The movements of the fingers of a pianist are each caused by an act of choice, in distinction from an act of self-determination to an ultimate end. There are thousands of volitions exerted in a few moments. Volition is also seen in insects, and is inconceivably rapid in them. Volition here is innervation. Excitement of the nerve results in excitement of the muscle. If the molecular theory of vitality were true, volition in insects would be rightly defined as Haeckel defines will: namely, "the habit of molecular motion." It would be the molecular process in the nervous-muscular system. A gnat, according to a French naturalist, vibrates its wings five hundred times in a second. The vibrations of the wings of the common fly, according to an English naturalist, are as many as six hundred in a second. Pouchet: Universe, p. 112. These are each and every one of them volitionary, not voluntary acts; choice, not self-determination; and are the same in kind with those by which the pianist plays a tune, or a drummer beats a tattoo. For if the vibrations of the gnat's wing were not caused by volitions, it could not stop flying. The motion would be mechanical, and animals

[1] Hartmann, in his Philosophy of the Unconscious, makes will synonymous with *vitality* Animal growth, animal instinct, animal lust, equally with human inclination and volition, are alike modes of will, according to this theorist The distinction between nature and spirit, matter and mind, is denied, and the whole universe is converted into a blind pantheistic movement of physical appetite and bestial desire, called "will."

would be machines as Descartes asserted in his curious theory. Naturalists are now distinguishing between vegetable or passive life, and active or wilful life. The vegetable puts forth no volitions; the animal does.

But volition in the animal or the insect has something behind it as its ground and cause, as volition in man has. This back-ground and originating source in the animal is *instinct*. This takes the place of self-determination or inclination, in man. All the volitions of an animal or an insect are exerted for the purpose of attaining the end prescribed by animal instinct, just as the volitions of a man are exerted for the purpose of reaching the end prescribed by his moral inclination. Volitionary action in man is responsible, because the disposition or inclination prompting it is self-moved. But in the animal, volitionary action is irresponsible, because instinct is not self-moved. Instinct is the necessitated motion of physical substance, in accordance with physical properties and laws. Inclination is the free motion of mental and spiritual substance, which is not controlled by physical law.

6. Inclination or self-determination is inherited; volitions or choices are not. The bias of the will is born with the individual. His choices or volitions are not born with him, and do not begin until self-consciousness begins. The sinful self-determination began in Adam, prior to birth; sinful volitions begin in the individual, after birth.

7. Inclination is free, because it is self-determined; volition is necessitated, because it is determined in its morality by the inclination of which it is the executive. The selfishly inclined drunkard may drink or not drink in a particular instance, and thus seems to be free in regard to volition, but in either case, his volition is selfish like his inclination. Apparently and formally it is free, but really, it is necessitated. No volition can be holy, if it is the executive of a sinful inclination; or sinful, if it is the executive of a holy inclination. Hence man's freedom must be

sought for in his *inclination*, not in his volitions. Moral necessity can be predicated of volitions, but not of inclination. There is a necessary connection between volitions and the foregoing inclination of which they are the index and executive; but no such necessary connection exists between an inclination and a foregoing inclination, or between an inclination and a foregoing volition. It is improper to say, that a person *must incline* in a certain manner, but proper to say that he *must choose* in a certain manner. If he has an evil inclination, his choices are necessarily evil; but his inclination itself is not necessarily evil. Inclination has no antecedent, but constitutes an absolute beginning ex nihilo; but a volition does not.

This is what Kant means, when he asserts that the will as noumenon, or "thing in itself," is free, but as phenomenon is necessitated. Practical Reason. Abbott's Trans., 269–289. The law of cause and effect, or of the antecedent causing the consequent, operates in regard to the phenomenal series of volitions in time, but not in regard to the abiding inclination which underlies them, and which is referable to no particular moment of time. The inclination is not a series, but a unit. There is only one inclination (noumenon), but myriads of volitions (phenomena). The inclination is not caused either by an antecedent inclination, or by a volition, but is self-caused. And the inclination is the real will of the man: the Ding an sich. Ritschl (History of Justification, VII.) states Kant's doctrine as follows: "Freedom denotes the will as unconditioned causality out of time, in distinction from the phenomena of will that run on in time, and are subject to natural necessity. The reason why every recollection of an act committed long ago calls forth sorrow is, that reason in all that pertains to our moral existence recognizes no distinctions of time, but asks only if the action was really mine." Edwards teaches the same truth in his doctrine of moral necessity—according to which, the volition in its moral quality necessarily follows the inclination. M. Hopkins, also, says that "choice" is free, but "volition" is necessary. Study of Man, 212, 231, 257.

8. Self-determination is causative, and originative of character. It starts a bias or disposition in the will. Volition is unproductive of character and disposition. A volition leaves the man's inclination exactly as it found it. It makes no alteration in the bias of the will. This is seen in the futile attempt of the moralist to change his inclination by volitionary resolutions. Inclination is a positive determination of the will in one direction, and towards one final end. Volition or choice is the selection of one out of two or more things, not from any interest in one rather than another, but because it is best adapted to the end in view. A volitionary choice is indifferent towards the thing chosen. If the drunkard could gratify his selfish inclination to physical pleasure better by water than by alcohol, he would choose water.

9. Inclination is spontaneous; volition is nervous and often spasmodic. Inclination is easy and genial; volition is more or less an effort, whether exerted against the inclination, or in accordance with it. When the drunkard by a volition refuses the cup because of his selfish inclination in the form of shame or fear, this volition costs him a great effort. When the drunkard by a volition takes the cup because of his selfish inclination in the form of desire of sensual pleasure, the volition is still an effort, though not a great one. He is, at least, compelled to exert his will sufficiently to move his muscles and limbs. Volition moves the body; and this requires a distinct and separate resolution of the will back of the bodily movement. Inclination moves the will itself; but this does not require a distinct and separate resolution of the will back of the mental and voluntary movement. The inclining is itself the mental activity; the cause and the effect are one and the same thing. But the volition is not itself the muscular bodily

action; the cause and the effect are two different things. When a person loves or hates, he does not need to resolve to do it. But when he picks up a pin, or applies his mind to a geometrical proposition, he must resolve to do so. Love and hatred are easy because spontaneous; volitions are more or less an effort.

To recapitulate, then, we say that the total action of the Will is to be distinguished into *voluntary* and *volitionary* action, according as we speak of the central abiding inclination, or the superficial momentary choice. "Voluntary" action both *originates*, and *is* inclination, according as the action is viewed as subjective or objective; as *originans* or *originata*. It has only three points at which it may begin. 1. The instant of creation, when a holy inclination commenced by being con-created in the will of the *specific* Adam. 2 The instant of apostasy, when a sinful inclination commenced in the will of the *specific* Adam, by solitary self-determination without Divine co-operation. 3. The instant of regeneration, when a holy inclination is re-originated in the sinful will of the *individual* man, by the Holy Ghost. The beginning of a self-determined inclination is consequently an *epoch* in the history of the human will, and epochs are infrequent and rare from the nature of the case. Creation, apostasy, and regeneration are the great epochal points in man's existence.[1] But volitions are beginning continually, and are numberless. "Volitionary" action has innumerable points of beginning, and in every instance supposes a prior inclination to an ultimate end.[2]

---

[1] "The subject of the Paradise Lost is the origin of evil—an era in existence; an event more than all others dividing past from future time, an isthmus in the ocean of eternity." Campbell Essay on English Poetry

[2] Of American writers, Hopkins, in his Outline Study of Man, distinguishes between "choice" and "volition" in a manner that approximates to the distinction between inclination and volition. "Rational choice is the fundamental, the voluntary, the moral part of the will; volition is the executive part of the will," p 224 "The point of freedom is in choice, and in that only Choice being made, volition follows of course. The one is the essential element of freedom manifesting itself in the spiritual realm, and is the immediate ob-

This distinction, between "voluntary" and "volitionary" action, or between inclination and choice, is marked in German, by Wille and Wilkuhr; in Latin, by voluntas and arbitrium; and in Greek by θέλημα and βουλή. Compare Cicero: Tusc. Quaest., IV. 6. The neglect of the distinction results in confusion and misunderstanding. If he who makes this distinction asserts that "original sin is voluntary, but not volitionary," he is understood to say that original sin is the inclination of a man, and not a successive series of single choices; that it is the constant and central determination of the will to self and sin, and not the innumerable outward transgressions that proceed from this. But if one who does not make this distinction between voluntary and volitionary action asserts that "original sin is voluntary," he may be understood to mean that there is no sin but that of volitions; that original sin is the product of a volition, and can be removed by a volition.

Theologians who in fact agree with each other, appear to disagree in case the distinction is not recognized. Owen, for example, remarks (Indwelling Sin, XII,) that "the will is the principle, the next seat and cause of obedience and disobedience. Moral actions are unto us, or in us, so far good or evil as they partake of the consent of the will. He spake truth of old who said: 'Every sin is so voluntary, that if it be not voluntary it is not sin.'" In this statement, "will" is employed in the comprehensive sense as antithetic to the understanding, and "voluntary" does not mean "volitionary." Owen would not say that "every sin is so volitionary, that if it be not volitionary it is not sin." Hodge

ject of the divine government, the other simply instrumental and executive, and is that of which human governments chiefly take cognizance," p 225. Compare pp 212, 231, 257. Hickok also tends towards the distinction between inclination and volition, in his threefold discrimination of "immanent preference," "governing purpose," and "desultory volition," and in his definition of "spiritual susceptibility" and "spiritual disposition" Empirical Psychology, pp. 282-292 But both Hopkins and Hickok adopt the classification of intellect, sensibility, and will

(Theology, I. 403), on the other hand, asserts that "freedom is more than spontaneity," and that "the affections are spontaneous, but not free. Loving and hating, delighting and abhorring do not depend upon the will." This agrees with the modern psychology, not with the elder. For by "will," Hodge here means the volitionary power, and by "freedom" the power to the contrary in the exercise of single choices.[1] If this is the true psychology, and freedom means the power of contrary choice, then it is correct to say that "the affections are not free;" because they are most certainly not the product of volitions. Yet Hodge holds that evil affections are guilty and punishable. But this requires that they be free in the sense of inclination or disposition; that they are not the product of compulsion and necessity. And in saying that "the affections are spontaneous," he implies that they are from the will (ex sponte). For spontaneity in a rational being is free will. Spontaneity in an animal, is mere physical instinct; but in man, it is rational self-determination. Leibnitz (De Libertate, Ed. Erdmann, 669) says, "libertas est spontaneitas intelligentis, itaque, quod spontaneum est in bruto vel alia substantia intellectus experte, id in homine vel in alia substantia intelligente, altius assurgit et liberum appellatur."[2] Instinct in a brute is necessitated, because it is grounded wholly in sense and animal nature; inclination in man is free, because it is grounded in reason and a spiritual essence. Inclination is the subject of command, and prohibition. Man is bidden to have a good inclination, and forbidden to have an evil one. The command to love (Deut. 6:5; Lev. 19:18; Matt. 28:39, 40), to "make the tree good" (Matt 12:33),

[1] Hodge (Theology, II 307) defines a self-determined will, as "acting independently of reason, conscience, inclinations, and feelings" This is the Arminian volitionary self-determination, which is accompanied with the power to the contrary

[2] Owen (Arminianism, XII ) defines freedom, with Prosper, as "a spontaneous appetite of what seemeth good unto it. liberum arbitrium est rei sibi placitae spontaneus appetitus."

to love not (1 John 2 : 15), to lust not (Ex. 20 : 17), are examples.

The great question in anthropology, and in reference to sin and holiness, relates to inclination rather than volition. How does an inclination begin—either a holy or a sinful inclination—is the true subject of inquiry. Had unfallen man power to change his holy inclination? Has fallen man power to change his sinful inclination? That man has power over his volitions is undisputed.

## CHAPTER IV.

### MAN'S PROBATION AND APOSTASY.

Augustine: City of God, XIII. Gangauf: Psychologie des Augustinus, VI § 5, 6. Anselm: De Casu Diaboli, XXVI. Calvin: Institutes, II. i. Ursinus. Christian Religion, Qu. 7. Witsius: Covenants, I. ii. 10. Charnocke: Holiness of God, 476, 477. Ed. Bohn. Turrettin: Institutio, IX. vii. viii. Howe: Oracles, II. xxii.; Man Created Mutable. Owen: Perseverance of Saints, I. Muller: Sin, IV. iii, iv. Dorner: Christian Doctrine, § 74–75. Macdonald Creation and the Fall. Shedd: History of Doctrine, II. 56 sq.

"Our first parents, being left to the freedom of their own will, through the temptation of Satan transgressed the commandment of God in eating the forbidden fruit, and thereby fell from the estate wherein they were created. Gen. 3:6–8, 13. Eccl. 7:29. 2 Cor. 11:3." Westminster L. C., 21. In this statement, it is not meant that the external act of eating the forbidden fruit was the whole of the first transgression, and constituted the whole of human apostasy. A part is put for the whole. The full statement would be, that "our first parents transgressed the commandment of God, by *lusting* after, and eating the forbidden fruit. This is evident from the proof text cited by the Westminster divines: "When the woman saw that the tree was a tree to be *desired* to make one wise, she took of the fruit thereof, and did eat," Gen. 3:6. According to the inspired account, the first sin began with a lustful desiring of the heart, which is the same thing as a sinful inclining of the will.

The possibility of such a lustful desiring, or wrong inclining in Adam's will supposes its mutability. "God created man male and female, with righteousness and true holiness, having the law of God written in their hearts, and power to fulfil it: and yet under a possibility of transgressing, being left to the liberty of their own will, which was *subject unto change*." Westminster Confession, IV. 2; L. C. 17.

Adam was holy by creation, but not indefectibly and immutably so The inclination of his will, though conformed to the moral law, was mutable, because his will was not omnipotent. When voluntary self-determination is an infinite and self-subsistent power, as it is in God, the fall of the will is impossible. But when voluntary self-determination is a finite and dependent power, as it is in man or angel, the fall of the will is possible. A will determined to good with an omnipotent energy is not "subject to change;" but a will determined to good with a finite and limited force is so subject. By reason of the restricted power of his created will, Adam might lose the righteousness with which he was created, though he was under no necessity of losing it. His will had sufficient power to continue in holiness, but not so much additional power as to make a lapse into sin impossible. By the terms of the covenant of works, perseverance and indefectibility in holiness were made to depend upon Adam's own decision. In this respect they differed from the believer's perseverance and indefectibility under the covenant of grace, which are infallibly secured by the operation of the Holy Spirit. The regenerate man is "kept from falling." Jude 24; Eph. 1:10; John 10:28, 29; 1 Thess 4:17; Rev. 21:4. God imparted such a measure of grace to holy Adam as enabled him to continue inclined to the Creator, if he would; but not such a measure of grace as to preclude inclining to the creature if he would. The power to the contrary; the *possibilitas peccandi*, or power to originate sin; belonged to Adam's will because of its finiteness. The use of this power was left wholly to himself. He might continue to believe and trust in God, in which case he would persevere in holiness, and obtain indefectibility as his reward; or he might believe and trust in Satan, in which case he would apostatize and lose holiness. The already existing power to incline rightly, and to persevere in this inclination was real and true freedom, and did not need this additional power to incline wrongly, in order to be such. The power to originate sin was not requisite in order to make Adam a free agent, but to make him a *probationary* agent.

Consequently, the paradisiacal state, though a holy and happy state, was not equal to the heavenly state. It had not the safety and security of the latter. Eden differed from heaven, as holiness differs from indefectibility of holiness; as a mutable perfection differs from an immutable. The perfection of holy Adam was relative, not absolute. It differed from that of God, who by reason of his omnipotence and infinity cannot fall from holiness, James 1:13; from that of the elect angels, who were kept from falling by a special measure of grace that was not granted to the fallen angels, whose perseverance like that of Adam was left to themselves; and from that of redeemed men, who like the elect angels are preserved by special grace. Howe: Man Created Mutable, vi.

God created man with relative perfection, or the possibility of sinning, for the purpose of placing him in probation. Had the Creator given Adam indefectibility in the outset, by bestowing upon him that extraordinary measure of grace which infallibly secures perseverance in holiness, Adam's own strength of will would not have been tested. In this case, God would have prevented the use of the power to the contrary, by intensifying the existing self-determination to holiness. Adam would have been kept from falling by God, and would not have kept himself.[1]

---

[1] The possibility of sinning must not be confounded with the *tendency* to sin The possibility of sinning is merely the power to originate sin ex nihilo, by the act of self-determination. The tendency to sin implies that the originating or

The object of this probation was, that Adam, by resisting Satan's temptation and persevering in holiness, might secure by his own work indefectibility, or immutable perfection. This was to be an infinite reward for standing the trial of his faith and obedience. God did not place Adam in a state of probation from mere curiosity to see if he would fall; or from malevolence to cause him to fall; but from the benevolent desire that Adam, in the exercise of the ample power with which he was endowed, might merit and obtain, as the recompense of his fidelity, a final and everlasting deliverance from the possibility of sinning The possibility of sinning is in itself an evil. It is one of the perils of finite freedom. To be delivered from it, is an infinite and eternal good. The cry in Wesley's hymn, "Take away the love of sinning," is the cry of the Christian heart. A will that is so strongly determined to holiness, by its union with the Divine will, that it is beyond the hazard of apostasy, is a greater good than a will which though holy is exposed to this hazard. Everlasting holiness is better than temporary; immutable perfection is more desirable than mutable; heaven is more blessed than paradise.

The righteousness which Adam had by creation did not merit indefectibility. God owed nothing at the instant of creation to a creature whom he had just originated from nonentity, to whom he had given holiness, and whom he was upholding by his power. He had a right to terminate Adam's existence, and reduce him to nonentity again if he so pleased A creature, from the very definition of a creature, cannot bring the Creator under an obligation, except so far as the latter by covenant and promise permits him to do so. Witsius (Covenants, I. iv. 12) cites "Durandus's

---

self-determining power has been *inwardly* exerted, though it may not have been externally. A tendency to sin is an inclination to sin It is a propensity of the heart, and a disposition of the will. The possibility of sinning is innocent, the tendency to sin is sinful.

reasoning, which Bellarmine was unable to refute: 'What we are, and what we have, whether good acts, habits, or practices, are all of them from the bounty of God, who both gives freely and preserves them. And because no one after having given freely is obliged to give more, but rather the receiver is the more obliged to the giver; therefore from good habits, acts, or practices given us by God, God is not bound by any debt of justice to give anything more.'" Says Calvin (Inst., I. xv. 8), "Adam could have stood if he would, since he fell merely by his own will, because his will was flexible to either side, and he was not endued with constancy to persevere. If any object, that he was placed in a dangerous situation on account of the imbecility of his will, I reply, that the station in which he was placed was sufficient to deprive him of all excuse. For it would have been unreasonable that God should be confined to this condition, to make man so as to be altogether incapable either of choosing or of committing any sin. It is true that such a nature would have been more excellent; but to expostulate with God as though he had been under any obligation to bestow this upon man, were unreasonable. Why he did not sustain him with the power of perseverance, remains concealed in his own mind Yet there is no excuse for man; he received so much, that he was the voluntary procurer of his own destruction; but God was under no necessity to give him any other than a mutable will, midway between sin and indefectibility (medium et caducam)."

God graciously entered into a covenant with holy Adam, and with his posterity in him, to the effect, that if he obeyed the command not to eat of the forbidden fruit, he should receive as his reward indefectibility of holiness and blessedness. This is proved by Gen. 2:17, "In the day thou eatest thereof thou shalt surely die;" which implies the converse, "If thou dost not eat thereof, thou shalt surely live." The "life" here implied and promised is a good *additional* to what Adam already had; otherwise it would not be a reward. Adam already had spiritual life, namely holiness and happiness; but it was mutable. The additional good, therefore, must have been immutable holiness and happiness. He was to have had spiritual life as *indefectible.* He was to have passed beyond all possibility of apostasy and misery.

This covenant is denominated "the covenant of works" Gal. 4:24, "These women are [represent] the two covenants:" one of works, and the other of grace. Rom. 9·4. Hosea 6:7, "But they like man (margin, Adam) have transgressed the covenant"

The consent implied in the covenant of works was by acquiescence on the part of man; like that between child and parent, and between the citizen and the state. Assent cannot be righteously or wisely refused to that which is both equitable and advantageous. Adam, being holy, would not refuse to enter into a righteous engagement with his maker; and being intelligent, would not decline an improvement in his condition. See Howe: Man Created Mutable (sub fine).

The merit to be acquired under the covenant of works was pactional Adam could claim the reward, in case he stood, only by virtue of the promise of God; not by virtue of the original relation of a creature to the creator. Upon the latter basis, he could claim nothing, as Christ teaches in Luke 17:10

The probationary statute was a positive precept. It was not sinful per se to eat of the tree of knowledge, but only because God had forbidden it. The Eden statute was, thus, a better test of implicit faith and obedience than a moral statute would have been, because it required obedience for no reason but the sovereign will of God. At the same time, disobedience of this positive statute involved disobedience of the moral law. It was contempt of authority; disbelief of God and belief of Satan; discontent with the existing state; impatient curiosity to know; pride and ambition. Anselm: Cur Deus Homo, I. xxi.

The "tree of knowledge" was an actual tree bearing fruit in the garden. It might have been a date-tree, or any other kind of tree, and still have been the tree of the knowledge of good and evil. Because, when once God had selected a particular tree in the garden, and by a positive statute had forbidden our first parents to eat of it, the instant they did eat of it they transgressed a Divine command, and then *knew* consciously and bitterly what evil is, and how it differs from good. The tree thus became "the tree of the knowledge of good and evil," not because it was a particular species of tree, but because it had been selected as the tree whereby to test the implicit obedience of Adam.

The first sin was unique, in respect to the statute broken by it. The Eden commandment was confined to Eden. It was never given before or since. Hence the first Adamic transgression cannot be repeated. It remains a single solitary transgression; the "one" sin spoken of in Rom. 5:12, 15–19

The first sin was wilful and wanton in a high degree, because committed under circumstances that made it easy not to commit it. Charnocke: Holiness of God, 477. Ed. Bohn. Adam was holy, and had full power to remain so. And, still more, the temptation that assailed him was much weaker than that which now assails his posterity. Fallen man is now tempted by solicitation addressed both to innocent desire and susceptibility, and to *sinful* desire and susceptibility: but unfallen man was tempted by a solicitation addressed only to innocent desire and susceptibility. Holy Adam had no rebellious inward lust to which Satan could appeal; none of that selfish and sinful desire which St. James speaks of, when he says that a man "is tempted when he is drawn away of his own lust and enticed" (James 1:14). The only subjective susceptibility in Adam which Satan could address, was the natural and innocent desire for the fruit of the tree of knowledge considered as "good for food, and pleasant to the eyes" (Gen. 3 : 6). This was a desire and susceptibility founded in the created relation between the nature of man and that of the tree. The other desire for the fruit as "*making wise like the gods*" (Gen. 3 : 6) was forbidden desire, and forbidden desire is sin (Gen. 20 : 17 ; Matt. 5 : 28 ; Rom. 7 : 7). Forbidden and sinful desire was not provided for in the creative act, and the established relation between man's nature and the outward object, as permitted and innocent desire was. Adam was not created with a desire for that knowledge of good and evil which would make him like the "gods": that is, like Satan and his angels. Such a kind of knowledge as this is falsehood, not truth, and to desire it is wrong and sinful. "Thou shalt not covet," is a command that prohibits such a species of desire. On the contrary, Adam was created with a desire for *true* knowledge, and this desire was satisfied by the knowledge of God which he possessed as made in his Maker's image. He was created "in [true] knowledge, and true holiness." If Adam was already lusting after the spurious knowledge of good and evil, and was already proudly desiring to be like the "gods," when Satan suggested the temptation to eat of the fruit, this would have proved that he was already fallen, and would have very greatly increased the force of the temptation, and made it far more difficult for him to refrain from eating of it. But he was not lusting after and desiring this kind of knowledge, when Satan proposed that he should eat of the fruit. This kind of rebellious, disobedient desire required to be *originated* by Adam himself, as something not previously existing in his submissive heart and obedient will. God had not implanted any such wrong desire as this. This proud and selfish lust for a false and forbidden knowledge had to be *started* by Adam himself, as something entirely new and aboriginal. It was not a primary God-created desire of the finite will, but a secondary self-originated one. It was not the product of the creative act, but of voluntary self-determination.

Such being the facts in the case, it is evident that inward lust, or sinful desire, did not contribute to the force of temptation in the instance of unfallen Adam, as it does in that of his fallen posterity, nor can it be postulated as helping to explain his fall. Sinful desire was *begun* by an act of pure self-determination, and therefore could not have been the cause of this act. Unfallen Adam was not "drawn away of his own lust and enticed," as his fallen posterity now are. He wilfully and wantonly yielded to an *external* suggestion of Satan which had by no means the violent strength of an *internal* desire. To disobey the command of God under the stress of no greater temptation than this, was wilfulness and wickedness in a high degree. That a holy and happy being, not dragged down in the least by inward lust, with full power to remain holy and happy, should by an act of sheer self-determination convert himself into a sinful and miserable being, under a moderate temptation like that in Eden, was strange and not to be expected. The fall of Adam was intrinsically improbable. A spectator would have prophesied that the holy and happy man would continue in holiness and happiness, and not plunge into sin and misery.

Hence, the origin of sin has somewhat of the characteristic of *caprice*. It was not a natural, or a rational act; but unnatural and irrational. Sin is "the *mystery* of iniquity." The fall of man cannot be rationalized: that is, explained on natural and rational grounds. This would require that it be accounted for not by pure self-determination, but by the operation of the law of cause and effect. In the physical world, a fact can be explained and made to look rational, by pointing to a foregoing cause for it that is *different* from the fact itself. But the fact of sin cannot be so explained and rationalized. There was no prior sinful act or sinful inclination of Adam, by which to account for the fact of his apostasy. The sinful self-determination of Adam's will was both the cause of the first sin and the first sin itself. Sin is *self*-caused, and therefore cannot be an effect proper of a cause proper, because an effect is different from its cause. "Let no one," says Augustine (City, XII. 7), "look for an efficient cause of the evil will; for it is not efficient, but deficient, since the evil will itself is not an effecting of something, but a defect. To seek for an efficient cause of sin [out of the will, and other than the will], is like attempting to see darkness, or hear silence." Again he says (City, XIV. ii.), "God made man upright, and consequently with a good inclination. The good inclination, then, is the work of God. But the first evil inclination, which preceded all of man's evil acts, was rather a kind of falling away from the good work of God to its own work, than any positive work; the will now not having God, but the will itself, for its end." See, also, De Libero Arbitrio, II. xx.

And this action of Adam's will in apostatizing was not only self-determination, but self-determination with no good and sufficient reason. The good reasons were all against it. Self-determination to evil is contrary to pure reason. Sin is the divorce of will from reason. Says Muller (Sin, II. 173–175), "we must acknowledge that evil is in its nature inconceivable and incomprehensible; that is to say, is the product of arbitrariness (Wilkuhr), and arbitrariness is a violation of right reason and true sequence. The inexplicableness of evil is contained in the very conception of evil. The incomprehensibleness of its origin arises not so much from the limitedness of our knowledge, as from the nature of evil itself. Hence its inexplicableness does not dwindle and disappear with the increase of our knowledge; and at no future stage of development and growth in wisdom do we pass from this incomprehensibleness, to an insight into a higher necessity of evil. On the other hand, the purer and more perfect our moral and religious knowledge becomes, the more attentively we listen to the solemn voice of our inmost consciousness and to the word of divine revelation, the more thoroughly do we perceive evil to be contrary to nature and to reason, and thoroughly unaccountable and groundless."

The death threatened in Gen. 2 : 17 was physical, spiritual, and eternal. That it was physical, is proved by Gen. 3 : 19, "Unto dust thou shalt return." Rom. 5 : 14, "Death reigned from Adam to Moses." Gen. 5 : 5, "Adam died." Physical death as a mortal principle befell Adam immediately, though he did not actually die on the day he sinned. When a man is smitten with mortal disease he is a dead man, though he may live some months. Adam's body immediately became a mortal body. Symmachus translates the Hebrew by θνητός ἔσῃ, "thou shalt become mortal." Compare Edwards: Original Sin, Works, II. 403.

That the body of Adam was not mortal by creation, is proved by the *threatening* of death in Gen. 2 : 17; which implies that as things then were, there was no liability to death. No sin, then no death. Also by Gen. 3 : 22, God "drove out the man from the garden, lest he take of the tree of life and live forever." This implies that in the original plan provision was made for the immortality of the body. After the transgression, it was necessary to prevent the immortality of the body by a special act of God. "In my opinion," says Augustine (De Peccatorum Meritis, I. 3), "Adam was supplied with sustenance against decay from the fruit of the various trees, and with security against old age from the tree of life." In Rev. 2 : 7, the Holy Spirit promises to him "that overcometh," the privilege of "eating of the tree of life which is in the midst of the paradise of God." Complete redemption places man beyond the possibility of death, either physical or spiritual. See also Rom. 8 : 11, 23, where the glorified body is connected with the sinless perfection of the soul. The perfection of unfallen Adam's body, also, excluded an inherent mortality.

The difference between the immortal body of holy Adam and the mortal body of fallen Adam is, that prior to the fall the human body was not liable to death from internal causes, but only from external. It had no latent diseases, and no seeds of death in it. Neither had it inordinate and vicious physical appetites, such as craving for stimulants, gluttonous appetite for food, licentious sexual appetite, etc., all of which tend to destroy the body. It could, however, be put to death. If it were deprived of food, or air, it would die. It was not a celestial body like that of the glorified saints, but a body of flesh and blood. The question was raised in the Patristic church, whether Christ's body previous to his resurrection was like that of unfallen Adam, or of fallen. Smith's Hagenbach, § 103; Schaff: History, § 143. Christ was weary, and hungry, and thirsty; but it is never said that he was sick with any bodily disease. And he certainly had no inordinate physical appetites. That he might have had a diseased and dying body, is compatible with his sinless perfection. For although a sinless soul like that of our Lord *deserves* an undying and immortal body, yet he might have voluntarily submitted to that part of the "curse" of sin which consists in a diseased and dying body, without thereby becoming a partaker of sin itself. Gal. 3:13.

This original immortality of the body, like Adam's moral perfection, was mutable and relative only. It might be lost. In case he fell from holiness, his body would be affected by his sin. The seeds of mortality would be implanted, the organism would begin to die from the moment of its birth, and the temperate physical appetite would become intemperate and inordinate. On the contrary, if Adam stood probation, that possibility of being put to death (posse mori) which was associated with Adam's relative perfection would become an impossibility (posse non mori), like that connected with the glorified body of Christ and the resurrection-body of believers. These latter not only have no seeds of death in them, but they cannot be put to death by external agency. Says Augustine (De peccatorum meritis, I. 2), "If Adam had not sinned, he would not have been divested of his body, but would have been clothed upon with immortality and incorruption, that 'immortality might have been swallowed up of life;' that is, that he might have passed from the natural body into the spiritual body."

The mere possibility of death is not the same as a tendency to death. Unfallen Adam might have the former, but not the latter. A tendency implies the germinal base or seed of the thing. There is a possibility that every man may have all the physical diseases; but there is no tendency to all of them in every man.

That the death threatened was spiritual, is proved by Rom. 5.18, where it is opposed to "spiritual life." So also in Rom. 5:21; 6:23; 2 Tim. 1:10. The description of the consequences of apostasy discloses mental characteristics that belong to spiritual death; namely, terror and shame before God. Gen. 3:8, 10, 24.[1]

That the death was endless, is proved by the texts that represent it as the contrary of life; because the life is unquestionably endless. Rom. 5:18, 21; 6:23. Also by the texts that prove endless punishment. See Eschatology, pp. 677 sq.

Adam and Eve fell from the state of holiness by an act of self-determination, as the efficient cause. "Being left to the freedom of their own will, our first parents transgressed, and thereby fell." Westminster L. C., 21. They also fell by the external temptation of Satan addressed to their innocent susceptibility, as the occasional cause. "Through the temptation of Satan, they transgressed."

---

[1] Wesley held that the death caused by the first sin was spiritual, not physical; yet that it brought physical death upon the brutes Southey. Wesley, Ch. XX.

Westminster L. C., 21. On the freeness of the first sin, see Charnocke: Holiness of God, pp. 476, 477. Ed. Bohn.

Adam and Eve were already holy, and did not need to originate holiness. In being holy, that is enlightened in their understanding and rightly inclined in their will, they had plenary power to continue and persevere in holiness. The temptation by Satan had no power to force their decision. To fall under these circumstances, was as free and unnecessitated an act of self-determination as can be conceived of. As previously remarked, it was a species of voluntary caprice which cannot be made to look rational or natural. All sin after the first sin is explicable by selfish inclination and strong evil propensities concurring with outward temptation. But the first sin had not these antecedents. There was nothing but an external temptation addressed to an innocent susceptibility. "This sin was aggravated in being committed when man had full light in his understanding; a clear copy of the law in his heart; when he had no vicious bias in his will, but enjoying perfect liberty; and when he had a sufficient stock of grace in his hand to withstand the tempting enemy; in being committed after God had made a covenant of life with him, and given him express warning of the danger of eating the forbidden fruit." Fisher: Catechism, Q. 15.[1]

If the will of Adam and Eve had been in a state of indifference, the probability of the fall would have been far greater, because the resistance of an undetermined will is less than that of a determined holy will. Under the circumstances, the fall of the holy pair was unlikely. That it occurred, proves that it was a very wilful act: wanton and gratuitous. It was also an extremely guilty act, because of being committed against great light, and under no great stress of temptation.

[1] Compare, Howe. Oracles II, xxiv. Augustine City of God, XIV xii. xiv; XXI. xii. xv

The trial of man upon the Pelagian and Semi-Pelagian theories was very disadvantageous, compared with his trial upon the Augustinian and Calvinistic. An indifferent and undecided will is extremely liable to succumb to temptation. A will positively inclined to holiness can very readily resist temptation. It is, therefore, a defect in Muller's theory (Sin, II. 70), and also in Howe's, that the human will at the instant of its creation is regarded as "created without any determination to good; it was made in that state of liberty as to be in a certain sort of equipoise, according as things should be truly or falsely represented to it by the mind or understanding." Howe: Oracles, II. xxii. If this was the original condition of Adam when subjected to temptation and probation, he was unfavorably placed by his Creator.

"Sin is any want of conformity unto, or transgression of the law of God." Westminster L. C., 14 Rom. 3:23, "All have sinned, and come short of the glory of God." Rom. 3:12, "All have deviated" (ἐξέκλιναν). 1 John 3: 4, "Sin is lawlessness" (ἀνομία). Gal. 5:19–21, Sin is "the work of the flesh." Rom. 8:7, Sin is "the carnal mind, and enmity toward God."

The intrinsic and inmost characteristic of sin is its *culpability* or guilt. Guilt is desert of punishment. Sin is damnable and punishable before the moral law Consequently sin must be the product of free agency. Necessitated sin is a contradiction. The primary source and seat of sin, therefore, is the *will*, because this is the causative and originating faculty of the soul. "Our first parents being left to the freedom of their will fell." From this inmost centre of the soul, it passes into the understanding, and through the entire man The inclination and affections having become contrary to what they were by creation, the understanding is darkened, and the conscience benumbed.

Some theologians explain the origin of sin by the understanding, rather than the will. Eve was deceived, 1 Tim.

2 : 14. Deception is cognitive. The human mind by creation was enlightened so that it knew God and divine things spiritually. But it was not omniscient. It was capable therefore of being deceived by an apparent good: namely, the knowledge of good and evil. The tempter addresses his temptation to the understanding: "Ye shall be as gods, knowing good and evil." This was a plausible temptation to a creature already knowing much, and capable of knowing more. But this does not account for the first sin. For this temptation through an apparent good ought to have been repelled, and might have been, by an act of the *will* Eve ought to have remained content with the knowledge she already possessed by creation. By self-determination, she should and could have continued to be satisfied with her Maker's arrangement, and *refused* this promised increase of knowledge. Had she done so, she would have remained unfallen and sinless. In this way, it appears that the proximate and efficient cause of the first sin was the will rather than the understanding. It was not necessary that unfallen Eve should incline, or self-determine in accordance with an apparent good. Even though her understanding did perceive a species of good in the forbidden knowledge of good and evil, yet her still holy will could have rejected it Her understanding had no power to compel her will by means of an apparent, or seeming good. This is expressed in the lines of Dante:

> "Then through the glowing air was sweetly sent
> A strain so ravishing to mortal sense,
> It made me Eve's audacity lament
> That when both heaven and earth obedient were,
> Woman alone, and she but just created,
> *Refused* the veil of ignorance to bear;
> To which had she submitted patiently,
> O how extended, how much antedated
> Had been these joys ineffable."
>
> PURGATORY, XXIX. 22.

The deception of the understanding is a mis-judgment of the understanding that does not of necessity carry the will with it. Free will can reject a seeming good, as well as a real good; can decide against a false judgment, as well as against a true one. Furthermore, a deceived understanding is rather an *effect* of an evil will, than its cause. A false judgment results from a sinful inclination, rather than the converse. Error in the head comes from error in the heart. When the will has once substituted self and the creature for God and the creator, as its ultimate end, then false judgments respecting what is good, and what is happiness, and what is true knowledge, immediately arise Then finite objects take on a false appearance, and are deemed to be the summum bonum. "When once man surrenders himself to the sway of that perverted principle which makes his own satisfaction the aim of all his endeavors, there will necessarily spring from this foul root a multitude of erroneous notions as to what this satisfaction consists in." Muller: Sin, I. 165. But if the will continues true in its primary created determination to God as the chief end, the understanding is not thus hoodwinked, but sees through all the deceptions of temptation, and rejects them

Still less is the origin of sin to be sought for in the sensuous nature of man—a theory at one time considerably current in Germany, and which has received a thorough examination by Muller. Sin, I. 295–334. The great objection to it is, that it finds the source of sin outside of the voluntary faculty. Man's sensuous nature is not his will; *σάρξ* is not *πνεῦμα*. Sense is not causative and originative, in its working. Consequently, sin does not begin in the lower physical nature and ascend to the will and reason; but vice versa. The will and reason fall first in the order. The soul sins, and then the body becomes vitiated.

In respect to its having no sinful antecedent out of which it is made, sin is origination ex nihilo. Sin is the beginning of something from nothing, and there is this resemblance between it and creation proper. In holy Adam, there was no sinful inclination or corruption that prompted the first transgression. Adam started the wicked inclination itself ex nihilo, by a causative act of self-determination. The first sin was an act of origination, not of selection or choice. If the first sinful act were one of choice between good and evil, this would require an existing indifference towards both, and the absence of inclination. But if it was a self-determining and causative act, this would be compatible with an existing holy inclination. The will, in this case, passed or "lapsed" from one inclination to another, by the inherent energy of self-motion that originated something new. As in regeneration, a new holy inclination originated by the Holy Spirit expels the existing sinful inclination, so in apostasy, a new sinful inclination originated by the human will expels the existing holy inclination. See p. 135 sq.

But sin differs from creation proper, in that it is not a *substance*. Creation originates beings and things ; but sin is neither a being nor a thing. Yet it is not "nothing," in every sense of the term "nothing" Anselm denominated it "essentia," and denied that it is "substantia." But "essentia" is too strong a term for sin. "Habit" and "accident" are better terms. These are the terms employed by the Reformed theologians. Inasmuch as sin is a habitus inhering in the will and infecting the understanding, it is not a strict nonentity. To commit sin, is not to do nothing. To do evil, is to do something. Compare Turrettin, IX. i. Neither is sin a "property" of a substance, because properties *necessarily* belong to a substance. Sin is an "accident:" that is, a characteristic that may or may not belong to a spiritual substance. "When we say that God is the cause of all things, we mean of all such things as have a *real* existence [i.e. *substances*] ; which is no reason why those things themselves should not be the cause of some *accidents*, such as actions are. God created man, and some other intelligences superior to man, with a liberty of acting; which liberty of acting is not itself evil, but may be the cause of something that is evil." Grotius: Christian Religion, I. viii. "Peccatum non est quid substantiale, ut Flacius Illyricus, haud procul a Manichaeismo, saltem de originale labe statuebat. Materia peccati proxima est ipsamet vel ἕξις vel actio vitiosa" Maresius: Systema, VI. 6, 8. The term ἕξις is used by Plato and Aristotle to denote the habitual disposition of a faculty of the mind, in distinction from the substance of the faculty itself. "Sin," says Calvin (Inst., II. i. 11), "is rather an adventitious quality or accident, than a substantial property originally innate."

The first sin of man, though proximately and formally the violation of the Eden statute, was ultimately and implicitly the violation of the whole moral law. The contempt of the Divine authority in transgressing the commandment not to eat of the tree of knowledge, was the contempt of Divine authority generally. "He that offendeth in one point is guilty of all," James 2:10. Hence sin is defined as "the transgression of law," or lawlessness. 1 John 3:4.

The moral law violated by the free will of man is both written, and unwritten: the law of nature, and the decalogue. Rom. 2:14–16. The points of difference between them have been specified under the head of Revelation. Vol. I., p. 62 sq. The two laws are originally and essentially the same. The ethics of man's rational nature as he came from the Creator's hand, and of the decalogue, are identical. The now existing difference between the two is due to apostasy. "The natural law," says Ursinus (Christian Religion, Quest 92), "doth not differ from the moral in nature *not corrupted;* but in nature *corrupted,* a good part of the natural law is darkened by sins, and but a little part only concerning the obedience due to God was left remaining in man's mind after the fall: for which cause, also, God hath in his church repeated again and declared the whole sentence and doctrine of his law in the decalogue. Therefore the decalogue is a restoring and re-entering or reinforcing of the law of nature; and the law of nature is a part only of the decalogue." Such being the connection between the unwritten and written law, it follows that sin in the heathen is the same in *kind* with sin in Christendom. Free and responsible human will, in both instances, transgresses a common law and ethics. The difference between the violation of the unwritten law and the written, is one of degree only. "As many as have sinned without law, shall also perish without law; and as many as have sinned in the law, shall be judged by the law," Rom. 2:12.

# CHAPTER V.

## ORIGINAL SIN.

Augustine: City of God, XIV. xii. xiii.; De natura et gratia; Contra Julianum, Opus imperfectum contra Julianum. Anselm: De Conceptu virginali et originali peccato. Aquinas. Summa, II. (1) lxxix.-lxxxvii. Lombard. Sententiarum, II. xxii. 12. Calvin: Institutes, II. i.-v. Ursinus: Christian Religion, Qu. 7-9. Turrettin: Institutio, IX viii-xii Placaeus. De Imputatione. Burgess: Original Sin. Charnocke: Attributes (Holiness). Owen: Vindiciae, VI; Arminianism, VII. VIII. Howe: Oracles, II. xxiii.-xxvii; Temple, II viii Episcopius: Opera, II vii. (Apologia). John Taylor: Original Sin. Jeremy Taylor: Original Sin. Davenant: Justification, Ch. XIV. Usher: Original Sin. Butler: Sermons on Human Nature. Edwards. Original Sin. King Origin of Evil Nitzsch: Christian Doctrine, § 107, 111. Wiggers: Augustinianism and Pelagianism (Emerson's Tr) Watson: Institutes, Pt. II. Ch. xviii. Baur: Gegensatz (Lehre von der Sunde). Gangauf: Aug. Psychologie, VI. 7, 8. Heppe: Dogmatik der Evangelish-Reformirten Kirche; Dogmatik des Deutschen Protestantismus. Schweitzer: Glaubenslehre der Evangelisch-Reformirten Kirche. Rivetus Testimonia de Imputatione. Landis. Original Sin and Gratuitous Imputation. Princeton Essays: On Imputation Fisher: Discussions (Augustinian and Federal Theories). Muller: Sin, I. i. ii.; IV. i. ii. Shedd: History of Doctrine, II. 50-177; Theological Essays (Original Sin).

"The sinfulness of that estate [status, or condition] whereinto man fell consists in the guilt of Adam's first sin, the want of original righteousness, and the corruption of the whole nature: which is commonly called original sin; together with all actual transgressions which proceed from it." Westminster Shorter Catechism, 18.

According to this doctrinal statement, there are three

particulars under the general head of Sin. 1. The guilt of the first sin. 2. The corruption of nature resulting from the first sin. 3. Actual transgressions, or sins of act, which result from corruption of nature.

1. The first part of the sinfulness of man's estate or condition is the guilt of the first sin. The first sin of Adam, strictly and formally considered, was the transgression of the particular command not to eat of the tree of knowledge. This was a positive statute, and not the moral law. It tested obedience more severely than the moral law does, because the latter carries its own reason with it, while the former containing no intrinsic morality appealed to no reason except the mere good pleasure of God. To disobey it, was to disregard the authority of God, and involved disobedience of all law. The guilt of Adam's first sin is the guilt of transgressing the law of Eden explicitly, and the moral law implicitly. "The rule of obedience revealed to Adam, besides a special command not to eat of the fruit of the tree of knowledge, was the moral law." Westminster L. C., 92.

The first sin of Adam was twofold: (*a*) Internal; (*b*) External. The internal part of it was the originating and starting of a wrong inclination. The external part of it was the exertion of a wrong volition prompted by the wrong inclination. Adam first inclined to self instead of God, as the ultimate end. He became an idolater, and "worshipped and served the creature more than the creator," Rom. 1:25. Then, in order to gratify this new inclination, he reached forth his hand and ate of the forbidden fruit. "Our first parents fell into *open* disobedience, because already they were secretly corrupted; for the evil act had never been done had not an evil inclination (voluntas) preceded it. And what is the origin of our evil inclination but pride? And what is pride but the craving for undue exaltation? And this is undue exaltation, when the soul abandons Him to whom it ought to cleave as its end, and becomes an end to *itself*. The wicked desire to please himself secretly existed in Adam, and the open sin was but its consequence." Augustine: City of God, XIV. xiii. Edwards (Original Sin, Works, II. 385) directs attention to the internal part of Adam's first sin, in the following manner. His opponent Taylor had said that "Adam could not sin [externally] without a sinful inclination." Edwards replies that "this is doubtless true; for although there was no natural sinful inclination in [holy] Adam, yet an inclination to that sin of eating the forbidden fruit was *begotten* in him by the delusion and error he was led into, and this inclination to eat the forbidden fruit must precede his actual eating." The rising of this sinful desire and inclination, Edwards considers to be the firsts in itself. There was not a first sin prior to it of which the sinful inclination was the effect; but the very inclining away from God to the creature was Adam's fall itself, and that of his posterity in him. "I am humbly of the opinion," he says (Original Sin, Works, II. 481), "that if any have supposed the children of Adam to come into the world with a *double* guilt, one the guilt of Adam's sin, another the guilt arising from their having a corrupt heart, they have not so well conceived of the matter. The guilt a man has upon his soul at his first [individual] existence, is one and simple, viz., the guilt of the original apostasy, the guilt of the sin by which the *species* first rebelled against God. This, and the guilt arising from the first corruption or depraved disposition of the heart, are not to be looked upon as *two* things, *distinctly* imputed and charged upon men in the sight of God. It is true that the guilt that arises from the corruption of the heart as it remains a *confirmed principle*, and appears in its *subsequent operations*, is a distinct and additional guilt; but the guilt arising from the *first existing* [the start, or origination] of a depraved disposition in Adam's posterity, I apprehend is *not* distinct from their guilt of Adam's first sin. For so it was not in Adam himself. The first evil disposition or inclination of the heart of Adam to sin was not properly *distinct* from his first sin, but was *included* in it. The external act he committed was no otherwise his, than as his heart was in it, or as that action proceeded from the wicked inclination of his heart. Nor was the guilt he had *double*, as for two distinct sins: one, the wickedness of his heart and will in that affair; another, the wickedness of the external act caused by his heart. His guilt was all truly from the act of his *inward* man; exclusive of which, the motions of his body were no more than the motions of any lifeless instrument. His sin consisted in wickedness of heart, fully sufficient *for*, and entirely amounting *to* all that appeared in the act he committed." [1]

The internal part of Adam's first sin was the principal part of it. It was the real commencement of sin in man. It was the origination from nothing, of a sinful disposition in the human will. There was no previous sinful disposition to prompt it, or to produce it. When Adam inclined away from God to the creature, he exercised an act of pure self-determination. He began sinning by a real beginning, analogous to that by which matter begins to be from nothing. In endowing Adam with a mutable holiness, God made it possible, but not necessary, for Adam to originate a sinful inclination, and thereby expel a holy one. The finite will can fall from holiness to sin, if it is not "kept from falling" (Jude 24) by God's special grace, because it is finite. The finite is the *mutable*, by the very definition.

Since this first inclining of the human will had no sinful

---

[1] Hodge (Princeton Essays, I 150, 168) thinks that Edwards here "abandons" the doctrine of immediate imputation which "he maintains in two-thirds of his work on Original Sin," and adopts mediate imputation But Edwards, in this place, explicitly imputes the guilt of the *first rising* of evil desire as well as of the corruption resulting from it, and this rising of evil desire he says was the first sin, which was inseparable from its consequence, namely, corruption of nature. Had Edwards asserted that only the corruption as the effect, but not the rising of evil desire itself as the cause of the effect, is imputed, he would have been liable to the charge of holding mediate imputation.

antecedent, it is denominated "original" sin. There is no sin before it, by which to explain it. "If it be asked," says Lombard (Liber II., Distinctio xxii. 12), "whether inclination (voluntas) preceded that first sin, we answer, in the first place, that inasmuch as that first sin consisted both of inclination (voluntas) and of outward act (actus), inclination preceded outward act, but another evil inclination did not precede the evil inclination itself; and, secondly, that through the persuasion of Satan, and by the arbitrary decision (arbitrio) of Adam, that evil inclination was produced by which he deserted righteousness and began iniquity. And this inclination (voluntas) itself was iniquity." The following dialogue in Anselm's De Casu Diaboli, Cap. 27, is to the same effect. "Disciple. Why did the wicked angel will what he ought not to have willed? Master. No cause preceded this wrong act, except it were that the angel could so will. Disciple. Did he then will wickedly because he was able to? Master. No, because the good angel had the same power, but did not will wrongly. No one wills wrongly merely because he can so will. Disciple Why then does he will wrongly? Master. Only because he will. The wicked will has no other cause but this, why it determines to sin. It is both an efficient and an effect in one."

The internal part of Adam's first sin was "voluntary," not "volitionary." It was will as desire, not will as volition; will as inclining, not will as choosing. The fall was the transition from one form of self-motion to another form of self-motion, and not the beginning of self-motion for the first time. The fall was a self-determining to evil expelling an existing self-determination to good. It was inclining away from one ultimate end to another, not choosing between two ultimate ends to neither of which was there any existing inclination. Adam before he fell was self-determined to God and goodness. Consequently, in the garden of Eden, he had not to choose either good or evil as two contraries to both of which his will was *indifferent*. By creation, he was positively inclined to good. The question put before him in the probation and temptation was, whether he would remain holy as he was, or begin a new inclination to evil; not whether, having no inclination at all, he would choose either good or evil. His act of apostasy, if it occurred, was to be an act of new and wrong desire in place of the existing holy desire; of new and wrong self-determination, in place of the existing and right self-determination. The fall was a change of inclination, not the exertion of a volition.

The internal part of Adam's first sin is described in Gen. 3:1–6. According to this narrative, Eve first listened to the crafty query of Satan, whether God could have given such a command; then she entered into a discussion with him; then she believed him. All this internal agency of the soul occurred prior to plucking and eating the forbidden fruit But this listening, discussing, and believing on the part of Eve, occurred because she was secretly *desiring* the forbidden knowledge by which she would "be as the gods," Gen. 3:5. *Lust* for that false knowledge which Satan had promised, explains these mental processes. Dalliance with temptation always implies a *desire* for the tempting object. Had Eve continued to desire and to be content with that *true* knowledge which she had by creation, she would have *abhorred* the false knowledge proposed by the Tempter, and this abhorrence would have precluded all parleying with him, and all trust in him.

A comparison of the manner in which our Lord dealt with the same Tempter is instructive. Christ, in the wilderness, entered into no parley and debate with Satan, as Eve did in paradise. He did not dally with temptation, because no *desire* for what God had forbidden arose within him. The second Adam did not lust, like the first Adam, after the false good presented by the Tempter. The first two of Satan's suggestions he instantaneously rejects, giving reasons therefor in the decisive language of Scripture.

And the third and more blasphemous suggestion, he thrusts away with the avaunt of abhorrence. There was not the slightest swerving from God, the faintest hankering after prohibited good, in the most secret soul of our Lord. His will from centre to circumference, both as inclination and volition, both in desire and act, remained steadfast in holiness. Christ met Satan's temptation with aversion and loathing. Eve met it with inclination and liking.

The history of the rise of evil desire or lust is given by Divine inspiration. Along with the listening, the debating, and the believing on the part of Eve, there was, according to the narrative in Genesis, a yet more important activity that occurred in the soul of Eve, prior to the eating of the forbidden fruit. "The woman saw that the tree was good for food, and that it was pleasant to the eyes, and a tree *to be desired to make one wise*," Gen 3 : 6. Eve looked upon the tree of knowledge not only with *innocent*, but with *sinful* desire She not only had the natural created desire for it as producing nourishing food, and as a beautiful object to the eye, but she came to have, besides this, the unnatural and *self-originated* desire for it as yielding a kind of *knowledge* which God forbade man to have. She "lusted" after that "knowledge of good and evil" which eating of the fruit would impart. This knowledge was not the true wisdom and spiritual knowledge which Adam and Eve already had by creation, and which is the intellectual side of holiness, but it was the false knowledge which "the gods," that is Satan and his angels, had acquired by apostasy.[1] This lusting of Eve for a knowledge

[1] If it be objected to this explanation of the term "gods" in this place, that in Gen 3 : 22 the knowledge is described as like that of God himself ("one of *us*"), the reply is, that there are two ways of knowing evil : the one as Satan knows it, namely, by personal sinfulness and self-consciousness ; the other as God knows it, namely, by the intuition of omniscience without personal sinfulness and self-consciousness The knowledge can therefore be spoken of from either point of view As prohibited, it must have been as a *bad* knowledge : that is, the knowledge of "the gods" in the bad sense, the knowledge which Satan and his angels had.

that God had *prohibited* was her apostasy. This was the self-determining and inclining of her will away from God as the chief end and chief good, to self and the creature as the chief end. To desire what God has forbidden is to prefer self to God, and this is to sin. This concupiscence was the beginning of sin in her will. It was the same thing, in kind, with the concupiscence which God forbids in the tenth commandment. The command not to covet, or lust, is a command not to *desire* anything that God has forbidden. God has forbidden theft. To inwardly desire another man's property is theft. God has forbidden murder. To be inwardly angry at a fellow-man is murder. God has forbidden adultery. To inwardly desire another man's wife is adultery. In like manner, God had forbidden to Adam Satanic knowledge of good and evil. To inwardly desire it, was the first sin. Achan's sin began with inward desire, or lust. "When I saw among the spoils a goodly Babylonish garment, and two hundred shekels of silver, and a wedge of gold, then I *coveted* them, and took them," Joshua 7 : 21.

All this internal action of the soul of Eve, then, occurred prior to the outward act of plucking and eating Says Fisher (Catechism, Q. 3), "Were not our first parents guilty of sin before eating the forbidden fruit? Yes: they were guilty in hearkening to the devil, and believing him before they actually ate it. Why, then, is their eating of it called their *first* sin? Because it was the first sin *finished.* James 1:15." "The first sin," says Pictet (Theology, IV. 2), "commenced when Eve began to *doubt* whether she had rightly understood the intention of God in forbidding the fruit of the tree. Afterwards, when she ought to have consulted God upon this subject, she *believed* the devil, who said that they should not die; in the next place, she was flattered with the hope held out to her by Satan of *knowing* all things, and being equal to God; and at last, she reached forth her hand to the fruit." "From the account in Genesis," says

Hodge (Theology, II. 128), "it appears that doubt, unbelief, and pride, were the principles which led to this fatal act of disobedience. Eve doubted God's goodness; she disbelieved his threatening; she aspired after forbidden knowledge."[1]

The account given in Gen. 3:1–6 favors the supposition that Eve had the colloquy with Satan by herself, as Milton represents it in his poem. The woman alone entered into the discussion with Satan of a subject that ought not to have been discussed at all. "And when," continues the narrative, "the woman saw that the tree was good for food, and that it was pleasant (תַּאֲוָה) to the eyes, and a tree to be desired (נֶחְמָד) to make one wise, she took of the fruit thereof and did eat; and gave also unto her husband, and he did eat," Gen. 3:6. St. Paul (1 Tim. 2:14) affirms that "Adam was not deceived [by Satan], but the woman being deceived by him fell into the transgression (ἐν παρά-βασει γέγονε)." This implies that Adam did not believe the tempter's assertion that a good would follow the eating of the forbidden fruit, and that death would not be the consequence. According to St. Paul, Adam was seduced by his affection for Eve, rather than deceived by the lie of Satan. He fell with his eyes wide open to the fact that if he ate he would die. But in loving his wife more than God, he "worshipped and served the creature instead of the Creator," and like Eve set up a different final end from the true one

The account in Gen. 3:6 describes: (*a*) The *innocent physical desire* of man's unfallen nature for the fruit of the tree of knowledge; (*b*) The rising of *sinful moral desire* for it. "The woman saw that the tree was good for food, and that it was pleasant (a desire, תַּאֲוָה) to the eyes." This denotes merely the correlation between the created qualities of man's physical constitution and this particular product of God's creation. It was not wrong, but perfectly

[1] The lustful looking of Eve is indicated in Luther's version of Gen. 3:6. Lange, in loco

innocent, to perceive that the tree was good for *food* and to desire it as such, and to be pleasantly affected by the *beauty* of it. This Divinely established relation between man's physical nature and that of the tree of knowledge, constituted the subjective basis for the temptation. Had the tree been repulsive to the sight and taste, its fruit would not have been employed by Satan as a means of solicitation. Up to this point in the description, the phraseology is the same as that in Gen. 2 : 9, respecting all the trees in the garden. "Out of the ground, made the Lord God to grow every tree that is pleasant (נֶחְמָד) to the sight, and good for food." All the physical products of God, the tree of knowledge included, were agreeable and pleasant objects for the newly created and sinless man.

But the account in Gen. 3 : 6 further adds, that the tree of knowledge came to be for Eve a tree "to be desired (נֶחְמָד), *to make one wise*." The sinful moral desire, here mentioned, is different from the innocent physical desire spoken of in the preceding part of the verse. It was a mental hankering after the fruit *as imparting to the eater a kind of knowledge which God had forbidden to man.* This is something new, and different from the innocent craving belonging to man's sensuous nature. To desire the fruit simply as food, and as a beautiful object, was innocent. But to desire a knowledge of good and evil such as the "gods" had, which the eating of it would communicate, was rebellious and wicked, because this kind of knowledge had been prohibited. The word נֶחְמָד, descriptive of Eve's longing after the prohibited knowledge, is the same employed in the tenth commandment (Ex. 20 : 17), which the Seventy render by ὄυκ ἐπιθυμήσεις. Eve's evil desire was also the same in kind with the ἐπιθυμία of St. Paul, which he declares to be ἁμαρτία. Rom. 7 : 7. It was also the same in kind with the ἐπιθυμία mentioned in James 1 : 14, "Every man is tempted when he is drawn away by his own lust and enticed."

*The self-willed origination and rising of this desire for a knowledge that God had forbidden, was the fall of Eve.* It was a new inclination of her will to self, directly contrary to that inclination to God with which she had been created. As regeneration is denominated a "birth" of the soul because of the *totality* of the moral change, so apostasy may be called a "birth" of the soul for the same reason. By the fall, the children of God became the children of Satan. John 8:44; Matt. 13:38. Each "birth" alike is an entire revolution in human character; one upward the other downward. As regeneration is the origination by the Holy Spirit of holy desire and inclination, so apostasy was the origination by Adam of sinful desire and inclination. God had not forbidden the existence of the desire for the fruit as "good for food and pleasant to the eye," and had this continued to be the only desire in Eve in regard to the tree, she would have remained sinless as she was created. But God had forbidden the desire for the fruit as fitted "to make one wise" with the knowledge of good and evil. The instant the desire "to be as gods" arose in Eve's heart, she sinned. God's command, in its full form, was: "Thou shalt not lust after but *abhor* the knowledge of good and evil; thou shalt not choose but *refuse* it." The prohibition in the instance of the Eden statute, as in that of the tenth commandment, included both the inward desire and the outward act; both inclination and volition. If a man hates his brother, he violates the sixth commandment, even if he does not actually kill him. Matt. 5:22. So, too, if when Eve had *desired* the forbidden knowledge, she had been prevented from reaching out the hand and plucking the fruit, she would still have transgressed the Eden statute. For obedience to God required that she *abhor* and *reject* the knowledge proffered by Satan. But to *lust* after it, was to prefer and love it. Even, therefore, if she had been forcibly stopped from completing, or as St James (1:15) phrases it "finishing" the sin of desiring, by the outward act of eating, she would still have been guilty of disobeying God. For the Divine command is, to choose the good and *refuse* the evil. Deut. 30 : 19. The holiness of Immanuel, which is true holiness, is described as "*refusing* the evil and choosing the good." Isa 7 : 16. But whoever *desires* the evil that is prohibited "chooses" it, and thereby *refuses* the good that is commanded. Had Eve continued to desire and love the true knowledge which she already had by her creation in the Divine image, this desire and love would have been the rejection and abhorrence of the false knowledge offered in the temptation. But when she began to desire and love the false knowledge, this was the rejection and hatred of the true knowledge. And this was apostasy. Neutrality or indifference was impossible in the will of Eve, or any will whatever. For her to incline to self, was to disincline to God; to desire false knowledge, was to dislike true knowledge; to choose the evil, was to refuse the good; to love the creature, was to hate the Creator. The rising of her evil desire, consequently, was the expulsion of her holy desire; the starting of her new sinful self-determination, was the ousting of her existing holy self-determination. She could not have two contrary desires or inclinations simultaneously. Hence the universal command, "Thou shalt not covet:" that is, "Thou shalt not desire anything that God has forbidden;" because this is the same thing as to dislike and hate what God has commanded.

This evil inclining and desiring is denominated "concupiscence," in the theological nomenclature. In the Augustinian and Calvinistic anthropology, it includes mental as well as sensual desire; in the Pelagian anthropology, it is confined to sensual appetite. "Man," says Calvin, II. i. 9, "has not only been ensnared by the inferior appetites, but abominable impiety has seized the very citadel of his mind, and pride has penetrated into the inmost recesses of his heart; so that it is weak and foolish to restrict the corruption which has proceeded thence to what are called the sensual appetites. In this the grossest ignorance has been discovered by Peter Lombard, who when investigating the seat of it says it is in the flesh according to the testimony of Paul, Rom. 7:18, not indeed exclusively, but because it principally appears in the flesh; as though Paul designated only a part of the soul, and not the whole of our nature which is opposed to supernatural grace Now Paul removes every doubt by informing us that the corruption resides not in one part only, but that there is nothing pure and uncontaminated by its mortal infection. For, when arguing respecting corrupt nature, he not only condemns the inordinate motions of the appetites, but principally insists on the blindness of the mind, and the depravity of the heart, Eph. 4:17, 18" Says Luther, On Galatians 5:17, "When Paul says that the flesh lusteth against the spirit, and the spirit against the flesh, he admonishes us that we must feel the concupiscence of the flesh, that is to say, not only carnal lust but also pride, wrath, slothfulness, impatience, unbelief, and such like" See Heppe: Reformirter Dogmatik, Locus XV., for definitions from the elder Calvinists.

Concupiscence is different from natural created appetency or desire. Hunger and thirst are not evil concupiscence. They are instinctive, constitutional, and involuntary. Gluttony on the contrary is voluntary, not constitutional. It is not pure instinctive craving for food There is will in it It is the inclining and desire of the will for a more intense pleasure from eating food, than the natural healthy appetite provides for. Innocent hunger makes use of the appointed food, and when satisfied it rests. If a man simply quiets his hunger with bread convenient for it, he does not have or exhibit concupiscence. But if he craves sensual pleasure from eating, and gratifies the craving by tickling the palate, he has and exhibits concupiscence or evil desire.

Concupiscence is not natural and innocent appetite intensified. It is not a difference in degree, but in kind. A starving man is not concupiscent, though his desire for food is intense to the very highest degree. His famine-struck craving for food is not a gluttonous craving for sensual pleasure. It is purely physical. But gluttony is the mental in the physical. Gluttony is the will's selfish inclination manifested in a bodily appetite. It is the will in the senses

These remarks apply to thirst, and the sexual appetite. As created and constitutional, neither of these is evil concupiscence. But as mixed with will and moral inclination—the form in which they appear in drunkards who "shall not inherit the kingdom of God," and "whoremongers and adulterers whom God will judge"—they are sinful concupiscence.[1] Concupiscence is not confined to the sensuous nature. There is concupiscence or lust of the *reason*, as well as of the sense. Pride and ambition is a lust of the mind. "We had our conversation in times past, in the lusts of our flesh, fulfilling the desires (θελήματα) of the flesh and of the *mind*" (τῶν διανοιῶν), Eph. 2 : 3. According to 2 Cor. 7 : 1, there is a "filthiness of the flesh and the *spirit*" (πνεύματος).

The external part of Adam's first sin was the act of eating the fruit of the tree of knowledge. After the sinful inclination had arisen, a sinful volition followed. "When the woman saw that the tree was to be desired to make one wise, she took of the fruit thereof and did eat," Gen. 3 : 6.

This first sin in both of its parts, internal and external, is imputed to Adam and his posterity as sin and guilt, because they committed it. The evil desire and the evil act were the desiring and acting of the human nature in the first human pair. The Biblical proof of this fundamental and much disputed position is found in Rom. 5 : 12, "Death passed upon all men, for that all have sinned." Rom. 5 : 15, "Through the offence of one (man) many be dead" (ἀπέθανον)

[1] Compare Heppe · Reformirter Dogmatik, II 249 Augustine Opus Imperfectum, V , De natura sana, et vitiata.

Rom. 5 : 16, "The judgment was by one (offence) unto condemnation." Rom. 5 : 17, "By one man's offence (or, by one offence) death reigned by one." Rom. 5 : 18, "By the offence of one (one offence, Lachm. Tisch.), judgment came upon all men to condemnation." Rom. 5 : 19, "By one man's disobedience many were made sinners." 1 Cor. 15 : 22, "In Adam (τῷ 'Αδὰμ) all die."

The very important discussion of St. Paul in Rom 5 : 12–19 teaches: 1. That the death which came upon all men as a punishment came because of *one* sin, and only one; and 2. That this sin was the one committed by Adam and his posterity as a *unity*. Three explanations have been given of ἥμαρτον, in this passage. 1. It is active in its meaning, and denotes the first sin of Adam and his posterity as a unity: his posterity being one with him by natural union, or else by representation, or by both together. 2. It is active in its meaning, and denotes the first sin of each individual after he is born. In this case, ἥμαρτον does not denote Adam's first sin. 3. It is passive in its meaning, signifying, either, "to be sinful," or, "to be reckoned as having sinned." Shedd: On Romans, 5 : 12–19.

That ἥμαρτον is active in its signification is proved: (*a*) By the fact, that ἐφ' ᾧ πάντες ἥμαρτον means the same as δὶα τῆς ἁμαρτίας in the preceding context; and ἁμαρτίας is active in signification. (*b*) By the invariable use of the word ἥμαρτον elsewhere. Matt. 27 : 4; Luke 15 : 18; John 9 : 2; Acts 25 : 8; Rom. 2 : 12; 3 : 23; 5 : 14, 16; 6 : 15; 1 Cor. 7 : 28; Eph 4 : 26; 1 Tim. 5 : 20; 1 Pet. 2 : 20. (*c*) By the invariable signification of the substantive ἁμαρτία. A verb has the same meaning as its noun. (*d*) By the interchange of ἁμαρτία with παράπτωμα, which is active in meaning. Rom 5 : 16–21.

Turrettin (Institutio, IX. ix. 16) denies that ἥμαρτον signifies "to be sinful" "Verbum ἥμαρτον proprie non protest trahi ad habitum peccati, vel ad corruptionem habitualem et inhaerentem, sed proprie peccatum aliquod actuale notat, idque praeteritum, quod non potest aliud esse quam ipsum Adami peccatum ; aliud quippe est peccatorem esse vel nasci, aliud vero reipsa peccare." So also Witsius: Covenants, I. viii. 31. Edwards (Original Sin, Works, II. 448) denies that ἥμαρτον signifies "to be regarded as sinners." "There is no instance wherein the verb 'sin,' which is used by the apostle when he says, 'all have sinned,' is anywhere used in our author's [Taylor's] sense, for being brought into a state of suffering, and that not as a punishment for sin, or as anything arising from God's displeasure. St. Paul is far from using such a phrase, to signify a being condemned without guilt or any imputation or supposition of guilt. Vastly more, still, is it remote from his language, so to use the verb 'sin,' and to say, man 'sinneth,' or 'has sinned,' hereby meaning nothing more nor less than that he by a judicial act is condemned."

Unless, therefore, St. Paul departed from the invariable Scripture use of the word ἥμαρτον, when he asserts that death, as a just punishment, passed upon all men "because all sinned," he employs the word "sinned" actively. And if he does depart here from the invariable Scripture meaning of ἥμαρτον, he is the only inspired writer that does so; and this is the only instance in his own writings in which he does so—his use of the verb ἁμαρτάνειν in scores of other instances being the ordinary use.

But while ἥμαρτον in Rom. 5:12 is active in signification, it does not denote the transgressions of each individual subsequent to birth, and when no longer in Adam, but the transgression of Adam and Eve inclusive of their posterity. This is proved by the following considerations: 1. *One*, and but one sin is specified as the ground of the penalty of death This is asserted five times over, in succession, in Rom 5:15–19. In Rom. 5:12, ἥμαρτον unquestionably refers to the same sin that is spoken of in Rom. 5:15–19.

2. In Rom. 5:14, some who die, namely, infants, "did

not sin after the *similitude* of Adam's first transgression." That is, they did not *repeat* the first sin. They must, therefore, have sinned in some other manner, because they are a part of the "all" (πάντες) who sinned, and because they experience the death which is the wages of sin. The only other conceivable manner of sinning is that of participation in the first sin itself. But participation in Adam's first sin is not the repetition of it by the individual.

From these considerations, it is evident that the word "sinned" in Rom. 5:12 is active in its signification; but the action is specific, not individual: the action of the common nature in Adam prior to any conception and birth, and not the action of the individuals one by one after conception and birth.

The passive signification given to ἥμαρτον, is twofold: (*a*) To be sinful (Calvin). (*b*) To be reckoned as having sinned (Chrysostom). The first has never had much currency. The last has been extensively adopted by Semi-Pelagian and Arminian theologians, and also by many Later-Calvinists. The objections to this explanation are the following: 1. It is contrary to invariable usage. This would be the only instance in the New Testament in which the verb ἁμαρτάνω would have such a meaning. 2. Had St. Paul intended to bring in the notion of regarding or treating as sinners, this would require the combination of ἁμαρτάνειν with εἰναὶ, and he would have used the compound form, πάντες ἡμαρτηκότες ἦσαν: as does the Septuagint in Gen. 43·9; 44:32 (ἡμαρτηκὼς ἔσομαι); 1 Kings 1:21 (ἔσομαι ἐγω καὶ Σάλωμων ἁμαρτολοί) 3. The passive signification excludes Adam and Eve from the πάντες who sinned. They, certainly, were not "reckoned" to have sinned. 4. According to the passive signification, ἥμαρτον would denote God's action, not man's: God's act of imputing sin, not man's act of committing it. But it is the sinner's act, not that of the judge, which is the reason for punishment. 5. It destroys the logic. All die, because all are reckoned to deserve death. This is one reason for death, but not the particular one required here. The argument demands a reason founded upon the act of the criminal, not of the judge. To say that all die because all are condemned to die, is to give no sufficient reason for death. For the question immediately arises, why are they condemned to die? 6 It tends to empty *θάνατος* of its plenary Biblical meaning as including hell-punishment. A qualified meaning is given to it, in order to make it agree with the qualified meaning given to *ἥμαρτον*. The withdrawment of grace is said by some Later-Calvinists to be the only penalty inflicted upon original sin; the positive pains of hell being due only to actual transgression. Historically, this passive signification was forced upon *ἁμαρτάνω* by those (Chrysostom and the Greek Fathers) who asserted that the first sin was not imputed as culpable. Arminian writers, like Whitby and John Taylor, follow Chrysostom.

The *total* guilt of the first sin, thus committed by the entire race in Adam, is imputed to each individual of the race, because of the *indivisibility* of guilt. If two individual men together commit a murder, each is chargeable with the whole guilt of the act. One-half of the guilt of the murder cannot be imputed to one, and one-half to the other. Supposing that the one human nature which committed the "one offence" (Rom. 5:17, 18) became a family of exactly a million individuals by propagation, it would not follow that each individual would be responsible for only a millionth part of the offence. The whole undivided guilt of the first sin of apostasy from God would be chargeable upon each and every one of the million individuals of the species alike For though the one common nature that committed the "one offence" is divisible by propagation, the offence itself is not divisible, nor is the guilt of it. Consequently, one man is as guilty as another of the whole first sin; of the original act of falling from God The individual Adam and Eve were no more guilty of this first act, and of the whole of it, than their descendants are; and their descendants are as guilty as they.

The same principle applies also to the indivisibility of *merit.* The merit of Christ's obedience is indivisible, and the *whole* of it is imputed to every individual believer alike. A million of believers do not each obtain by imputation a millionth part of their Redeemer's merit. One believer is as completely justified by gratuitous imputation as another, because all alike receive by faith the total worthiness and desert of their Lord's obedience, not a fractional part of it. As the unmerited imputation of Christ's obedience conveys the total undivided merit of this obedience to each and every believer, so the merited imputation of Adam's disobedience conveys the total undivided guilt of this disobedience to each and every individual of the posterity

The first sin of Adam, being a *common*, not an individual sin, is deservedly and justly imputed to the posterity of Adam upon the same principle upon which all sin is deservedly and justly imputed: namely, that it was committed by those to whom it is imputed. "All men die, because all men sinned," says St. Paul. Free agency is supposed, as the reason for the penalty of death: namely, the free agency of all mankind in Adam. This agency, though differing in the manner, is yet as real as the subsequent free agency of each individual.

The imputation either of Adam's sin or of Christ's righteousness must rest upon a *union* of some kind. It is just to impute the first sin of Adam to his posterity, while it would be unjust to impute it to the fallen angels, because Adam and his posterity were a unity when the first sin was committed, but Adam and the fallen angels were not. "Haud justum fuisset unius angeli crimen alteri imputari, vel unius hominis peccatum alterius censeri, posito quod singuli seorsim essent creati sicut angeli. Sed est unitas naturae, cui unitas foederalis erat innixa." Leydecker: Synopsis, 164, in Heppe: Reformirter Dogmatik, Loc. XV. The fact that the fallen angels have committed individual transgressions of their own, would not justify imputing a common race-transgression to them. Again, it is just to impute Christ's righteousness to a believer, but not just to impute it to an unbeliever, because the former has been united to him by faith, and the latter has not.

The popular explanation of the imputation of Adam's sin, by the fact that under the Divine government children inherit the poverty and disease of their vicious parents, is inadequate. The Divine government does not *punish* the children of vicious parents for their inherited poverty and disease. If Adam's posterity merely inherited moral corruption, but were not punished for it, this explanation would be pertinent. But inherited corruption is visited with Divine *retribution*, according to Eph. 2:3. And this requires participation in the origin of it. Men must sin in Adam, in order to be justly punished for Adam's sin. And participation requires union with Adam.

There is a similar fallacy in citing the Biblical instances in which innocent individuals suffer for the sins of guilty individuals, in proof that Adam's posterity though innocent of his sin are punishable for it. To *suffer* in consequence of the sin of another, is not the same as to be *punished* for it. The sufferings that came upon the descendants of Ham because of his individual sin were not *retributive*, like those which come upon the whole human race because of the one specific sin of Adam, or like those which come upon an individual for his own transgressions. Ham's descendants have suffered for centuries on account of their ancestor's sin, but have not been under eternal condemnation on account of it. They are exposed to eternal death, in common with the rest of mankind, because of the sin in Adam and of their own individual sins, but not because of the *individual* sin of Ham. The same is true of the sin of Korah, in relation to his family. In reference to all individual transgressions, Ezekiel

(18 : 20) asserts that "the son shall not bear the iniquity of his father;" that is, he shall not be *punished* for it, though he may *suffer* for it. Suffering and affliction are sovereign acts of God, and may or may not be connected with the individual sin of a secondary ancestor, according to his good pleasure; but punishment is a judicial act that is necessary, and necessarily connected with the specific sin of the first ancestor, and the individual sins of the person himself.

The imputation of Adam's sin rests upon a different kind of union from that upon which the imputation of Christ's righteousness rests. The former is founded upon natural union: a union of constitutional nature and substance. The possibility of an existence, a probation, and a free fall in Adam has been considered under the head of traducianism. The entire human species, as an invisible but substantial nature, acts in and with the first human pair. Traducianism is true only in anthropology, and with reference to apostasy. It has no application at all to soteriology and redemption. There is no race-unity in redemption. All men were in Adam when he disobeyed; but all men were not in Christ when he obeyed. All men are propagated from Adam, and inherit his sin. No man is propagated from Christ, or inherits his righteousness. Apostasy starts with the race. Redemption starts with the individual All men fall. Some men are redeemed. Union in Adam, is substantial and physical; in Christ, is spiritual and mystical (L C. 66); in Adam, is natural; in Christ, is representative; in Adam, is by creation, in Christ, is by regeneration; in Adam, is with man as a species; in Christ, is with man as an individual; in Adam, is universal; in Christ, is particular and by election. Shedd: On Romans 5 : 19.

The theory of Schleiermacher, Rothe (Steinmeyer: History of Christ's Passion, p. 15), and Nevin as criticised by Hodge, supposes that Christ united himself with the *entire* human nature. This is an error. In the incarnation, the

Logos assumed into union with himself only a fractional *part* of human nature: namely, that flesh and blood which was derived from the Virgin There was no union, in the incarnation, with the human race as a whole. This would have required the Logos to have united with the human nature as it was in Adam, prior to any division and individualization of it. Furthermore, in regeneration, Christ is united with only a particular individual who has been elected and separated (Gal. 1:15) from all other individuals.

The principal objection to the tenet of the participation of the posterity in the first sin is, that the individual has no self-conscious recollection of such an event, and that he cannot be held responsible for an act of which he is not self-conscious and cannot remember.

The reply to this is: 1 That upon any theory, no individual man is self-conscious of and remembers the first act of sin. Neither Pelagianism nor Semi-Pelagianism, neither Socinianism nor Arminianism, has any advantage in this respect over Augustinianism and Calvinism. Neither does creationism have any advantage over traducianism. Upon any theory that recognizes the fact of sin in man, the first act of sin is not observed by self-consciousness at the time of its occurrence. No man remembers the time when he was innocent, and the particular first act by which he became guilty before God.

2 Guilt is caused by self-determination, not by self-consciousness. Self-consciousness is not *action*, but *vision;* and it is action, not the sight of an action that constitutes crime A man is wrongly inclining all the time to self and the creature, but he is not self-conscious all the time that he is wrongly inclining. If it be said, that he might *become* self-conscious that he is so inclining, this does not prove that such a self-consciousness is necessary in order to responsibility for the wrong inclining. Even if he does not become self-conscious of his wrong inclining (as he may not for days and weeks), this does not destroy the fact that he

*is* so inclining. It is the inclining, not the self-consciousness of inclining, which constitutes the free action of his will; and it is this free action which constitutes the sin and guilt. This is true also of the momentary volition, as well as of the abiding inclination. If a man commits a murder, it is not necessary that at the time when he stabs his victim he should have that clear apprehension of the enormity of the act which he subsequently has, in order to be chargeable with murder. Sins of thoughtlessness are as truly sinful, as deliberate sins. Leviticus 5 : 17, 18, Luke 12 : 48. Men generally are not self-conscious of the "secret sins" (Ps. 19: 12; 90 : 8) of feeling and desire which they are committing inwardly all the time. The purpose of preaching the law is to produce the self-consciousness of sin. The "darkness" in which, according to St. Paul (Eph. 4: 18), men "walk," is the thoughtless unconsciousness in which they live and act. It is a proverb, that man sins the more, the less God and sin are in his thoughts. The clearness of the self-consciousness is not the measure of the intensity of the self-determination. The two may be in inverse proportion. The will may be vehemently resolute and determined to a particular end, and yet the understanding be very blind to the will's activity. It is frequently the case, that great strength and energy in voluntariness are accompanied with great obtuseness and stupidity in moral perception. The most wicked and devilish men are oftentimes the most apathetic and hardened of men. The will is awake and full of force, but the conscience is asleep. When the sinner is convicted by the truth and Spirit of God, he does not excuse or extenuate his guilt on the ground of his past unconsciousness in sin. Even the heathen, when convinced of the abominations of idolatry and of selfish lust in its varied forms, do not plead "the ignorance that was in them because of the blindness of their hearts," in excuse for having "given themselves over to work all uncleanness with greediness." Eph. 4 : 17.

It is on this ground, that Samuel Hopkins contends that infants are moral agents. "Many have supposed," he says (Works, I. 233), "that none of mankind are capable of sin, or moral agency, before they can distinguish between right and wrong. But this wants proof which has never yet been produced. And it appears to be contrary to divine revelation. Persons may be moral agents and sin without knowing what the law of God is, or of what nature their exercises are, and while they have no consciousness." Hamilton (Bowen's Ed, xiii., xiv.) contends that there are agencies of the soul deeper than self-consciousness. Pascal, in the fourth of his Provincial Letters, shows the consequences of the position of the Jesuit, that "nothing is voluntary but what is accompanied with deliberation, and clear consciousness of the nature of the act."[1]

3. There was, comparatively, more self-consciousness attending the first sin for the posterity, if it was committed by them in Adam, than can be found upon any other theory. The first sin of every man must have been committed either: (*a*) In Adam. (*b*) In the womb. (*c*) In infancy. We cannot conceive of any relation to, or connection with self-consciousness, in the last two cases. We can in the first For the individuals Adam and Eve were self-conscious So far as they were concerned, the first sin was a very deliberate and intensely wilful act. The human species existing in them at that time *acted* in their act, and *sinned* in their sin, similarly as the hand or eye acts and sins in the murderous or lustful act of the individual soul. The hand or the eye has no separate self-consciousness of its own, parallel with the soul's self-consciousness. Taken by itself, it has no consciousness at all. But its *union* and *oneness* with the self-conscious soul, in the personal union of soul and body, affords all the self-consciousness that is possible in the case. The hand is co-agent with the soul, and hence is

[1] See Ritschl · History of Justification (Black's Tr ), 390–410. Shedd . Theological Essays, 243–254.

particeps criminis and has a common guilt with the soul.

In like manner, the psychico-physical human nature existing in Adam and Eve had no separate self-consciousness parallel with that of Adam and Eve. Unlike the visible hand or eye, it was an invisible substance or nature capable of being transformed into myriads of self-conscious individuals; but while in Adam, and not yet distributed and individualized, it had no distinct self-consciousness of its own, any more than the hand or eye in the supposed case. But *existing*, and *acting* in and with these self-conscious individuals, it participated in their self-determination, and is chargeable with their sin, as the hand, and eye, and whole body is chargeable with the sin of the individual man. As in the instance of the individual unity, everything that constitutes it, body as well as soul, is active and responsible for all that is done by this unity, so in the instance of the specific unity, everything that constitutes it, namely, Adam and the human nature in him, is active and responsible for all that is done by this unity.

2. The second part of "the sinfulness of that estate whereinto man fell," consists in "the want of original righteousness, and the corruption of the whole nature." This part of human sinfulness stands to the first, in the relation of effect to cause. Human nature in Adam and Eve inclined from holiness to sin, and as a consequence that nature became destitute of its original righteousness and morally corrupt

It is easy to see how this negative destitution of righteousness and positive inclination to evil, with all the moral corruption attending it, should be imputed as guilt, provided it be conceded that the first sin is really committed and righteously imputed. If it is just to impute the cause, it is certainly just to impute the effect. But, on the contrary, it is impossible to see why the corruption of nature should be imputed as sin, if the first sin is not. It is improper to impute the effect when the cause cannot be imputed.[1]

It is here that the illogical character of the theory of mediate imputation is apparent. This was first advanced by Placaeus, in 1640. To relieve, as he supposed, the Calvinistic doctrine of original sin of some of its difficulties, he maintained that the corruption of nature which is inherited from Adam is chargeable upon each individual as sin and guilt, but the act of transgressing the probationary statute given in Eden is not chargeable. This is to be imputed only to Adam and Eve as individuals. A man is guilty and punishable for his evil heart, but not for Adam's first sin. His own personal corruption is imputable, because it is personal; but the act of another person is not imputable, because it is another's act. Placaeus would impute Adam's sin as a state, but not as an act; the "corruption of nature," but not the "guilt of the first sin," in the Westminster formula.

This theory made a greater difficulty than it relieved. The corruption of nature, according to Placaeus himself, is the effect of Adam's first sin. Why should the effect be imputed, and not the cause? Such a kind of imputation looked unreasonable, and, as the Formula Consensus says, "imperilled the whole doctrine of original sin." It would be difficult to retain the imputation of the corruption of nature, by this method; and both the first sin and corruption would cease to be imputed.

The Synod of Charenton, in 1644, condemned the view of Placaeus, and also charged him with denying the imputation of Adam's sin. He objected to this, saying that he did not deny the imputation of Adam's sin, *altogether*, but only when stated *in a certain manner*. "Illis enim verbis [in the decree of the synod] aut exposita non est Placaei

---

[1] "Sin," as Müller (Sin, II 163) remarks, "must begin, not in a state, but in an act" Yet the first act of sin, it must be remembered, causes and produces a state of sin.

sententia, aut male exposita est. Is enim primi peccati Adae imputationem nunquam simpliciter negavit, nunquam negatam voluit Cum igitur imputationem primi illius peccati quandam affirmet, quandam neget, non exponitur ejus sententia, si dicitur simpliciter, et *nulla distinctione adhibita*, primi peccati Adae imputationem negare." Placaeus: De Imputatione, I. iii

The criticism of Turrettin (IX. ix. 5) upon this is as follows: "To break the force of the statement of the Synod of Charenton, Placaeus distinguished between *immediate* or *antecedent* imputation, and *mediate* or *consequent* imputation. The former he calls that imputation [of Adam's sin] by which the first act of Adam was imputed immediately to all his posterity, Christ only excepted, and antecedently to any inherent corruption. The latter, he calls that imputation [of Adam's sin] which follows upon seeing in the posterity that hereditary corruption derived to them from Adam, and which is brought about by it [hereditary corruption], as the means or medium [of the imputation]." The first "immediate" imputation Placaeus rejects, the second "mediate" imputation he accepts; and upon this ground contends that he does not reject the imputation of Adam's sin absolutely, and without qualification.

But, as Turrettin proceeds to say, "this distinction does in fact do away with the imputation of Adam's [first] sin altogether. For if the sin of Adam is imputed to us only in this *mediate* manner, according to which we are constituted guilty before God, and made liable to penalty, on account of an hereditary corruption which we derive from Adam, there is no real and proper imputation of Adam's [*first*] sin, but only of inherent corruption. This the synod intended to prevent and proscribe, by distinguishing original sin into two parts: namely, inherent corruption, and imputation proper [i.e., the imputation of the *first* sin itself] —a thing that could not be done, if imputation cannot be except upon the ground of a foregoing corruption of nature.

For it is one thing to be exposed to the wrath of God on account of inherent and hereditary corruption, and quite another thing to be exposed to this wrath on account of Adam's first act of sin."

The phrase "original sin," in the Westminster statement (S. C., 18), comprises both the first sin and the corruption of nature: Adam's sin both as an act, and a resulting state of the will. Edwards (Original Sin, in initio) remarks that original sin "is vulgarly understood in that latitude, as to include not only the depravity of nature, but the imputation of Adam's first sin." The whole truth of the doctrine of original sin includes the imputation of both the first sin and the ensuing corruption. The first sin of Adam and his posterity is immediately imputed to them as sin, antecedently, in the order of nature, to inherent corruption, because it was their voluntary act. And then the resulting inherent corruption is imputed as sin; not, however, as in Placaeus's theory, through *itself* as the medium of the imputation, but through the medium of the *first sin*, because this was the cause of it. Both the cause and the effect, both the first sin and the corruption caused by it, are imputed to Adam and his posterity.

The phrase "original sin" is sometimes employed to denote only the corruption of nature, in distinction from the sins of act that proceed from it. In this use of the term, original sin is equivalent to the Scripture phrases: The "evil treasure of the heart," Mark 12:35; the "corrupt tree," Mark 12:33; the "heart from which proceed evil thoughts," Mark 7:21; the "stony heart," Ezek. 11:19; the "carnal mind," Rom. 8:7; the "flesh," Rom. 8:4, et alia.

It is also equivalent to the theological phrases: The "corrupt nature;" the "sinful inclination;" the "evil disposition;" the "apostate will." When the term "nature" is applied to sin, it does not denote "nature" in the primary but the secondary sense. In the primary sense, "nature" denotes a substance, and one that is created by God. In this sense, Augustine denies that sin is "nature," and asserts that it is "intentio." Shedd: History of Doctrine, II. 82; Theological Essays, 220. Howe (Oracles, II. xxiv.) remarks that "that evil heart, that nature, not as it is nature but as it is depraved nature, is now transmitted." When "nature" signifies created substance, it is improper to call sin a nature. Aristotle (Politics, I ii) says: "What every being is in its *perfect* state, that certainly is the nature of that being, whether it be a man, a horse, or a house." Sin is imperfection, and therefore not "nature" in this sense. But there is a secondary meaning of the word In this use of it, "nature" denotes "natural inclination," or "innate disposition." In this sense, sin is a "nature," and the adjective "natural" is applicable to the corruption of sin. In the same sense, holiness is called a "nature," in 2 Pet. 1:4 Believers are "partakers of a divine nature," by being regenerated and coming to possess a holy disposition or inclination "It is true that sin is a nature, but then it is a second nature, a state of degeneration." Nitzsch: Christian Doctrine, § 107. Calvin, on Eph. 2:3, says: "Since God is the author of nature, how comes it that no blame attaches to God if we are lost by nature? I answer, there is a twofold nature: The one produced by God, and the other is corruption of it. We are not born such as Adam was at first created." See Formula Concordiae, I. xii.; Calvin: Institutes, II. ii. 12.

1. Viewed as natural corruption, original sin may be considered with respect to the *understanding*. (*a*) It is blindness. Is. 42:7, "A light to open blind eyes." Luke 4.18, "Recovering of sight to the blind." Rev. 3:17, "Knowest not that thou art blind." 2 Cor 4:4, "The god of this world hath blinded their minds." All texts that speak of regeneration as "enlightening." 2 Cor. 4:6; Eph. 5:14; 1 Thess. 5:5; Ps 97:11, etc All texts that call sin "darkness." Prov. 4:19; Is. 60:2; Eph. 5:11; Col.

1:13; 1 John 2:11; 1 Thess. 5:4; Eph. 4:18, "Having the understanding (διάνοια) darkened;" Rom. 1:28, "Reprobate mind (νοῦν)"

Sin blinds and darkens the understanding, by destroying the *consciousness* of divine things. For example, the soul destitute of love to God is no longer conscious of love; of reverence, is no longer conscious of reverence, etc. Its knowledge of such affections, therefore, is from hearsay, like that which a blind man has of colors, or a deaf man of sound. God, the object of these affections, is of course unknown for the same reason. The spiritual discernment, spoken of in 1 Cor. 2:6, is the immediate consciousness of a renewed man. It is experimental knowledge. Sin is described in Scripture as voluntary ignorance. "This they willingly are ignorant of, that by the word of God the heavens were of old," 2 Pet. 3:5. Christ says to the Jews: "If I had not come and spoken unto them they had not had sin:" the sin, namely, of "not knowing him that sent me," John 15:21, 22. But the ignorance, in this case, was a willing ignorance. They desired to be ignorant

Another effect of original sin upon the understanding as including the conscience is: (*b*) Insensibility. It does not render conscience extinct, but it stupefies it. 1 Tim 4:2, "Having cauterized their own conscience." (*c*) Pollution. Titus 1:15, "Even their reason (νοῦς) and conscience (συνείδησις) are polluted," or stained (μεμίανται). Rom. 1:21, "They became vain in their reasonings," or speculations (διαλόγισμους). The pollution of reason is seen in the foolish speculations of mythology. The myths of polytheism are not pure reason. The pollution of conscience is seen in remorse. The testifying faculty is spotted with guilt. It is no longer a "good conscience:" spoken of in Heb. 13:18 (καλήν συνείδησιν); 1 Pet. 3:16, 21; 1 Tim. 1:5, 19; Acts 23:1 (συνείδησιν ἀγαθήν); nor a "pure conscience:" mentioned in 1 Tim. 3:9 (συνείδησις κάθαρα) It is an "evil conscience" (πονήρα συνείδησις): a conscience needing cleansing by atoning blood "from dead works," Heb. 9·14. Dead works, being no fulfilment of the law, leave the conscience perturbed and unpacified.

2. Considered with respect to the *will*, original sin is: (*a*) Enmity. Rom 8:6; James 4:4, "The friendship of the world is enmity towards God;" Deut. 1.26, "They rebelled against God;" Job 34:37; Is. 1:1; 30:9; 45: 2; Ezek. 12:2. (*b*) Hatred. Rom. 1:29; Ps. 89:23; 139:21; Ex. 20:5; Prov. 1:25; 5:12; John 7:7; 15: 18, 23, 24 (*c*) Hardness of heart, or insensibility. Ex. 7: 14, 22, 2 Kings 17:14; Job 9:4; Is. 63:17, Dan. 5. 20; John 12:20; Acts 19:9; Heb. 3:8, 15; 4:7. (*d*) Aversion. John 5:40, "Ye will not" (ὀυ θέλητε), ye are disinclined; Rev 2:21. (*e*) Obstinacy. Deut. 31: 27, "stiff necked;" Ex. 32:9, Ps. 75:5; Is. 26:10; 43:4; Acts 7:51; Rom 10.21. (*f*) Bondage. Jer. 13: 23; Mark 3:23; John 6.43, 44; 8:34; Rom. 5:6, 6:20; 7:9, 14, 18, 23; 8:7, 8; 9:16; 2 Pet 2:14.

Original sin, considered as corruption of nature, is sin in the sense of *guilt*. "Damnant Pelagianos et alios, qui vitium originis negant esse peccatum." Augsburg Confession, II. "Every sin, both original and actual, being a transgression of the righteous law of God doth in its own nature bring guilt upon the sinner, whereby he is bound over to the wrath of God, and made subject to death, temporal and eternal" Westminster Confession, VI. vi. "Corruption of nature doth remain in those that are regenerated, and although it be through Christ pardoned and mortified, yet both itself and all the motions thereof are truly and properly sin" Westminster Confession, VI. v. The Semi-Pelagian, Papal, and Arminian anthropologies differ from the Augustinian and Reformed, by denying that corruption of nature is guilt. It is a physical and mental disorder leading to sin, but is not sin itself.[1]

---

[1] Shedd History of Doctrine, II 35–42; 180–186, On Romans, 7:15–17 Muller Sin, II. 400

Corruption of nature is guilt because: (*a*) The scriptures do not distinguish between sin proper, and improper. Ἁμαρτία, as denoting the principle of sin, is exchanged with παράπτωμα, denoting the act of sin, and vice versa. Rom. 5:13, 15, 16, 17, 19, 21 (*b*) Ἁμαρτία is the equivalent of ἐπιθυμία and σάρξ. Rom 7:7, "I had not known sin, except the law had said, Thou shalt not lust." Rom. 8:3, 5. (*c*) The remainders of corruption in the regenerate are hated as sin by the regenerate himself, Rom. 7:15; and by God, who slays them by his Spirit, Rom. 8:13 (*d*) Evil desire is forbidden in the tenth commandment, Ex. 20:17. Compare 1 John 2:16. The tenth commandment, which the Septuagint renders ὄυκ ἐπιθυμήσεις, prohibits that internal lusting which is the chief characteristic of the corrupt nature It is also forbidden by Christ in his exposition of the seventh commandment. Matt. 5:28. 1 John 3:15, "Whosoever hateth his brother is a murderer." (*e*) Corruption of nature is guilt, because it is the inclination of the will. It is "voluntary" though not "volitionary." It is conceded that the inclination to murder is as truly culpable as the act of murder. "The thought (purpose, זִמָּה) of foolishness is sin," Prov. 24:9. (*f*) Corruption of nature is guilt, upon the principle that the cause must have the same predicates as its effects. If actual transgressions are truly and properly sin, then the evil heart or inclination which prompts them must be so likewise. If the stream is bitter water, the fountain must be also. If the murderer's act is guilt, then the murderer's hate is. (*g*) If corruption of nature, or sinful disposition is not guilt, then it is an extenuation and excuse for actual transgressions These latter are less blameworthy, if the character which prompts them and renders their avoidance more difficult is not self-determined and culpable. (*h*) If corruption of nature is not culpable, it is impossible to assign a reason why the dying infant needs redemption by atoning blood Christ came "by water and blood;" that is, with both expiating and sanctifying power. 1 John 5:6. But if there be no guilt in natural depravity, Christ comes to the infant "by water only," and not "by blood;" by sanctification, and not by justification. Infant redemption implies that the infant has guilt as well as pollution. The infant has a rational soul; this soul has a will; this will is inclined; this inclination, like that of an adult, is centred on the creature instead of the Creator. This is culpable, and needs pardon. It is also pollution, and needs removal. (*i*) God forgives original sin as well as actual transgression, when he bestows the "remission of sins." The "carnal mind," or the enmity of the heart is as great an offence against his excellence and honor, as any particular act that issues from it. Indeed, if there be mutual good-will between two parties an occasional outward offence is less serious. "Suppose," says Thirlwall (Letters, p. 46), "two friends really loving one another, but liable now and then to quarrel. They may easily forgive the occasional offence, because their habitual disposition is one of mutual good-will; but should the case be the reverse—hatred stifled, but occasionally venting itself by unfriendly acts—how little would it matter though they should forget the particular offence, if the enmity should continue at the bottom of the heart." This illustrates the guilt of sin as a state of the heart towards God, and the need of its forgiveness and removal.

With the Scriptures, the theologians assert that corruption of nature is sin. "We must not only abstain from evil deeds, but even from the desire to do them. Christ commanded not only to abstain from things forbidden by the law, but even from longing after them. Our Lord forbade concupiscence itself, as well as the act of adultery." Irenaeus: Contra Haereses, IV. xiii. "The command not to lust condemns the beginnings of sin, that is, unruly desires and wishes, no less than overt acts" Tertullian: De Pudicitia. Augustine, according to Turrettin (IX. i. 3), defines sin to be "aliquid concupitum, dictum, factum, contra legem dei." Augustine, according to Calvin (Institutes III. iii. 10), "sometimes denominates concupiscence infirmity, teaching that it becomes sin in cases where action or consent is added to the conception of the mind; but sometimes he denominates it sin; as when he says, 'Paul gives the appellation of sin to this from which all sins proceed; that is, to carnal concupiscence.'" "If lust which wars against the soul (1 Pet. 2:11) be already sin (Ex. 20:17, Matt. 5:28), then must the act of sin be regarded as augmenting its degree." Nitzsch: Christian Doctrine, § 111. "By the precept concerning the tree of knowledge, man was taught that God is Lord of all things, and that it is unlawful even to desire, but with his leave. Man's true happiness is placed in God alone, and nothing is to be desired but with submission to him." Witsius: Covenants, I. iii. 21. Hales, quoted by Davenant (Allport's Trans., II. 214), says that "the irregular pleasure proceeding from the sensualized mind, inasmuch as it is corrupt, is sin; because it ought to have been subject to reason, and moves in an undue manner contrary to reason." Owen (Justification, XVII.) says: "To root out the pernicious error of self-righteousness, our Lord gives the spiritual intention of the law, and declares: 1. That the law had regard to the regulation of the heart with all its first motions and actings. For he asserts that the first motions of concupiscence, though not consented to, much less actually accomplished, are directly forbidden in the law. This he doth in his exposition of the seventh commandment. 2. He declares the penalty of the law upon the least sin to be hell-fire, in his assertion of causeless anger to be forbidden in the sixth commandment." "Have we," says Calvin (Institutes, II. viii. 58), "felt any evil desire in our heart? we are already guilty of concupiscence, and are become at once transgressors of the law; because the Lord forbids us not only to plan and attempt anything that would prove detrimental to another, but even to be stimulated and agitated with concupiscence. The curse of God always rests on the transgression of the law. We have no reason, therefore, to exempt even the most trivial emotions of concupiscence from the sentence of death." Says Bullinger: "Lex 'ne concupiscito' inquit. Itaque et si cupiditate, quae te incendit, non assentiaris, ipse tamen carnis tuae impetus peccatumest."

The position that original sin is *voluntary inclination* has been maintained in anthropology, from the beginning of speculation upon the subject. Augustine argues as follows with Julian: "Says Julian, 'If sin is from will, then it is an evil will that produces sin; but if from nature, then an evil nature produces sin.' I quickly reply that sin is from will. Then he asks, 'whether original sin is also from will?' I answer, certainly, original sin also; because this was transmitted from the will of the first man" De Nuptiis, II. xxviii. 2. Turrettin defines sin as "inclinatio, actio, vel omissio pugnans cum lege dei." Institutio, IX i 3. Ursinus, speaking of corruption of nature in infants, says that "infants want not the faculty of will, and though in act they do not will sin, yet they will it by inclination" Christian Religion, Original Sin, Q 7 Rivetus asserts that "concupiscentia est inclinatio voluntaria" Explicatio Decalogi, verse 15. William of Auxerre, quoted by Davenant (Allport's Trans., II. 214), asserts that "the movement of wrong desire in man is a voluntary act, and it is sin, even when it moves before the reason has had time to exercise its judgment." Says Charnocke (Holiness of God, p. 476), "there is no sin but is in some sort voluntary; voluntary in the root, or voluntary in the branch; voluntary by an immediate act of the will [volition], or voluntary by a general or natural inclination of the will [self-determination]. That is not a crime, to which a man is violenced without any concurrence of the faculties of the soul to that act." Says Owen (Vindiciae, VI.): "Original sin, as peccatum originans, was voluntary in Adam; and as it is originatum in us, is in our wills habitually [as a habitus], and not against them, in any actings of it or them. The effects of it, in the coining of sin and in the thoughts of men's hearts, are all voluntary." Compare Indwelling Sin, VI. xii. Says Howe (Oracles, II. xxiv.), "We must understand that an evil inclination, or a depraved nature, is that which doth first violate the law of God; and so that it is not infelicity only to be ill-inclined, but it is sin: sin in the highest and most eminent sense thereof. It is the habitual frame and bent of the soul which the law of God doth in the first place direct. So that the empoisoned nature of man, the malignity of the heart and soul, is that which makes the first and principal breach upon the law of God."

It must be remembered that sin in its entire history is *inclination* and *self-determination.* While it is true that the first sin of Adam is the fall of the human race, and decides its eternal destiny apart from redemption, yet it must not be supposed that after the first act of Adam, all self-determination ceases. Original sin, as corruption of nature in each individual, is only the *continuation* of the first inclining away from God. The self-determination of the human will from God to the creature, as an ultimate end, did not stop short off with the act in Eden, but goes right onward in every individual of Adam's posterity, until regeneration reverses it. As progressive sanctification is the continuation of that holy self determination of the human will which begins in its regeneration by the Holy Spirit, so the progressive depravation of the natural man is the continuation of that sinful self-determination of the human will which began in Adam's transgression.

In connection with the doctrine that the corruption of nature is the same as the free inclination of the will, a position of Edwards is sometimes misunderstood and misapplied. Edwards (Will, IV. i.) asserts that "the virtuousness or viciousness of a disposition consists not in the origin or *cause* of it, but in the *nature* of it." This position cannot be understood without taking into view the error which Edwards was combating. He was opposing the view of Arminian writers, Taylor, Whitby and others, that a disposition or inclination cannot be chargeable as guilt unless it has been originated by a *volitionary* act preceding it. Their doctrine of the will implied that inclination can be produced by volition, and must be, in order to responsibility for the inclination. This Edwards denies. "It is agreeable," he says, "to the natural notions of mankind that moral evil, with its desert of dislike and abhorrence, and all its other ill-deservings, consists in a certain deformity in the *nature* of certain dispositions of the heart and acts of the will; and not in the deformity of *something else*, diverse from the very thing itself which deserves abhorrence, supposed to be the cause of it." That is to say, the disposition of the heart, or inclination of the will, is in its own quality and nature an evil disposition, and does not get its evil quality from "something else"—namely a volition that went before it, and caused it. If a man is inclined or disposed to sin, this inclination or disposition is itself sin. It is not necessary that he should, previously to the inclining, *resolve* to incline, or *choose* to incline, in order that the inclination should be sinful. The inclining itself is sin and guilt. "Thus, for instance," he says, "ingratitude is hateful and worthy of dispraise, according to common sense, not because something as bad, or worse than ingratitude, was the cause that produced it; but because it is hateful in itself by its own inherent deformity. So the love of virtue is amiable, and worthy of praise, not merely because something else went before this love of virtue in our minds which caused it to take place there (for instance our own choice [volition]—we chose to love virtue, and by some method or other wrought ourselves into the love of it), but because of the amiableness and condecency of such a disposition and inclination of the heart." In other words, Edwards here teaches that a man does not choose to incline, but he inclines; he does not choose to love, but he loves. The first thing in the order is not a volition, and then after this a disposition or inclination; but the first thing is a disposition or inclination, and then a volition.

Now it is only with reference to *the relation of a volition to a disposition or inclination*, that Edwards lays down the position that "the virtuousness or viciousness of a disposition lies not in the origin of it, but in the nature of it." He does not carry the position any further than this. When the volition is left out of the account, and only the *disposition* or *inclination* is considered, Edwards teaches that *this* must have a free origin, or else it is not sin. The whole purpose of his celebrated argument to prove that Adam and his posterity were one agent in the origin of sin is, to show how the sinful disposition is the working of spontaneity, or unforced inclination. When it comes to that act of will by which man *inclines* to sin, Edwards affirms that man is the self-moved and guilty actor and author of it. In his treatise on the Will (IV. i.), he remarks as follows: "If any shall still object and say: Why is it not necessary that the cause should be considered in order to determine whether anything be worthy of blame or praise? Is it agreeable to reason and common sense, that a man is to be praised or blamed for that which he is not the cause or author of, and has no hand in? I answer, such phrases as 'being the cause,' 'being the author,' 'having a hand in,' and the like, are ambiguous They are most vulgarly understood for being the designing voluntary [volitionary] cause, or cause by *antecedent choice:* and it is most certain that men are not in *this* sense the causes or authors of the first act of their wills [i.e., of their inclination, or disposition], in any case; as certain as anything is or ever can be; for nothing can be more certain than that a thing is not before it is, nor a thing of the same kind before the first thing of that kind; and so no choice before the first choice. As, however, the phrase 'being the author' may be understood, not of being the producer by an antecedent act of will [i.e, a volition]; but as a person may be said to be the author of the act of the will itself by his being the *immediate agent*, or *the being that is acting*, or *in the exercise of that act;* if the phrase 'being the author' is used to signify *this*, then doubtless common sense requires men's being the authors of their own acts of will, in order to their being esteemed worthy of praise or dispraise on account of them. And common sense teaches that they must be the authors of *external* actions in the former sense, namely, their being the causes of them by an act of will or choice [volition], in order to their being justly blamed or praised; but it teaches no such thing in respect to the *internal* acts of will themselves."[1] In this last remark, Edwards concedes that a volition precedes an *outward* act, and is the cause of it. The Arminian position in respect to volitionary action is true up to this point. An *external* act is not sinful or holy unless preceded by a volition. But with reference to that *internal* action of the will which is denominated its inclination or disposition, he holds that the Arminian position is not true. There is no need of a volition to precede *this* in order to make it sinful or holy; but it is so in its own nature, because it is the spontaneity of the man; because it is the action of "the immediate agent, or the being that is acting, or in the exercise of the act."[2]

---

[1] Edwards defines inclination as the "*leading* act" of the will See ante, p. 121

[2] The Arminian and the Calvinistic view of freedom are contrasted in the following statement of Edwards "Natural sense does not place the moral evil of volitions and dispositions in the cause of them, but the nature of them An evil thing's being *from* a man in the sense of from something *antecedent* in him, is not essential to the original notion we have of blameworthiness, but it is its being the choice of the *heart* When [on the other hand] a thing is *from* a man in the sense that it is from his will or choice, he is to blame for it because his will is *in it*: so far as the will is *in it* blame is *in it*, and no further Neither do we go any further in our notion of blame, to inquire whether the bad will be

When the question is asked: Is man the responsible author of his sinful inclination not by an antecedent volition to incline, but by a present actual inclining, Edwards answers in the affirmative. "As a person may be said to be the author of the act of the will itself, not by an antecedent act of will [i.e., by a foregoing volition], but by his being the *immediate agent*, or the being that is acting, or in the exercise of that act; if the phrase 'being the author' is used to signify this, then, doubtless, common sense requires men's being the authors of their own acts of will, in order to their being esteemed worthy of praise or dispraise on account of them."

Edwards's objection to the doctrine that the will chooses to choose, or chooses its choices: namely, that it supposes "a choice before the first choice," and that this is as absurd as that "a thing is before it is," or that there is "a thing of the same kind before the first thing of the same kind," implies that there *is* such a thing as a "first choice." But since he employed the term "choice" indiscriminately to include all the action of the will, the *first* choice with him meant an inclination or disposition of the will, not a volition (proper). There is no action of the will that precedes its inclination or disposition. Consequently this is the primary action, the "first choice" of the will The other action of the will in volitions (proper) is second choice. This "first choice" of the will in spontaneously inclining, Edwards denominates a "*leading* act," an "*original* act," the "*first determining* act." Will, III. iv. The word "act" in this instance means *activity*, or self-motion, or self-determination: not in the Arminian sense of self-determination, which is a volition coupled with power to the contrary, and is really indetermination not self-determination, but self-determination in the Calvinistic sense of spontaneously in-

---

*from* a bad will there is no consideration of the original of that bad will. because, according to our natural apprehension, blame originally consists in it" [i.e., the bad will]. Will, sub fine: Works, II 174

clining, or in the sense of "the immediate agent, or the being that is acting, or in the exercise of the act," as Edwards phrases it.

Again, that Edwards held the inclination or disposition of the will to be voluntary agency, is proved by his position that the inclination or disposition is an object either of command or of prohibition. A man is commanded to have a holy inclination, and forbidden to have a sinful one. He is so commanded, when he is commanded to love God with all his heart. Love is inclination. He is prohibited from having a sinful inclination, when he is prohibited from lust in any form. The tenth commandment prohibits a sinful inclination But commands and prohibitions are addressed to the will, and require or forbid something that is truly voluntary. The following is the phraseology of Edwards upon this point: "The will itself [i.e., the inclination of the will], and not only those actions which are the effects of the will [inclination], is the proper object of precept or command. That is, such or such a *state* or act of men's wills is in many cases properly required of them by command; and not merely those alterations in the state of their bodies or minds only that are consequences of volition." Again he remarks, "the will itself [i.e , the inclination] may be required, and the being of a good will is the most proper, direct, and immediate subject of command." Will, III. iv.; IV. xiii.

It is important to notice, by reference to the connection, in what sense Edwards uses the term "choice" or "volition." Sometimes the term denotes volition in distinction from inclination; sometimes it denotes inclination considered as voluntary agency. Had he appropriated the terms "choice" and "volition" to only one form of the will's activity, he would have been less liable to misapprehension. The charge of fatalism urged by some against Edwards arises from a failure to observe, that while Edwards taught that volitions necessarily agree with the inclination and have no power over it, he also taught that the inclination itself is free not necessitated agency. In the instance of a holy inclination, it was either created, or re-created by God. In the instance of a sinful inclination, it was self-originated in the fall of Adam. The inclination of the will is free spontaneity in both instances. In the former, it results from God working in the will to will; in the latter, it is the will in its solitary self-motion.

The dictum of Edwards to which we have referred is misapplied, sometimes, by writers whose view of sin and the will is substantially that of Edwards. They agree that a man is responsible for his sinful volitions, because they issue from his sinful inclination; but when asked why a man is responsible for his sinful inclination, instead of answering that this had a free and self-determined origin in Adam, they take refuge in the dangerous position that the sinfulness of an inclination does not depend upon its origin, but upon its nature, and that it is of no consequence how it originated "Malignity is evil, and love is good, whether *concreated*, innate, acquired, or *infused.* A malignant being is a sinful being, if endowed with reason, whether he was so *made* or so *born*" Hodge: Theology, II. 808. In this statement, holiness and sin are made to hold precisely the same relation to God and the human will, when in fact they hold totally different relations. All four of these adjectives will apply to "love," but only two of them to "malignity:" namely, "innate" and "acquired." God creates a holy inclination or disposition, whenever he creates a holy will in man or angel; and he re-creates a holy inclination whenever he regenerates a sinner. Holiness is good and meritorious, "whether concreated, innate, acquired, or infused." But then it is meritorious only in a *relative* sense. Since God is the ultimate author of holiness in both the creation and the regeneration of the will, to him belongs the glory of it. Man is not the originating agent, when holy inclination is the instance. God works in him to will. But the case is wholly different in the instance of an *evil* disposition or inclination. Man is the sole author, here. The demerit here is absolute, not relative. The doctrine of created holiness is true, but not of created sin; of infused holiness, but not of infused sin. To say that God can "create" and "infuse" a malignant inclination, is to contradict the explicit teaching of Scripture which asserts that God cannot sin, and that he hates sin with an infinite hatred. God cannot create and infuse what he hates and punishes And it shocks alike the moral sentiment of the natural man, and the holy reverence of the renewed man. An evil inclination may be "innate," and "acquired." But it cannot be "created" or "infused" There may be a created merit, but not a created demerit. God can create and infuse holiness, but not sin.

The testimony of Scripture and of consciousness is to this effect. When David, in the fifty-first psalm, is brought to a sense of the wickedness of his heart, or sinful disposition, he never dreams of referring this disposition to God as its creator and author. He imputes his inborn depravity to himself. He acknowledges that the demerit of it is absolute. It is the creature's agency, and the creature's only. He describes it as "innate," but not as "created" or "infused" by God. He derives it from his mother, but not from his Maker. But when David rejoiced over his own holy disposition, and that of the people, to honor God in the erection of a temple, his utterance is very different. "Who am I, and what is my people that we should be able to offer so willingly after this sort? For all things come of thee, and of thine own have we given thee." 1 Chron. 29: 14.

Because holiness can be created and infused, it does not follow that sin can be, unless it can be shown, first, that the demerit of sin is only a relative demerit, as the merit of holiness is only a relative and gracious merit, and, secondly, that God's creative agency can be exerted in the origination of sin in the same manner that it is in the origination of holiness: namely, by direct spiritual efficiency and operation.

When it is said that "malignity is evil," it is meant of course that it is morally evil, i.e., damnable and punishable. The punishableness of it, is what constitutes it evil. It is not evil in the sense that poverty or sickness are evils To say, therefore, that such a form of evil as sin can be understood without looking at the origin of it, is self-contradictory. A malignant disposition is morally evil, that is damnable and punishable, only in case it is *guilt.* If it is misfortune, it is not moral evil at all. If therefore it is not the product of the human will solely, but the product of God working in the human will; if it is "created" and "infused;" it is certainly neither damnable nor punishable. Auctor mali non ultor mali. It is no answer to say that a holy disposition is commendable and rewardable, and yet this is created and infused. The merit in this case, we repeat, is gracious and pactional, and does not rest upon any absolute and primary obligation in God to reward God in this case rewards his own grace, and his own work in his creature. But the demerit of a sinful disposition is absolute, and its reward necessary; that is, resting upon an absolute and primary obligation in God as just to punish sin. God in this case does not punish his own co-operating agency in a creature's will, or visit with judicial infliction his own work.

Thus it appears that the "nature" of man's *sinful* inclination or disposition cannot be determined except by knowing its "origin." If it originates in one way, it is not sin; if in another, it is sin Suppose that a judge should say to a jury: "You are not to look at the origin of this act of killing, but only at the nature of it; killing a man, is killing a man, whatever may be the source from which the act originated." The reply would be, that it is impossible to determine the nature of the act in this instance, without tracing it to its origin. Killing is of the nature of murder, only in case it originates in a murderous inclination and purpose. The nature depends upon the origin In like manner, it is impossible to decide that a particular human disposition or inclination is of a culpable and damnable nature, until it has been decided whether God or man is the author of it The very epithet "original," applied to Adam's first sin, implies that its *origin* is a feature that is vital to the understanding of it; that its nature cannot be determined but by examining its first source. The term "original," when applied to sin, implies that it originates in man. But the very same term, when applied to righteousness, implies that it originates in God. "In all agency, whether of good or evil, much is wont to be attributed to this: who was *first* in it? In point of good, the blessed God hath no competitor; he is the undoubted first fountain of all good, and is therefore acknowledged the Supreme Good. In point of evil (viz. moral) there is none prior to the devil, who is therefore eminently called the evil or wicked one." Howe: Living Temple, II., viii.

Original sin is to be distinguished from indwelling sin. The latter is the remainder of original sin in the regenerate. Its workings are described in Rom. 7:14—8:27. Shedd: Commentary, in loco It is not, like original sin, a dominant and increasing principle in the believer, but a subjugated and diminishing one. Indwelling sin is the minuendo movement of sin "It hath a dying fall." Original sin is the crescendo movement. "Original sin does not remain in the same manner after regeneration as it remained before; for there are two remarkable differences. In the unregenerate, it occupies all the faculties of the soul *peaceably*, and *rules* in their mind, will, and affections; but in the regenerate, it neither dwells peaceably, because grace from above is infused into them, which daily opposes this disease, and more and more expels it from every faculty of the soul; nor does it rule over them, because grace prevailing and predominating restrains it and sends it as it were under the yoke. The other difference is, that in the unregenerate it has the guilt of eternal death annexed to it; but in the regenerate it is absolved from this fruit, for the sake of Christ the mediator." Davenant: Justification, XV. Says Luther (Table Talk, Of Sins), "Original sin after regeneration is like a wound that begins to heal; though it be a wound, yet it is in course of healing, though it still runs, and is sore. So, original sin remains in Christians until they die, yet itself is mortified and continually dying Its head is crushed to pieces, so that it cannot condemn us." Indwelling sin is denominated "the law in (not *of*) the members," Rom. 7:23; original sin is denominated "the law of sin and death," Rom. 8:2.

The bondage of sin is defined in the Westminster Larger Catechism, 25. It describes the corruption of nature, called original sin in distinction from actual transgression, as that corruption "whereby man is utterly indisposed, disabled, and made opposite to all that is spiritually good." The Westminster Confession describes this corruption as that "whereby we are utterly indisposed, disabled, and made opposite to all good, and wholly inclined to all evil." The symbols of the Lutheran and Calvinistic churches are equally explicit upon this point.[1] For the Scripture proof, see ante, p. 109.

This introduces the subject of the *inability to good* of the apostate will, respecting which the following particulars are to be noted. (*a*) The inability relates to *spiritual* good. (*b*) The inability is *self-caused* and *voluntary*.

1. In the Westminster statement, the inability and opposition of the will relates to all that is "spiritually good." Spiritual good is holiness, and holiness is supreme love of God and equal love of man. The creed-statement there-

---

[1] Calvin Institutes, II ii v Shedd. History of Doctrine, II. 164-177, Theological Essays, 235-243; Sermons to the Natural Man, Sermon XI.

fore is, that apostate man, alone and of himself, is unable to love God with all his soul, and his neighbor as himself. He cannot start such an affection as this in his heart. He cannot originate within his will an inclination, or disposition that is "spiritually good" The inability relates to voluntary action, in distinction from volitionary; to self-determination to an ultimate end, in distinction from the choice of particular means.

The doctrine in question does not imply that fallen man is unable to be moral; but that he is unable to be spiritual, holy, and religious. St. Paul teaches (Rom. 2:14) that some unregenerate pagans practise morality; that they "do by nature the things contained in the law." that is, *some* things contained in the law (τὰ τοῦ νόμου), not all things.[1] Their obedience is fractional and imperfect. Under the natural stimulus of conscience, they refrain more or less from vice, and live more or less virtuously, as compared with others around them. But this morality is not supreme love of God, and perfect obedience of his law. St Paul denies that these virtuous heathen are spiritually good and holy, when he affirms that, if tested by the law that requires supreme love of God, "every mouth must be stopped, and all the world become guilty before God," Rom. 3:19; that "all have sinned and come short of the glory of God," Rom. 3:23; and that "there is none righteous, no, not one," Rom. 3:10.

Again, this inability and opposition to all that is "spiritually" good, does not imply that fallen man is destitute of certain natural and instinctive affections that are attractive and beneficent.[2] First in the list, are the family affections. The love of the parent for the child, of the children for the parents, of brothers and sisters for each other, is an amiable

---

[1] Had St Paul intended to teach that these virtuous heathen do all things required by the law, he would have said τὸν νόμον ποιῇ, as in Gal 5 3

[2] On the natural instincts, and the moral and religious affections, see ante, p 119 sq

sentiment, and oftentimes leads to great self-sacrifice. But the self-sacrifice is for the brother or sister, not for God. Family affection may and often does exist without any supreme love of God. It may and often does lead to disobedience of God. The workings of natural affection must be subordinated to the claims of Christ, in order to become religious affection, or "spiritually good." "He that loveth father or mother more than me is not worthy of me," Matt. 11:37. When the two come in conflict, the instinctive human affection if allowed sway is positively idolatrous and irreligious

Secondly, there are the social affections. Man is instinctively interested in his fellow-man, and performs many acts of self-sacrifice and generosity towards him The sailor will share his last crust with his fellow-sailor; the fireman will risk his own life for a fellow-creature whom he never saw before, and will never see again. But both actions may be performed, and often have been, by one who takes the name of God in vain, and breaks every other commandment of the decalogue whenever he is tempted to it. The self-sacrifice in this instance, also, is for man, not for God. The act in this case is one of gallantry, or courage, and the common sense of man never denominates it a spiritual and holy act. Men call it "noble," and reward it by some token of admiration: a silver cup, or a purse of money. They would not think of so rewarding a spiritual or holy act, like that of the martyr who dies for his faith in Christ, or of the missionary who lays his bones among the savages to whom he has preached the gospel.

Thirdly, there are the civil affections. Man is by his constitution a political animal, as Aristotle denominates him. He is interested in the nation and country to which he belongs, by reason of his birth. This patriotic feeling, like the social and family affections, rises up instinctively and uniformly in every man, the unregenerate as well as regenerate. This, too, like the others, is not spiritual and holy in its nature. The most intense patriotism may be accompanied with atheism, and unbelief, and immorality. Such patriotism is expressed in the sentiment: "My country, right or wrong."

Fourthly, the aesthetic feeling is not spiritual or religious. A love for the beautiful in art has nothing of holy virtue in it. "Who will affirm that a disposition to approve of the harmony of good music, or the beauty of a square, or equilateral triangle, is the same with true holiness, or a truly virtuous disposition of mind." Edwards: Nature of Virtue. Good taste is not piety and religion. A refined voluptuary is oftentimes a good judge in fine art; and even a coarse sensualist may be. Turner, one of the first painters that England has produced, was an example of the latter. Good taste may be spiritualized and elevated, by being associated with and subordinated to a higher affection. But until this is done, it is of the earth earthly. It terminates only on that which is finite and temporal; and anything that terminates solely upon earth and time is unspiritual and unreligious. The same is true of the love of literature and science. Human discipline and culture is not holiness of heart, and spirituality of mind.

In all these instances, we have to do with a portion of man's constitution that is outside of the voluntary nature. We are concerned with *instinct*, using the term in a wide sense, not with will. In its narrow and common signification, instinct signifies only the impulse of animal nature in brutes. But it may be used to denote all the constitutional impulses of human nature. Man did not lose aesthetic impulse and feeling by the apostasy of his will; neither did he lose the family, the social, or the civil affections. When he inclined away from God he did not incline away from art, from science, from the family-state, from society, from government and country. His instinctive and constitutional interest in all these objects continued after the apostasy. His will was revolutionized, but not his instinctive nature. His love of God was gone, but not his love of family, of country, of beauty. Man continued to take pleasure in finite objects and relations, but lost delight in infinite and eternal objects and relations.

The foundation of all these affections is *natural instinct*, not will. They are constitutional, not voluntary; physical, not moral. Their source and basis is physical, using the term etymologically and broadly, to denote that which belongs to the φύσις, or created nature of man. The family affection is founded in blood and lineage A father does not love and toil for another man's son. The patriotic affection springs from flesh and birth. An Englishman will not lay down his life for a Frenchman. Aristotle notices this. He founds the state upon the family, and the family he founds upon the sexual relation and affection, which manifests itself "not through voluntary choice, but by that natural impulse which acts both in plants and animals, namely, the desire of leaving behind them others like themselves." Politics, I. ii. The aesthetic feeling, also, is founded in the created constitutional nature, but in the mental not the animal side of it. It does not depend, like the family and patriotic affection, on affinity in blood and birth.

There is nothing voluntary in the love of a parent for his child; in the love of a citizen for his country; in the love of the artist for beauty. They are not the inclination of the will. This is proved by the fact that the apostasy of the will does not radically change them. If they belonged to the will, they would be converted into their contraries when the will is. When man began to be destitute of love to God, he would begin to be destitute of love for his family, and his nation. In becoming an enemy of God and holiness, he would become an enemy of his family, of society, and of culture and art. In becoming disinclined and averse toward the Creator, he would become disinclined and averse toward these forms of the creature also.

2. In the Westminster statement, the disability or inability is connected with the disposition and inclination of the will. Man is "indisposed to all spiritual good, and inclined to all [spiritual] evil" It follows from this, that the cause and seat of the inability in question is in the action and state of the voluntary faculty. It is *moral* or *willing* inability. "Nam servit voluntas peccato, non nolens sed volens. Etenim voluntas non noluntas dicitur." Second Helvetic Confession, IX.

In denominating it "moral" inability, it is not meant that it arises merely from habit, or that it is not "natural" in any sense of the word nature. A man is sometimes said to be morally unable to do a thing, when it is very difficult for him to do it by reason of an acquired habit, but not really impossible. This is not the sense of the word "moral" when applied to the sinner's inability to holiness He is really and in the full sense of the word impotent. And the cause of this impotence is not a habit of doing evil which he has formed in his individual life, but a natural disposition which he has inherited from Adam The term "moral," therefore, when applied to human inability denotes that it is *voluntary*, in distinction from created. Man's impotence to good does not arise from the agency of God in creation, but from the agency of man in apostasy.

Whether, therefore, it can ever be called "natural" inability, will depend upon the meaning given to the term "nature." (*a*) If "nature" means that which is created by God, there is no natural inability to good in fallen man. But if "nature" means "natural disposition," or "natural inclination," there is a "natural" inability to good in fallen man. (*b*) Again, "natural" sometimes means something which is born with man, in distinction from that which he acquires after birth; something in man *at* birth, yet not *caused by* birth. In this sense, man's inability to good is "natural" It is innate inability The Scriptures sometimes employ the word in this sense. 1 Cor. 2:14, "The natural man receiveth not the things of the Spirit of God, neither can he know them." Eph. 2:3, "And were by nature (φύσει, by birth) children of wrath." Ps. 51:5, "Conceived in sin and shapen in iniquity." In this last passage, "conceived" is not synonymous with "created," and must be carefully distinguished from it. So, also, in Rom. 9:11, "The children being not yet born," does not mean, "The children being not yet created." As opposed, therefore, to what is natural in the sense of created by God, man's inability is moral, not natural; but as opposed to what is moral in the sense of acquired by habit, man's inability is natural When "natural" means "innate," we assert that inability is "natural" When "natural" means "created," we assert that inability is "moral," that is, voluntary.

Owing to this ambiguity in the signification of the terms "natural" and "moral," the elder Calvinistic theologians did not use either term exclusively, to denote the sinner's inability to good. Sometimes they employ one and sometimes the other, and explain their meaning. The symbols of the Lutheran and Calvinistic churches frequently use the word "natural," and assert entire inability with great decision and unanimity. "When God converts a sinner, he freeth him from his natural bondage under sin." Westminster Confession, IX. iv.[1]

The elder Edwards differs from the old Calvinists in two particulars. 1. In refusing to denominate the bondage of the human will "natural inability," 2. In denying that "moral inability," by which term exclusively he designates the sinner's bondage, is "inability proper." As these positions bring Edwards into contradiction with himself, and open the way for a different anthropology from that contained in his writings generally, and particularly in his treatise on Original Sin, we direct attention to them His view is contained in the following statements: "Natural

[1] Compare Formula Consensus Helvetici, Ed. Niemeyer, 737 For Turrettin's account of the distinction, see Institutio, X iv. 39

inability alone is properly called inability." Will, Works, II. 104 "No inability which is merely moral is properly called by the name inability." Will, Works, II. 103[1]

In his treatise on the Will (Works, II. 104), Edwards defines "natural inability" as the want of the requisite mental faculties. Consequently "natural *ability*," for him, is the possession of the requisite mental faculties viewed *apart* from their moral state and condition. In so viewing them, he differs from the elder Calvinists, who regarded a mental faculty and its moral condition as inseparable. Edwards conceives of the will abstractly and separate from its inclination, and as so conceived contends that it is "naturally able" to obey the law of God. The elder Calvinists denied that the will can be so conceived of.

"Natural inability," says Edwards, "arises from the want of natural capacity, or from external hindrance." A man would be naturally unable to obey the divine law, if he were destitute of any of the faculties of the human soul, or if he were prevented from obeying the divine law by external force. Now, argues Edwards, inasmuch as man is not destitute of either understanding or will, and is not compelled to sin by outward circumstances or by another being, it cannot be said that man is naturally unable to obey the divine law. This is true of the fallen man as well as of the unfallen.

Again, Edwards defines "natural inability" with reference to inclination or disposition. If a man is inclined to do a thing and is prevented, he is naturally unable. "We are said," he remarks (Will, Works, II. 15), "to be naturally unable to do a thing when we cannot do it if we will [i.e., are inclined], because what is most commonly called nature does not allow of it, or because of some impeding

[1] On page 102 (Works, II ), Edwards, however, speaks doubtfully on this point · "*If* moral inability can truly be called inability " Compare his doubt whether it is proper to call God a part of "being in general." See Nature and Definition of God. Vol. I. p. 91 sq.

defect or obstacle that is extrinsic to the will, either in the faculty of understanding, constitution of body, or external objects."

There are two criticisms to be made upon this statement. 1. In the first place, if "the impeding defect or obstacle in the faculty of understanding" should amount to the total absence of reason, it would not be possible for a man to have an inclination to obey. An idiot or an insane person is not a moral agent, and is incapable of moral inclination. If, however, Edwards means only a deficiency in intelligence that hinders the man in acting out his inclination—as when a man, though inclined to a right course, does not know what is the best means of accomplishing it—then, in this case, the will or inclination would be taken for the deed, and this would not be an instance of inability.

2. In the second place, if a man is inclined to obey God, but is prevented in a particular instance from performing the outward service, by sickness, or by imprisonment—by "constitution of body," or by "external objects"—he is regarded by God, who always looks upon the truth or reality of things, as an obedient servant. "If there be a willing mind (προθυμία), it is accepted according to what a man hath, and not according to what he hath not," 2 Cor. 8 : 12. The inclination is the obedience; and Edwards supposes the inclination. This case, also, is not an instance of inability to obey the divine law. "The very willing is the doing," says Edwards himself Will, Works, II. 17.

Edwards's denial of "natural inability" is equivalent *inferentially* and *indirectly* to the assertion of "natural ability." But he nowhere formally and directly asserts "natural ability," and in one instance directly and explicitly denies and combats it. "It will follow," he remarks (Original Sin, Works, II. 464), "on our author's principles, that redemption is needless, and Christ is dead in vain. For God [according to him] has given a sufficient power and ability, in all mankind, to do all their duty and wholly to avoid sin. Yea, this author insists upon it that when men have not sufficient power to do their duty, they have no duty to do. These things fairly imply that men have in their own *natural ability* sufficient means to avoid sin, and to be perfectly free from it; and so from all the bad consequences of it. And if the means are sufficient, then there is no need of more; and therefore there is no need of Christ's dying, in order to it"

The explanation is this. Edwards was combating the doctrine of Whitby and Taylor, that apostate man has plenary power to keep the divine law. Consequently, he had no motive to advocate the doctrine of ability in any form. His great object in the controversy was to establish the doctrine of *inability*. When, however, he is pushed by his opponents with the objection, that if there be no power in fallen man to keep the divine law there is no obligation to keep it, instead of recurring, as the elder Calvinists did, to the fall in Adam and the loss of ability by a free act of will,[1] Edwards meets the objection by asserting that fallen man is under no "natural *inability*" to keep the divine law, and in this way implies that he has a "natural *ability*" to keep it. But when his definition of the "natural ability" thus indirectly attributed to fallen man is examined, it proves not to be efficient and real power, but only a quasi-ability that is incapable of producing the effect required in the objection, namely, perfect obedience. In this way, he evades the objection of his opponent, rather than answers it. "It is easy," he says (Will, Works, II. 17), "for a man to do the thing if he will [is inclined], but the very willing [inclining] is the doing. Therefore, in these things

[1] So Ursinus argues "Objection 5 They who cannot but sin, are unjustly punished, but the unregenerate cannot but sin therefore God doth unjustly punish them Answer They who necessarily sin are unjustly punished, except that necessity come *voluntarily*, and *by their own will.* But men have drawn upon them that necessity voluntarily in the first parents, and themselves do willingly sin Therefore God doth justly punish them" Christian Religion. Question 8.

to ascribe a non-performance to the want of power or ability, is not just, because the thing wanting is not a being able, but a being willing. There are faculties of mind, and capacity of nature, and everything sufficient but a disposition; nothing is wanting but a will [inclination]." But this amounts only to the truism that the sinner is able to obey the law of God, if he is inclined to obey it, and avoids the point in dispute. For the real question is, whether the sinner can originate the "thing that is wanting" in order to obedience: namely, "a being willing," or a disposition to obey. Edwards always and everywhere asserts that he cannot; but for the purpose of meeting the objection that if the sinner is unable to obey he is not obligated to obey, he contends that it is improper to call the inability to "be willing" or inclined, an inability, because the mere existence of the faculty of will without the power to change its disposition constitutes ability. "To ascribe a non-performance," says Edwards, "in these things, to the want of power is not just; because the thing wanting is not a being able, but a being willing. There are faculties of mind, and a capacity of nature, and everything sufficient but a *disposition*" But the absence of a disposition to obey is fatal. The presence of a disposition to obey is necessary in order to obedience. No man can obey the divine law without being willing or inclined to obey it; and Edwards asserts over and over again that the sinner is unable to incline himself to obedience. A man destitute of an inclination to obey the divine law, cannot obey it merely because he has the abstract faculty of will. Volitionary acts can be performed, but since they do not proceed from a right inclination, they are not obedience. The sinner's so-called "natural ability," consisting of everything except a "disposition" to obey, consists of everything necessary to efficient power except efficiency itself. The ability to obey is an ability to *incline*, because it is the inclination of the will that constitutes true obedience. Consequently, if inclining to good is not within the competence of the sinner, he is unable to obey.

In order, therefore, that a man destitute of an inclination to obey the divine law may be said without any equivocation to be "able" to obey, he must be able to *originate* such an inclination. The question that settles the question respecting "ability," and precludes all evasion, is this: Has fallen man the ability to start and begin that right inclination of will which is the essence of obedience, and without which it is impossible to obey the law of God? If so, he has without any ambiguity the "ability" to perfectly obey the divine law. But if not, he is unable to obey it, and this impotence is properly called inability. In answering this question, Edwards is explicit in the negative, and stands upon the position of Augustine and Calvin, in respect to the bondage and helplessness of the apostate will. See Edwards, Will, Works, II. 101; Endless Punishment, Works, I. 615, 616, et alia.

Pascal (Provincial Letters, II.) illustrates this equivocation respecting "natural ability" (a distinction employed by the Jesuits) in the following manner: "A man setting out on a journey is encountered by robbers who wound him, and leave him half dead. He sends for aid from three neighboring surgeons. The first on examining his wounds pronounces them mortal, and tells him that God alone can restore him. The second tells him that he has strength enough to carry him back to his dwelling, and that he will recover by the force of his system. The patient, perplexed between the two, calls upon the third surgeon. This latter after examination sides with the second surgeon, and ridicules the opinion of the first. The patient naturally supposes that the third surgeon agrees with the second; and in fact receives in reply to his inquiries an assurance that he has strength sufficient to prosecute his journey. The poor man, however, conscious of his weakness, asks on what his conclusions are founded? 'Because,' said he, 'you still have your legs, and the legs are the natural organs for walking.' 'But,' says the sick man, 'have I strength to make use of them; for they seem to me useless, in my state of weakness?' 'Certainly not,' replied the doctor; 'and in reality you never will walk, unless God shall send you supernatural aid to sustain and lead you.' 'What!' cries the patient, 'have I not then in myself sufficient strength for walking?' 'Very far from it,' replied the surgeon. 'Your opinion then is entirely *opposed* to the second surgeon respecting my state?' 'I confess it is,' he replied"

When "ability" is attributed to the human will, it is naturally understood to mean the power to *use* and *control* the energetic force of the faculty. Inclining to an ultimate end is the energy of the will, and its most important activity. But if the sinful will is unable to incline to God as the supreme end and good, it is improper to say that it has a "natural ability" to do this. Because, "ability" properly denotes efficient power. The man, in Pascal's illustration, who "still had his legs," but had lost the power to use them, could not properly be said to be able to walk; and the man who "still has a will," but is unable to incline it to good, cannot properly be said to be able to obey. If when Edwards replied to his opponent that "it is easy for a man to do the thing if he will," he had added that "it is easy for a man to will," this would have been an unequivocal assertion of ability. But Edwards not only denied that it is easy for the sinner to will rightly, but asserted that it is impossible.

Ability must not be confounded with *capability*, or power with *capacity*. The sinner is capable of loving God supremely, but not able to love him supremely; and probably this is all that is intended by many who assert "natural ability." Capacity implies possibility only; as when it is said that man has the capacity for all the diseases to which flesh is heir. But something more than capacity is requisite to warrant the assertion that he is able to have them all. The ability to have all the diseases of the human body would require the germ of them all. A man is not able to have the small-pox, unless he has the contagion, or been inoculated with it. But he is capable of having the small-pox, without either contagion or inoculation. Adam before the fall had the capacity to sin, rather than the ability; the possibility, not the propensity. It is, therefore, more strictly proper to say that it was possible for holy Adam to sin, than to say that he had the ability to sin. Accurately speaking, the ability to sin, is inward sin itself; and the ability to be holy, is inward holiness itself. Hence Augustine attributed to the unfallen Adam the *posibilitas* peccandi, and denied the *potestas*. In moral things, the ability implies the inclination and tendency.

Consequently, in ethics and religion, *moral* ability is the only kind of power that is properly designated by the term "ability." In reference to obedience and disobedience, holiness and sin, if there is not moral or voluntary ability, there is no ability at all. And moral or voluntary ability cannot be separated from inclination. No inclination, no ability. If inclination, then ability A man who is able to love God supremely, is inclined to love Him. A man who is able to steal, is inclined in his heart to theft. In common parlance we say of a bad man: "He can do anything; he can lie, he can steal." This is the same as saying: "He *is* a thief, he *is* a liar" If we say that he is capable of lying, we do not say so much, as when we say he is able to lie.

"Natural ability" is, properly, only *physical* force It is the power of matter, not of mind. A man has the natural ability to lift one hundred pounds. This is the power of matter; of his body. But we can think of this kind of power as not exerted, and as never exerted. The man may have this species of ability, and yet never lift a hundred pounds weight. In the case of natural ability, we can abstract and separate the faculty from its exercise and use. The faculty, in the instance of natural ability, is the body of the man. We say that there is in this body the ability or power to lift one hundred pounds weight. Whether this ability shall be exerted or not, depends not upon the body but upon the man's will. But the man's body and the man's will are distinct and separate substances and faculties. We can therefore conceive of this natural or physical ability as *inactive*, and doing nothing, until a volition employs it. We can conceive of natural power or ability without any *effect* produced by it.

But in the instance of moral or voluntary power or ability, we cannot thus abstract and separate the faculty from its use and exercise, and conceive of it as inert and producing no effect. The faculty in this case is not the body, but the will itself. But the will cannot be inactive and inert, as matter may be. It is inclined and active by its very idea and definition. There is no conceivable separation, therefore, in this instance, between the faculty and its use and exercise, as there is in the instance of the body and the volition that uses the body. Moral or voluntary power is necessarily in exercise. A man may be naturally able to lift a hundred pounds, and yet not do it. But a man may not be morally able to love God, and yet not do it. The ability to an act in this latter case, is one with the act itself. Ability to incline, is inclination itself. Ability to love, is love itself. Ability to hate, is hatred itself.

In the instance of natural ability or physical power, the ability is in one subject, and the use or exercise of it in another subject. The natural force is in the bodily limbs, and the moral force that exerts and uses it is in the will. But in the instance of moral ability or voluntary power, there is only one subject, namely, the human will. The will is the faculty, and the inclining of the will is the use and exercise of the faculty. We cannot, therefore, conceive of the will as being inert and inactive until another agent *makes* it active. Neither can we conceive of the will as inactive until some act of its own *makes* it active. Edwards was unquestionably correct, in denying that the will can be started out of indifference and inaction by its own antecedent volition. But we can conceive of this, in the instance of natural or physical power. We can conceive of the body as inert and inactive until another agent than itself, namely the soul, *makes* it active by an antecedent volition. In the instance of moral ability, the faculty of will and its use and exercise are inseparable. If there be a will, it is necessarily in action; it is necessarily inclined. We cannot say that it is able to incline, not yet having inclined It can pass from one inclination to another; but it cannot exist an instant with no inclination at all. Consequently, if the will is able to do a thing, it is doing it. But in the instance of natural ability, the faculty and its exercise are separable. If there be a body, it is not necessarily exerting its physical force. In this case, we can say that it is able to do a thing, and yet is not doing it.

It is ambiguous and misleading, therefore, to apply the term "natural ability" to a moral faculty like the will; as it confessedly would be to apply the term "moral ability" to a physical faculty like the human body. No one would attribute to the human body a moral ability to swim; and no one should attribute to the human will a natural ability to love or obey, because a natural ability may not be in use and exercise. Andrew Fuller (Memoir, 15, Bohn's Ed.) quotes from Gill the distinction between a thing "being in the power of our hand, and in the power of our heart." Natural ability is the power of the hand; moral ability is the power of the heart Referring to Des Cartes' distinction between the act of the will that terminates on the will itself, and the act of the will that terminates on the body, natural ability would designate the latter, and moral ability the former. Obedience of the divine command, "Thou shalt love the Lord thy God with all thy heart," is the product of moral, not of natural ability.

Edwards asserts "moral inability," and defines it to be either the absence of right inclination, or the presence of wrong inclination. "A man may be said to be morally unable to do a thing; when he is under the influence or prevalence of a contrary inclination, or has a want of inclination. Moral inability consists either in want of inclination, or the strength of a contrary inclination. It may be said, in one word, that moral inability consists in the opposition or want of inclination. A man is truly morally unable to choose[1] contrary to a present inclination A child of great love to his parents may be unable to be willing to kill his father." Will, Works, II. 15, 16, 101, 102.

This is the inability that is meant in the Westminster statement, that "man is utterly indisposed and disabled to all that is spiritually good." And this species of inability is *real* inability. It is not a figure of speech, but an impotence as helpless and insuperable by the subject of it, as natural inability. The substantive "inability" has its full and strict meaning. The adjective "moral" does not convert the notion of impotence into that of power, but only denotes the species of impotence. It is true that the "cannot" is a "will not," but it is equally true that the "will not" is a "cannot." The sinful will is literally unable to incline to good, apart from grace.

Notwithstanding his assertion that moral inability is improperly called inability, Edwards strenuously maintains that moral inability is *utter* and *helpless impotence.* This is the self-contradiction in his theory. "By reason of the total depravity and corruption of man's nature, he is utterly unable, without divine grace, savingly to love God, believe in Christ, or do anything truly good." Works, II. 177 He

---

[1] "To choose," here means "to incline," or "to be willing." It does not mean, "to exert a volition," for a man is able to exert a volition "contrary to a present inclination."

also asserts the same thing in his doctrine of *moral necessity.* "Moral necessity," he says, "may be as absolute as natural necessity—that is, the [moral] effect may be as perfectly connected with its moral cause, as a natural necessary effect is with its natural cause. When I use this distinction of moral and natural necessity, I would not be understood to suppose, that if anything comes to pass by the former kind of necessity, the nature of things is not concerned in it, as well as in the latter." Will, I. iv. Edwards means that the connection between the volition and the inclination is as necessary, or as much founded in the nature of things, as that between a physical effect and its physical cause. Given a wrong inclination, and wrong volitions must follow. If the disposition of the will be vicious, the volitions of the will cannot be virtuous, any more than the fruit can be grapes if the root is that of the thistle.

Now in thus asserting that moral necessity is properly called *necessity*, Edwards is inconsistent in denying that moral inability is properly called *inability*. For the sinner's moral necessity of sinning is the very same thing as his moral inability to obedience. If, therefore, Edwards was willing to say that moral necessity is as real and absolute as natural necessity, he should have been willing to say that moral inability is as real and absolute as natural inability. If the term "necessity" is properly applicable to moral necessity, the term "inability" is properly applicable to moral inability. Necessity is a stronger term than inability, and it is singular that while Edwards was not afraid to employ the former in connection with voluntary action, he should have shrunk from the latter. The same general argument that proves that moral necessity, taken in its full unambiguous sense, is consistent with the freedom of the will, would prove that moral inability, taken in its full unambiguous sense, is likewise consistent with it. The nature of Edwards's answer to the Arminian objection that if there is not ability in the sinful will there is no obligation resting upon it, explains the inconsistency. Instead of denying, with the Calvinistic creeds generally, the Arminian premise that all inability however brought about is inconsistent with obligation, he concedes it, and endeavors to show that there is ability.

Moral necessity is asserted by Augustine and Calvin. It means that necessity in the moral character of the volitions which arises from a habitus of the will; from a bias or disposition of the voluntary faculty. A holy will has a holy habitus, and is thereby under a moral necessity of exerting holy volitions. "A good tree cannot bring forth evil fruit" Hence St. Paul denominates the spiritual man "a servant (slave) of righteousness," Rom. 6:18. St. John asserts that "whosoever is born of God cannot sin," 1 John 3:9. A sinful will has a sinful habitus, and is thereby under a moral necessity of exerting sinful volitions. "Ye were servants (slaves) of sin," Rom. 6:17. "Whosoever committeth sin is the servant (slave) of sin," John 8:34. A holy will is unable to disobey; and a sinful will is unable to obey.

Fatalism has been charged upon this doctrine of moral necessity, but erroneously. Were the sinful *disposition* of the will itself necessitated, the charge would be well founded. Were the sinful *inclination* the necessary effect of some antecedent act or arrangement of God, as the volition is the necessary effect of the antecedent inclination, man would not be responsible for sin. But it is not. The sinful inclination is the abiding self-determination of the human will. Its origin is due to an act of freedom in Adam; and its continuance is due to the unceasing self-determination of every individual of the posterity. Each individual man prolongs and perpetuates in himself the evil inclination of will that was started in Adam. Sinful inclination began freely in the one sin of the whole race, and is continued freely in the millions of individual inclinations in the millions of individuals of the race. Had sinful inclination been created and infused by God, then as the sinful volitions are referred to the inclination as their cause, the sinful inclination must have been referred to God as its cause. The doctrine of moral necessity means only that the volitions must necessarily be like the inclination. It does not mean that the inclination itself is originated and necessitated by God.

A habitus or disposition in the will intensifies and confirms free voluntary action, instead of weakening or destroying it. For a habitus is a vehement and total self-determination. But that which promotes determination by the *self*, of course precludes compulsion by that which is not self. Hence the bondage of the will to sinful inclination does not destroy either the voluntariness, or the responsibility of the will. The enslaved will is still a self-determining faculty; the bondage of sin is a responsible and guilty bondage, because proceeding from the ego, not from God. Calvin (Institutes, II. ii. 5) maintains this in the following manner: "Bernard subscribing to what is said by Augustine, thus expresses himself: 'Among all the animals, man alone is free; and yet by the intervention of sin, he also suffers a species of violence; but from the *will*, not from nature, so that he is not thereby deprived of his innate liberty.' For what is voluntary is also free. And a little after, Bernard says, 'The will being, by I know not what corrupt and surprising means, changed for the worse, is itself the *author of the necessity* to which it is subject; so that neither necessity, being *voluntary*, can excuse the will, nor the will, being fascinated (illecta), can exclude necessity.' For this necessity is in some measure *voluntary*. Afterwards he says, that we are oppressed with a yoke, but no other than that of a *voluntary* servitude; that therefore our servitude renders us miserable, and our will renders us inexcusable; because the will, when it was free, made itself the slave of sin. At length he concludes, 'Thus the soul, in a certain strange and evil manner, under this kind of voluntary and free yet pernicious necessity, is both enslaved and free; enslaved by necessity, free by its will [inclination]; and, what is more wonderful and more miserable, it is guilty because free; and enslaved wherein it is guilty; and so therein enslaved wherein it is free.' From these passages, the reader clearly perceives that I am teaching no novel doctrine, but what was long ago advanced by Augustine, with the universal consent of pious men, and which for nearly a thousand years after was confined to the cloisters of monks. But Lombard, for want of knowing how to distinguish necessity from coercion, gave rise to a pernicious error."

The moral inability of the sinner, then, is the inability to incline rightly from a wrong state of the will; to convert sinful into holy inclination. He is already sinfully inclined This sinful inclination is moral spontaneity, or self-determination to an ultimate end. From the standpoint and starting-point of evil, it is impossible to incline or self-determine to God. The sinner may exert volitions, and make resolutions, in hope of producing another inclination, but they are failures. A holy inclination cannot be originated by this method. This is moral inability. What are the grounds of it?

1. The finiteness and limitation of the created will is a ground. Holy inclination, we have seen (ante, p 99 sq), must be given in creation. Neither man's nor angel's will can be first created without character, and from this involuntary state originate holy inclination. The beginning, therefore, of holiness must *always* proceed from God. It can no more be originated by the creature, than the spiritual substance itself of the will can be. But if this is true of man as finite, and of angel as finite, it is still more so of man as sinful. When he is already preoccupied by a sinful inclination, it would be still more impossible for him to originate a holy inclination.

The mutability of the finite will is the possibility of falling from holiness to sin, not the possibility of rising from sin to holiness. If the will of man or angel becomes evil, it is evil immutably, apart from regenerating grace. When holy, it can change its inclination by its own energy without the co-agency of God. But when sinful, it cannot do this. The finite will is mutably holy, but immutably sinful, so far as its own force is concerned.

2. The derivative nature of finite holiness is a second ground of moral inability. Holiness is a concreated quality of man, like intelligence, or rationality. But concreated qualities are incapable of self-origination. We perceive immediately that man cannot be the author of his own intellectuality. He cannot be created without the ideas of space and time, of God and self; in brief, without innate ideas; and then originate them by his own power. He cannot come from the creative hand an idiot without reason, and then rationalize himself. Rationality and intelligence are derived characteristics, and therefore they are beyond man's power to produce. In like manner, holiness is a derived characteristic, and therefore cannot be man's product. The creature cannot do the Creator's work. It would be absurd to say that matter can be created lacking one of the necessary properties of matter, say impenetrability, and can then originate for itself the lacking property. But it would be a like absurdity, to affirm that man or angel can be created lacking one of the necessary characteristics of moral perfection, namely, holiness, and can then originate it.

This reasoning does not hold good in regard to sin. Man can be created without sin, and afterwards originate it himself, for three reasons: (*a*) Because sin is not a derivative quality. Sin starts in the finite will, not in the Infinite. If it were derived from God, it would not be damnable, and therefore not sin. (*b*) Because sin is not an element in moral perfection. Everything that comes from the Creator's hand must be perfect after its kind. A created moral being must have created moral perfection. This implies holiness, and excludes sin. (*c*) Because sin is not a primary and normal characteristic of human nature. It does not enter into the idea and ideal of man. Sin, unlike holiness, does not belong to man as man. The human will can originate sin, because it is a secondary and abnormal quality. God is the author of the normal, but the creature is the originator of the abnormal. All that belongs to man as ideal and perfect must come from God; but all that belongs to man as fallen and imperfect must come from man himself. Hence man can originate sin, but not holiness.

3. The adorableness of a self-originated holiness is a third proof of moral inability. If man or angel were the sole and ultimate author of holiness in himself, his holiness would be underived and self-subsistent, and he would deserve the glory due to such holiness. Strictly self-originated holiness is worthy of worship. But the testimony of the Christian experience is against this. "By the grace of God I am what I am," 1 Cor. 15:10. The testimony of the angelic consciousness is also against this. The seraphim cried "Holy, holy, holy is the Lord of Hosts," Is. 6:3. The trisagion attributes absolute and original holiness only to God. The testimony of Christ is against this "None is good but one," Luke 18:19. If man or angel should begin a holy inclination, his merit before God and law would be absolute and not relative. This contradicts Luke 17:10, "When ye shall have done all those things that are commanded you, say, We are unprofitable servants" God in this case would be under an original and primary obligation to the creature

4. The reflex action of sin upon the will itself is a fourth ground of moral inability. Self-determination to evil destroys self-determination to good. The voluntary faculty, like every other faculty of the soul, cannot escape the consequences of its own action. Self-determination to sin reacts upon the will and renders it unable to holiness. The slavery of the will is an effect of the will upon its self. Whosoever commits sin, in and by this very voluntary act

becomes the slave of sin. John 8 : 24. Says Augustine (Confessions, VIII. v.), "My will the enemy held, and thence had made a chain for me, and bound me. For of a perverse will comes lust; and a lust yielded to becomes custom; and custom not resisted becomes necessity. By which links, as it were, joined together as in a chain, a hard bondage held me enthralled. And that new will, to serve Thee freely and to enjoy Thee, O God, which had begun to be in me, was not able to overcome my former long-established wilfulness. In these spiritual things, ability is one with will, and to will is to do; and yet the thing is not done. Whence is this strange anomaly (monstrum)? The mind commands the *body*, and it obeys instantly; the mind commands *itself*, and is resisted. The mind commands the hand to be moved, and such readiness is there that command is scarce distinct from obedience. The mind commands the mind, its own self, to will; and yet it doth not will. It commands itself, I say, to will, and would not command unless it willed; and yet what it commands is not done. But it willeth not *entirely;* therefore doth it not command entirely. For it commandeth only so far forth as it willeth. The will commandeth that there be a *will* [inclination]; not another's will, but its own will But it doth not command *entirely;* therefore, what it commandeth does not take place."

"It is certain," says Samuel Hopkins (Works, I. 233–235), "that every degree of inclination contrary to duty, which is and must be sinful, implies and involves an equal degree of difficulty and inability to obey. For indeed, such inclination of the heart to disobey, and the difficulty or inability to obey, are precisely one and the same. The kind of difficulty, or inability, therefore, always is great according to the strength and fixedness of the inclination to disobey; and it becomes total and absolute [inability], when the heart is totally corrupt and wholly opposed to obedience. Nothing but the opposition of the heart or will of man to coming to Christ, is or can be in the way of his coming So long as this continues, and his heart is wholly opposed to Christ, he cannot come to him; it is impossible, and will continue so, until his unwillingness, his opposition to coming to Christ, be removed by a change and renovation of his heart, by divine grace, and he be willing in the day of God's power."

The excess of will to sin is the same as defect of will to holiness. The degree of intensity with which any being inclines to evil, is the measure of the amount of power to good which he has thereby lost. If the intensity be total, the loss is entire. Sin is the suicidal action of the human will. To do wrong destroys the power to do right. This is illustrated in the effect of a vicious habit in diminishing a man's ability to resist temptation. But habit is the continual repetition of wrong self-decisions, every one of which reacts upon the will as a faculty, and renders it less strong and energetic to good. No man can do a wrong act, and be as sound in his will, and as spiritually strong, after it as he was before it.

Again, the *totality* of the depravity of the will destroys moral ability, or ability to good. The whole and not a mere part of the will is determined. Consequently, when a self-determination to a final end has occurred, there is no remainder of uncommitted power in reserve, as it were, behind the existing determination, by which the direction of the will may be reversed. This total and intense determination to evil is inability to good.

The *debilitating* effect of self-determination upon the will itself is too often overlooked. When cause and effect are in different subjects, the impotence of the cause itself after its own action is always taken into account; but when, as in the case of a sinful inclination, cause and effect are in one and the same subject, viz, the human will, the impotence of the cause itself after its own action is not always noticed, or is practically denied. If, for illustration, one man kill another man, all know that the murderer cannot restore the murdered man to life. The cause cannot undo its effect when they are in different subjects. But the same is true when a man kills himself. Here the cause and the effect are in one and the same subject. Now this is true also of the human will, in reference to the sin of which it is the cause. Sin is the effect of free will as the cause; and because the will originates sin, it is assumed that the will can nullify sin; can destroy what it originated. But the effect in this instance is as much beyond the power of the cause, when once the cause has acted, as in any other instance. A man certainly cannot undo the guilt of his sin, and neither can he undo the inclination to sin.

"A certainty," says the younger Edwards (Against Chauncey, XIII.), "that has been established by the will of man with respect to the will itself, as effectually binds that will, and is equally inconsistent with its liberty [to the contrary], as if that certainty were established by any other cause. Suppose the will of any man shall establish in itself a certain and unfailing bias to any particular action or series of actions; it cannot be pretended that this fixed bias already established is any more consistent with liberty [to the contrary], and moral agency [?], in the man in whom the bias exists, than if it had been established by any other cause. If a man were to cut off his own leg, though he might be more blamable for the act of cutting it off than he would be for the same act performed by another, yet the effect, as to his subsequent ability to walk, would be the very same." [1]

But if man, either unfallen or fallen, cannot begin a holy inclination, how is it that he can begin an evil one? If he cannot be the ultimate and meritorious author of holiness, how can he be the ultimate and ill-deserving author of sin?

---

[1] Shedd Sermons to the Natural Man, XI. and XIV.

Why may there be a power to the contrary downward from a holy position, but no power to the contrary upward from a sinful position?

1. Because of the difference between self-determination to holiness, and self-determination to sin. The first is relative, the last is absolute self-determination. Relative self-determination is self-determination with a Divine element in it; absolute self-determination is self-determination without a Divine element in it. The former is self-determination under the Divine impulse and actuation; the latter is solitary self-determination without the Divine impulse and actuation. Holiness in man is Divine-human: the product of God working in the creature to will and to do. Sin in man is human simply and only: the product of the finite will uninfluenced and unimpelled. Augustine, as quoted by Calvin (Inst., II. ii. 4), defines liberum arbitrium as "a power of reason and will by which good is chosen when grace assists, and evil is chosen when grace is wanting." Aquinas, as quoted by Neander (History, IV. 481), says that holy "free will is not an independent causality. God works in the finite will in the way that the nature of it requires that he should; although, therefore, he changes the inclination of man to another direction, nevertheless, by his almighty power he causes that man should freely will the change which he experiences; and thus all constraint is removed. For to suppose otherwise, that the man willed not the change which is a change in his will, would be a contradiction."

The difference between the two kinds of self-determination is marked in language. The noun "sin" has a verb active to correspond with it; the noun "holiness" has none. Sin is "sinning," or "to sin;" but holiness is not "holying," or "to holy." Only the passive is employed in the latter case: "to be holy," or, "to become holy." But both the active and passive are employed in the former. Man is willing in holiness; and he is willing in sin. But the willingness in the first case is complex. God works in man to will. Phil. 2 : 13. The willingness in the second case is simple. Man works alone In the first instance, the human will harmonizes with the Divine; in the second, it antagonizes. In the first instance, the voluntariness is recipient 1 Cor. 4 : 7, "What hast thou that thou didst not receive?" Rom. 8 : 15, "Ye have received the spirit of adoption." In the second instance, the voluntariness is originant.

The question arises whether the Divine element in holy self-determination does not, in reality, destroy the *self*-determination If God creates voluntary spontaneity when he creates a holy man, or re-creates it when he regenerates him, is it in either case real and genuine spontaneity? Must not the human will act *alone* and *independently*, in order to act voluntarily; and is not the sinful will the only free will, because it is not influenced by God in its action? The answer is in the negative: (*a*) Because revelation teaches this agency of God in and on the finite will, and at the same time teaches that the resulting holiness is true freedom. John 8 : 36, "If the Son shall make you free, ye shall be free indeed." (*b*) Because consciousness reports that the holy inclination is spontaneous, and unforced. (*c*) Because if the human will in order to act freely must not experience any influence or impulse from God, then all Divine influence is necessitating. And the same is true of human influence.

2 Man can originate sin, because sin is imperfection. The Infinite will cannot originate imperfection. Deut. 32 : 4, "God's work is perfect." 2 Sam. 22 : 31; Ps. 18 : 30. This is one of the differentia between the Creator and the creature. Infinite, uncreated, and eternal will cannot cause any defective thing; but finite, created, and temporal will can. Sin is defective, because it has less of being in it than holiness has. There was once a time when it was not; but holiness always was. Sin has no

positive and eternal right to be; holiness has such a right. Sin is not necessary in the universe of God; had God so decreed, the created will would never have originated it. But holiness is necessary. Because of these facts, the schoolmen defined sin as a negation; a defect rather than an effect. To originate it, is not the sign of power, but of weakness. Hence the possibility of sinning is not an excellence, but a deficiency. It is one of the limitations of the finite. That it does not belong to God does not prove that God is not free, or that he has less power than a man or angel has, any more than the impossibility of having a physical disease, or of dying, proves that God is inferior to man. The possibility of doing an evil thing is weakness rather than power.

The foundation of man's obligation to perfectly obey the Divine law, was the holiness and plenary power to good with which he was endowed by his Creator. Because God made man in his own image, he was obliged to sinless obedience. Moral obligation rested upon the union and combination of the so-called "natural ability" with the "moral." It did not rest upon the first alone. Not a will without any inclination, but a will with a holy inclination, was the basis of the requirement of sinless obedience. The possession of a will undetermined would not constitute man a moral agent. God did not make man without moral character, and then require perfect obedience from him. When man was created and placed under law, he was endowed not only with the faculties of a man, but with those faculties in a normal condition. The understanding was spiritually enlightened, and the will was rightly inclined. He had both "natural" and "moral" ability. He had real and plenary power to obey the law of God. In the beginning of man's moral existence, ability must equal obligation. And the ability did equal it. Kant's dictum: "I ought, therefore I can," was true of holy Adam and his posterity in him. If at the instant man came from the hand of God he had been unable to obey, he would not have been obligated to obey. "The law was not above man's strength when he was possessed of original righteousness, though it be above man's strength since he was stripped of original righteousness. The command was dated before man had contracted his impotency, when he had a power to keep it, as well as to break it. Had it been enjoined to man only after the fall, and not before, he might have had a better pretence to excuse himself, because of the impossibility of it; yet he would not have had sufficient excuse, since the impossibility did not result from the nature of the law, but from the corrupted nature of the creature. It 'was weak through the flesh' (Rom. 8:3), but it was promulged when man had a strength proportioned to the commands of it." Charnocke: The Holiness of God.

Obligation being thus founded upon the Creator's gifts, cannot be destroyed by any subsequent action of the creature. If he destroys his ability, he does not destroy his obligation. If man by his own voluntary action loses any or all of the talents entrusted to him, he cannot assign this loss as a reason why any or all the talents, together with usury, should not be demanded of him in the final settlement See Christ's parable of the talents. "Praecepta dei non sunt mensura virium, sed regula officii; non docent quid nunc possumus, sed quid debeamus, et quod *olim* potuerimus." Turrettin, Institutes, X. iv. 23. The Heidelberg Catechism thus represents the subject. Q. 9. "Does not God, then, wrong man by requiring of him in his law that which he cannot perform? A. No; for God so made man that he could perform it; but man through the instigation of the devil, by wilful disobedience deprived himself and all his posterity of this power."

1. It is objected, that if man is unable to keep the law, he is not obligated to keep it. This depends upon the *nature* of the inability, and its *cause*.

If man were destitute of reason, conscience, will, or any of the faculties of a moral being, he would not be obligated. If he were internally wrought upon by an almighty being, and prevented from obeying, he would not be obligated. If he were prevented by any external compulsion, he would not be obligated. If he had been created sinful, he would not be obligated. If he had been created indifferent either to holiness or sin, he would not have been obligated. None of these conditions obtain in the case of man. He was created holy, with plenary power to keep perfectly the moral law, and therefore was obligated to keep it. At the point of creation, ability and obligation were equal.

But if after creation in holiness and plenary power, any alteration be made in the original ratio between ability and obligation by the creature's voluntary agency, this cannot alter the original obligation If ability is weakened by an act of self-determination, obligation is not weakened. If ability is totally destroyed by self-determination, obligation is not destroyed. The latter is the fact in the case. There is a total inability, but it is not an original or created inability. It came to be by man's act, not by God's. "Man's inability to restore what he owes to God, an inability brought upon himself, does not excuse man from paying the satisfaction due to justice; for the result of sin cannot excuse the sin itself." Anselm: Cur deus homo, I xxiv.

The principle, that if a moral power once possessed is lost by the voluntary action of the possessor he is not thereby released from the original duty that rested upon it, is acknowledged by writers upon ethics. Aristotle (Ethics, III. v.) remarks that it is just in legislators "to punish people even for ignorance itself, if they are the cause of their own ignorance; just as the punishment is double for drunken people. For the cause is in themselves; since it was in their own power not to get drunk, and drunkenness is the cause of their ignorance. And they punish those who are ignorant of anything in the laws which they ought to know, and which it is not difficult to know; and likewise in all other cases in which they are ignorant through negligence; upon the ground that it was in their own power to pay attention to it. But perhaps a person is unable to give his attention? But he himself is the cause of this inability, by living in a dissipated manner. Persons are themselves the causes of their being unrighteous, by performing bad actions; and of being intemperate, by passing their time in drunken revels and such-like. When a man does those acts by which he becomes unjust, he becomes unjust voluntarily [that is by the action of his own will]. Nevertheless, he will not be able to leave off being unjust and to become just, whenever he pleases. For the sick man cannot become well whenever he pleases, even though it so happen that he is voluntarily sick owing to an incontinent life, and from disobedience to physicians. At the time indeed, it was in his own power not to be sick; but when he has once allowed himself to become sick, it is no longer in his power not to be sick; just as it is no longer in the power of a man who has thrown a stone to recover it. And yet the throwing of it was in his own power; for the origin of the action was in his own power. In like manner, in the beginning it was in the power of the unjust and the intemperate man not to become unjust and intemperate; and therefore they are so voluntarily. But when they have become so, it is no longer in their power to avoid being unjust and intemperate. . . . And not only are the faults of the soul voluntary, but in some persons those of the body are so likewise, and with these we find fault For no one finds fault with those who are disfigured and ugly by birth; but only with those who are so through neglect of gymnastic exercise, or through carelessness The case is the same with bodily weakness and mutilation. For no one would blame a man who is born blind, or who is blind from disease or a blow; but would rather pity him. But everybody would blame the man who is blind from drunkenness, or any intemperance. For those faults of the body which are in our own power originally, and which result from our own action, we are blamable."

The assertion of Plato (Laws, V 731) that "the unjust man is not unjust of his own free will; because no man of his own free will would choose to experience the greatest of evils," if it were true, would relieve the unjust man of obligation. The ethics of Plato in such an assertion is defective. He, however, contradicts himself; because elsewhere he teaches the guiltiness of the unjust man. Even in this very connection (Laws, V. 734), he reasons in a self-contradictory manner. The temperate life, he says, is pleasant, and the intemperate is painful, "and he who would live pleasantly cannot possibly choose to live intemperately. If this be true, the inference clearly is that no man is voluntarily intemperate; but that the whole multitude of men lack temperance in their lives, either from ignorance, or from want of self-control, or both." But "want of self-control" is voluntariness. The probability is, that Plato in the above extract employs "voluntary" in the sense of "volitionary."

In secular commercial life, the loss of ability does not release from obligation. A man is as much a debtor to his creditors after his bankruptcy, as he was before. The loss of his property does not free him from indebtedness He cannot say to his creditor, "I owed you yesterday, because I was able to pay you, but to-day I owe you nothing, because I am a bankrupt." It is a legal maxim, that bankruptcy does not invalidate contracts.

That obligation remains fixed and immutable under all the modifications of ability introduced by the action of the human will, is proved by the case of the drunkard, and the habit which he has formed. The drunkard is certainly *less* able to obey the law of temperance than the temperate man is. But this law has precisely the same claim upon him that it has upon the temperate. The diminution of ability has not diminished the obligation. If obligation must always keep pace with the changes in the ability, then there are degrees of obligation. The stronger the will is, the more it is obliged; the weaker it is, the less is it bound by law. In this case, sin rewards the sinner by delivering him from the claims of law. The most vicious man would be least under obligation to duty.

2. It is objected, that if the apostate will is unable to perfectly obey the divine law, it is not free. The reply to this objection requires a definition of finite freedom, both negatively and positively. Negatively, finite freedom is not: (*a*) The freedom of omnipotence Owen: Arminianism, XII There are many things out of man's power, but this does not prove that he is necessitated within his own proper sphere of action. (*b*) Nor the freedom of independence. This species of freedom requires self-existence and self-sustentation It is beyond the reach of an influence from another being. It is pure aseity (aseitas), or self-sufficiency (*c*) Nor freedom from the internal consequences of voluntary action. The formation of a habit is voluntary; but when the habit has been voluntarily formed, it cannot be eradicated by a volition. (*d*) Nor freedom from the external consequences of voluntary action. The objective fact caused by the will cannot be destroyed by the will. The suicide cannot restore himself to life; the homicide cannot reanimate his victim. (*e*) Nor freedom from action itself. The will is not free not to act at all. The will must will something, as the mind must think something. Inaction of the will is impossible, like inaction of the understanding. (*f*) Nor freedom from the regulation and restraint of law. Even in God, freedom is not unbridled almightiness unregulated by other attributes. God can do all that he wills to do, but there are some things which he cannot will because certain of his attributes prevent: for example, logical contradictions, and sinful acts. Freedom in God is rational freedom. Kant denominates the practical reason the will, be-

cause, ideally, the will is one with reason. "Subjection (δουλεία) to righteousness" (Rom. 6:19) is "obedience from the heart," or spontaneity, (Rom. 6:17); and also "glorious liberty," Rom. 8:21. The moral law is "a law of liberty," James 2:25. The believer is "free indeed," John 8:34. (*g*) Nor the possibility of willing contrary to what is already being willed. The possibility of willing the contrary is an accident, not the substance of freedom. It may be associated, temporarily, with an existing self-determination, for the purpose of testing the strength of it, but not for the purpose of making the self-determination any more *self*-determined than it already is in its own nature. Freedom is the present actual willingness, and not the power to will something else in *addition* to the present actual willingness Suppose, for illustration, that a man thinks of only one single act, say, to walk to a certain tree before him. No other act is in his mind. He walks spontaneously to this tree. Here, he does not choose between two actions, but he self-determines to one action. He walks to the tree, and is free in so doing, not because he could have walked away from the tree if the thought of so doing had occurred to him, but because he actually walked to the tree proprio motu, and without compulsion (*h*) Nor indifference, or freedom from a bias or inclination. A bias or inclination of the will is the central and dominant self-determination of the will. The stronger the bias, the more intense is the self-determination, and hence the intenser the freedom. The more the will is self-determined and inclined, the farther off it is from indifference; and hence indifference is not the characteristic of freedom (*i*) Nor the mere liberty of performing an outward act. Edwards, in his polemics against the Arminian, finds the substance of freedom in this.[1] According to this, a man is free to worship God only when he is permitted to act out

[1] Will, Works II 17 So also does Locke Understanding, II. 8, 21; and Hobbes Works, II. 410.

his inclination and to worship externally; and if he is not so permitted, he is not free to worship God. But the truth is, that if he has the inclination to worship he is a free worshipper, whether he is allowed to put his inclination into volition and act, or not. He is the Lord's freeman, and a true worshipper, by virtue of his spontaneous inclination itself "Fool," says the lady in Comus,

> "Fool do not boast:
> Thou canst not touch the freedom of my mind
> With all thy charms, although this corporal rind
> Thou hast immanacled, while Heaven sees good"

The same truth is embodied in the fine lines of Lovelace, written while confined in prison:

> "Stone walls do not a prison make,
> Nor iron bars a cage,
> Minds innocent and quiet take
> That for an hermitage.
>
> If I have freedom in my love,
> And in my soul am free,
> Angels alone, that soar above,
> Enjoy such liberty."—PERCY: Reliques.

And on the other hand, if a man has an evil inclination, say to earthly ambition and power, he is free in sin, that is self-determinedly sinful, whether he is permitted to carry it out in volition and act or not. Shut him in prison, so that he can take no part in earthly affairs, he is still Satan's freeman, by virtue of the inclination of his will.

And the reason of this is the fact, that the *subjective energy* of the human will is all that a man can call his own, and be responsible for. The realization of this personal inward energy in outward act depends upon others, and especially upon the providence of God, and not upon the man himself. The circumstances of a man are no part of his spontaneous self-determination, and he is not responsible for them. He is not free in regard to them. As in the case supposed, a man may have the inclination to worship God, but his surroundings prevent. These surroundings are no part of his voluntary agency, and ought not to be taken into account, in determining whether he is a free agent. If the subjective personal energy of his own will, as seen in his inclination, is truly free from compulsion and really spontaneous, he is free, whether he can give it outward form in a particular act or not. Says Calvin (Inst., II. iv. 8), "The ability of the human will is not to be estimated from the *event* of things, as some ignorant men are accustomed to do. For they imagine that they disprove the freedom of the human will, because even the greatest monarchs have not all their desires fulfilled. But the ability of which we are speaking is to be considered as *within* man, and not to be measured by external success. For in the dispute concerning free will, the question is not whether a man notwithstanding external impediments can perform and execute whatever he may have determined in his mind, but whether in every case his understanding exerts freedom of judgment (judicii electionem), and his will freedom of inclination (affectionem voluntatis). If men possess both of these, then Attilius Regulus when confined in the small extent of a cask stuck round with nails, will possess as much free will as Augustus Cæsar when governing a great part of the world with his rod." To the same effect, Edwards (Will, III. iv.) remarks, that "if the will [inclination] fully complies, and the proposed effect does not prove, according to the laws of nature, to be connected with his [executive] volition, the man is perfectly excused; he has a natural inability to the thing required. For the will [inclination] itself, as has been observed, is all that can be directly and immediately required by command; and other things only indirectly, as connected with the will If, therefore, there be a full compliance of will [inclination], the person has done his duty; and if other things do not prove to be connected with his [executive] volition that is not owing to him." Compare Reid: Intellectual Powers, III. iv. 1.

Defining positively, finite freedom is (*a*) Self-determination in the sense of moral spontaneity; not self-determination *and* power to the contrary, but self-determination alone, pure, and simple. The first is true, the last is spurious self-determination, and should be denominated indetermination. (*b*) Freedom from compulsion, either internal or external. "God hath indued the will of man with that natural liberty, that it is not *forced* to good or evil." Westminster Confession, IX. i (*c*) Freedom from physical necessity, or the operation of the law of cause and effect. "God hath indued the will of man with that natural liberty, that it is not by any absolute *necessity of nature* determined to good or evil." Westminster Confession, IX. i. Physical necessity is seen in the sequences of physical cause and effect. There is no freedom in such a series of sequences, because there is no true beginning and first start. The cause is itself an effect of a foregoing cause, and this again is the effect of another foregoing cause, and so backward indefinitely. Causa causae causa causati. No responsible cause can be found in such a line of antecedents and consequents, because as fast as the responsibility is found in a particular cause, it is thrown back upon the cause of this cause. No real and true *author* or *beginner* is found until the chain terminates in God, who is not a part of the chain, but the creator of it. All physical and material events and phenomena must be referred to the Prime Mover. There is no real author, and no first cause, within the chain of nature itself. But in the sphere of mind, the case is different. The law of cause and effect, operating in matter, has no operation in the human will. This latter is the faculty of *self*-motion. Even when the Holy Spirit works in it "to will and to do," the motion is still self-motion—spiritual not physical, voluntary not necessitated. In the origin of sin, the will cannot refer its action back to a physical cause, and thus convert it into a mere effect, and transfer its responsibility to a foregoing cause of its agency. In respect to *sin*, it is itself a true originating cause It begins its own movement ab intra, by an act of self-determination. There is a first inclining of the will to the creature, and away from the creator, which is not the effect of a foregoing sin, but is the original nisus or start of self-will. And in the origin of holiness, though the will must refer its action back to God, yet not to him as a *physical* cause producing a physical effect Holy inclination is the activity of mind, not of matter. It is not produced by the operation of the law of cause and effect, because the Divine Spirit works in the human will in accordance with the nature of mind, not of matter.

If this be the true definition of freedom, it follows that the apostate will is free in being inclined or self-determined, and that this inclination to evil constitutes an inability to good The sinner is at once voluntary in sin, and impotent to holiness. He is enslaved by himself to himself. He cannot love God supremely, because he loves himself supremely. He cannot incline rightly, because he is inclining wrongly. He is spontaneously and freely evil, and therefore is unable to be spontaneously and freely good. Self-determination is a hazardous endowment. It may be an evil as well as a good When free-will is wicked will, it is a curse.

The answer to the question, "Can the sinner repent if he will?" depends on the meaning of the term "will:" whether it denotes inclination or volition. "Can the sinner repent if he *incline?* Yes. But the inclining is the repentance itself. So that this answer is the truism, "He can repent, if he repents." "Can the sinner repent, if he *choose*, or *resolve?*" No. A volition of the will cannot produce an inclination of the will If a man inclines to repent, he repents in so inclining; but if a man resolves to repent, he does not repent in so resolving.

3. It is objected, that if the sinner has no power to obey the law, he has nothing to do in the matter of religion. He may say with Macbeth,

> "If chance will have me king, why let chance crown me,
> Without my stir"

This does not follow. Because the sinner cannot do the primary work, it does not follow that he cannot do the secondary. He has a very important work to do; namely *to discover his inability*. A wide field is open here for his agency. (*a*) He can compare his character and conduct with the requirements of the law; this tends to convince him of his inability to perfectly obey the law. "I have seen an end of all perfection; thy commandment is exceeding broad," Ps. 119 : 96. (*b*) He can try to obey the law; this will convince him of his inability still more.

A sinner has power under common grace to find out that he has no power to the "spiritually good" This is a preparative work to regeneration. The discovery that he is "without strength" leads to the discovery that "Christ died for the ungodly," Rom. 5 : 6. When he is weak then he is strong. God has appointed certain means to be employed by common grace prior to his exercise of regenerating grace; not meritoriously, but as congruous or adapted to the end. The sinner is to use them. Says Howe (Decrees, III. 7), "Where there is not as yet the light of a *saint*, there is that of a *man*, and that is to be improved and made use of in order to our higher light; and if there be that self-reflection to which God has given to every man a natural ability, much more may be known than usually is. It belongs to the nature of man to turn his eyes inwards. Men can reflect and consider this with themselves: Have I not an aversion towards God? Have not worldly concernments and affairs, by the natural inclination of my own mind, a greater room and place there than heaven and the things of heaven? Are not other thoughts more grateful? And have they not a more pleasant relish with me than thoughts of God? Men, I say, are capable of using such reflections as these. And therefore of considering: This can never be well with me. If there remain with me an habitual aversion to God, who must be my best and eternal good, I cannot but be eternally miserable. If I cannot think of and converse with him with inclination and pleasure, I am lost. If my blessedness lie above, in another world, and my mind is carried continually downward towards this world, I must have a heart attempered to heaven, or I can never come there. Well, then, let me try if I can change the habit of my own mind, make the attempt, make the trial. The more you attempt and try, the more you will find that of yourselves you cannot; you can do nothing of yourselves, you do but lift a heavy log, you attempt to move a mountain upwards, when you would lift at your own terrene hearts. Then is this consideration obvious: I must have help from Heaven, or I shall never come there. Therefore fall a-seeking, fall a-supplicating, as one that apprehends himself in danger to perish and be lost, if he have not another heart, a believing heart, a holy heart, a heavenly heart"[1]

4. It is objected, that if the sinner's ability to keep the moral law depends upon the sovereign grace of God, he must wait God's time. The reply is, that God's time is *now*, and therefore excludes waiting for it. 2 Cor. 6:2, "God saith, I have heard thee in a time accepted, and in the day of salvation have I succored thee: behold now is the day of salvation." Heb. 4:7, "God limiteth (ὁρίζει) a certain day: saying, To-day if ye will hear his voice harden not your hearts." God promises to give the Holy Spirit as a regenerating Spirit this very instant, but confines

[1] See also Howe: Blessedness of the Righteous, XVIII; Boston: Fourfold State, II. iii. 1–3; and especially, Owen: Holy Spirit, III. ii.

the promise to this very instant. Nowhere in revelation does God promise to pardon sin or regenerate the soul at a *future* time. This work is always described as to be done in the sinner's heart, now, this very moment. No *future* redemption is promised.

5. The sinner excuses himself from faith and repentance, by saying, "I cannot believe I am unable to repent." He is to be made to *feel the truth* of his statement, not to be told that his statement is untrue. He needs to become *conscious* of that inability which in words he asserts, but not in sincerity. The difficulty in the instance in which this objection of inability is urged is, that the sinner does not really believe what he says. He does not realize his inability; but he perceives that to urge it is a good verbal objection, an argumentum ad hominem for the preacher. In this case, the work of the preacher is to make the objector eat his own words, and seriously feel the truth of what he says. And in doing this, he will bring out the important fact that the sinner's inability is guilty, because self-originated; that the sinner is the sole author of the inability.

6. It is objected that the doctrine of inability is incompatible with commands and exhortations to believe, repent, and obey the law of God. It is said that we would not command a dead man to rise from the grave, or a man without legs to walk. To this it is to be replied, that we would so command, if God bade us to utter this commandment in a given instance, and promised to accompany the word from our lips with his own *omnipotent* and *creative* power. Christ's command to preach the gospel to men "dead in trespasses and sins," and who "cannot come unto the Son except the Father draw them" (John 6 . 44), is coupled with the promise to accompany the truth with the Holy Spirit.

The doctrine of the sinner's *ability* is exposed to great objections. 1. It contradicts consciousness The process of "conviction" is a growing sense of inability to everything spiritually good in heart and conduct Sinful man cannot be made conscious of ability. This form of consciousness has never been in the human soul.

2. The tenet undermines the doctrine of atonement. It is conceded that the sinner has no ability to make atonement for his guilt; it would follow from this theory of ability that he is not obligated to make one, in other words, that punitive justice has no claims upon him.

3. The tenet conflicts with the doctrine of endless punishment. If the power to the contrary belongs inalienably to the apostate will, self-restoration in the future world is possible, and endless punishment is not certain. The Alexandrine theologians, Clement and Origen, founded their denial of endless punishment upon this view of the will. If the sinner is able at all times to believe and repent, he may do so at any time, and under the impressions of the other world it is probable that he will. Clement and Origen founded the final recovery of Satan and his angels, together with fallen man, in the future world, upon the abiding existence of free will to good. It is no reply to this objection, to say that the lost man can, but certainly never will repent. If latent power be given in the premise, the natural inference is that it will be used, not that it will not be. Suppose that previous to the fall it had been said, "Adam has the power to sin, but he certainly never will sin" Suppose that it were said, "Gunpowder has the inherent power of self-explosion, but it certainly never will explode." To say that it was certain that Adam would use his power to sin, because it was decreed that he would use it, is not to the point; because this is inferring the certainty as relative to the Divine decree, not as relative to the power of the human will, which is the matter in dispute.

4. The tenet of ability encourages the sinner to procrastination, and neglect of the gospel offer. If he believes that from the very nature of free will he has the power to believe and repent at any moment, he will defer faith and

repentance. A sense of danger excites; a sense of security puts to sleep. A company of gamblers in the sixth story are told that the building is on fire. One of them answers, "We have the key to the fire-escape," and all continue the game. Suddenly one exclaims, "The key is lost;" all immediately spring to their feet, and endeavor to escape. While there was the belief of security, there was apathy; the instant there was a knowledge of insecurity, there was action.

5 If the law can be perfectly obeyed by "natural ability," or by will without right inclination, then "moral ability" is superfluous. But if the law cannot be obeyed except by the union of natural and moral ability, or by will with right inclination, then either alone is insufficient.

The following propositions comprise the substance of the Augustino-Calvinistic doctrine of inability. 1. There is a free self-determination or inclining to evil, in the sinner's will. 2. There is an inability of the sinner to self-determine or incline to good, that results from his self-determining or inclining to evil. This inability is culpable, because it is the product of the sinner's agency. 3. The Holy Spirit re-originates self-determination or inclination to good, in the sinner's will. 4. The sinner's will is wholly, not partially, dependent upon the Divine Spirit for a holy self-determination or inclination. 5. God has elected an immense "multitude whom no man can number," to be the subjects of his regenerating power.

Actual transgressions are the particular sins that proceed from original sin They are the individual's sins of act, in distinction from his inherited nature and inclination. Original sin is one; actual sin is manifold. "Actual" in this connection is not the contrary of "imaginary." Actual transgressions are accompanied with more or less of self-consciousness.

Actual transgressions are: (*a*) Interior, namely, a particular conscious doubt in the mind, or a particular conscious lust in the heart. These are single manifestations of the general inclination. The worship of the creature, or idolatry (Rom. 1 : 25), is the generic corruption, and an internal actual transgression is the outworking of this in a particular ambitious purpose, or a proud aspiration, or a malignant emotion, etc (*b*) Exterior, namely, a theft, a lie, a homocide, a suicide, etc.

The depravity or corruption of nature is total. Man is "wholly inclined to evil, and that continually." Westminster L. C, 25 Gen. 6 : 5, "God saw that every imagination of the thoughts of man was only evil continually." There can be but a single dominant inclination in the will at one and the same time; though with it there may be *remnants* of a previously dominant inclination. Adam began a new sinful inclination. This expelled the prior holy inclination. He was therefore totally depraved, because there were no *remainders* of original righteousness left after apostasy, as there are remainders of original sin left after regeneration. This is proved by the fact that there is no struggle between sin and holiness, in the natural man, like that in the spiritual man. In the regenerate, "the flesh lusteth against the spirit, and the spirit against the flesh," Gal. 5 : 17. Holiness and sin are in a conflict that causes the regenerate to "groan within themselves," Rom 8 · 23 But there is no such conflict and groaning in the natural man. Apostasy was the fall of the human will, with no remnants of original righteousness. Regeneration is the recovery of the human will, with some remnants of original sin.

Total depravity means the entire absence of holiness, not the highest intensity of sin. A totally depraved man is not as bad as he can be, but he has no holiness, that is, no supreme love of God. He worships and loves the creature rather than the creator, Rom. 1 : 25.

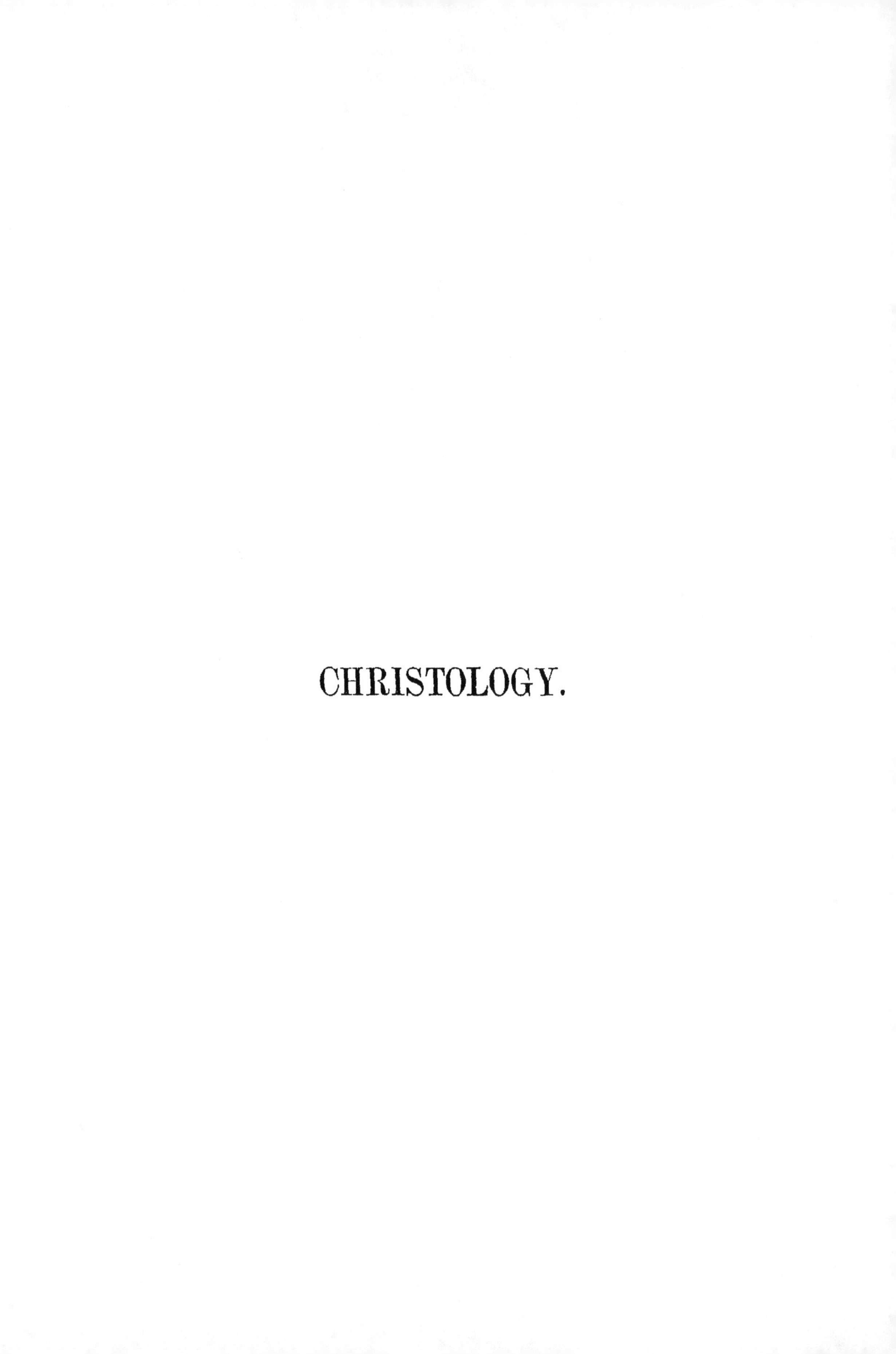

# CHRISTOLOGY.

# CHRISTOLOGY.

---

## CHAPTER I.

### CHRIST'S THEANTHROPIC PERSON.

Athanasius: Third Discourse against the Arians. Augustine: Letter cxxxvii. (To Volusianus). Anselm: Cur Deus Homo, II. vii-ix Aquinas Summa, III. i.-xxxv. Petavius: De Incarnatione. Calvin. Institutes, II. xii.-xiv Ursinus: Christian Religion, Qu. 35. Paraeus: Corpus Doctrinae, Qu 35 Witsius: Apostles' Creed, Diss XIV. De Moor: Commentarius, Caput XIX. § xiv. Turrettin: Institutio, XIII. iv-xiv Gerhard· Loci, IV. xii. Usher. On the Incarnation. Hooker: Polity, V. li lii. Van Mastricht. I. x. 5, 6. Pearson: Creed, Art III Owen· Person of Christ, XVIII.; Vindiciae, VIII. XIII. XIX.; Holy Spirit II. iii. iv. Bunyan: On Imputed Righteousness. Edwards: On the Will, II ii. Hopkins: System, Vol I. 283. Fisher: On the Catechism, Qu. 21, 22. Dorner. Person of Christ. Hagenbach· History of Doctrine, § 64-67, 98-105, 179, 266, 267, 299. Hase· Hutterus, § 94-98 Neander: History, II 478-616 Hengstenberg Christology of the Old Testament. Martensen: Dogmatics, § 125-147. Ullman: Sinlessness of Jesus Schaff History, III. 705-772 Shedd: History of Doctrine, I. 392-408 Gess Person of Christ. Bruce· Humiliation of Christ (Kenotic Theories) Briggs: Messianic Prophecy. Dod· On the Incarnation Wilberforce On the Incarnation. Liddon. Divinity of Our Lord Leathes· Witness of O. T. and N. T to Christ Delitzsch Messianic Prophecies. Riehm: Messianic Prophecy

Christology (Χριστοῦ λόγος) is that division of theological science which treats of the Person of the Redeemer

As the doctrine of the Trinity is found in the Old Testament, so is that of the Redeemer. As there is an Old Testament Trinitarianism, so there is an Old Testament

Christology. Both doctrines, however, are less clearly revealed under the former economy than under the latter. Christ is explicit in asserting that the doctrine of his person is found in the Old Testament. "Many prophets and righteous men have desired to see those things which ye see," Matt. 13 : 17. "Abraham saw my day, and was glad," John 8 : 56. Compare John 12 : 41; Luke 24 : 27. 1 Pet 1 : 10–12, "The prophets searched diligently what the Spirit of Christ which was in them did signify, when it testified beforehand the sufferings of Christ, and the glory that should follow."[1]

The Redeemer is announced under several names in the Old Testament. The earliest designation is the "Seed of the woman," Gen. 3 : 15. Christ himself adopts this designation in the title "Son of man," employed by himself but never by his apostles. The next name in order is Shiloh, Gen. 49 : 10. Luther, Gesenius, Rosenmuller, Hengstenberg, and others, explain this to mean the "Peacemaker." This is favored by other Messianic texts. In Isaiah 9 : 6, Messiah is denominated "prince of peace" In Micah 5 : 5, of the Redeemer it is said, "This man shall be our peace." In Zech. 9 : 10, he is denominated the "speaker of peace;" and in Eph. 2 : 14, "our peace."[2] Others explain the term Shiloh to mean "the desired One" (Haggai 2 : 7); "he who shall be sent;" "his son" (Calvin); "he whose right it is" (Sept. Aquila, Symmachus, Onkelos); "the place Shiloh" (Eichhorn, Bleek, Hitzig, Ewald, Delitzsch, Kalisch).[3] In Isaiah 7 . 14, the Re-

---

[1] The Patristic and Reformation divines find both the Trinity and the God-man in the Old Testament. Irenaeus (Adversus Haereses, IV xxxiii xxxiv) makes ample quotations in proof of both doctrines For the Lutheran and Reformed citations, see Gerhard, Chemnitz, Hase, Heppe, and Schweitzer, in locis

[2] See Kitto Dictionary; Speaker's Commentary Genesis 49 10, and Newton Prophesies, Dissertation IV

[3] The connection is strongly against this last interpretation "Probably the town Shiloh did not exist in Jacob's time, and Judah neither acquired nor lost the pre-eminence over the other tribes at Shiloh. He was not the leader in the

deemer is called Immanuel; in Daniel 9 · 25, Messiah; in Zech. 6:12, the Branch; in Malachi 3:1, the Messenger of the Covenant. The designation of the Redeemer that was most common among the Jews was Messiah, or the Annointed One (מָשִׁיחַ), rendered in the Septuagint by Χρίστος. It is found 39 times in the Old Testament. See Alexander on Isa. 52:13.

The time of the Redeemer's advent is distinctly foretold in Gen. 49:10. "The sceptre shall not depart from Judah, nor a lawgiver from between his feet, until Shiloh come." Historically, the sceptre, that is, self-government, did not depart from the Hebrew nation, represented by the tribe of Judah (Judaei, Jews), until the destruction of Jerusalem, A.D. 70 The time is again specified very particularly in Daniel 9.24–27. "Seventy weeks are determined upon thy people, and upon thy holy city, to finish the transgression, and to make an end of sins, and to make reconciliation for iniquity, and to bring in everlasting righteousness, and to seal up the vision and prophecy, and to anoint the Most Holy." In this prophecy, a day stands for a year; seventy weeks denoting 490 years The prophet announces that in seven weeks, that is 49 years, from the end of the captivity, Jerusalem should be rebuilt, that in sixty-two weeks, that is 434 years from the rebuilding, Messiah should appear; and that in one week, that is 7 years from his appearance, he should "confirm the covenant," and should be "cut off" "in the midst of the week."[1] In the different calculations of exegetes

wilderness, for the people were led by Moses and Aaron, nor did he gain any fresh authority at Shiloh Every ancient version, paraphrase, and commentator, makes Shiloh, not the objective case after the verb, but the nominative before the verb" Speaker's Commentary, in loco.

[1] "It is supposed that John the Baptist began his ministry about three and a half years before Christ; so that John's ministry and Christ's put together made seven years, which were the last of Daniel's weeks Christ came in the midst of the week, as Daniel foretold · 'And in the midst of the week he shall cause the sacrifice and oblation to cease.'" Edwards. Work of Redemption, Works, I 407.

there is a difference of only ten years. The difficulty is to know exactly when the seventy weeks begin. Hales says that they begin from the twentieth year of Artaxerxes Longimanus. W Smith supposes that "the *final* and effectual edict of Artaxerxes was the commencing date, and that this was issued in B C. 457. Exactly 490 years may be counted from this to the death of Christ in A D. 33."

That the Jesus Christ of the New Testament is the Messiah promised in the Old Testament, is proved by the agreement between the descriptions of the personage in each. In both he is: (*a*) The seed of the woman, Gen 3:15; Ps. 22:10; Micah 5:3; Gal. 4:4; 1 Tim. 2:15; Rev. 12·15. (*b*) Born of a virgin, Isa. 7:14; Matt. 1:23; Luke 1:26–35. (*c*) Of the family of Shem, Gen. 9:26–27. (*d*) Of the Hebrew race, Ex. 3:18. (*e*) Of the seed of Abraham, Gen. 12:3; 18:18; Matt. 1:1; John 8:56; Acts 3:25. (*f*) Of the line of Isaac, Gen. 17:19; Rom. 9:7; Gal. 4:23–28; Heb. 11:8. (*g*) Of the line of Jacob or Israel, Gen 28:4–14; Numbers 24:5–17; Isa. 41:8; Luke 1:68; 2:32; Acts 28:20. (*h*) Of the tribe of Judah, Gen 49:10; 1 Chron. 5:2; Micah 5:2; Matt. 2:6; Heb. 7:14; Rev. 5:5 (*i*) Of the house of David, 2 Sam 7:12–15; 1 Chron. 17:11–14; Ps 89:4–36; Isa. 9:7; Matt 1:1; Luke 1: 69; 2:4; John 7:42; Acts 2:30; Rom. 1:3; 2 Tim. 2:8; Rev. 22:16. (*j*) Born at Bethlehem, Micah 5:2; Matt. 2:6; Luke 2:4; John 7:42. (*k*) To suffer an agony, Gen. 3:15; Ps. 22:1–18; Isa. 53:1–12; Zech 13:6, 7; Matt. 26:37, Luke 24:26 (*l*) To die, and in a peculiar manner, Isa. 53:9; Dan. 9:26; Numbers 21:9 compared with John 3:14; Ps. 22·18 compared with John 19:24. (*m*) To be embalmed and entombed, Isa. 53:9; Matt 27:57: Luke 23:56; John 19:38–41. (*n*) To rise from the dead, Ps. 16·10; Acts 3:15. (*o*) To ascend into heaven, Ps. 68:18 compared with Eph. 4:8; Ps. 110:1; Luke 24:51. (*p*) To come a second time spiritually in regeneration,

Isa. 40 : 10; 62 : 11; Jer. 23 : 5, 6; Hosea 3 : 5; Micah 5 : 4; Dan. 7 : 13, 14; John 14 : 3, 18, 23; 16 : 23, 26. (*q*) To come a second time visibly, Job 19 : 25; Ps. 50 : 1–6; Dan. 12 . 1, 2; Matt. 25 : 31; 1 Cor. 15 : 23; 1 Thess. 1 : 10; Rev. 20 : 11 sq.

The Biblical representations of the person of the Redeemer make him to be a *complex* person, constituted of two natures. He is not merely God, or merely man; but a union of both. He is a God-man. The Westminster statement defines him as follows: "The Redeemer of God's elect is the Lord Jesus Christ, who being [originally] the eternal Son of God became man, and so was, and continueth to be, God and man in two distinct natures and one person, forever," S. C., 21. The principal proof texts are John 1 : 1, 14, The "Word was God," and "The Word was made flesh;" Phil 2 : 6, 7, "Who being in the form of God took upon him the form of a servant;" Gal. 4 . 4; Luke 1 : 35; Rom. 9 : 5; Coloss. 2 : 9; Rom. 1 : 3, 4; 1 Tim. 2 : 5.

In order to a self-consistent scheme of Christ's complex person, the following particulars are to be marked:

1. The divine nature in Christ's person is the second person of the Godhead, the Eternal Son, or Logos. This is asserted in John 1 : 14, "The Word was made flesh." Neither God the Father, nor God the Spirit, became man. The Godhead did not become incarnate, because the Godhead is the divine essence in all three modes; and the essence in all three modes did not become incarnate. Says Turrettin (XIII vi 4), "non ipsa trinitas bene incarnata dicatur, quia incarnatio non terminatur ad naturam divinam absolute, sed ad personam τοῦ Λογοῦ relate." And Aquinas (III ii. 1, 2) remarks, that "it is more proper to say that a divine person assumed a human nature, than to say that the divine nature assumed a human nature." It was only the divine essence in that particular mode of it which constitutes the second trinitarian person, that was united with

man's nature. There was, consequently, something in the triune Godhead which did not enter into Christ's person. This something is the personal characteristic of the Father, and of the Holy Spirit. The paternity of the first person, and the procession of the third person, do not belong to Jesus Christ.

The following reasons for the incarnation of the second person, rather than of the first or third, are mentioned by Paraeus (Notes on the Athanasian Creed): First, that by the incarnation the names of the divine persons should remain unchanged; so that neither the Father nor the Holy Spirit should have to take the name of a Son Secondly, it was fitting that by the incarnation men should become God's adopted sons, through him who is God's natural Son. Thirdly, it was proper that man, who occupies a middle position between angels and beasts, in the scale of creatures, should be redeemed by the middle person in the trinity. Lastly, it was proper that the fallen nature of man which was created by the Word (John 1:3) should be restored by him. In addition to these reasons, it is evident that it is more fitting that a father should commission and send a son upon an errand of mercy, than that a son should commission and send a father.

2. Incarnation must be distinguished from transmutation, or transubstantiation. The phrase "became man" does not mean that the second person in the trinity ceased to be God. This would be transubstantiation. One substance, the divine, would be changed or converted into another substance, the human; as, in the Papal theory, the substance of the bread becomes the substance of Christ's body. See Anselm: Cur deus homo, II. vii.

In saying that "the Word was made flesh" (John 1:14), it is meant that the Word came to possess human characteristics in *addition* to his divine, which still remained as before. The properties of the divine nature cannot be either destroyed or altered. A human nature was united with the divine, in order that the resulting person might have a human form of consciousness as well as a divine. Previous to the assumption of a human nature, the Logos could not experience a human feeling because he had no human heart, but after this assumption he could; previous to the incarnation, he could not have a finite perception because he had no finite intellect, but after this event he could; previous to the incarnation, the self-consciousness of the Logos was eternal only, that is, without succession, but subsequent to the incarnation it was both eternal and temporal, with and without succession. This twofold consciousness may be illustrated by the union between the human soul and body. Prior to, or apart from its union with a material body, a man's immaterial soul cannot feel a physical sensation or a sensuous appetite; but when united with it in a personal union, it can so feel. In like manner, prior to the incarnation, the second person of the Trinity could not have human sensations and experiences; but after it he could. The unincarnate Logos could think and feel only like God; he had only one form of consciousness. The incarnate Logos can think and feel either like God, or like man; he has two modes or forms of consciousness.

When, therefore, it is said that "God became man," the meaning is that God united himself with man, not that God changed himself into man. Unification of two natures, not transmutation of one nature into another is meant We might say of the union of soul and body, in the instance of a human person, that "spirit becomes matter;" that is, is materialized or embodied. We would not mean by this phrase, that spirit is actually changed into matter, but that it is united with matter in that intimate manner which is denominated personal union. In the incarnation, God is humanized, as in ordinary human generation, spirit is materialized or embodied. Each substance, however, still retains its own properties. In an ordinary man, spirit remains immaterial, and body remains material; and in the God-man, the divine nature remains divine in its properties, and the human remains human.

3 The distinctive characteristic of the incarnation is the union of two diverse natures, a divine and a human, so as to constitute one single person. A single person may consist of one nature, or of two natures, or of three. A trinitarian person has only one nature: namely, the divine essence. A human person has two natures: namely, a material body, and an immaterial soul. A theanthropic person has three natures: namely, the divine essence, a human soul, and a human body. By the incarnation, not a God, not a man, but a God-man is constituted. A theanthropic person is a trinitarian person *modified* by union with a human nature, similarly as a trinitarian person is the Divine essence *modified* by generation, or spiration. A theanthropic person is constituted, consequently, in the same general manner in which an ordinary human person is: namely, by the union of diverse natures. In the case of a human individual, it is the combination of one material nature and one immaterial that makes him a person. Says Howe (Oracles, II xxxvii), "the production of a human creature [individual] doth not lie in the production of either of the parts, but only in the *uniting* of them substantially with one another It neither lies in the production of the soul, nor doth it lie in the production of the matter of the body; but it lies in the beginning of these into a substantial union with one another." Says Hooker (V. liv.), "the incarnation of the Son of God consisteth merely in the union of natures, which union doth add perfection to the weaker, to the nobler no alteration at all." The divine-human person, Jesus Christ, was produced by the union of the divine nature of the Logos with a human nature derived from a human mother Before this union was accomplished, there was no theanthropic person There was the divine person of the Logos existing in the Trinity

before this union, and there was the unindividualized substance of Christ's human nature existing in the virgin Mary before this union; but until the two were united at the instant of the miraculous conception, there was no God-man. The trinitarian personality of the Son of God did not begin at the incarnation, but the *theanthropic* personality of Jesus Christ did.

4. It is the divine nature, and not the human, which is the base of Christ's person. The second trinitarian person is the root and stock into which the human nature is grafted. The wild olive is grafted into the good olive, and partakes of its root and fatness.

The eternal Son, or the Word, is personal per se. He is from everlasting to everlasting conscious of himself as distinct from the Father, and from the Holy Spirit. He did not acquire personality by union with a human nature. The incarnation was not necessary in order that the trinitarian Son of God might be self-conscious. On the contrary, the human nature which he assumed to himself acquired personality by its union with him. By becoming a constituent factor in the one theanthropic person of Christ, the previously impersonal human nature, "the seed of the woman," was personalized. If the Logos had obtained personality by uniting with a human nature, he must have previously been impersonal. The incarnation would then have made an essential change in the Logos, and thereby in the Trinity itself. But no essential change can be introduced into the triune Godhead, even by so remarkable an act as the incarnation.

(*a*) If the human nature and not the divine had been the root and base of Christ's person, he would have been a man-God and not a God-man. The complex person, Jesus Christ, would have been anthropotheistic, not theanthropic. This was the error of Paul of Samosata, Photinus, and Marcellus; according to whom, Christ was an ἄνθρώπος ἔνθεος, a deified man: the base of the complex person being the human nature. Christ is humanized deity, not deified humanity.

(*b*) That the personality of the God-man depends primarily upon the divine nature, and not upon the human, is also evinced by the fact that this complex theanthropic personality was not destroyed by the death of Christ. At the crucifixion, the union between the human soul and the human body was dissolved temporarily, but the union between the Logos and the human soul and body was not. Christ's human soul and body were separated from each other during the "three days and three nights," in which he "lay in the heart of the earth." This was death. The humanity of Christ was thus dislocated for a time, and its complete personality was interrupted. For a soul without its body is not a full and entire human person, although it is the root and the base of the person. Between death and the resurrection, when the human soul and body are separated, although there is self-consciousness in the disembodied spirit, and so the most important element in personality, yet there is an incomplete human personality until the resurrection of the body restores the original union between soul and body.

But there was no such interruption and temporary dissolution of the unity of Christ's *theanthropic* personality, caused by the crucifixion. The divine nature was of course unaffected by the bodily dissolution; and although the human soul and body were separated from one another by the crucifixion, they were neither of them separated from the *Logos*, by this event. Between Christ's death and resurrection, both the human soul and the human body were still united with the Logos. That the body was still united to the Logos, is evinced by the fact that it "did not see corruption," Acts 2:31. "The divine and the human natures," says Hooker (V. 53), "from the moment of their first combination, have been and are forever inseparable. For even when Christ's human soul forsook the tabernacle of his body, his deity forsook neither body nor soul. If it had, then could we not truly hold, either that the *person* of Christ was buried, or that the *person* of Christ did raise up himself from the dead. For the body separated from the Word can in no true sense be termed the person of Christ; nor is it true to say, that the Son of God in raising up that body did raise up himself, if the body were not both with him, and of him, even during the time it lay in the sepulchre. The like is also to be said of the soul; otherwise we are plainly and inevitably Nestorians. The very person of Christ, therefore, forever one and the self-same, was only touching bodily substance concluded within the grave, his soul only from thence severed; but by personal union his deity still inseparably joined with both." Turrettin (XIII. vi. 9) makes the same statement: "Naturalis unio animae et corporis in unam naturam humanam est separabilis, quae soluta fuit morte Christi; personalis unio duarum naturarum, divinae et humanae, in unam personam est inseparabilis, quia quod semel Λόγος assumpsit nunquam deposuit." Owen also affirms (Holy Spirit, II. iii.) that the theanthropic personality of Christ "was necessary and indissoluble, so that it was not impeached, nor shaken in the least, by the temporary dissolution of the humanity by the separation of the soul and body. For the union of the soul and body in Christ did not constitute him a [theanthropic] person, so that the dissolution of them should destroy his [theanthropic] personality; but he was a [theanthropic] person by the uniting of both into the Son of God."[1] Compare Belgic Confession, Art. 19.

The unification, then, of the three factors, the Logos, the human soul, and the human body, which was effected in the miraculous conception, and which continued through

[1] In a similar manner, the body and soul of a believer, though separated from each other between death and the resurrection, are both as truly united to Christ during this disembodied period as they were before it Westminster L C, 86 But in this case the union is mystical, not theanthropic.

the whole earthly life of our Lord, was not interrupted by the crucifixion. The God-man existed between the crucifixion and the resurrection, notwithstanding the separation between the human soul and body, as truly as he did before, or as he does this instant. And this, because it was the immutable divinity, and not the mutable humanity, which constitutes the foundation of his personality.

(*c*) That the divinity and not the humanity is dominant and controlling in Christ's person, is proved by the fact that his acts of power were regulated by it. If the Logos so determined, Jesus Christ was powerless; and if the Logos so determined, Jesus Christ was all-powerful. When the divine nature withdrew its support from the human, the latter was as helpless as it is in an ordinary human creature. And when the divine nature imparted its power, the human nature became "mighty in word and deed."[1] When the Logos so pleased, Jesus of Nazareth could no more be taken by human hands and nailed to the cross, than the eternal Trinity could be; and when the Logos so pleased, he could be arrested without any resistance, and be led like a lamb to the slaughter. This is taught repeatedly in the Gospels, when it is related that no man could lay violent hands upon him, "because his hour had not come." Jesus Christ, the Son of Mary, speaking generally, had so much power, and only so much, as the divine nature in his complex person pleased to exert in him. Sometimes, consequently, he was almighty in his acts, and sometimes he was "a worm, and no man," Ps. 22 : 6.

(*d*) Again, the knowledge of the God-man depended upon the divine nature for its amount, and this proves that the divinity is dominant in his person. The human mind of Jesus Christ stood in a somewhat similar relation

[1] It did not become strictly omnipotent, according to the Later-Lutheran doctrine, for this would be, in so far, the conversion of the human nature into the divine But it became powerful enough to do anything which the Logos willed it to do.

to the Logos, that the mind of a prophet does to God. Though not the same in all respects, because the Logos and the human mind in the instance of Jesus Christ constitute one person, while the Holy Spirit and the inspired prophet are two persons, yet in respect to the point of dependence for knowledge, there is an exact similarity. As the prophet Isaiah could know no more of the secret things of God than it pleased the Holy Spirit to disclose to him, so the human mind of Christ could know no more of these same divine secrets than the illumination of the Logos made known. And this illumination, like that of the material sun, was dimmed by the cloud through which it was compelled to penetrate. The finite and limited human nature hindered a full manifestation of the omniscience of the deity. This was a part of the humiliation of the eternal Logos. He condescended to unite himself with an inferior nature, through which his own infinite perfections could shine only in part. When deity does not work as simple deity untrammelled, but works in "the form of a servant," it is humbled. The Logos in himself knew the time of the day of judgment, but he did not at a particular moment make that knowledge a part of the human consciousness of Jesus Christ. In so doing, he limited and conditioned his own *manifestation* of knowledge in the theanthropic person, by the ignorance of the human nature. The same is true respecting the retention of knowledge. Though the Logos himself cannot forget anything, yet he might permit the human nature to forget many things for a season, and afterwards bring them to remembrance. The Gospels, however, mention no instance of Christ's ignorance excepting that respecting the day of judgment: supposing this to be an instance of ignorance. See note on p. 13.

The difficult subject of the ignorance of Christ, and his growth in wisdom and knowledge, has light thrown upon it, by distinguishing between the *existence* of the Logos in

Christ's person, and the *manifestation* of this existence. This is the key to the doctrine of the kenosis. The Logos constantly existed in Jesus Christ, but did not constantly act through his human soul and body. He did not work miracles continually; nor did he impart to the human soul of Christ the whole of his own infinite knowledge.

Compare the infancy of Jesus Christ with his manhood. When Christ lay in the manger at Bethlehem, the eternal Logos was the root and base of his person as much, and as really, as it was when he appeared at the age of thirty on the banks of the Jordan and was inaugurated to his office. Christ in the manger was called the messianic King, and was worshipped as such by the Magi. Even the theanthropic embryo (*τὸ γεννώμενον*) is denominated the "Son of God," Luke 1:35. In Heber's hymn, the "infant Redeemer" is styled "Maker, and Monarch, and Saviour of all." But the Logos, though present, could not properly and fittingly make such a *manifestation* of knowledge through that infant body and infant soul, as he could through a child's body and a child's soul, and still more through a man's body and a man's soul. It would have been unnatural, if the Logos had empowered the infant Jesus to work a miracle, or deliver the sermon on the Mount. The repulsive and unnatural character of the apocryphal gospels, compared with the natural beauty of the canonical gospels, arises from attributing to the infant and the child Jesus acts that were befitting only a mature humanity.

During all these infantile years of the immature and undeveloped human nature, the Logos, though present, was in eclipse in the person of Jesus Christ.[1] By this is meant,

---

[1] The term occultatio is used by Zanchius, Heidegger, Ursinus, and others, to denote the self-emptying (*ἑαυτὸν ἐκένωσε*) of the Logos spoken of by St Paul, in Phil 2 7 The exinanition related to the use and manifestation of divine excellences, not to their possession Traces of this are seen in Ambrose (De Incarnatione, I.), who employs the terms retentio and retraxit Van Mastricht

that the Logos made no *manifestation* of his power through the human nature he had assumed, because this human nature was still infantine. When the infant Jesus lay in the manger, the Logos was present and united with the human nature as really and completely as he is this instant, but he made no exhibition of himself. There was no more thinking going on in the infant human mind of Jesus, than in the case of any other infant. The babe lay in the manger unconscious and inactive. Yet the eternal Logos was personally united with this infant There was a God-man in the manger as truly as there was upon the cross

It will not follow, however, that because there was no thinking going on in the human mind of the infant Jesus, there was none going on in the Logos. For it must be remembered, that though the Logos has condescended to take "the form of a servant," he has not ceased to exist in "the form of God." While he voluntarily submits to the limitations of human infancy, and will do no more in the sphere of the *finite infant* with the feeble instrument which he has condescended to employ than that instrument is fitted to perform, yet in the other infinite sphere of the *Godhead* he is still the same omniscient and omnipotent person that he always was. The Son of man was on earth and in heaven, at one and the same instant, John 3:13. Because the Logos was localized and limited by a human body on the earth, it does not follow that he did not continue to exist

---

uses subducere with occultare Francis Junius says "In humana natura, gloriam et majestatem apud homines non exercuerit Christus ut post resurrectionem et ascensionem, sed veluti represserit et occultam continuerit vel (uti loquitur Irenaeus) quieverit, ut humana natura tentari et mori possit, quamvis interim divinae naturae quaedam vindicia ad fidei confirmationem prodierint." Theses Theologicae (De Humiliatione Christi) The words of Irenaeus are the following "As Christ became man in order to undergo temptation, so also was he the Word that he might be glorified, the Word remaining quiescent, that he might be capable of being tempted, dishonored, crucified, and suffering death" Adv Hæreses, III. xix. Paraeus quotes this passage Doctrinae Christianae, Quaest xxxvii

and act in heaven. And because the Logos did not think in and by the mind of the infant Jesus, it does not follow that he did not think in and by his own infinite mind. The humanity of Jesus Christ, then, knew as much, and only as much as the Logos pleased to disclose and manifest through a human mind. Says Beza: "Ipsa θεότητος plenitudo sese, prout et quatenas ipsa libuit, humanitati assumtae insinuavit." Grotius, on Mark 13:32, says: "Videtur mihi, hic locus non impie posse exponi hunc in modum; ut dicamus divinam sapientiam menti humanae Christi effectus suos impressisse pro temporum ratione" Says Tillotson: "It is not unreasonable to suppose that the Divine Wisdom, which dwelt in our Saviour, did communicate itself to his human soul according to his pleasure, and so his human nature might at some time not know some things." Christ's knowledge was, and ever is, dependent upon the amount of information vouchsafed by the deity in his person He did not know the time of the day of judgment, "quia Verbum hoc illi non releverat," says Turrettin, XIII. xiii. 5.[1] He could therefore "increase in wisdom" (Luke 2:52) as a child and a youth, because from the unfathomable and infinite fountain of the divine nature of the Logos there was inflowing into the human understanding united with it a steady and increasing stream. But that infinite fountain was never emptied. The human nature is not sufficiently capacious to contain the whole fulness of God

The ignorance of Jesus Christ may still further be illus-

[1] Bengel, on Mark 13 32, adopts the explanation favored by Augustine "Christ's words may be understood to mean, that he does not know the time of the judgment day, because it was not among his instructions from the Father to *declare* the time. An apostle was able both to know and not to know one and the same thing, according to the different point of view ('I know that I shall abide' Phil 1·25) · how much more Christ?" In Cor 2 2, to "know" means to "make known" "I determined not to know anything among you but Christ, and him crucified" The same is the meaning of "know,' in Gen 22:12 "Now I know that thou fearest God seeing thou hast not withheld thy son from me." God had made Abraham's faith to be known, by this trial.

trated by the forgetfulness of an ordinary man. No man, at each and every instant, holds in immediate consciousness all that he has ever been conscious of in the past. He is relatively ignorant of much which he has previously known and experienced. But this forgetting is not absolute and total ignorance. This part of his consciousness may re-appear here upon earth; and will all of it re-appear in the day of judgment. But he cannot recall it just at this instant. He is ignorant, and must say: "I do not know." Similarly, if we suppose that Christ when he spoke these words to his disciples was ignorant of the time of the judgment, he may subsequently have come to know it as his human nature increased in knowledge through the illumination of the Divine Says Bengel, "The stress in Matt. 24: 36 is on the present tense, 'No man *knoweth*.' In those days, no man did know, not even the Son. But *afterwards* he knew it, for he revealed it in the Apocalypse." Christ was relatively ignorant, not absolutely, if he was destined subsequently to know the time of the judgment day. It is more probable that the glorified human mind of Christ on the mediatorial throne now knows the time of the day of judgment, than that it is ignorant of it.

The dawning of Christ's messianic consciousness, as seen in the incident of the youth in the temple with the doctors, illustrates the gradual illumination and instruction of the humanity by the divinity in his person. It is not necessary, in order to explain this occurrence, to suppose that the Virgin Mother had informed Jesus respecting his miraculous conception. On the contrary, as she did not feel authorized to inform her husband of the fact but left its disclosure to God, so neither did she feel authorized to inform her child of it. Christ's self-consciousness of his theanthropic person and mediatorial office was formed gradually, as he passed from youth to manhood, by the increasing illumination of the humanity by the divinity, similarly as in an ordinary human person, the self-consciousness gradually forms and increases by the interpenetration of the lower sensuous nature by the higher rational.

(*e*) That the divinity is the dominant factor in Christ's complex person, is proved by the fact that the degree of his happiness was determined by it. The human nature had no more enjoyment than the divine permitted. The desertion of the humanity by the divinity is implied in the cry: "My God, why hast thou forsaken me?" The Logos at this moment did not support and comfort the human soul and body of Jesus. This may be regarded equally as desertion by the Father or by the Logos, because of the unity of essence. In the promise: "If ye shall ask anything [of the Father] in my name I will do it" (John 14: 14), the official work of the first person is attributed to the second As God the Father raised Christ from the dead, and Christ also raised himself from the dead, so also God the Father deserted the human nature, and God the Logos also deserted it.

(*f*) That the foundation of Christ's complex personality is the divine nature, is proved by his immutability. "Jesus Christ is the same yesterday, and to-day, and forever," Heb. 13:8. What has been said concerning the effect of the crucifixion upon the theanthropic personality will apply here. Christ is immutably the God-man, notwithstanding the temporary separation between his human soul and body

5. The theanthropic personality of the Redeemer began in time The God-man was a new person, as well as a unique one. There was no God-man until the moment when the incarnation began. This beginning is to be placed at the instant of the miraculous conception, and this at the instant of the salutation, when the angel Gabriel uttered the words: "Hail thou that art highly favored, the Lord is with thee; blessed art thou among women," Luke 1:28. At this punctum temporis, the eternal Logos united

with a portion of human nature in the Virgin Mary. The union was embryonic in its first form. Previous to this instant, the only person existing was the second trinitarian person: the human nature existing in the Virgin Mary being yet unpersonalized. This trinitarian person was not complex, but simple; God the Son, but not God-man; the unincarnate Logos (*Λόγος ἄσαρκος*), not the incarnate (*Λόγος ἔνσαρκος*). Jesus Christ is not the proper name of the unincarnate second person of the trinity, but of the second person incarnate. "Thou shalt conceive and bring forth a son, and shalt call his name Jesus," Luke 1:31. Prior to the incarnation, the trinity consisted of the Father, the unincarnate Son, and the Holy Ghost; subsequent to the incarnation, it consists of the Father, the incarnate Son, and the Holy Ghost Yet it would not be proper to alter the baptismal formula, and baptize "in the name of the Father, and of Jesus Christ, and of the Holy Ghost," because the incarnate Christ is the *mediator* between the triune God and sinful man, so that the primary trinitarian designation Son, not the secondary mediatorial designation Christ, is the fitting term in the baptismal formula.

6. Though beginning in time, the theanthropic personality of the Redeemer continues forever. This is taught in Rom. 9:5, "Of whom as concerning the flesh Christ came, who is over all God blessed forever;" in Col. 2:9, "In him dwelleth [now and forever] all the fulness of the Godhead, bodily;" in Heb. 13:8, "Jesus Christ, the same yesterday, to-day, and forever;" in Eph. 2:6, "Believers sit together in heavenly places in Christ Jesus;" in Heb. 4: 14, 15, "We have a great high priest who hath passed into the heavens."

7. The incarnation makes no change in the constitution of the Trinity. It leaves in the Godhead, as it finds in it, only three persons. For the addition of a human nature to the person of the Logos, is not the addition of another person to him. The second trinitarian person, though so much

modified by the incarnation as to become a God-man, is not so much modified as to lose his proper trinitarian personality, because incarnation is not the juxtaposition of a human person with a divine person, but the assumption of a human nature to a divine person. The incarnation produces a change in the humanity that is assumed, by exalting and glorifying it, but no change in the deity that assumes. "The divine nature," says Bull (De Subordinatione, IV. iv. 14), "flows through (immeat) the human nature, but the human nature does not flow through the divine." If the Logos had united himself with a distinct and separate individual, the modification of the Logos by incarnation would have been *essential*, and a fourth person, namely a human person, would have thereby entered into the Godhead; which would have been an alteration in the constitution of the trinity, making it to consist of four persons instead of three. "We must consider," says Usher (Incarnation, Works, I. 580), "that the divine nature did not assume a human person, but the divine person did assume a human nature; and that of the three divine persons, it was neither the first nor the third that did assume this nature, but it was the middle person who was to be the middle one [mediator] that must undertake the mediation between God and us. For if the fulness of the Godhead should have thus dwelt in any human person, there should have been added to the Godhead a fourth kind of person; and if any of the three persons besides the second had been born of a woman, there should have been two Sons in the Trinity. Whereas, now, the Son of God and the Son of the Blessed Virgin, being but one person, is consequently but one Son; and so, no alteration at all made in the relations of the persons of the Trinity." See Hooker, V. liv.

The Logos, by his incarnation and exaltation, marvellous as it seems, took a human nature with him into the depths of the Godhead. A finite glorified human nature is now eternally united with the second trinitarian person, and a God-man is now the middle person of the Trinity.

> "No Paean there, no Bacchic song they raise,
> But the three Persons of the Trinity,
> And the two natures joined in one they praise."
>
> DANTE: Paradise xiii. 25–27.

Yet the Trinity itself is not altered or modified by the incarnation Only the second person is modified. The Trinity is not divine-human; nor is the Father; nor is the Holy Spirit. But the Eternal Son is. For this reason, the Son stands in a nearer relation to redeemed man than either the Father or the Spirit can. Neither of them is the "elder brother" of the redeemed. Neither of them is the "head" of which the church is the "body." Neither of them is the divine person of whom it can be said, "We are members of his body, of his flesh, and of his bones," Eph. 5:30.

The union of the Logos with a human nature does not disturb either the trinitarian relation of the Logos, or his relation to the created universe. When the Logos consents to unite with a human nature, he consents to exist and act in "the form of a servant." But, as previously remarked, this does not imply that he ceases to exist and act "in a form of God." Incarnation is not transubstantiation. Consequently, when incarnate, the Logos is capable of a *twofold* mode of existence, of consciousness, and of agency. Possessing a divine nature, he can still exist and act as a divine being, and he so exists and acts within the sphere of the infinite and eternal Godhead without any limitation. Possessing a human nature, he can also exist and act as a human being, and he so exists and acts within the sphere of finite and temporal humanity and under its limitations. The Son of man was in heaven, and upon earth simultaneously, John 3:13. In heaven he was in glory; on earth he was in sorrow and death. The God-man is both unlimited and limited, illocal and local. He has consequently a twofold consciousness: infinite and finite. He thinks like God; and he thinks like man. He has the eternal, all-comprehending, and successionless consciousness of God; and he has the imperfect, gradual, and sequacious consciousness of man. In this way, the trinitarian relations of the second person remain unchanged by his incarnation. The divine nature, though it condescends to exist and act in and through a human soul and body, and to be trammelled by it, at the same time is existing and acting in an untrammelled manner throughout the universe of finite being, and in the immensity of the Godhead.

Consider, for illustration, Christ's relations to space. He lived a double life in this reference, when he lived in Palestine eighteen centuries ago. He subsisted in both forms—that of God, and that of a servant—at one and the same moment. He was simultaneously the absolute and eternal Spirit, unlocalized, filling immensity; and he was also that same Spirit localized, dwelling in and confined to the soul and body of Jesus of Nazareth. Because the Logos voluntarily confined and limited himself to the latter, it does not follow that he could not also continue to be unconfined and unlimited God Because the sun is shining in and through a cloud, it does not follow that it cannot at the same time be shining through the remainder of universal space unobscured by any vapor whatever. The omnipresence of the Logos is that of the infinite Spirit. Consequently he is *all* in every place, and at every point. He is *all* in the human soul and body of Jesus of Nazareth, and simultaneously he is *all* at every other point of space. His total presence in the man Christ Jesus did not prevent his total presence throughout the universe. He was therefore, both omnipresent, and locally present. Says Calvin (Institutes, II. xv), "although the infinite essence of the Logos is united in one person with the nature of man, yet we have no thought of its incarceration or confinement. For the Son of God miraculously descended from heaven, yet in such a manner that he never left heaven: he chose to be miraculously conceived in the womb of the Virgin, to live on earth, and to be suspended on the cross; and yet he never ceased to fill the universe in the same manner as from the beginning." "Who will say," says Paraeus (Upon Hunnius, XXI.), "that the deity of the Word was only where his body was, say, in the mother's womb, in the temple, on the cross, in the sepulchre, and was absent in other places where his body was not? Who will say that he did not fill heaven and earth; that he was not at Rome, at Athens, and everywhere outside of Judea, at the same time when his body was within the limits of Judea alone?" "The Word of God," says Augustine (Letter 137, To Volusianus), "did so assume a body from the Virgin, and manifest himself with mortal senses, as neither to destroy his own immortality, nor to change his eternity, nor to diminish his power, nor to relinquish the government of the world, nor to withdraw from the bosom of the Father, that is from the secret place where he is with him and in him." Says Aquinas (III. v. 2), "Christus dicitur de coelo descendisse ratione divinae naturae, non ita quod natura divina in coelo desierit; sed quia in infimis novo modo coepit, scilicet secundum naturam assumptam."

As the inspiration of a prophet by the Holy Spirit, or his indwelling in a believer, does not interfere with the trinitarian relations of the third person, so neither does the incarnation interfere with those of the second. The Holy Spirit makes intercessions that cannot be uttered, and thereby unites himself to a certain degree to a particular man, but is still the same distinct person in the trinity. Moreover, this intercession of the Holy Ghost in the soul of the believer does not disturb or prevent the single self-consciousness of the believer. Here are two distinct persons, confessedly, and yet only one self-consciousness in the believer. But if a single self-consciousness is not dualized and destroyed in the instance when the Divine nature and the human, the Holy Ghost and the believer, do not constitute a God-man, still less need it be when they do. The two different modes or forms of consciousness, the divine and the human, in the God-man, do not constitute two *self*-consciousnesses, or two persons, any more than two or more different forms of consciousness in a man constitute two or more self-consciousnesses or persons. A man at one moment has a sensuous form of consciousness, and at another moment a spiritual form; but he is one and the same person in both instances, and has but a single self-consciousness.

8. In the incarnation, the Logos does not unite himself with a human *person*, but with a human *nature*. This is taught in Scripture. Heb. 2:16, Christ "took upon him the seed (σπέρμα) of Abraham." Rom. 1:3, Christ "was made of the seed of David." In the first promise (Gen. 3:15), the Redeemer is denominated the "seed of the woman." Heb. 2:14, "Forasmuch as the children were partakers of flesh and blood, he also himself likewise took part of the same."

The terms "seed," "flesh and blood," imply that the humanity which the Logos laid hold upon, and assumed into personal union with himself, was not yet personalized. At the instant when it was assumed, it was human nature unindividualized, not a distinct individual person. This is the interpretation of the Scripture statement which is found in the symbols generally. More particular attention was turned to the distinction between a nature and a person by the Nestorian controversy, and ever since that time the creeds have been careful to state that the Logos united a human nature with himself, but not a human person.

The orthodox statement in the Patristic church is made in the following extract from John of Damascus (De Orthodoxa Fide, III. ii.): "The Logos was not united with a flesh which previously existed by itself as an individual man, but, in and by his own infinite person dwelling in the womb of the holy Virgin, he personalized (ὑπεστησάτο) of the chaste blood of the Ever-Virgin a flesh enlivened with a rational and intellectual soul; the Logos thereby assuming the first-fruits of the human lump, and becoming a [divine] person in the flesh."

The Westminster Confession (VIII. ii ) accords with the Ancient, Mediaeval, and Reformed Christology, in its statement that "the Son of God, the second person in the Trinity, did take upon him man's *nature* with all the essential properties thereof; so that the two whole perfect and distinct natures, the Godhead [Godhood] and the manhood, were inseparably joined together in one person." The Athanasian symbol (29) denominates Christ "homo ex *substantia* matris in saeculo natus." In the theological nomenclature, "nature" is designated by "substance," and person by "subsistence."

Hooker (V. lii ) enunciates the doctrine in the following language: "The Son of God did not assume a man's person into his own person, but a man's nature to his own person; and therefore he took semen, the seed of Abraham, the very first original element of our nature before it was come to have any personal human subsistence." In similar terms, Owen (Holy Spirit, II iii.) expresses himself. He remarks that the Son of God took the nature formed and prepared for him in the womb of the Virgin, by the operation of the Holy Ghost, "to be his own, in the instant of its formation, thereby preventing [going before] the singular [single] and individual subsistence of that nature in and by itself" Again (ut supra) he says, that "as it is probable that the miraculous conception was immediate upon the angelical salutation, so it was necessary that nothing of the human nature of Christ should exist of itself antecedently unto its union with the Son of God." By the phrase "exist of itself," Owen here means "exist by itself" as constituted and formed into a distinct and separate *individual person.* That the human nature as bare nature existed antecedently to its union with the Logos, Owen abundantly teaches in all that he says of the work of the Holy Ghost in preparing and forming the human nature as it existed in the Virgin mother. In another passage (Trinity Vindicated), Owen is still more explicit. "The person of the Son of God, in his assuming human nature to be his own, did not take an individual person of any one into a near conjunction with himself, but preventing the personal subsistence of human nature in that flesh which he assumed, he gave it its subsistence (i.e. its personality) in his own person, whence it hath its individuation, and distinction from all other persons whatever. This is the personal union." Again, Owen (Vindiciae, XIX.) says: "Jesus Christ the Mediator, *θεάνθρωπος*, God and man, the Son of God, having assumed *ἅγιον τὸ γεννώμενον*, Luke 1:35, that holy thing that was born of the Virgin, *ανυπόστατον*, having no subsistence of its own, into personal subsistence with himself, is to be worshipped with divine religious worship, even as the Father." See Owen. Person of Christ, Ch. XVIII. Says Charnocke (Wisdom of God), "Christ did not take the person of man, but the nature of man into subsistence with himself. The body and soul of Christ were not united in themselves, had no [personal] subsistence in themselves, till they were united to the [trinitarian] person of the Son of God. If the *person* of a man were united to him, the human nature would have been the nature of the person so united to him, and not the [human] nature of the Son of God, according to Heb. 2:14, 16. The [trinitarian] Son of God took 'flesh and blood' to be his own [human] nature, perpetually to subsist in the person of the Logos; which must be by a personal union, or no way: the deity united to the humanity, and both natures to be one person."

Turrettin (XIII. vi. 18) says: "Although the human nature of Christ is a spiritual and intelligent substance, and perfect in respect to the existence and properties of such a substance, yet it is not at first (statim) a person;[1] because it has not that peculiar incommunicable property which constitutes a subsistence as distinguished from a substance [or a person as distinguished from a nature]. Just as soul (anima) taken by itself is a particular intelligent substance, yet not a person, because it is an incomplete part of a greater whole It requires to be joined to a body, before there can be an individual man. It does not derogate from the reality and perfection of Christ's human nature to say that before it was assumed into union with the Logos it was destitute of personality, because we measure the reality and dignity of a human nature by the *essential properties* of the nature, and not by the characteristic of *individuality* subsequently added to it. These essential properties belong to it by creation, but the individual form is superinduced after creation by generation. The definition of substance or nature, consequently differs from the definition of subsistence or person. Personality is not an integral and essential part of a nature, but is, as it were, the terminus to which it tends[2] (nec pars integralis nec essentialis naturae, sed quasi terminus); and Christ's human nature acquired a more exalted and perfect personality by subsisting in the Logos, than it would had it acquired personality by ordinary generation." Similarly, Quenstedt (Hase: Hutterus, p. 233) asserts that "subsistentia non ad essentiam hominis pertinet, sed ad terminationem humanitatis." He also remarks (Hase: Hutterus, p. 232) "non enim persona (alioquin duae essent in Christo personae), sed natura humana, propria personalitate destituta, assumpta est." Calovius teaches that Christ as man was "natus e massa seminali;" Hollaz says, "e semine animato;" Baier says, "e massa sanguinea virginis."

---

[1] It is noticeable that in this place Turrettin describes Christ's "human nature," *while existing in the Virgin Mother*, as a "spiritual" and "intelligent" substance, and not as merely physical. This is inconsistent with the creationist view, adopted by Turrettin.

[2] This agrees with Aristotle's, "materia appetit formam"

An American theologian, Samuel Hopkins, I. 283, adopts the catholic Christology "The personality of Jesus Christ is in his divine nature, and not in the human. Jesus Christ existed a distinct, divine person from eternity, the second person in the adorable trinity. The human nature which this divine person, the Word, assumed into a personal union with himself is not and never was a distinct person by itself, and personality cannot be ascribed to it, and does not belong to it, any otherwise than as united to the Logos, the Word of God. The Word assumed the human nature, not a human person, into a personal union with himself, by which the complex person exists, God-man. Hence, when Jesus Christ is spoken of as being a man, 'the Son of man, the man Christ Jesus,' etc, these terms do not express the personality of the manhood, or of the human nature of Jesus Christ; but these personal terms are used with respect to the human nature as united to a divine person, and not as a mere man [i.e. as merely human nature]. For the personal terms, He, I, and Thou, cannot with propriety or truth be used by, or of, the human nature considered as distinct from the divine nature of Jesus Christ."[1]

In a similar manner, Hodge explains the subject. After remarking (Theology, II. 391) that "though realism may not be a correct philosophy, the fact of its wide and long-continued prevalence may be taken as a proof that it does not involve any palpable contradiction," he proceeds to make use of realism, in the statement that "human nature although endowed with intelligence and will may be, and in fact is, in the person of Christ, impersonal.[2] That it is

---

[1] The human nature of Christ, viewed by itself, and prior to the union with the Logos, must be designated by the impersonal pronoun, "It." We could not call it "He;" nor could we address it as "Thou" In Luke 1 35, the neuter is employed τὸ γεννώμενον, "that holy thing which shall be born," or rather, "which is being conceived"

[2] The more accurate statement would be, that the human nature in the *Virgin Mother*, antecedent to the assumption of it by the Logos, is impersonal Strictly speaking, the human nature when once "in the person of *Christ*" is

so, is the plain doctrine of Scripture, for the Son of God, a divine person, assumed a perfect human nature, and nevertheless remains one person."

Van Mastricht (Theologia, V. iv. 7) defines the hypostatical union as, "ineffabilis quaedam relatio divinae personae ad humanam naturam per quam haec humana natura peculiariter est humana natura secundae personae deitatis." Wollebius (I. xvi.) says that "Christ assumed not man, but the humanity; not the person, but the nature." John Bunyan (On Imputed Righteousness) says that "the Son of God took not upon him a particular person, though he took to him a human body and soul; but that which he took was, as I may call it, a lump of the common nature of man. 'For verily he took not on him the nature of angels, but he took on him the seed of Abraham.'"[1]

Since much depends in Christology upon the important distinction between "nature" and "person," or "substance" and "subsistence," we shall enlarge somewhat upon it.

When we speak of a human nature, a real *substance* having physical, rational, moral, and spiritual *properties* is meant. This human nature, or substance, is capable of becoming a human person, but as yet is not one. It requires

---

no longer impersonal, because it has been personalized by the union As Owen says, the Logos "gave it its subsistence in his own person, whence it hath its individuation, and distinction from all other persons whatever"

[1] Dorner (Christian Doctrine, § 93) objects to "the *anhypostasia*, or impersonality of the human nature," and asserts that "it has passed into no creed, and is only to a moderate extent the doctrine of theologians" The extracts given above disprove the latter assertion Dorner's objection to the tenet is, that "if a divine ego is supposed to take the place of the human, there is an abridgment of the humanity, according to its complete idea—a more subtle kind of Apollinarism." But the divine ego does not take the place of the human ego, for the reason that there is no human ego There is at the moment of the assumption, only the seed, or unindividualized substance of the Virgin. Dorner assumes that a human nature without a human individuality is "abridged" and incomplete humanity But all the essential *properties* of humanity are in this nature Only it has not been constituted a particular person, by conception in the womb. This personalizing, which in the case of Christ's humanity is produced miraculously by its union with deity, adds no new properties to the human nature It only gives it a new form.

to be personalized, in order to be a self-conscious individual man. A human person is a fractional part of a specific human nature or substance which has been *separated* from the common mass, and formed into a distinct and separate individual, by the process of generation. Prior to this separation and formation, this fractional portion of the common human nature has all the qualities of the common mass of which it is a part, but it is not yet individualized It is potentially, not actually personal. It has all the properties that subsequently appear in the particular individual formed of it, such as spirituality, rationality, voluntariness —viewing the nature upon the psychical side of it—and sensuousness with general adaptation to a visible and material world—viewing the nature upon the physical side.[1]

Accordingly, the Westminster Confession (VIII. ii) affirms that "the second person in the trinity did take upon him man's nature with all the essential *properties* thereof." It does not say, with the individual *form* thereof. The fact that the nature has all the properties of man, though it has not as yet the form of an individual man, is sufficient to make it human nature. A brute's nature does not have all the properties of human nature; and neither does an angel's nature. Therefore, the Logos "took not upon him the nature of angels, but he took on him the seed (σπέρμα) of Abraham," Heb. 2:16.

Saint Paul's figure of the potter's clay, and the vessels to be shaped from it, may be employed in illustration. A lump of clay has all the properties of matter that belong to the vessel of honor or dishonor. But it has not as yet the individual form of the vessel. An act of the potter must intervene, whereby a piece of clay is separated from the lump and moulded into a particular vase having its own peculiar shape and figure. In like manner, human nature as an entire whole existing in Adam possessed all the ele-

[1] This description is traducian The creationist concedes only one side to the nature, namely the sensuous, and finds only physical properties

mentary properties that are requisite to personality, though it was not yet personalized. And in like manner, any *portion* of this entire human nature, when transmitted from Adam and existing in nearer or remote ancestors, is also possessed of all the properties requisite to personality, though it is not yet, in Owen's phrase, "individuated," or transformed from a nature to a person. The difference, then, between nature and person is virtually that between *substance* and *form*. As a material substance may exist without being shaped in a particular manner, so a human nature may exist without being individualized. See Anthropology, pp. 71 sq

Thus it appears, that although a human nature is not actually personal, that is, a distinct person, it is nevertheless potentially personal; that is, it is capable of becoming a separate self-conscious individual man. Every individual of Adam's posterity has precisely the same properties or qualities in his person, that there are in the specific nature of which he is a part and portion. He is physical, rational, intelligent, and voluntary, only because the human nature out of which he is formed is a physical, rational, intelligent, and voluntary substance created by God on the sixth day when he created the species man. It is the *properties* of a substance that make it what it is, not the particular individual form which it may assume. As Turrettin says, in the extract previously quoted, "We measure the reality and dignity of a human nature by the essential properties of the nature, not by the characteristic of individuality subsequently added to it. Personality is not an integral and necessary part of a nature, but, as it were, the terminus to which it tends."

It is evident, then, from this discussion, that the term "nature" is a more impersonal term than the term "person." A human nature, though not absolutely impersonal, like a brute-nature, or like inorganic matter, is yet less personal than a human person. This may be illustrated by considering the divine nature, and the trinitarian persons. In the discussion of the doctrine of the Trinity, we have seen that if we abstract from the divine essence its trinality, we have nothing left but the impersonal substance of pantheism, or the unreflecting unit of deism. It is only when the divine nature is contemplated, as it is in Scripture, as "subsisting," or "modified," or, if we may so speak, metamorphosed in the eternal Three, Father, Son, and Holy Ghost, that we have full and clear personality. This is what is meant in Phil 2:6 by *μόρφη Θεοῦ*. This is not the same in every respect with *οὐσια Θεοῦ* or *φύσις Θεοῦ*. It is a personal "form" of the *οὐσια* or *φύσις Θεοῦ*. God is self-conscious, self-knowing, and self-communing, in other words is personal, because he subsists in three individual distinctions. As an untrinalized nature merely and only, he is the impersonal unit of deism or pantheism; but as a nature in three persons, or a nature *personalized* by trinality, he is a unity: the self-conscious and "living" God of Abraham, Isaac, and Jacob. The eternal trinitarian processes of generation and spiration personalize the divine nature, as ordinary generation analogously individualizes the human nature. The one human nature, or species, is personalized gradually in time by division into millions of human individuals; and the one divine nature is personalized simultaneously in eternity by subsisting indivisibly and wholly in three divine hypostases. If the human nature were never individualized by ordinary generation; if it remained a mere nature in Adam; though it would be human nature still, and not brutal nature or inorganic matter, yet it would be impersonal for our minds. It would have no history, and none of the interest and impression of individuality. And if the divine nature had no trinality in it; if there were no Father, Son, and Holy Ghost, but only the one substance of pantheism or deism; the deity would peresent no prsonal characteristics appealing to a man's personal feelings and wants.

To apply all this to the subject of Christ's theanthropic person: we say, that in the act of incarnation, the Logos, who is already a conscious trinitarian person, takes into personal union with himself a human nature—what the Scripture denominates the "seed of David," the "seed of Abraham," the "seed of a woman," the "flesh and blood," of man. This human nature previous to this assumption is not a person ("for the personal being which the Son of God already had, suffered not the substance which he took to be a person," says Hooker), yet it is capable of being personalized, and becoming an individual man. It is actually personalized, and made to have an individual life and history, by being miraculously quickened, formed, and sanctified by the Holy Ghost in the womb of the Virgin Mother, and assumed by the eternal Logos into union with himself. Hence Athanasius (Contra Arianos, III. li.) defines Christ as "a man impersonated into God;" and describes Christ's human body and soul as an instrument which the Logos appropriates personally (*ὄργανον ἐνυπόστατον ἴδιοποιησε*). Witsius: Creed, Dissertation XVI. The human nature thus becomes an integrant constituent of one complex person, the God-man, Jesus Christ. In the phraseology of Owen (Person of Christ, XVIII.) "assumption is unto [in order to] personality; it is that act whereby the Son of God and our nature become one person." Francis Junius (Theses Theologicae, XXVII.) similarly remarks: "Natura humana, prius *ἀνυπόστατος*, in unitatem personae assumpta est a *Λόγῳ* et facta *ἐνυπόστατος*." Aquinas (III. ii. 2) contends that the human nature of Christ, by being personalized through assumption into union with a trinitarian person, obtained a more exalted personality in this way than it would have obtained by being personalized by ordinary generation; just as the animal soul, when personalized by its union with a rational soul, in the case of a man, is more excellent than when, as in the case of a dog, or any mere animal, it is not personalized at all by union with a rational soul.

Still another point of difference between a "nature" and a "person" is the fact that a nature cannot be distinguished from another nature, but a person can be from another person. One fractional portion of human substance has no marks by which it can be discriminated from another portion. It is not until it has been individualized by generation, that it has a personal peculiarity of its own that differentiates it. When human "flesh and blood" has acquired personal characteristics, it can then be distinguished from the parents, and from the species. "Human nature," says Owen (Person of Christ, XVIII), "in itself is ἀνυπόστατος: that which hath not a subsistence of its own which should give it individuation, and distinction from the same nature in any other person." Says Hooker (V. lii.), "We cannot say, properly, that the Virgin bore, or John did baptize, or Pilate condemn, or the Jews crucify, the *nature* of man; because these are all personal attributes. Christ's person is the subject which receiveth them, his nature that which maketh his person capable or apt to receive."

In the case of an ordinary human person, the body or the material nature is personalized by the soul or the spiritual nature within it. The body as a mere corpse, and separate from the soul, is impersonal. Similarly, the human nature of Christ considered as the substance of the Virgin is personalized by the Logos uniting with it. "Humana natura, ut Damascenus dicit, habet suam personalitatem in Christo." Aquinas: Summa, III. ii. 3. Viewed merely as the substance, the "blood" and "seed" of the Virgin prior to its assumption, it was impersonal. It could not be distinguished as the particular individual man Jesus of Nazareth, until the miraculous conception had individualized it. As the mere "substance" and "seed" of the Virgin, it had nothing to distinguish it from the "substance" and "seed" of any other woman; or from other "substance" of Mary herself, who could have conceived still other sons by ordinary generation.

9. In the incarnation, the Logos did not unite himself with the *whole* human nature, but with only a *part* of it. The term "human nature" may signify the entire human species as it existed in Adam, or only a part of it as it exists in near or remote ancestors. In the first case, it is *the* human nature; in the second, it is *a* human nature. The proper statement is, that the Logos united himself with *a* human nature, not with *the* human nature. Whenever there is any conception of human nature, either ordinary or miraculous, there is abscission of substance. Turrettin (XIII. xi. 10) speaks of Christ's humanity as "materiam ex beatissimi Virginis substantia decisam." The union between God and man, in the incarnation, is not a union with the human species as an entirety. At the time of the incarnation of the Logos, the human nature considered as an entire whole had been in the process of generation and individualization for four thousand years, and millions of separate and distinct individuals had been formed out of it. The Logos did not unite himself with this already propagated part of the human nature or species. Neither did he unite with that whole remainder of the common nature which had not yet been individualized by generation. This latter was latent and unindividualized, in the population existing at the time of the incarnation. The Logos united with only a fraction of this remainder; namely with that particular portion of human nature which he assumed from the virgin mother. The Eternal Word took into a personal union with himself, not the whole human nature both distributed and undistributed, individualized, and unindividualized, but only a transmitted fractional part of the undistributed remainder of it, as this existed in the Virgin Mary.[1]

---

[1] It is at this point that the strongest objection to the traducian theory arises How can unextended substance be subdivided? How can that have parts which has none of the geometrical dimensions? See Anthropology, pp. 83 sq

That theory of universal redemption which rests upon the hypothesis of a union of the Logos with the whole human species finds no support in Scripture, and we may add in reason or the nature of the case. The humanity of Christ was not a specific whole, but only a part of a specific whole. "Dicendum quod Verbum Dei non assumpsit humanam naturam in *universali* sed in *atomo*, id est, in individuo, sicut Damascenus ait, Orthod. Fid., III. vii.; alioquin oporteret quod cuilibet homini conveniret esse Dei Verbum, sicut convenit Christo." Aquinas: Summa: III. ii. 2.

10. The human nature assumed into union with the Logos was miraculously sanctified, so as to be sinless and perfect. John 1:14, "The Word was made flesh and dwelt among us full of grace and truth." John 3:34, "God giveth not the Spirit by measure unto him." Is. 11:2, "The Spirit of the Lord shall rest upon him, the spirit of wisdom and understanding, the spirit of council and might, the spirit of knowledge and of the fear of the Lord." Heb. 4:15, "Christ was in all points tempted like as we are, yet without sin."[1] Heb. 7:26, "Such an high priest became us, who is holy, harmless, undefiled, separate from sinners." Luke 1:35, "That holy thing which shall be born": literally, "which is being conceived" (τὸ γεννώμενον). Isa. 7:14, 15, "Butter and honey shall Immanuel eat, that he may know to refuse the evil and choose the good." Heb. 10:5, "A body hast thou prepared for me." Matt. 3:17, "This is my beloved Son in whom I am well pleased." 1 John 3:5, "In him is no sin."

In accordance with these texts, the symbols affirm the perfect sanctification of the human nature, in and by the incarnation. The Westminster Larger Catechism, Q. 37, teaches that "the Son of God became man by being con-

[1] In this passage, χωρὶς ἁμαρτίας qualifies πεπειρασμένον: showing that all of Christ's temptations were sinless He was not "tempted and drawn away by inward lust," James 1.14

ceived by the power of the Holy Ghost in the womb of the Virgin Mary, of her substance, and born of her, yet without sin." The Formula Concordiae (De peccato originis, Hase, 574), after saying that the Son of God assumed the "seed of Abraham," adds: "eandam humanam nostram naturam (opus videlicet suum) Christus redemit, eandam (quae ipsius opus est) sanctificat, eandam a mortuis resuscitat, et ingenti gloria (opus videlicet suum) ornat."

With these statements of the symbols, the theologians agree. They assert the sinfulness of the Virgin Mary, the consequent sinfulness of human nature as transmitted by her, and the necessity of its being redeemed and sanctified, in order to be fitted for a personal union with the Logos. Says Augustine (Letter 164), "If the soul of Christ be derived from Adam's soul, he, in assuming it to himself, cleansed it so that when he came into this world he was born of the Virgin perfectly free from sin either actual or transmitted. If, however, the souls of men are not derived from that one soul, and it is only by the flesh that original sin is transmitted from Adam, the Son of God created a soul for himself, as he creates souls for all other men, but he united it not to sinful flesh, but to the 'likeness of sinful flesh,' Rom. 8 : 3. For he took, indeed, from the Virgin the true substance of flesh; not however 'sinful flesh,' for it was neither begotten nor conceived through carnal concupiscence, but was mortal and capable of change in the successive stages of life, as being like unto sinful flesh in all points, sin excepted." See also Enchiridion, xxxvi. xxxvii. Athanasius (Contra Arianos, II. lxi.) explains the clause, "first-born of every creature," Col. 1 : 5, as meaning the same as "first-born among many brethren," Rom. 8 : 29; and adds that Christ "is the first-born of us in this respect, that the whole posterity of Adam lying in a state of perdition by the sin of Adam, the human nature of Christ was first redeemed and sanctified (ἐσώθη καὶ ἠλευθερώθη), and so became the means of our regeneration, redemption, and sanctification, in consequence of the community of nature between him and us." John of Damascus (De Fide, III. ii.) teaches the same doctrine. Says Anselm (Cur deus homo, II. 17), "Christ's mother was purified by the power of his death. The virgin of whom he was born could be pure only by true faith in his death." Anselm supposes that the Virgin Mother was perfectly sanctified, but does not hold the later dogma of the immaculate conception of the Virgin. Yet he prepares the way for it, by teaching her immaculateness by regeneration. Says Paraeus (Corpus Doctrinae, Q. 35.), "Non conveniebat Λογῳ, filio dei, assumere naturam pollutam peccato. Quicquid enim natum est ex carne, peccatrice scilicet et non sanctificata, caro est, mendacium et vanitas. Spiritus Sanctus optime novit separare peccatum a natura hominis; substantiam ab accidente. Peccatum enim non est de natura hominis, sed aliunde a diabolo naturae accessit. Separavit a foetu omnem impuritatem, et contagionem peccati originalis." Says Ursinus (Christian Religion, Quest. 35), "Mary was a sinner; but the mass of flesh which was taken out of her substance was, by the operation of the Holy Ghost, at the same instant sanctified when it was taken." Says Pearson (Creed, Art. III.), "The original and total sanctification of the human nature was first necessary to fit it for the personal union with the Word, who out of his infinite love humbled himself to become flesh, and at the same time out of his infinite purity could not defile himself by becoming sinful flesh. Therefore the human nature, in its first original, without any precedent merit, was formed by the Spirit, and in its formation sanctified, and in its sanctification united to the Word; so that grace was co-existent and in a manner co-natural with it." Says Owen (Holy Spirit, II. iv.), "The human nature of Christ, being thus formed in the womb by a creating [supernatural] act of the Holy Spirit, was in the instant of its conception sanctified and filled with grace according to the measure of its receptivity." Owen adds that the human nature, "being not begotten by natural generation, derived no taint of original sin or corruption from Adam, that being the only way or means of its propagation." Says Quenstedt (III. iii.), "Idem Spiritus, singularissima praesentia et virtute, Mariam semper virginem ad concipiendum mundi Salvatorem foecundam reddidit, semen prolificum ex castis ejus sanguinibus elicuit, ab omni adhaerente peccato purgavit, ipsique Mariae virtutem praebuit qua conciperet ipsum Dei Filium."

Usher (Incarnation, Works, IV. 583) speaks of the effect of the incarnation upon the human nature of Christ, not merely in sanctifying it, but in preserving it from certain innocent defects. "As the Son of God took upon him not a human person but a human nature, so it was not requisite that he should take upon him any personal infirmities such as madness, blindness, lameness, and particular kinds of diseases which are incidental to some individuals only, and not to all men generally; but those infirmities which do accompany the whole nature of manhood, such as are hungering, thirsting, weariness, grief, pain, mortality." Says Gill (Divinity, p. 165), "Christ was made of a woman, took flesh of a sinful woman, though the flesh he took of her was not sinful, being sanctified by the Spirit of God, the former of Christ's human nature." Turrettin (XIII. xi. 10), describing the operation of the Holy Spirit in respect to the incarnation, remarks that "the Holy Spirit must prepare the substance abscided from the substance of the blessed Virgin by a suitable sanctification, not only by endowing it with life and elevating it to that degree of energy which is sufficient for generation without sexual connection, but also by purifying it from all stain of sin (ab omni peccati labe) so that it shall be harmless and undefiled, and thus that Christ may be born without sin. Hence there is no need of having recourse to the doctrine of the immaculate conception of Mary. For although there is no created power which can bring a clean thing from an unclean (Job

14 : 4), yet the Divine power is not to be so limited. To this there is nothing impossible. This calls things which are not, as if they were." Wollebius (I. xvi.) says that "the material cause of Christ's conception was the blood of the blessed Virgin. The formal cause of Christ's conception consisteth in the preparing and sanctifying of the Virgin's blood by the virtue of the Holy Ghost." Edwards (Excellency of Christ) remarks that "though Christ was conceived in the womb of one of the corrupt race of mankind, yet he was conceived without sin."

Marck (Persona Christi, XI. xiv.) teaches that the Virgin's substance was preserved from original sin. After saying "carnem humanam habuit Christus ex substantia virginis Mariae, cum ejus filius, Luc. 11 : 7, et ex muliere factus, Gal. 4 : 5, dicatur," he adds respecting the miraculous conception : "Actio Spiritus fere triplex fuit ; foecundatio seminis virginei, humanae naturae formatio, et ab omni labe praeservatio ; quae inde bene derivari potest, quod Christus, supernaturaliter generatus, culpa Adamica non tenetur, hinc labe illius infici non potest." Here nothing is said respecting positive sanctification, but only of preservation from corruption. De Moor, however, in his commentary upon Marck (XIX. xiv.), adopts the statement of Alting in the following terms : "Altingius observat 'semen illud, ex quo corpus Christi formatum est, ut a peccatrice decisam, sic peccato, saltem quoad dispositionem, fuit infectum. At Spiritus Sanctus praeparando illud repurgavit ab omni labe inhaerente ; atque etiam principia infirmitatum, toti speciei communium, quae manserunt, ab *ἀνομία καὶ ἀταξία* secrevit.'" Van Mastricht tends to the Semi-Pelagian anthropology, in asserting that the Virgin's seed was cleansed from physical not from moral corruption. In IV. x. 5, 6, he remarks that the Holy Spirit "semen illud virgineum *quasi* defoecavit, non quidem ab impuritate *morali* seu peccato, utpote cui semen necdum animatum non est obnoxium ; sed ab intemperie *physica*, a qua, suo tempore, peccatum potuisset resultare, aut saltem nativitatem ab omni impuritate praeservavit, ad hoc, ut quod ex eo nasceretur esset sanctum. Luc. 1 : 35." In IV. x. 6, he says, "istud autem semen, licet per *peccatores* ad Mariam fuerit propagatum; *peccato* tamen, seu malitiae morali, non fuit obnoxium, cum malitia ista non cadat in inanimatum et irrationale, licet intemperiem naturalem possit habere, quae postmodum peccato possit occasionem praebere, quam hinc, a semine Mariano, per Spiritum Sanctum sublatam diximus"[1]

That the human nature derived from Mary, in itself and apart from the agency of the Holy Ghost in the incarnation, was corrupt, is proved by Rom. 8 : 3, "God sent his own Son in the likeness of sinful flesh." This means that the "flesh" as it existed in the mother, and before its sanctification in the womb, was sinful. John 3 : 6, "That which is born of the flesh is flesh." Job 14 : 4, "Who can bring a clean thing out of an unclean? Not one." Job 25 : 4, "How can he be clean that is born of a woman?" The Formula Concordiae (De peccato originis, Hase, 644) says that "in primo conceptionis nostrae momento, ipsum semen ex quo homo formatur peccato contaminatum et corruptum est" It also condemns the Anabaptists who asserted "quod Christum carnem et sanguinem suum non e Maria virgine assumpserit, sed e caelo attulerit."[2]

---

[1] The impossibility of harmonizing the Augustino-Calvinistic tenet that original sin as *culpability* is transmitted by propagation, with creationism, is here virtually acknowledged by Van Mastricht. Only physical corruption can be inherited, if only the body is propagated, but physical corruption without moral, as Van Mastricht teaches, is not *peccatum* And the cleansing from it is *quasi* cleansing In IV x 24, Van Mastricht assigns as the principal reason for the absence of original sin from the human nature of Christ, that this nature though "naturaliter in Adam, velut in capite et radice naturae humanae," was not "foederaliter" in him But, in his reasoning, he apparently confounds the simple humanity of Christ with the composite θεανθρώπος, who of course was neither naturally nor federally in Adam See Dorner Person of Christ, II. 308, 341, Note

[2] Even if the Romish dogma of the immaculate conception of Mary were true, it would not follow that a human nature transmitted by her would also be immaculate Regeneration and sanctification by the Holy Ghost are confined to

In the Adoptian controversy, in the 8th century, Felix of Urgellis maintained that the Logos united with a human nature that was unsanctified ; that Christ had a corrupted nature though he never committed actual transgression. He thought this to be necessary, in order that Christ might be tempted in all points like as we are, yet without sin. But this implies that corruption of nature is not sin He was opposed by Alcuin. See Guerike's Church History, § 107. The theory was revived, about 1830, in Germany by Menken, and in Great Britain by Irving.[1] Schleiermacher (Glaubenslehre, § 97) departs from the catholic doctrine, in holding that Christ had an earthly father, but that by a

---

the individual. They do not affect the specific nature in him See Anthropology, p 91 sq

[1] Irving's view is, that Christ's human nature after its union with the Logos was still fallen and "sinful flesh" (Rom 8 · 3) as it was before the union, but that by means of the indwelling of the Holy Spirit Christ repressed all stirrings of this sinful flesh, so that he not only never committed an outward transgression, but never exercised a sinful desire At the same time, Irving contends that Christ experienced *all* the temptations which sinful man experiences His words are as follows Christ's humanity "was flesh in the fallen state, and liable to all the temptations to which [fallen] flesh is liable, but the soul of Jesus, thus anointed with the Holy Ghost, did ever resist the suggestions of evil I wish it to be clearly understood, that I believe it to be necessary unto salvation, that a man should believe that Christ's soul was so held in possession by the Holy Ghost, and so supported by the Divine Nature, as that it never assented unto an evil suggestion, and never originated an evil suggestion" Irving · On the Incarnation (Its Method, Pt. I.) This last assertion is inconsistent with the assertion that Christ "was liable to *all* the temptations to which sinful flesh is liable" If his human nature "never originated an evil suggestion," he could not have been tempted by inward lust, which is one species of temptation that sinful man experiences, according to James 1 . 14.

Irving's view of Christ's holiness seems to be that of spiritual regeneration by the Holy Spirit as in the case of a believer, rather than of a supernatural transformation by the miraculous conception Only, the regeneration in Christ's case *completely* subjects the inward corruption, while in the believer it imperfectly subjects it According to the catholic doctrine, the corruption is entirely extirpated from the human nature of Christ, according to Irving's doctrine, it remains, but is repressed and subdued. "They argue for an inherent holiness ; we argue for a holiness maintained by the person of the Son through the operation of the Holy Ghost The substance of our argument is, that Christ's human nature was holy in the only way in which holiness under the fall exists or can exist, namely, through inworking or energizing of the Holy Ghost." Irving Works, V 564

supernatural operation on the embryo it was cleansed from original sin.

The possibility of a perfect sanctification of the human nature of Christ appears from considering the mode of his conception, and comparing it with that of an ordinary man. The individualizing of a portion of human nature is that process by which it becomes a distinct and separate person, and no longer an undistinguishable part of the common species. A part of human nature becomes a human person by generation. In all instances but that of Jesus Christ, the individualization of a portion of human substance is accomplished through the medium of the sexes, and is accompanied with sensual appetite. By ordinary generation, human nature is transmitted and individualized without any change of its characteristics, either physical or moral. The individual has all the qualities both of soul and body which fallen Adam had. There is no sanctification of the nature possible by this mode. Ordinary generation transmits sin. "That which is born of the flesh [in this manner] is flesh" But in the instance of the conception of Jesus Christ, the God-man, there was no union of the sexes, and no sensual appetite. The quickening of a portion of human nature in the Virgin Mother was by the creative energy of God the Holy Ghost. This miraculous conception, consequently, was as pure from all sensuous quality as the original creation of Adam's body from the dust of the ground, or of Eve's body from the rib of Adam. As the dust of the ground was enlivened by a miraculous act, and the result was the individual body of Adam, so the substance of Mary was quickened and sanctified by a miraculous act, and the result was the human soul and body of Jesus Christ.[1]

[1] Here, we notice an important point of difference between traducianism and creationism According to the former theory, both the soul and body of Christ were formed simultaneously, and by one act of the Holy Spirit, out of the psychico-physical substance of the mother According to the latter, only the body was formed out of the Virgin's merely physical substance, the soul being subsequently created ex nihilo, and infused into the body Turrettin

The miraculous quickening of the substance of the Virgin Mother is not sufficient, alone and by itself, to account for its sanctification. As her substance, it was a part of the fallen and corrupt human species. Merely to quicken or vitalize it, even though miraculously, would not change its moral quality. Hence we must postulate a *renewing* and *sanctifying* operation of the Holy Spirit, in connection with his quickening energy. Witsius (Covenants, II. iv. 11) quotes Cloppenburg as saying, "that the miraculous impregnation of the Virgin's womb, of itself alone, could not secure, in the least, an exemption to the flesh of Christ from the inheritance of sin; for the origin of sin is not derived from the male sex alone, or male seed; nor did the apostle, in Rom. 5, so understand one man Adam as to exclude Eve: which is the leading error of some." Similarly, Calvin (Inst., II. xiii. 4) remarks that "they betray their ignorance, in arguing that if Christ is perfectly immaculate and was begotten of the seed of Mary by the secret operation of the Spirit, then it follows that there is no impurity in the seed of women, but only in that of men. For we do not represent Christ as perfectly immaculate merely because he was born of the seed of a woman unconnected with any man, but because he was sanctified by the Spirit, so that his generation was pure and holy, such as it would have been before the fall of Adam." The doctrine of the sinlessness of Christ is, thus, necessarily connected with the doctrine of the miraculous conception by the Holy Ghost. The one stands or falls with the other. "It is," says Howe (Oracles, II. xxxvii.), "a mighty confirmation of the natural descent of sin with the nature of man in the ordinary way, that when God designed the incarnation of his own

presents this view, in Inst XIII xi 11–15. As in the creation of Adam, God first made his body out of the substance of the earth, and then by a second act created and imbreathed his soul, so, according to the creationist, in the origination of the humanity of our Lord two acts must be postulated: one by which his human body was conceived out of the substance of the Virgin, and another by which his human soul was created from nothing.

Son, to avoid the corruption of nature descending to him, he then steps out of the ordinary course; a consideration that hath that weight with it, that if any one allow himself to think, it must overbear his mind, in that matter, that surely there is some secret profound reason in the counsel of God, whether obvious to our view, or not obvious, that the descent of corrupt nature was in the ordinary way unavoidable: that when God had a design to incarnate his own Son, when it was intended God should be manifested in the flesh, to avoid that contagion and corruption which in the ordinary course is transmitted, he doth in this single instance recede and go off from the ordinary natural course. Because the human nature had been corrupted if it had descended in the ordinary way, therefore the ordinary course of procreation is declined and avoided: a most pregnant demonstration that in the ordinary course sin is always naturally transmitted."

Although the human nature of Christ was individualized and personalized by a miraculous conception, and not by ordinary generation, yet this was as really and truly a conception and birth as if it had been by ordinary generation. Jesus Christ was really and truly the Son of Mary. He was bone of her bone, and flesh of her flesh. He was of her substance, and of her blood. He was consubstantial with her, in as full a sense as an ordinary child is consubstantial with an ordinary mother. And she was the mother of his human soul, as well as of his human body. All the stages in the process of generation and growth are to be found, from the embryo up to the mature man. The union of deity with humanity was first embryonic, then foetal, then infantine, then that of childhood, then that of youth, and lastly that of manhood. The God-man was conceived in the womb, grew in the womb, was an infant, a child, a youth, and a mature man.

Contemplating the mystery of the God-man in this way, as pointed out in Scripture, it is easier to see how only one person and one self-consciousness shall result. If we do not distinguish between nature and person—if we assume that there is no such reality as an unindividualized, or non-individualized nature, and that we must think of a distinct individual or we must think of nothing—then we must say that the Logos united with a human person. This person must be a self-conscious ego, and when united with the second person of the Godhead, which is likewise a self-conscious ego, must still have its own distinct self-consciousness. The God-man, consequently, must be two persons with two *self*-consciousnesses.

But when it is said that the trinitarian person of the Logos assumes unto union with himself a portion of human nature, which portion is not yet a distinct ego, but is capable by reason of its properties of becoming one, then the problem of the single self-consciousness of the God-man becomes much easier of solution. The human nature possessing, on the psychical side, all the properties requisite to personality, such as spirituality, rationality, and voluntariness, upon being assumed into union with the eternal Son is thereby personalized, that is to say, individualized. The properties of finite reason and finite will, potential in the human nature, now manifest themselves actively in the single self-consciousness of the God-man. He reasons like a man, thinks like a man, feels like a man, and wills like a man. These are truly personal acts and operations of Jesus Christ. But, unlike the case of an ordinary man, these are not the *whole* of his personal acts and operations. Over and besides these, there is in his complex theanthropic person another and higher series of acts and operations which spring from another and higher nature in his person. He thinks, and feels, and wills like God. And these are also, and equally with the others, the personal acts of Jesus Christ.

In the one person of Jesus Christ, consequently, there are two different kinds of consciousness or experience: one divine and one human. But these two kinds of consciousness do not constitute two persons, any more than the two kinds of experience or consciousness, the sensuous and the mental, in a man, constitute him two persons. There can be two general forms or modes of conscious experience in one and the same person, provided there enter into the constitution of the person two natures that are sufficiently different from each other to yield the materials of such a twofold variety. This was the case with the God-man. If he had had only one nature, as was the case previous to the incarnation, then he could have had only one general form of consciousness: the divine. But having two natures, he could have two corresponding forms of consciousness. He could experience either divine feeling, or human feeling; divine perception, or human perception. A God-man has a twofold variety of consciousness or experience, with only one self-consciousness When he says "I thirst," and "I and my Father are one," it is one theanthropic ego with a finite human consciousness in the first instance, and an infinite divine consciousness in the second.

A man can have two forms of consciousness, yet with only one self-consciousness. He can feel cold with his body, while he prays to God with his mind. These two forms of conscious experience are wholly diverse and distinct. He does not pray with his body, or feel cold with his mind. Yet this doubleness and distinctness in the consciousness, does not destroy the unity of his *self*-consciousness. So, also, Jesus Christ as a theanthropic person was constituted of a divine nature and a human nature. The divine nature had its own form of experience, like the mind in an ordinary human person; and the human nature had its own form of experience, like the body in a common man. The experiences of the divine nature were as diverse from those of the human nature, as those of the human mind are from those of the human body. Yet there was but one person who was the subject-ego of both of these experiences. At the very time when Christ was conscious of weariness and thirst by the well of Samaria, he also was conscious that he was the eternal and only-begotten Son of God, the second person in the trinity. This is proved by his words to the Samaritan woman: "Whosoever drinketh of the water that I shall give him shall never thirst; but the water that I shall give him shall be in him a well of water springing up into everlasting life. I that speak unto thee am the Messiah" The first-mentioned consciousness of fatigue and thirst came through the human nature in his person; the second-mentioned consciousness of omnipotence and supremacy came through the divine nature in his person. If he had not had a human nature, he could not have had the former consciousness; and if he had not had a divine nature, he could not have had the latter. Because he had both natures in one person, he could have both.[1]

---

[1] Shedd. Presbyterian Review, July 1881, pp. 618–621.

## CHAPTER II.

### CHRIST'S DIVINITY.

The subject of the Divinity of Christ has been examined under the head of Theology (Doctrine of God). See Vol. I. pp. 312–328. All Scripture texts and data prove the deity of Christ that prove his Trinitarian position and relations. The act and process of incarnation makes no essential change in the Logos. The incarnate Word has all the properties of the unincarnate Word. To the God-man are ascribed in Scripture, the divine names, attributes, works, and adorableness.

There is a class of texts which taken by themselves would imply an inferiority to God, in Jesus of Nazareth. They are such as describe his acts and experiences from the side of the humanity in his person, and of his estate of mediatorial humiliation. This inferiority may run all the way from the comparatively exalted view of the Semi-Arian, to the low humanitarian view of the Socinian. All of these parties really contemplate Jesus Christ only *κατὰ σάρκα*, omitting that aspect of him presented in the other class of passages which describe him *κατὰ πνεῦμα ἁγιωσύνης* (Rom. 1: 4), as *ὁ ὢν ἐπὶ πάνίων* (Rom. 9:5), as *ἐν μορφῇ θεοῦ ὑπάρχων* (Phil. 2:6), and as *θεὸς* (John 1:1).

Strictly speaking, none of these parties accept the *theanthropic* personality of Christ. The divine nature is left out in the constitution of his person, so that it is really only anthropic. For although the Semi-Arian conceded a complex personality in Christ composed of two natures, one of which was immensely higher than the other and in reference to which he cherished a feeling akin to adoration, yet since there is no true mean between the infinite and finite, the creator and the creature, this exalted higher nature must fall into the same finite class with the lower one. Such a Christology cannot be harmonized with the Scripture representations, except by omitting those passages which attribute to Jesus of Nazareth a nature to which the divine titles, attributes, and works are ascribed, and which is the object of worship both in heaven and on earth.

## CHAPTER III.

### CHRIST'S HUMANITY.

CHRIST'S Humanity is undisputed, being demonstrable from all the desciiptions of him given in the Gospels. Some of the more important of the numerous texts are: Gen. 3:15, "The seed of the woman." Matt. 13:37, "The Son of man." Isa. 7:14, "A virgin shall conceive and bear a son, and shall call his name Immanuel." Luke 1:32, "God shall give unto him the throne of his father David." Luke 3:23–38, Christ was "the son of David, of Abraham, and of Adam." Gal. 4:4, Christ was "made of a woman." Rom. 1:3, "Jesus Christ concerning the flesh was made of the seed of David." 1 Tim. 2:5, "The man Christ Jesus." Christ was born and died, hungered and thirsted, grew from infancy to childhood and manhood, was subject to the alternations of pleasure and pain, was tempted and struggled with temptation—in short, had all the experiences of man excepting those which involve sin. Luke 2:52; 24:36–44; Matt. 4:1; John 11:33, 35; 13:23; Heb. 4:15; 5:8; Phil. 2:7, 8.

What is implied in humanity has never been a dispute within the Church; but as some heretical parties have asserted a defective or mutilated humanity in Christ, the Church has specified particulars.

1. Christ had "a true body." Westminster L. C., 37. This was maintained in opposition to the Docetae (*δοκεῖν*), who asserted that Christ's body was seeming only, and spectral, a phantom of ghostlike appearance and not solid

flesh and blood. This heresy is refuted by Luke 24:39, "A spirit hath not flesh and bones, as ye see me have." John 20:27, "Reach hither thy hand, and thrust it into my side." Luke 24:43, "He did eat before them."

2. Christ had "a rational soul." Westminster L. C., 37. This was held in opposition to Apollinarism; which would find the rational element for the human nature in the eternal reason of the Logos. Apollinaris at first asserted that the Logos united with a human body only. Afterwards he modified this, by asserting that he united with a body and an irrational animal soul. Socrates: History, II. lxvi. Texts that disprove this are: Matt. 26:38, "My soul is sorrowful." Mark 6:6, Jesus "marvelled." Matt. 8:10. Luke 7:9. Sorrow and wonder are rational emotions, proper to man, but not to God. Apollinaris, from the account given of him by Gregory of Nyssa (Adv. Apollinarem), seems to have blended and confused the human and divine natures even in the Godhead; for he asserted a human element in the divine essence itself. The Divine, he contended, is also *essentially* and *eternally* human. There is, thus, an eternal humanity. The Divine nature necessarily tends to the human form; inherently yearns to become man, and is unsatisfied until it is incarnate. This is the worst feature in Apollinaris's scheme, who was nevertheless a strong advocate of the Athanasian trinitarianism against the Arians. Apollinaris also held that the mental suffering of Christ was suffering of the divine nature; otherwise it could not be a real atonement. See Dorner: Person of Christ.

The rational objections to Apollinarism are the following:

(*a*) A human nature destitute of finite reason would be either idiotic or brutal. If the Logos assumed into union only the body and the animal soul—the *σῶμα* and *ψυχή*, and not the *πνεῦμα*, in St. Paul's classification in

1 Thess. 5 : 23—he did not unite himself with a rational nature. (*b*) In this case, also, he did not unite with a complete, but a defective humanity. Some of the essential properties of human nature, namely, rationality and voluntariness, would have been wanting. (*c*) In this case, none of Christ's mental processes could have been of a finite kind. Nothing but infinite and divine reason could have been manifested in his self-consciousness. The same would be true of his voluntary action. This must have been infinite only. There could have been no exhibition of finite human will, or of finite human reason in his earthly life.

3. Christ "continues to be God and man in two distinct natures." Westminster L. C., 36. This statement is in opposition to Eutychianism, which asserts that the union of the Logos with a human nature results in a *single nature* of a third species, which nature is neither divine nor human, but theanthropic. Eutychianism is contradicted by Rom. 1 : 3, 4, which describes Christ *κατὰ σάρκα* and *κατὰ πνεῦμα ἁγιωσύνης*; and by Rom. 9 : 5, which describes him *κατὰ σάρκα* and as *ἐπὶ παντῶν Θεός*. Christ, in these and similar passages, is represented as having two natures, not one only. A nature is necessarily incomplex and simple. A person may be incomplex, like a trinitarian person who has only one nature, or complex, like a human person who has two natures, and a theanthropic person who has three natures A person may have two or more heterogeneous natures, but a nature cannot have two or more classes of heterogeneous properties. A substance or nature is homogeneous as to its qualities. A theanthropic *nature*, therefore, such as Eutyches supposed, having two classes of heterogeneous properties, the divine and the human, is inconceivable. We cannot think of a substance composed of both immaterial and material properties; a substance which is both mind and matter. This is Spinoza's error. But we can think of a person so composed. We cannot logically conceive of a

divine-human nature. It would be like an immaterial-material nature. But a person may be immaterial-material. Man is such.[1]

---

[1] Dorner (Christian Doctrine, III. 280) is Eutychian, in asserting that Christ had "a God-human nature," and in denominating "the God-human personality" "a God-humanity." This is confounding and mixing the natures. A "God-human nature" would be a theanthropic nature There is a "God-human," or theanthropic *person* having two natures, but not a "God-human," or theanthropic *nature* having two sets of properties, divine and human. A "God-humanity," strictly speaking, would be a Divine humanity that is, a human *nature* that is divine. But this is very different from a Divine-human *person*.

## CHAPTER IV.

### CHRIST'S UNIPERSONALITY.

THAT the two natures, the divine and the human, constitute only one person, is proved by the following Scripture texts: Rom. 1 : 3. Here, the one person called "Jesus Christ our Lord" is said to be "made of the seed of David according to the flesh," and "declared to be the Son of God, according to the spirit of holiness." This latter phrase, being antithetic to the phrase "according to the flesh," means "according to the divinity." Shedd: On Romans 1 : 4. Christ is described by St. Paul, *κατὰ σάρκα* and *κατὰ πνεῦμα ἁγιωσύνης*; the first denoting the human nature, the last the divine. Rom. 9 : 5. Here, Christ is represented as "God over all, blessed forever," and as having also a descent from the fathers of the Jewish nation. Phil. 2 : 6–11; 1 Tim. 3 : 16; Heb. 1 : 6–9 compared with Heb. 2 : 14; John 1 : 14; 1 John 1 : 1–3; 4 : 3; Gal. 4 : 4. Usher (Incarnation, Works, IV. 580) combines the Scripture data as follows: "He 'in whom dwelleth all the fulness of the Godhead bodily' is the *person;* that fulness which so doth dwell in him is the *natures.* Now, there dwelleth in him not only the fulness of the Godhead, but the fulness of the manhood also. For we believe him to be both perfect God, begotten of the substance of his Father before all worlds; and perfect man made of the substance of his mother in the fulness of time. And therefore we must hold that there are two distinct natures in him; and two so distinct that they do not make one compounded nature; but still remain uncompounded and unconfounded together. But he in whom the fulness of the manhood dwelleth is not one person, and he in whom the fulness of the Godhead dwelleth, another person; but he in whom the fulness of both these natures dwelleth is one and the same Immanuel, and consequently it must be believed as firmly that he is but one person."

That the two natures constitute only one person, is also proved by the fact that in Scripture human attributes are ascribed to the person as designated by a divine title; and divine attributes are ascribed to the person as designated by a human title. This interchange of titles and of attributes in respect to one and the same person proves that there are not two different persons, each having its own particular nature and attributes, but only one person having two natures and two classes of attributes in common.

1. Passages in which human attributes are ascribed to the person designated by a divine title are: Acts 20:28, The "blood of God."[1] Rom. 8:32, "God spared not his own son" (ἰδίου υἱοῦ). 1 Cor. 2:8, "They crucified the Lord of glory." Coloss. 1:13, 14, "Redemption through the blood τοῦ υἱοῦ τῆς ἀγάπης αὐτοῦ." Matt. 1:33, "A virgin shall bring forth a son, and they shall call his name Immanuel." Luke 1:31, 32, "The Son of the Highest is conceived in the womb."

2. Passages in which divine attributes are ascribed to the person designated by a human title are: John 3:13, "No man hath ascended up to heaven, but the Son of man which is in heaven." John 6:62, "What and if ye shall see the Son of man ascend up where he was before?" Rom. 9:5, "As concerning the flesh Christ came, who is God over all." Rev. 5:12, "Worthy is the Lamb that was slain to receive power."

From these Biblical representations, therefore, it follows that both human and divine qualities and acts may be attributed to the God-man under any of his names. If the

[1] The reading θεοῦ is supported by א B, Vulg Syr Rec Hort, κυρίου is supported by A C D E, Sahidic, Coptic, Tisch, Lachm.

God-man be called Jesus Christ, then it is proper to say that Jesus Christ raised the dead, and Jesus Christ died; that Jesus Christ is God, and Jesus Christ is man. If the God-man be called the Redeemer, then it is proper to say that the Redeemer created all things, and the Redeemer hungered and thirsted; that the Redeemer existed before Abraham, and the Redeemer was born eighteen centuries after Abraham. If the God-man be called Messiah, then it is proper to say that Messiah is seated upon the eternal throne, and Messiah was crucified, dead, and buried. In 1 Cor. 15, the God-man is called "Man," the "Second Man," and the "Last Adam," and divine acts are attributed. "By Man came also the resurrection of the dead." "The second Man is the Lord from heaven." "The last Adam was made a quickening spirit." It would be correct to say: "The last Adam groaned and wept: and the last Adam will judge the world." In Acts 20:28, the God-man is called "God," and human characteristics are attributed: viz., blood, and the pains of death. "Feed the church of God, which he hath purchased with his own blood." The term "God" here denotes *incarnate* God: a complex person, not an incomplex nature. In this use, the ecclesiastical phrase "God's blood" is proper.[1] So also is the expression, "God the mighty Maker died;" because "God" here designates the theanthropic person having two natures —God in the flesh—not the one abstract divine nature. It would be improper to say, "God's nature died," because this can have but one meaning. But it is proper to say "God died," because this may mean either "God's nature," or the "God-man;" either unincarnate or incarnate God; either the Logos or Jesus Christ. It would be proper to speak of the blood of Immanuel. But Immanuel means "God with us."

[1] "Virgo Maria non nudum aut merum hominem, sed verum dei filium, concepit et genuit. unde recte mater dei appellatur" Formula Concordiae, viii

The humanity assumed by the Logos is the Logos's or God's humanity; just as the body is the soul's body. When, therefore, the humanity suffers, it is as proper to say that it is "God's suffering," as it is when the body suffers, to say that is the "soul's suffering"—not meaning, thereby, the suffering of the soul considered separately as an immaterial substance, but of the soul as put for the total person. We speak of "the blood of souls," because the soul is united with a body that bleeds. Similarly, Scripture speaks of "the blood of God," because God is united with a humanity that has blood. "The matter of which the human body is composed does not subsist by itself, is not under all those laws of motion to which it would be subject if it were mere inanimated matter; but by the indwelling and actuation of the soul it has another spring within it, and has another course of operations According to this then, to 'subsist by another' is when a being is acting according to its natural properties but yet in a constant dependence upon another being; so our bodies subsist by the subsistence of our souls. This may help us to apprehend how that as a body is still a body, and operates as a body, though it subsists by the indwelling and actuation of the soul, so in the person of Jesus Christ, the human nature was entire, and still acting according to its own character, yet there was such an union and inhabitation of the Eternal Word in it, that there did arise out of that such a communication of names and characters as we find in the Scriptures. A man is called tall, fair, and healthy, from the state of his body; and learned, wise, and good, from the qualities of his mind; so Christ is called holy, harmless, and undefiled, is said to have died, risen, and ascended up into heaven, with relation to his human nature. He is also said to be in the form of God, to have created all things, to be the brightness of the Father's glory, with relation to the divine nature." Burnet: Thirty-nine Articles (Art. II.).

In accordance with this complex constitution of Christ's person, we find that his consciousness, as expressed in language, is sometimes divine and sometimes human. When he spoke the works: "I and my Father are one" (John 10: 30), the form of his consciousness at that instant was divine. The divine nature yielded the elements in this particular experience. When he spoke the words: "I thirst" (John 19 : 28), the form of his consciousness at that instant was human, or an experience whose elements were furnished by the human nature. When he said: "Now, O Father, glorify thou me with thine own self, with the glory which I had with thee before the world was" (John 17 : 5), his mode of consciousness at that instant was that of the eternal Word who was in the beginning with God. When he said: "My God, my God, why hast thou forsaken me?" (Matt. 27 : 46), his mode of consciousness was that of a finite creature deserted of his Creator.

In each of these instances, it was one and the same person, viz, Jesus Christ, who possessed the consciousness. The ego denoted by "I," in the phrase, "Which I had with thee before the world was," is the very same ego denoted by "I," in the phrase, "I thirst." There is no alteration in the person, but there is in the form of the consciousness. And this alteration arises from the fact that there are two natures in the person which furnish the materials of consciousness. Had Christ possessed, like an ordinary man, only a human nature, there could not have been this variety in the modes of his consciousness. A brute can have some of the forms of human consciousness. He can feel hunger, and thirst, and physical pain, like a man, because he has a physical nature like that of man. But he cannot experience religious emotions like joy in God, or aesthetic emotions like delight in beauty, or rational perceptions like the intuitions of geometry, because he has no rational nature like man. These modes of consciousness are precluded in his case, because there does not belong to his constitution that rational, aesthetic, and moral nature which alone can furnish the materials of such a consciousness. Man has two general forms of consciousness, the animal and the rational, because he is complex in his constitution; but the brute has only one form of consciousness, the animal, because he is simple in his constitution.

Similarly, there arise in the person of the God-man two general forms of consciousness, the divine and the human, because there are two distinct and specific natures in his person. When the human nature yields the matter of consciousness, Jesus Christ hungers, thirsts, sorrows, rejoices, and expresses his consciousness accordingly. When the divine nature yields the matter of consciousness, the very same Jesus Christ commands the raging sea to be still and it obeys; commands the dead Lazarus to rise and he obeys; says, "My Father worketh hitherto and I work;" "Before Abraham was, I am;" "I say unto you, that in this place is One greater than the temple"

This fluctuation of consciousness in the identity of a person is occurring continually in the sphere of human life. When a man says, "I am thirsty," the elements and form of his consciousness, at this particular instant, are furnished from his material and physical nature. When the same man says, with David, "I love the Lord, because he hath heard my voice and my supplications" (Ps. 116:1), the elements and form of his consciousness issue from his mental and spiritual nature. The difference between these two modes of consciousness, the sensuous and the spiritual, is as real and marked, though it is not as great, as between the divine and the human consciousness in the person of the God-man. And yet there is no schism in the person, or duplication of the person. It is the very same individual man who says, "I thirst," and "I love God."[1]

[1] When St Paul says "I hate what I do," and "with the mind I myself serve the law of God, but with the flesh I myself serve the law of sin" (Rom 7 15, 25), the two modes of consciousness spring out of one nature, viz., the

These varying modes and forms of consciousness chase each other over the field of human personality like the shadows of the clouds over a landscape. At one moment, the man's experience is sensuous. At another, perhaps the very next moment, it is intensely spiritual. If the nature of the individual person should be inferred from the sensuous consciousness in him, we should say that he is nothing but an animal; if only from the spiritual consciousness in him, we should say that he is nothing but a spirit. Putting the two together, we say that the person who has these different modes of conscious experience is "human." We do not say, using terms strictly, that he is a sensuous person, though he has a sensuous nature. We do not say that he is a spiritual person, though he has a spiritual nature. "Human" is the proper denomination of the person.

In like manner, in the complex person of Christ there was a continual fluctuation of consciousness, according as the divine or the human nature was uppermost, so to speak, in the self-consciousness. At one moment, he felt and spoke as a weak, dependent, and finite creature; at the next instant, he felt and spoke as an almighty, self-existent, and infinite being. The finite and infinite, man and God, the creature and creator, time and eternity, met and mingled in that wonderful Person who was not divine solely, or human solely, but divine-human "There is," says Bengel, on Mark 13 : 32, "an admirable variety in the motions of the soul [i.e., in the self-consciousness] of Christ. Sometimes he had an elevated feeling, so as hardly to seem to remember that he was a man walking on the earth; sometimes he had a lowly feeling, so that he might almost have seemed to forget that he was the Lord from heaven. And he was wont always to express himself according to his mental feeling for the time being; at one time, as he who was one with the Father; at another time, again, in such a manner as if

mental or spiritual, and are both alike mental This would not illustrate the difference in the consciousness that arises from two diverse natures

he were only of that condition in which are all ordinary and human saints. Often, these two are blended together in wonderful variety."

At this point, it is proper to notice the effect of Christ's exaltation upon his humanity. When the humiliation of Christ ends and his exaltation begins, the human nature, though still unchanged in its essential properties, no longer yields certain elements of consciousness which it previously yielded. Christ on the mediatorial throne hungers no more, and suffers no more. Certain *accidental* properties are left behind, but all *essential* properties of humanity are retained. The exalted human nature still keeps its finiteness. It is not invested with infinite properties. It does not acquire omnipotence, omniscience, and omnipresence by Christ's exaltation. It is man's nature still. The change which occurs in the instance of the perfected nature of a redeemed man illustrates the alteration in Christ's human nature. "Flesh and blood cannot inherit the kingdom of God," and yet the redeemed are as really and truly men as they ever were. But there will be certain modes of consciousness which the redeemed experienced when upon earth that will be impossible to them in heaven. Not because they are different persons in heaven from what they were upon earth, but because there has been a change wrought in their physical nature by the resurrection and glorification of their bodies, so that this nature, though human and physical still, does not need meat and drink as it did while upon earth, and is not liable to sickness, suffering, and death, as it was here below. Those modes of consciousness which involved pain and suffering, which man was capable of here upon earth by reason of the state and condition of his body while here upon earth, are no longer possible to him as redeemed and glorified in heaven. And so, likewise, those experiences of earthly suffering and sorrow which Christ passed through in his state of humiliation, will constitute no part of his self-consciousness in his state of exaltation.

While, in this way, the acts and qualities of either nature may be attributed to the one theanthropic *person*, the acts and qualities of one *nature* may not be attributed to the other nature. It would be erroneous to say, that the divine nature suffered, or that the human nature raised the dead; as it would be erroneous to say that the human body thinks, or that the human soul walks. The man, or "person" whose is the body and whose is the soul, both thinks and walks; but the natures by whose instrumentality he performs these acts do not both of them think and walk. One thinks, and the other walks.

Properties belong to a nature, and are confined to it. Hence properties are always homogeneous. A material nature or substance can have only material properties. It cannot be marked partly by material and partly by immaterial properties. Natures, on the other hand, belong to a person, and may be heterogeneous. A nature must be composed wholly of material, or wholly of immaterial properties; but a person may be composed partly of a material, and partly of an immaterial nature. Hence two, or even three kinds of natures may be ascribed to a person, but only one kind of properties may be attributed to a nature.

By overlooking the difference between person and nature, the Later-Lutherans have partially revived the ancient error of Eutyches, of confounding or mixing the natures in Christ's person. They distinguish three kinds of "communicatio idiomatum," or communication of properties: namely, genus idiomaticum—the attribution of the properties of either nature to the person; genus apotelesmaticum—the attribution of the mediatorial acts to either nature; and genus majestaticum The last of these is of such an exalted species as to amount to a communication of the properties of one nature to the other. It is founded upon those texts in which, according to Hase's definition of this genus, the Scriptures speak of "the human nature as exalted by divine attributes: quibus natura humana attributis divinis effertur," Hutterus, p. 238. The texts in which this is supposed to be done are such as John 3:13, "The Son of man is in heaven;" John 5:27, "The son of man has authority to execute judgment;" Matt. 28:18, 20, "All power is given unto me. I am with you alway;" Rom. 9:5, "Concerning the flesh, Christ is God over all, blessed forever;" Phil. 2:10, "At the name of Jesus, every knee shall bow." In these passages, the titles "Son of man," "Jesus," and "Christ," according to the advocate of the genus majestaticum, denote, not the theanthropic *person*, but the human *nature;* and this human nature is exalted by the divine attributes of omnipresence—being upon earth and in heaven simultaneously; of sovereignty—being the judge of mankind; of omnipotence—having all power in heaven and earth; of absolute deity—being God over all.

The foundation for this view is laid in the Formula Concordiae, though this creed is somewhat wavering and contradictory, and not so pronounced as later individual theologians. It affirms that by the glorification of the human nature, after Christ's resurrection, this human nature received, in addition to its own natural essential properties, certain "supernatural, inscrutable, ineffable, and celestial prerogatives of majesty, glory, virtue, and power above everything that is named in time or eternity," Hase: Libri Symbolici, 774. This, however, is guarded by the affirmation that "hae duae naturae in persona Christi nunquam confunduntur, vel altera in alteram mutatur," Hase: Libri Symbolici, 762; that "unius naturae proprietates essentiales nunquam alterius naturae proprietates essentiales fiunt," Hase: Libri Symbolici, 763; "that in hac unione, utraque natura essentiam et proprietates suas retinet." Hase: Libri Symbolici, 765. But these statements, again, are modified, and seemingly contradicted, by the affirmation that Christ "non tantum ut deus, verum etiam ut *homo*, ubique praesens dominatur et regnat a mari ad mare, et usque ad terminos terrae;" and that Christ's promise to be continually with his apostles, co-operating with them, and confirming their word with attending miraculous signs, was fulfilled "not in an earthly manner (non terreno modo), but as Luther was wont to say, after the manner and method of God's right hand: which certainly does not mean a certain circumscribed locality in heaven, as the Sacramentarians claim, but denotes the omnipotent energy (virtus) of God, which fills heaven and earth, into possession of which Christ according to his *humanity* (juxta humanitatem suam) really and truly came, yet without any confusion or equalizing of the natures," Hase: Libri Symbolici, 768. This last clause is contradictory to preceding statements in the creed, unless it can be shown that Christ's human nature can have the attributes of omnipresence and omnipotence without any equalizing of the natures, and without causing any essential property of the divine nature to become a property of the human nature.[1] In a similar contradictory manner, Brentz (De incarnatione Christi, p. 1001) affirms that the humanity of Christ is omnipotent and omnipresent, and yet is not omnipotence itself. Quoted by Bruce: Humiliation of Christ, p. 113.

Later Lutheran theologians are more explicit and self-consistent, than the Formula Concordiae. Hollaz defines the "genus majestaticum" as that mode "quo filius dei idiomata divinae suae naturae humanae naturae, propter unionem personalem, vere et realiter communicavit, ad communem possessionem, usurpationem, et denominationem," Hase: Hutterus, p. 238. He asserts that "subjectum, cui data est majestas divina, est Christus secundum *humanam naturam*, vel quod idem est, humana natura in ὑπόστασιν τοῦ Λογόυ assumpta," Hase: Hutterus, p. 238. He defines the communicatio idiomatum in the following terms: "Communi-

---

[1] A similar self-contradiction is found in the Formula Concordiae, respecting the doctrine of predestination and election. See Muller: Sin, II. pp. 228–230. Urwick's Trans.

catio naturaram in persona Christi est mutua divinae et humanae Christi naturae participatio, per quam natura divina τοῦ Λογόυ particeps facta humanae naturae, hanc permeat, perficit, inhabitat, sibique appropriat; humana vero particeps facta divinae naturae, ab hac permeatur, perficitur et inhabitatur," Hase: Hutterus, p. 234. According to this Lutheran definition, the "communication of idioms," or of properties, means far more than the Reformed divines meant by it. The latter intended by it only the communication of the properties of both natures to the *person* constituted of them. In the Lutheran use, it denotes the communication of the properties of one nature to the other *nature.* It is thus the communication of a nature to a nature, rather than of properties to a person.[1] Similarly, Hahn (Hase: Hutterus, p. 238) says: "Genus majestaticum continet propositiones quibus de natura humana idiomata naturae divinae praedicantur." Gerhard (Loci IV. xii.) says: "We teach that the [human] soul of Jesus in the very first moment of the incarnation was personally enriched, as with other excellences, so also with the proper omniscience of the Logos, through, and in virtue of, the intimate union and communion with the Logos. But as he did not always use his other excellences in the state of exinanition, so also the omniscience personally communicated to him he did not always exercise." Quoted by Bruce: Humiliation of Christ, p. 143.

The principal motive for the Lutheran tenet of the ubiquity of Christ's humanity is, to explain the presence of the *entire* Christ. The God-man promises to be with his disciples upon earth, "alway, even unto the end of the world," Matt. 28: 20. The Reformed explanation is, by the *conjunction* and *union* of the limited and local humanity with the illocal and omnipresent divinity. "Presence by way of conjunction is in some sort presence," says Hooker (V. lv.). The divine

[1] Dorner so understands it "The Reformed disown the communication of essence, of the Lutherans" Christian Doctrine, § 93, 95.

nature of Christ is present with his human nature wherever the latter may be, though his human nature is not, as the Lutheran contends, present with his divine nature wherever the latter may be. But this continual presence of the deity with the humanity is *equivalent* to the presence of the humanity with the deity. The humanity is in effect ubiquitous, because of its personal connection with an omnipresent nature, and not because it is in itself so immense as to be ubiquitous. Christ's deity never is present anywhere in isolation and separation from his humanity, but always as united with and *modified* by his humanity. But in order to this union and modification, it is not necessary that his humanity should be locally present wherever his deity is. Distance in space is no bar to the personal union between the Logos and his human nature. Suppose, for illustration, the presence of the divine nature of Christ in the soul of a believer while partaking of the sacrament in London. This divine nature is at the same moment conjoined with, and present to, and modified by the human nature of Christ which is in heaven, and not in London. This conjunction between both is equivalent to the presence of both. The whole Christ is present in this London believer's soul, because, though the human nature is in heaven and not in London, it is yet personally united with the divine nature which is both in heaven and in London. There is no separation between the two natures; so that whatever influence or effect the divine nature exerts in the believer's soul as he receives the sacrament is a *divine-human* influence—an influence proceeding from the union of the divine with the human in Jesus Christ.

The union of the two natures in Christ's person is denominated *hypostatical*, that is personal. The two natures, or substances (*οὐσίαι*), constitute one personal subsistence (*ὑπόστασις*). A common illustration employed by the Chalcedon and later fathers is, the union of the human soul and body in one person, and the union of heat and iron, neither of which loses its own properties. Formula Concordiae, Hase: Libri Symbolici, p. 765.

The doctrine of the two natures implies the doctrine of *two wills* in Christ. Either nature would be incomplete and defective, without the voluntary quality or property in it. Each nature, in order to be whole and entire, must have all of its essential elements. A human nature without voluntariness would be as defective as it would be without rationality.

The Monothelite party regarded the two natures as having only one *theanthropic* will between them: *μία θεανδρίκη ἐνεργεῖα.* From the union of the two natures there resulted a will that was not divine solely, nor human solely, but divine-human. The Monothelite contention was, that "the one Christ works that which is divine, and that which is human, by one divine-human mode of agency." Neander: History, III. 177. This was in reality a conversion of the two natures, so far as the voluntary property in the nature is concerned, into a third species which is neither divine nor human. It was thus a modified Eutychianism.

In opposition to this error, the catholic theologians asserted two wills in order to the completeness of each nature, and met the objection of the Monothelites that there must then be two persons, by affirming that by reason of the intimate personal union of the two natures neither will works without the other's *participation* in the efficiency. If the human will acts, the divine will submits and co-acts. This is the humiliation of the divine. If the divine will acts, the human will submits and co-acts. This is the exaltation of the human. One and the same Christ, therefore, performs the divine or the human action, as the case may be, although each action is wrought in accordance with the distinctive qualities of the will that corresponds with it, and takes the lead in it. Moreover, as the human will in Christ was sinless, there was no antagonism between it and the will of the Logos. This is taught in the words, "Nevertheless, not my will, but thine be done," Luke 22 : 42. Thus, in any agency of the God-man, although there are two wills concerned in it, a divine and a human, there is but one resulting action. Two wills are not incompatible with a single self-consciousness, even when they are not hypostatically united in one person. The divine will works in the regenerate will "to will and to do," and yet there is not duality in the self-consciousness of the regenerate man.

We have already observed, that the personalizing of the human nature by its union with the Logos is seen in the fact, that the activities of the human nature appear as factors in the single self-consciousness of the God-man. He is conscious of finite inclination, and finite volitions; this proves that there is voluntariness in the human nature that has been individualized. He is conscious also of finite and limited perceptions, judgments, and conclusions; this proves that there is rationality in the human nature that has been individualized. These two elements or properties of human nature, the rational and the voluntary, are no longer dormant, as they are in all non-individualized human nature, but are active and effective in the one self-conscious person Jesus Christ. And one of them is as necessary as the other, to the wholeness and completeness of the human nature. To omit the will from the humanity, is as truly an error as to omit the reason; and therefore the Monothelites deviated from the true doctrine as really as did the Apollinarians.

## CHAPTER V.

### CHRIST'S IMPECCABILITY.

THE doctrine of Christ's person is not complete without considering the subject of his impeccability. That he was sinless is generally acknowledged [1] But the holiness of the God-man is more than sinlessness. The last Adam differs from the first Adam, by reason of his impeccability. He was characterized not only by the posse non peccare, but the non posse peccare. He was not only able to overcome temptation, but he was unable to be overcome by it.

An impeccable will is one that is so mighty in its self-determination to good that it cannot be conquered by any temptation to evil, however great. A will may be positively holy and able to overcome temptation, and yet not be so omnipotent in its holy energy that it cannot be overcome. The angels who fell could have repelled temptation with that degree of power given them by creation, and so might Adam. But in neither case was it infallibly certain that they would repel it. Though they were holy, they were not impeccable. Their will could be overcome, because it was not omnipotent, and their perseverance was left to themselves and not made sure by extraordinary grace. The case of Jesus Christ, the second Adam, was different, in that he was not only able to resist temptation, but it was infallibly certain that he would resist it. The holy energy

---

[1] Neander Life of Christ, p 77 sq. Ed. Bohn Jeremy Taylor: Life of Christ, Sect. iii. Ullmann Sinlessness of Jesus, III. i. ii. Trench · Studies in the Gospels (The Temptation) Ullmann is profound and thoughtful upon Christ's sinlessness, but deficient on the subject of his impeccability. Edwards (Will, III. ii ) asserts Christ's impeccability.

of his will was not only sufficiently strong to overcome, but was so additionally strong that it could not be overcome.

The Scripture proof of Christ's impeccability is the following:

1. The immutability of Christ, taught in Heb. 13:8, pertains to all the characteristics of his person. His holiness is one of the most important of these. If the God-man, like Adam, had had a holiness that was mutable and might be lost, it would be improper to speak of him in terms that are applicable only to the unchangeable holiness of God. He would not be "holy, harmless, and undefiled, yesterday, to-day, and forever."

2. A mutable holiness would be incompatible with other divine attributes ascribed to the God-man. (*a*) The possibility of being overcome by temptation is inconsistent with the omnipotence of Christ. It implies that a finite power can overcome an infinite one. All temptation to sin must proceed from a created being: either man, or fallen angel. Temptation proper, in distinction from God's paternal trial, must always be finite. God tempts no man, in the strict sense of the term (James 1:13). But if a finite temptation is met by an infinite power of resistance, the result must be the failure of the temptation, and not the defeat of the tempted person. (*b*) The success of temptation depends, in part, upon deceiving the person tempted. "Adam was not deceived, but the woman being deceived was in the transgression," 1 Tim. 2:14. A finite intelligence may be deceived, but an infinite intelligence cannot be. Therefore, the omniscience which characterizes the God-man made his apostasy from good impossible.

3. A mutable holiness is irreconcilable with the fact that the God-man is the author of holiness. He is the "author and finisher of our faith," Heb. 12:2. He is denominated the "last Adam" in distinction from the first, and as such he is "a quickening spirit," 1 Cor. 15:45. This means that unlike the first Adam he is the fountain of spiritual and

holy life for others; and this implies the unchangeable nature of his own holiness. In Rom. 1:4, the divine nature of Christ is described as "a spirit of holiness." The genitive, here, is not equivalent to an adjective, but denotes that the noun which it limits is a source of the quality spoken of.

In accordance with these statements of Scripture respecting the person of Christ, the symbols and theologians have generally affirmed his impeccability.[1] Augustine and Anselm attribute this characteristic to him. Neander: History, IV. 495, 496.

The truth and self-consistence of the doctrine of Christ's impeccability appear, also, from a consideration of the constitution of his person.

Christ's person is constituted of two natures: one divine, and the other human. The divine nature is both intemptable, and impeccable. "God cannot be tempted with evil," James 1:13. "It is impossible for God to lie," Hebrews 6:18. The human nature, on the contrary, is both temptable and peccable. When these two natures are *united* in one theanthropic person, as they are in the incarnation, the divine determines and controls the human, not the human the divine. See pp. 269 sq. The amount of energy, therefore, which the total complex person possesses to resist temptation, must be measured not by the human nature but by the divine; and the amount of energy to resist temptation determines the peccability or impeccability of the person. Jesus Christ, consequently, is as mighty to overcome Satan and sin, as his mightiest nature is. His strength to prevent a lapse from holiness is to be estimated by his divinity, not by his humanity, because the former and not the latter is

[1] It is remarkable, that a theologian of such soundness and accuracy as the elder Hodge should deny the impeccability of the God-man "The sinlessness of our Lord," he says (Theology, II. 457), "does not amount to absolute impeccability It was not a non potest peccare Temptation implies the possibility of sin. If from the constitution of his person it was impossible for Christ to sin, then his temptation was unreal and without effect, and he cannot sympathize with his people."

the base of his personality, and dominates the whole complex person.

Consequently, what might be done by the human nature if *alone*, and by itself, cannot be done by it in this *union* with omnipotent holiness. An iron wire by itself can be bent and broken in a man's hand; but when the wire is welded into an iron bar, it can no longer be so bent and broken. And yet iron, whether in a bar or in a wire, is a ductile and flexible metal; and human nature, whether in a God-man or a mere man, is a temptable and fallible nature. A mere man can be overcome by temptation, but a God-man cannot be. When, therefore, it is asked if the person named Jesus Christ, and constituted of two natures, was peccable, the answer must be in the negative. For in this case the divine nature comes into the account. As this is confessedly omnipotent, it imparts to the person Jesus Christ this divine characteristic. The omnipotence of the Logos preserves the finite human nature from falling, however great may be the stress of temptation to which this finite nature is exposed. Consequently, Christ while having a peccable human *nature* in his constitution, was an impeccable *person*. Impeccability characterizes the God-man as a totality, while peccability is a property of his humanity.

But it may be asked, If the properties of either nature may be attributed to the person of the God-man, why may not both peccability and impeccability be attributed to the person of the God-man. We say that Jesus Christ is both finite and infinite, passible and impassible, impotent and omnipotent, ignorant and omniscient, why may we not also say that he is both peccable and impeccable? If the union in one person of the two natures allows of the attribution of contrary characteristics to the one God-man in these former instances, why not also in this latter?

Because, in this latter instance, the divine nature cannot *innocently* and *righteously* leave the human nature to its own finiteness without any support from the divine, as it can in the other instances. When the Logos goes into union with a human nature, so as to constitute a single person with it, he becomes responsible for all that this person does through the instrumentality of this nature. The glory or the shame, the merit or the blame, as the case may be, is attributable to this one person of the God-man. If, therefore, the Logos should make no resistance to the temptation with which Satan assailed the human nature in the wilderness, and should permit the humanity to yield to it and commit sin, he would be implicated in the apostasy and sin. The guilt would not be confined to the human nature. It would attach to the whole theanthropic person. And since the Logos is the root and base of the person, it would attach to him in an eminent manner. Should Jesus Christ sin, incarnate God would sin.

In reference, therefore, to such a characteristic as *sin*, the divine nature may not desert the human nature and leave it to itself. In reference to all other characteristics, it may. The divine nature may leave the human nature alone, so that there shall be ignorance of the day of judgment, so that there shall be physical weakness and pain, so that there shall be mental limitation and sorrow, so that there shall be desertion by God and the pangs of death. There is no sin or guilt in any of these. These characteristics may all attach to the total person of the God-man without any aspersion upon his infinite purity and holiness. They do, indeed, imply the humiliation of the Logos, but not his culpability. Suffering is humiliation, but not degradation or wickedness. The Logos could consent to suffer in a human nature, but not to sin in a human nature. The God-man was commissioned to suffer (John 10 : 18), but was not commissioned to sin.

Consequently, all the innocent defects and limitations of the finite may be attributed to Jesus Christ, but not its culpable defects and limitations. The God-man may be weak, or sorrowful, or hungry, or weary; he may be crucified, dead, and buried; but he may not be sinful and guilty. For this reason, the divine nature constantly supports the human nature under all the temptations to sin that are presented to it. It never deserts it in this case. It empowers it with an energy of resistance that renders it triumphant over the subtlest and strongest solicitations to transgress the law of God. It deserts the humanity so that it may suffer for the atonement of sin, but it never deserts the humanity so that it may fall into sin itself. When Christ cried, "My God, why hast thou forsaken me?" the desertion of the finite by the infinite nature occurred in order that there might be suffering, not that there might be sin. The divine nature, at the very moment of this agony and passion, was sustaining the human nature so that it should not sinfully yield to what was the most powerful temptation ever addressed to a human nature: namely, the temptation to flee from and escape the immense atoning agony, which the God-man had covenanted with the Father to undergo. This is implied in Christ's words, "If it be possible, let this cup pass; nevertheless, not my will but thine be done. The cup that my Father giveth me, shall I not drink it?"

Again, the impeccability of Christ is proved by the relation of the two wills in his person to each other. Each nature, in order to be complete, entire, and wanting nothing, has its own will; but the finite will never antagonizes the infinite will, but obeys it invariably and perfectly. If this should for an instant cease to be the case, there would be a conflict in the self consciousness of Jesus Christ similar to that in the self-consciouness of his apostle Paul. He too would say, "The good that I would, I do not; but the evil which I would not, that I do. It is no more I that do it, but sin that dwelleth in me. O wretched man that I am, who shall deliver me?" Rom 7:19, 20, 24. But there is no such utterance as this from the lips of the God-man. On the contrary, there is the calm inquiry of Christ: "Which of you convinceth me of sin?" John 8:46; and the confident affirmation of St. John: "In him was no sin," 1 John 3:5. There is an utter absence of personal confession of sin, in any form whatever, either in the conversation or the prayers of Jesus Christ. There is no sense of indwelling sin. He could not describe his religious experience as his apostle does, and his people do: "The flesh lusteth against the spirit, and the spirit against the flesh," Gal. 5:17

It is objected to the doctrine of Christ's impeccability that it is inconsistent with his temptability. A person who cannot sin, it is said, cannot be tempted to sin.

This is not correct; any more than it would be correct to say that because an army cannot be conquered, it cannot be attacked. Temptability depends upon the constitutional *susceptibility*, while impeccability depends upon the *will*. So far as his natural susceptibility, both physical and mental, was concerned, Jesus Christ was open to all forms of human temptation excepting those that spring out of lust, or corruption of nature. But his peccability, or the possibility of being overcome by these temptations, would depend upon the amount of voluntary resistance which he was able to bring to bear against them. Those temptations were very strong, but if the self-determination of his holy will was stronger than they, then they could not induce him to sin, and he would be impeccable. And yet plainly he would be temptable.

That an impeccable being can be tempted, is proved by the instance of the elect angels. Having "kept their first estate," they are now impeccable, not by their own inherent power, but by the power of God bestowed upon them. But they might be tempted still, though we have reason to believe that they are not. Temptability is one of the necessary limitations of the finite spirit. No creature is beyond the possibility of temptation, though he may, by grace, be beyond the possibility of yielding to temptation. The only being who cannot be tempted is God. ὁ γὰρ Θεὸς ἀπείραστος, James 1:13. And this, from the nature of an Infinite Being. Ambition of some sort is the motive at the bottom of all temptation. When the creature is tempted, it is suggested to him to endeavor to "be as gods." He is incited to strive for a higher place in the grade of being than he now occupies. But this, of course, cannot apply to the Supreme Being. He is already God over all and blessed forever. He, therefore, is absolutely intemptable.

Again, redeemed men in heaven are impeccable through the grace and power of Christ their head. Yet they are still temptable, though not exposed to temptation. Redemption, while it secures from the possibility of a second apostasy, does not alter the finite nature of man. He is still a temptable creature.

And, in like manner, Christ the God-man was temptable, though impeccable. But his impeccability, unlike that of the elect angels and redeemed men, is due not to grace but to the omnipotent and immutable holiness of the Logos in his person. One of the reasons mentioned in Scripture (Heb. 2:14–18) for the assumption of a human nature into union with the second person of the Trinity is, that this person might be tempted. The Logos previous to the incarnation could not be tempted. The human nature was the avenue to temptation; but the divine nature so empowered and actuated the human, the divine will so strengthened the human will, that no conceivable stress of temptation could overcome Jesus Christ, and bring about the apostasy of the second Adam.

The temptability of Christ through his human nature may be illustrated by the temptability of a man through his sensuous nature. A man's body is the avenue of sensual solicitation to his soul. A certain class of human temptations are wholly physical. They could not present themselves through the mental, or immaterial part of man. Take away the body, and the man could not be assailed by this class of temptations. These, it is true, do not constitute the whole of human temptations. Fallen man is tempted through his soul, as well as through his body. But we can distinguish between the two inlets of temptation. Now, as the mind of man, which may be called his higher nature, is approached by temptation through the body, which is his lower nature, so the divinity of Christ, which is his higher nature, was approached by temptation through his humanity, which is his lower nature. The God-man was temptable through his human nature, not though his divine; and he was impeccable because of his divine nature, not because of his human.

Temptability and peccability may be in inverse proportion to each other, and this proves that the two things are entirely distinct and diverse. There may be a great temptation with little possibility of its succeeding, owing to the great strength of character, and the great voluntary resistance that is made. Here, there is great temptability, and little peccability. A very strong temptation is required to overcome a very virtuous person. The God-fearing man must be plied with far more solicitation than the irreligious man, in order to bring about a fall into sin. Some saintly men repel a species and stress of solicitation, which, if it were applied to some vicious men, would cause them to sin immediately. To such apply the lines of Watts:

> "Nor can a bold temptation draw
> His steady soul aside."

The patriarch Joseph was as strongly tempted as ever Charles II. was, but there was less possibility of yielding to temptation, that is, less peccability. A godly poor man with a suffering family whom he tenderly loves may be as strongly tempted to steal, or embezzle, for the sake of his family, as an ungodly poor man in a similar case, but the peccability of the former is less than that of the latter. And for the reason that has been mentioned, namely that the temptability is in the susceptibility, but the peccability is in the will. And while the susceptibility, or sensibility to the solicitation, may be the same in two men, the wills of the two men have become very different from each other. The will of one has been renewed, and endowed with a divine energy of resistance, while the other possesses only the power of a self-enslaved faculty.

Upon the same principle, there may be the very greatest degree of temptation, where there is no possibility at all of its succeeding; there may be the highest temptability and absolute impeccability. Such we suppose to have been the case of the God-man. He had a perfectly pure human nature which was exceedingly sensitive, because of this purity, to all innocent desires and cravings. No human being ever felt the gnawings of hunger as he experienced them after the forty days' fast, during which he was miraculously kept alive "and was *afterwards* an hungered," Matt. 3 : 4. No human being ever felt a deeper sorrow under bereavement, than he felt at the death of Lazarus, when the God-man wept. No human soul was ever filled with such an awful agony of pain, as that which expressed itself in the words, "My God, why hast thou forsaken me?" and which had previously forced the globules of blood through the pores of the flesh. "The Lord Jesus endured most grievous torments immediately in his soul, and most painful sufferings in his body." Westminster Confession, VIII iv. It is to this extreme sensibility, and susceptibility, and temptability, that our Lord alludes, when he says (Luke 22 : 28, 29), "Ye are they which have continued with me in my temptations. And I appoint unto you a kingdom, as my Father hath appointed unto me, that ye may eat and drink at my table in my kingdom, and sit on thrones judging the twelve tribes of Israel." And when he says (Matt 26 : 41) with the deepest emphasis, because of the experience he had just passed through, and of the experience which he knew he was yet to have, "Watch and pray that ye enter not into temptation; the spirit indeed is willing but the flesh is weak." And when, in reference to this whole subject, he both permits and commands tempted man to pray, "Lead us not into temptation, but deliver us from evil."

The fact is, that as there may be the most violent attack upon a strategic point where there is an invincible power of resistance, so there may be the most extreme and powerful of temptations addressed to a person in whom there is absolute impeccability. A holy God-man, who can meet Satan's solicitation with an almighty energy of opposition, will be assailed by a fiercer trial than an irresolute sinful man would experience. A far heavier ordnance will be brought to bear upon Gibraltar than upon a packet-boat. Christ was exposed to a severer test and trial than the first Adam was. And this, for the very reason that his resistance was so steady, and so mighty. Had he showed signs of yielding, or had he succumbed in the outset, the stress of the temptation would have been far less than it actually was. Had the first temptation in the wilderness succeeded, it would not have been followed by the second and third. But the more the God-man baffled the tempter, the more the tempter returned to the charge, and intensified his attack.

Neither let it be supposed that our Lord's temptations were slight, because they were sinless. An innocent temptation may be greater in its force than a sinful one. Christ was solicited by sinless temptation more strongly than any man ever was by sinful temptation No drunkard, or sensualist was ever allured by vicious appetite so fiercely as Christ was by innocent appetite, when after the forty days "he was a hungered." For the stress of the appetite was supernaturally heightened in this instance. A natural appetite may be stronger, and more difficult to control, than an unnatural and vicious one. The craving of the glutton for artificial sauces, and highly seasoned food, is not so intense as the hunger of the traveller in the desert who is upon the brink of starvation. The thirst of the inebriate, great as it is, is not so dreadful and overpowering as that of an English soldier in the Black Hole of Calcutta, or of a negro slave in the middle passage.

Furthermore, the innocent temptations of Christ were made more stringent and powerful, by reason of the steady resistance which he offered to them. Temptations that are accompanied with struggle and opposition against them are fiercer than those that are not so accompanied. The good man, in this way, often feels the distress of temptation far more than the bad man. The latter yields supinely, and making no opposition does not experience the anguish of a struggle. The former is greatly wearied and strained by his temptation, though he is not conquered by it. Christ "resisted unto blood, striving against sin, and offered up prayers and supplications with strong crying and tears unto him that was able to save him from death." But his people "have not so resisted." Heb 12:4; 5:7.

At this point, it is necessary to notice the difference between the temptability of Christ, and that of a fallen man; for while there is a resemblance, there is also a dissimilarity between them Christ's temptations were all of them *sinless*, but very many of the temptations of a fallen man are *sinful:* that is, they are the hankering and solicitation of forbidden and wicked desire. The desire to steal, to commit adultery, to murder, is sinful, and whoever is tempted by it to the act of theft, or adultery, or murder, is sinfully tempted. St. James (1:14) refers to this species of temptation, when he says that "a man is tempted, when he is drawn away by his own lust and enticed." The *ἐπιθυμία* here spoken of is the same which St. Paul mentions in Rom. 7:7, as the equivalent of *ἁμαρτία*. It is also the same thing that is forbidden in the tenth commandment, "Thou shalt not lust"—which Luther (Von Gerlach's Ed, V. 25) renders: "Du sollst nicht bose Begierden haben." St. James (1:2, 3) bids the believer to "count it all joy when he falls into divers [innocent] temptations" by the will and providence of God, "knowing this, that the trial of his faith worketh patience," but he does not bid him to count it all joy when he is tempted and drawn away by his own lust.

A man, for illustration, is sinfully tempted, when he is solicited to perform a certain outward act, say to preach a sermon, by the craving of pride or ambition. This craving or inward lust after human applause is itself sin (John 5:44; 12:43; Rom. 1:25), and to be tempted by it, is to be sinfully tempted. It is idolatry, or creature-worship, in the heart. Even if he does not perform the outward act to which his pride or ambition tempted and urged him, he must repent of his wicked lust or pride of heart, and obtain forgiveness for it. This is taught in Acts 8:21, 22. "Thy heart is not right in the sight of God. Repent, therefore, of this thy wickedness [of heart], and pray God if peradventure the thought (*ἐπίνοια*, purpose) of thine heart may be forgiven thee." Simon Magus's particular lust was avarice; it was wickedness (*κακία*), and needed the exercise of mercy. Had it been an innocent desire, he might have continued to have it, and needed not to repent of it.

When, again, a man is solicited by the lust of gluttony to perform the external act of intemperate eating of food for the sake of the sensual pleasure of eating, he is not innocently but sinfully tempted. This is wholly different from the solicitation of the natural and innocent appetite for food, such as a famishing sailor on a wreck experiences; such as our Lord felt when having "fasted forty days and forty nights he was afterwards a hungered." The craving of gluttony is vicious, and whoever is tempted by it is sinfully tempted. Gluttony is not merely and only physical appetite, but contains also a mental and voluntary element. It *thinks* of eating as enjoyment, and *calculates* for this. Hunger, pure and simple, on the contrary, is physical merely, not mental and voluntary. Gluttony is a part of original sin; it is the corruption of human nature as respects the body.

Now our Lord was not tempted by the sinful lusts of pride, ambition, envy, malice, hatred, anger, jealousy, avarice, gluttony, voluptuousness, drunkenness; in short by evil desire or "concupiscence" of any kind. He never felt the hankering of pride and vain-glory so common to man, but was always in his inmost spirit meek and lowly. The appeal of Satan, in the last of the three temptations, to a supposed pride and ambition in Christ, was met with the avaunt: "Get thee hence, Satan" Christ had no sinful lust of any sort. This is taught in Christ's own words: "The prince of this world cometh, and hath nothing in me," John 14:30. It is also taught in Heb. 4:15, "We have a high priest who was in all points tempted like as we are, yet without sin." This text teaches that the temptations of Christ were "without sin" in their *source* and *nature*, and not merely, as the passage is sometimes explained, that they were "without sin" in their *result*. The meaning is not, that our Lord was tempted in every respect exactly as fallen man is—by inward lust, as well as by other temptations—only he did not outwardly yield to any temptation; but that he was tempted in every way that man is, excepting by that class of temptations that are sinful because originating in evil and forbidden desire.[1] This is evident, because, in the original, *χωρὶς ἁμαρτίας* qualifies *πεπειρασμένον*. Christ was tempted without sin, or sinlessly, in all points like as we are."[2]

[1] When the Westminster Larger Catechism, 37, affirms that "Christ was born of the Virgin Mary, yet without sin," the meaning is not that he "was born of the Virgin Mary, yet did not commit sin," but that he "was born sinless of the Virgin Mary"

[2] The preposition *χωρὶς* denotes entire separation (*χωρίζειν*) The author of this Epistle frequently uses it Heb 7 21, "Those priests were made without an oath" (*χωρὶς ὁρκωμοσίας*). Their consecration was oathless Heb 9:18, "The first testament was not dedicated without blood" (*χωρὶς αἵματος*). The

Temptations from evil desire have a different moral quality from those presented through innocent desire. The former are δὶ ἁμαρτίας, or ἐξ ἁμαρτίας, not χωρὶς ἁμαρτίας. A temptation from pride, envy, or malice, is plainly different in its nature from the temptation from hunger experienced by our Lord in the wilderness; or from the desire to be acknowledged as the Messiah; or from the dread of suffering experienced by him in the garden of Gethsemane. "When a temptation comes from *without*," says Owen (Indwelling Sin, VI.), "it is unto the soul an indifferent thing, neither good nor evil, unless it be consented to. But the very proposal from *within*, it being the soul's own act, is its sin. Christ had more temptations from Satan and the world than ever had any of the sons of men; and yet in all of them he had to do with that which came from without. But let a temptation be proposed to a *man*, and immediately he hath not only to do with the temptation as outwardly proposed, but also with his own heart about it." Again he remarks (Holy Spirit, II. iii), "Although Christ took on him those infirmities which belong unto our human nature as such, and are inseparable from it until it be glorified, yet he took none of our particular infirmities which cleave unto our persons, occasioned either by the vice of our constitutions, or irregularity in the case of our bodies. Those natural [and innocent] passions of our minds which are capable of being the means of affliction and trouble, as grief, sorrow, and the like, he took upon him; and also those infirmities of nature which are troublesome to the body, as hunger, thirst, weariness, and pain. Yea, the purity of his holy constitution made him more highly sen-

---

dedication was not bloodless Heb. 9:22, "There is no remission without shedding of blood" (χωρὶς αἱματεκχυσίας) Remission is not bloodless So, too, any temptation that is χωρὶς ἁμαρτίας is sinless wholly separate from sin, either internal or external Had the writer omitted χωρὶς ἁμαρτίας, the passage would read "Tempted in all points (κατὰ πάντα) like as we are" In adding this, he modifies κατὰ πάντα, so that it reads. "all points, sin excepted." See Ebrard, on Heb. 4:15.

sible of these things than any of the children of men. But as to our bodily diseases, and distempers, which personally adhere unto us upon the disorder and vice of our constitutions, he was absolutely free from them." If Christ, like fallen man, were subject to that class of forbidden appetences and selfish desires mentioned in Gal. 5 : 19, 21, namely, "idolatry, hatred, emulation, envyings, murder, wrath, uncleanness, drunkenness, and such like," the dignity and perfection of his character would be gone, and he could not be looked up to with the reverence that he is. The words of the dead kings to the fallen king of Babylon would apply: "Art thou also become weak, as we? art thou become like unto us?" Isa. 14:10.

The reasons why Christ was tempted are the following: 1. The suffering involved in his temptations was a part of his humiliation and satisfaction for sin. A tempted being is, in so far, a sufferer. Hence we have reason to believe that no temptation is experienced in the heavenly world. 2. In submitting to temptation, Christ sets an example to his disciples, of constancy in obedience and resistance to evil. Believers are bidden to "look unto Jesus, who for the joy that was set before him endured the cross despising the shame," and to "consider him that endured such contradiction of sinners against himself lest they be wearied and faint in their minds," Heb. 12 : 2, 3.

The fact that Christ was almighty and victorious in his resistance, does not unfit him to be an example for imitation to a weak and sorely tempted believer. Because our Lord overcame his temptations, it does not follow that his conflict and success was an easy one for him. His victory cost him tears and blood. "His visage was so marred more than any man," Isa. 52 : 14. There was "the travail of his soul," Isa. 52 : 14. In the struggle he cried, "O my Father, if it be possible let this cup pass from me!" Matt. 26 : 39. Because an army is victorious, it by no means follows that the victory was a cheap one "One more such victory," said Pyrrhus after the battle of Asculum, "will ruin me." The physical agony of the martyr is not diminished in the least by the strength imparted to him by God to endure it. The fire is as hot, and the pain as great, in his case as in that of an unbeliever. Divine grace does not operate like chloroform, and deaden pain. The bereavement of a believer by the death of a beloved object is none the less sore and heavy, because of the grace which helps him to bear it. The promise is, "Cast thy burden on the Lord and he shall sustain *thee*"—not the burden. Such facts show that victory over a temptation does not imply that the temptation is a slight one; that because Christ could not be overcome by temptation, therefore his temptation must have been less severe than that of his people.

On the contrary, Christ's human nature, while it was supported and strengthened by the divine, was *for this very reason* subjected to a severer strain than an ordinary human nature is. Suppose that an additional engine should be put into a vessel that is adapted to carry only one, and that a safe passage is guaranteed to it. When it comes into port after boring through three thousand miles of billows, it will show marks of the strain such as an ordinary ship, under ordinary pressure, will not. "Gemuit sub pondere cymba" Aeneid VI., 413. The traditions of the Church, and the representations of the old painters, founded upon the Scripture statements, present Christ's humanity as weighed down and worn by the awful burden of that heavy cross which the finite nature supported by the infinite was compelled to bear, and which without that support it could not have borne. For "it was requisite that the mediator should be God, that he might sustain and keep the human nature from sinking under the infinite wrath of God, and the power of death." Westminster Larger Catechism, 38.

3. By this almighty and victorious resistance of temptation, Christ evinced his power to succor those that are

tempted, and to carry them through all temptation. He showed that he is Lord and conqueror of Satan, and his kingdom. Coloss 2:15, "Having spoiled principalities and powers, he made a show of them openly, triumphing over them" Ps. 2:2, 4, "The kings of the earth set themselves against the Lord's anointed. He that sitteth in the heavens shall laugh; the Lord shall have them in derision" 1 Cor. 15:25, "He must reign till he hath put all enemies under his feet." Heb. 2:10, "It became him for whom are all things, to make the captain of their salvation perfect through sufferings." The "perfection" spoken of here is not sanctification from sin; but a suitable preparation and accomplishment for his mediatorial office and work by trial and grief, whereby he is able to sympathize with those that are tempted. Hence *τελιῶσαι* and not *ἁγιάζειν* is the word employed.

1. In the first place, then, the Redeemer of sinful men must be truly human, not weakly human; unfallen man, not fallen; the ideal man, not the actual; temptable not peccable. He must be truly human, in order to be assailable by temptation and thereby able to sympathize with every tempted man. In order to sympathize with a person, it is not necessary to have had exactly the same affliction that he has. It is only necessary to have been afflicted. A different kind of affliction may make a man all the more sympathetic. Because Christ was sinlessly tempted, he feels a deeper and more tender sympathy with sinfully tempted man, than he would had he been lustfully and viciously tempted. And this, for three reasons. (*a*) Lustful desire deadens the sensibility, and blunts the tenderness and delicacy of the nature. (*b*) There is much selfishness in the sympathy of vice with vice; of one drunkard with another. Misery loves company. But the sympathy of a benevolent temperate man for a drunkard is disinterested. (*c*) The strength and reality of sympathy are seen in the amount of self-sacrifice that one is willing to

make for the miserable, rather than in the mere fact that one has felt precisely the same misery himself. Tested by this, Christ has infinitely more sympathy for man than any man has had, or can have. "Greater love hath no man than this, that a man lay down his life for his friends," John 15 : 13. One man may know very vividly from personal experience how another man feels, and yet not be willing to undergo any suffering for him, for the purpose of delivering him from suffering. Drunkards have a common feeling of misery, but they do not make sacrifices for one another. On the contrary, they "bite and devour one another," Gal. 5 : 15. Satan well knows from personal experience what remorse is, and how his fellow-angels suffer from remorse, but he has no disposition to help them at his own expense.

2. Secondly, the Redeemer of man must not be weakly and peccably human, because he must be "mighty to save, travelling in the greatness of his strength," Isa. 63 : 1. He must have power to overcome all temptation when it assails himself personally, in order that he may be able "to succor them that are tempted," Heb. 2 : 18. Fallen and helpless man cannot trust himself to one who is himself liable to fall from God. The second Adam must be mightier to repel temptation than the first Adam. And certainly if good and evil were so proportioned to each other in Christ that they trembled in the balance, as they sometimes do in his disciples, no fallen man could go to him with confidence of victory over evil. After the cry, "O wretched man that I am: who shall deliver me from the body of this death?" there would not be the exulting shout, "I thank God through Jesus Christ our Lord." If Christ could meet all the temptations that approached him through his innocent and sinless human nature, from the wiles of Satan, and from suffering positively inflicted by eternal justice upon the sinner's voluntary substitute; if Christ could meet this vast amount of temptation with only a feeble finite will not reinforced and strengthened

by an infinite will; he would not be "mighty to save," nor would he "travel in the greatness of his strength." The Monophysite error, which makes Christ to be nothing but God, is not so great and discouraging as the Socinian, which makes him to be nothing but man. For it would be possible for a helpless sinner fainting in the conflict with sin and death to trust in a merely infinite person, but not in a merely finite one.

# SOTERIOLOGY.

# SOTERIOLOGY.

## CHAPTER I.

### CHRIST'S MEDIATORIAL OFFICES.

Calvin: Institutes, II xv. Ursinus· Christian Religion, Q 29-31. Turrettin. Institutio, XIV. i.-vii, xv.-xvii. Witsius Apostles' Creed, Dissertation X Van Oosterzee: Dogmatics, § cviii.-cxiii. Martensen· Dogmatics, § 148-180. Hodge: Theology, II 455-608.

SOTERIOLOGY (σωτηρίας λόγος) treats of the Work of the God-man, and its application to individuals by the Holy Spirit.

When we pass from the complex constitution of Christ's person to the work which he wrought for man's redemption, we find him represented in Scripture as a Mediator. "There is one God, and one mediator between God and man, the man Christ Jesus," 1 Tim 2: 5. In this passage, the term "man" denotes the entire theanthropic person Jesus Christ, not the human nature. The human nature is not the Mediator. Man, here, designates the God-man under a human title, and is like the title "Son of man," or "last Adam" (1 Cor. 15: 45); or "second man" (1 Cor. 15: 47). Again, the God-man is described in Scripture as being appointed and consecrated to the work of human redemption by God the Father as the representative of the Trinity. Hence the incarnate Word is also denominated the Messiah, the Anointed One. Dan. 9· 25; Ps. 2. 2; 45: 7.

Speaking generally. Messiah is the Old Testament term

for the Redeemer, and Mediator is the New Testament term. The word Christ which translates Messiah is generally a proper name in the New Testament, not an official title. Sometimes, however, the God-man is denominated Jesus "the Christ," or "that Christ." Matt 16:20; Luke 9:20; John 1:25; 6:29 The Christian church prefers the New Testament designation of Mediator, to the Old Testament designation of Messiah. The Westminster Larger Catechism (Q. 36) denominates Christ "the only Mediator of the convenant of grace."

There are several characteristics of Christ as the Mediator that must be carefully noted, in order to avoid misconception.

1. The mediator between God and man cannot be God only, or man only. This is taught in Gal 3:20, "A mediator is not of one, but God is one." A mediator supposes two parties between whom he intervenes; but God is only one party. Consequently, the mediator between God and man must be related to both, and the equal of either He cannot be simply God, who is only one of the parties, and has only one nature. Therefore the eternal Word must take man's nature into union with himself, if he would be a mediator between God and man As a trinitarian person merely, he is not qualified to mediate between them. The same truth is taught in 1 Sam. 2:25, "For if one man sin against another, the judge shall judge him; but if a man sin against the Lord, who shall entreat for him;" and in Job 9:33, "There is not any days-man betwixt us, to lay his hand upon us both;" and in Heb 10:5, "Therefore when he [the mediator] cometh into the world, he saith, A body hast thou prepared for me."

2. Secondly, the office of a mediator between God and man is one of condescension and humiliation: (*a*) Because it involves the assumption of a human nature by a divine person. This is taught in Phil. 2:5, 8, "Let this [lowly] mind be in you which was also in Christ Jesus, who being

in the form of God made himself of no reputation, and took upon him the form of a servant." To unite the finite with the infinite is to humble the infinite. Incarnate deity is a step down from unincarnate deity. The latter is wholly unconditioned; the former is conditioned by the inferior nature which it has assumed. (*b*) Because to be a mediator between God and man implies a condition of dependence. When the second person in the Trinity agrees to take the place of a mediator between the Trinity and rebellious man, he agrees to be commissioned and sent upon a lowly errand. He consents to take a secondary place. A king who volunteers to become an ambassador to his own subjects condescends, and humbles himself. The office of a commissioner sent to offer terms to rebels is inferior to that of the king. This is taught in many passages of scripture. Matt. 11 : 27, "All things are given me of my Father;" Matt. 28 . 18, "All power is given to me in heaven, and in earth;" John 17: 2, "Thou has given unto him power over all flesh;" Col. 1: 19, "It pleased the Father that in him all fulness should dwell;" Rev. 1 : 1, "The revelation of Jesus Christ, which God gave unto him to show unto his servants;" Phil. 2 : 8, "He became obedient unto death;" Gal. 4: 4, The Son of God "was made under the law;" Eph. 1 · 22, 23, "He put all things under his feet, and gave him to be head over all things" This class of texts is cited by Socinus to disprove the doctrine of Christ's original deity. But it has reference to Christ in his capacity and office of mediator, which is an assumed not an original office. These texts do not describe the Logos prior to his incarnation, but subsequent to it. When Christ speaks of his pre-existent and eternal place in the Trinity, he does not employ such phraseology. He says, "I and my Father are one," John 10: 30; "Glorify thou me with the glory which I had with thee before the world was," John 17 : 5; "Before Abraham was I am," John 8 : 58; "My Father worketh hitherto, and I work," John 5 : 17; "The Son of man is Lord of the Sabbath," Luke 6: 5; "I am the resurrection and the life," John 11: 25; "I am the living bread which came down from heaven," John 6: 51; "Whoso eateth my flesh, and drinketh my blood hath eternal life," John 6: 54. But when Christ refers to his incarnate and mediatorial position, he says, "My Father is greater than I," John 14: 28; "Say ye of him whom the Father hath sanctified and sent into the world, Thou blasphemest: because I said, I am the Son of God?" John 10: 36; "I came down from heaven not to do mine own will, but the will of him that sent me," John 6: 38; "I have finished the work which thou gavest me to do," John 17: 4; "Then shall the Son be subject unto him that put all things under him, that God may be all in all," 1 Cor. 15: 28. Accordingly, the Westminster Confession, VIII. iii., speaking of Christ's office of mediator, says that "this office he took not unto himself, but was thereunto called by his Father; who put all power and judgment into his hand, and gave him commandment to execute the same." (*c*) Because the office of mediator is temporary. It begins to be exercised in time, and a time will come when it will cease to be exercised. This is taught in 1 Cor 15: 24, 28 "Then cometh the end [of the economy of redemption], when he shall have delivered up the kingdom to God, even the Father, when he shall have put down all rule, and all authority and power. And when all things shall be subdued unto him, then shall the Son also himself be subject unto him that did put all things under him, that [the triune] God may be all in all" As there was once a time when there was no mediatorial work of salvation going on, so there will be a time when there will be none. The Logos was not actually and historically a mediator until he assumed human nature. It is true that in the Old Testament church the second trinitarian person discharged the office of a mediator by anticipation, and men were saved by his mediatorial work; but it was in view of his future advent, and future performance of that work.

Types and symbols stood in the place of the incarnate Word. Not however until the miraculous conception, was there actually a God-man; and not until then, was there an actual historical mediator. And although there will now always be a God-man, yet there will not always be a mediatorial work going on. The God-man will one day cease to redeem sinners. St. Paul is explicit in saying that a day will come when Christ will deliver up and return his mediatorial commission to the Father, from whom as the representative of the Trinity he received it. There will then "remain no more [available] sacrifice for sin," Heb. 10 : 26; and there will be no longer an access to a holy God for sinful men through Christ's blood. Hence it is said: "Now is the accepted time, and now is the day of salvation;" "To-day if ye will hear his voice, harden not your hearts;" "He limiteth a certain day, saying, To-day, if ye will hear his voice," Heb. 3: 13, 15, 18; 4: 1, 7.[1] But a function that begins in time and ends in time, when discharged by a Divine person is evidently one of condescension and secondary nature. The second person of the Trinity as a creator holds no position of condescension and humiliation, and performs no function that is secondary and temporary in its nature. He is a creator by reason of his absolute and eternal deity, and is so from everlasting to everlasting. There never was a time when he was not a creator, and there never will be a time when he will cease to be a creator. He never was commissioned to the office of creator; he never assumed this office; and he will never lay it down. It belongs to him by virtue of his divinity. Creation is a primary, not a secondary function. But the second person as mediator assumes an office and takes a position which is not necessarily implied in his deity. He might be God the Son, without being God the mediator; but he could not be God the Son without being God the creator. (*d*) Because the office of mediator is one

[1] See also Christ's parables of the foolish virgins, Matt. 25, and the wedding garment, Matt. 22. Compare Witsius: Apostles' Creed, X 42–44, XXVI. 76

of reward. The condescension and humiliation of the Logos in assuming a finite nature, and executing a commission, is to be recompensed. It is a self-sacrifice that merits a return from the person who commissioned and sent the mediator upon this service. This is taught in Phil. 2: 5–11. "Christ Jesus took upon him the form of a servant; *wherefore* God also hath highly exalted him and given him a name which is above every name; that at the name of Jesus every knee should bow, of things in heaven, and things in earth, and things under the earth; and that every tongue should confess that Jesus Christ is Lord, to the glory of God the Father." This is not a reward for that which the Logos was and did as unincarnate, and as the second person of the Trinity, but of what he was and did as the incarnate Logos, and as the commissioned mediator between God and man. A Divine person, as such, cannot be either exalted or rewarded. This phraseology of St. Paul refers not to the eternal and pre-existent state and position of Jesus Christ, but to his post-existent state and condition. It does not relate to the "form of God" which he had originally and from all eternity, but to the "form of a servant" which he assumed in time, and which he retains forever. The same truth is taught in Heb. 2: 9, "We see Jesus, who was made a little lower than the angels [i.e. was made a man, ver. 7.], for the suffering of death crowned with glory and honor;" and in Rev. 3: 21, "To him that overcometh will I grant to sit with me in my throne, even as I also overcame and am set down with my Father in his throne." (*e*) Because the Son of God enters into a convenant with the Father to take a mediatorial office and position. But if he were originally in a subordinate position, he could not covenant or agree to become subordinate.

Jesus Christ is represented in Scripture as the mediator of a covenant. Heb. 12: 24, "Jesus the mediator of the new covenant;" Heb. 8: 6, "He is the mediator of a better covenant;" Malachi 3: 1, "The Lord whom ye seek shall suddenly come to his temple, even the messenger of the covenant;" Luke 22: 20, "This cup is the new covenant (διαθήκη) in my blood." Compare Matt. 14: 24; 26 : 28. Accordingly, the symbols so represent him. "The only mediator of the covenant of grace is the Lord Jesus Christ." Westminster L C. 36.

A difference in the Scripture representations has given rise to a distinction between the covenant of grace, and the covenant of redemption. The covenant of grace is made between the Father and the elect. This is taught in those passages which speak of Christ as the mediator of the covenant. Heb. 9: 15, "For this cause, he is the mediator of the new covenant;" Heb. 8: 6, "He is the mediator of a better covenant." This implies that the promises of the covenant are made by God the Father to his people, and that Christ stands between the two parties. The same is taught in Gal. 3: 16, "Now to Abraham and his seed were the promises made. He saith not, And to seeds, as of many [seeds]; but as to one [seed], And to thy seed, which is Christ" The contracting parties here are the Father and the elect "seed." This also has its type in the Sinaitic theocratic covenant between Jehovah and the Hebrews as a chosen nation, of which national covenant Moses was the mediator. Gal. 3: 19, "The law was ordained by angels in the hands of a mediator." The following passages mention the covenant of God the Father with the elect church: Isa 43: 1–6, "Fear not, O Israel, for I have redeemed thee: thou art mine. When thou passest through the waters, I will be with thee; and through the rivers, they shall not overflow thee;" Isa. 59: 21, "This is my covenant with them, saith the Lord: My spirit that is upon thee, and my words which I have put in thy mouth, shall not depart out of thy mouth, nor out of the mouth of thy seed, saith the Lord, from henceforth and for ever."[1]

[1] "Israel, as well as the Messiah, and in due dependence on him, was to be the light of the Gentiles, the redeemer of apostate nations" Alexander on Isa. 59.

The covenant of redemption is made between the Father and the Son. The contracting parties here are the first and second persons of the Trinity; the first of whom promises a kingdom, a glory, and a reward, upon condition that the second performs a work of atonement and redemption.[1] The following are passages in which it is spoken of. Isa. 42: 1–6, "Behold my servant whom I uphold. He shall not cry, nor lift up, nor cause his voice to be heard in the street. I the Lord have called thee, and will hold thy hand, and will keep thee, and will give thee for a light of the Gentiles, to open the blind eyes;" Luke 22: 29, "I appoint [διατίθεμαι, covenant] unto you a kingdom, as my father hath appointed unto me;" Isa 53: 10–12, "When thou shalt make his soul an offering for sin, he shall see his seed;" Isa. 49: 6, "I will give thee for a light to the Gentiles, that thou mayest be my salvation unto the ends of the earth;" Ps. 89: 34–36, "My covenant will I not break Once have I sworn, that I will not lie unto David. His seed shall endure forever;" Ps. 2: 8, "Ask of me, and I will give thee the heathen for thine inheritance, and the uttermost parts of the earth for thy possession."

Though this distinction is favored by the Scripture statements, it does not follow that there are two separate and independant covenants antithetic to the covenant of works The covenant of grace and that of redemption are two modes or phases of the one evangelical covenant of mercy. The distinction is only a secondary or subdistinction. For when, as in Isa. 43: 1–6, the elect are spoken of as the party with whom God the Father makes a covenant, they

---

21 In Isaiah, the "servant of the Lord" is sometimes national, i e the Church; and sometimes personal, i e the Messiah This is the key to the interpretation

[1] Christ is the mediator of the covenant of redemption as well as of grace, for though no one mediates between the Father and the incarnate Son, yet as the elect are one with him in the former covenant as well as the latter, he is a mediator in respect to *them* in the former case as well as in the latter All the benefits that come to the church from the covenant between the Father and the Son are mediated to it through the Son.

are viewed as in Christ and one with him. The covenant is not made with them as alone and apart from Christ. This is taught in Gal. 3 : 16, "To Abraham and his seed were the promises made;" but this seed "is Christ." The elect are here (as also in 1 Cor. 12 : 12) called "Christ," because of the union between Christ and the elect. And in like manner, when Christ, as in Isa. 42 : 1–6, is spoken of as the party with whom the Father covenants, the elect are to be viewed as in him As united and one with him, his atoning suffering is looked upon as their atoning suffering, Gal. 2 : 20, "I am crucified with Christ;" his resurrection involves their resurrection, Rom. 6 : 5, "Grown together in the likeness of his resurrection;" his exaltation brings their exaltation, Matt. 19 : 28, "Ye shall sit on thrones judging the twelve tribes of Israel;" 1 Cor. 6 : 3, "We shall judge angels." The covenant of redemption is not made with Christ in isolation, and apart from his people. It is with the Head and the members. Eph. 1 : 22, 23, "He gave him to be the head over all things to the church, which is his body, the fulness of him that filleth all in all"

The following statement, then, comprises the facts There are only two general covenants, the legal, and the evangelical. "These are the two covenants, the one from Mount Sinai which gendereth to bondage," Gal. 4 : 24. The first in order is the legal covenant of works. It is founded upon the attribute of justice. Its promise is, "Do this and thou shalt live" This covenant failed upon the part of man, in the fall of Adam. The second is the evangelical covenant, founded upon the attribute of mercy. Its promise is two-fold: (*a*) To the Mediator. "Make thy soul an offering for sin, and I will give thee the heathen for thine inheritance, and the uttermost parts of the earth for thy possession," Isa. 53 : 10; Ps. 2 : 8. (*b*) To the elect. "Fear not, for I have redeemed thee, I have called thee by thy name; thou art mine. When thou passest through the waters, I will be with thee; and through the rivers, they shall not overflow

thee" Isa. 55: 1, 2; "Believe on the Lord Jesus Christ and thou shalt be saved, and thy house," Acts 16: 31. The evangelical covenant, as opposite to the legal covenant, may therefore be called the covenant of redemption when Christ and his offices are the principal thing in view; and the covenant of grace, when the elect and their faith and obedience are the principal thing under consideration.

Respecting the validity of the distinction there is some difference of opinion, though the weight of authority is in favor of it. Turrettin (XII. ii. 12) adopts it; also Witsius, Covenants II. ii. 1; and Hodge, Theology II. 358. Fisher, on the Catechism (Q. 20, § 57) asserts that the Westminster "standards make no distinction between a covenant of redemption and a covenant of grace." The phrase "covenant of redemption" is not found in them. In the Larger Catechism Q. 31, it is said that "the covenant of grace was made with Christ, and in him with all the elect." This would be the covenant of redemption. In the Westminster Confession VII. iii, it is stated that "the Lord was pleased to make a second covenant, commonly called the covenant of grace, wherein he freely offereth unto sinners life and salvation by Jesus Christ, requiring of them faith in Him that they may be saved, and promising to give unto all those that are ordained unto life his Holy Spirit, to make them willing and able to believe." Here the covenant is made with the elect. The phraseology in the twentieth question of the Shorter Catechism is somewhat ambiguous: "God having elected some to everlasting life, did enter into a covenant of grace, to deliver them out of the estate of sin and misery, and to bring them into an estate of salvation by a Redeemer." Whether the "covenant" mentioned is made with the elect, or with the mediator, is not to be indisputably determined from the wording of the statement.

The evangelical covenant as the opposite of the legal covenant is essentially one and the same under the Old dispensation and the New. The difference is only in the mode of administration. In the Old dispensation, comprising the Patriarchal and Jewish churches, it was administered through animal sacrifices and visible types and symbols; in the New dispensation, by the advent and sacrifice of Christ. The old administration was ceremonial and national; the new is spiritual and universal. This difference is mentioned in 2 Cor. 3:14. "Moses put a vail [of types and ceremonies] over his face, that the children of Israel could not steadfastly look to the end of that which is abolished; but their minds were blinded; for until this day, remaineth the same vail untaken away in the reading of the old testament; which vail is taken away in Christ." In Heb. 8:6-13, the "first covenant" is the covenant of grace made "with their fathers when God took them by the hand to lead them out of Egypt," administered by types and symbols; and the "second covenant" is the covenant of grace under the administration of Christ personally, who is "the mediator of a better covenant." Heb. 9:15 speaks of the "new covenant" in distinction from the "first covenant" (which had "ordinances of divine service, and an earthly sanctuary"), and of the "redemption of transgressions under the first covenant." This shows that the "first covenant" was a gracious one.[1]

[1] The difference between these two phases of one and the same evangelical covenant, is marked in the authorized version of the New Testament by the translation of διαθήκη. It is generally rendered "covenant" when it refers to the administration of mercy in the Old dispensation, and "testament" when it refers to the administration of mercy in the New. But the only passage in which it can with any plausibility mean "testament," is Heb. 9:16, 17; and in this, "covenant" might be used, in accordance with the following rendering: "For where a covenant is, the death of the covenanter (τοῦ διαθεμένου) of necessity is implied (φέρεσθαι). For a covenant is valid (βεβαία) over dead victims (νεκροῖς); since it is never of force while the covenanter (ὁ διαθέμενος) liveth. Wherefore, neither the first covenant was inaugurated without blood [i.e. without a slain victim]." The phrase, "death of the covenanter," is natural from the Hebrew point of view. In the biblical conception, the covenanter is identified with his substituted offering. The death of the offering is equivalent, before the divine tribunal, to the death of the offerer. The cove-

Christ, the God-man, as the mediator of the evangelical covenant, discharges three offices; those of prophet, priest, and king. "Our mediator was called Christ, because he was anointed with the Holy Ghost above measure; and so set apart and fully furnished with all authority and ability, to execute the offices of prophet, priest, and king of his church, in the estate both of his humiliation and exaltation." Westminster L. C., 42. His prophetical office is taught in Deut. 18:15, 18; Acts 3:22, "The Lord thy God will raise up unto thee a prophet from the midst of thee, of thy brethren, like unto me;" Isa. 16:1; Luke 4:18, "The spirit of the Lord God is upon me; because the Lord hath anointed me to preach good tidings" His priestly office is taught in Ps. 110:4; Heb. 5:5, 6, "Thou art a priest forever after the order of Melchisedec;" Heb. 4:14, 15, "We have a great high priest that is passed into the heavens." His kingly office is taught in Isa. 9:6, 7, "He shall be called the prince of peace;" Ps. 2:6, "I have set my king upon my holy hill of Zion."

These offices were each and all of them executed by the mediator before, as well as after his advent. Westminster Confession, VII. v.; VIII. vi. This is proved by Rev. 13: 8, "The Lamb slain from the foundation of the world," Gen. 3:15, "The seed of the woman shall bruise the serpent's head;" Rom. 3:25, "To declare his righteousness for the remission of sins that are past;" Heb. 9:15, "He is the mediator of the new testament, that by means of death for the redemption of the transgressions that were under the first testament, they which are called might receive the promise of eternal inheritance;" Gal 3:8, 14, 16–18, compared with Gen 17:7; 22:18; Acts 15:11, "We believe that through the grace of Christ we shall be saved even as they" [the fathers]; Acts 10:43, "To him

nantor is reckoned to have died, when his vicarious victim dies Such a phrase as "the death of the covenantor," would not have seemed strange in the least to the Hebrews, to whom the epistle was addressed.

give all the prophets witness that through his name whosoever believeth in him shall receive remission of sins;" Heb. 10:1–10, "For the law [Jewish dispensation] having a shadow of good things to come;" Coloss. 2:17, The Jewish ordinances "are a shadow of things to come; but the body is of Christ;" Isa. 53; Isa. 42:6, "I the Lord have called thee, and will give thee for a light of the Gentiles;" Heb. 4:2, "Unto us was the gospel preached, as well as unto them."

Faith in the Mediator was the unmeritorious, but indispensable condition of salvation,[1] before the advent as well as after it. "The just [i.e. the justified] shall live by faith," Hab. 2:4. This is quoted by St. Paul in Rom. 1:17. "Blessed are all they that put their trust in him," Ps. 2:12. "Abraham believed God and it was counted to him for righteousness," Rom. 4:3. "David saith, Blessed is the man to whom the Lord will not impute sin," Rom. 4:8. "These all died in faith," Heb. 11:13. Enoch "pleased God" by his faith, Heb. 11:5. "The Old Testament is not contrary to the New: for both in the Old and New Testament everlasting life is offered to mankind by Christ, who is the only mediator between God and Man," Thirty-nine Articles, Art. VII. Says Calvin, on Gal. 4: 1–7, "We learn from this passage, that the fathers under the Old Testament had the same hope of the inheritance which we have at the present day, because they were partakers of the same adoption. Notwithstanding their outward servitude, their consciences were still free. Though bearing the yoke of the [ceremonial] law upon their shoulders, they nevertheless with a free spirit worshipped God. More particularly, having been instructed concerning the free pardon of sin, their consciences were delivered from the tyranny of sin and death. They held the same doctrine, were joined with us in the true unity of faith, placed re-

[1] On the use of the term "condition," applied to the covenant of grace, see Witsius: Apostles' Creed, Vol. I., Note xliv.

liance on one Mediator, called on God as their Father, and were led by the same Spirit. Hence it appears, that the difference between us and these ancient fathers lies not in substance, but in accidents or circumstantials"

The Old Testament believer had both the penitent consciousness of sin, and of the remission of sin The account of the religious experience of Abraham, Moses, David, and Isaiah, discloses a contrite spirit before the absolute holiness of God. The Old Testament saint cast himself upon the Divine mercy. Ps. 32 : 1–11 ; Ps. 51 ; Ps. 103 : 2, 3. And this mercy he expected through the promised "seed of the woman," the Messiah ; and through an atonement typified by the Levitical sacrifices. The forgiveness of sin was both promised and received under the Old dispensation

The *Prophetical* office of Christ is thus described in the Westminster Larger Catechism, Q. 43 : "Christ executeth the office of a prophet in revealing to the church, in all ages, by his Spirit and word, the whole will of God in all things concerning edification and salvation." The prophetical function of Christ is not confined to the prediction of future events. The idea is wider than that of mere vaticination, though it includes this. Christ, as "that prophet that should come into the world" (John 6 : 14 ; John 1 : 21 ; Luke 24 : 19), is the source and teacher of truth ; and particularly of that truth which relates to human redemption. This is implied in the names that are given to him in Scripture. He is called the Counsellor, Isa 9 : 6 ; the Witness, Isa. 55 : 4 ; the Interpreter, Job 33 : 23 ; the Apostle, Heb. 3 : 1 ; the Word, John 1 : 1 ; the Truth, John 14 : 6 ; and Wisdom, Prov. 8 In the Logos-doctrine of St. John, all the previous statements respecting the prophetical or teaching function of the Mediator are summed up, and more fully unfolded He is "the light of men," John 1 : 4 ; the "light of the world," John 9 : 5 ; the "true light which coming into the world lighteth every man," John 1 : 9 ; "the light to lighten the Gentiles," Luke 2 : 32 ; Isa.

60 : 3; "the Word dwelling among us full of truth," John 1 : 14; the "Christ in whom are hid all the treasures of wisdom and knowledge," Coloss 2 : 3. Hence the voice from heaven to mankind, "This is my beloved Son, hear ye him," Matt. 17 : 5.

The great characteristic of Christ as a prophet is his consciousness of infallibility "He spake as one having authority, and not as the scribes," Mark 1 : 22; "But *I* say unto you," Matt. 5 : 34. Merely human prophets, like Isaiah (Ch. 6), are abashed in the presence of deity when receiving communications from him. Christ never shows the least trace of such a feeling "No man knows the Father but the Son, and no one knows the Son but the Father," Matt. 11 : 27. This implies co-equality with the Father in the knowledge of the mystery of the Trinity. Christ speaks out of the fulness of his own immediate intuition. He never says, "The word of the Lord came unto me" From the omniscience of his own divine nature he draws all his teachings, as a prophet. "In him dwelleth all the fulness of the Godhead bodily," Coloss. 2 : 9. He is the source to others of prophetical knowledge. He "opened the understanding of his disciples that they might understand the scriptures," Luke 24 : 45. The Old Testament prophets "prophesied of the grace that should come, searching what, or what manner of time, the Spirit of Christ which was in them did signify, when it testified beforehand the sufferings of Christ, and the glory that should follow," 1 Pet. 1 : 10, 11.

1. Christ executes the office of prophet personally and directly. This he did: (*a*) In all the theophanies of the Old Testament. The appearances of Jehovah to individuals before the flood, to the patriarchs and Moses after the flood, to the prophets of Israel and Judah, were a discharge of the prophetical function of the Mediator. These were all harbingers and adumbrations of his incarnation (*b*) In his incarnation itself. This was as direct and personal teaching as is possible. The second person of the Trinity when in-

carnate upon earth spoke as never man spake, and spoke face to face to man. And his teaching was not confined to his words, though most of his instruction was so conveyed. The works of Christ as well as his words, and especially his miraculous works, taught man. "If I do not the works of my Father, believe me not. But if I do, though ye believe not me, believe the works," John, 10 : 37, 38. His disciples describe him as "a prophet mighty in deed and word before the people," Luke 24 : 19. This prophetical office continues to be discharged personally by the incarnate Word, in his state of exaltation. In the description of the heavenly world, the "Lamb" is said to be "the light thereof," Rev. 21 : 23.

2. Christ executes the office of prophet mediately: (*a*) Through the Holy Spirit. All the truth that was conveyed previous to the advent through the inspired prophets of the Old Testament, and subsequent to it through the apostles of the New Testament, comes to man in the discharge of the prophetical function of the Mediator. Hence it is said (1 Pet. 1 : 10–12) that it was "the Spirit of Christ" that was in the prophets "who prophesied of the grace that should come," and who "testified beforehand the sufferings of Christ." By this same Holy Spirit, Christ "preached unto those that were disobedient in the days of Noah," and who are now and forevermore "in prison" for their disobedience. 1 Pet. 3 : 19, 20. See Eschatology p. 000. Christ as prophet is thus the source of all revelation, unwritten and written. The truths of natural religion come to man through him. He is the "light of men," in the sense that what "may be known of God" is an unwritten and internal revelation to them. Rom. 1 : 19. And he is the "light of the world," in the sense that all that higher and more perfect knowledge respecting God and human salvation which constitutes the written word has him for its author. "The only begotten Son which is in the bosom of the Father, he hath declared him," John 1 : 18. (*b*) Through the instrumentality of the Christian

ministry and church. Christ, in the first place, commissioned his apostles as inspired agents both to teach and to preach the gospel. Their writings are the infallible documents by which the church is to be instructed and guided. Matt. 28: 19, 20, "Go ye and teach all nations," John 15: 13, 14, "The Spirit of truth will guide you into all truth; he shall glorify me, for he shall receive of mine and show it unto you." Again, secondly, Christ provided for successors to the apostles considered as preachers and ministers of the word, and through this ministry he instrumentally executes his prophetical office. The supernatural gifts of inspiration and miracles which the apostles possessed were not continued to their ministerial successors, because they were no longer necessary. All the doctrines of Christianity had been revealed to the apostles, and had been delivered to the church in a written form. There was no further need of an infallible inspiration. And the credentials and authority given to the first preachers of Christianity in miraculous acts, did not need continual repetition from age to age. One age of miracles well authenticated is sufficient to establish the divine origin of the gospel In a human court, an indefinite series of witnesses is not required. "By the mouth of two or three witnesses," the facts are established. The case once decided is not reopened. With the exception, therefore, of the two supernatural gifts of inspiration and miracles, the ministry who took up the work of preaching the word had the same preparation for the work that the apostles had. They were like them regenerated, sanctified, and enlightened by the Holy Spirit. This is taught in Eph. 4: 11, 12. Having "ascended far above all heavens," and being seated upon the mediatorial throne, the Mediator "gave some to be apostles, and some to be prophets, and some to be evangelists, and some to be pastors and teachers: for the perfecting of the saints, for the work of the ministry, for the edifying of the body of Christ." Accordingly, the preaching of the gospel by his ministers is called Christ's preaching. Acts 13 : 12, "Then the deputy Sergius Paulus, when he saw what was done to Elymas the sorcerer, believed, being astonished at the doctrine [teaching] of the Lord [through Paul]." In 1 Cor. 1: 6, and Rev. 1 : 2, the preaching of the gospel is denominated "the testimony of Christ." In 2 Cor. 5 : 20, Paul represents himself and his co-laborers as ambassadors for Christ, and beseeches men in Christ's stead to be reconciled to God. In 1 Pet. 3 : 19, and Eph 2 : 17, the preaching of Noah and the apostles is called Christ's preaching.

Again, the mass of the church, as well as the Christian ministry, are represented as an agency by which the Mediator executes his prophetical office. After the death of Stephen, all the church "excepting the apostles" were scattered by persecution, and "went everywhere preaching the word," Acts 8 : 4. The church is represented as "a chosen generation, a royal priesthood," to "show forth the praises of him who hath called it out of darkness into his marvellous light," 1 Pet. 2 : 9. The Holy Spirit dwelling in the church, in all the fulness of his graces and gifts, enriches it with wisdom and knowledge, so that it is capable both by word and example of proclaiming Christ crucified to the sinful world of which it is said to be the light. Matt. 5 : 14–16. The superiority of the church to the secular world, in regard to the comprehension of religious truth and of everything relating to the eternal destiny of mankind, is boldly and strongly asserted by St. Paul. "We speak wisdom among them that are perfect [saints enlightened]; even the hidden wisdom of God which none of the princes of this world knew. The natural man cannot know the things of the Spirit of God, because they are spiritually discerned. He that is spiritual judgeth all things, yet he himself is judged of no man," 1 Cor. 2 : 6–15. The Christian mind is qualified to be a critic of secular knowledge; but the secular mind is not qualified to be a critic of Christianity. Christ crucified is foolishness to the Greek;

yet this foolishness of God is wiser than men. 1 Cor. 1 : 23, 25.

The *Priestly* office of Christ is thus defined in the Westminster Larger Catechism, Q. 44 : "Christ executeth the office of a priest, in his once offering himself a sacrifice without spot to God, to be a reconcilation for the sins of his people; and in making continual intercession for them." The function of a priest is described in Heb. 5 : 1. "Every high priest is ordained for men in things pertaining to God, that he may offer both gifts, and sacrifices for sins."[1] The priest is a mediator in religion, as an ambassador is one in politics. He is appointed to officiate between God and man, in religious matters. And since the fact of sin is a cardinal fact in the case of man, the function of a mediating priest for man must be mainly expiatory and reconciling. Since "every high priest is ordained to offer gifts and sacrifices, it is of necessity that Jesus Christ have somewhat to offer," Heb. 8 : 3.

Accordingly, we find the expiatory priest in existence long before the Mosaic institute. Noah, at the cessation of the deluge, nearly a thousand years before the exodus of the Israelites, officiated as the priest of his household. "Noah builded an altar unto the Lord; and took of every clean beast, and of every clean fowl, and offered burnt offerings on the altar. And Jehovah smelled a sweet savour," Gen. 8 : 20. This implies that the system of sacrifices was then in existence. There was an altar, and a victim. The distinction between clean and unclean beasts and birds was made, a distinction which has its principal significance in reference to a piacular offering. Not any and everything may be offered as an atonement, but only that which is specified.

Still more than this, there is evidence in the first chapters

[1] Compare article "Priest," in Kitto· Encyclopaedia, Lowman Hebrew Ritual, Outram On Sacrifice; Kurtz· The Mosaic Sacrifices: Cave On Sacrifice, Blunt Coincidences, 14–22.

of Genesis that atoning sacrifices, and an officiating priest to offer them, were instituted immediately after the apostasy, and in connection with the promise of a Mediator. It was a common Jewish opinion that Adam was the first human priest. The correctness of this opinion is favored by the following considerations. The permission to eat vegetable food is given to Adam in Gen. 1 : 29, but nothing is said of animal food. The permission to eat both vegetable and animal food is given to Noah, in Gen 9 : 3. Yet animals were slain by Adam; for "the Lord God made coats of skins and clothed both Adam and Eve," Gen 3 : 21. It is a natural explanation of this fact, to suppose that animals had been killed and offered in sacrifice by Adam. For even if it be assumed that animal food was permitted to Adam, the narrative respecting the coats of skins implies that more animals were slain than would be required for the food of Adam and Eve. Again, in Gen. 4 : 3, 4, both Cain and Abel are represented as offering sacrifices; the former, the bloodless eucharistic offering of the fruit of the ground, the latter, the bloody expiatory offering of the firstlings of the flock. They are described as "bringing" their offering (Gen. 4 : 3, 4); and to a locality which is described as the "face of the Lord," and the "presence of the Lord" (Gen. 4 : 14, 16). This looks like a sacred place appointed for the offering of sacrifice, and a sacred person to officiate, namely Adam the head and priest of his family, as Noah was of his. The words of God to Cain (Gen. 4 : 7) teach that a piacular offering for sin had been appointed. "If thou doest not well, sin [a sin offering] lieth at the door." Subsequently, the lamb or goat was to be brought "to the door of the tabernacle." Again, the prohibition, in Gen. 9 : 4, 16, to eat blood, given to Noah, is the same that is afterwards given to the Israelites, in Leviticus 17 : 10, 12; and the reason assigned when the command is laid upon the Israelites is, that the blood is the life of the flesh, and is to be poured upon the altar "to make atonement for your souls."

From this it follows with great probability, that the statute as given to Moses was only a re-enactment of the statute as given to Noah, and given for the same reason; namely, that the blood of animals must be used only for piacular purposes. Even under the Levitical law, the use of animal food was considerably restricted. The blood and fat were interdicted in all cases. The sin offering and trespass offering were to be eaten only by the priests; and the more solemn sin offerings could not be eaten even by them. The burnt offerings, the most numerous of all, were wholly consumed.

Similar proofs of the institution of an expiatory sacrifice, and an officiating priest, are found in the history of Abraham and the other patriarchs. On first entering Canaan, Abram "built an altar and called upon the name of the Lord," Gen 12 : 7, 8. When he returned from his victory over the kings, he is congratulated and blessed by Melchisedec the Canaanite king of Salem, who is called "the priest of the most high God," Gen 14 : 18, 19. Isaac builds an altar, Gen. 26 : 25. Jacob offers sacrifice, Gen. 31 : 54.

The indications of a priest and a sacrifice are plain in the book of Job. It was the "continual" custom of this patriarch, who probably lived between the deluge and Abraham, as the head of his family to "offer burnt offerings according to the number of them all," Job 1 : 5. The Septuagint rendering of Job 12 : 19 is, "He leadeth priests [A. V. 'princes'] away spoiled" In Job 33 : 23, 24, the idea of one who furnishes a ransom is presented. The rite of sacrifice under the Old Testament taught that God is both just and merciful: just, in that his law requires death for sin; merciful, in that he permits and provides a vicarious death for sin. In this way it deepened fear, and inspired hope; fear of the divine holiness, and hope in the divine mercy.

The priestly office of the Mediator, unlike his prophetical, is not administered mediately but directly. The priests of the Old dispensation, both Patriarchal and Mosaic, were *types* of Christ, not his agents or delegates. The human priests "were many, because they were not suffered to continue by reason of death;" but the divine high priest is one and alone, "because he continueth ever, and hath an unchangeable priesthood," Heb. 7 : 23, 24. And because he constantly discharges his priestly office, he does not delegate it to others. This unique and solitary character of Christ's priesthood is taught in the comparison of him to Melchisedec, in Heb. 7. The king of Salem was the only one of his class. He was "without father, without mother, without descent (ἀγενεαλόγητος), having neither beginning of days nor end of life." That is, he was not one of a line of priests having predecessors and successors In this respect he was like the Son of God, who was also alone and solitary in his priesthood.

The Romish theory of an ecclesiastical priesthood acting, since Christ's ascension, as the delegates and agents of the great high priest, has no support in scripture. Had Christ intended to discharge his sacerdotal office through a class of persons in his church, he would have appointed and commissioned such a class, and provided for its continuation. He did this in regard to his prophetical office. He appointed "apostles, prophets, evangelists, pastors, and teachers, for the perfecting of the saints and the work of the ministry," Eph. 4 : 11, 12. But he did not appoint any to be priests to "offer both gifts and sacrifices for sins," Heb. 5 : 1. On the contrary, he abolished the earthly priesthood, when he formally assumed his own priestly office. The substance having appeared, the shadow disappeared. The antitype makes the type useless, Heb. 9 : 23–26. The earthly sacrifice was done away, and the earthly priest with it.

The two parts of Christ's priestly work are: (*a*) Atonement. Heb. 9 : 14, 28, "How much more shall the blood of Christ purge your conscience." Christ "was once offered to bear the sins of many." John 1: 29, "The lamb of God which taketh away the sin of the world." Heb. 2: 17, "A merciful and faithful high priest to make reconciliation for the sins of the people." Matt. 20: 28, "A ransom for many." Luke 22: 19, "My blood is shed for you." 2 Cor. 5: 21, "He made him to be sin for us." Gal. 3: 13, "Christ was made a curse for us." 1 Pet. 3: 18, "Christ suffered for our sins the just for the unjust." 1 John 2. 2, "He is the propitiation for our sins." Isa. 53: 10, "He made his soul an offering for sin." Rom. 8: 32, "He spared not his own Son, but delivered him up for us" Rom. 5: 11, "By him we have received the atonement." Rom. 5: 6, 7, "Christ died for us; scarcely for a righteous man will one die." Eph. 5: 2, "Christ hath loved us, and given himself for us, an offering and a sacrifice to God." (*b*) Intercession. 1 John 2. 1, "If any man sin, we have an advocate with the Father, Jesus Christ the righteous." Heb. 7: 25, "Wherefore he is able to save them to the uttermost, seeing he ever liveth to make intercession for them." John 17: 9, 20, "I pray for them which thou hast given me; neither pray I for these alone, but for them also which shall believe on me through their word."

The intercession of Christ is intimately connected with his atoning work. The Westminster Confession (VIII. viii.), after saying that Christ "effectually applies and communicates redemption to those for whom he has purchased it," adds that "he makes intercession for them." Compare Larger Catechism, Q. 44. This is in accordance with the Scriptures. The apostle John (1 John 2 : 1, 2) asserts that "if any man sin, we have an advocate with the Father," and adduces as the ground of his success as an advocate two facts: that he is "Jesus Christ the righteous," and is "the propitiation for our sins." The apostle Paul, in Rom. 8: 34, states that Christ is "at the right hand of God making intercession for us," and mentions as the reason why he is fitted for this work, the fact that he "died, and is risen again." In Heb. 4:14–16, believers are encouraged to "come boldly unto the throne of grace," because they "have a great high priest who is passed into the heavens, and is touched with the feeling of their infirmities." Again, in Heb. 7:24, 25, Christians are assured that because Christ has an "unchangeable priesthood, he is able to save them to the uttermost that come unto God by him, seeing he ever liveth to make intercession for them." In Heb. 9:7–12, the writer reminds the reader that the Jewish "high priest went alone once every year into the second tabernacle, not without blood, which he offered for himself and the errors of the people," and then states that Christ, "a high priest of good things to come, by his own blood entered in once into the holy place, having obtained eternal redemption for us."

Still further proof of the close connection of Christ's intercessory work with his atoning work, is found in that class of texts which represent the gracious influence of the Holy Spirit as being procured by Christ's intercession. These teach that that plenary effusion of the Holy Ghost which is the characteristic of the Christian economy, is owing to the return of the Mediator to the Father, and his session upon the mediatorial throne Matt. 3:11, "I indeed baptize with water; he shall baptize you with the Holy Ghost." John 7:39, "Jesus spake this of the Spirit, which they that believe on him should receive, for the Holy Ghost was not yet given, because that Jesus was not yet glorified." John 16:7, "It is expedient for you that I go away; for if I go not away, the Comforter will not come unto you; but if I depart I will send him unto you." In John 14:16–26; 15:26, Christ assures his disciples that after he has left them and returned to the Father "where he was before," he "will pray the Father, and he will give them another Comforter, that he may abide with them, even the Spirit of truth," and furthermore that he will himself "send the Comforter unto them from the Father."

In accordance with these statements of Christ, we find Peter referring the outpouring of the Holy Spirit on the day of Pentecost to the mediatorial agency and intercession of Christ. Acts. 2:33, "Therefore being by the right hand of God exalted, and having received of the Father the gift of the Holy Ghost, he hath shed forth this which ye now see and hear." And the whole book of Acts contains frequent allusions and references to the person and work of the Holy Spirit, in a manner and to a degree which are not seen in the four Gospels, showing that immediately after the ascension of Christ a more powerful agency and influence of the third trinitarian Person began to be experienced in the church. This descent and gift of gracious operation and influence was directly connected with Christ's presence and intercession in heaven. And this intercession rested for its ground and reason of success, upon that atoning work which he had performed upon earth.

The same connection between Christ's atonement and Christ's intercession is noticed in the Epistles. Christ was "made a curse for us, that we might receive the promise of the Spirit, through faith," Gal. 3:13, 14. The Holy Spirit is "shed on us abundantly through Jesus Christ our Saviour," Titus 3:5, 6. When Christ "ascended up on high, he received gifts for men," Eph. 4:8. The intercession of Christ relates: (*a*) To the application of his own atonement to the individual; (*b*) To the bestowment of the Holy Spirit as enlightening and sanctifying the believer. Compare Smith: Theology, 481–490.

## CHAPTER II.

### VICARIOUS ATONEMENT.

Anselm : Cur deus homo (Bib Sacra, 1844–5). Aquinas : Summa, III. xlvi.-xlix. Calvin : Institutes, II. xvi.,xvii. Ursinus Christian Religion, Q 37–43. Turrettin Institutio, XIV. viii.-xiv., De necessitate satisfactionis Christi. Grotius. De satisfactione. Witsius : Apostles' Creed, Diss XV, XVI, XVIII. Owen · Divine Justice; Vindiciae, XX -XXV. Bates Harmony of Attributes in Redemption. Pearson. Creed, Art IV. Howe: Living Temple, II. v.-xi. Outram: On Sacrifice. Magee On Atonement Cave. On Sacrifice. Crawford · On Atonement Smeaton. On Atonement. Kurtz: Mosaic Sacrifices. Lowman: Hebrew Ritual. Blunt Coincidences of Old and New Testament (pp. 14–22). Baur Versohnungslehre (pp. 142–282); Critique of Grotius. tr in Bib. Sacra, 1852. Watson . Institutes, II. xx.-xxii Dorner: Theology, § 112–122. Hodge: Theology, II. 464–591 Dabney. Theology, XLII., XLIII. Smith. Theology, 442–461. Wines · Laws of the Hebrews Shedd: On Atonement (Theol Essays); History of Doctrine, II. 201–386. Candlish: On Atonement Wardlaw · Nature and Extent of the Atonement. Symington: On Atonement. Hill: Theology, IV. (Extent of the Atonement). Maurice · The Doctrine of Sacrifice. Bushnell: Vicarious Sacrifice. Campbell: Nature of the Atonement Park: Collection of Essays on Atonement. Van Oosterzee: Dogmatics, II. 594–597.

THE atonement of Christ is represented in Scripture as *vicarious.* The satisfaction of justice intended and accomplished by it is for others, not for himself. This is abundantly taught in Scripture Matt. 20 : 28, "The Son of man came to give his life a ransom for (ἀντὶ) many." Matt. 10 : 45, "This is my body which is given for (ἀντὶ) you." In these two passages the preposition ἀντὶ indisputably denotes substitution. Passages like Matt. 2 : 22, "Archelaus reigned in the room (ἀντὶ) of his father Herod;" Matt 5: 38, "An eye for an eye;" Luke 11: 11, "Will he for a fish give him a serpent," prove this.

In the majority of the passages, however, which speak of Christ's sufferings and death, the preposition ὑπὲρ is employed. Luke 22: 19, 20, "This cup is the new covenant in my blood which is shed for (ὑπὲρ) you." John 6. 51, "The bread that I will give is my flesh which I will give for the life of the world." John 15: 13, "Greater love hath no man than this, that a man lay down his life for his friends." Rom. 5: 6–8, "Christ died for the ungodly; while we were yet sinners Christ died for us." Rom. 8: 32, "He delivered him up for us all." 2 Cor. 5: 14, 15, "If one died for all then all died." 2 Cor. 5: 21, "He made him to be sin for us." Gal. 3: 13, "Being made a curse for us." Eph. 5: 2, 25, "Christ gave himself for us, an offering and a sacrifice to God." 1 Tim 2: 5, 6, "The man Christ Jesus gave himself a ransom for all." Heb. 2: 9, Christ "tasted death for every man." 1 Pet 3: 18, Christ "suffered the just for the unjust."

The preposition ὑπὲρ, like the English preposition "for," has two significations. It may denote advantage or benefit, or it may mean substitution. The mother dies for her child, and Pythias dies for Damon. The sense of "for" in these two propositions must be determined by the context, and the different circumstances in each instance Christ (John 15. 13) lays down the proposition: "Greater love hath no man than this, that a man lay down his life for (ὑπὲρ) his friends." The preposition ὑπὲρ, here, may mean either "for the benefit of," or "instead of." In either case, the laying down of life would be the highest proof of affection. The idea of substitution, therefore, cannot be *excluded* by the mere fact that the preposition ὑπὲρ is employed; because it has two meanings. In 2 Cor. 5: 20, 21, ὑπὲρ is indisputably put for ἀντὶ. "Now then we are ambassadors for Christ, as though God did beseech you by us; we pray you in Christ's stead (ὑπὲρ Χριστοῦ), be ye reconciled to God. For he hath made him who knew no sin to be sin for us (ὑπὲρ ἐμῶν)." In Philemon 13, ὑπὲρ is clearly equivalent to ἀντὶ. "Whom I would have retained with me, that in thy stead (ὑπὲρ σοῦ) he might have ministered unto me." In 2 Cor. 5: 14, it is said that "the love of Christ constraineth us; because we thus judge that if one died for all (ὑπὲρ πάντῶν), then all died (πάντες ἀπέθανον)." Here, the notion of substitution is plain. If Christ died in the room and place of the "all," then the "all" are reckoned to have died. The vicarious atonement of Christ is regarded as the personal atonement of the believer. It would be nonsense to say, that "if one died for the benefit of all, then all died."

There is also abundant proof from classical usage that ὑπὲρ may be used in the sense of ἀντὶ. Magee (Atonement, Dissertation XXX) quotes the following· Xenophon (Anabasis, VII iv) relates that the Thracian prince Seuthes asked Episthenes if he would be willing to die, instead of the young lad who had been captured in war (ἦ καὶ ἐθέλοις ἄν, ὦ 'Επίσθενες, ὑπὲρ τουτοῦ ἀποθανεῖν;). The same use of ὑπὲρ is seen in Xenophon's Hellenica, and De Venatione; also in Plato's Symposium, 180 and 207; also in the Alcestis of Euripides, 446, 540, 732, compared with 155, 156, 698, 706, 715–717. In the first three lines, ἀντὶ is employed, and in the remainder ὑπὲρ, in respect to the same subject; showing that classical usage allows of their being interchanged. Demosthenes (in De Corona) says, ἐρωτησόν τούτους, μαλλὸν δὲ ἐγω τουθ' ὑπὲρ σοῦ ποιήσω. Winer (Grammar, Thayer's ed. p. 383) remarks, that "ὑπὲρ is sometimes nearly equivalent to ἀντὶ: instead of, loco. See especially Euripides, Alcestis, 700; Thucydides, I 141; Polybius, III. 67; Philemon, 13." De Wette, on Rom 5.7, says: "ὑπὲρ kann anstatt heissen. 2 Cor. 5: 20." Baur (Paulus der Apostel, p. 168) says: "Wenn auch in vielen Stellen das ἀποθάνειν ὑπὲρ nur ein Sterben zum besten Anderer ist, so kann doch wohl in den Stellen, Rom. 4: 25; Gal. 1: 4; Rom. 8: 3; 1 Cor. 15: 3; 2 Cor. 5: 14, der Begriff der Stellvertretung, wenigsten der Sache nach, nicht zuruckgewiesen werden."

The meaning, therefore, of ὑπὲρ must be determined by the context. Since both classical and New Testament usage permit of its being employed to signify either benefit or substitution, it is plain that it cannot be confined to either signification. It would be as erroneous to assert that it uniformly means "for the advantage of," as to assert that it uniformly means "in the place of." The remark of Magee (Dissertation XXX.) is just. "The word 'for,' or the Greek words ἀντὶ, ὑπὲρ, διὰ, περὶ, of which it is the translation, admitting of different senses, may of course be differently applied, according to the nature of the subject, and yet the doctrine remain unchanged. Thus it might be proper to say that Christ suffered instead of us (ἀντὶ ἡμῶν), although it would be absurd to say that he suffered instead of our offences (ἀντὶ τῶν ἁμαρτημάτων ἡμῶν). It is sufficient if the different applications of the word carry a consistent meaning. To die 'instead of us,' and to die 'on account of our offences,' perfectly agree.[1] But this change of the expression necessarily arises from the change of the subject. And, accordingly, the same difficulty will be found to attach to the exposition proposed by these writers (Sykes and H. Taylor): since the word 'for,' interpreted 'on account of,' i.e. 'for the benefit of,' cannot be applied in the same sense in all the texts. For although dying 'for our benefit' is perfectly intelligible, dying 'for the benefit of our offences' is no less absurd than dying 'instead of our offences.'"

In the light of these facts, it is easy to see why the New Testament writers employ ὑπὲρ so often, rather than ἀντὶ,

[1] The first of these statements might be either ὑπὲρ ἡμῶν, or ἀντὶ ἡμῶν, the second might be ὑπὲρ τῶν ἁμαρτημάτων ἡμῶν, or περὶ, or διὰ, but not ἀντὶ. The preposition ἀντὶ has only the one meaning of substitution; the others have more than this meaning.

to denote the relation of Christ's death to man's salvation. The latter preposition excludes the idea of benefit or advantage, and specifies only the idea of substitution. The former may include both ideas. Whenever, therefore, the sacred writer would express both together and at once, he selects the preposition ὑπὲρ. In so doing, he teaches both that Christ died in the sinner's place, and for the sinner's benefit.

Vicariousness implies *substitution*. A vicar is a person deputed to perform the function of another. In the case under consideration, the particular function to be performed is that of atoning for sin by suffering. Man the transgressor is the party who owes the atonement, and who ought to discharge the office of an atoner; but Jesus Christ is the party who actually discharges the office, and makes the atonement, in his stead. The idea of vicariousness or substitution is, therefore, vital to a correct theory of Christ's priestly office. Man the transgressor would make his own atonement, if he should suffer the penalty affixed to transgression. So far as the penalty is concerned, retributive justice would be satisfied if the whole human race were punished forever.[1] And if God had no attribute but retributive justice, this would have been the course that he would have taken. A deity strictly and simply just, but destitute of compassion for the guilty, would have inflicted the penalty of the violated law upon the actual transgressor He would not have allowed of a substituted satisfaction of justice, and still less would he have provided one. It is important to notice this fact, because it shows the senselessness of a common objection to the doctrine of vicarious atonement, namely, that it is incompatible with mercy. If God, it is asked, insists upon satisfying justice by allowing his Son to suffer

[1] The law as *precept*, however, would not be satisfied This proves that endless punishment is not excessive punishment It still leaves the sinner in debt According to strict justice, the law could require from the lost an *active* as well as a passive obedience, perfect obedience in the present and future, as well as suffering of penalty for past disobedience.

in the place of sinners, where is his mercy? The ready answer is, that it is mercy to the criminal to permit the substitution of penalty, and still more to provide the substitute after the permission. If God had no compassionate feeling towards the sinner, he would compel the sinner himself to satisfy the demands of the law which he has transgressed. But in permitting, and still more in providing a substitute to make that satisfaction which man is under obligation to make for himself, God manifests the greatest and strangest mercy that can be conceived of. For, the vicarious atonement of Christ is the Sovereign and the Judge putting himself in the place of the criminal.

It is important, at this point, to mark the difference between *personal* and *vicarious* atonement. (*a*) Personal atonement is made by the offending party; vicarious atonement is made by the offended party. The former is made by the sinner; the latter is made by God: "our great God and Saviour, Jesus Christ," Titus 2:13. (R. V.) If a citizen pays the fine appointed by the civil law, he satisfies justice for his own civil transgression. If the murderer is executed, he atones for his own crime before the human law, though not before the divine. And when a sinner suffers endless punishment, he personally satisfies eternal justice for his sin. (*b*) Personal atonement is given by the criminal, not received by him; but vicarious atonement is received by the criminal, not given by him. This is indicated in the scripture phraseology In Rom. 5:11, it is said that the believer "receives the atonement" vicariously made for him by Christ. If he had made an atonement for himself, he would have given to justice the atonement, not received it. (*c*) Personal atonement is incompatible with mercy, but vicarious atonement is the highest form of mercy. When the sinner satisfies the law by his own eternal death, he experiences justice without mercy; but when God satisfies the law for him, he experiences mercy in the wonderful form of God's self-sacrifice. (*d*) Personal atonement is incompatible with the eternal life of the sinner, but vicarious atonement obtains eternal life for him. When the sinner suffers the penalty due to his transgression, he is lost forever, but when God incarnate suffers the penalty for him, he is saved forever.

Vicarious atonement in the Christian system is made by the *offended* party. God is the party against whom sin is committed, and he is the party who atones for its commission. Vicarious atonement, consequently, is the highest conceivable exhibition of the attribute of mercy. "Herein is love, that God sent his Son to be the propitiation for *our* sins," 1 John 4 : 10. For God to remit penalty without inflicting suffering upon God incarnate, would be infinitely less compassion than to remit it through such infliction In one case, there is no self-sacrifice in the Godhead; in the other there is. The pardon in one case is inexpensive and cheap; in the other, costly and difficult of execution.

The Socinian objection that vicarious atonement is unmerciful because it involves the full and strict satisfaction of justice, has no force from a Trinitarian point of view. It is valid only from a Unitarian position. If the Son of God who suffers in the sinner's stead is not God but a creature, then of course God makes no self-sacrifice in saving man through vicarious atonement In this case, it is not God the offended party who makes the atonement. The Trinitarian holds that the Son of God is true and very God, and that when he voluntarily becomes the sinner's substitute for atoning purposes, it is very God himself who satisfies God's justice. The penalty is not inflicted upon a mere creature whom God made from nothing, and who is one of countless millions; but it is inflicted upon the incarnate Creator himself. The following extract from Channing (Unitarian Christianity) illustrates this misconception "Unitarianism will not listen for a moment to the common errors by which this bright attribute of mercy is obscured. It will not hear of a vindictive wrath in God which must be quenched by blood, or of a justice which binds his mercy with an iron chain, until its demands are satisfied to the full. It will not hear that God needs any foreign influence to awaken his mercy." The finger must be placed upon this word "*foreign.*" The Trinitarian does not concede that the influence of Jesus Christ upon God's justice is an influence "foreign" to God. The propitiating and reconciling influence of Jesus Christ, according to the Trinitarian, emanates from the depths of the Godhead; this suffering is the suffering of one of the Divine persons incarnate. God is not propitiated (1 John 2 : 2; 4 : 10) by another being, when he is propitiated by the only begotten Son. The term "foreign," in the above extract, is properly applicable only upon the Unitarian theory, that the Son of God is not God, but a being like man or angel alien to the Divine essence.

This fallacy is still more apparent in the following illustration from the same writer "Suppose that a creditor, through compassion to certain debtors, should persuade a benevolent and opulent man to pay in their stead? Would not the debtors see a greater mercy, and feel a weightier obligation, if they were to receive a free gratuitous release?" (Unitarian Christianity). Here, the creditor and the debtors' substitute are entirely different parties The creditor himself makes not the slightest self-sacrifice in the transaction, because he and the substitute are not one being, but two. Consequently, the sacrifice involved in the payment of the debt is confined wholly to the substitute. The creditor has no share in it. But if the creditor and the substitute were one and the same being, then the pecuniary loss incurred by the vicarious payment of the debt would be a common loss Upon the Unitarian theory, God the Father and Jesus Christ are two beings as different from each other as two individual men. If this be the fact, then indeed vicarious atonement implies no mercy in God the Father. The mercy would lie wholly in Jesus Christ, because the self-sacrifice would be wholly in him. But if the Trinitarian theory is the truth, and God the Father and Jesus Christ are two persons of one substance, being, and glory, then, the self-sacrifice that is made by Jesus Christ is not confined to him alone, but is a real self-sacrifice both on the part of God the Father and also of the entire Trinity. This is taught in Scripture. "God [the Father] so loved the world, that he gave his only begotten Son," John 3:16. "He spared not his own Son, but delivered him up for us all," Rom. 8:32. [The Triune] "God commendeth his love toward us, in that while we were yet sinners, Christ died for us," Rom 5:8[1]

Though it was God the Son, and not God the Father, who became incarnate, and suffered, and died, it by no means follows that the first person of the Trinity made no self-sacrifice in this humiliation and crucifixion of the incarnate second person. He gave up to agony and death, his "dear," and "beloved" son. He passed the sword, as Zechariah (13:7) says, through "the man who was his fellow" Such scriptures imply that the redemption of sinful man caused God the Father a species of sorrow: the

---

[1] The following are the principal points of difference between Unitarianism and Calvinism, respecting the subject of Christ's redemption Unitarianism contends (*a*) That God is inherently and spontaneously merciful (*b*) That justice is only a form of benevolence, and opposes no obstacles to the exercise of God's inherent and spontaneous mercy. (*c*) That Christ was not God, but an exalted creature sent to announce the Divine mercy, set a holy example, and proffer spiritual assistance to imitate it. It was no part of his mission to satisfy legal claims and harmonize justice with mercy, because there is no need of harmonizing them (*d*) That the doctrine of vicarious atonement implies that God is not inherently merciful, but needs to be made so by the agency of another being, namely, Christ. Channing's Life, I 294, 344, 349, 354. Calvinism contends: (*a*) That God is inherently and spontaneously merciful (*b*) That justice is an attribute distinct from benevolence, requiring satisfaction for sin, and prohibiting the exercise of mercy until this requirement is met (*c*) That Jesus Christ was incarnate God himself, who suffered vicariously for sinners in order to satisfy the legal claims which obstructed the exercise of the Divine mercy (*d*) That this vicarious satisfaction of justice by God himself is the way in which God shows his inherent and spontaneous mercifulness, and not a means employed by a third party, other than God, to make him merciful.

sorrow of "bruising and putting to grief" (Isa. 53:10) the Son of his love; the Son who is "in the bosom of the Father," John 1:18. The self-sacrifice, therefore, that is made by the Son in giving himself to die for sinners, involves a self-sacrifice made by the Father in surrendering the Son for this purpose. No person of the Godhead, even when he works officially, works *exclusively* of the others. The unity of being and nature between Father and Son makes the act of self-sacrifice in the salvation of man common to both. "He that hath seen me hath seen the Father. I and my Father are one," John 14:9; 10:30. "The Mediator," says Augustine (Trinity, IV. xix.), "was both the offerer and the offering; and he was also one with him to whom the offering was made." See South: Sermon XXX.

And this does not conflict with the doctrine that the Divine essence is incapable of suffering. The Divine impassibility means that the Divine nature cannot be caused to suffer from any *external* cause. Nothing in the created universe can make God feel pain or misery.[1] But it does not follow that God cannot *himself* do an act which he feels to be a sacrifice of feeling and affection, and in so far an inward suffering. When God gave up to humiliation and death his only begotten Son, he was not utterly indifferent, and unaffected by the act. It was as truly a sacrifice for the Father, to surrender the beloved Son, as it was for the Son to surrender himself. The Scriptures so represent the matter. "God so loved the world that he gave his only begotten Son." "God spared not his own Son, but freely gave him up." When the Father, in the phrase of the prophet, "awoke the sword against the man who was his fellow," he likewise pierced himself.

Vicarious atonement, unlike personal atonement, cannot be made by a creature. Ps. 49:7, "None of them can by

---

[1] The Divine wrath against sin, we have seen (Vol. I p 176 sq ), causes no unhappiness or misery in God, because of its righteousness and legitimateness

any means redeem his brother, nor give to God a ransom for him" Micah 6:7, "Shall I give my first-born for my transgression?" Matt. 16:26, "What shall a man give in exchange for his soul?" This is acknowledged in the province of human law. No provision is made in human legislation for the substitution of penalty. In the case of capital punishment, one citizen may not be substituted for another; in the case of civil penalty such as fine or imprisonment, the state cannot seize upon an innocent person and compel him to suffer for the guilty. And even if there should be a willingness upon the part of the innocent to suffer for the guilty, legislation makes no provision for the substitution. The state would refuse to hang an innocent man, however willing and urgent he might be to take the place of the murderer. The state will not fine or imprison any but the real culprit.

The reason for this is twofold. First, each citizen owes duties towards man that could not be performed if he should assume the obligations of another citizen. There are debts to the family, to society, and to the commonwealth, of which these would be defrauded, if the life or property of one person should be substituted for that of another. Secondly, each individual owes duties towards God which would be interfered with by the substitution of one man for another within the sphere of human relations. And the state has no right to legislate in a manner that interferes with God's claims upon his creatures.

The instances in Pagan or Christian communities in which there seems to be substitution of penalty are exceptional, and irregular. They are not recognized as legitimate by Pagan authorities, and still less by Christian jurists. When, as in the early Roman history, an individual citizen was allowed to devote himself to death for the welfare of the state, this was an impulse of the popular feeling. It was not regularly provided for and legitimated by the national legislature. It was no part of the legal code. And human sacrifices among savage nations cannot be regarded as parts of the common law of nations.

That vicarious atonement cannot be made by a created being within the province of divine law, will be made evident when we come to consider the nature of Christ's substituted work At this point, it is sufficient to observe, that if within the lower sphere of human crimes and penalties one man cannot suffer for another, it would be still more impossible in the higher sphere of man's relations to God. No crime against man is of so deep a guilt as is sin against God; and if the former cannot be expiated by a human substitute, still less can the latter be.

It should be remembered, however, that the reason why a creature cannot be substituted for a creature for purposes of atonement is not that substitution of penalty is inadmissible, but that the creature is not a proper subject to be substituted, for the reasons above mentioned. Substitution is sometimes allowed within the province of commercial law. One man may pay the pecuniary debt of another, if this can be done without infraction of any rights of other parties. If, however, it cannot be, then vicarious payment is inadmissible A man would not be permitted to take money due to one person to pay the debt of another. A man is not allowed in the State of New York to leave all his property to benevolent purposes, if he has a family dependent upon him.

The priestly office of Christ cannot be understood without a clear and accurate conception of the *nature* of atonement.

The idea and meaning of atonement is conveyed in the following statements in Leviticus 6:2–7, and 4:13–20[1] "If a soul sin and commit a trespass against the Lord, he

---

[1] "It was in China that a Baptist missionary found his converts slow to appreciate the value of Christ's atoning blood, until the book of Leviticus threw light upon the sacrificial offering, and showed the relation between shedding of blood and remission." Bible Society's Record, Nov. 21, 1878.

shall bring his trespass offering unto the Lord, a ram without blemish, and the priest shall *make an atonement* for him before the Lord, and it shall be *forgiven* him." This is individual atonement for individual transgression. "If the whole congregation of Israel sin and are guilty, then the congregation shall offer a young bullock for the sin, and the elders of the congregation shall lay their hands upon the head of the bullock, and the bullock shall be killed, and the priest shall *make an atonement* for them, and it shall be *forgiven* them." This is national atonement for national transgression. Two particulars are to be noticed in this account. (*a*) The essence of the atonement is in the *suffering*. The atoning bullock or ram must bleed, agonize, and die. And he who offers it must not get any enjoyment out of it. It must be a loss to him, and so far forth a suffering for him. He must not eat any of the trespass offering. The sin offering must be wholly burned: "skin, flesh, and dung," Lev. 16:27. In harmony with this, our Lord lays stress upon his own suffering, as the essential element in his atonement. "The son of man must suffer many things," Luke 9:22; Matt. 16:21, et alia. "It behoved Christ to suffer," Acts 3:18; Luke 24:26. Christ refused the anodyne of "wine mingled with gall" that would have deadened his pain. Matt. 27:34.[1] (*b*) The forgiveness is the *non-infliction of suffering* upon the transgressor. If the substituted victim suffers, then the criminal shall be released from suffering. In these and similar passages, the Hebrew word כָּפַר, which in the Piel is translated "to make an atonement," literally signifies "to cover over" so as not to be seen. And the Hebrew word סָלַח, translated

---

[1] Bahr, in his Symbolik des Mosaischen Cultus, denies that there is anything piacular in the Levitical sin-offering The slain victim is emblematic of self-consecration and self-sacrifice, not of penal satisfaction. The death of the lamb or goat teaches, not that the offerer deserves to die for his past transgression, but that he ought to live for future consecration to obedience This interpretation lies under all the moral theories of the atonement Its inconsistency is apparent in making the shedding of blood, or death, the symbol of life.

"to forgive," has for its primary idea that of "lightness, lifting up," perhaps "to be at rest or peace." Gesenius in voce.

The connection of ideas in the Hebrew text appears, then, to be this: The suffering of the substituted bullock or ram has the effect to *cover over* the guilt of the real criminal, and make it invisible to the eye of God the holy. This same thought is conveyed in Ps. 51: 19, "Blot out my transgressions. Hide thy face from my sins;" in Is. 38: 17, "Thou hast cast all my sins behind thy back;" in Micah 7: 19, "Thou wilt cast all their sins into the depths of the sea." When this covering over is done, the conscience of the transgressor is at *rest*.

These Hebrew words, however, are translated in the Septuagint by Greek words which introduce different ideas from "covering" and "resting." The word כָּפַּר is rendered by *ἐξιλάσκομαι*, which means to "propitiate" or "appease;" and the word סָלַח is translated by *ἀφίημι*, to "release," or "let go." The connection of ideas in the Greek translation appears, therefore, to be this: By the suffering of the sinner's atoning substitute, the divine wrath at sin is *propitiated*, and as a consequence of this propitiation the punishment due to sin is *released*, or not inflicted upon the transgressor. This release or non-infliction of penalty is "forgiveness," in the Biblical representation This is conceded by the opponents of the evangelical system. Says Wegscheider (Institutiones, § 140), "*Venia* sive condonatio peccatorum, ex vulgari et biblica dicendi consuetudine, est *abolitio poenae* peccatis contractae, et restitutio benevolentiae divinae erga peccatorem." In the Lord's prayer, the petition for forgiveness is *ἄφες ἡμῖν τὰ ὀφειλήματα ἡμῶν*, Matt. 6: 12. Christ assures the paralytic that his sins are forgiven, in the words, *ἄφεωνταί σοι ἅι ἁμαρτίαι σοῦ*, Matt. 9: 2. The preaching of the gospel is the preaching of the "release of sins" (*ἄφεσις ἅμαρτιῶν*), Acts 13: 38.

It is highly important to notice that in the Biblical representation, *the "forgiveness" is inseparably connected with the "atonement,"* and *the "remission" with the "propitiation."* The former stands to the latter in the relation of effect to cause. The Scriptures know nothing of forgiveness, or remission of penalty, in isolation. It always has a foregoing cause or reason. It is because the priest has offered the ram, that the individual transgression is "forgiven:" that is, not punished in the person of the individual. It is because the priest has offered the bullock upon whose head the elders have laid their hands, that the national sin is "forgiven:" that is, not visited upon the nation. Without this vicarious shedding of blood, there would be no remission or release of penalty, Heb. 9: 22. Not until the transgression has been "covered over" by a sacrifice, can there be "peace" in the conscience, of the transgressor. Not until the Holy One has been "propitiated" by an atonement, can the penalty be "released." Neither of these effects can exist without the antecedent cause. The Bible knows nothing of the remission of punishment arbitrarily: that is, without a ground or reason. Penal suffering in Scripture is released, or not inflicted upon the guilty, because it has been endured by a substitute. If penalty were remitted by sovereignty merely, without any judicial ground or reason whatever; if it were inflicted neither upon the sinner nor his substitute; this would be the *abolition* of penalty, not the remission of it.

According to the Biblical view, the Divine mercy is seen more in the cause than in the effect; more in the "atonement" for sin than in the "remission" of sin; more in "expiation" than in "forgiveness;" more in the vicarious infliction than in the personal non-infliction. After the foundation has been laid for the release of penalty, it is easy to release it. When a sufficient reason has been established why sin should be pardoned, it is easy to pardon. It is the first step that costs. This is taught by St. Paul in Rom. 5: 10. "If when we were enemies we were reconciled to God by the death of his Son, *much more* being reconciled we shall be saved by his life." The greater includes the less. If God's mercy is great enough to move him to make a vicarious atonement for man's sin, it is certainly great enough to move him to secure the consequences of such an act. If God's compassion is great enough to induce him to lay man's punishment upon his own Son, it is surely great enough to induce him not to lay it upon the believer. If God so loves the world as to atone vicariously for its sin, he certainly so loves it as to remit its sin.

In looking, therefore, for the inmost seat and centre of the Divine compassion, we should seek it rather in the work of atonement than in the act of forgiveness; rather in the cause than in the effect. That covenant-transaction in the depths of the Trinity, in which God the Father commissioned and gave up the Only-Begotten as a piacular oblation for man's sin, and in which the Only-Begotten voluntarily accepted the commission, is a greater proof and manifestation of the Divine pity, than that other and subsequent transaction in the depths of a believer's soul in which God says, "Son, be of good cheer, thy sin is forgiven thee." The latter transaction is easy enough, after the former has occurred. But the former transaction cost the infinite and adorable Trinity an effort, and a sacrifice, that is inconceivable, and unutterable. This is the mystery which the angels desire to look into. That a just God should release from penalty after an ample atonement has been made, is easy to understand and believe. But that he should himself make the atonement, is the wonder and the mystery. "Hereby perceive we the love of God, because he laid down his life for us," 1 John 3 : 16.

It follows from this discussion, that atonement is *objective* in its essential nature. An atonement makes its primary impression upon the party to whom it is made, not upon the party by whom it is made When a man does a wrong to a fellow man, and renders satisfaction for the wrong, this satisfaction is intended to influence the object, not the subject; to produce an effect upon the man who has suffered the wrong, not the man who did the wrong. Subjective atonement is a contradiction. Atoning to one's self is like lifting one's self.[1] The objective nature of atonement is wrought into the very phraseology of Scripture, as the analysis of the Biblical terms just made clearly shows. To "cover" sin, is to cover it from the sight of God, not of the sinner. To "propitiate," is to propitiate God, not man.

The Septuagint idea of "propitiation," rather than the Hebrew idea of "covering over," is prominent in the New Testament, and consequently passed into the soteriology of the Primitive church, and from this into both the Romish and the Protestant soteriology. The difference between the two is not essential, since both terms are objective; but there is a difference. The Hebrew term כִּפֶּר denotes that the sacrificial victim produces an effect upon sin. It covers it up. But the corresponding Septuagint term ἱλάσκομαι denotes that the sacrificial victim produces an effect upon God. It propitiates his holy displeasure. When St. John (1 John 2:2; 4:10) asserts that "Jesus Christ the righteous is the propitiation (ἱλασμός) for our sins," and that God "sent his Son to be the propitiation for our sins," the implication is that the Divine nature is capable of being conciliated by some propitiating act. This propitiating act under the Old dispensation was, typically and provisionally, the offering of a lamb or goat as emblematic of the future offering of the Lamb of God; and under the New dispensation it is the actual offering of the body of Jesus Christ, who takes the

---

[1] If it be objected that in the statement of the doctrine of vicarious atonement it is maintained that God atones to God (pp. 399 sq.), the reply is, that Jesus Christ does not make satisfaction to himself as Jesus Christ, but to the Trinity. The incarnate Word satisfies the justice of the God-*head*. The relation of his death is therefore objective. It has reference to the Divine Nature, not to his own theanthropic personality.

sinner's place and performs for him the propitiating and reconciling act

The objective nature of atonement appears, again, in the New Testament term καταλλαγή and the verb καταλλάσσειν. These two words occur nine times in the New Testament, with reference to Christ's atoning work. Rom. 5 : 10, 11, 15; 2 Cor. 5 : 18–20. In the authorized version, καταλλαγή is translated "atonement" in Rom. 5 : 11; but in the other instances, "reconciliation" and "reconcile" are the terms employed. The verb καταλλάσσειν primarily signifies, "to pay the exchange, or difference," and secondarily "to conciliate, or appease." The following from Athenaeus (X. 33) brings to view both meanings of the word. "Why do we say that a tetradrachma καταλλάττεται, when we never speak of its getting into a passion?" A coin is "exchanged," in the primary signification; and a man is "reconciled," in the secondary. Two parties in a bargain settle their difference, or are "reconciled," by one paying the exchange or balance to the other. In like manner two parties at enmity settle their difference, or are "reconciled," by one making a satisfaction to the other. In each instance the transaction is called in Greek καταλλαγή. The same usage is found in the Anglo-Saxon language The Saxon bot, from which comes the modern boot, denotes, first, a compensation paid to the offended party by the offender; then, secondly, the reconciling effect produced by such compensation; and, lastly, it signifies the state of mind which prompted the boot or compensation, namely repentance itself. Bosworth : Anglo-Saxon Dictionary, sub voce.

The term "reconciliation" is objective in its signification. Reconciliation terminates upon the object, not upon the subject. The offender reconciles not himself but the person whom he has offended, by undergoing some loss and thereby making amends. This is clearly taught in Matt. 5 : 24. "First, be reconciled to thy brother" (διαλλάγηθι τῷ ἀδελφῷ). Here, the brother who has done the injury is the one who is to make up the difference. He is to propitiate or reconcile his brother to himself, by a compensation of some kind. Reconciliation, here, does not denote a process in the mind of the offender, but of the offended. The meaning is not: "First conciliate thine own displeasure towards thy brother," but, "First conciliate thy brother's displeasure towards thee" In the Episcopalian Order for the Holy Communion, it is said: "If ye shall perceive your offences to be such as are not only against God, but also against your neighbors; then ye shall *reconcile yourselves* unto them: being ready to *make restitution* and *satisfaction*, according to the uttermost of your powers, for all injuries and wrongs done by you to any other." The Biblical phraseology, "Be reconciled to thy brother," agrees with that of common life, in *describing* reconciliation from the side of the offending party, rather than of the offended. We say of the settlement of a rebellion, that "the subjects are reconciled to their sovereign," rather than that "the sovereign is reconciled to the subjects;" though the latter is the more strictly accurate, because it is the sovereign who is reconciled by a satisfaction made to him by the subjects who have rebelled. In Rom. 5:10, believers are said to be "reconciled to God by the death of his Son." Here the reconciliation is described from the side of the offending party; *man* is said to be reconciled. Yet this does not mean the subjective reconciliation of the sinner toward God, but the objective reconciliation of God towards the sinner. For the preceding verse speaks of God as a being from whose "wrath" the believer is saved by the death of Christ. This shows that the reconciliation effected by Christ's atoning death is that of the divine anger against sin. Upon this text, Meyer remarks that "the death of Christ does not remove the wrath of man towards God, but it removes God's displeasure towards man." Similarly, De Wette remarks that "the reconciliation must mean the removal of the wrath of God; it is that reconciliation of God to man which not only here, but in Rom. 3 : 25 ; 2 Cor. 5 · 18, 19 ; Coloss. 1 : 21 ; Eph. 2 : 16, is referred to the atoning death of Christ." [1]

The priestly work of Christ is also represented in Scripture under the figure of a price or ransom. This, also, is an objective term. The price is paid by the subject to the object. Matt. 20 : 28, "The Son of man is come to give his life a ransom (*λύτρον*) for (*ἀντὶ*) many." Acts 20 : 28, "The church of God which he hath purchased (*περιεποιήσατο*) with his own blood" Rom 3 : 24, "The redemption (*ἀπολυτρώσις*) that is in Jesus Christ." 1 Cor. 6 : 20, "Ye are bought (*ἠγοράσθητε*) with a price." Gal. 3 : 13, "Christ hath redeemed (*ἐξηγόρασεν*) us from the curse." Eph. 1 : 7 ; Col. 1 : 14, "Redemption through his blood." 1 Tim 2 : 6, "Who gave himself a ransom (*ἀντίλυτρον*) for all." The allusion in the figure is sometimes to the payment of a debt, and sometimes to the liberation of a captive. In either case, it is not Satan but God who holds the claim. Man has not transgressed against Satan, but against God. The debt that requires cancelling is due to a divine attribute, not to the rebel archangel. The ransom that must be paid, is for the purpose of delivering the sinner from the demands of justice, not of the devil. Satan cannot acquire or establish legal claims upon any being whatever.

Some of the early fathers misinterpreted this doctrine of a "ransom," and introduced a vitiating element into the patristic soteriology, which however was soon eliminated, and has never reappeared. They explained certain texts which refer to sanctification, as referring to justification. In 2 Tim. 2 : 26, sinful men are said to be "taken captive by the devil at his will." In 1 Tim. 1: 20, Hymenaeus and Alexander are "delivered unto Satan." In 1 Cor. 5 : 5, St. Paul commands the church to "deliver over" the incestuous member "to Satan for the destruction of the flesh." In these passages, reference is had to the power

[1] See Magee : Dissertation XX. ; Owen Vindiciae, Ch. XXI., Shedd Theological Essays, 265–273.

which Satan has over the creature who has voluntarily subjected himself to him. The sinner is Satan's captive upon the principle mentioned by Christ in John 8 : 34, "Whosoever committeth sin is the servant (δοῦλος) of sin ;" and by St. Paul in Rom. 6 : 16, "Know ye not, that to whom ye yield yourselves servants (δούλους) to obey, his servants ye are to whom ye obey; whether of sin unto death, or of obedience unto righteousness?" There is in these passages no reference to any legal or rightful *claim* which the devil has over the transgressor, but only to the strong and tyrannical grasp which he has upon him. This captivity to Satan is related to the work of the Holy Spirit, more than to the atoning efficacy of Christ's blood; and deliverance from it makes a part of the work of sanctification, rather than of justification. This deliverance is preceded by another. In the order of nature, it is not until man has been first redeemed by the atoning blood from the claims of justice, that he is redeemed by the indwelling Spirit from the captivity and bondage of sin and Satan.

When, therefore, the efficacy of Christ's death is represented as the payment of a ransom price, the same objective reference of Christ's work is intended as in the previous instances of "propitiation" and "reconciliation." By Christ's death, man is ransomed from the righteous claims of another being than himself. That being is not Satan, but God the holy and just. And these claims are vicariously met. God satisfies God's claims in man's place. God's mercy ransoms man from God's justice.

We have thus seen from this examination of the Scripture representations, that Christ's priestly work has an objective reference: namely, that it affects and influences the Divine Being Christ's atonement "covers sin" from God's sight. It "propitiates" God's wrath against sin. It "reconciles" God's justice toward the sinner. It "pays a ransom" to God, for the sinner. None of these acts terminate upon man the subject, but all terminate upon God the object. Christ does not "cover sin" from the sinner's sight. He does not "propitiate" the sinner's wrath. He does not "reconcile" the sinner to the sinner. He does not "pay a ransom" to the sinner. These acts are each and all of them outward and transitive in their aim and reference. They are directed toward the Infinite, not the finite; toward the Creator, not the creature. Whatever be the effect wrought by the vicarious death of the Son of God, it is wrought upon the Divine nature. If it *appeases*, it appeases that nature; if it *propitiates*, it propitiates that nature; if it *satisfies*, it satisfies that nature; if it *reconciles*, it reconciles that nature. It is impossible to put any other interpretation upon the Scripture ideas and representations. A merely subjective reference, which would find all the meaning of them within the soul of man, requires a forced and violent exegesis of Scripture, and a self-contradictory use of the word "atonement."

At the same time, revelation plainly teaches that the *author* of this atoning influence and effect upon the Divine Being is the Divine Being himself. God propitiates, appeases, satisfies, and reconciles God. None of these are the acts of the creature. In all this work of propitiation, reconciliation, and redemption, God himself is the originating and active agent. He is therefore both *active* and *passive;* both *agent* and *patient* God is the Being who is angry at sin, and God is the Being who propitiates this anger. God is the offended party, and he is the one who reconciles the offended party. It is Divine justice that demands satisfaction, and it is the Divine compassion that makes the satisfaction. God is the one who holds man in a righteous captivity, and he is the one who pays the ransom that frees him from it. God is the holy Judge of man who requires satisfaction for sin; and God is the merciful Father of man who provides it for him. This fact relieves the doctrine of vicarious atonement of all appearance of severity, and evinces it to be the height of mercy and compassion. If it were man and not God who provided the atonement, the case would be otherwise. This peculiarity of the case is taught in Scripture. In 2 Cor. 5:18,19, it is said that "God hath reconciled us to *himself* (ἑαυτῷ, his own self), by Jesus Christ;" and that "God was in Christ, reconciling the world unto *himself* (ἑαυτῷ)." The statement is repeated in Coloss. 1: 20, "It pleased the Father through the blood of Christ's cross, to reconcile all things unto *himself*." According to this, in the work of vicarious atonement God is both subject and object, active and passive. He exerts a propitiating influence when he makes this atonement, and he receives a propitiating influence when he accepts it. He performs an atoning work, and his own attribute of justice feels the effect of it. Says Augustine (Trinity, IV. xiv. 19), "The same one and true Mediator reconciles us *to* God by the atoning sacrifice, remains one *with* God to whom he offers it, makes those one in himself *for* whom he offers it, and is himself both the offerer and the offering." Similarly, Frank (Christian Certainty, 352) remarks that "freedom from guilt is possible for man, because it has been provided for by God, and this provision rests upon a transaction of God with himself, whereby as other [i.e. as Son] he has made satisfaction to the claims of his own justice upon the sinner."

This doctrine of Scripture has passed into the creeds and litanies of the Church. In the English litany there is the petition: "From thy wrath and from everlasting damnation, Good Lord, deliver us." Here, the very same Being who is displeased is asked to save from the displeasure The very same holy God who is angry at sin is implored by the sinner to deliver him from the effects of this anger. And this is justified by the example of David, who cries (Ps. 38:1), "O Lord, rebuke me not in thy wrath, neither chasten me in thy hot displeasure;" and by the words of God himself addressed to his people through the prophet Isaiah (60:10), "In my wrath I smote thee, but in my favor have I had mercy upon thee." The prophet Hosea

(6:1) says to the unfaithful church: "Come and let us return unto the Lord: for he hath torn, and he will heal us; he hath smitten, and he will bind us up." In Zechariah 1: 2–4, Jehovah is described as "sore displeased," and yet at the same time as exhibiting clemency towards those with whom he is displeased. "The Lord hath been sore displeased with your fathers. Therefore say thou unto them, Thus saith the Lord of hosts, Turn ye unto me, saith the Lord of hosts, and I will turn unto you, saith the Lord of hosts" Also (Job 42: 7, 8), "The Lord said to Eliphaz, My wrath is kindled against thee, and against thy two friends. Therefore take unto you seven bullocks and seven rams, and offer up for yourselves a burnt offering, lest I deal with you after your folly." Here, the very same God who was displeased with Job's friends devises for them a method whereby they may avert the displeasure. Upon a larger scale, God is displeased with every sinful man, yet he himself provides a method whereby sinful man may avert this displeasure. This is eminently the case with the believer. "When," says Calvin (Inst., III. ii. 21), "the saints seem to themselves to feel most the anger of God, they still confide their complaints to him; and when there is no appearance of his hearing them, they still continue to call upon him." Says Anselm (Meditatio II.), "Respira, o peccator, respira; ne desperes, spera in eo quem times. Affuge ad eum a quo aufugisti. Invoca importune quem superbe provocasti."

The doctrine of vicarious atonement, consequently, implies that *in God there exist simultaneously both wrath and compassion.* In this fact, is seen the infinite difference between Divine and human anger. When God is displeased with the sinner, he compassionately desires that the sinner may escape the displeasure, and invents a way of escaping it. But when man is displeased with his fellow-man, he does not desire that his fellow-man may escape the displeasure, and devises no way of escape. The Divine wrath issues from the constitutional and necessary antagonism between the Divine holiness and moral evil. The Divine compassion springs from the benevolent interest which God feels in the work of his hands. The compassion is founded in God's paternal relation to man; the wrath is founded in his judicial relation to him. God as a creator and father pities the sinner; as a judge he is displeased with him. Wrath against sin must be both felt and manifested by God; compassion towards the sinner must be felt, but may or may not be manifested by Him. Justice is necessary in its exercise, but mercy is optional. The righteous feeling of wrath toward sin is immutable and eternal in God, but it may be propitiated by the gracious feeling of compassion toward the sinner, which is also immutable and eternal in God. God the father of men may reconcile God the judge of men. Whether this *shall* be done, depends upon the sovereign pleasure of God. He is not obliged and necessitated to propitiate his own wrath for the sinner, as he is to punish sin; but he has mercifully determined to do this, and has done it by the atonement of Jesus Christ. By the method of vicarious substitution of penalty, God satisfies his own justice and reconciles his own displeasure towards the transgressor. That moral emotion in the Divine essence which from the nature and necessity of the case is incensed against sin, God himself placates by a self-sacrifice that inures to the benefit of the guilty creature. Here, the compassion and benevolent love of God propitiates the wrath and holy justice of God. The two feelings exist together in one and the same Being. The propitiation is no oblation ab extra: no device of a third party, or even of sinful man himself, to render God placable towards man. It is wholly ab intra: a self-oblation upon the part of the deity himself, in the exercise of his benevolence towards the guilty, by which to satisfy those constitutional imperatives of the divine nature which without it must find their satisfaction in the personal punishment of the transgressor, or else be outraged by arbitrary omnipotence.

Upon this point, Augustine (Tractatus in Joannem, cx. 6), remarks: "It is written, 'God commendeth his love towards us, in that while we were yet sinners Christ died for us.' He loved us, therefore, even when in the exercise of enmity towards him we were working iniquity. And yet it is said with perfect truth, 'Thou hatest, O Lord, all workers of iniquity.' Wherefore, in a wonderful and divine manner, he both hated and loved us at the same time. He hated us, as being different from what he had made us; but as our iniquity had not entirely destroyed his work in us, he could at the same time, in every one of us, hate what we had done, and love what he had created. In every instance it is truly said of God 'Thou hatest nothing which thou hast made; for never wouldst thou have made anything, if thou hadst hated it.'" Calvin, after quoting the above from Augustine, remarks (Institutes, II. xvi. 3) that "God who is the perfection of righteousness cannot love iniquity, which he beholds in us all. We all, therefore, have in us that which deserves God's hatred Wherefore, in respect to our corrupt nature and the consequent depravity of our lives, we are all really offensive to God, guilty in his sight, and born to the damnation of hell. But because God is unwilling to lose that in us which is his own, he still finds something in us which his benevolence (benignitas) can love. For notwithstanding that we are sinners by our own fault, we are yet his creatures; though we have brought death upon ourselves yet he had created us for life."

Turrettin (De veritate satisfactionis Christi, I. i.) distinguishes between "compassion" and "reconciliation." Because God is compassionate in his own excellent and perfect nature, he can become reconciled towards a transgressor of his law. If he were inherently destitute of compassion, he would be incapable of reconciliation. Compassion is a feeling, reconciliation is an act resulting from it. The former is inherent and necessary; the latter is optional and sovereign. If God were not compassionate and placable, he could not be propitiated by the sacrifice of Christ. An implacable and merciless being could not be conciliated, and would do nothing to effect a reconciliation. God is moved by a feeling of compassion and a benevolent affection towards sinners, prior to and irrespective of the death of Christ. "When we were yet sinners, Christ died for us," Rom. 5:8. The death of Christ did not make God compassionate and merciful. He is always and eternally so. But God's holy justice is not *reconciled* to sinners, unless Christ die for their sin. The compassion is prior in the order of nature to the death of Christ; the reconciliation of justice is subsequent to it. "Before the death of Christ, God was already compassionate (misericors), and placable. This moved him to provide salvation and redemption for man. But he was actually reconciled and propitiated, only upon the condition and supposition of that death of Christ which was required by eternal justice."

In this manner, compassion and wrath coexist in God. "To us indeed," says Turrettin (ut supra), "it seems difficult to conceive that the same person who is offended with us should also love us; because, when any feeling takes possession of us we are apt to be wholly engrossed with it. Thus if our anger is inflamed against any one, there is usually no room in us for favor towards him; and on the other hand, if we regard him with favor, there is often connected with it the most unrighteous indulgence. But if we could cast off the disorders of passion, and clothe ourselves in the garments of righteousness, we might easily harmonize these things with one another. A father offended with the viciousness of his son loves him as a son, yet is angry with him as being vicious. A judge, in like manner, may be angry and moved to punish, yet not the less on this account inclined by compassion to pardon the offender, if only some one would stand forth and satisfy the claims of justice for him. Why then, should not God, who is most righteous and benevolent, at once by reason of his justice demand penalty, and by reason of his compassion provide satisfaction for us?" Turrettin quotes in proof of this view the following from Aquinas (III. xlix. 4). "Non dicimur reconciliati quasi deus de novo amare incipiret, nam aeterno amore dilexit, sed quia per hanc reconciliationem sublata est omnis odii causa, tum per ablutionem peccati, tum per recompensationem acceptabilioris boni." He also remarks that "scholastici loquntur, dilexit deus humanum genus quantum ad naturam quam ipse fecit; odit quantum ad culpam quam homines contraxerunt."

In all that is said, consequently, respecting the wrath of God, in Christian theology, it is of the utmost importance to keep in view the fact that *this wrath is compatible with benevolence and compassion* This is the infinite difference in kind between divine and human anger. At the very moment when God is displeased, he is capable of devising kind things for the object of his displeasure. "While we were yet sinners Christ died for us," Rom. 5:8. And at the very instant when guilty man is conscious that the Divine wrath is resting upon him, he may address his supplication for a blessing to the very Being who is angry with his sin, and may pray: "From thy wrath, good Lord, deliver me." And the great and ample warrant and encouragement for men to do this, is found in the sacrifice of the Son of God. For in and by this atoning oblation, the Divine compassion conciliates the Divine wrath against sin. In the death of the God-man, "righteousness and peace, justice and mercy, kiss each other," Ps. 85: 10. The mercy vicariously satisfies the justice; the Divine compassion in the sinner's stead receives upon itself the stroke of the Divine wrath; God the Father smites God the Son, in the transgressor's place "Awake, O sword, against the man that is my fellow, saith the Lord of hosts," Zechariah 13: 7.[1]

[1] The same principle applies to the afflictions of life The strength and comfort must come from the very same Being who afflicts God is the source of affliction, and he is the God of all comfort God wounds, and God heals the

This subject is elucidated still further, by noticing the difference between the holy wrath of God and the wicked wrath of man. "The wrath of man worketh not the righteousness of God," James 1 : 20. When man is angry at man, this feeling is absolutely incompatible with the feeling of compassion and benevolent love. Selfish human anger and benevolence cannot be simultaneous. They cannot possibly co-exist. When a man, under the impulse of sinful displeasure, says to his brother man, "Raca," or "Thou fool" (Matt. 5 : 22); when he feels passionate and selfish wrath; he cannot devise good things for his brother man. On the contrary, he devises only evil things. He plots his neighbor's destruction. The wrath of the human heart is not only incompatible with benevolence, but is often intensely malignant. It is even increased by the moral excellence that is in the object of it. Holiness in a fellow-creature sometimes makes wicked human anger hotter and more deadly. The Jews gnashed their teeth in rage at the meekness and innocence of Christ. "The hatred of the wicked," says Rousseau (Confessions, IX.), "is only roused the more from the impossibility of finding any just grounds on which it can rest; and the very consciousness of their own injustice is only a grievance the more against him who is the object of it." "Oderint quem laeserint," says Tacitus. This kind of wrath requires complete eradication, before compassion can exist. "Better it were," says Luther (Table Talk, Of God's Works), "that God should be angry with us, than

---

wound. See Pascal's Letter to his brother-in-law, on the death of his own father. The same truth is expressed in the lines of George Herbert.

"Ah, my dear, angry Lord!
Since Thou dost love, yet strike;
Cast down, yet help afford;
Sure, I will do the like

I will complain, yet praise;
I will bewail, approve;
And all my sour-sweet days,
I will lament, and love."

that we be angry with God, for he can soon be at an union with us again, because he is merciful; but when we are angry with him, then the case is not to be helped."

Still further elucidation of this subject is found in the resemblance there is between the holy wrath of God, and the righteous anger of the human *conscience*. The sinful feeling of passionate anger to which we have just alluded is an emotion of the heart; but the righteous feeling of dispassionate anger to which we now allude is in the conscience. This is a different faculty from the heart[1] Its temper towards sin is unselfish and impartial, like the wrath of God. And this feeling can exist simultaneously with that of benevolence. When a man's own conscience is displacent and remorseful over his own sin, there is no malice towards the man himself, "for no man ever yet hated his own flesh," Eph. 5 : 29. At the very moment when a just and righteous man's conscience is offended and incensed at the wickedness of a fellow-man, he can and often does devise good things towards him. The most self-sacrificing philanthropists are those whose conscience is the most sensitive towards the moral evil which they endeavor to remove, and whose moral displeasure against sin is the most vivid and emphatic It is not the sentimental Rousseau, but the righteous Calvin who would willingly lay down his life, if thereby he could save men from eternal retribution. The conscience of Rousseau was dull and torpid, compared with the keen and energetic conscience of Calvin; but the desire of the latter for the spiritual and eternal welfare of sinful men was a thousand times greater than that of the former, supposing that there was in Rousseau any desire at all for the spiritual and eternal welfare of man. When St. Paul says respecting Alexander the coppersmith, "The Lord reward him according to his works" (2 Tim. 7 : 14),

[1] "La conscience est la voix de l'âme, les passions sont la voix du corps" Rousseau. Émile, IV. This is borrowed from Des Cartes: Les passions de l'âme, Art XVIII. XIX.

he gives expression to the righteous displeasure of a pure conscience towards one who was opposing the gospel of Christ, and the progress of God's kingdom in the earth. It was not any personal injury to the apostle that awakened the desire for the Divine retribution in the case, but a zeal for the glory of God and the welfare of man. Could St. Paul by any self-sacrifice on his own part have produced repentance and reformation in Alexander, he would gladly have made it. As in the instance of his unbelieving Jewish kindred, he would have been willing to be "accursed from Christ," for this purpose. Rom. 9 : 3. But when a profane man angrily says to his fellow-man: "God damn you," this is the malignant utterance of the selfish passion of the human heart, and is incompatible with any benevolent feeling.[1]

We find, then, that in the exercise of Christ's priestly office the agency is wholly within the Divine Nature itself. The justice and the mercy, the wrath and the compassion, are qualities of one and the same Eternal Being. It follows, consequently, that the explanation of the great subject of the Divine reconciliation lies in the doctrine of the Trinity. The doctrine of vicarious atonement stands or falls with that of the Triune God. If God the Father, Son, and Holy Ghost are three distinct persons, each one of them really objective to the others, then one of them can do a personal work not done by the others, that shall have an effect upon the Godhead. And if God the Father, Son, and Holy Ghost are also one undivided Being in nature and essence, then this effect, whatever it be, is not limited and confined to any one of the persons exclusive of the others, but is experienced by the one whole undivided nature and essence itself. The God*head*, and not merely God the Father, or God the Son, or God the Spirit, is reconciled to guilty man by the judicial suffering of one of the persons of

[1] On the difference between divine and human anger, see Shedd: Theological Essays, 269–284.

the Godhead, incarnate. The Son of God is a person distinct from, and objective to the Father and the Spirit. Hence, he can do a work which neither of them does. He becomes incarnate, not they. He suffers and dies for man, not they. And yet the efficacy of this work, which is his work as a trinitarian person, can terminate upon that entire divine nature which is all in God the Father, and all in God the Spirit, as it is all in God the Son. "Christ," says Frank (Christian Certainty, 366), "experienced as a [vicarious] sinner both subjection *to* God, and rejection *by* God; but yet as one who can call the God who has rejected him, *his* God, and who while the wrath of God goes forth upon him and delivers him up to the punitive infliction, nevertheless can pray: 'Not my will, but thine be done'"

Before leaving the subject of vicarious atonement, it is in place here to notice *its relation to the soul of man.* For, while Christ's atonement has primarily this objective relation to the Divine nature, it has also a secondary subjective relation to the nature of the guilty creature for whom it is made. The objective atonement is intended to be subjectively appropriated by the act of faith in it.

1. In the first place, the priestly work of Christ has an influence upon the human *conscience* similar to that which it has upon the divine justice. Man's moral sense is pacified by Christ's atonement. Peace is everywhere in Scripture represented as the particular effect produced by faith in Christ's blood. "Therefore being justified by faith, we have peace with God," Rom 5:1 "We are made nigh to God by the blood of Christ, for he is our peace," Eph. 2:13, 14. "Having made peace through the blood of his cross," Coloss. 1:20. "Peace I leave with you, my peace I give unto you," John 14:27. "The peace of God passeth all understanding," Philip. 4:7.

The human conscience is the mirror and index of the divine attribute of justice. The two are correlated. What therefore God's justice demands, man's conscience demands. "Nothing," says Matthew Henry, "can pacify an offended conscience but that which satisfied an offended God" The peace which the believer in Christ's atonement enjoys, and which is promised by the Redeemer to the believer, is the subjective experience in man that corresponds to the objective reconciliation in God. The pacification of the human conscience is the consequence of the satisfaction of the divine justice. God's justice is completely satisfied for the sin of man by the death of Christ. This is an accomplished fact. "Jesus Christ the righteous is the propitation for the sins of the whole world," 1 John 2: 2. The instant any individual man of this world of mankind *believes* that divine justice is thus satisfied, his conscience is at rest. The belief of a fact is always needed in order to a personal benefit from it. Belief is not needed in order to establish the fact. Whether a sinner believes that Christ died for sin or not, will make no difference with the fact, though it will make a vast difference with him. "If we believe not, yet he abideth faithful: he cannot deny himself," 2 Tim. 2: 13. Unbelief cannot destroy a fact. Should not a soul henceforth believe on the Son of God, it would nevertheless be a fact that he died an atoning death on Calvary, and that this death is an ample oblation for the sin of the world. But it must be remembered that the *kind* of belief by which a man obtains a *personal* benefit from the fact of Christ's death is experimental, not historical, or hearsay. A man may believe from common rumor that the death of Christ satisfies divine justice for the sin of the world, and yet experience no benefit and no peace from his belief; even as a blind man may believe from common rumor that there is a mountain in front of him, and yet have none of the pleasing sensations and personal benefits that accompany the vision of it. The blind man may have no doubt of the fact that there is a mountain before him; he may even argue to prove its existence; and still have all the wretched sensations of blindness, and obtain no personal advantage from his hearsay belief. And a sinful man may have no skeptical doubt that the death of Christ on mount Calvary has completely expiated human guilt, and may even construct a strong argument in proof of the fact, and still have all the miserable experience of an unforgiven sinner; may still have remorse, and the fear of death and the damnation of hell The belief by which men obtain personal benefit, namely, mental peace and blessedness, from the fact of Christ's atonement involves *trust* and *reliance* upon Christ. A man may believe Christ, and yet not believe *on* him. Christ himself marks the difference between historical or hearsay belief, and experimental faith, in Matt. 13: 13–15. "Seeing, they see not; and hearing, they hear not, neither do they understand. In them is fulfilled the prophecy of Esaias, which saith, By hearing ye shall hear, and shall not understand; and seeing ye shall see, and shall not perceive." Whenever there is an experimental belief of the actual and accomplished fact of Christ's atonement, there is a subjective pacification of the conscience corresponding to the objective reconciliation of the divine justice. But this subjective effect of Christ's death is neither the primary nor the whole effect of it. It presupposes the objective satisfaction or propitiation. In this instance, as in all others, the object is prior to the subject and determines its consciousness.

2. Secondly, the subjective appropriation of Christ's atonement is the evidence and test of genuine repentance. An unselfish godly sorrow for sin is shown by a willingness to suffer *personally* for sin. In Leviticus 26: 41, 43, the truly penitent are described as "accepting the punishment of their iniquity." The criminal who complains of punishment, or resists it, or endeavors to escape from it, evinces by this fact that he cares more for his own happiness than he does for the evil and wickedness of his act. If he were certain of not being punished, he would repeat his transgres-

sion. There is of course no genuine sorrow for sin in such a temper. If, on the contrary, a wrong-doer approves of, and accepts the punishment denounced against his crime, and voluntarily gives himself up to suffer for his transgression, he furnishes the highest proof of true sorrow. He does not make his own happiness the first thing, but the maintenance of justice. With Angelo (Measure for Measure, V. i.), he says:

> " So deep sticks it in my penitent heart,
> That I crave death more willingly than mercy;
> 'Tis my deserving, and I do entreat it."

With the penitent thief, he says, " We are in this condemnation justly, for we receive the due reward of our deeds," Luke 23 . 41. " No one can deny," says Dorner (Christian Doctrine, I. 302), " that true penitence includes the candid acknowledgment of actual desert of punishment, and that the denial of this desert and the unwillingness to suffer punishment and to surrender to the disgrace of justice, is the most certain proof of a mere semblance of penitence. And it is not essentially different, when repentance and the resolution to live a better life are put in the place of that suffering which constitutes satisfying atonement, and gives a title to remission of sin. Such views are a poisoning of penitence, which, in order to be genuine, must stand the test of being ready to suffer punishment and approve of the retribution of justice."

The first impulse consequently of true penitence is, to make a *personal* atonement. This distinguishes penitence from remorse; the godly sorrow from the sorrow of the world, 2 Cor. 7 : 10. Mere remorse has no desire or impulse to suffer and make amends for what has been done. Its impulse and desire is wholly selfish, namely, to escape suffering. Remorse leads to suicide, penitence never. The suicide's motive is to put an end to his misery. He supposes that he will be happier by dying, than by continuing to live. This was the motive of the impenitent Judas.[1] But the broken and contrite heart is willing to do and to suffer anything that would really satisfy God's holy law. This is taught in Psalm 51 : 16. David in his genuine sorrow for his great transgression says: "Thou desirest not sacrifice, else would I give it." He perceives that any expiation which he could make for his sin would be unequal to what justice requires; but this does not render him any the less ready to make it if he could. And when the true penitent perceives that another competent person, Divinely appointed, has performed that atoning work for him which he is unable to perform for himself, he welcomes the substitution with joy and gratitude. Any aversion, therefore, to Christ's vicarious atonement, evinces that there is a defect in the supposed sorrow for sin. The lust of self is in the experience. The individual's happiness is in the foreground, and the divine holiness is in the background. And the positive and deliberate rejection of Christ's atonement, upon the same principle, is absolute and utter impenitence. A hostile and polemic attitude towards the blood of Christ as atoning for human guilt, is fatal hardness of heart. Christ refers to it in his awful words to the Pharisees: "If ye believe not that I am he, ye shall die in your sins," John 8 : 24. Impenitence shows itself both in unwillingness to make a personal atonement for sin, and to trust in a vicarious atonement for it.

It becomes necessary now, to consider the question: How does the suffering of Christ meet the requisitions

---

[1] Suicide, if the act of sanity, is ipso facto proof of insubmission and rebellion towards God, and impenitence in sin. Socrates (Phaedo, 61) contends that to take one's own life, is to defraud and dishonor the Creator. "The gods," he says, "are our guardians, and we are a possession of theirs. If one of your own possessions, an ox or an ass, for example, took the liberty of putting himself out of the way when you had given no intimation of your wish that he should die, would you not be displeased with him, and would you not punish him if you could?" It was upon this view of suicide, that the self-murderer was denied burial by the Church in consecrated ground.

involved in the case of substitution of penalty, or vicarious atonement? We have seen that suffering is the inmost essence of an atonement. The sacrificial victim must agonize and die. Without shedding of blood there is no remission of penalty. Even in cases where physical suffering does not take place, a suffering of another kind does. A citizen, within the province of civil law, is said to make amends for his fault when he pays a fine and suffers a loss of money as the compensation to civil justice. What, then, is suffering?

Suffering is of three kinds: 1. Calamity. 2. Chastisement. 3 Punishment, or penalty.

1. *Calamity* does not refer to sin and guilt. It is a kind of suffering that befalls man by the providence of God for other reasons than disciplinary or judicial. Calamitous suffering, however, it should be noticed, occurs only in a sinful world Consequently it is never found isolated, and by itself alone. It is associated either with chastisement: as when a calamity falls upon a child of God; or with punishment: as when it falls upon the impenitent sinner. Calamity is therefore rather an element in suffering, than the whole of the suffering. When, for illustration, some of the Galilaeans had been cruelly put to death by Herod (Luke 13.1-5), our Lord distinctly told those who informed him of this fact, that these Galilaeans "were not sinners *above* all the Galilaeans because they suffered such things." They were sinners, but not the worst of sinners In other words, he taught them that the *whole* of this suffering was not penal. As sinners, they deserved to suffer; and some of this suffering was for their sins. But as they were not greater sinners than other Galilaeans, they did not deserve a suffering that was so much greater than that of the Galilaean people as a whole. A part of this extraordinary suffering, therefore, was calamity, not punishment As such, it had no reference to the guilt of the Galilaeans. If it had, it would have been a proof that they "were sinners above

all the Galilaeans." Our Lord then repeats and emphasizes the same truth, by an allusion to the fall of the tower in Siloam upon some of the inhabitants of Jerusalem This event did not prove that these few persons were sinners "above all men that dwelt in Jerusalem." There was therefore a calamitous as well as a penal element, in this fall of the tower. The same doctrine is taught by the extraordinary sufferings of the patriarch Job Job's friends contended that these were *all* and *wholly* penal. They inferred that Job had been guilty of some extraordinary sin which merited this extraordinary punishment, and they urged him to confess it. The patriarch, though acknowledging himself to be a sinner, and deserving to suffer for sin (Job 42 : 5, 6), was not conscious of any such extraordinary act of transgression as his friends supposed he must have committed, and cannot understand why he should have been visited with such enormous afflictions. Both he and they are finally informed by God himself, out of the whirlwind, that the *extraordinariness* of the suffering is due to the will of God; that it is of the nature of calamity, not of penalty. Jehovah resolves the mystery in the uncommon treatment of Job, into an act of almighty power by an infinitely wise being who gives no reason for his procedure in this instance. Job, Chapters 38–41. Elihu, the youngest of the speakers, seems to have had an intimation in his own mind that this was the true explanation of the dark problem. "I will answer thee that God is greater than man. Why dost thou strive against him? For he giveth not account of any of his matters," Job 33 : 12, 13.

2. The second species of suffering is *chastisement.* This is spoken of in Heb. 12 : 6. "For whom the Lord loveth, he chasteneth (παιδεύει, treats like a child)." Chastisement and punishment are distinguished from each other in 1 Cor. 11 : 32, "When we are judged, we are chastened of the Lord, that we should not be condemned with the world." The purpose of chastisement is discipline and moral im-

provement. The reason for it is not secret and unknown, as in the case of calamity. It is adapted to reform It is administered by parental affection, not by judicial severity. It is the form which suffering assumes within the family. The parent does not cause the child to feel pain for the satisfaction of justice, but for personal improvement. The suffering does indeed remind the child of his guilt, and is suggestive of penalty, but it is not itself penal. Family discipline is not of the nature of retribution.

Hence analogies drawn from the family do not apply to the civil government, and still less to the Divine government, when guilt and retribution are the subjects under consideration. Guilt and retribution are not res domi; they are not family affairs. The family was not established for the purpose of punishing criminals, but of educating children. Because a human father may forgive a child, that is, may forego the infliction of suffering for an offence, without any satisfaction being rendered for him by a substitute, and without any reference to the claims of law, it does not follow that the state can do this, or that the Supreme Ruler can. Within the sphere of family life, there is nothing judicial and retributive. There is, therefore, no analogy between the two spheres. There can be no legitimate arguing from a sphere in which the retributive element is altogether excluded, such as that of the father and the child, over into a sphere in which the retributive is the prime element, such as that of God the just and man the guilty. It is μετάβασις ἐις ἄλλο γένος. A parent is at liberty, in case he judges that in a particular instance the child will be morally the better for so doing, to forego chastisement altogether. He can pass by the transgression without inflicting any pain at all upon the child. But the magistrate has no right to do this, in the instance of crime against the state. He must cause each and every transgression to receive the penalty prescribed by the statute. Furthermore, since chastisement has no reference to crime, it is not graduated by justice and the degree of the offence, but by expediency and the aim to reform. Sometimes a small fault in a child may be chastised with a severe infliction, and a great fault with a mild one. The object not being to weigh out penalty in exact proportion to crime, but to discipline and reform the character, the amount of suffering inflicted is measured by this aim and object. A very slight offence, if there is a tendency frequently to repeat it on the part of the child, may require a heavy chastisement, so that the habit may be broken up And on the other hand, a very grave offence which is exceptional in its nature, and to which there is no habitual tendency on the part of the child, may be best managed with a slight infliction of pain, or even with none at all. A rebuke merely may be better adapted to promote the reformation of the offender. All this is illustrated in God's dealings with his own children. A Christian of uncommon excellence to human view sometimes experiences a great affliction, while one of less devoutness, apparently, is only slightly afflicted, or perhaps not at all. This difference is not caused by the degree of demerit in each instance, but by what the Divine eye sees to be required in each case in order to the best development of character.

Now the relation of a believer to God, is like that of the child to the earthly father. Man enters into God's heavenly family by the act of faith in Christ. All the suffering that befalls him in this sphere is therefore of the nature of chastisement, not of punishment or retribution. It is not intrinsically endless and hopeless, as Divine retribution is. "I will visit their transgression with the rod; nevertheless my loving kindness I will not utterly take from him." "He will not always chide; neither will he keep his anger forever." Ps. 89: 31-34; 103: 9; Jer. 10: 24. The penalty due to the believer's sin has been endured for him by his Redeemer, and therefore there is no need of his enduring it Justice does not exact penalty twice over.

Consequently, whenever the believer suffers pain from any cause or source whatever, he is not suffering retributive punishment for purposes of law and justice, but corrective chastisement for purposes of self-discipline and spiritual improvement: ἐπὶ τὸ συμφέρον, Heb. 12:10. This suffering, though for the present moment not joyous but grievous, yet after it has been submissively endured, works out the peaceable fruit of righteousness, Heb. 12:11. Even death itself, which is the climax of suffering, it not penal for a believer. Its sting, that is, its retributive quality, is extracted, 1 Cor. 15:55, 56. Suffering is penal when it is intended and felt to be such; and is chastisement when it is not so intended and felt. God intends a benefit, not a punishment, when he causes a believer in Christ to suffer the pains of dissolution; and the believer so understands it. He feels that it is fatherly discipline. When a penitent believer dies, God supports and comforts the departing soul; but when an impenitent unbeliever dies, the soul is left to itself without support and comfort from God. The tranquillizing presence of God converts death into chastisement, the absence of such a presence makes it penalty.

The relation of a rebellious and unbelieving man to God is like that of a rebellious citizen to the state. All that such a citizen can expect from the government under which he lives is justice, the due reward of his disobedience. The state is not the family, and what is peculiar to the one is not to the other. The disobedient citizen cannot expect from the magistrate, the patient forbearance, and affectionate tuition which the disobedient child meets with from a parent with a view to his discipline and moral improvement. The citizen is entitled only to justice, and if he gets it in the form of the righteous punishment of his crime he must be silent. No man may complain of justice, or quarrel with it. To do so is an absurdity, as well as a fault. By creation, man was within the circle both of the Divine government and the Divine family. Holy Adam was at once a subject and a child. By apostasy and rebellion, he threw himself out of the circle of God's family, but not out of the circle of God's government. Sinful man is invited and even commanded to re-enter the Divine family, when he is invited and commanded to believe on the Lord Jesus Christ for the remission of his sins. But so long as he is an unbeliever, he has not re-entered it, and is not an affectionate or "dear" child of God. The phraseology in Jer. 31 : 20, Ephraim is "my dear son;" in Eph. 5 : 1, "Be ye followers of God as dear children;" in Rom 8 : 16, 17, "The Spirit itself beareth witness with our spirit that we are the children of God, and if children, then heirs;" in Gal. 3 : 26, "Ye are the children of God by faith in Christ Jesus;" and in Matt. 5 : 9, "The peacemakers shall be called the children of God"—this and the like phraseology is not applicable to men indiscriminately, but only to believers. The childhood and the fatherhood in this case is special, because it is founded in redemption.

There is a providential fatherhood and childhood, spoken of in scripture, which is not sufficient to constitute fallen man a member of God's *heavenly* family. In Acts 17 : 28, all men are called the "offspring" of God; and in Malachi 2 : 10, the question is asked, "Have we not all one father?" This providential fatherhood and childhood is founded in creation. This is proved by a second question in Malachi 2 : 10, which follows the one already cited and explains it: "Hath not one God created us?" And in Acts 17 : 26, the reason given why all nations are the offspring of God is, that they are "made of one blood" by their Creator. Creation is a kind of paternity. In Job 38 : 28, 29, this is extended even to the inanimate creation. "Hath the rain a father? or who hath begotten the drops of the dew? Out of whose womb came the ice? And the hoary frost of heaven, who hath gendered it?" In Deut. 2 : 27, idolatrous Israel is represented as "saying to a stock, Thou art my father: and to a stone, Thou hast brought me forth."

In acknowledging a false God to be their maker, they acknowledged him to be their providential father. In accordance with this, God says to a wicked generation "whose spot is not the spot of his children," who are not "dear" children in the special sense, "Do ye thus requite the Lord, O foolish people and unwise? Is not he thy father that bought thee? Hath he not made thee, and established thee?" Deut. 32 : 6. Our Lord (Matt. 7 : 11) teaches that "evil" men have a "father in heaven," and explains this fatherhood by God's readiness to bestow "good things" in his general providence. This association of paternity with creation and providence is found also in secular literature. Plato (Timaeus, 9) says that "to discover the creator and father of this universe is indeed difficult." Horace (Carminum I. 12) speaks of "the Father of all, who governs the affairs of men and gods." Creation, together with providence and government which are necessarily associated with creation, is a solid basis for this kind of paternity. It implies benevolent care and kindness towards its objects, and these are paternal qualities. God's providential and governmental goodness towards all his rational creatures is often referred to in Scripture. Matt. 5 : 45, "Your Father which is in heaven maketh his sun to rise on the evil and the good, and sendeth rain upon the just and the unjust." Acts 14 : 17, "He left not himself without witness, in that he did good, and gave us rain from heaven and fruitful seasons, filling our hearts with food and gladness."

The fact, then, that God creates man after his own image a rational and immortal being, that he continually upholds him and extends to him the blessings of a kind and watchful providence, and still more that he compassionates him in his sinful and guilty condition, and provides for him a way of salvation—all this justifies the use of the term "father" in reference to God, and the term "child" in reference to man. But the fatherhood and childhood, in this case, are different from those of redemption and adoption.

The former may exist without the latter. God as the universal Parent, while showing providential benevolence and kindness to an impenitent sinner, "filling his mouth with food and gladness" all the days of his earthly existence, may finally punish him forever for his ungrateful abuse of paternal goodness, for his transgression of moral law, and especially for his rejection of the offer of forgiveness in Christ. And this lost man is still, even in his lost condition, one of God's "offspring." Abraham, speaking in the place of God, calls Dives in hell a child of the universal Parent. "Son, remember that thou in thy lifetime receivedst thy good things," Luke 16 : 25. And Dives recognizes the relationship, when he says, "Father Abraham, have mercy on me," Luke 16 : 24. The providential fatherhood of God is thus shown to be consistent with the punishment of a rebellious son. It is also consistent with the refusal to abate the merited punishment. Dives asks for a drop of water to cool his tongue, and is refused Dives was an *impenitent* man. He did not confess his sin, or implore its forgiveness. He only asked for deliverance from suffering. He lacked the spirit of the prodigal son, and of the penitent thief. He did not say, "Father, I have sinned, and am no more worthy to be called thy son, make me as one of thy hired servants. I am in this condemnation justly. I am receiving the due reward of my deeds"

The universal fatherhood and childhood may exist without the special; but not the special without the universal. There may be creation, providence and government, without redemption; but not redemption without the former. A man may experience all the blessings of God's general paternity without those of his special; but not the blessings of God's special fatherhood without those of his general. Christ speaks of those who are not God's children in the special sense, when he says, in reply to the assertion of the Jews, "We have one Father, even God," "If God were your Father, ye would love me. Ye are of your father, the devil," John 8 : 41–44. St. John refers to the same class in the words, "In this the children of God are manifest, and the children of the devil," 1 John 3 : 10.

When men universally are commanded to say "Our Father which art in heaven," they are commanded to do so with the heart, not with the lips merely. They have no permission to employ the terms of the family from the position of a rebel. Says Christ, "Why call ye me Lord, Lord, and do not the things which I say?" Luke 6 : 46. In like manner God says, "A son honoreth his father: If I be a father, where is mine honor?" Malachi 1 : 6. The fact of the providential fatherhood, as previously remarked, is not sufficient to constitute *fallen* men members of God's heavenly family. Unfallen man was a member of the heavenly family merely by the fatherhood of creation and providence; but after his rebellion and apostasy this ceased to be the case. Redemption was needed in order to restore him to membership. The whole human family are not now God's heavenly family. Only a part of it are the dear children of God. Those only are members of God's family who are members of Christ, "of whom the whole family in heaven and earth [the church above and below] is named," Eph. 3 : 15. All others "are bastards, and not sons," Heb. 12 : 8.[1]

3. The third species of suffering is *punishment*. This is pain inflicted because of guilt. The intention of it is the satisfaction of justice. Retributive justice is expressed in the saying, "An eye for an eye, and a tooth for a tooth." This is the lex talionis, or law of requital.[2] Our Lord, in the Sermon on the Mount, did not abolish this law, but placed its execution upon the proper basis. "That which was addressed to the judges," says Calvin (Henry's Life, I. 287), "private individuals applied to themselves, and it was this abuse which our Lord Jesus Christ would correct."

[1] See the excellent treatise of Crawford: The Fatherhood of God

[2] See the explanation and defence of it by Kalisch On Ex. 21 22–25.

The private person may not put out the eye of him who has put out an eye, but the government may. Retribution is not the function of the individual. It belongs to God, and to the government, which is ordained of God. "Dearly beloved, avenge not yourselves; for it is written, Vengeance is mine, I will repay, saith the Lord," Rom. 12:19. This retributive function is delegated by God to the magistrate, "for he is the minister of God, an avenger to execute wrath upon him that doeth evil," Rom. 13:4. When the private individual takes the lex talionis into his own hands, it is revenge. Christ forbade this. When God or the government administers it, it is vengeance. Christ did not forbid this. The former is selfish and wrong; the latter is dispassionate and right.

That particular amount and kind of suffering which is required by the law of requital is punishment. Its primary aim is the satisfaction of justice, not utility to the criminal. The criminal is sacrificed to justice. His private interest is subservient to that of law and government, because the latter is of more importance than the former. Even if he derives no personal benefit from the retribution which he experiences, the one sufficient reason for it still holds good, namely, that he has voluntarily transgressed and deserves to suffer for it. Both the quantity and the quality of the suffering must be considered, in order to penalty. (*a*) In the first place, the amount of the suffering must be *proportionate* to the offence. To take human life for a petty larceny would be unjust. To take money as an offset for murder would be unjust. (*b*) In the second place, suffering must be *intended* as penal and *felt* to be penal, in order to be penal. It must have this retributive quality. Two men might suffer from God precisely the same amount of suffering, and in one case it might be retribution, and in the other chastisement, because in the one case his intention was the satisfaction of law, in the other the correction of his child. Physical death in the case of a wicked man is penal evil, because it is designed as a punishment on the part of God, and is felt to be such by the man. God grants no comfort to the wicked in his death; the sting is not extracted, and death is remorseful and punitive. But the very same event of death, and the same suffering in amount, is chastisement and not punishment for a believer, because it is accompanied with inward strength from God to endure it, and is known to be the means of entrance into heaven.

The sufferings of Christ the mediator were vicariously *penal*, or *atoning*, because the intention, both on the part of the Father and the Son, was that they should satisfy justice for the sin of man. They were not calamity, for their object is known. The reason for calamitous suffering is secret. And they were not disciplinary, because Christ having no sin could not pass through a process of progressive sanctification. Scripture plainly teaches that our Lord's sufferings were vicariously retributive; that is, that they were endured for the purpose of satisfying justice in the place of the actual transgressor. 1 Pet. 3:18, "Christ hath once suffered for sins, the just for the unjust." Gal. 3:13, "Christ was made a curse for us." Isa. 53:5, "Immanuel was wounded for our transgressions, and bruised for our iniquities." Rom. 4:25, "Jesus our Lord was delivered for our offences." 2 Cor 5:21, "He hath made him to be sin [a sin-offering] for us, who knew no sin." 1 John 2:2, "He is the propitiation for our sins" John 1:29, "Behold the Lamb of God which taketh away the sins of the world." Rom. 8:32, "He spared not his own Son, but delivered him up for us all." With this, compare 2 Pet. 2:4, "He spared not the angels that sinned, but cast them down to hell" Penalty in the case of Christ was vicarious; in that of the fallen angels was personal.

The penal and atoning sufferings of Christ were twofold: (*a*) Ordinary. (*b*) Extraordinary The first came upon him by virtue of his human nature. He hungered, thirsted, was weary in body, was sad and grieved in mind, by the operation of the natural laws of matter and mind. All that Christ endured by virtue of his being born of a woman, being made under the law, living a human life, and dying a violent death, belongs to this class. The extraordinary sufferings in Christ's experience came upon him by virtue of a positive act and infliction on the part of God. To these belong, also, all those temptations by Satan which exceeded in their force the common temptations incident to ordinary human life. Through these Christ was caused to suffer more severely than any of his disciples have. And that this was an intentional and preconceived infliction on the part of God, for the purpose of causing the sinner's substitute to endure a judicial suffering, is proved by the statement that "Jesus was led up of the *Spirit* into the wilderness, to be tempted of the devil," Matt 4:1. These severe temptations from Satan occurred more than once. "The devil departed from him for a season," Luke 4:13. But still more extraordinary was that suffering which was caused in the soul of Christ by the immediate agency of God, in the garden and on the cross. That agony which forced the blood through the pores of the skin, and wrung from the patient and mighty heart of the God-man the cry, "My God, why hast thou forsaken me!" cannot be explained by the operation of natural laws. There was positive desertion and infliction, on the part of God. The human nature was forsaken, as the words of Christ imply. That support and comfort which the humanity had enjoyed, in greater or less degree, during the life of the God-man upon earth, was now withdrawn utterly and entirely. One consequence of this was, that the physical suffering involved in the crucifixion was unmitigated. Christ had no such support as his confessors have always had in the hour of martyrdom. But this was the least severe part of Christ's extraordinary suffering. The pain from the death of crucifixion was physical only. There was over and above this a mental distress that was far greater. This is indicated in the terms employed to describe the spiritual condition of Christ's soul, in the so-called "agony" in the garden. "He began to be sore amazed, and to be very heavy, and saith unto them, My soul is exceeding sorrowful unto death," Mark 14 · 33, 34. The words ἐκθαμβεῖσθαι and ἀδημονεῖν imply a species of mental distress that stuns and bewilders. This mental suffering cannot be explained upon ordinary psychological principles, but must be referred to a positive act of God. Christ was sinless and perfect. His inward distress did not result from the workings of a guilty conscience. The agony in the garden and on the cross was not that of remorse; though it was equal to it. Neither was it the agony of despair; though it was equal to it.[1]

The positive agency of God, in causing a particular kind of suffering to befall the Mediator which could not have befallen him by the operation of natural causes, is spoken of

---

[1] Christ felt that he was forsaken of God, but not, like a despairing person, that he was *eternally* forsaken. The desertion was only temporary The comforting presence of God returns to Christ, as is indicated in the statement of Luke (23 46) that "Jesus cried with a loud voice, saying, Father, into thy hands I commend my spirit." Again, the agony of Christ was not despair, because in this very cry he says, "*My* God." A despairing man or angel would say, "*O* God," and would not expostulate, saying, "*Why* hast thou forsaken me?" Again, Christ did not experience despair, because he knew that the union between the divine and human natures was indissoluble He also knew that the covenant of redemption between him and the Father could not fail His distress did not relate to either of these two particulars. It arose (*a*) From his view of the nature of the curse upon sin which he had vicariously come under, (*b*) Because the comforting influences from the union of the divine with the human nature were temporarily restrained, (*c*) From temporary desertion of God, (*d*) From positive infliction when the "sword was awakened" against him Owen Third Sacramental Discourse The words, "Why hast thou forsaken me?" express *wonder*, not ignorance, or unbelief, or complaint. Christ well knew why he was deserted at this hour, had perfect faith and confidence in his Father, and was entirely submissive to his will. But he was *amazed* and *paralyzed* at the immensity of the agony "Why," is not interrogative, but exclamatory The words are equivalent to "How thou hast forsaken me!" This is Hugh St Victor's explanation See Hooker, V xlviii When a Christian exclaims, "Why am I so unbelieving and sinful?" it is only another way of saying, "How unbelieving and sinful I am!" He is not asking for information. He well knows the reason why.

in Isa. 53 : 5, 6, 10 "He was wounded for our transgressions, he was bruised for our iniquities. The Lord hath laid on him the iniquity of us all. It pleased the Lord to bruise him." And again in Zechariah 13 : 7, "Awake, O sword, against my shepherd, and against the man that is my fellow, saith the Lord of hosts; smite the shepherd" This language teaches, that the incarnate second person of the Trinity received upon himself a stroke inflicted by the positive act of another divine person. The Son of God was bruised, wounded, and smitten by God the Father, as the officer and agent of Divine justice, and the effects of it appear in that extraordinary mental distress which the Mediator exhibited, particularly during the last hours of his earthly life. "While he was buffeted, scourged, and nailed to the cross, we hear nothing from him; but like a lamb before the shearers, he was dumb. But when God reached forth his hand, and darted his immediate rebukes into his very soul and spirit, then he cries out, My God, my God, why hast thou forsaken me!"[1]

The nature of this suffering is inexplicable, because it has no parallel in human consciousness. The other forms of Christ's suffering are intelligible, because they were like those of men. Thirst, hunger, weariness, grief at the death of a friend, were the same in Christ that they are in us. But that strange and unique experience which uttered itself in the cry, "My God, why hast thou forsaken me?" belongs to the consciousness of the God-man. Only he who occupied the actual position of the sinner's substitute can experience such a judicial stroke from eternal justice, and only he can know the peculiarity of the suffering which it produces. Suffering is a form of consciousness, and consciousness can be known only by the possessor of it.

There are some particulars respecting this positive infliction upon the Mediator which must be carefully noted. 1.

---

[1] South Sermon on Messiah's Suffering Edwards· Excellency of Christ. Works, IV. 189

Though the Father "smote," "wounded," and "bruised" the Son, he felt no *emotional* anger towards the person of the Son The emotional wrath of God is revealed only against personal unrighteousness, and Christ was holy, harmless, undefiled, and separate from sinners. The Father smote his "beloved Son, in whom he was well pleased," Matt. 3:17. At the very instant when the Father forsook the Son, he loved him emotionally and personally with the same infinite affection with which he had loved him "before the world was." When it is said that Christ experienced the "wrath of God," the meaning is, that he experienced a judicial suffering caused by God. The "wrath" of God in this instance is not a divine *emotion*, but a divine *act* by which God the Father caused pain in Jesus Christ for a particular purpose. This purpose is judicial and penal, and therefore the act may be called an act of wrath. "Ira dei est voluntas puniendi" Anselm: Cur deus homo, I. 6. In Rom. 13:4, the infliction of suffering by the magistrate upon the criminal is denominated an act of "wrath." "He is the minister of wrath." But the magistrate has no emotional anger towards the criminal. God the Father could love the Son, therefore, at the very instant when he visited him with this punitive act. His emotion might be love, while his act was wrath. Nay, his love might be drawn forth by this very willingness of the Son to suffer vicariously for the salvation of man. "We do not admit," says Calvin (Inst., II. xvi 11), "that God was ever hostile or [emotionally] angry with him. For how could he be angry with his beloved Son in whom his soul delighted? or how could Christ by his intercession appease the Father for others, if the Father were incensed against him? But we affirm that he sustained the weight of the divine severity; since being smitten and afflicted of God, he experienced from God all the *tokens* of wrath and vengeance." Says Witsius (Covenants, II vi 38), "To be the beloved Son of God, and at the same time to suffer the wrath of God, are not such contrary things as that they cannot stand together. For, as Son, as the Holy One, while obeying the Father in all things, he was always the beloved; and indeed most of all when obedient to the death of the cross; for that was so pleasing to the Father that on account of it he raised him to the highest pitch of exaltation, Phil. 2:9; though as charged with our sins he felt the wrath of God burning not against himself, but against our sins which he took upon himself."

2 Secondly, the Son of God understands the judicial infliction which he undergoes, in this sense. God the Son knows that the blow which he experiences from God the Father is not for sin which he has himself committed. The transaction between the two Divine persons is of the nature of a covenant between them. The Son agrees to submit his person, incarnate, to a penal infliction that is required by the attribute of justice. But this attribute is as much an attribute of the Son as it is of the Father. The second trinitarian person is as much concerned for the maintenance of law as is the first. The Son of God is not seized an unwilling victim, and offered to justice by the Father. The Son himself is willing and desires to suffer. "I have," he says, "a baptism to be baptized with, and how am I straitened till it be accomplished," Luke 12:50. This explains the fact that Christ everywhere represents himself as voluntarily giving up his life. "No man taketh my life from me, I lay it down of myself," John 10:18 In some instances he employs his miraculous power to prevent his life from being taken, because "his hour was not yet come." But when the hour had come, though in the full consciousness that "twelve legions of angels" were at his command, he suffers himself to be seized by a handful of men, to be bound, and to be nailed to a cross. So far as the feature of mere voluntariness is concerned, no suicide was ever more voluntary in the manner of his death than was Jesus Christ.

A distinction is made between Christ's active and passive obedience.[1] The latter denotes Christ's sufferings of every kind; the sum-total of the sorrow and pain which he endured in his estate of humiliation. The term "passive" is used etymologically. His suffering is denominated "obedience," because it came by reason of his submission to the conditions under which he voluntarily placed himself, when he consented to be the sinner's substitute. He vicariously submitted to the sentence, "The soul that sinneth, it shall die," and was "obedient unto death," Phil. 2 : 8.

Christ's passive, or suffering obedience is not to be confined to what he experienced in the garden and on the cross. This suffering was the culmination of his piacular sorrow, but not the whole of it. Everything in his human and earthly career that was distressing belongs to his passive obedience. It is a true remark of Edwards, that the blood of Christ's circumcision was as really a part of his vicarious atonement, as the blood that flowed from his pierced side. And not only his suffering proper, but his humiliation, also, was expiatory; because this was a kind of suffering. Says Edwards (Redemption, II. i. 2), "The satisfaction or propitiation of Christ consists either in his suffering evil, or his being subject to abasement. Thus Christ made satisfaction for sin, by continuing under the power of death while he lay buried in the grave, though neither his body nor soul properly endured any suffering after he was dead. Whatever Christ was subject to that was the judicial fruit of sin, had the nature of satisfaction for sin. But not only proper suffering, but all abasement and depression of the state and circumstances of mankind [human nature] below its primitive honor and dignity, such as his body remaining under death, and body and soul remaining separate, and other things that might be mentioned, are the judicial fruits of sin."

Christ's active obedience is his perfect performance of

---

[1] Philippi: Der thatige Gehorsam Christi.

the requirements of the moral law. He obeyed this law in heart, and in conduct, without a single slip or failure. He was "holy, harmless, and undefiled," Heb. 7:26. Some theologians confine Christ's atonement to his passive obedience, in such sense that his active obedience does not enter into it and make a part of it.[1] Since atonement consists in suffering, and since obedience of the divine law is not suffering but happiness, they contend that Christ's active obedience cannot contribute anything that is strictly piacular or atoning. This would be true in reference to the active obedience of a mere creature, but not in reference to the active obedience of the God-man. It is no humilation for a created being to be a citizen of the Divine government; to be made under the law, and to be required to obey it. But it is humiliation for the Son of God to be so made, and to be so required to obey. It is stooping down, when the Ruler of the universe becomes a subject, and renders obedience to a superior. In so far as Christ's active obedience was an element in his *humiliation*, it was an element also in his expiation. Consequently, we must say that both the active and the passive obedience enter into the sum-total of Christ's atoning work. Christ's humiliation confessedly was atoning, and his obedience of the law was a part of his humiliation. The two forms of Christ's obedience cannot therefore be so entirely separated from each other, as is implied in this theory which confines the piacular agency of the Mediator to his passive obedience.

But while there is this atoning element in Christ's active obedience, it is yet true that the principal reference of the active obedience is to the law as precept, rather than to the law as penalty. It is more meritorious of reward than it is

[1] Piscator was the first formally to present this view. John Taylor of Norwich went to an opposite extreme, and held that the active obedience was the sole cause of man's salvation. He denied any piacular effect of Christ's death, and held that as a reward of Christ's active obedience alone the remission of sin was given to man, as the eminent services of a soldier are rewarded by the monarch by benefits to his family

piacular of guilt. The chief function of Christ's obedience of the moral law is, to earn a title for the believer to the rewards of heaven. This part of Christ's agency is necessary; because, merely to atone for past transgression would not be a complete salvation. It would, indeed, save man from hell, but it would not introduce him into heaven. He would be delivered from the law's punishment, but would not be entitled to the law's reward. "The man which *doeth* the things of the law shall live by them," Rom. 10:5. Mere innocence is not entitled to a reward. Obedience is requisite in order to this. Adam was not meritorious until he had obeyed the commandment, "Do this" Before he could "enter into life," he must "keep the commandment," like every subject of the divine government and candidate for heavenly reward. The Mediator, therefore, must not only suffer for man, but must obey for him, if he would do for man *everything* that the law requires Accordingly, Christ is said to be made of God unto the believer, "wisdom" and "sanctification," as well as "righteousness" and "redemption," 1 Cor. 1:30. Believers are described as "complete" in Christ, Coloss. 1:10; that is, they are entitled to eternal blessedness, as well as delivered from eternal misery. Christ is said to be "the end (τέλος) of the law for righteousness, to every one that believeth," Rom. 10:4. This means that Christ *completely* fulfils the law for the believer; but the law requires obedience to its precept as well as endurance of its penalty. Complete righteousness is conformity to the law in both respects. Rom. 5:19, "By his obedience, shall many be made righteous" Isa. 53:11, "By his knowledge, shall my righteous servant justify many." Jer. 23:6, "The Lord our righteousness." Jer. 45:24, "In the Lord have I righteousness." Rom. 8:4; Phil. 3:9; 2 Cor. 5:21.

The imputation of Christ's active obedience is necessary, also, in order to hope and confidence respecting the endless future. If the believer founds his expectation of an eternity of blessedness upon the amount of obedience which he has himself rendered to the law, and the degree of holiness which he has personally attained here upon earth, he is filled with doubt and fear respecting the final recompense. He knows that he has not, by his own work, earned and merited such an infinite reward as "glory, honor, and immortality." "We cannot by our best works merit eternal life at the hand of God, by reason of the great disproportion between them and the glory to come." Westminster Confession, XVI. v.[1] But if he founds his title to eternal life, and his expectation of it, upon the obedience of Christ for him, his anxiety disappears.

A distinction is made by some theologians between "satisfaction" and "atonement." Christ's satisfaction is his fulfilling the law both as precept and penalty. Christ's atonement, as antithetic to satisfaction, includes only what Christ does to fulfil the law as penalty. According to this distinction, Christ's atonement would be a part of his satisfaction. The objections to this mode of distinguishing are: (*a*) Satisfaction is better fitted to denote Christ's piacular work, than his whole work of redemption. In theological literature, it is more commonly the synonym of atonement. (*b*) By this distinction, atonement may be made to rest upon the passive obedience alone, to the exclusion of the active. This will depend upon whether "obedience" is employed in the comprehensive sense of including all that Christ underwent in his estate of humiliation, both in obeying and suffering.

Another distinction is made by some, between "satisfaction" and "merit." In this case, "satisfaction" is employed in a restricted signification. It denotes the satisfaction of retributive justice, and has respect to the law as penalty. Thus employed, the term is equivalent to "atonement" "Merit" as antithetic to "satisfaction" has re-

[1] See on this point, Paley: Sermon on Heb 9·26, Pt II

spect to the law as precept, and is founded upon Christ's active obedience. Christ vicariously obeys the law, and so vicariously merits for the believer the reward of eternal life. Respecting this distinction, Turrettin (Institutio XIV. xiii. 12) remarks that "the two things are not to be separated from each other. We are not to say as some do, that the "satisfaction" is by the passive work of Christ alone, and the "merit" is by the active work alone. The satisfaction and the merit are not to be thus viewed in isolation, each by itself, because the benefit in each depends upon the *total* work of Christ. For sin cannot be expiated, until the law as precept has been perfectly fulfilled; nor can a title to eternal life be merited, before the guilt of sin has been atoned for. Meruit ergo satisfaciendo, et merendo satisfecit." There is some ambiguity in this distinction, also. The term "merit" is often applied to Christ's passive obedience, as well as to his active. The "merit of Christ's blood" is a familiar phrase. The Mediator was meritorious in reference to the law's penalty, as well as to the law's precept.[1]

Having thus considered the nature of atonement, and the sufferings of the Mediator as constituting it, we proceed to notice some further characteristics of it

1. In the first place, atonement is correlated to justice, not to benevolence. Some have maintained that retributive justice is a phase of benevolence. They would reduce all the moral attributes to one, ultimately, namely, the divine love. This theory is built upon the text, "God is love." But there are texts affirming that "God is light," 1 John 1:5, and that "God is a consuming fire," Heb. 12:

---

[1] Owen (Justification, Ch X) endorses the distinction as made by Grotius "Whereas we have said that Christ hath procured two things for us, freedom from punishment, and a reward, the ancient church attributes the one of them to his satisfaction, the other to his merit" Edwards adopts it "Whatever in Christ had the nature of satisfaction, it was by virtue of the suffering or humiliation in it. But whatever had the nature of merit, it was by virtue of the obedience or righteousness that was in it." Redemption, Works, I. 402.

29 The affirmation, "Holy, holy, holy is the Lord of Hosts" (Isa. 6:3), is equivalent to, "God is holiness." Upon the strength of these texts, it might be contended that all the divine attributes may be reduced to that of wisdom, or of justice, or of holiness.[1] The true view is, that each of the attributes stands side by side with all the others, and cannot be merged and lost in any other. Justice is no more a phase of benevolence, than benevolence is a phase of justice. Each attribute has a certain distinctive characteristic which does not belong to the others, and by which it is a different attribute. The fact that one divine attribute affects and influences another, does not convert one into another. Omnipotence acts wisely, but this does not prove that omnipotence is a mode of wisdom. God's justice acts benevolently, not malevolently, but this does not prove that justice is a mode of benevolence. God's benevolence acts justly, not unjustly, but this does not prove that benevolence is a mode of justice. The divine attributes do not find a centre of unity in any one of their own number, but in the divine *essence*. It is the divine nature itself, not the divine attribute of love, or any other attribute, in which they all inhere.

Accordingly, the atoning sufferings and death of Christ are related to the attribute of justice, rather than to any other one of the divine attributes. They manifest and exhibit other attributes, such as wisdom, omnipotence, benevolence, and compassion, nay, all the other attributes, but they are an *atonement* only for retributive justice. Christ's death does not propitiate or satisfy God's benevolence, nor his wisdom, nor his omnipotence; but it satisfies his justice. Atonement cannot be correlated to benevolence, any more than creation can be correlated to omniscience. It is true that the creation of the world supposes omniscience, but

[1] Bengel composed his Syntagma de Sanctitate, to prove that all the attributes of God are *implied* in the Hebrew קָדוֹשׁ. But he did not hold that all *are* holiness.

creation is an act of power rather than of knowledge, and is therefore referred to omnipotence, rather than to omniscience. In like manner, Christ's atonement supposes benevolence in God, but benevolence is not the particular attribute that requires the atonement. It is retributive justice that demands the punishment of sin. If there were in God mere and isolated benevolence, there would be neither personal nor vicarious punishment; just as there would be no creation, if there were in God mere and isolated omniscience. Benevolence alone, and wholly disconnected from justice, would not cause pain but pleasure. It would relieve from suffering, instead of inflicting it. St. Paul, in Rome 5 : 7, teaches the diversity between the attribute of justice and that of benevolence, in saying that "scarcely for a just man will one die; yet peradventure for a benevolent man some would even dare to die." [1]

2. Secondly, an atonement for sin, of one kind or the other, if not personal then vicarious, is necessary, not optional. The transgressor must either die himself, or some one must die for him. This arises from the nature of that divine attribute to which atonement is a correlate. Retributive justice, we have seen (Vol. I., pp. 373–380), is necessary in its operation. The claim of law upon the transgressor for punishment is absolute and indefeasible. The eternal Judge may or may not exercise mercy, but he must exercise justice. He can neither waive the claims of law in part, nor abolish them altogether. The only possible mode, consequently, of delivering a creature who is obnoxious to the demands of retributive justice, is to satisfy them for him. The claims themselves must be met and extinguished, either personally, or by substitution. Fiat justitia ruat coelum. And this necessity of an atonement is absolute, not relative. It is not made necessary by divine decision,

[1] Butler (Nature of Virtue, Dissertation II. sub fine), contends that "the *whole* of virtue does not consist in promoting happiness" This is the same as contending that all moral qualities cannot be resolved into benevolence.

in the sense that the divine decision might have been otherwise. It is not correct to say, that God might have saved man without a vicarious atonement had he been pleased so to do. For this is equivalent to saying, that God might have abolished the claims of law and justice had he been pleased to do so.

3. In the third place, an atonement, either personal or vicarious, when made, naturally and necessarily cancels legal claims. This means that there is such a natural and necessary correlation between vicarious atonement and justice, that the former supplies all that is required by the latter. It does not mean that Christ's vicarious atonement naturally and necessarily *saves* every man; because the relation of Christ's atonement to divine justice is one thing, but the relation of a particular person to Christ's atonement is a very different thing. Christ's death as related to the claims of the law upon all mankind, cancels those claims wholly. It is an infinite "propitiation for the sins of the whole world," 1 John 2:2. But the relation of an impenitent person to this atonement, is that of unbelief and rejection of it. Consequently, what the atonement has effected objectively in reference to the attribute of divine justice, is not effected subjectively in the conscience of the individual. There is an infinite satisfaction that naturally and necessarily cancels legal claims, but unbelief derives no benefit from the fact.

In like manner, a personal atonement naturally and necessarily cancels legal claims. When the prescribed human penalty has been personally endured by the criminal, human justice is satisfied, and there are no more outstanding claims upon him. And this, by reason of the essential nature of justice. Justice insists upon nothing but what is due, and when it obtains this, it shows its righteousness in not requiring anything further, as it does in not accepting anything less. Consequently, personal atonement operates inevitably, and we might almost say mechanically. If a criminal suffers the penalty affixed to his crime, he owes nothing more in the way of penalty to the law. He cannot be punished a second time. Law and justice cannot now touch him, so far as this particular crime and this particular penalty are concerned. It would be unjust to cause him the least jot or tittle of further retributive suffering for that crime which by the supposition he has personally atoned for. The law now owes him immunity from suffering anything more. It is not grace in the law not to punish him any further, but it is debt. The law itself is under obligation not to punish a criminal who has once been punished. St. Paul says respecting grace and debt, in the case of active obedience, that "to him that worketh is the reward not reckoned of grace but of debt; otherwise work is no more work," Rom. 4:4; 11:6. In like manner, it may be said that, "to him who atones for sin, the legal consequence of atonement is not reckoned of grace but of debt; otherwise atonement is no more atonement."

This reasoning applies to vicarious atonement equally with personal. Justice does not require a second sacrifice from Christ, in addition to the first. "Christ was once offered to bear the sins of many," Heb. 10:28. This one offering expiated "the sins of the whole world," and justice is completely satisfied in reference to them. The death of the God-man naturally and necessarily cancelled all legal claims. When a particular person trusts in this infinite atonement, and it is imputed to him by God, it then becomes his atonement for judicial purposes as really as if he had made it himself, and then it naturally and necessarily cancels his personal guilt, and he has the testimony that it does in his peace of conscience. Divine justice does not, in this case, require an additional atonement from the believer. It does not demand penal suffering from a person for whom a divine substitute has rendered a full satisfaction, which justice itself has *accepted* in reference to this very person. By accepting a vicarious atonement for a particular individual, the Divine justice precludes itself from requiring a personal atonement from him. Accordingly, scripture represents the non-infliction of penalty upon the believer in Christ's atonement, as an act of justice to Christ, and also to the believer viewed as one with Christ. "If we confess our sins, he is faithful and *just* to forgive us our sins," 1 John 1:9. "Who shall lay anything to the charge of God's elect? Who is he that condemneth? It is Christ that died," Rom. 8:33, 34. The atoning Mediator can demand upon principles of strict justice, the release from penalty of any sinful man in respect to whom he makes the demand. And if in such a case we should suppose the demand to be refused by eternal justice, we should suppose a case in which eternal justice is unjust. For, by the supposition, justice has inflicted upon the Mediator the full penalty due to this sinner, and then refuses to the mediator that release of this sinner from penalty which the mediator has earned by his own suffering, and which is now absolutely due to him as the reward of his suffering. "It is," says Edwards (Wisdom in Salvation, Works, IV. 150), "so ordered now, that the glory of the attribute of divine justice requires the salvation of those that believe. The justice of God that [irrespective of Christ's atonement] required man's damnation, and seemed inconsistent with his salvation, now [having respect to Christ's atonement] as much requires the salvation of those that believe in Christ, as ever before it required their damnation. Salvation is an absolute debt to the believer from God, so that he may in justice demand it on the ground of what his Surety has done." See also Edwards: God's Sovereignty, Works, IV. 552. Similarly Anselm (Cur deus homo, II. 20) asks, "Can anything be more just than for God to remit all debt, when in the sufferings of the God-man he receives a satisfaction greater than all the debt?" Says Ezekiel Hopkins (Exposition of the Lord's Prayer), "The pardon of sin is not merely an act of mercy, but also an act of justice. What abundant cause of comfort may this be to all believers, that God's justice as well as his mercy shall acquit them; that that attribute of God at the apprehension of which they are wont to tremble, should interpose in their behalf and plead for them! And yet, through the all-sufficient expiation and atonement that Christ hath made for our sins, this mystery is affected, and justice itself brought over, from being a formidable adversary, to be of our party and to plead for us." Shedd: Theological Essays, 310–316.

It may be asked, If atonement naturally and necessarily cancels guilt, why does not the vicarious atonement of Christ save all men indiscriminately, as the Universalist contends? The substituted suffering of Christ being infinite is equal in value to the personal suffering of all mankind; why then are not all men upon the same footing and in the class of the saved, by virtue of it? The answer is, Because it is a natural impossibility. Vicarious atonement without faith in it is powerless to save. It is not the *making* of this atonement, but the *trusting* in it, that saves the sinner. "By *faith* are ye saved. He that *believeth* shall be saved," Eph. 2:8; Mark 16:16. The making of this atonement merely satisfies the legal claims, and this is all that it does. If it were made, but never imputed and appropriated, it would result in no salvation. A substituted satisfaction of justice without an act of trust in it, would be useless to sinners. It is as naturally impossible that Christ's death should save from punishment one who does not confide in it, as that a loaf of bread should save from starvation a man who does not eat it. The assertion that because the atonement of Christ is sufficient for all men, therefore no men are lost, is as absurd as the assertion that because the grain produced in the year 1880 was sufficient to support the life of all men on the globe, therefore no men died of starvation during that year. The mere fact that Jesus Christ made satisfaction for human sin, alone and of itself, will save no soul. Christ, conceivably, might have died precisely as he did, and his death have been just as valuable for expiatory purposes as it is, but if his death had not been followed with the work of the Holy Ghost and the act of faith on the part of individual men, he would have died in vain. Unless his objective work is subjectively appropriated, it is useless, so far as personal salvation is concerned. Christ's suffering is sufficient to cancel the guilt of all men, and in its own nature completely satisfies the broken law. But all men do not make it their own atonement by faith in it; by pleading the merit of it in prayer, and mentioning it as the reason and ground of their pardon. They do not regard and use it as their own possession, and blessing. It is nothing for them but a historical fact. In this state of things, the atonement of Christ is powerless to save. It remains in the possession of Christ who made it, and has not been transferred to the individual. In the scripture phrase, it has not been *imputed.* There may be a sum of money in the hands of a rich man that is sufficient in amount to pay the debts of a million of debtors; but unless they individually take money from his hands into their own, they cannot pay their debts with it. There must be a personal act of each debtor, in order that this sum of money on deposit may actually extinguish individual indebtedness. Should one of the debtors, when payment is demanded of him, merely say that there is an abundance of money on deposit, but take no steps himself to get it and pay it to his creditor, he would be told that an undrawn deposit is not a payment of a debt. "The act of God," says Owen (Justification, Ch. X.), "in laying our sins on Christ, conveyed no title to us to what Christ did and suffered. This doing and suffering is not immediately by virtue thereof ours, or esteemed ours; because God hath appointed something else [namely, faith] not only antecedent thereto, but as the means of it."

The supposition that the objective satisfaction of justice by Christ saves of and by itself, without any application of it by the Holy Spirit, and any trust in it by the individual man, overlooks the fact that while sin has a resemblance to a pecuniary debt, as is taught in the petition, "Forgive us our debts," it differs from it in two important particulars. (*a*) In the instance of pecuniary indebtedness, there is no need of a consent and arrangement on the part of the creditor, when there is a vicarious payment. Any person may step up and discharge a money obligation for a debtor, and the obligation ceases ipso facto. But in the instance of moral indebtedness to justice, or guilt, there must be a consent of the creditor, namely, the judge, before there can be a substitution of payment. Should the Supreme Judge refuse to permit another person to suffer for the sinner, and compel him to suffer for his own sin, this would be just. Consequently, substitution in the case of *moral* penalty requires a consent and covenant on the part of God, with conditions and limitations, while substitution in the case of a pecuniary debt requires no consent, covenant, or limitations. (*b*) Secondly, after the vicarious atonement has been permitted and provided, there is still another condition in the case: namely, that the sinner shall confess and repent of the sin for which the atonement was made, and trust in the atonement itself.

Another error, underlying the varieties of Universalism, is the assumption that because an atonement sufficient for all men has been made, all men are *entitled* to the benefits of it. This would be true, if all men had made this atonement. But inasmuch as they had nothing to do with the making of it, they have not the slightest right or title to it. No sinner has a claim upon the expiatory oblation of Jesus Christ. It belongs entirely to the maker, and he may do what he will with his own. He may impute it to any man whom he pleases; and not impute it to any man whom he pleases, Rom. 9:18. Even the act of faith does not by its intrinsic *merit* entitle the believer to the benefits of Christ's satisfaction. This would make salvation a debt which the

Redeemer owes because of an act of the believer. It is only because Christ has promised, and thereby bound himself to bestow the benefits of redemption upon everyone that believeth, that salvation is certain to faith.

It is objected that it is unjust to exact personal penalty from any individuals of the human race, if a vicarious penalty equal in value to that due from the whole race has been paid to justice. The injustice alleged in this objection may mean injustice toward the individual unbeliever who is personally punished; or it may mean injustice in regard to what the Divine law is entitled to, on account of man's sin. An examination will show that there is no injustice done in either respect. (*a*) When an individual unbeliever is personally punished for his own sins, he receives what he deserves; and there is no injustice in this. The fact that a vicarious atonement has been made that is sufficient to expiate his sins, does not estop justice from punishing him personally for them, unless it can be shown that he is the *author* of the vicarious atonement. If this were so, then indeed he might complain of the personal satisfaction that is required of him. In this case, one and the same party would make two satisfactions for one and the same sin: one vicarious, and one personal. When therefore an individual unbeliever suffers for his own sin, he "receives the due reward of his deeds," Luke 23 : 24. And since he did not make the vicarious atonement "for the sins of the whole world," and therefore has no more right or title to it, or any of its benefits, than an inhabitant of Saturn, he cannot claim exemption from personal penalty on the ground of it. Says Owen (Satisfaction of Christ, sub fine), "The satisfaction of Christ made for sin, being not made by the sinner, there must of necessity be a rule, order, and law-constitution, how the sinner may come to be interested in it, and made partaker of it. For the consequent of the freedom of one by the sacrifice of another is not natural or necessary, but must proceed and arise from a law-constitution, compact, and agreement. Now the way constituted and appointed is that of *faith*, as explained in the Scriptures. If men believe not, they are no less liable to the punishment due to their sins, than if no satisfaction at all were made for sinners."

(*b*) The other injustice alleged in the objection, relates to the divine law and government. It is urged that when the unbeliever is personally punished, after an infinite vicarious satisfaction for human sin has been made, justice, in this case, gets more than its dues; which is as unjust as to get less. This is a mathematical objection, and must receive a mathematical answer. The alleged excess in the case is like the addition of a finite number to infinity, which is no increase. The everlasting suffering of all mankind, and still more of only a part, is a *finite* suffering. Neither the sufferer, nor the duration, is mathematically infinite; for the duration begins, though it does not end. But the suffering of the God-man is mathematically infinite, because his person is absolutely infinite. When, therefore, any amount of finite human suffering is added to the infinite suffering of the God-man, it is no increase of value. Justice, mathematically, gets no more penalty when the suffering of lost men is added to that of Jesus Christ, than it would without this addition. The law is more magnified and honored by the suffering of incarnate God, than it would be by the suffering of all men individually, because its demand for a strictly infinite satisfaction for a strictly infinite evil is more completely met. In this sense, "Where sin abounded, grace did much more abound," Rom. 5:20.

It is for this reason, that finite numbers, small or great, are of no consequence when the value of Christ's oblation is under consideration. One sinner needs the whole infinite Christ and his whole sacrifice, because of the infinite guilt of his sin. And a million of sinners need the same sacrifice, and no more. The guilt of one man in relation to God is infinite; and the infinite sacrifice of Christ cancels it. The guilt of a million of men is infinite—not, however, because a million is a larger number than one, but because of the relation of sin to God—and the one infinite sacrifice of Christ cancels it. If only one man were to be saved, Christ must suffer and die precisely as he has; and if the human race were tenfold more numerous than it is, his death would be ample for their salvation. An infinite satisfaction meets and cancels infinite guilt, whether there be one man or millions.

4. Fourthly, the vicarious satisfaction of justice is a mode or form of *mercy*. It is so, because it unites and harmonizes the two attributes in one Divine act: namely, the suffering of incarnate deity for human guilt When the Supreme Judge substitutes himself for the criminal, his own mercy satisfies his own justice for the transgressor. This single act is, therefore, both an exercise of mercy, and an exercise of justice. It is certainly mercy to suffer for the sinner; and it is certainly justice to suffer the full penalty which he deserves. The *personal* satisfaction of justice, on the contrary, is not a mode or form of mercy, because in this case the Supreme Judge inflicts the suffering required by the violated law upon the criminal himself. Personal satisfaction of justice is justice without mercy. It is the "severity" spoken of by St. Paul, in Rom 11:22.

Vicarious atonement is both evangelical and legal—gospel with law; personal atonement is merely legal—law without gospel. The former is complex: both merciful and just; the latter is simple: just, not merciful. In the legal sphere of ethics and natural religion, where personal satisfaction rules, justice and mercy are entirely separated attributes, unblended, and unharmonized. Justice obstructs the exercise of mercy by presenting its unsatisfied claims, and "mercy stands silent by." There is "no eye to pity, and no arm to save," Is 59·16; 63:5. But in the evangelical sphere of revealed religion, the two attributes are united and harmonized.

"Mercy and truth meet together; righteousness and peace kiss each other," Ps 85:10. Divine mercy now satisfies divine justice, and divine justice accepts the satisfaction. The mercy is now infinitely just, and the justice is now infinitely merciful. The two co-ordinate and distinct attributes, which, outside of the gospel, and apart from the incarnation, are separate—the one forbidding the exercise of the other—are now blended; the one meeting all the demands of the other, and both concurring in the salvation of the guilty sinner, for whose advantage all this costly sacrifice is made by the adorable Trinity.

5. Fifthly, the vicarious satisfaction of justice is the *highest* mode or form of mercy, because it is mercy in the form of self-sacrifice. A comparison of the different modes of the divine mercy will show this. When the Creator bestows temporal blessings in his providence upon the sinner; when he makes his rain to fall and his sun to shine upon him; this is a form of mercy greatly inferior to that shown in Christ's atonement. There is no loss on the part of the giver involved in the gifts of providence. They do not cost the deity any sacrifice. Again, should we conceive it possible for God to waive the claims of law by a word, and to inflict no penal suffering upon either the sinner or a substitute, this would be a lower form of mercy than that of vicarious atonement, for the same reason as in the previous instance. There is no suffering and no death undergone in the manifestation of such a species of compassion. This would be the easiest and cheapest of all methods of deliverance from punishment. Again, should we conceive of God, in the exercise of ownership and sovereignty, as taking one of his creatures, say an archangel, and making him a vicarious substitute for man, this too would be a low species of mercy, and for the same reason as in the previous cases. It involves no self-sacrifice upon the part of God. The transaction does not affect anything in the Divine essence. There is no humiliation, and no suffering of God

incarnate. But when justice is satisfied for man by the extraordinary method of substituting God for man; by the method of incarnating, humiliating, and crucifying a person of the Trinity; we see the highest conceivable form of divine compassion and pity. It is so strange and stupendous, that it requires very high testimony and proof to make it credible.

The vicarious satisfaction of justice is then the highest form of mercy, because: (*a*) The offended party permits a substitution of penalty; (*b*) The offended party provides the substitute; and (*c*) The offended party substitutes himself for the offender. The infinite and eternal Judge allows, prepares, and is, a substitute for the criminal. "How hast thou loved us," says Augustine (Confessions, X. 43), "for whom he that thought it no robbery to be equal with thee was made subject even to the death of the cross, for us, both victor and victim, and victor because victim; for us, both priest and sacrifice, and priest because sacrifice." Aquinas (I. xxi 3) remarks of the self-sacrificing pity of God: "Misericordia non tollit justitiam, sed quaedam justitiae plenitudo est." Similarly, Wessel (De caussis incarnationis, xvii.) describes the vicarious atonement in the words: "Ipse deus, ipse sacerdos, ipse hostia, pro se, de se, sibi satisfecit." Pascal (Thoughts) expresses the same truth, in the remark that in the Christian redemption "the Judge himself is the sacrifice." And Livingston (Last Journals, August 5, 1872) cries from the heart of Africa: "What is the atonement of Christ? It is himself: it is the inherent and everlasting mercy of God made apparent to human eyes and ears. The everlasting love was disclosed by our Lord's life and death. It shows that God forgives because he loves to forgive He works by smiles if possible; if not by frowns; pain is only a means of enforcing love"

In this fact that the vicarious satisfaction of justice is self-sacrificing mercy, we have the answer to the objection that if justice is satisfied there is no exhibition of mercy. There would be none, if the satisfaction were made personally by the sinner. But when it is made vicariously by the Eternal Judge himself, it is the acme of mercy and compassion. Says the Westminster Larger Catechism (Q 71): "Although Christ by his obedience and death did make a full satisfaction to God's justice in the behalf of them that are justified, yet inasmuch as God accepteth the satisfaction from a surety which he might have demanded of them, and did provide this surety, their justification is to them of free grace."

This truth is made still more evident by remarking the distinction between mercy and *indulgence*. The first is founded in principle; the latter is unprincipled. Mercy has a moral basis; it is good ethics. Indulgence has no moral foundation; it is bad ethics. Indulgence is foolish good nature. It releases from punishment without making any provision for the claims of law. Its motive is sensuous, not rational. It suffers, itself, from the sight of suffering, and this is the reason why it does not inflict it. It costs an effort to be just, and it does not like to put forth an effort. Indulgence, in the last analysis, is intensely selfish. Mere happiness in the sense of freedom from discomfort or pain is the final end which it has in view. Consequently, the action of indulgence as distinguished from mercy is high-handed. It is the exercise of bare power in snatching the criminal away from merited suffering It is might, not right. A mob exercises indulgence, when it breaks open a prison, and drags away the criminal merely because the criminal is suffering. No member of this mob would take the criminal's place, and suffer in his stead This would be real mercy, and mercy in its highest form of vicarious satisfaction. Should God deliver man from the claims of law without the substitution of penalty, it would be a procedure the same in principle with that of the mob in the case supposed. It would be indulgence, not mercy.

In Rom. 3 : 25, indulgence in distinction from mercy is referred to. St. Paul mentions as a secondary reason why Christ was set forth as a propitiation for sin, the fact that in the past history of the sinful world of mankind God had been indulgent towards those who deserved immediate and swift retribution. He had "passed by" and omitted to punish. Instead of inflicting penalty, he had bestowed "rain and fruitful seasons" upon rebellious men, and had "filled their hearts with food and gladness" He had "suffered (*εἴασε*) all nations to walk in their own ways," and had "winked at," that is, overlooked (*ὑπεριδών*), "the times of this ignorance." Acts 14 : 16, 17 ; 17 : 30. St. Paul does not designate this indulgent treatment of sinful men by *χάρις*, the usual and proper term for forgiving mercy, but by *ἀνοχή*. It is not mercy, but "forbearance." It is in itself irregular, and requires to be legitimated. And it is explained and set right, by the piacular offering of the Son of God. Because the vicarious atonement of Christ is sufficient to atone for the sins of the whole world, therefore it is that the sins of the whole world experience the forbearance of the Holy One ; therefore it is that the whole world receives many temporal blessings instead of swift retribution ; therefore it is that God "overlooks" the times of guilty ignorance and disobedience, and delays punishment.[1]

This "pretermission" of trangressions differs from their "remission," in being only temporary. This forbearance, even though explained and legitimated by the propitiation of Christ, is not to be eternal. Justice will finally assert its claims, and those whose unrepented trangressions have met

[1] That this is the correct interpretation, is proved by the use of the preposition διὰ, in Rom 3 25. God set forth Jesus Christ "to be a propitiation, to declare his righteousness *on account of* (διὰ) the pretermission of sins" Had the act of pretermission been the final cause, or chief end of the propitiation, the preposition employed would have been *εἰς*. The main and ultimate purpose of Christ's death is always denoted in the New Testament by *εἰς ἄφεσιν ἁμαρτιῶν*. The phrase *διὰ πάρεσιν ἁμαρτημάτων* occurs only this once in the New Testament

with this temporary indulgence and delay of punishment, on account of Christ's atonement, will in the end receive the just punishment of sin. St. Paul, in this passage, does not say that these sins had been eternally pardoned by divine grace (χάρις), but had been only temporarily passed by through divine forbearance (ἀνοχῇ).

6. In the sixth place, the vicarious satisfaction of justice is the only mode of exercising mercy that is possible to a just Being. This follows from the nature of justice, and its relation to other divine attributes. If it be conceded that legal claims must be met at all hazards, and cannot be either waived in part or abolished altogether, then it is evident that the great problem before the Divine mercy is, how to meet these claims in behalf of the object of mercy. The problem is not how to trample upon justice in behalf of the criminal, but how to satisfy justice for him. And if this problem cannot be solved, then there can be no manifestation of mercy at all by a just Being. The penalty must be endured by the actual criminal, and the matter end here. God is a perfectly just Being, and therefore cannot forever exercise mere forbearance and indulgence towards a transgressor. The mercy of the Supreme Being must be ethical; that is, must stand the test and scrutiny of moral principle and righteousness. If therefore the merciful God desires to release a transgressor from the suffering which he deserves, he must find some one who is fitted and willing to undergo this suffering in his place. And there is in the whole universe no being who is both fitted and willing to do this, but God himself. A creature might be willing, but he is unfit for the office of substitute. The language of Milton (Paradise Lost, III. 209–212) respecting the transgressor, is theology as well as poetry.

> "Die he, or justice must, unless for him
> Some other able, and as willing, pay
> The rigid satisfaction, death for death."

Respecting the possibility of the substitution of penalty, it is to be observed: 1. In the first place, that the punishment inflicted by justice is aimed, strictly speaking, not at the *person* of the transgressor, but at his *sin.* The wrath of God falls upon the human soul considered as an *agent*, not as a *substance.* The spiritual essence or nature of man is God's own work, and he is not angry at his own work, and does not hate anything which he has created from nothing. Man's substance is not sin. Sin is the activity of this substance; and this is man's work. God is displeased with this activity, and visits it with retribution. Consequently, justice punishes the sin rather than the sinner, the agency rather than the agent, the act rather than the person. It does not fix its eye upon the transgressor as this particular *entity*, and insist that this very entity shall suffer, and prohibit any other entity from suffering for him. Justice, it is true, is not obliged to allow substitution, but neither is it obliged to forbid it. If it were true that the penalty must be inflicted upon the transgressor's very substance and person itself, as well as upon the sin in his person, then there could be no substitution. The very identical personal essence that had sinned must suffer, and justice would be the only attribute which God could manifest towards a sinner.

2. Secondly, justice is dispassionate and unselfish. It bears no malice towards the criminal. It is not seeking to gratify a grudge against him personally, but only to maintain law and righteousness. It inflicts pain not for the sake of inflicting it upon a particular individual, but for the sake of a moral principle. Hence if the *sin* can be punished in another way than by causing the sinner to be punished; if the claims of law can be really and truly satisfied by a vicarious method; there is nothing in the spirit and temper of justice towards the sinner's person, or soul, to forbid this. "The aspect of the law upon a sinner," says Bates (On Forgiveness), "being without passion, it

admits of satisfaction by the sufferings of another." And the same truth is condensed in the schoolman's dictum: "Impersonaliter poenam necessario infligi omni peccato, sed non personaliter omni peccatori."

3. Thirdly, the substitution of penalty is implied in the Divine sovereignty in administering government. If God from his very nature could not permit a proper person to take the place of a criminal, but were necessitated in every single instance to inflict the penalty upon the actual transgressor, his government would be just, but not sovereign. He could make no changes in the mode of its administration—which is what is meant by a sovereign government. But God may vary the mode of administering justice, provided the mode adopted really satisfies justice, and there be no special reason in his own mind why in a particular instance the variation may not be permitted. There were such special reasons, apparently, in the case of the fallen angels, but not in the case of fallen men. This exercise of sovereignty in permitting substitution of penalty is by some Calvinistic theologians called a "relaxation" of justice; not in respect to the *penalty* demanded, but to the person enduring it. Justice relaxes its demands to the degree of permitting a vicar to suffer for the actual criminal, but not to the degree of abating the amount of the suffering. The vicar must pay the debt to the uttermost farthing Owen uses the term "relaxation" in the sense of substitution, but describes our Lord's suffering as the strict and full satisfaction of retributive justice. "To see him," he says (Communion with the Trinity, I. ii.), "who is the wisdom of God, and the power of God, always beloved of the Father; to see him, I say, fear, and tremble, and bow, and sweat, and pray, and die; to see him lifted up upon the cross, the earth trembling under him, as if unable to bear his weight, and the heavens darkened over him, as if shut against his cry, and himself hanging between both, as if refused by both, and all this because our sins did meet upon him; this

of all things doth most abundantly manifest the severity of God's vindictive justice. Here, or nowhere, is it to be learned." This is very different from Scotus's and Grotius's "relaxation" The latter is a relaxation in respect to the amount of the penalty, as well as to the person enduring it.

In case the administrative sovereignty of God decides to permit and provide a substituted penalty, the following conditions are indispensable; not by reason of any external necessity, but by reason of an internal necessity springing from the divine nature and attributes. 1. First, the suffering substituted must be *penal* in its nature and purpose, and of *equal value* with the original penalty. The theory of Duns Scotus, afterwards perfected by Grotius, according to which God's administrative sovereignty is so extended that he can by a volitionary decision accept a substituted penalty of inferior value, is the same in principle with the later theory of Socinus. This scheme, denominated "acceptilation" from a term of the Roman law, logically carried out is fatal to the doctrine of vicarious atonement. For the same arbitrary sovereignty which compels justice to be content with less than its dues, can compel it to be content with none at all. If a government has power and authority to say that fifty cents shall pay a debt of a dollar, it has the power to extinguish debts entirely, by a positive decision of the same kind. The principle of justice being surrendered in part, is surrendered altogether.

An illustration sometimes employed, taken from the instance of Zaleucus and his son, contains the false ethics of the theory of acceptilation. This Locrian lawgiver had decreed that a person guilty of adultery should be made blind His own son was proved to be an adulterer. He ordered one of his son's eyes and one of his own to be put out. Ælian: Historiae Variae, XIII. xxiv. This was an evasion, not a satisfaction of the law. The penalty threatened, and intended to be threatened against adultery, was total blindness. In a substitution of this kind, no one was made blind. Two eyes were put out, but not the two eyes of one man. Had Zaleucus ordered both of his own eyes to be put out, the case would have been a proper illustration of Christ's vicarious atonement. As the case actually stood, the lawgiver had principle enough to acknowledge the claims of justice, but not principle enough to completely satisfy them. That he was willing to lose one eye proves that he felt the claims of law; but that he was unwilling to make himself totally blind in the place of his son, shows that he preferred to sacrifice justice to self rather than self to justice.

In saying that the suffering substituted for that of the actual criminal must be of equal value, it is not said that it must be *identical* suffering. A substituted penalty cannot be an identical penalty, because identical means the same in every respect. Identity is inconsistent with any *exchange* whatever. To speak of substituting an identical penalty is a contradiction in terms. The identical punishment required by the moral law is personal punishment, involving personal remorse; and remorse can be experienced only by the actual criminal. If, in commercial law, a substituted payment could be prevented, a pecuniary debtor would be compelled to make an identical payment. In this case, he must pay in person and wholly from his own resources. Furthermore, he could not pay silver for gold, but gold for gold; and not only this, but he must pay back exactly the same pieces of gold, the ipsissima pecunia, which he had received. Identical penalty implies sameness without a difference *in any particular.* Not only is the quantity the same, but the quality is the same. But substituted penalty implies sameness with a difference in some particular. And in the case before us, that of Christ's satisfaction, the difference is in the *quality:* the quantity being unchanged. The vicarious suffering of Christ is of equal value with that of all mankind, but is not the same in kind.

*Equivalency*, not identity, is the characteristic, therefore, of vicarious penalty. The exchange, implied in the term substitution, is of quality not of quantity. One kind of judicial suffering; that is, suffering endured for the purpose of satisfying justice; is substituted for another kind. Christ's sufferings were of a different nature or quality from those of a lost man.[1] But there was no difference in quantity, or value. A less degree of suffering was not exchanged for a greater degree. The sufferings of the mediator were equal in amount and worth to those whose place they took. Vicarious penalty then is the substitution of an *equal quantity*, but a *different quality* of suffering. The mediator suffers differently from the lost world of sinners, but he suffers equally.

Equivalency satisfies justice as completely as identity. One hundred dollars in gold extinguishes a debt of one hundred dollars as completely as does one hundred dollars in silver. If the sufferings of the mediator between God and man are of equal value with those of the world of mankind, they are as complete a satisfaction of justice as the eternal death of mankind would be, although they do not, in their nature or quality, involve any of that sense of personal wickedness and remorse of conscience which enters into the punishment of a lost man. They get their value from the nature of the God-man, and it is the value of what is substituted which justice looks at.

The following extract from Samuel Hopkins (System of Doctrine, Works, I. 321) enforces this truth. "The mediator did not suffer precisely the same *kind* of pain, in all respects, which the sinner suffers when the curse is execut-

---

[1] Witsius (Covenants, I. iv) finds four elements in the pains of hell: 1. Privation of the divine love. 2 Sense of the divine hatred 3. The worm of conscience. 4. Despair of God's favor. The second, third, and fourth elements did not enter into Christ's experience The first did, temporarily.

ed on him. He did not suffer that particular kind of pain which is the necessary attendant or natural consequence of being a sinner, and which none but the sinner can suffer. But this is only a circumstance of the punishment of sin, and not of the essence of it. The whole penalty of the law may be suffered, and the evil may be as *much* and as *great*, without suffering that particular sort of pain. Therefore, Christ, though without sin, might suffer the *whole penalty*; that is, as *much* and as *great evil* as the law denounces against transgression."

2. Secondly, the penalty substituted must be endured by a person who is not himself already indebted to justice, and who is not a subject of the government under which the substitution takes place If he be himself a criminal, he cannot of course be a substitute for a criminal And if he be an innocent person, yet owes all his own service to the government, he cannot do a work of supererogation such as is implied in vicarious satisfaction An earthly state could not righteously allow an innocent citizen to die for another, even if he were willing so to die, because there are claims upon the person and life of every citizen which must go undischarged if his life should be taken. These are the claims of family, of society, of the commonwealth, and of God. "It is impossible," says Owen (Person of Christ, XVI), "that by anything a man can do well, he should make satisfaction for anything he hath done ill For what he so doeth is due in and for itself. And to suppose that satisfaction can be made for a former fault, by that whose omission would have been another fault had the former never been committed, is madness. An old debt cannot be discharged with ready money for new commodities; nor can past injuries be compensated by present duties which we are anew obliged unto" Says Anselm (Cur deus homo, I. 20), "Cum reddis aliquid quod debes deo, non debes computare hoc pro debito quod debes pro peccato. Omnia enim debis deo." The words of the Jew-

ish elders to Christ respecting the Roman centurion illustrate the point under consideration. They besought Christ to heal his servant, saying that the centurion was worthy of such a favor; "for he loveth our nation, and he hath built us a synagogue," Luke 7: 5. The centurion had acquired merit, because as a Roman citizen he was under no obligation to build a Jewish synagogue.

The sufferings of Christ meet all these conditions. 1. First, they were *penal* in their nature and intent, since they were neither calamitous nor disciplinary. They were a judicial infliction voluntarily endured by Christ, for the purpose of satisfying the claims of law due from man; and this *purpose* makes them penal. "It pleased the Lord to bruise him. He was wounded for our transgressions," Isa. 53: 5, 10. "Christ was made a curse for us," Gal. 2: 13. "No man taketh my life from me, but I lay it down of myself," John 10: 17, 18.

Some writers, while defending the doctrine of vicarious atonement, object to applying the terms "penal" and "penalty" to Christ's sufferings. Magee (Atonement, Dissertation XIII.) does so. "The idea of punishment cannot be abstracted from [personal] guilt. Christ's sufferings are a judicial infliction, and may perhaps be figuratively denominated punishment, if thereby be implied a reference to the actual transgressor, and be understood that suffering which was due to the offender himself; and which if inflicted upon him would then take the name of punishment. In no other sense, can the suffering inflicted on account of the transgressions of another be called a punishment." Ebrard (quoted by Van Oosterzee, II. 603, who agrees with Ebrard) says: "If I endure the infliction due to another instead of him, this suffering which for him would have had the moral quality of a punishment has not the moral quality of a punishment for me, because I am an innocent person. For the idea of a punishment contains, besides the objective element of suffering inflicted by the judge, also in addition the subjective element of the sense of guilt, or an evil conscience possessed by the guilty." This last assertion is the point in dispute. *Does* the idea of a punishment "contain, besides the objective element of suffering inflicted by the judge, also the subjective element of the sense of guilt?" The question is, whether the simple *purpose* and *aim* of the suffering in a given instance is sufficient to constitute it punishment. If a person suffers with a view to satisfy the claims of law, be he guilty himself or not, is this a "penal" suffering? Is such a "judicial infliction," as Magee calls it, properly denominated "penalty?" Does the existence of the objective element alone, apart from the subjective element, in the case of suffering for the purpose of atonement for sin, warrant the use of the terms "penal" and "penalty?" There are three reasons why it does. (*a*) There is no other term but this, by which to designate a suffering that is endured for the sole purpose of satisfying justice. It cannot be denominated either calamity or chastisement. (*b*) When a commercial debt is vicariously paid by a friend of the debtor, it is as truly a "payment" as if paid personally, and the term "payment" is applied to it in the strict sense of the word But if there is no valid objection to denominating the vicarious satisfaction of a pecuniary claim a "payment," there is none to denominating the vicarious satisfaction of a moral claim a "punishment." (*c*) A third reason for the use of the term punishment, or penalty, in this connection, is found in the use of the corresponding term "atonement." No objection is made to calling Christ's suffering an *atonement*. But atonement and punishment are kindred in meaning. Both alike denote judicial suffering. There is, consequently, no more reason for insisting that the term "punishment" be restricted to personal endurance of suffering for personal transgression, than there would be in insisting that the term "atonement" be restricted to personal satisfaction for personal sin. But the vicarious sufferings of Christ are as truly an atonement for sin as would be the personal sufferings of the sinner himself, and are as freely called so. It is as proper, therefore, to denominate Christ's suffering a vicarious punishment, as to denominate it a vicarious atonement. The objection of Magee and Ebrard is met by the qualifying term "vicarious," invariably joined with the term "punishment" when Christ's sufferings are denominated a punishment. No one asserts that they were a "personal" punishment. Anselm (Cur deus homo, I. 15) marks the difference, by denominating the infliction when laid upon the sinner, "poena;" and when laid upon the substitute, "satisfactio."[1]

2. Secondly, the vicarious sufferings of Christ were *infinite in value.* In the substitution, the amount is fully equal to that of the original penalty. A smaller suffering, an inferior atonement, was not put in the place of a greater and superior. The worth of any suffering is determined by the *total subject* who suffers, not by the particular nature in the subject which is the seat of the suffering. Physical suffering in a brute is not so valuable as it is in a man, because a brute has only an animal nature, while a man has an animal united with a rational nature. Yet the nature which is the sensorium or seat of the physical pain, is the same in both cases. But one hour of human suffering through the physical sentiency, is worth more than days of brutal suffering through the physical sentiency; as "one hour of Europe is worth a cycle of Cathay." When animal life and organization suffer in a man's person, the agony is human, and rational. It is high up the scale. It has the

[1] While there may be vicarious as well as personal punishment, because punishment is suffering endured for a judicial purpose, and this purpose can be fulfilled by a substitute as well as by the criminal, there can be no vicarious confession of sin, and no vicarious repentance for it Confession and repentance are necessarily personal acts The Scriptures never represent Christ as vicariously confessing the sins of his people, or as vicariously repenting of them. Yet McLeod Campbell, while dissatisfied with the catholic doctrine of vicarious atonement, has set forth the theory that Christ has made a perfect confession of human sin, and that this is an adequate satisfaction for sin. See Crawford: On Atonement; and on The Fatherhood of God, Lecture IV.

dignity and greatness of degree which pertain to man. But when animal life and organization suffer in an ox or a dog, the agony is brutal, and irrational. It is low down the scale. It has nothing of the worth and dignity that belong to the physical agony of the martyr and confessor. To apply this reasoning to the case before us: When a human nature suffers in an ordinary human person, the suffering is human, and rational, but finite. No mere man's suffering can be infinite in value, because the total subject or person is finite. Whatever a man suffers in either of his natures, body or mind, gets its value from his personality. Measured by this, it is limited suffering. But when a human nature suffers in a theanthropic person, the suffering is divine and infinite, because of the divinity and infinity of such a person. The suffering of the human nature, in this instance, is elevated and dignified by the union of the human nature with the divine, just as the suffering of an animal nature in an ordinary man is elevated and dignified by the union of the animal nature with the rational. The suffering of a mere man is human; but the suffering of a God-man is divine. Yet the divine nature is not the sensorium or seat of the suffering, in the instance of the God-man, any more than the rational nature is the sensorium or seat of the suffering, in the instance of physical suffering in the man. A man's immaterial soul is not burned when he suffers human agony in martyrdom, and the impassible essence of God was not bruised and wounded when Jesus Christ suffered the divine agony. Hence it is said that Christ "suffered in the *flesh*:" that is, in his human nature. 1 Pet. 4:1.

It has been objected that the sufferings of Christ, not being endless, cannot be of equal value with those of all mankind. But when carefully examined and strictly computed, they will be found to exceed in value and dignity the sufferings for which they were substituted. The suffering of the God-man during a section of time is more exactly and mathematically infinite, than would be the suffering of the human race in endless time. The so-called "infinitude" of human suffering is derived from the length of its duration, not from the dignity of the sufferer. It is the suffering of a finite creature, in a duration that is eternal only a parte post. This would not yield strict eternity. The suffering of the whole human race in an endless duration would, consequently, be only relatively infinite. But the vicarious suffering of the God-man obtains its element of infinitude from the person, not from the duration. And this person is absolutely, not relatively infinite. The suffering of an absolutely infinite person in a finite duration is, therefore, a greater suffering in degree and dignity, than is the suffering of a multitude of finite persons in an endless but not strictly infinite time. God incarnate is a greater Being, and a greater sufferer, than all mankind collectively; and his crucifixion involved a greater guilt upon the part of the perpetrators and a more stupendous sacrifice, than would the crucifixion of the entire human family. "If," inquires Anselm (Cur deus homo, II. 14) of his pupil Boso, "that God-man were here present before you, and (you having a full knowledge of his nature and character) it should be said, Unless you slay that Person, the whole world and the whole created universe will perish, would you put him to death in order to preserve the whole creation?" To this question the pupil makes answer, "I would not, even if an infinite number of worlds were spread out before me."

Another proof that the vicarious work of Christ is of greater value in satisfying the claims of the divine law, than would be the endless punishment of the whole human race, is the fact that Christ not only suffered the penalty but obeyed the precept of the law. In this case, law and justice get their *whole* dues. But when lost man only suffers the penalty but does not obey the precept, the law is defrauded of a part of its dues. No law is *completely* obeyed, if only its penalty is endured. The law does not give its subjects an option either to obey, or to suffer punishment. It does not say to them, "If you will endure the penalty, you need not keep the precept." It requires *obedience* primarily and principally; and then it *also* requires suffering in case of disobedience. But this suffering does not release from the primary obligation to obey. The law still has its original and indefeasible claim on the transgressor for a sinless obedience, at the very time that it is exacting the penalty of disobedience from him. Consequently, a sinner can never *completely* and *exhaustively* satisfy the divine law, however much or long he may suffer; because he cannot at one and the same time endure the penalty and obey the precept. He "owes ten thousand talents, and has nothing wherewith to pay," Matt 18:24. But Christ did both; and therefore he "magnified the law and made it honorable" (Isa. 42:21), in an infinitely higher degree than the whole human family would have done, had they all personally suffered for their sins. Compare Edwards: Redemption, Works, I. 406.

3. Thirdly, the vicarious sufferings of Christ were not due from him as from a guilty person. He was innocent, and retributive justice had no claims upon him. What he voluntarily suffered could, therefore, inure to the benefit of another than himself. The active obedience of Christ was also a work of supererogation, as well as his passive obedience. For although his human nature as such owed obedience, yet it owed only a *human* and *finite* obedience. But the obedience which the mediator actually rendered to the moral law was not that of a mere man, but of a God-man. It was *theanthropic* obedience, not merely human. As such, it was divine and infinite. It could, therefore, like the passive obedience of an innocent person, inure to the benefit of another, and earn for him a title to eternal life and reward. And lastly, the God-man, not being a mere creature, but also the Creator and Lord of all things, could rightfully dispose of himself and his agency, as he pleased.

He asserted this sovereign lordship over himself in the words, "No man taketh my life from me, but I lay it down of myself: I have power and authority (ἐξουσίαν) to lay it down, and I have power to take it again," John 10 : 18.

The above-mentioned grounds and reasons for the substitution of penalty abundantly demonstrate its harmony with the principles of law and justice; but should they still be disputed, the whole question may be quickly disposed of by asking, Who objects? Objections to any method of administering a government can be urged only by some party whose rights and claims have been disregarded, or trampled upon. In the instance of the vicarious atonement of the Son of God, no objection is raised by God the Father, for he officially proposed and planned the method. No objection is raised by God the Son, for he not only consents to be a party in the transaction, but to be the sacrificial victim required by it And no objection is raised by God the Spirit, for he likewise is a party in the transaction, and co-operates in its execution and application. This substitution of penalty is, therefore, a method devised and authorized by the entire Godhead. It is a Trinitarian transaction. Nothing is urged against it from this quarter.

And when we pass from the Divine Being to angels and men, and ask for objections from one having real grounds of complaint, there must be of course a dead silence. No angelic or human rights have been interfered with. Objections to the method of vicarious atonement from the world of mankind especially, would be not merely unthankful but absurd That the criminal, who has no claims at all before the law which he has transgressed, and under whose eternal condemnation he lies in utter helplessness; that the criminal in whose behalf Eternal Pity has laid down its own life should object to the method, would deserve not only no reply, but everlasting shame and contempt.

Having considered the nature and value of Christ's atonement, we are prepared to consider its *extent*.[1]

Some controversy would have been avoided upon this subject, had there always been a distinct understanding as to the meaning of words. We shall therefore first of all consider this point. The term "extent" has two senses in English usage. (*a*) It has a passive meaning, and is equivalent to value The "extent" of a man's farm means the number of acres which it contains. The "extent" of a man's resources denotes the amount of property which he owns In this signification of the word, the "extent" of Christ's atonement would be the intrinsic and real value of it for purposes of judicial satisfaction. In this use of the term, all parties who hold the atonement in any evangelical meaning would concede that the "extent" of the atonement is unlimited. Christ's death is sufficient in value to satisfy eternal justice for the sins of all mankind. If this were the only meaning of "extent," we should not be called upon to discuss it any further. For all that has been said under the head of the nature and value of the atonement would answer the question, What is the extent of the atonement? Being an infinite atonement, it has an infinite value.

(*b*) The word has an active signification. It denotes the act of extending. The "extent" of the atonement, in this sense, means its personal application to individuals by the Holy Spirit. The extent is now the intent. The question, What is the extent of the atonement? now means: To whom is the atonement effectually extended? The inquiry now is not, What is the value of the atonement? but, To whom does God purpose to apply its benefits?[2]

The active signification is the earlier meaning of the

[1] Hill Theology, Book IV Candlish · On Atonement, I ii. Cunningham · Historical Theology, II 323–370.

[2] To "extend" the atonement might be understood to mean, to "offer" the atonement But this is not the meaning in this connection To extend, in the sense now being considered, is not only to offer the atonement but also to render it personally efficacious by regenerating grace

word, in English literature The following are a few out of many instances in which "extent" means extending, or putting to use.

> " Let my officers of such a nature,
> Make an extent [levy] upon his house and lands."
> SHAKESPEARE. As You Like It, III i.

> " Let thy fair wisdom, not thy passion, sway
> In this uncivil and unjust extent [attack]
> Against thy peace.
> SHAKESPEARE. Twelfth Night, IV. i.

> " But both his hands, most filthy feculent,
> Above the water were on high extent [extended],
> And fayned to wash themselves incessantly;
> Yet nothing cleaner were for such intent"
> SPENSER: Fairy Queen, II vii.

> "Second him
> In his dishonest practices; but when
> This manor is extended [applied] to my use,
> You'll speak in an humble way and sue for favor"
> MASSINGER: New Way to Pay Old Debts, IV i.

"The rule of Solon, concerning the territory of Athens is not extendible [applicable] unto all; allowing the distance of six foot unto common trees, and nine for the fig and olive." BROWNE: Cyrus's Garden, IV.

The following are examples of the use of the term in the active signification, in the older theologians and doctrinal statements: "The rest of mankind God was pleased, according to the unsearchable counsel of his own will, whereby he extendeth or withholdeth mercy as he pleaseth, to pass by." Westminster Confession, III. vii. "According to the unsearchable counsel of his own will, God extendeth or withholdeth favor as he pleaseth." Larger Catechism, 13. In these passages, to "extend" mercy means, to effectually apply Christ's redemption, not merely to offer it. Because, in the latter sense God does not "withhold" mercy from any man. "Is grace impaired in its extent? We affirm it to be extended to everyone that is, or was, or ever shall be delivered from the pit." Owen: Against Universal Redemption, IV. vii Here, to "extend" grace is to actually save the soul, by effectual calling.

In modern English, the term "extent" is so generally employed in the passive signification of value that the active signification has become virtually obsolete, and requires explanation. Writers upon the "extent" of the atonement have sometimes neglected to consider the history of the word, and misunderstanding has arisen between disputants who were really in agreement with each other.

Accordingly, in answering the question as to the "extent" of Christ's atonement, it must first be settled whether "extent" means its intended application, or its intrinsic value, whether the active or the passive signification of the word is in the mind of the inquirer. If the word means value, then the atonement is unlimited; if it means extending, that is, applying, then the atonement is limited.

The dispute also turns upon the meaning of the preposition "for." One theologian asserts that Christ died "for" all men, and another denies that Christ died "for" all men. There may be a difference between the two that is reconcilable, and there may be an irreconcilable difference The preposition "for" denotes an *intention* of some kind. If, in the case under consideration, the intention is understood to be the purpose on the part of God, both to offer and apply the atonement by working faith and repentance in the sinner's heart, by the operation of the Holy Spirit, then he who affirms that Christ died "for" all men is in error, and he who denies that Christ died "for" all men holds the truth. These two parties are irreconcilable

But he who asserts that Christ died "for" all men may understand the intention signified by the preposition to be the purpose on the part of God only to offer the atonement, leaving it to the sinner whether it shall be appropriated through faith and repentance. The intention, in this latter case, does not include so much as in the former, and the preposition is narrower in meaning. When the word "for" is thus defined, the difference between the two parties is reconcilable. The latter means by "for," "intended for offer, or publication;" the former means, "intended for application."

Again, the preposition "for" is sometimes understood to denote not intention, but *value* or *sufficiency*. To say that Christ died "for" all men then means, that his death is sufficient to expiate the guilt of all men. Here, again, the difference is possibly reconcilable between the parties. The one who denies that Christ died "for" all men, takes "for" in the sense of intention to effectually apply. The other who affirms that Christ died "for" all men, takes "for" in the sense of value. As to the question, Which is the most proper use of the word "for?" it is plain that it more naturally conveys the notion of intention, than of sufficiency or value. If it be said to a person, "This money is for you," he does not understand merely that it is sufficient in value to pay his debt, but that it actually inures to his benefit in paying it. In the scripture statement that Christ "gave himself a ransom for all" (1 Tim. 2 : 6), if the word "for" be made to denote value, so that the text reads, Christ "gave himself a ransom sufficient for all," a circumlocution is introduced. The preposition "for" does not express the idea of sufficiency or value directly, but through an explanation; but it expresses the idea of intention immediately, and without circumlocution And this agrees better with the term "ransom," which denotes subjective redemption rather than objective satisfaction. This remark applies to such a text as that Christ "tasted death for every man" (Heb. 2 : 9), which is explained by "many sons" in verse 10. If we interpolate, and say that Christ tasted a death that is sufficient for every man, we indeed state a truth, but we inject into the preposition "for" a larger meaning than accords with the strictly idiomatic use of it.

The distinction between the "sufficiency" of the atonement, and its "extent" in the sense of "intent" or effectual application, is an old and well-established one. It is concisely expressed in the dictum, that Christ died "sufficienter pro omnibus, sed efficaciter tantum pro electis." The following extracts from Owen (Universal Redemption, IV. i) illustrate it. "It was the purpose and intention of God that his Son should offer a sacrifice of infinite worth, value, and dignity, sufficient in itself for the redeeming of all and every man, if it had pleased the Lord to employ it for that purpose; yea, and of other worlds, also, if the Lord should freely make them, and would redeem them. Sufficient we say, then, was the sacrifice of Christ for the redemption of the whole world, and for the expiation of all the sins of all and every man in the world. This is its own true internal perfection and *sufficiency;* that it should be *applied* unto any, made a price for them, and become beneficial to them, according to the worth that is in it, is external to it, doth not arise from it, but merely depends upon the intention and will of God. It was in itself of infinite value, and sufficiency, *to have been made* a price to have bought and purchased all and every man in the world. That it did formally *become* a price for any, is solely to be ascribed to the purpose of God intending their purchase and redemption by it. The intention of the offerer and acceptor [of the sacrifice] that it should be *for such, some,* or *any,* is that which gives the formality of a price unto it; this is external [to the sacrifice]. But the value and fitness of it to be made a price ariseth from its own internal sufficiency." In respect to such phraseology as a "ransom-price for all" (1 Tim. 2:6), Owen remarks that it must be understood to mean that Christ's blood was sufficient *to be made* a ransom for all, *to be made* a price for all; but that the terms "ransom" and "ransom-price" more properly denote the application than the value of Christ's sacrifice. He adds that "the expression, 'to die *for* any person,' holds out the *intention* of our Saviour in the laying down of the price, to be their *redeemer*."

Atonement must be distinguished from *redemption*. The latter term includes the *application* of the atonement. It is the term "redemption," not "atonement," which is found in those statements that speak of the work of Christ as limited by the decree of election. In the Westminster Confession, VIII. viii, it is said that "to all those for whom Christ hath purchased *redemption*, he doth certainly and effectually apply and communicate the same." In chapter VIII. v. it is stated that "the Lord Jesus hath purchased not only *reconciliation*, but an everlasting *inheritance* in the kingdom of heaven, for all those whom the Father hath given unto him" Since redemption includes reconciliation with God and inheritance in the kingdom of heaven, it implies something subjective in the soul: an appropriation by faith of the benefits of Christ's objective work of atonement. Reconciliation and inheritance of heaven are elements and parts of redemption, and are limited to those who have believed; and those who have believed are those who have been called and chosen. Eph. 2:9, "Faith is the gift of God." 1 Cor. 3:5, "Ye believed, even as the Lord gave to every man." Acts 3:48, "As many as were ordained to eternal life believed." Accordingly the Scriptures limit redemption, as contradistinguished from atonement, to the Church. Christ "makes reconciliation for the sins of his people," Heb 2:17. His work is called "the redemption of the purchased possession," Eph. 1:14. He is "the mediator of the New Testament, that by means of his death they which are called might receive an eternal inheritance," Heb. 9:15. He "hath visited and redeemed his people," Luke 1:68. David, addressing Jehovah, says, "Remember thy congregation which thou hast purchased of old, the rod of thine inheritance which thou hast redeemed," Ps. 74 : 2. The elders of Ephesus are commanded to "feed the church of God which he hath purchased with his own blood," Acts 20 : 28. "He sent redemption unto his people," Ps. 3 : 9. "O Israel, fear not, for I have redeemed thee," Isa. 43 : 1. "He shall save his people from their sins," Matt. 1 : 21. Christ is "the Saviour of his body the church," Eph. 5 : 23. "He said, surely they are my people: so he was their Saviour," Isa. 63 : 8. "I will save my people from the east country and from the west country," Zech. 8 : 7. See the Old Testament passages in which Jehovah is called the Saviour of Israel; and the New Testament passages in which God is called "our Saviour," that is, of the church.

Since redemption implies the application of Christ's atonement, *universal* or *unlimited* redemption cannot logically be affirmed by any who hold that faith is wholly the gift of God, and that saving grace is bestowed solely by election. The use of the term "redemption," consequently, is attended with less ambiguity than that of "atonement," and it is the term most commonly employed in controversial theology.[1] Atonement is unlimited, and redemption is limited. This statement includes all the Scripture texts: those which assert that Christ died for all men, and those which assert that he died for his people He who asserts unlimited atonement, and limited redemption, cannot well be misconceived. He is understood to hold that the sacrifice of Christ is unlimited in its value, sufficiency, and publication, but limited in its effectual application. But he who asserts unlimited atonement, and denies limited redemption, might be understood to hold either of three views: 1, The doctrine of the Universalist, that Christ's atonement, per se, saves all mankind; or, 2, the doctrine of the Arminian, that personal faith in Christ's atonement is necessary to salvation, but that faith depends partly upon

[1] Owen, in his treatise against Arminianism, presents "Arguments against Universal Redemption."

the operation of the Holy Spirit, and partly upon the decision of the sinful will; or, 3, the doctrine of the school of Saumur (Hypothetic Universalism), that personal faith in Christ's atonement in the first arrangement of God depended in part upon the decision of the sinful will, but since this failed, by a second arrangement it now depends wholly upon the work of the Spirit, according to the purpose of election.

The tenet of limited redemption rests upon the tenet of election, and the tenet of election rests upon the tenet of the sinner's bondage and inability. Soteriology here runs back to theology, and theology runs back to anthropology. Everything in the series finally recurs to the state and condition of fallen man. The answer to the question, How is the atonement of Christ savingly appropriated? depends upon the answer to the question, How much efficient power is there in the sinful will to savingly trust in it? If the answer be, that there is efficient power, either wholly or in part, in the sinful will itself to believe, then faith is either wholly or in part from the sinner himself, and is not wholly the gift of God, which is contrary to Eph. 2:8; and justification does not depend wholly upon electing grace, which is contrary to 1 Pet. 1:2; and redemption is not limited But if the answer be, that there is not efficient power in the sinful will itself, either wholly or in part, to savingly believe, then faith is wholly the gift of God; is wholly dependent upon his electing grace; and redemption is limited by election, as is taught in 1 Cor. 3.5: "Who then is Paul, and who is Apollos, by whom ye believed, even as the Lord gave to every man;" and in Rom. 9:16: "It is not of him that willeth, nor of him that runneth, but of God that showeth mercy"

The difference between the Calvinist and the Arminian appears at this point. Both are *evangelical*, in affirming that salvation is solely by faith in Christ's atoning blood. This differentiates them from the legal Socinian, who denies the doctrine of vicarious atonement, and founds salvation from condemnation on personal character and good works. But they differ regarding the *origin of faith.* The Calvinist maintains that faith is *wholly* from God, being one of the effects of regeneration; the Arminian, that it is *partly* from God and partly from man. The Calvinist asserts that a sinner is *unconditionally* elected to the act of faith, and that the Holy Spirit in regeneration inclines and enables him to the act, without co-operation and assistance from him. The Arminian asserts that a sinner is *conditionally* elected to the act of faith, and that the Holy Spirit works faith in him with some assistance and co-operation from him. This co-operation consists in ceasing to resist, and yielding to the operation of the Spirit. In this case, the Holy Spirit does not overcome a totally averse and resisting will, which is the Calvinistic view, but he influences a partially inclining will.

The Calvinist contends that unconditional election and total inability agree best with the Scripture representations, and that the Arminian really adopts them when he sings with Charles Wesley:

> "Other refuge have I none,
> *Hangs* my helpless soul on thee."

Conditional election is inconsistent with the Biblical texts which describe God as *independent* and *sovereign*, in bestowing faith and salvation. It is no sufficient reply to say that *plenary* ability to appropriate the atonement of Christ is not attributed to the fallen soul, but only a *partial* ability; that it is not contended that sinful man can exercise faith in the atonement without any aid at all from God, but only that he can and must contribute a certain degree of voluntary power which if united with that of God the Spirit will produce faith, and that the exercise of this is the condition of election. This position of partial ability or synergism comes to the same result with that of plenary ability, so far as the Divine independence and sovereignty are concerned. For it is this decision of the sinner to contribute his quota, to "do his part" in the transaction, which conditions the result. It is indeed true, upon this theory, that if God does not assist, the act of faith is impossible ; but it is equally true, that if the sinner does not assist, the act of faith is impossible. Neither party alone and by himself can originate faith in Christ's atonement. God is as dependent in this respect, as man. In this case, therefore, it cannot be said that faith depends wholly upon the divine purpose, or that redemption is regulated and limited by election.

The middle theory of partial ability, and conditional election, is found in the Greek anthropology, and the Semi-Pelagian fathers generally; and is opposed by Calvin (Inst, III. xxiv. 1) as follows: "The proposition of Paul, 'It is not of him that willeth, nor of him that runneth, but of God that showeth mercy,' is not to be understood in the sense of those who *divide* saving power between the grace of God and the will and exertion of man; who indeed say that human desires and endeavors have no efficacy of themselves unless they are rendered successful by the grace of God, but also maintain that with the assistance of his blessing these things have their share in procuring salvation. To refute their views, I prefer Augustine's words to my own: 'If the apostle only meant that it is not of him that wills, or of him that runs, without the assistance of the merciful Lord, we may retort the converse proposition, that it is not of [God's] mercy alone without the assistance of [man's] willing and running. But it is certain that the apostle ascribes everything to the Lord's mercy, and leaves nothing to our wills or exertions.'" Again (Institutes, III. xxiv. 13), Calvin marks the difference between Augustine and Chrysostom in the following terms: "Let us not hesitate to say with Augustine that God could convert to good the will of [all] the wicked, because he is omnipotent. Why then does he not? Because he would not. Why he would not, remains with himself For we ought not to aim at more wisdom than becomes us That would be much better than adopting the evasion of Chrysostom, 'that God draws those who are willing, and who stretch out their hands for his aid,' so that the difference may not appear to consist in the decree of God, but in the will of man." Luther took the same ground with Calvin. "Some allege that the Holy Spirit works not in those that resist him, but only in such as are willing and give consent thereto, whence it follows that free will is a cause and helper of faith, and that consequently the Holy Ghost does not alone work through the word, but that our will does something therein. But I say it is not so; the will of man works nothing at all in his conversion and justification; non est efficiens causa justificationis sed materialis tantum. It is the matter on which the Holy Ghost works (as a potter makes a pot out of clay), equally in those that resist and are averse, as in St. Paul. But after the Holy Ghost has wrought in the wills of such *resistants*, then he also manages that the will be consenting thereunto." Table Talk, Of Free Will.[1]

In saying that Christ's atonement is limited in its application, and that redemption is particular not universal, it is meant that the number of persons to whom it is effectually applied is a fixed and definite number. The notion of definiteness, not of smallness, is intended. In common speech, if anything is "limited," it is little and insignificant in amount. This is not the idea when the redemptive work of Christ is denominated a "limited" work. The circle of election and redemption must indeed be a circumference, but not necessarily a small one. No man is redeemed outside of the circle. All the sheep must be within the fold. But the circle is that of the heavens, not

[1] Compare Dabney. Theology, 580, 581, Watson· Institutes, II. 395 sq

of the earth The fold is that of the Great Shepherd, not that of an under-shepherd The Biblical representation is to this effect. Matt. 6 : 13, "Thine is the kingdom, and the power, and the glory." 1 Cor. 15 : 25, "Christ must reign till he hath put all enemies under his feet." Ps. 103 : 21, "The Lord hath prepared his throne in the heavens and his kingdom ruleth over all." Rev. 21 : 3, "The tabernacle of God is with men, and they shall be his people." Rev. 14 : 6, "The angel having the everlasting gospel to preach to every nation, kindred and tongue." Rev. 19 : 6, "The voice of a great multitude, and as the voice of many waters" Rev 29 : 16, The new Jerusalem "lieth foursquare, and the length is as large as the breadth." Rom. 5 : 20, "Where sin abounded, grace did much more abound" Ps. 68 : 17, "The chariots of God are twenty thousand, even thousands upon thousands."

Although Christ's atonement, in the discussion of its value and sufficiency, can be separated from the intention to apply it, yet in the Divine mind and decree the two things are inseparable The atonement and its application are parts of one covenant of redemption, between the Father and Son. The sacrifice of Christ is offered with the intention that it shall actually be successful in saving human souls from death. It is not rational to suppose that God the Father merely determined that God the Son should die for the sin of the world, leaving it wholly, or in part, to the sinful world to determine all the result of this stupendous transaction ; leaving it wholly, or in part, to the sinful world to decide how many or how few this death should actually save Neither is it rational to suppose that the Son of God would lay down his life upon such a peradventure ; for it might be that not a single human soul would trust in his sacrifice, and in this case he would have died in vain. On the contrary, it is most rational to suppose that in the covenant between the Father and Son, the making of an atonement was inseparably connected with the purpose to apply it : the purpose, namely, to accompany the atoning work of the Son with the regenerating work of the Holy Spirit. The Divine Father, in giving the Divine Son as a sacrifice for sin, simultaneously determined that this sacrifice should be appropriated through faith by a definite number of the human family, so that it might be said that Christ died for this number with the distinct intention that they should be personally saved by this death.

This is taught in Scripture. "The good shepherd layeth down his life for the sheep," John 10 : 15. "Greater love hath no man than this, that a man lay down his life for his friends," John 15 : 13. "Being high priest that year he prophesied that Jesus should die for that nation; and not for that nation only, but that also he should gather together in one, the children of God that were scattered abroad," John 11 : 51, 52. "Christ loved the church, and gave himself for it," Eph. 5 : 25. The annunciation to Joseph respecting the miraculous conception, described the Saviour as one who "should save his people from their sins," Matt. 1 : 21. Furthermore, in accordance with this fact of an intention to apply the atonement at the time when the atonement is provided, we find that believers are said to have been "chosen in Christ before the foundation of the world," Eph. 1 : 4; that they have been given to Christ by the Father, John 10 : 29; that Christ knows them as so given, John 10 : 27; that he claims them as his sheep before they have actually believed, and even before they have been born, saying, "Other sheep I have which are not of this fold, them also I must bring, and they shall hear my voice, and there shall be one flock (ποίμνη), and one shepherd," John 10 : 16 And when Paul was at Corinth, Christ encouraged his apostle to continue his labors, notwithstanding that little success had thus far attended them, by saying, "I have much people in this city," Acts 18 : 9.

That the atonement, in the mind of God, was inseparable from his purpose to apply it to individuals, is proved:

(*a*) By the fact that atonement in and by itself, separate from faith, saves no soul. Christ might have died precisely as he did, but if no one believed in him he would have died in vain. Hence it is said, that "God hath set forth Christ to be a propitiation through *faith* in his blood," Rom. 3: 25. It is only when the death of Christ has been actually confided in as an atonement, that it is completely "set forth" as God's propitiation for sin. In like manner, Christ is said to have been "delivered for our offences, and raised again for our justification," Rom. 4 : 25 If Christ had not risen from the dead, he could not have been believed in. A dead and buried Christ could not have been an object of personal trust and confidence. Consequently, although it was the suffering and death of Christ, and not his resurrection and exaltation, that properly constitutes the atoning sacrifice, yet this sacrifice in itself, and apart from its vital appropriation, is useless In order therefore to man's justification, Christ must not only be delivered to death for offences, but raised again from death so that he might be an object of faith. "It cannot be said," says Owen (Justification, IX), "that Christ's satisfaction was made in such a way as to render it uncertain whether it should save or not. Such an arrangement might be just in pecuniary payments. A man may lay down a sum of money for the discharge of another, on such a condition as may never be fulfilled. For on the failure of the condition, his money may and ought to be returned to him; whereupon, he hath received no injury or damage. But in penal suffering for crime and sin, there can be no righteous arrangement that shall make the event and efficacy of it to depend on a condition absolutely uncertain, and which may not be fulfilled. For if the condition fail, no recompense can be made to him that hath suffered. Wherefore the application of the satisfaction of Christ unto them for whom it was made, is sure and steadfast in the purpose of God."
(*b*) If in the mind of God the death of Christ was sep-

arate from the intention to apply it, then it would be as true that Christ died for lost angels as for lost men; because his atonement, being infinite, is sufficient in value to atone for their sin as well as that of mankind. When it is said that Christ died for the sin of the *world*, it is implied that he did not die for any sin but that of man. The offer of Christ's atonement is confined to the human race, and not made to the angelic world. Now as the divine intention accompanies the *providing* of an atonement, in respect to the difference between angels and men, so it accompanies the *application* of the atonement, in respect to the difference between elect and non-elect men. As the atonement of Christ is not intended to be offered to the angels though it is sufficient for them, so it is not intended to be applied to non-elect men though it is sufficient for them. (*c*) If in the mind of God the purpose that Christ should die had not been accompanied with the purpose that his death should be effective for individuals, the former purpose would have been an unproductive and useless one. It would have accomplished nothing, because of man's unbelief and rejection of the gospel offer. But no purpose of God is unproductive and useless. (*d*) The analogy of the typical atonement under the Mosaic economy shows that Christ's atonement is intended for application only to believers. The lamb offered by the officiating priest was offered for the particular person who brought it to the priest to be offered. Each man had his own lamb, and there was no lamb that belonged to no one in particular, but to every one indiscriminately. (*e*) The atoning work of Christ in its intended application is no wider than his intercessory work. He pleads the merit of his death for those to whom the Father purposed to impute it, and only for those. "I pray not for the world, but for them which thou hast given me," John 17:9. This was Christ's intercessory prayer. He here teaches that he does not discharge the particular office of intercessor, for the non-elect (the "world"), as distinguished from those whom the Father had given him. It is logical therefore to conclude that he does not discharge the particular office of priest for them.

There are Biblical passages which are cited to teach unlimited redemption. Heb 2 : 9, Christ "tasted death for every man." 1 John 2 : 2, Christ is the "propitiation not for our sins only, but for the sins of the whole world" 1 Tim. 2 : 6, Christ "gave himself a ransom for all." John 1 : 29, The lamb of God "taketh away the sins of the world" John 3 · 16, 17, "God so loved the world that he gave his only begotten son." Respecting this class of passages, the following particulars are to be noticed. 1. Scripture must be explained in harmony with Scripture. Texts that speak of the universal reference of Christ's death must, therefore, be interpreted in such a way as not to exclude its special reference 1 Tim. 4 : 10, "God is the Saviour of all men, specially of those that believe" Heb 2 : 17, Christ "makes reconciliation for the sins of his people." Eph. 5 : 23, "Christ is the Saviour of his body, the church" Luke 1 : 68, Christ "hath visited and redeemed his people." Matt. 20 : 28, Christ "gives his life a ransom for many." Matt. 1 : 21, "Jesus shall save his people from their sins." Ps. 74 : 2; 111 : 9. Isa. 63 : 8. Matt. 26 · 28. Heb. 9 : 28.

2. The word "world," in Scripture, frequently denotes a part of the world viewed as a collective whole, and having a distinctive character; as we speak of the scientific, or the religious world (*a*) Sometimes it is the world of believers, the church. Examples of this use are: John 6 : 33, 51, "The bread of God is he which giveth life to the world" [of believers]. Rom 4 : 13, Abraham is "the heir of the world" [the redeemed]. Rom 11 : 12, "If the fall of them be the riches of the world." Rom. 11 : 15, "If the casting away of them be the reconciling of the world." In these texts, "church" could be substituted for "world." (*b*) Sometimes the word "world" denotes the

contrary of the church. Ps. 7 : 14, "Men of the world." John 1 : 10, "The world knew him not" John 7 : 7, "The world cannot hate you, but me it hateth." John 14 : 17, 22, 27; 15 : 18, 19; 16 : 20, 33; 17 : 9, "I pray not for the world." John 17 : 14, 16, 25; 1 Cor. 2 : 12; 1 John 2 : 15–17; 3 : 1; 4 : 5; 5 : 4. (*c*) Sometimes the term "world" means all mankind, in distinction from the Jews. Matt. 26 : 13, "This gospel shall be preached in the whole world" Matt. 13 : 38, "The field is the world." John 3 : 16, "God so loved the world." 1 Cor. 1 : 21, "By wisdom the world knew not God." 2 Cor. 5 : 19, "Reconciled the world unto himself." 1 John 2 : 2, "Propitiation for the sins of the whole world." These texts teach that redemption is intended for all races, classes, and ages of men.

Similarly the word "all" sometimes has a restricted signification, denoting all of a particular class. 1 Cor. 15 : 22, "As in Adam all die, so in Christ shall all be made alive" The "all" in Adam is a larger aggregate than the "all" in Christ, because Scripture teaches that all men without exception are children of Adam, and that not all without exception are believers in Christ. 2 Cor. 5 : 14, "If one died for all, than all died" [with that one]. The "all" here denotes the body of believers, because it is described as "the living" (ὅι ζῶντες, ver. 15). Rom 5 : 18, "As the judgment came upon all men to condemnation, even so the free gift came upon all men unto justification." The "all" in one instance is described (ver. 17) as "receiving abundance of grace," but not in the other.[1]

---

[1] As a specimen of exegesis that throws out the qualifying words and explanatory statements of the author, consider the following from Farrar (St. Paul, II 201) "The word *all* is the governing word in the Epistle to the Romans *All*—for whatever may be the modifications which may be thought necessary, St. Paul does not himself make them—*all* are equally guilty, *all* are equally redeemed *All* have been temporarily rejected, *all* shall be ultimately received *All* shall be finally brought into living harmony with that 'God who is above all, and through all, and in all,' Eph 4 6." The words of St Paul in Eph. 4 . 6, are "God who is in *you* all"—the reference being to believers.

The passage, 1 Cor. 8 : 11, "Shall the weak brother perish for whom Christ died?" and also Heb. 6 : 4–10; 10 : 26–30, is a supposition, for the sake of argument, of something that does not and cannot happen: like 1 Cor. 13 : 1–3; Gal. 1 : 8 The influence and natural tendency of the conduct spoken of is to spiritual death. It is not said that the actual result will be the death of the "weak brother." On the contrary, it is said that "God shall hold him up," Rom. 14 : 4. In the text, 2 Pet. 2 : 1: "Denying the Lord that bought them," the "false teachers" are described according to their own profession, not as they are in the eye of God. They claim to have been bought by the blood of Christ, and yet by their damnable heresies nullify the atonement. Turrettin explains the "purchase" in this case, as redemption from the errors of paganism. See verse 20, "Escaped the pollutions of the world." Only the outward call is meant. Turrettin defends this, by the use in the passage of δεσπότης instead of σωτῆρα, and of ἀγοράζειν instead of λυτροῦσθαι. In 2 Pet. 3 : 9, "The Lord is not willing that any should perish, but that all should come to repentance," the will is that of *decree*, and the reference is to believers only. The Greek shows this: μὴ βουλόμενος τινας ἀπολέσθαι—"not purposing that any [of us] should perish." The preceding clause: "long-suffering to *us*-ward" (εἰς ἡμᾶς), shows that τινας refers to God's children. The true rendering of εἰς μετάνοιαν χωρῆσαι is: "should go on to repentance"—μετάνοιαν here denoting the process of sanctification or renewing (Eph. 4 : 23), and χωρῆσαι a progressive motion or advance, as in Matt. 15 : 17; 19 : 12 The passage, Isa 5 : 4, "What could have been done more unto my vineyard?" does not teach that God *could* not realize his desire that all men should "turn and live." It is not the idea of power, but of patience and long-suffer-

---

The uncials omit ὑμῖν, but the preceding verse contains it, and the succeeding verse implies it.

ing, that is contained in this text. Calvin and Gesenius explain: "What more was there to be done, or was I bound to do?" Alexander in loco

The question arises, If the atonement of Christ is not intended to be universally applied, why should it be universally offered?

The gospel offer is to be made to every man because: 1. It is the divine command. Matt. 16 : 5. God has forbidden his ministers to except any man, in the offer. 2. No offer of the atonement is possible, but a universal offer. In order to be offered at all, Christ's sacrifice must be offered indiscriminately. A limited offer of the atonement to the elect only, would require a revelation from God informing the preacher who they are. As there is no such revelation, and the herald is in ignorance on this point, he cannot offer the gospel to some and refuse it to others. In this state of things there is no alternative but to preach Christ to everybody, or to nobody. 3. The atonement is sufficient in value to expiate the sin of all men indiscriminately; and this fact should be stated because it is a fact There are no claims of justice not yet satisfied; there is no sin of man for which an infinite atonement has not been provided. "All things are now ready." Therefore the call to "come" is universal. It is plain, that the offer of the atonement should be regulated by its intrinsic nature and sufficiency, not by the obstacles that prevent its efficacy. The extent to which a medicine is offered is not limited by the number of persons favorably disposed to buy it and use it. Its adaptation to disease is the sole consideration in selling it, and consequently it is offered to everybody. 4. God opposes no obstacle to the efficacy of the atonement, in the instance of the non-elect. (*a*) He exerts no direct efficiency to prevent the non-elect from trusting in the atonement. The decree of reprobation is permissive. God leaves the non-elect to do as he likes. (*b*) There is no compulsion from the external circumstances in which the providence of God has placed the non-elect. On the contrary, the outward circumstances, especially in Christendom, favor instead of hindering trust in Christ's atonement. And so, in a less degree, do the outward circumstances in Heathendom. "The goodness, forbearance, and long-suffering of God [tend to] lead to repentance," Rom. 2 : 4; Acts 14 : 17; 17 : 26–30. (*c*) The special grace which God bestows upon the elect does not prevent the non-elect from believing, neither does it render faith any more difficult for him. The non-elect receives common grace, and common grace would incline the human will if it were not defeated by the human will. If the sinner should make no hostile opposition, common grace would be equivalent to saving grace.[1] Acts 7 : 51, "Ye stiff-necked and uncircumcised in heart and ears, ye do always resist the Holy Ghost." 2 Tim. 3 : 8, "As Jannes and Jambres withstood Moses, so do these also withstand the truth." See Howe's remarks on common grace. Oracles, II. ii. 5. The atonement of Christ is to be offered indiscriminately, because God desires that every man would believe in it. "God," says Turrettin (IV. xvii. 33), "delights in the conversion and eternal life of the sinner, as a thing pleasing in itself, and congruous with his infinitely compassionate nature, and therefore demands from man as a duty due from him (tanquam officium debitum) to turn if he would live." Substitute in this passage "faith and repentance" for "conversion and eternal life," and it is equally true. It is the divine delight in faith and repentance, and the divine desire for its exercise, that warrants the offer of the benefits of Christ's atonement to the non-elect. Plainly, the offer of the atonement ought to be regulated by the divine desire, and not by the aversion of the non-elect. God in

---

[1] To say that common grace if not resisted by the sinner would be equivalent to regenerating grace, is not the same as to say that common grace if *assisted* by the sinner would be equivalent to regenerating grace In the first instance, God would be the sole author of regeneration; in the second he would not be.

offering his own atonement should be guided by his own feeling, and not by that of sinful man. Because the non-elect does not take delight in faith and repentance is surely no reason why God, who does take delight in it, should be debarred from saying to him, "Turn ye, turn ye, for why will ye die?" May not God express his sincere feeling and desire to any except those who are in sympathy with him, and have the same species of feeling? If a man has a kind and compassionate nature, it is unreasonable to require that he suppress its promptings in case he sees a proud and surly person who is unwilling to accept a gift. The benevolent nature is unlimited in its desire. It wishes well-being to everybody, and hence its offers are universal. They may be made to a churlish and ill-natured man and be rejected, but they are good and kind offers nevertheless, and they are none the less sincere, though they accomplish nothing.

The universal offer of the benefits of Christ's atonement springs out of God's will of complacency. Ezek. 33:11, "I have no pleasure in the death of the wicked, but that the wicked turn from his evil way and live." God may properly call upon the non-elect to do a thing that God delights in, simply because he does delight in it. The divine desire is not altered by the divine decree of pretention. Though God decides not to overcome by special grace the obstinate aversion which resists common grace, yet his delight in faith and repentance remains the same. His desire for the sinner's faith and repentance is not diminished in the least by the resistance which it meets from the non-elect, nor by the fact that for reasons sufficient he does not decide to overcome this resistance. 6. It is the non-elect himself, not God, who prevents the efficacy of the atonement For the real reason of the inefficacy of Christ's blood is impenitence and unbelief. Consequently the author of impenitence and unbelief is the author of limited redemption. God is not the cause of a sinner's impenitence and unbelief, merely because he does not overcome his impenitence and unbelief. If a man flings himself into the water and drowns, a spectator upon the bank cannot be called the cause of that man's death. Non-prevention is not causation. The efficient and responsible cause of the suicide is the suicide's free will In like manner, the non-elect himself, by his impenitence and unbelief, is the responsible cause of the inefficacy of Christ's expiation. God is blameless in respect to the limitation of redemption; man is guilty in respect to it.[1] God is only the indirect and occasional cause of it; man is the immediate and efficient cause of it. This being the state of the case, there is nothing self-contradictory in the universal offer of the atonement upon the part of God. If either of the following suppositions were true, it would be fatal to the universal offer: (*a*) If at the time of offering Christ's atonement God was actively preventing the non-elect from believing, the offer would be inconsistent. (*b*) If at the time of offering it God were working upon the will of the non-elect to strengthen his aversion to the atonement, the offer would be inconsistent. (*c*) If God were the efficient author of that apostasy and sinfulness which enslaves the human will and renders it unable to believe in Christ without special grace, then the offer of the atonement unaccompanied with the offer of special grace would be inconsistent. But none of these suppositions are true. 7. The offer of the atonement is universal, because, when God calls upon men universally to believe, he does not call upon them to believe that they are elected, or that Christ died for them in particular. He calls upon them to believe that Christ died for sin, for sinners, for the world; that there is no other name under heaven given among men whereby we must be saved; that the blood of Christ cleanseth from all sin; and that there is no condemnation to them that are in Christ Jesus. The atonement is not offered to an individual either as an elect

---

[1] See Owen. Works, XIV. 411 Russell's Ed.

man, or as a non-elect man ; but as a man, and a sinner, simply. Men are commanded to believe in the sufficiency of the atonement, not in its predestinated application to themselves as individuals. The belief that Christ died for the individual himself is the assurance of faith, and is more than saving faith. It is the end, not the beginning of the process of salvation. God does not demand assurance of faith as the first act of faith. "Assurance of grace and salvation not being of the essence of faith, true believers may wait long before they obtain it." L. C. 81. "In whom, after ye believed, ye were sealed with that Holy Spirit of promise," Eph. 1 : 13.[1] 8. The atonement is to be offered to all, because the preacher is to hope and expect from God the best and not the worst for every man.[2] He is consequently to expect the election of his hearer, rather than his reprobation. The fact of the external call favors election, not reprobation. The external call embraces the following particulars : (*a*) Hearing the word. (*b*) Religious education by parents and friends. (*c*) Common grace, experienced in conviction of sin, fear of death and judgment, general anxiety, and dissatisfaction with this life. Upon such grounds as these, the individual is to be encouraged to believe that God's purpose is to elect him rather than to reprobate him. If a person fears that he is of the non-elect, he should be assured rather that he is mistaken in this fear than that he is correct in it ; because God has done more for him that tends to his salvation than to his perdition. 9. The atonement is to be offered to all men, because even those who shall prove in the day of judgment to be non-elect do yet receive benefits and blessings from it. Turrettin, (XVI. xiv. 11) mentions the following benefits: (*a*) The preaching of the gospel, whereby paganism with its idolatry, superstition, and wretchedness is abolished. (*b*) The extremes of human depravity are restrained. (*c*) Many tem-

[1] Owen · Display of Arminianism, IV. i viii.

[2] Zanchius. On Predestination, p. 67. Toplady's Tr

poral blessings and gifts of providence are bestowed. Rom. 2:4; Acts 14:7. (*d*) Punishment is postponed and delayed. Acts 17:30; Rom. 3:25. "The grace of the Redeemer," says Bates (Eternal Judgment, II.), "is so far universal, that upon his account the indulgent providence of God invited the heathen to repentance. His renewed benefits that sweetened their lives, Rom. 2:4, and his powerful patience in forbearing so long to cut them off, when their impurities were so provoking, was a testimony of his inclination to clemency upon their reformation, Acts 14:17. And for their abusing his favors, and resisting the methods of his goodness, they will be inexcusable to themselves, and their condemnation righteous to their own conscience."

The reasons for the universal offer of the atonement, thus far, have had reference to *God's* relation to the offer. They go to show that the act upon his part is neither self-contradictory, nor insincere. But there is another class of reasons that have reference to *man's* relation to the offer. And these we now proceed to mention. 1. The atonement is to be offered to every man, because it is the duty of every man to trust in it. The atonement is in this particular like the decalogue. The moral law is to be preached to every man, because it is every man's duty to obey it. The question whether every man will obey it has nothing to do with the universal proclamation of the law. It is a fact that the law will have been preached in vain to many persons, but this is no reason why it should not have been preached to them. They were under obligation to obey it, and this justified its proclamation to them. Still more than this, the moral law should be preached to every man even though no man is able to keep it perfectly in his own strength. The slavery of the human will to sin is no reason why the primary and original duty which the human will owes to God should not be stated and enjoined, because this slavery has been produced by man, not by God. In like manner faith in Christ's atonement should be required as a duty from every man, nothwithstanding the fact that "no man can come unto Christ except the Father draw him," John 6:44; that "faith is not of ourselves, but is the gift of God," Eph. 2:8; and that Christ is "the author and finisher of faith," Heb. 12:2. Man's inability, without the grace of God, to penitently trust in Christ's atonement, being self-caused like his inability to perfectly keep the moral law without the same grace, still leaves his duty in the case binding upon him. The purpose of God to bestow grace is not the measure of man's duty. Neither is the power that man has as fallen the measure of man's duty. Only the power that man had as unfallen, and by creation, is the measure of it. 2. The offer of Christ's atonement for sin should be universal, because it is the most impressive mode of preaching the law In exhibiting the nature of Christ's sacrifice, and its sufficiency to atone for all sin, and especially in showing the necessity of it in order to the remission of any sin whatever, the spirituality and extent of the divine law are presented more powerfully than they can be in any other manner. The offer of the atonement is consequently a direct means of producing a sense of guilt and condemnation, without which faith in Christ is impossible. 3. The offer of the atonement to an unbeliever is adapted to disclose the aversion and obstinacy of his own will. This method of forgiving sin displeases him It is humbling. If he were invited to make a personal atonement, this would fall in with his inclination. But to do no atoning work at all, and simply to trust in the atoning work of another, is the most unwelcome act that human pride can be summoned to perform. Belief in vicarious atonement is distasteful and repulsive to the natural man, because he is a proud man. When, therefore, a man is informed that there is no forgiveness of sin but through Christ's atonement, that this atonement is ample for the forgiveness of every man, and that nothing but unbelief will prevent any man's forgiveness, his attention is immediately directed to his own disinclination to trust in this atonement, and aversion to this method of forgiveness. But this experience is highly useful. It causes him to know his helplessness, even in respect to so fundamental an act as faith. The consequence is, that he betakes himself to God in prayer that he may be inclined and enabled to believe. Larger Catechism, 59, 67.

## CHAPTER III.

### REGENERATION.

Augustine : De predestinatione sanctorum; Contra duas epistolas Pelagianorum, Lib. IV.; De gratia et libero arbitrio, De correptione et gratia. Calvin. Institutes, III. i. ii. Ursinus Christian Religion, Q. 89, 90 Witsius · Covenants, III. vi. Charnocke : On Regeneration. Owen. Holy Spirit, III. Leighton. On Regeneration. Howe : On Regeneration (Sermons xxxviii.-xlix.) Turrettin : Institutio, XV. i.-xi. (De Vocatione). Witherspoon · On Regeneration. Edwards: On Spiritual Light. Faber Primitive Doctrine of Regeneration. Hodge. Theology, II. 639-732, III. 3-40. Shedd : History of Doctrine, II. 102-110, 186-194 (Synergism).

In the Westminster symbol (S. C., 30, 31), the application of redemption is attributed to a particular work of God denominated Effectual Calling. "The Spirit applieth to us the redemption purchased by Christ, by working faith in us, and thereby uniting us to Christ in our effectual calling;" and this effectual calling is defined to be "the work of God's Spirit, whereby convincing us of our sin and misery, enlightening our minds in the knowledge of Christ, and renewing [Larger Catechism, 67, adds, "and powerfully determining"] our wills, he doth *persuade* and *enable* us to embrace Jesus Christ freely offered to us in the gospel." According to this definition, the effectual call produces: (*a*) Conviction of conscience; (*b*) Illumination of the understanding; (*c*) Renovation of the will; (*d*) Faith in Christ's atonement. Everything in redemption runs back, ultimately, to God. "His divine power hath given unto us *all* things that pertain unto life and godliness," 2 Pet. 1 : 3,

But such effects in the soul as conviction, illumination, renovation, and faith, imply a great change within it. These are fruits and evidences of that spiritual transformation which in Scripture is denominated a "new birth," a "new creation," a "resurrection from the dead," a "death to sin and life to righteousness," a "passage from darkness to light." Consequently, effectual calling includes and implies regeneration. Hence it is said in the Westminster Confession, XIII. i., that "they who are effectually called and *regenerated*, having a new heart and a new spirit created in them, are farther sanctified" In the Westminster Confession, X. ii., effectual calling is made to include regeneration, because man is said to be "altogether passive, until he is enabled to answer the call." [1]

The term "regeneration" has been used in a wide, and in a restricted sense. It may signify the whole process of salvation, including the preparatory work of conviction and the concluding work of sanctification. Or it may denote only the imparting of spiritual life in the new birth, excluding the preparatory and concluding processes. The Romish Church regards regeneration as comprehending everything in the transition from a state of condemnation on earth to a state of salvation in heaven, and confounds justification with sanctification. The Lutheran doctrine, stated in the Apology for the Augsburg Confession and in the Formula Concordiae, employs regeneration in the wide meaning, but distinguishes carefully between justification and sanctification. In the Reformed Church, the term regeneration was also employed in the wide signification. Like the Lutheran, while carefully distinguishing between justification and sanctification, the Reformed theologian brought under the term "regeneration" everything that pertains to the development as well as to the origination of the new spiritual life. Regeneration thus included not only the new birth,

[1] In the older theological treatises, Regeneration commonly does not constitute a separate topic, but is discussed under the head of Vocation.

but all that issues from it. It comprised the converting acts of faith and repentance, and also the whole struggle with indwelling sin in progressive sanctification. Thus Calvin (Institutes, III. iii. 9) remarks: "I apprehend repentance (poenitentiam) to be regeneration (regenerationem), the end of which is the restoration of the divine image within us. In this regeneration, we are restored by the grace of Christ to the righteousness of God from which we fell in Adam. And this restoration is not accomplished in a single moment, or day, or year; but by continual even tardy advances the Lord destroys the carnal corruptions of his elect." Here, regeneration is employed to denote not merely the instantaneous act of imparting life to the spiritually dead, but also the processes of conversion and sanctification that result from it.

This wide use of the term passed into the English theology. The divines of the seventeenth century very generally do not distinguish between regeneration and conversion, but employ the two as synonyms. Owen does this continually: On the Spirit, III. v. And Charnocke likewise: Attributes, Practical Atheism. The Westminster symbol does not use the term regeneration. Instead of it, it employs the term vocation, or effectual calling. This comprises the entire work of the Holy Spirit in the application of redemption Under it, belongs everything pertaining to the process of salvation, from the first step of conviction of sin to the act of saving faith in Jesus Christ. Compare Fisher: On the Catechism, 31, 32.

The wide and somewhat vague use of the term regeneration was suggested by a few scripture texts. The apostle, in Eph. 4:22–25, gives the injunction: "Put off the old man," "put on the new man," and "be renewed (*ἀνανεοῦσθαι*) in the spirit of your minds" In Rom. 12:2, he exhorts Christians to "be transformed by the renewing (*ἀνακαινώσει*) of their mind." In 2 Cor. 4:16, he says that the "inward man is renewed (*ἀνακαινοῦνται*) day by day."

In these instances, as the use of ἀνανεόω and ἀνακαινόω, instead of γεννάω, shows, the notion of moulding or forming, rather than that of regenerating, is in St. Paul's mind. He is addressing those in whom the principle of the new life has been implanted; who have been born again; and now urges them to the exercise and nurture of the new life. Similarly, the prophet Ezekiel (18:31), addressing the house of Israel, the church of God, says: "Make you a new heart, and a new spirit." Here, the return from backsliding, and the reformation and culture of the spiritual life, not the actual regeneration of the soul, are what is demanded. Neither of these two texts refers to regeneration in the restricted signification of the term. God does not, in either of them, command man to quicken himself; to create life from the dead; to command the light to shine out of darkness; to call things that be not as though they were. 2 Cor. 4:6; Rom. 4:17 In them both, he exhorts regenerate but backsliding man, as he does the church at Ephesus, to "repent, and do the first works," Rev. 2:5. In the New Testament, the renewing of regeneration is denoted by κτίζειν, γεννάν, ζωοποιέιν; and that of sanctification, by ἀνανεοῦσθαι, Eph. 4:23, ἀνακαινοῦνται, 2 Cor 4·16, ἀνακαίνωσις, Rom 12:2.

But this wide use of the term regeneration led to confusion of ideas and views As there are two distinct words in the language, regeneration and conversion, there are also two distinct notions denoted by them. Consequently, there arose gradually a stricter use of the term regeneration, and its discrimination from conversion. Turrettin (XV. iv. 13) defines two kinds of conversion, as the term was employed in his day. The first is "habitual" or "passive" conversion. It is the production of a habit or disposition in the soul. "Conversio habitualis seu passiva fit per habituum supernaturalium infusionem a Spiritu Sancto" The second kind is "actual" or "active" conversion. It is the acting out in *faith* and *repentance* of this implanted habit or disposition "Conversio actualis seu activa fit per bonorum istorum habituum exercitium, quo actus fidei et poenitentae, et dantur a deo, et homine eliciuntur." After thus defining, Turrettin remarks that the first kind of conversion is better denominated "regeneration," because it has reference to that new birth by which man is renewed in the image of his Maker; and the second kind of conversion is better denominated "conversion," because it includes the operation and agency of man himself. De Moor on Marck (XXIII ii), after distinguishing between conversio activa and passiva, says that the latter is synonymous with vocation.

We shall adopt this distinction between regeneration and conversion. Regeneration, accordingly, is an act; conversion is an activity, or a process. Regeneration is the origination of life; conversion is the evolution and manifestation of life. Regeneration is wholly an act of God; conversion is wholly an activity of man. Regeneration is a cause; conversion is an effect Regeneration is instantaneous; conversion is continuous

The doctrine of regeneration was taught by Christ to Nicodemus John 3:3, 6, "Except a man be born again, he cannot see the kingdom of God. That which is born of the Spirit is spirit." John 1:13, "The sons of God are born not of the will of man, but of God" It had previously been taught in the Old Testament. Ezek 11:19, "I will put a new spirit within you; and I will take the stony heart out of your flesh, and will give you an heart of flesh." Ezek. 36:26, "A new heart will I give you" Jer. 31:33, "I will put my law in their inward parts, and write it in their hearts" The vision of dry bones (Ezek. 37) taught the doctrine symbolically. Moses taught the doctrine in Deut. 30:6. "The Lord thy God will circumcise thine heart, and the heart of thy seed, to love the Lord thy God with all thine heart and with all thy soul" Compare Ps. 51:10.

Respecting regeneration, the following characteristics are to be noted: 1. Regeneration is solely the work of God. The terms employed in Scripture prove this "Creating anew," Eph. 4 24. "Begetting," James 1 : 18. "Quickening," John 5 : 21; Eph. 2 · 5. "Calling out of darkness into light," 1 Pet. 2 : 9. "Commanding the light to shine out of darkness," 2 Cor. 4 : 6. "Alive from the dead," Rom. 6 : 13. "New creature," 2 Cor. 5 . 17 "Born again," John 3 : 3–7. "God's workmanship," Eph. 2 : 10. These terms denote a work of omnipotent power. The origination of life is impossible to the creature. He can receive life; he can nurture life; and he can use and exert life. But he cannot create life.

2. Regeneration as the creative and life-giving act of God produces an effect on the human *understanding.* It is "illumination:" "enlightening the mind," Westminster L. C., 67. "God, who commanded the light to shine out of darkness, hath shined in our hearts to give the light of the knowledge of the glory of God in the face of Jesus Christ," 2 Cor 4 : 6. 1 Cor 2 : 12, 13 "The eyes of your understanding being enlightened," Eph. 1 : 18 Phil 1 : 9. Coloss. 3 : 10. 1 John 4 . 7, 5 : 20. John 17 : 3. Ps. 19 : 7, 8; 43 : 3, 4. The distinguishing peculiarity of the knowledge produced by regeneration is, that it is experimental By this is meant, that the cognition is that of *immediate consciousness.* This is the highest and clearest form of cognition. When, for example, the truth that God is merciful is stated in language, the natural man understands the language grammatically and logically, but nothing more. He has no accompanying consciousness of God's mercy. In common phrase, he does not feel that God is merciful. But a knowledge that is destitute of inward consciousness is an inferior species. It is a blind man's knowledge of color. The blind man understands the phraseology by which the color is described. It conveys logical and self-consistent notions to his understanding; but it is unattended with

*sensation.* Such a knowledge of color is inadequate, in reality is ignorance, compared with that of a man possessed of vision. It is the knowledge of a sensuous object without any sensation. It is quasi-knowledge; such as Christ refers to, when he says of the natural man: "Seeing he sees not; and hearing he hears not."

Illumination, or instruction by the Holy Spirit, implies then the production of an experimental consciousness of religious truth. In this respect, it differs from human teaching. This is alluded to in John 6 : 63, "The words I speak unto you, they are spirit, and they are life:" that is they are spiritual life Vital and conscious knowledge of religious truth is the effect of the operation of the Holy Spirit in the human understanding One man can teach religious truth by grammatical propositions to another, but he cannot illumine his mind in respect to it. He can tell a man that God is holy; is love; that sin is hateful, and virtue is lovely; but he cannot impart the consciousness that God is holy; that God is love, that sin is hateful; that virtue is lovely. The production of an *experience* upon such subjects is the prerogative of God.

Hence all the unexperimental knowledge of the natural man upon religious subjects is denominated "ignorance," in Scripture. Said Christ to the Jews, "Ye neither know me nor my Father," John 8 : 19. To his disciples he said, "It is given to you to know the mysteries of the kingdom of Heaven," Matt. 13 : 11. "This is life eternal to know thee, the only true God and Jesus Christ whom thou hast sent," John 17 : 3 "No man knoweth the Father save the Son, and he to whomsoever the Son will reveal him," Matt. 11 : 27. The books of Proverbs and Ecclesiastes are filled with the praise of a kind of knowledge which they represent sinful man to be destitute of, and which is the gift of God. Christ the great high-priest "has compassion upon the ignorant," Heb. 5 : 2. Scoffers are "willingly ignorant," 2 Pet. 3 : 5. Unbelieving Jews were "ignorant of

God's righteousness," Rom. 10 : 3. Before regeneration, men fashion themselves "according to their lusts in ignorance," 1 Pet. 1: 14. The sinful condition of the pagan world is called a "time of ignorance" which God in his forbearance temporarily overlooked, Acts 17 : 30. Sin is often denominated folly. The Psalmist mourning over the remainders of sin exclaims: "So foolish was I, and ignorant," Ps. 73: 32.

St. Paul explains the difference between the knowledge of the natural man and that of the regenerate, in 1 Cor. 2 : 14. "The natural man receiveth not the things of the Spirit of God, for they are foolishness unto him." "There is a wide difference," says Owen (Holy Spirit, III. iii), "between the mind's receiving doctrines *notionally*, and its receiving the things taught in them *really*. The first, a natural man can do. It is done by all who, by the use of outward means, do know the doctrine of Scripture in distinction from human ignorance, and error. Hence men unregenerate are said 'to know the way of righteousness,' 2 Pet. 2 : 21." This true and real reception of divine truth, according to Owen, denotes: (*a*) An apprehension that these "spiritual things" agree with the divine attributes, and express them. The doctrine of gratuitous justification, for example, when received by the regenerate mind is perceived to accord with all the attributes of God, and thus to be a manifestation of the glory of God. (*b*) An apprehension that the particular "spiritual thing" is suited to the end proposed. The death of Christ, for example, is adapted in every way to meet the demands of God's holy nature, and of man's sinful nature. It is not "foolishness," but wisdom, or an adaptation of means to ends, and is so perceived and understood by the spiritual man, but not by the natural. That there is this power of illuminating the understanding, is proved by the fact that good men pray that it may be exercised. Ps. 119 : 34, "Give me understanding and I shall keep thy law." Ps. 119 : 68, "Teach me thy statutes."

3. Regeneration with respect to the human *will* is "renewal." The Westminster Larger Catechism (Q. 67) describes one part of effectual calling, as the "renewing and powerfully determining" of the will. Biblical texts that prove this are: Ezek. 11:19, "I will put a new spirit within you: and I will take away the stony heart out of their flesh, and will give them a heart of flesh." Ezek. 36: 26, 27. Ps. 51:10, "Renew a right spirit within me." Heb 13:21, "May the God of peace make you perfect to do his will, working in you that which is well pleasing in his sight." Rom. 9:16, "It is not of him that willeth, but of God that showeth mercy." Phil. 2:13, "God worketh in you to will." Ps. 110: 3, "Thy people shall be willing in the day of thy power." 2 Thess. 3:5, "The Lord direct your hearts into the love of God." Those texts, also, which describe regeneration as a "quickening" prove that the will is renewed.

Recurring to the distinction which we have made between "inclination," and "volition" or "choice," regeneration is to be defined as the origination of a new inclination by the Holy Spirit, not as the exertion of a new volition, or making a new choice by the sinner[1] Keeping this distinction in mind, we say that in regeneration God inclines man to holiness, and disinclines him to sin. This change of the disposition of the will is attributable solely to the Holy Spirit. The sinner discovers, on making the attempt, that he is unable to reverse his determination to self and the creature. He cannot start a contrary disposition of his will. He is unable to incline himself to God as the chief end of

---

[1] Edwards denominates it the origination of a new "principle" "By a principle," he says, "I mean that foundation which is laid for any particular kind of exercise of the faculties of the soul A new holy disposition of heart is not a new faculty of will, but a foundation laid for a new kind of exercise of the faculty of will." Affections, III 1. Similarly, Owen remarks "As the principle of holiness hath the nature of a habit, so also hath it the properties thereof. And the first property of a habit is, that it *inclines* and *disposeth* the subject wherein it is unto acts of its own kind." On the Spirit, IV 1.

his existence. He can choose the antecedents or preparatives to inclining, but cannot incline. By a volition he can read his Bible. This is a preparative or antecedent to supreme love of God, but it is not supreme love, and cannot produce it. By volitions he can listen to preaching, and can refrain from vicious actions. These also are preparatives or antecedents to a holy inclination of the will, but are not this inclination itself, and cannot produce it. It is a fact of consciousness, that while the sinner can put forth single volitions, or particular choices, that are favorable to a new voluntary disposition because they evince the need of it, he cannot begin the new disposition itself. He cannot incline himself by any volition whatsoever. "The will," says Edwards (Will, III. iv.), "in the time of a leading act or inclination that is opposite to the command of God, is not able to exert itself to the contrary The sinful inclination is unable to change itself; and for this plain reason that it is unable to incline to change itself." To employ a phrase of Edwards, the unregenerate is "unable to *be willing*" in the direction of holiness. The reason and ground of this inability has been explained in Anthropology. The inability is voluntary, in the sense that it is the consequence of an act of self-determination, and this act was the sin in Adam by which the human will became sinfully inclined.

By the operation of the Holy Spirit in regeneration, the man is *enabled* to incline to holiness instead of sin. In the Scripture phraseology, he is "made willing," Ps. 110 : 3. God "works in him to will," Phil. 2 : 13. In the phraseology of the Westminster statement (L. C., 67), he is "powerfully determined." By renewing the sinful and self-enslaved will, the Holy Spirit empowers it to self-determine or incline to God as the chief good and the supreme end. This new self-determination expels and takes the place of the old sinful self-determination. From this new self-determination, or inclination, or disposition, or principle, holy volitions or choices proceed, and from the holy choices, holy actions

That God the Spirit possesses the power to originate an inclination to holiness in the human will, is proved by the Biblical representations. David frequently asks God to exert this power. Ps. 119 : 36, "Incline my heart unto thy testimonies." Ps. 119 : 35, "Make me to go in the path of thy commandments." Ps. 119 : 37, "Turn away mine eyes from beholding vanity." Ps. 51 : 10, "Create in me a clean heart." Ps. 51 : 15, "Open thou my lips and my mouth shall shew forth thy praise." Isa. 64 : 8, "We are the clay, and thou our potter." Acts 16 : 14, "The Lord opened the heart of Lydia, that she attended to the things which were spoken by Paul." The assurance of Christ that the Holy Spirit shall be given to every one that asks, implies the power of the Spirit to incline the human will.

While the operation of the Holy Spirit upon the human will is inexplicable (John 3 : 8), yet certain particulars are clear: (*a*) The influence of the Spirit is distinguishable from that of the truth; from that of man upon man; and from that of any instrument or means whatever. His energy acts *directly* upon the human soul itself. It is the influence of spirit upon spirit; of one of the trinitarian persons upon a human person. Neither the truth, nor a fellow-man, can thus operate directly upon the essence of the soul itself. It is in this respect, that theologians have defined the influence of the Holy Ghost upon the human will to be "physical."[1] The φύσις, or essence, of the Holy Spirit operates upon the φύσις of the human spirit. In regeneration, there is immediate contact between God and man. Spiritual essence touches spiritual essence. Yet there is no mingling or confusion of substance God and man are two distinct and different beings, yet in regeneration they approach closer to each other than they do either

---

[1] Owen: Works, II. 357 sq Russell's Ed.

in creation, or providence. This fact is supported by the metaphors which describe the intimacy of the union between the believer and Christ. The one is the head, and the other is a member of the same body. Christ is the very life of the regenerate soul. In two instances the church is called "Christ:" Gal. 3:16, "To thy seed, which is Christ;" 1 Cor. 12:12. Christ is "formed in the believer," Gal. 4:19. It is also supported by the Biblical statements respecting the working of the Holy Spirit in the soul. Rom. 8:26, 27, "The Spirit maketh intercession." The operation of the Spirit is so intimate, that his working cannot in consciousness be distinguished from that of the soul itself. The believer is a "temple" of the Holy Spirit, 1 Cor. 6:19. That the influence of the Holy Spirit is directly upon the human spirit, and is independent even of the word itself, is further proved by the fact that it is exerted in the case of infants without any employment of the truth. John the Baptist was "filled with the Holy Ghost even from his mother's womb," Luke 1:15.[1] (*b*) By reason of this peculiarity in the operation of the Holy Spirit, it does not force the human will. It is purely spiritual agency exerted upon a spiritual being. If matter could operate by contact and directly upon mind, the consequence would be compulsion. The two things are heterogeneous. But when God operates directly upon man, the two beings are homogeneous. It is a scholastic maxim, that "quicquid recipitur, recipitur in modum recipientis." Sensuous organs, alone, are adapted to receive sensuous impressions from objects of sense; the immaterial spirit, alone, is adapted to receive an impression from the Eternal Spirit. Man's body cannot experience spiritual influences, and his soul cannot be affected by matter. (*c*) The operation of the Holy Spirit is *in* the will; that of the truth, and of man upon man, is

[1] Meyer, in loco, explains ἔτι literally "*Still* from his mother's womb" After birth, he was still the subject of the Holy Spirit's influences as he was before it.

*on* the will. The more interior an influence is, the farther is it from being compulsory. It is better able to work in accordance with the nature and constitution of that within which it works. If it were operating ab extra, it would be more apt to work across or against the constitutional structure. "Proprium est dei movere voluntatem, maxime interius eam inclinando." Aquinas: Summa, I. cv. 4.

4. Man is passive in regeneration. He cannot actively originate spiritual life. His relation to regeneration is that of a recipient. This is a part of the meaning of "passivity" in this connection. In that particular instant when the divine and holy life is implanted, the soul of man contributes no energy or efficiency of any kind. Being dead in sin, it cannot produce life to righteousness. A corpse cannot originate animal life. Lazarus was passive at that punctum temporis when his body was reanimated. The same is true of the soul of man, in respect to regeneration. But since regeneration is instantaneous, the sinner's passivity is instantaneous also. Man is passive only for a moment, during the twinkling of an eye. God's regenerating act is like the sounding of the last trumpet. The resurrection of dead bodies is instantaneous, and the regeneration of dead souls is so likewise. The doctrine that the sinner is passive in regeneration does not imply that the passivity extends over a great length, or even any length of time in his existence. On the contrary, it is only a punctum temporis in his history. Up to that point of time, he is active: active in enmity to God. After that point of time he is active: active in submission to God. The carnal mind is enmity; the spiritual mind is love. Enmity and love are activities of the soul. Between the carnal mind and the spiritual mind, there is nothing but the instant of regeneration. In this instant when the new life is imparted, the activity is solely that of God the Holy Ghost.

5. Man cannot co-operate in regeneration. This follows logically from the fact that he is passive in regeneration.

A dead man cannot assist in his own resurrection. It also follows from the fact that co-operation implies some agreement between the parties. God and the sinner must harmonize, before they can work together. Two forces cannot co-operate unless they are co-ordinate and co-incident forces. But up to the instant of regeneration, man is hostile to God. "The carnal mind is enmity toward God," Rom. 8 : 7 Enmity cannot co-operate with love.

Upon the Semi-Pelagian, the Tridentine, and the Arminian theory of depravity, there may be co-operation, but not upon the Augustinian and Calvinistic. According to the former theories, there are slight remainders of holiness in the natural man which, though feeble, yet afford a point of contact, and an element of force in his regeneration. Calvin (Inst., III. xxiv. 13) attributes synergism to Chrysostom; and also to Bernard and Lombard, in Institutes, II. ii. 6. "Lombard, in order to establish the position that the human will performs its part in regeneration, informs us that two sorts of grace are necessary. One he calls operative, by which we efficaciously will what is good; the other co-operative, which attends as auxiliary to a good will. This division I dislike, because, while he attributes an efficacious desire of what is good to the grace of God, he insinuates that man has of his own nature, antecedent though ineffectual desires after what is good; as Bernard asserts that a good will is the work of God, but yet allows that man is self-impelled to desire such a good will. But this is very remote from the meaning of Augustine, from whom, however, Lombard claims to have borrowed this distinction." Synergism is enunciated in the canons of the council of Trent (vi. 4). Regeneration is explained as taking place by some co-operation of the human will with the divine. The will is said to be "excited and assisted" by divine grace. Similarly, Limborch (Theologia, IV xiv. 21) says that "grace is not the *solitary*, yet it is the *primary* cause of salvation; for the co-operation of free will is due to grace as a primary cause; for unless the free will had been *excited* (excitatum) by prevenient grace, it would not be able to co-operate with grace." These are not the terms which the Scriptures employ. To "excite" and "assist" sinful man is not the same as to "quicken" and "renew" him. To excite the human will is to stimulate it, not to impart life. Excitement supposes some vitality which is in low tone and requires a tonic. Assistance implies that the will already has some force in the right direction which only needs to be added to This is very different from the view presented in Ezek. 37:14, "I will put my spirit in you, and ye shall live" If there be some spiritual life in the natural man, he can co-operate in regeneration. But if he is "dead in trespasses and sins" (Eph. 2:11) he cannot. The truth upon this subject is well stated in the Westminster Confession, X. ii. "This effectual call is of God's free and special grace alone, not from anything at all foreseen in man, who is altogether passive therein, until being quickened and renewed by the Holy Spirit, he is thereby enabled to answer the call, and to embrace the grace offered and conveyed in it." According to this statement, man is passive until he is quickened; after which Divine act he is actively holy.

It is said by some, that the sinful will has the power to *cease* self-determination to evil, though it has not the power to self-determine or incline to good. It can stop resistance to God, though it can do nothing more. But this would involve a cessation of all action in the will, both sinful and holy action, at the instant of regeneration, and this would make the will characterless at this instant. But in Anthropology (pp 99, 109, 227) we have shown that the will cannot be inactive or destitute of an inclination, either good or evil. The will must be incessantly inclined, in order to be a will, as the understanding must be incessantly intelligent, in order to be an understanding. Consequently, the cessation of sinful inclination must be caused by the origination of holy inclination. Sin does not first stop, and then holiness comes into the place of sin; but holiness positively expels sin. Darkness does not first cease, and then light enters; but light drives out darkness. Sin goes out, as Chalmers phrases it, by "the expulsive power of a new affection." Consequently, the regeneration of the will is the only way to stop the evil inclination of the will. Again, it is said that there is *receptivity* for holiness in the fallen will, though there is no energy to produce it. But receptivity is more than capacity. It is a faint desire or inclination. Hence St. Paul says that "the natural man receiveth not the things of the Spirit of God, for they are foolishness unto him," 1 Cor. 2:14. There is repulsion, not recipiency, in the natural man. "The carnal mind (*φρόνημα*) is enmity against God," Rom. 8:7. When Christ (Luke 18:42) said to the blind man: "Receive thy sight," there was no receptivity in the eye, no *favoring* condition of the organ, that facilitated the restoration of sight. The causing of vision was wholly miraculous. Simultaneously with the words, "Receive thy sight," there was the exertion of creative power upon the sightless eye, enabling it to the act of vision.

6. Regeneration is a work of God in the human soul that is below consciousness. There is no internal sensation caused by it. No man was ever conscious of that instantaneous act of the Holy Spirit by which he was made a new creature in Christ Jesus. And since the work is that of God alone, there is no necessity that man should be conscious of it. This fact places the infant and the adult upon the same footing, and makes infant regeneration as possible as that of adults. Infant regeneration is taught in scripture. Luke 1:15, "He shall be filled with the Holy Spirit, even from his mother's womb." Luke 18:15, 16, "Suffer little children to come unto me; for of such is the kingdom of God." Acts 2:39, "The promise is unto your children." 1 Cor. 7:14, "Now are your children holy." Infant re-

generation is also taught symbolically. (*a*) By infant circumcision in the Old Testament; (*b*) By infant baptism in the New Testament.

7. Regeneration is not effected by the use of means, in the strict signification of the term "means." The Holy Spirit employs means in conviction, in conversion, and in sanctification, but not in regeneration. The appointed means of grace are the word, the sacraments, and prayer. None of these means are used in the instant of regeneration; first, because regeneration is instantaneous, and there is not time to use them; secondly, because regeneration is a *direct* operation of the Holy Spirit upon the human spirit. It is the action of Spirit upon spirit, of a Divine person upon a human person, whereby spiritual life is imparted. Nothing, therefore, of the nature of means or instruments can come between the Holy Ghost and the soul that is to be made alive. God did not employ an instrument or means, when he infused physical life into the body of Adam. There were only two factors: the dust of the ground, and the creative power of God which vivified that dust. The Divine omnipotence and dead matter were brought into direct contact, with nothing intervening. The dust was not a means or instrument by which God originated life. So in regeneration there are only two factors: the human soul destitute of spiritual life, and the Holy Spirit who quickens it. The dead soul is not an instrument by which spiritual life is originated, but the subject in which it is originated.

When Christ restored sight to the blind man, he did it by creative energy alone, without the use of means or instruments. The light of day was not a means. It contributed nothing to the result. Nor was the blind eye a means of originating vision. When Christ anointed the eyes of the blind man with clay mixed with spittle, the act was symbolical, probably; but certainly the spittle was not a means employed by him to work the miracle. In like manner, the word and truth of God, the most important of all the means of grace, is not a means of regeneration, as distinct from conviction, conversion, and sanctification. This is evident, when it is remembered that it is the office of a means or instrument to excite or stimulate an *already existing* principle of life. Physical food is a means of physical growth; but it supposes physical vitality. If the body is dead, bread cannot be a means or instrument. Intellectual truth is a means of intellectual growth; but it supposes intellectual vitality. If the mind be idiotic, secular knowledge cannot be a means or instrument. Spiritual truth is a means of spiritual growth, in case there be spiritual vitality. But if the mind be dead to righteousness, spiritual truth cannot be a means or instrument. Truth certainly cannot be a means unless it is apprehended. But "the natural man receiveth not the things of the Spirit of God, neither can he know them because they are spiritually discerned," 1 Cor. 2: 14.

That regeneration is not effected by the use of means, will appear from considering those cases in which means are employed. 1. First, the word and truth of God is a means of *conviction*, because there is in the human conscience a kind of vitality that responds to the truth as convicting and condemning. The apostasy did not kill the conscience stone-dead. If it had, no fallen man could feel remorse. Adam's fall has benumbed and stupefied the conscience, but there is still sufficient vitality left in it for it to be a distressing witness to man. Consequently, the Holy Spirit employs truth as a means of exciting and stimulating the human conscience, not of regenerating it in the strict sense of the term. The conscience is not "made alive from the dead," in the sense that the will is. It has not lost all sensibility to moral truth. It possesses some vitality that only needs to be stimulated and toned up. This is done in conviction, and by the use of truth as an instrument. 2. Secondly, the word and truth of God is a means of *conversion*, because regeneration has preceded, and has imparted spiritual life to the soul.[1] There is now a spiritual vitality that can respond to the truth. The understanding having been enlightened by regeneration, when the particular truth that the blood of Christ cleanseth from all sin is presented, it is apprehended. This truth is now spiritually understood and is no longer "foolishness" to the mind. And the will having been renewed, and "powerfully determined" or inclined, this same cardinal truth is believed savingly. The doctrine of vicarious atonement thus becomes a means of faith in Christ, and faith in Christ works by sorrow for sin and love of holiness. Faith and repentance are converting acts. They are the substance of conversion, and are brought about by the use of the appropriate means: by the presentation of evangelical truth to a soul in which the Holy Spirit has operated with regenerating grace. 3. Thirdly, the word and truth of God is a means of *sanctification*, upon the same principle. Regeneration and conversion precede sanctification. By regeneration, spiritual life is originated; by conversion, spiritual life is put in action and manifested. Of course, then, the means of sanctification find a spiritual vitality in the soul, to which they are correlated. The Holy Spirit employs the word, sacraments and prayer, afflictions and all the discipline of life, as instruments by which he excites and induces the renewed man to struggle with indwelling sin, and to endure unto the end.

But when we consider regeneration itself, and look into the soul for a principle of life and power to be correlated to means or instruments of regeneration, we do not find any. The unenlightened understanding is unable to apprehend, and the unregenerate will is unable to believe. Vital force is lacking in these two principal faculties What is

---

[1] In the case of an adult, the precedence of regeneration to conversion is of order and nature only, not of time Regeneration immediately exhibits its fruit in the converting acts of faith and repentance. In the case of infant regeneration, there is an interval of time between regeneration and conversion.

needed at this point is, life and force itself. Consequently, the Author of spiritual life himself must operate directly, without the use of means or instruments, and outright give spiritual life and power from the dead: that is, ex nihilo. The new life is not implanted because man perceives the truth, but he perceives the truth because the new life is implanted. A man is not regenerated because he has first believed in Christ, but he believes in Christ because he has been regenerated. He is not regenerated because he first repents, but he repents because he has been regenerated.[1]

8. Regeneration is the cause of conversion. The Holy Spirit acts in regeneration, and as a consequence the human spirit acts in conversion. And as the act of regeneration is not divisible between God and man, neither is the act of conversion. The converting activity of the regenerate soul moves in two principal directions: (*a*) Faith, which is the converting or turning of the soul to Christ as the Redeemer from sin (*b*) Repentance, which is the converting or turning of the soul to God as the supreme good. Regeneration

---

[1] The words in James 1 18 are sometimes quoted to prove that the truth is a means of regeneration "Of his own will, begat he us with the word of truth" The original is, *βουληθεὶς ἀπεκύησεν ἡμᾶς λόγῳ ἀληθείας.* "According to his purpose, he brought us forth by the word of truth" (R V.) Ἀποκυεῖν denotes the maternal, not the paternal act; as יָלַד primarily does in Ps. 2 7, "I have begotten thee" And *λόγος ἀληθείας* means the gospel, as in Eph 1 13, "After that ye heard the word of truth, the gospel of your salvation," and in Coloss 1 5, "Whereof ye heard before, in the word of the truth of the gospel, which is come unto you as it is in all the world" The teaching, then, of St. James in this text is, that "in accordance with the Divine purpose man is born a child of God, under the gospel dispensation" There is a similar statement in 1 Pet. 1.23, "Being born again (*ἀναγεγεννημένοι*) not of corruptible seed, but of incorruptible, by the word of God" The "word of God," here, is not the "incorruptible seed" itself from which the birth proceeds The Holy Ghost is this. But it is the sphere within which the birth takes place It denotes the gospel dispensation, like the "word of truth" in James 1 18. Christians are born again of incorruptible seed, namely of the Holy Spirit, under the Christian dispensation The Revised rendering of this verse is: "Having been begotten again, not of corruptible seed, but of incorruptible, through the word of God."

is instantaneous, conversion is continuous. Faith is gradual and unceasing, and so is repentance; but regeneration is effected completely and once for all.

In connection with the doctrine that God is the sole author of regeneration, several particulars are to be noticed. 1. The reason for expecting the regeneration of men is found in God's promise to bestow regeneration, not in man's power to produce it. In his discourse on the day of Pentecost, Peter assigns as a reason for "repenting and being baptized for the remission of sins," the fact that God "has promised remission to as many as *he had called*," Acts 2:38, 39. He expected to see men repent under his preaching, because "God had exalted Jesus to be a Prince and a Saviour for *to give repentance*," Acts 5:31; and because "God also to the Gentiles had *granted repentance unto life*," Acts 11:18. Similarly, Paul exhorts Timothy to "be gentle unto all men, in meekness instructing those that oppose themselves, if God peradventure *will give them repentance* to the acknowledging of the truth," 2 Tim. 2:24 The preacher should confidently expect faith and repentance to follow from his preaching, because of God's purpose and promise to bestow regenerating grace in connection with preaching. In order to this expectation, it is not necessary that he should know who are the particular persons whom God has elected It is enough to know that God has made an immense election; that he has formed a purpose to regenerate "a multitude which no man can number, out of all nations, and kindreds, and peoples, and tongues," Rev. 7:9. 2 A second ground of hope and expectation that sinners will be regenerated, is the fact that under the gospel dispensation God's regenerating grace is being continually exerted. The Holy Ghost actually accompanies the faithful preacher of the word. The prophets "preached the gospel unto you with the Holy Ghost sent down from heaven," 1 Pet. 1:12. The Holy Spirit as a regenerating spirit is actually poured out among mankind. There is not a moment in which he does not regenerate many souls. Men are being born spiritually all the time, as men are being born physically all the time. 3. A third reason for the expectation that sinners will be regenerated, is the fact that God has promised to pour out the regenerating Spirit in answer to the prayers of the church. The church can obtain the Holy Spirit for the sinful world. "Bring ye all the tithes into the storehouse, and prove me, saith the Lord of hosts, if I will not open you the windows of heaven, and pour you out a blessing," Malachi 3 : 10. "If ye being evil know how to give good gifts unto your children, how much more shall your heavenly Father give the Holy Spirit to them that ask him," Luke 11 : 13. The outpouring of the Spirit at Pentecost was an answer to the prayer of the church.

The question here arises, What is man's relation to regeneration? The answer is, that his agency is not in regeneration itself, but in the work of *conviction* which is preparatory or antecedent to regeneration

The term "preparative," as used by the Augustinian and Calvinist, is very different from its use by the Semi-Pelagian and Arminian. The former means by it, conviction of sin, guilt, and helplessness. The latter employs it in the sense of a preparative *disposition*, or a favoring state of heart. This is referred to in the Westminster Confession, IX. 3 "A natural man is not able to convert himself, or prepare himself thereto." The tenth of the Thirty-nine Articles, also, excludes the Semi-Pelagian "preparatives" to regeneration. "We have no power to do good works acceptable to God, without the grace of God by Christ preventing us that we may have a good will, and working with us when we have that good will." In the Semi-Pelagian use, a "preparative" denotes some faint desires and beginnings of holiness in the natural man upon which the Holy Spirit, according to the synergistic theory of regeneration, joins. Having this sense of the term in view,

Witsius (Covenants, III. vi. 27), says: "Let none think it absurd that we now speak of means of regeneration, when but a little before (III vi. 10, 12) we rejected all preparatives for it." Owen, on the other hand, denies "means," and asserts "preparatives" of regeneration. Yet Owen and Witsius agree in doctrine In the Calvinistic system, a "preparative" to regeneration, or a "means" of it, is anything that demonstrates man's total lack of holy desire and his need of regeneration. It is consequently not a part of regeneration, but something prior and antecedent to it. There is a work performed in the soul previous to the instantaneous act of regeneration, as there is a work performed in the body previous to the instantaneous act of death. A man loses physical life in an instant, but he has been some time in coming to this instant. So man gains spiritual life in an instant, though he may have had days and months of a foregoing experience of conviction and sense of spiritual death. This is the ordinary divine method, except in the case of infants.

John the Baptist was sent to preach the law, in order "to make ready a people *prepared* for the Lord," Luke 1: 17. Conviction of sin, in this instance, was an antecedent or preparative to the regenerating work of the Holy Spirit, but no part of regeneration itself. There is a grace of God that goes before regenerating grace, and makes the soul ready for it. It is common or prevenient grace Man's work in respect to regeneration is connected with this. Moved and assisted by common or prevenient grace, the natural man is to perform the following duties, in order to be convicted of sin, and know his need of the new birth.

1. Reading and hearing the divine word. Rom. 10:17, "Faith cometh by hearing." Matt. 13: 9, "Who hath ears to hear, let him hear." "The Spirit of God maketh the reading, but especially the preaching of the word, an effectual means of enlightening, convincing, and humbling

sinners, of driving them out of themselves, and drawing them unto Christ." L. C., 155.

2 Serious application of the mind, and examination of the truth in order to understand and feel its force. Luke 8:18, "Take heed how ye hear: for whosoever hath to him shall be given." Says Owen (Holy Spirit, II.), "Should men be as intent in their endeavors after knowledge in spiritual things, as they are to skill in crafts, sciences, and other mysteries of secular life, it would be much otherwise with them." The use of these means of conviction under common grace produces: (*a*) Illumination in regard to the requirements of the law, and failure to meet them. This is not the spiritual illumination of the regenerate mind (1 Cor. 2 : 14), but the legal illumination referred to in 2 Cor. 7: 10. (*b*) Conviction and distress of conscience.[1] (*c*) Reformation of the outward life.

3. Prayer for the gift of the Holy Spirit both as a convicting and a regenerating spirit, which is commanded by Christ in Luke 11 : 9, 13, "I say unto you, Ask and it shall be given you. If ye being evil know how to give good gifts unto your children, how much more shall your heavenly Father give the Holy Spirit to them that ask him" That prayer for regenerating grace is a duty and a privilege for the unregenerate man, is proved: (*a*) By the fact that the Holy Spirit is promised generally under the gospel, as a regenerating spirit. Ezek. 36 : 24, 27, "I will take you from among the heathen and gather you out of all countries, and I will put my Spirit within you. A new heart will I give you." Joel 2 · 28–32, "It shall come to pass that I will pour out my Spirit upon all flesh, and your sons and your daughters shall prophesy. And whosoever shall call upon the name of the Lord shall be delivered." This is quoted by Peter on the day of Pentecost. In ac-

[1] See Edwards respecting legal and evangelical humiliation. Affections, Pt III, Works, III 137 sq Howe Blessedness of the Righteous, Ch. XVII. Owen Works, II 309 sq. Russell's Ed.

cordance with these scriptures, the Westminster Confession (VII. iii.) teaches that "God promises to give unto all those who are ordained to life his Holy Spirit, to make them willing and able to believe." All men are to "call upon the name of the Lord" for the gift of the Holy Spirit thus promised, because no man has the right to assert that he is of the non-elect, or to affirm this of another man. As Christ's atonement is offered indiscriminately, so the Holy Spirit is offered indiscriminately; and this warrants every man in asking for what is offered. (*b*) By the fact that a man must obtain the gift of the Holy Spirit as a *regenerating* spirit, before he can obtain it as a *converting* and *sanctifying* spirit. The Holy Ghost is not given as a converting and a sanctifying spirit, until he has been given as a regenerating spirit. Regeneration is the very first saving work in the order, and this therefore is the very first blessing to be asked for. "Make the tree good, and his fruit good," Matt. 12:33. "Except a man be born again, he cannot see the kingdom of God," John 3:3 No man has any warrant or encouragement to pray either for conversion or for sanctification, before he has prayed for regeneration. Whoever, therefore, forbids an unregenerate man to pray for regenerating grace, forbids him to pray for any and all grace. In prohibiting him from asking God to create within him a clean heart, he prohibits him altogether from asking for the Holy Spirit. (*c*) By the fact that the church is commanded to pray for the outpouring of the Spirit upon unregenerate sinners, in order to their regeneration. It is not supposable that God would command the church to pray for a blessing upon sinners which sinners are forbidden to ask for themselves.

To recapitulate, then, we say that the sinner's agency in respect to regeneration is in the antecedent work of conviction, not in the act of regeneration itself. The Holy Spirit does not ordinarily regenerate a man until he is a *convicted* man; until, in the use of the means of conviction under common grace, he has become conscious of his need of regenerating grace. To the person who inquires: "How am I to obtain the new birth, and what particular thing am I to do respecting it?" the answer is: "Find out that you need it, and that your self-enslaved will cannot originate it. And when you have found this out, cry unto God the Holy Spirit, 'Create in me a clean heart, and renew within me a right spirit.'" And this prayer must not cease until the answer comes; as Christ teaches in the parable of the widow and the unjust judge, Luke 18 : 1–8. When men are convicted of sin and utter helplessness, they are "a people prepared for the Lord," Luke 1 : 17. A sense of guilt and danger is a "preparative" to deliverance from it. A convicted man is a fit subject for the new birth, but an unconvicted man is not. A person who denies that he is a guilty sinner before God, or that sin deserves endless retribution, or who has no fears of retribution, is not "prepared" for the regenerating work of the Spirit. It is true that the Holy Spirit, "who is free to work with means, without means, above means, and against means" (Westminster Confession, V. ii.), can convict a sinner without his co-operation, if he pleases. An utterly careless and thoughtless person is sometimes, by the power of God the Spirit, suddenly filled with remorse and terror on account of his sins. And sometimes a convicted person does his utmost to repress conviction, and get rid of moral anxiety, and the Divine Spirit will not permit him to succeed. But this is not to be counted upon. The sinner is commanded to *co-operate* with the Holy Spirit in the work of conviction "Quench not the Spirit" (1 Thess. 5 : 19), is enjoined upon him as well as upon the believer. He must endeavor to deepen, not to dissipate the sense of sin which has been produced in his conscience, or he is liable to be entirely deserted by the Spirit, and left to his own will, and be filled with his own devices. The sinner cannot co-operate in the work of regeneration, but he can in the work of conviction.

This "preparative" of conviction does not make the sinner deserving of regeneration. God is not obliged to overcome the sinner's self-determination to sin because the sinner knows that he cannot overcome it himself. The sinner's helplessness does not make him meritorious of salvation, because it is self-produced; but it does make him a suitable subject for the exercise of God's unmerited compassion in regenerating grace.

One thing is important, therefore, in giving advice to an unregenerate person: namely, to remind him of the danger of legality and self-righteousness. He must not suppose that by the use of the means of conviction—reading and hearing the word of God, avoiding all associations and practices that dissipate seriousness and quench conviction, and prayer that God would apply the truth to his conscience—he is doing a meritorious work that obliges God to the regenerating act. He must not imagine that "by doing his own part," as it is sometimes said, he can necessitate God to do his This would make regeneration a debt, not grace. It would make it depend upon the sinner's action, and not, as St. Paul says, upon God's "purpose according to election," Rom. 9:11. The sinner must not require beforehand an *infallible certainty* that he will be regenerated, as the condition of his using the means of common grace in conviction. He must not say to the Most High: "I will do my part, provided thou wilt do thine." He must proceed upon a *probability*, remembering all the while that he merits not, and has no claim to the new birth. After his best endeavors, he must look up as the leper did, saying, "Lord, if thou wilt, thou canst make me clean." He must do as the preacher does, in regard to the regeneration of his hearers. The preacher does not say to the Lord, "I will preach thy word, on condition that thou wilt regenerate every one to whom I preach." But he does as Paul bade Timothy: "In meekness instructing those that oppose themselves; if God *peradventure* will give them repentance, to the acknowleding of the truth," 2 Tim. 2:25. And as the preacher has ample encouragement to preach, because of the *general* promise that God's "word shall not return to him void," so every convicted sinner has ample encouragement to look up for God's grace in Christ for the new heart and right spirit which come only from this source, and which are promised *generally* under the gospel dispensation.

The language of Edwards (Pressing into the Kingdom, Works, IV. 392) accords with the Scripture representations. "Though God has not bound himself to anything that a person does while destitute of faith, and out of Christ, there is great *probability* that in a way of hearkening to this counsel you will live; and that by pressing onward and persevering, you will at last, as it were by violence, take the kingdom of heaven Those of you who have not only heard the directions given, but shall, through God's merciful assistance, practise according to them, are those that *probably* will overcome." Of the same tenor is the following from Davies (Sermons, I. 50, Ed. Barnes): "Men say to us, 'You teach us that faith is the gift of God, and that we cannot believe of ourselves, why then do you exhort us to it? How can we be concerned to endeavor that which it is impossible for us to do?' I answer to this, I grant that the premises are true; and God forbid that I should so much as intimate that faith is the spontaneous growth of corrupt nature, or that you can come to Christ without the Father's drawing you; but the conclusions you draw from these premises are very erroneous. I exhort and persuade you to believe in Jesus Christ, because it is while such means [as preaching the gospel] are used with sinners, and by the use of them, that it pleases God to enable them to comply, or to work faith in them. I would therefore use those means which God is pleased to bless to this end I exhort you to believe, in order to set you upon the trial [to believe]; for it is putting it to trial, and that only, which can fully convince you of your own inability to believe; and till you are convinced of this, you can never expect strength from God. I exhort you to believe, because sinful and enfeebled as you are, you are capable of using various *preparatives* to faith. You may attend upon prayer, preaching, and all the outward means of grace, with natural seriousness; you may endeavor to get acquainted with your own helpless condition, and as it were place yourself in the way of divine mercy; and though all these means cannot of themselves produce faith in you, yet it is only in the use of these means that you are to expect divine grace to work it in you; never was it yet produced in one soul while lying supine, lazy, and inactive." Compare Owen: Works, II. 272 sq. Ed. Russell.

The speculative difficulties connected with the doctrine of regeneration arise from the fact that men put their questions, and make objections, from the view-point and position of the unconvicted sinner. They deny that they are helpless sinners; or they deny that sin deserves endless punishment; or they deny that sin requires vicarious atonement in order to its remission. A mind that is speculatively in this state is not "prepared" for regenerating grace. These are not the antecedents of regeneration. Such opinions as these must be given up, and scriptural views must be adopted, before the Holy Spirit will create the new heart. Or even if there be no heterodoxy, yet if the orthodox truth be held in unrighteousness; if the person does not reflect upon the truth, and makes no effort to know his guilt and danger, but lives on in thoughtlessness and pleasure; this state of things must be changed. By a serious application to his own case of the law of God, the person must become an anxious inquirer, as a "preparative" to regeneration. The questions about man's relation to regeneration will give no serious trouble to any *convicted* man; to any one who honestly acknowledges that he is a guilty and helpless sinner, and seeks deliverance from the guilt and bondage of sin. The questions will then answer themselves.

1. It is objected that the prayer of the unregenerate is sinful. This proves too much, because it would preclude any action whatever by the unregenerate man The hearing of the word by the unregenerate is sinful. But the unregenerate is not forbidden to hear, upon this ground. The thinking of the wicked, like his ploughing, is sin. All the acts of the unregenerate are sinful, because none of them spring from supreme love to God, yet some of them are better "preparatives" for, or "antecedents" to, God's work of regeneration, than others. Attendance upon public worship is better adapted to advance a man in the knowledge of his spiritual needs, than attendance upon the theatre. Prayer is better adapted than prayerlessness, to bring a blessing to the soul. "Behold he prayeth," was mentioned as a hopeful indication in the case of Saul of Tarsus. "An act," says Owen, "may be good as to the matter of it, though sinful as to the form: for example, hearing the word by the unregenerate. And an act may be bad both as to the matter and the form: for example, pleasure-seeking on the Sabbath by the unregenerate. The former act is to be preferred, rather than the latter. The former act is positively commanded of God; the latter is positively forbidden" The Westminster Confession (XVI. vii.) teaches that "works done by unregenerate men, although for the matter of them they may be things which God commands, yet because they do not proceed from faith, are sinful, and cannot please God. And yet, their neglect of them is more sinful and displeasing unto God [than their performance of them]." If the presence of sin in the soul is a reason why an unregenerate man may not pray for regenerating grace, then it is a reason why the regenerate man may not pray for sanctifying grace. A regenerate man's prayer is mixed with sin. If, then, a person may not pray until he is regenerated, neither may he pray until he is perfectly sanctified.

If the existence of sin is a reason for not praying in one case, it is in the other.

2. It is objected, secondly, that only the prayer of faith is infallibly granted. But this is no reason why a prayer that will *probably* be granted should not be offered. Prayer for sanctification supposes previous regeneration. This is the prayer of faith, and is heard in every instance. But it does not follow that the prayer for regeneration, which God is able to answer, and which he encourages convicted sinners to hope that he will answer, should not be put up, because infallible certainty is not connected with the answer. Probability of an answer is good reason for asking for regenerating grace. The fact that the prayer of the unregenerate does not deserve an answer does not prove that God will not answer it. The prayer of the regenerate does not deserve an answer on the ground of merit.

(*a*) The first reason why prayer for sanctification is infallibly certain to be granted, while that for regeneration is not, is, that God has bound himself by a promise in the former case, but not in the latter. The former is connected with a covenant; the latter is not. God has promised to sanctify every believer without exception who asks for sanctification; but he has not promised to regenerate every convicted sinner without exception who asks for regeneration. Regeneration is according to the purpose of God in election; and election does not depend upon any act of the creature, be it prayer or any other act. Consequently the convicted sinner's prayer cannot *infallibly* secure regeneration, as the believer's prayer can sanctification. Whenever regenerating grace is implored, the sovereignty of God in its bestowment must be recognized. The words of St. Paul apply here: "If God peradventure will give them repentance to the acknowledging of the truth," 2 Tim. 2:25 The words of the prophets also: "Let every man cry mightily unto God; who can tell if God will turn and repent, that we perish not," Jonah 3 : 9. "Rend your heart, and turn unto the Lord your God, for he is gracious and merciful. Who knoweth if he will return and repent, and leave a blessing behind him," Joel 2 : 13, 14. The words of the leper must always be a part of the prayer for regenerating grace: "If thou wilt, thou canst make me clean," Mark 1:40. When it is said that "whosoever shall call upon the name of the Lord, shall be saved" (Joel 2:32; Acts 2:21; Rom. 10:13), the prayer of the convicted may be meant, and the *general* fact is that it will be answered.[1] Or the prayer of the regenerate for sanctification may be meant. Whosoever shall believingly and penitently call on the name of the Lord shall be saved.

(*b*) A second reason why the answer to prayer for regeneration is optional and sovereign, while that for sanctification is not, is, that in the latter instance it is a means to the end, while in the former it is not. The prayer for sanctification is a part of the process of sanctification, but the prayer for regeneration is not a part of regeneration. Prayer as a divinely appointed means infallibly secures its end; but prayer as an appointed antecedent, and not a means, is accompanied with probability, not absolute certainty.

Because God has not bound himself by a covenant to hear the prayer of every convicted sinner without exception, it by no means follows that he does not hear such a prayer, and that it is useless for such a person to pray. He has heard the cry of multitudes of this class It is his general rule under the gospel economy to hear this cry. The highest probability of success, therefore, attends the prayer of an anxious and convicted person for regenerating grace. And this is ample encouragement for him to call upon the

[1] Compare "If I be lifted up, I will draw all men unto me;" and, "My word shall not return unto me void" These texts do not mean that every single individual shall be saved, but describe the general and common effect of the gospel.

merciful and mighty God for what he needs, namely, a heart of flesh in place of the stony heart. It is not true, that God never granted the prayer of an unregenerate man. Such men in peril have called upon God to spare their lives, and have been heard. This is taught in Ps. 107 : 10–14. Convicted men, from a sense of danger and the fear of the wrath to come, have prayed for the salvation of their souls from perdition, and God has saved them. In such cases, God has granted the petition, not because it was a holy one, or because it merited to be granted, but because the blessing was needed, and because of his mercy to sinners in Christ. Calvin (III. xx. 15) mentions the prayers of Jotham (Judges 9 : 20), and of Samson (Judges 16 . 28), as instances in which "the Lord complied with some prayers, which, nevertheless, did not arise from a calm or well-regulated heart. Whence it appears that prayers not conformable to the rules of the Divine word are nevertheless efficacious."

But in addition to the fact that the prayer of a convicted sinner may have an effect upon God, and be answered favorably, it also has an effect on the person himself, and prepares for the regenerating act of God. No man can study the divine word, and receive legal illumination from it, without having some sense of danger awakened, and giving utterance to it in prayer. Even if the prayer be only the cry of fear, and is not accompanied with filial trust and humble submission, it is of use. The prayer, by its very defects, prepares for the new birth by showing the person his need of it. The person in distress asks for a new heart. The answer does not come immediately. The heart is displeased, is perhaps made more bitter and rebellious. By this experience, the Holy Spirit discloses to the unregenerate man more and more of the enmity of the carnal mind, and the impotence of the self-enslaved will. This goes towards preparing him for the instantaneous act of regeneration.

"It is," says Owen (Holy Spirit, IV. iii.), "in no way inconsistent that faith should be required previously unto the receiving of the Spirit as a spirit of sanctification; though it be not so as he is the author of regeneration." And the reason he assigns is, that in the instance of sanctification prayer is a means; while in the instance of regeneration prayer is not a means but a preparative. He discusses the point in the following manner: "May a person who is yet unregenerate pray for the Spirit of regeneration to effect that work in him? For whereas as such he is promised only to the elect, such a person not knowing his election seems to have no foundation to make such a request upon. Ans. 1. Election is no qualification on our part which we may consider and plead in our supplications, but is only the secret purpose on the part of God of what himself will do, and is known to us only by its effects. 2. Persons convinced of sin, and a state of sin, may and ought to pray that God, by the effectual communications of his Spirit unto them, would deliver them from that condition. This is one way whereby we 'flee from the wrath to come.' 3. The especial object of their supplications herein, is sovereign grace, goodness, and mercy as disclosed in and by Jesus Christ. Such persons cannot indeed plead any especial promise as made unto *them*. But they may plead for the grace and mercy declared in the promises as indefinitely proposed unto *sinners*. It may be that they can proceed no further in their expectations but unto that of the prophet, 'Who knoweth if God will come and give a blessing?' Joel 2: 14. Yet is this a sufficient ground and encouragement to keep them waiting at the throne of grace. So Paul, after he had received his vision from heaven, continued in great distress of mind praying until he received the Holy Ghost. Acts 9: 9, 17. 4. Persons under such convictions have really sometimes the seeds of regeneration communicated unto them, and then as they ought to so they will continue in their supplications for the increase and manifestation of it."[1] When our Lord (John 14: 17) asserts that "the world cannot receive the Holy Spirit because it seeth him not neither knoweth him," the reference is to the Holy Spirit as the spirit of *sanctification*. Christ is speaking of him as the "Comforter" who augments and strengthens already existing spiritual life. But if the "world," that is, the unregenerate, are incapable of receiving the Holy Ghost in his regenerating office, they cannot be regenerated.

There is the highest encouragement in the Word of God to pray for the regenerating grace of the Holy Ghost. It is a duty enjoined upon all men without exception, like that of hearing the word. "If ye, being evil, know how to give good gifts unto your children, how much more shall your heavenly Father give the Holy Spirit to them that ask him," Luke 11:14 "Thou, Lord, art plenteous in mercy unto all them that call upon thee," Ps. 86: 5. "The Lord is nigh to all them that call upon him," Ps 145: 18. "The Lord is rich unto all that call upon him," Rom. 10: 12. "Seek ye the Lord while he may be found, call ye upon him while he is near," Isa. 55: 6. "I will that men pray everywhere, lifting up holy hands without wrath and doubting," 1 Tim. 2: 8. "Behold he prayeth," Acts 9: 11. "Thou that hearest prayer, unto thee shall all flesh come," Ps. 65: 2. These and other similar texts relate to spiritual gifts They invite and command men universally and indiscriminately to ask God for the Holy Spirit in *any* of his operations, as the first and best of his gifts. "Prayer, being one special part of religious worship, is required by God of all men." Westminster Confession, XXI. iii.[2]

While regeneration is a sovereign act of God according to

---

[1] See Bunyan's account of his own experience, in Grace Abounding Edwards: Manner of Seeking Salvation, Works, IV. 386 sq; Pressing into the Kingdom, Works, IV 381 sq.

[2] See the admirable remarks of Calvin, on Prayer the Principal Exercise of Faith. Institutes, III. xx. 1-17.

election, it is an encouraging fact both for the sinner and the preacher of the word that God's regenerating grace is commonly bestowed where the preparatory work is performed. This is the rule, under the gospel dispensation. He who reads and meditates upon the word of God is ordinarily enlightened by the Holy Ghost, perhaps in the very act of reading, or hearing, or meditating. "While Peter yet spake these words, the Holy Ghost fell on all them which heard the word," Acts 10 : 44. He who asks for regenerating grace may be regenerated perhaps in the act of praying. God has appointed certain human acts whereby to make ready the heart of man for the divine act Without attentive reading and hearing of the word, and prayer, the soul is not a fit subject for regenerating grace. By "fitness" is not meant holiness, or even the faintest desire for holiness; but a conviction of guilt and danger, a sense of sin and utter impotence to everything spiritually good Such an experience as this "breaks up the fallow ground," to employ the Scripture metaphor. Jer. 4:3; Hosea 10:12. When the Holy Ghost finds this preparation, then he usually intervenes with his quickening agency. The effect of prevenient grace in conviction is commonly followed by special grace in regeneration; the fact of the outward call is a reason both for the sinner and the minister of the word, for expecting the inward call. Yet regeneration, after all the preparation that has been made by conviction and legal illumination, depends upon the sovereign will of God. "The wind bloweth where it listeth, so is every one that is born of the Spirit," John 3: 8. Regeneration rests upon God's election, and not upon man's preparative acts; upon special grace, and not upon common grace.

It follows, consequently, that the unregenerate man should be extremely careful how he deals with common grace. If he suppresses conviction of sin, and thus nullifies common grace, then God may withdraw all grace. This was the case with some of the Jews. "For they being [willingly] ignorant of God's righteousness, and going about to establish their own righteousness, did not submit themselves to the righteousness of God. And because of unbelief were broken off," Rom. 10:3; 11:20. The same is true of some nominal Christians. God has sovereignty and liberty in respect to regenerating grace. When a person has stifled conviction, God sometimes leaves him to his self-will forever. Yet observation shows that the Holy Spirit suffers long, and is very patient and forbearing with convicted men; that he does not hastily leave them, even when they disobey his admonitions, but continues to strive with them, and finally brings them to faith and repentance.

Upon this general fact in the economy of Redemption, that the right use of common grace is followed by regenerating grace, both the sinner and the preacher should act. In this respect, both are like other men. The farmer has no stronger motive than that of probable success, for sowing grain; the merchant, for sending out ships, the manufacturer, for erecting factories. Salvation is in the highest degree probable for any person who earnestly and diligently uses common grace, and the means of common grace It is to be confidently expected that a convicted man will be made a new man in Christ Jesus. Every lost man ought to be thankful for such an encouraging probability. But to insist beforehand upon infallible certainty—and especially a certainty that is to depend upon his own action—is both folly and sin. It is folly, to suppose that so weak and fickle a faculty as the human will can make anything an infallible certainty. And it is sin, to attempt to divide the glory of regenerating the human soul between the Holy Spirit and the soul itself.

3. It is objected, thirdly, that to pray for regeneration is to delay faith and repentance The sinner is commanded immediately to believe on Christ, and turn from his sin with godly sorrow; but praying for regeneration is dallying

with the use of means. It is an excuse for procrastination. To this it is to be replied: (*a*) That prayer for regeneration is a prayer that God the Holy Spirit would work *instantaneously* upon the heart, and would *immediately* renew and incline the will. There would be force in this objection, if the sinner were taught that there are *means* of regeneration, and were exhorted to supplicate God to regenerate him at some future time through his own use of these means. But he who truly prays for regenerating grace, despairs of all agency in the use of means, and precludes all procrastination, by entreating an immediate and instantaneous act on the part of God by which he shall, this very instant, be delivered from the death and bondage of sin, and be brought into the life and liberty of the gospel. He implores "God, who commanded the light to shine out of darkness, to shine in his heart, to give the light of the knowledge of the glory of God in the face of Jesus Christ," 2 Cor. 4: 6 He asks the Son of God, "who quickeneth whom he will" (John 5: 21), to enliven his spirit now "dead in trespasses and sins," Eph. 2: 1. Consequently, prayer for regenerating grace is an evidence that the convicted person has come to know that the word, sacraments, and prayer—all the means of grace—are inadequate to reanimate the soul and make it alive to righteousness. It is not until he has discovered that legal conviction, legal illumination, resolutions to reform, external reformation, reading and hearing the word, and prayer itself cannot change the heart, that he leaves all these behind him, and begs God immediately and instantaneously to do this needed work in his soul. The prayer for regenerating grace is, in truth, the most energetic and pressing act that the sinner can perform. It is the farthest removed of any from procrastination. It is an immediate act on the part of the sinner, and it entreats God to do an instantaneous work within him.

In this manner, prayer for the instantaneous gift of regenerating grace harmonizes with the gospel-call to immediate faith and repentance. Faith and repentance naturally and necessarily result from regeneration. Whoever is regenerated will believe and repent.[1] To pray therefore for instantaneous regeneration is, virtually, to pray for instantaneous faith and repentance, and vice versa. He who prays: "Help thou mine unbelief; take away the stony heart, and give the heart of flesh," prays that God would "renew and powerfully determine the will," which is the definition of regeneration. At the same time, prayer for regenerating grace must not be substituted for the act of faith and repentance. The direction is: "Believe on the Lord Jesus Christ." This is the Biblical answer to the question: "What must I do to be saved?" But when the convicted person discovers that the act of faith is hindered and prevented by the blindness of his understanding, and the bondage of his will to sin, and asks if he may implore the "enlightening and quickening energy of the Holy Spirit, to persuade and enable him to embrace Jesus Christ, freely offered in the gospel" (S. C, 31), he is to be answered in the affirmative. In imploring the regenerating grace of the Holy Spirit, he is "striving to enter in at the strait gate;" he is endeavoring to believe on the Lord Jesus Christ. The act of faith in the blood of Christ, *in its own nature*, is simple and easy. "My yoke is easy, and my burden is light," Matt. 11:30. But considered in reference to the pride and self-righteousness of the natural heart, faith is impossible without regeneration. Hence the frequent statement in Calvinistic creeds, that man needs to be *persuaded* and *enabled* to this act.[2]

---

[1] The regenerate child, youth, and man, believes and repents *immediately*. The regenerate infant believes and repents when his faculties will admit of the exercise and manifestation of faith and repentance. In this latter instance, regeneration is *potential* or *latent* faith and repentance

[2] Westminster Confession, VII iii; VIII viii.; IX. iv.; X i, XIV i. Larger Catechism, Q. 32; Q. 59, Q. 67, Q 72.

## CHAPTER IV.

### CONVERSION.

§ 1. *Faith.* Owen: Justification, XV. Turrettin: Institutio, XV. vii–xvii. Edwards: Observations concerning Faith. Romaine: On Faith. Halyburton: On Faith. Erskine: On Faith. Hodge: Theology, III. 41–111; Way of Life, VI. § 2. *Repentance.* Calvin: Institutes, III. iii. iv. Ursinus: Christian Religion, Q. 21. Jeremy Taylor: Unum Necessarium: or the Doctrine and Practice of Repentance.[1] Saurin: Sermon on Repentance.

Conversion is that action of man which results from regeneration. As the etymology implies, it is turning towards (con-verto) a certain point, and away from a certain point. Conversion consists of two acts: 1. Faith; 2. Repentance. Faith is turning to Christ as the ground of justification, and away from self as the ground. Repentance is turning to God as the chief end of existence, and away from the creature as the chief end. Faith and repentance are converting acts; the first having principal reference to justification, the second to sanctification; the first to the guilt of sin, the second to its corruption.

The Westminster Confession (XIV. ii.) defines *Faith* in Jesus Christ as "a saving grace, whereby we receive and rest upon him for salvation." There is a difference between belief (assensus), and faith (fiducia). The first is assent to testimony; the last is assent to testimony and also trust in the person who gives the testimony. "Justifying faith not

[1] This elaborate and eloquent treatise is somewhat vitiated by a legalizing element and tendency.

only assenteth to the truth of the promise, but receiveth and resteth upon Christ for pardon." L. C., 72. There may be belief without faith. A man may credit the statements made by Jesus Christ, and yet not rest in him for salvation. Faith is a "saving grace," but belief is not. All who are not skeptics believe the testimony of Christ and his apostles, but not all who are not skeptics have faith. Faith is accompanied with love; belief is not. "The devils believe and tremble." The natural man believes that God is merciful, but does not trust in his mercy.

This distinction is marked in the New Testament, by the use of the prepositions connected with the verb, or noun. *Πιστέυω* when used in reference to Christ is accompanied with *ἐν*, *ἔις*, and *ἐπὶ*, because the object is to denote rest and reliance upon his person. Paul said to the jailer, "Believe on (*πίστευσόν ἐπὶ*) the Lord Jesus Christ, and thou shalt be saved." He did not bid him merely to believe that the statements which he had heard from Paul respecting Christ were correct. He bade him do much more than this: namely, receive and rest on Christ himself as a living and personal Redeemer. Had he asked only for the assent of the mind to testimony, he would have said: "Believe the Lord Jesus Christ."

The same use of the prepositions is sometimes associated with the term "gospel," because of its connection with Christ. "Repent and believe (*πιστεύετε ἐν*) the gospel," Mark 1: 15. Even when there is no preposition, *πιστέυω* sometimes denotes trust. "Christ did not commit himself" (*οὐκ ἐπίστευεν ἑαυτὸν*), John 2 : 24. "Who will commit to your trust the true riches (*τίς πιστεύσει*)?" Luke 16 : 11. "Unto them were committed the oracles" (*ἐπιστεύθησαν*), Rom. 3 : 2. "The gospel of circumcision was committed to me," Gal. 2 : 7. "I know whom I have believed," or trusted in (*ᾧ πεπίστευκα*), 2 Tim. 1 : 12. An instance of mere belief in testimony is found in Mark 11 : 31, "Why did ye not believe him" (*διάτι ὀυκ ἐπιστεύσατε ἀυτῷ*)?

This fiducial or confiding nature of faith is taught in the phrases, "looking" to Christ, "receiving" Christ, "eating" his flesh, "drinking" his blood. The definition which makes faith merely belief in testimony, converts Christ into a witness only. He is this, but much more: a prince and saviour; a prophet, priest and king; a person not to be believed merely, but to be believed in and on.

Faith is an effect of which regeneration is the cause. This is taught in 1 John 5 : 1, "Whosoever believeth that Jesus is the Christ is born of God." Phil. 1 : 29, "Unto you it is given, in behalf of Christ, to believe on him." 2 Thess 1 : 11, "We pray that God would fulfil [in you] all the good pleasure of his goodness, and the work of faith with power." 1 Cor. 2 : 5, "That your faith should not stand in the wisdom of men, but in the power of God." John 6 : 44, 65, "No man can come to me except the Father which hath sent me draw him. No man can come unto me, except it were given him of my Father." 1 Pet. 1 : 21, "By him, do ye believe in God, that raised him up from the dead, and gave him glory; that your faith and hope might be in God." The order and connection between regeneration and faith is taught by our Lord. After announcing the doctrine of regeneration to Nicodemus, in John 3 : 3, "Except a man be born again, he cannot see the kingdom of God," he then, in John 3 : 14–18, proceeds to speak of his own atonement for sin, and of man's trust in it, "The Son of man must be lifted up, that whosoever believeth in him should not perish but have eternal life." That great change which Christ denominates being "born again," manifests itself first of all in an act of reliance upon Christ's blood of atonement. Saving faith in the person and work of the Redeemer follows regeneration, and always presupposes it.

The following particulars are to be noted.

1. Evangelical faith is an act of man. The active nature of faith in Christ is indicated in the Scripture phraseology,

which describes it as "coming" to Christ (Matt. 11:28), "looking" to Christ (John 1:29), "receiving" Christ (John 3:11), "following Christ (John 8:12). The object of the epistle of James, is to teach that faith is an active principle. "Dead faith," the epistle defines to be "faith without works:" that is, pretended faith that does not work. The hypocrite merely "*says*" that he has faith (James 2:14).

2. Evangelical faith is an act of both the understanding and the will. It is complex; involving a spiritual perception of Christ, and an affectionate love of him. (*a*) That faith is an intelligent act, is proved by John 6:44, 45, "They shall be all taught by God. Every man, therefore, that hath heard and hath learned of the Father, cometh unto me." 2 Cor. 3:14; 4:4. Eph. 1:17, 18, God giveth "the spirit of wisdom and revelation in the knowledge of Christ." 1 John 2:20, "Ye have an unction from the Holy One, and ye know all things." (*b*) That faith is an affectionate and voluntary act, is proved by Gal. 5:6, "Faith worketh by love." Eph. 6:23, "Peace be to the brethren, and love, with faith from God the Father." Eph. 3:17; 4:16; 5:2. Coloss. 2:2 1 Thess. 3:12; 5:8. 1 Tim. 1:14. 2 Tim. 1:13, "Hold fast the form of sound words, in faith and love which is in Christ Jesus."

3. Evangelical faith is the particular act that unites the soul to Christ. For this reason, it stands first in the order of the acts that result from regeneration. "The Holy Spirit applieth to us the redemption purchased by Christ, by working faith in us, and thereby uniting us to Christ in our effectual calling," S. C., 30. Penitence for sin, love of holiness, hope, long-suffering, patience, temperance, etc., are none of them acts by which Christ's atonement for sin is laid hold of and made personal. Trusting faith is the special exercise of the soul by which this is done, and hence faith is the first thing commanded. "Believe on the Lord Jesus Christ, and thou shalt be saved," Acts 16:13. "This

is the work of God, that ye believe on him whom he hath sent," John 6 : 29.[1]

The union with Christ by faith is not natural and substantial, like that between Adam and his posterity. Nor is it moral or social, like that between individuals in a corporation or state. Its characteristics are the following. (*a*) It is a spiritual union, because of its author, the Holy Spirit. 1 Cor. 6 : 17, "He that is joined unto the Lord is one spirit." 1 Cor. 12 : 13, "By one Spirit are we all baptized into one body." 1 John 3 : 24, "Hereby we know that he abideth in us, by the Spirit which he hath given us." 1 John 4 : 13. (*b*) It is a vital union, because it involves a divine and spiritual life derived from Christ. John 14 : 19, "Because I live, ye shall live also." John 11 : 25, "He that believeth in me though he were dead, yet shall he live." Gal. 2 : 20, "I live; yet not I, but Christ liveth in me." (*c*) It is an eternal union. John 10 : 28, "They shall never perish, neither shall any man pluck them

---

[1] The priority, in the order, of faith to all other acts, is illustrated by the following anecdote "In a beautiful New England village a boy lay very sick, drawing near to death, and very sad His heart longed for the treasure which was worth more to him now than all the gold of the western mines One day I sat down by him, took his hand, and looking in his troubled face asked him what made him so sad 'Uncle,' said he, 'I want to love God Won't you tell me how to love God?' I cannot describe the piteous tones in which he said these words, and the look of anxiety which he gave me I said to him: 'My boy, you must trust God first, and then you will love him without trying to at all' With a surprised look he exclaimed, 'What did you say?' I repeated the exact words again, and I shall never forget how his large, hazel eyes opened on me, and his cheek flushed as he slowly said, 'Well, I never knew that before I always thought that I must love God first before I had any right to trust him' 'No, my dear boy,' I answered, 'God wants us to trust him, that is what Jesus always asks us to do first of all, and he knows that as soon as we trust him we shall begin to love him. This is the way to love God, put your trust in him first of all' Then I spoke to him of the Lord Jesus, and how God sent him that we might believe in him, and how, all through his life, he tried to win the trust of men, how grieved he was when men would not believe in him, and every one who believed came to love without trying at all. He drank in all the truth, and simply saying, 'I will trust Jesus now,' without an effort put his young soul in Christ's hands that very hour; and so he came into the peace of God which passeth understanding, and lived in it calmly and sweetly to the end."

out of my hand." Rom. 8 : 35–39, "Who shall separate us from the love of Christ?" 1 Thess. 4 : 14, 17. (*d*) It is a mystical, that is, mysterious union. The elect are "mystically joined to Christ," L. C., 67. Eph. 5 . 32, "This is a great mystery ; I speak concerning Christ and the church." The spiritual union between Christ and his people is individual, not specific. It does not rest upon unity of race and nature. It results from regeneration, not from creation. Consequently it is not universal, but particular.[1] Upon this spiritual and mystical union, rests the federal and legal union between Christ and his people. Because they are spiritually, vitally, eternally, and mystically one with him, his merit is imputable to them, and their demerit is imputable to him. The imputation of Christ's righteousness supposes a union with him. It could not be imputed to an unbeliever, because he is not united to Christ by faith.

4. Saving faith terminates on Christ as its object; and upon Christ in all three of his offices: prophet, priest, and king. Since, however, guilt is a prominent fact in man's condition, the priestly office is prominent in relation to faith as described in Scripture. Under the Levitical economy, faith was indispensable. The typical sacrifice must be offered trusting in the promise of God concerning the Messiah. Merely to bring and slay a lamb, as an opus operatum, was not sufficient. There must be filial reverence for the Divine command, and confidence in the Divine promise of mercy through the coming Redeemer.

The second effect of regeneration is *Repentance.* The word *μετάνοια* denotes a change of the mind (*νοῦς*). But "mind" is employed in the sense of disposition, will or inclination, as in Rom. 7 : 25, "With the mind (*νοΐ*), I myself serve the law of God" It is an instance in which *νοῦς* is put for *καρδία*. See Anthropology, p. 130. The word *μεταμέλομαι* is sometimes employed to denote the

[1] For twelve points of difference between union with Adam and union with Christ, see Shedd . On Romans 5 19.

genuine sorrow that accompanies repentance. Matt. 21: 29, "Afterwards he repented and went." 2 Cor. 7:8, "Though I made you sorry, I do not repent though I did repent." Matt. 21:32, "And ye, when ye had seen it, repented not afterwards that ye might believe him." Heb. 7:21, "The Lord sware and will not repent." In Matt. 27:3, it denotes the impenitent remorse of Judas. But *μετάνοια*, not *μεταμέλεια*, is the technical term in the New Testament for repentance. The difference between penitence and remorse is described in 2 Cor. 7:9, 10. Penitence is "godly sorrow," and is one of the elements in repentance.

The definition of repentance in the Westminster Confession (XV. ii.) comprises the following particulars: (*a*) "A sense not only of the danger, but of the odiousness of sin." (*b*) "The apprehension of God's mercy in Christ." (*c*) "Grief for, and turning from sin."[1] (*d*) "The purpose and endeavor to walk in God's commandments." Ezek. 36:31, "Then shall ye remember your own evil ways, and shall loathe yourselves in your own sight, for your iniquities." Ps. 51:4, "Against thee, thee only, have I sinned; that thou mightest be justified when thou speakest, and clear when thou judgest." 2 Cor. 7:11, "That ye sorrowed after a godly sort, what carefulness is wrought in you, yea what indignation, what fear, what vehement desire, what zeal" Ezek. 18:30, 31. Joel 2:12, 13. Amos 5:15 Ps. 119:128. Jer. 31:18, 19, "I have heard Ephraim bemoaning himself thus: Thou hast chastised me as a bullock unaccustomed to the yoke; turn thou unto me, and I shall be turned; for thou art the Lord my God."

---

[1] Sorrow for sin must be carefully distinguished from shame on account of it. The impenitent experience shame for sin, and they "awake to shame and everlasting contempt," Dan 12.2 A person may feel degraded by his vices, and ashamed of them, without any sincere grief for them as committed against God Such feeling as this is selfish; while godly sorrow is disinterested. A man may be vexed and angry with himself, and despise himself, without any humble prostration of soul before God and confession of guilt. A sense of

Though faith and repentance are inseparable and simultaneous, yet in the order of nature, faith precedes repentance. Zech. 12: 10, "They shall look on me whom they have pierced, and they shall mourn for him as one mourneth for his only son." Acts 11 : 22, "A great number believed and turned unto the Lord." This order is evinced by the following particulars: (*a*) Faith is the means, and repentance is the end. Faith leads to repentance, not repentance to faith. The Scriptures present God's mercy in redemption as the motive to repentance. Jer. 3 : 14, "Turn, O blacksliding children, saith the Lord; for I am married unto you." Joel 2 : 13, "Turn unto the Lord your God, for he is gracious and merciful." (*b*) Repentance involves turning to God; but there can be no turning but through Christ. John 14: 6, "No man cometh unto the Father but by me." John 10 : 9, "I am the door." (*c*) If repentance precedes faith, then it stands between the sinner and Christ. The sinner cannot go to Christ "just as he is," but must first make certain that he has repented. (*d*) If repentance precedes faith, then none but the penitent man is invited to believe in Christ. This contradicts Rom. 5 : 6, "Christ died for the *ungodly*." Impenitent sinners are commanded to believe on the Lord Jesus Christ, in order to the remission of their sins. (*e*) The doctrine that repentance precedes faith tends to make repentance legal: that is, a reason why Christ should accept the sinner. (*f*) God out of Christ, and irrespective of faith in Christ, is a consuming fire, Deut. 4 : 24. Heb. 12 : 29. It is impossible to have godly sorrow with this view of God. Only remorse and terror are possible. In such passages as Mark 1: 15, "Repent ye, and believe the Gospel," and Acts 20: 21, "Testifying repentance toward God, and faith toward our Lord Jesus Christ," the end is mentioned first, and the means last. In a proposition, a term may have a position

---

the meanness and disgrace of sin is not the sense of its odiousness and ill-desert.

*verbally* which it has not logically. In Jer. 31 : 34, sanctification is mentioned before pardon. "They shall all know me, for I will forgive their iniquity."[1]

---

[1] "Melanchthon taught that repentance was the effect of the law, and anterior to faith, and used forms of expression which were thought to imply that good works or sanctification, although not the ground of justification, were nevertheless a causa sine qua non of our acceptance with God To this Luther objected; as true sanctification is the consequence, and in no sense the condition of the sinner's justification. We are not justified because we are holy, but being justified, we are made holy." Hodge. Theology, III. 238.

# CHAPTER V.

## JUSTIFICATION.

Augustine: Enarratio in Ps. 50. Luther: On Galatians. Calvin: Institutes, III. xi.–xviii. Bellarmin. Disputationes (De Justificatione). Ursinus: Christian Religion, Qu. 12–14, 21, 59–64 Turrettin: Institutio, XIV. x.–xiv. Gerhard: Loci, Tom. IV. Davenant. On Justification. Hooker: Polity, VI. v.; Discourse on Justification. Pearson: Creed, Art. X. Owen: On Justification; Holy Spirit, IV. Bunyan: Justification by Imputed Righteousness. Edwards: Justification by Faith; Wisdom displayed in Salvation Baur: Gegensatz (Lehre von der Rechtfertigung). Mohler: Symbolics. Dorner: Christian Doctrine § 132. Ritschl · Doctrine of Justification. Faber: Primitive Doctrine of Justification. Buchanan: On Justification (Lect. viii.–xv.). Hodge: Theology, III. 114–212; Princeton Essays (On Imputation). Shedd: History of Doctrine, II. 203–375.

Justification is one of the most important doctrines in the Christian system. It supposes faith, and faith supposes regeneration. "Whosoever believeth that Jesus is the Christ, is born of God," 1 John 5 : 1. "I will put my law in their inward parts, and write it in their hearts. For I will forgive their iniquity, and will remember their sin no more," Jer. 31 : 33, 34. This order is given in the Larger Catechism, Q. 67. The "mind being enlightened," and "the will being renewed," the person is "enabled to accept Christ as offered in the gospel." Faith unites with Christ, and union with Christ results in justification. This is defined in the Shorter Catechism (Q. 33) to be "an act of God's free grace wherein he pardoneth all our sins, and accepteth us as righteous in his sight, only for the righteousness of Christ imputed to us and received by faith." Acts

13 : 38, 39, "Through this man is preached unto you the forgiveness of sins. And by him, all that believe are justified from all things from which ye could not be justified by the law of Moses." Rom. 3 : 23, 24, "All have sinned and have come short of the glory of God; being justified freely by his grace, through the redemption that is in Christ Jesus." Rom. 4 : 5, "To him that worketh not, but believeth on him that justifieth the ungodly; his faith is counted for righteousness." Rom. 4 : 6–8; 5 : 17–19; 8 : 30. 1 Cor. 1 : 30, "Of God are ye in Christ Jesus, who of God is made unto us wisdom, and righteousness, and sanctification, and redemption." 2 Cor. 5 : 19, 21. Eph. 1 : 7; 2 : 8. Phil. 3 : 9. Jer. 23 : 6. Heb. 2 : 4, "The just [justified] shall live by his faith."

The justification of a *sinner* is different from that of a righteous person. The former is unmerited; the latter is merited. The former is without good works; the latter is because of good works. The former is pardon of sin and accepting one as righteous when he is not; the latter is pronouncing one righteous because he is so. The former is complex; the latter it simple.

The justification of the "ungodly" (Rom. 4 : 5; 5 : 6) includes both pardon and acceptance. Either alone would be an incomplete justification of the ungodly. In the case of a sinner, the law requires satisfaction for past disobedience and also perfect obedience. When a criminal has suffered the penalty affixed to his crime, he has done a part, but not *all* that the law requires of him. He still owes a perfect obedience to the law, in *addition* to the endurance of the penalty. The law does not say to the trangressor: "If you will suffer the penalty, you need not render the obedience." But it says: "You must both suffer the penalty and render the obedience." Sin is under a *double* obligation; holiness is under only a *single* one. A guilty man owes both penalty and obedience; a holy angel owes only obedience.

Consequently, the justification of a *sinner* must not only

deliver him from the penalty due to disobedience, but provide for him an equivalent to personal obedience. Whoever justifies the *ungodly* must lay a ground both for his delivery from hell, and his entrance into heaven. In order to place a transgressor in a situation in which he is δίκαιος, or right in *every* respect before the law, it is necessary to fulfil the law for him, both as penalty and precept. Hence the justification of a sinner comprises not only pardon, but a title to the reward of the righteous. The former is specially related to Christ's passive righteousness, the latter to his active. Christ's expiatory suffering delivers the believing sinner from the punishment which the law threatens, and Christ's perfect obedience establishes for him a right to the reward which the law promises. The right and title in both cases rest upon Christ's vicarious agency. Because his Divine substitute has suffered for him, the believer obtains release from a punishment which he merits; and because his Divine substitute has obeyed for him, the believer obtains a reward which he does not merit.

The meaning of the term "justify" must be determined by its Scripture use and connection, and not by the etymology merely. It may have two meanings, like "glorify" and "sanctify" To "glorify God," and to "glorify the body," are different significations of the word. The one signifies to declare to be glorious, the other, to make glorious. The clause, "Sanctify the Lord God in your hearts," employs the term "sanctify" differently from the clause, "Ye are sanctified." Similarly, "to justify" might mean to "make just" (justum facere), as well as to "pronounce just." But in Scripture, it never means to sanctify, or make inwardly holy.

In the New Testament, the verb δικαιόω signifies: (*a*) To pronounce, or declare to be just. Luke 7:29, "And the publicans justified God." Rom. 3:4, "That thou mightest be justified in thy sayings." (*b*) To acquit from condemnation. Acts 13:39, "Justified from all things from which ye could not be justified by the law of Moses." Rom. 4: 5–7; 5:1, 9; 8: 30–33; 1 Cor. 6:11; Gal. 2:16; 3:11. That δικαιόω does not mean sanctifying or making just, is proved by its antithesis to "condemning:" Deut. 25:1, Prov. 17:15, Isa. 5:23, 2 Chron. 18:6, 7; and by its equivalents, "imputing righteousness" and "covering sin," Rom. 4:3, 6–8; 2 Cor. 5:19, 21.[1]

In order to be justified, or pronounced righteous, a person must possess a righteousness (δικαιοσύνη) upon the ground of which the verdict is pronounced. There are two kinds of righteousness, upon the ground of which a person might be justified before the Divine law. (*a*) Legal righteousness, or that of the covenant of works. This is perfect personal conformity to the law. Rom. 10: 5, "Moses describeth the righteousness which is of the law, that the man which [perfectly] doeth those things shall live by them." A holy being is justified by this kind of righteousness. A sinner cannot be pronounced righteous upon the ground of legal righteousness, or perfect obedience, because he has not rendered it. Rom. 3: 20, "By the deeds of the law shall no flesh be justified." Rom. 3:10, "There is none righteous, no, not one." Rom. 3:23. Acts 13:39. Gal. 2:16. The impossibility of man's being justified by legal righteousness is relative, not absolute. If he had rendered perfect obedience, he would be pronounced just upon this ground. "The doers of the law shall be justified," Rom. 2:13. (*b*) Gratuitous or evangelical righteousness, or that of the covenant of grace. This is technically denominated "the righteousness of God." Matt. 6:33; Rom. 1:17; 3:5, 21, 22, 25, 26; 10:3; 2 Cor. 5:21; Phil. 3:9; 2 Peter 1:1. The

[1] Möhler (Symbolics, § xiii) contends that "justificare" means "to acquit" only when applied to the innocent and holy, and is inapplicable to a transgressor. "The forgiveness of sin," he says, "is undoubtedly a remission of the guilt and the punishment which Christ has borne upon himself, but it is likewise the *transfusion* of his Spirit into us." But St Paul expressly says that "God justifieth the *ungodly*," Rom. 4 5 So far as a person has *infused* righteousness, he is not ungodly.

Old Testament teaches it. "The Lord our righteousness," Jer. 23 : 6 ; 33 : 16. It is so denominated, to distinguish it from the ordinary ethical or legal righteousness which is the righteousness of man. In Rom. 10 : 3, this latter is called *ἰδίαν δικαιοσύνην* ; and in Phil 3 : 9, *ἐμὴν δικαιοσύνην*. If man should perfectly obey the law, the righteousness would be the result of his own agency. It would be "his own righteousness." But the "righteousness of God" is the result of God's agency solely. Hence it is described (Rom. 4 : 6) as *χωρὶς ἔργων* [sc. *ἀνθρώπου*]. Man is not the author of it, in any sense whatever.

The "righteousness of God" is the active and passive obedience of incarnate God. It is Christ's vicarious suffering of the penalty, and vicarious obedience of the precept of the law which man has transgressed. It is Christ's atoning for man's sin, and acquiring a title for him to eternal life. It is "gratuitous" righteousness, because it is something given to man outright, without any compensation or equivalent being required from him in return. "Ho, every one that thirsteth, come ye to the waters, and he that hath no money ; come ye, buy and eat ; yea, come, buy wine and milk without money and without price," Isa. 55 : 1. "Being justified gratuitously (*δωρεὰν*) by his grace," Rom. 3 : 24. Since this evangelical "righteousness of God" is not inherent and personal to man, like the legal or ethical "righteousness of the law," it has to be *imputed* to him. Rom. 4 : 6, "David describeth the blessedness of the man to whom God imputeth righteousness." Rom. 4 : 9, 10. Christ's atoning death for sin is not the sinner's atoning death for sin, but God imputes it to him : that is, he calls or reckons it his. Christ's perfect obedience which merits eternal life is not the sinner's perfect obedience, but God imputes it to him ; he calls or reckons it his. Gen. 15 : 6. Rom. 4 : 3, 5, " Abraham believed God, and it was counted (*ἐλογίσθη*) to him for righteousness. Now to him that worketh not, but believeth on him that justifieth the ungodly, his faith is counted for righteousness." James 2:23, "Abraham believed God, and it was imputed unto him for righteousness."

We have observed that in order that a person may be pronounced just, there must be a *reason* or *ground* for the verdict. Justification cannot be groundless, and without a reason. The "righteousness of God" is the ground or basis upon which a believing sinner is pronounced to be righteous. Because Christ has suffered the penalty for him, he is pronounced righteous before the law in respect to its penalty, and is entitled to release from punishment. Because Christ has perfectly obeyed the law for him, he is pronounced righteous before the law in respect to its precept, and is entitled to the reward promised to perfect obedience. To pardon a believer, and accept him as if he had rendered the sinless obedience which entitles to eternal reward, is to impute "the righteousness of God" to him.

The following particulars in connection with the justification of a sinner are to be noted. 1. Faith is the instrumental, not the procuring or meritorious cause of his justification. "God justifieth, not by imputing faith itself, the *act* of believing, but by imputing the obedience and satisfaction of Christ." Westminster Confession, XI. i. The reasons are: (*a*) Because faith is an internal act or work of man. If the sinner's act of faith merited the pardon of his sin, and earned for him a title to life, he would be pronounced righteous because of *his own* righteousness, and not because of God's righteousness. Faith is denominated a work. John 6:29, "This is the work of God, that ye believe." It is the activity of the man, like hope and charity, and can no more be meritorious of reward, or atoning for disobedience, than these acts can be. "In a right conception, fides est opus; if I believe a thing because I am commanded, this is opus."[1] Selden: Table Talk. (*b*)

[1] For the Tridentine view of justification adopted partially by a Protestant, see Jeremy Taylor's sermon. Faith working by Love. Coleridge refers to this

Because, as an inward act of the believer, faith is the gift of God, being wrought within him by the Holy Spirit. Eph. 2:8; Philip. 1:29. But a Divine gift cannot be used as if it were a human product, and made the ground of pardon and eternal reward. A debt to God cannot be paid by *man* out of God's purse; though it can be so paid by God himself. (*c*) Because the believer's faith is an imperfect act. As such, it cannot be either atoning or meritorious. (*d*) Because faith is not of the nature of suffering, and consequently cannot be of the nature of an atonement The believing sinner is "justified by faith" only instrumentally, as he "lives by eating" only instrumentally. Eating is the particular act by which he receives and appropriates food. Strictly speaking, he lives by bread alone, not by eating, or the act of masticating. And, strictly speaking, the sinner is justified by Christ's sacrifice alone, not by his act of believing in it.

2. The justification of a sinner is solely by Christ's satisfaction. "No man may look at his own graces as a part of his legal righteousness, in conjunction with Christ's righteousness as the other part. We must go wholly out of ourselves, and deny and disclaim all such righteousness of our own." Baxter: Spiritual Peace and Comfort. Bacon's Ed. I. 273. Justification does not depend partly upon the merit of Christ's work, and partly upon that of the believer. The Tridentine theory is heretical at this point, because it makes the believer's justification to rest upon Christ's satisfaction in combination with inward sanctification and outward works. Scripture explicitly teaches that justification is by faith alone: not by faith and works combined. "A man is justified by faith without the deeds of the law," Rom. 3:28. Paul's "faith alone," in this passage, must not be confounded with James's, "faith that *is*

---

defect in Jeremy Taylor. Works, V 195 Yet in an earlier period in his life, he fell into the same error himself See the Friend, Works, II. 288. Ed. Harper.

alone," James 2:17. The latter is spurious faith that produces no works, or "dead" faith.[1]

3. The justification of a sinner is instantaneous and complete. It is a single act of God which sets the believer in a justified state or condition. Rom. 8:1, "There is no condemnation to them that are in Christ Jesus." Rom. 8:33, 34, "Who shall lay anything to the charge of God's elect? Who is he that condemneth?" John 5:24, "He that heareth my word, and believeth on him that sent me, hath everlasting life, and shall not come into condemnation."

4. The justification of a sinner is an all comprehending act of God. All the sins of a believer, past, present, and future, are pardoned when he is justified. The sum-total of his sin, all of which is before the Divine eye at the instant when God pronounces him a justified person, is blotted out, or covered over, by one act of God. Consequently, there is no repetition in the Divine mind of the act of justification; as there is no repetition of the atoning death of Christ, upon which it rests. "Christ is not entered into the holy places made with hands, that he should offer himself often; for then must he often have suffered since the foundation of the world; but now once in the end of the world hath he appeared, to put away sin by the sacrifice of himself; and as he was once offered to bear the sins of many, unto them that look for him shall he appear the second time, without sin, unto salvation. For by one offering he hath perfected forever them that are sanctified," Heb. 9:24–28; 10:14.

While, however, there is no repetition of the Divine act of justification, yet the *consequences* of it in the soul of the believer are consecutive. In the believer's *experience*, God is continually forgiving his sins. The Divine mercy "is constantly absolving us by a perpetual remission of our

[1] Compare Calvin: Institutes, III. xiv. 11. Shedd: History of Doctrine, II. 318–332; Sermons to the Spiritual Man, 293–298.

sins." Calvin: Institutes, III. xiv. 10. The one eternal act of justification is *executed* successively in time, as the Divine decree is. "God doth from all eternity decree to justify all the elect; nevertheless, they are not [consciously] justified, until the Holy Spirit doth in due time actually apply Christ unto them." Westminster Confession, XI. iv.

When a justified man commits sin, though his sin deserves eternal death, yet he is not exposed to eternal death as an unbeliever is, and as he himself was prior to justification. But he experiences the withdrawal of the Divine favor, and God's paternal chastisement. This may be very severe and painful; and perhaps, sometimes, in the believer's experience may be almost equal to the distress of the unpardoned. David's experience during his backslidings was fearful in the extreme. Ps. 116 : 3, "The sorrows of death compassed me, and the pains of hell gat hold of me." Ps. 32 : 4, "Day and night thy hand was heavy upon me: my moisture is turned into the drought of summer." Ps. 42 : 7, "All thy waves and thy billows are gone over me." Here in this life, the believer oftentimes suffers more than the unbeliever does. God deals with the former as with a son, and causes him great mental distress for his soul's good; he deals with the latter as with a bastard and not a son. Heb. 12 : 8. Lazarus in this life suffered more than Dives did. At the same time, the true believer, under all this experience, is really and in the eye of God a justified and forgiven man. The believer himself may be in great doubt upon this point, and sometimes may be on the brink of despair; but he is not cast off by God. David himself, after those dreadful passages in his experience, is enabled to hope in the Divine pity. He never falls into the absolute despair of the lost. Ps. 71 : 3, "Thou hast given commandment to save me." Ps. 42 : 5, "Why art thou cast down, O my soul? hope thou in God; for I shall yet praise him for the help of his countenance."

Some writers, in this reference, distinguish between

"actual" and "declarative" justification. Cunningham and Buchanan make this distinction. Actual justification is the act in the divine mind; declarative justification is the announcement of the divine act in the consciousness of the believer. The believer's experience has its fluctuations and varieties; but the act of God is one and immutable. A person may be actually justified, with little or even no confident and joyful sense of it, in some chapters of his experience. Yet a justified man will not absolutely lose the hope of justification, and have the experience of blaspheming despair.

5. The justification of a sinner includes a title to eternal life, as well as deliverance from condemnation. This is denoted by the clause, "accepting as righteous," in the Westminster definition. Eternal life, as a reward, rests upon *perfect* obedience of the law. Had man rendered this obedience, he could claim the reward. He has not rendered it, and hence cannot claim it. Yet he must get a title to it, or he can never enjoy it. The rewards of eternity must rest upon some good basis and reason. They cannot be bestowed groundlessly. Christ, the God-man, has perfectly obeyed the law; God gratuitously (δωρέαν, χώρὶς ἔργων) imputes this obedience to the believer; and the believer now has a right and title to the eternal life and blessedness founded upon Christ's theanthropic obedience. This is the second part of justification; the first part being the right and title to exemption from the penalty of the law, founded upon Christ's atoning sacrifice. Justification thus includes the imputation of Christ's obedience as well as of his suffering; of both his active and his passive righteousness.

Piscator, Tillotson, Wesley, and Emmons denied the imputation of Christ's active obedience; contending that justification is "pardon" alone, without "acceptance," or a title to life. They maintain that after the pardon of the believer's sin, on the ground of Christ's passive obedience,

the end of it. For these two reasons, the believer cannot establish a valid title to an *infinite* and *eternal* reward upon the ground of his imperfect and halting service of God here in this life. He must therefore found it upon the perfect obedience of his Redeemer, and expect entrance into heaven because his Substitute has obeyed for him, even as he expects to escape retribution because his Substitute has suffered for him. The reason why the believer must press forward after perfect sanctification is, that he may be *fit* for heaven, not that he may *merit* heaven. Sinless perfection in the next life is not the ground and reason of the believer's future reward, but the necessary condition of his future blessedness. If there be remaining sin, there must be, so far, unhappiness.

Passages of Scripture that prove the imputation of Christ's active obedience are the following: Rom. 5:19, "Through the obedience of one shall many be made righteous." 1 Cor. 1:30, "Christ is made unto us wisdom, and righteousness, and sanctification." 2 Cor. 5:21, "He made him to be sin for us, that we might be made the righteousness of God in him." This "righteousness" is complete, and therefore includes a title to the reward of righteousness. Col. 2:10, "Ye are complete in him." Eph. 1:6, "He hath made us accepted in the beloved." Eph. 3:12, "In whom we have boldness, and access with confidence." The boldness and confidence imply that there is no deficiency in the justification effected for the believer by Christ. But if he were resting his title to eternal life upon his own character and works, he could be neither bold nor confident in the day of judgment, 1 John 4:17 John 3:16, "Whosoever believeth shall not perish"—this is pardon; "but shall have eternal life"—this is acceptance as righteous.

It is objected that the believer is represented as being rewarded for his works, and in proportion to his works, in the last day. The reply is: (*a*) The reward of the last day is gracious; resulting from a covenant and promise on the part of God. It is the recompense of a parent to a child, not the payment of a debtor to a creditor. God is not under an absolute indebtedness to the believer founded on an independent agency of the believer, but only a relative obligation established by himself and depending upon his assistance and support in the performance of the service. This is proved by the fact that the reward of a Christian is called an "inheritance." Matt. 55:34; Acts 20:32; Gal. 3:18; Eph. 5:5; Col. 1:12 The believer's reward is like a child's portion under his father's will. This is not wages and recompense, in the strict sense; and yet it is relatively a reward for filial obedience. If an angel under the legal covenant fails to keep the law in a single instance, he gets no reward; a redeemed man under the evangelical covenant, though he often fails, yet gets his reward. God graciously compensates the believer in Christ, because he is fatherly and compassionate towards his child, and not because the reward has been completely earned and is strictly due upon the principle of abstract justice "Where remission of sins," says Calvin (Inst., III. xvii. 8, 9), "has been previously received, the good works which follow are estimated by God far beyond their intrinsic merit; for all their imperfections are covered by the perfection of Christ, and all their blemishes are removed by his purity. Now if any one urge as an objection to the righteousness of faith, that there is a righteousness of works, I will ask him, whether a man is to be reputed righteous on account of one or two holy actions, while in all the other actions of his life he is a transgressor of the law. This would be too absurd to be pretended. I will then ask him, If a man is to be reputed righteous on account of many good works, while he is found guilty of any instance of transgression. This, likewise, my opponent will not presume to maintain in opposition to the law which pronounces a curse upon those who do not fulfil every one of its precepts. I will then further inquire, If there is any work of man which does not deserve the charge of impurity or imperfection. Thus he will be compelled to concede that there is not an absolutely good work to be found in man, that deserves the name of righteousness in the strict sense." Eternal life is called a "gift" in Rom. 6:23, while eternal death is called "wages." Again, the address of the judge in the last day to those who receive the reward of obedience is, "Come ye blessed." The reward is also a *blessing*. This would not be the language of a debtor who is discharging strict indebtedness to his creditors. The redeemed, also, when receiving their reward disclaim absolute merit: "When saw we thee an hungered, and fed thee? Or thirsty, and gave thee drink?"

(*b*) The object in considering the works of men in the final judgment is to evince the genuineness of faith in Christ, and discriminate true from false believers; not to show that man's works merit pardon and eternal life. Those who have done good works are described as humble, and surprised that they receive such an immense recompense for their poor service; while those who have not done good works are described as self-righteous and proud, and surprised that they are punished and not rewarded. Matt. 7:22, "Many shall say unto me in that day, Lord, Lord, have we not prophesied in thy name? and then will I profess unto them, I never knew you." Matt. 25:44, "Then those on the left hand shall answer him, saying, Lord when saw we thee an hungered, or athirst, or a stranger, or naked, or sick, or in prison, and did not minister unto thee?" The parable of the laborers, all of whom receive the same wages though hired at different hours, proves that the rewards of the last day are not regulated by the exact value of the obedience rendered. Since the reward is the consequence of a promise and not of an original obligation on the part of God, God may do as he will with his own. He never pays less than he has promised; thereby becoming himself a debtor. The lord in the parable did not. But he may pay more than is due, and does pay more.

An error of the Perfectionist, at this point, is to be noticed. It is confounding *imputed* sanctification with *inherent* sanctification. Imputed sanctification is mentioned in 1 Cor. 1:30: "Christ was, of God, made unto us sanctification." Inherent sanctification is inward holiness: as in 1 Cor. 6:11, "Ye are sanctified." In the former sense, a believer's "sanctification" is instantaneous and perfect; but not in the latter. When God imputes Christ's active obedience to the believer, Christ is "made sanctification" to him. It is a complete sanctification that is imputed, and his title to life founded upon it is perfect; but his inward sanctification, or cleansing from indwelling sin, is still imperfect. Sanctification as imputed is a part of justification; but sanctification as infused and inherent is the antithesis to justification. The Perfectionist overlooks this distinction.

6. Justification is a means to an end. Men are justified in order that they may be sanctified; not sanctified in order that they may be justified. Redemption does not stop with justification. Rom. 8:30, "Whom he justified, them he also glorified." John 8:11, "Neither do I condemn thee [i.e., I pardon thee]; go and sin no more." Pardon is in order to future resistance and victory over sin. The sense of forgiveness is accompanied with a hatred of sin, and hunger after righteousness. If the latter be wanting, the former is spurious. An unpardoned man could not be

sanctified, because remorse and fear of retribution would prevent struggle with sin. David prays first for forgiveness, in order that he may obey in future. Ps. 51:7, 13, "Purge [atone] me with hyssop; hide thy face from my sins; then will I teach transgressors thy ways."

## CHAPTER VI.

### SANCTIFICATION.

**Calvin: Institutes, III. vi.-x. xx.; IV. xiv.-xvii. Á Kempis: Imitation of Christ. Ursinus Christian Religion, Q. 89-91. Turrettin: Institutio, Locus XVII. Hooker: Polity, V. lvii. lviii. Owen. Indwelling Sin; Mortification; Saint's Perseverance. Jeremy Taylor: Holy Living and Dying. Scougal: Life of God in the Soul of Man. Bates. Spiritual Perfection. Charnocke: Attributes (Holiness). Flavel Keeping the Heart. Edwards: Religious Affections. Wesley: Christian Perfection. Watson: Institutes, II. xxix. Junkin: On Sanctification. Dabney: Theology, LVI.-LVII. Hodge: Theology, III. 466-709; Way of Life, IX. Faber: Operations of the Holy Spirit. Hare. Mission of the Comforter. Buchanan: Office and Work of the Holy Spirit.**

THE term "sanctify" (*ἁγιάζειν*) is employed in Scripture in two senses: (*a*) To consecrate, or set apart to a sacred service or use. John 10:36, "Whom the Father hath sanctified and sent." Matt. 23.17, "The temple that sanctifieth the gold." (*b*) To purify and make holy. 1 Cor. 6:11, "But ye are washed, ye are sanctified." Heb. 13:12. John 17:17, "Sanctify them through thy truth." The latter is the sense in which it is taken, when the doctrine of Sanctification is discussed. The Westminster Shorter Catechism (Q 35) defines as follows: "Sanctification is the work of God's free grace, whereby we are renewed in the whole man after the image of God, and are enabled more and more to die unto sin, and live unto righteousness." Eph. 1:4, "God hath chosen us that we should be holy." 1 Cor. 6:11, "Ye are washed, ye are sanctified by the Spirit of our God." 2 Thess. 2:13, "God hath chosen you to salvation, through sanctification of the Spirit." 1 Thess. 5 : 23, "The very God of peace sanctify you wholly."

1. Sanctification results from the continuation of the agency of the Holy Spirit, after the act of regeneration. (*a*) In strengthening and augmenting existing graces: faith, hope, charity, etc. (*b*) In exciting them to exercise, through reading and hearing the word, the sacraments, prayer, providences, afflictions, and chastisements. Hence it is often called "renewing," Ps. 51 : 10 ; 2 Cor. 4 : 16 ; Eph. 4: 23 ; Col. 3:10; Rom. 12:2; Titus 3 : 5. "Renewing," or renovation, in this use of the term, is not synonymous with "regeneration." When St. Paul exhorts the Ephesians (4: 23) to "be renewed in the spirit of their mind," he is not exhorting them to regenerate themselves, but to sanctify themselves. So also with the exhortation to "the house of Israel," "Make you a new heart," Ezek. 18: 31.

2. Sanctification includes the entire man. 1 Thess. 5 : 23, "The very God of peace sanctify you wholly; and I pray God your whole spirit, and soul, and body be preserved blameless."[1] Sanctification affects: (*a*) The higher rational and spiritual part of man's nature, the *πνεῦμα*, because this has been corrupted by the fall. Titus 1 : 15 ; Rom. 1: 28 ; Eph. 4 : 18. (*b*) The inferior intelligence, the *ψυχή*. (*c*) The body, *σῶμα*. As apostasy began in the *πνεῦμα*, and affected the other parts of human nature, so sanctification begins in the *πνεῦμα* and passes throughout the soul and body. A man can control his physical appetites, in proportion as he has a vivid spiritual perception of God and divine things. The intuition in the *πνεῦμα* restrains the appetites of the *ψυχή* and *σῶμα*. If spiritual perception be dim, the bodily appetite is strong. That the higher nature,

[1] See Shedd. On Romans 7 · 23 ; 8 · 10, for the meaning of this trichotomy.

denominated $\pi\nu\varepsilon\tilde{\upsilon}\mu\alpha$ or $\nu o\tilde{\upsilon}\varsigma$, is depraved, and needs to be sanctified, is proved by Rom. 1 : 28 ; 12 : 2. Eph. 4 : 17 ; 2 Tim. 3 : 8 ; Tit. 1 : 15 ; Mark 1 : 23 ; 1 Thess. 5 : 23.

3. Sanctification is gradual. "We are enabled more and more to die to sin." It is the conflict with, and victory over indwelling sin described in Rom. 7 : 14–8 : 28. The eighth chapter of Romans, as well as the seventh, speaks of the struggle and groaning of the still partially enslaved will. "Even we ourselves who have the first-fruits of the Spirit groan within ourselves, waiting for the adoption, to wit, the redemption of our body For we are saved by hope. Likewise the Spirit also helpeth our infirmities, and maketh intercession for us with groanings which cannot be uttered," Rom. 8 : 23, 24, 26.

4. The means of sanctification are : (*a*) Internal : namely, Faith. Gal. 5 : 6, "Faith worketh by love." Hope. Rom. 5 : 5, "Hope maketh not ashamed, because the love of God is shed abroad in our hearts." Joy. 1 Pet. 1 : 8, 9, "In whom ye rejoice with joy unspeakable, receiving the end of your faith, even the salvation of your souls." Peace. Phil. 4 : 7, "The peace of God shall keep your hearts and minds, through Christ Jesus." The *exercise* of any one of these Christian graces increases the holiness of the believer. (*b*) External : The Scriptures. John 17 : 17, "Sanctify them through thy truth." 1 Pet. 1 : 22, 23 ; 2 : 2, "Desire the sincere milk of the word, that ye may grow thereby." Prayer. John 14 : 13, 14, "Whatsoever ye shall ask in my name I will do it." Acts 2 : 42. Providential discipline. John 15 : 2, "Every branch in me that beareth not fruit, he purgeth." Rom. 5 : 3, 4 ; Heb. 12 : 5–11. The sacrament of the Supper. Acts 2 : 42, "They continued steadfastly in the apostles' doctrine and fellowship, and in breaking of bread, and in prayers."

5. The believer co-operates with God the Spirit in the use of the means of sanctification. Sanctification is both a

grace and a duty. 1 Cor. 16 : 13, "Watch ye, stand fast in the faith, quit you like men, be strong." Eph. 6 : 16, 18, "Take the shield of faith, the helmet of salvation, and the sword of the Spirit which is the word of God, praying always with all prayer and supplication in the Spirit, and watching thereunto with all perseverance." Phil. 2 : 12, 13, "Work out your own salvation, for it is God which worketh in you." Hence sanctification is the subject of a command. Eph 4 : 22, 23, "Put off the old man, and be renewed in the spirit of your mind." Ezek. 18 : 31, "Make you a new heart, and a new spirit." Regeneration, being the sole work of God, is a grace but not a duty. It is nowhere enjoined upon man as a duty, to regenerate himself.

6. Sanctification though progressive is not complete in this life. 1 John 1 : 8, 10, "If we say we have no sin, we deceive ourselves." Phil. 3 : 12–14, "Brethren, I count not myself to have apprehended, but I press toward the mark." Rom. 7 : 18, 23, "I know that in me, that is in my flesh, dwelleth no good thing. I see another law in my members, warring against the law of my mind." Gal. 5 : 7. Sanctification is completed at death. "The souls of believers at their death are made perfect in holiness," S. C., 37. Heb. 12 : 23, The heavenly Jerusalem contains "the spirits of just men made perfect." 1 John 3 : 2, "We shall be like him, for we shall see him as he is." 2 Cor. 5 : 8, "Absent from the body, and present with the Lord." Eph. 5 : 27, "Christ loved the church that he might sanctify it, and present it to himself a glorious church not having spot or wrinkle." 1 Cor. 13 : 12, "Now we see through a glass darkly; but when that which is perfect is come, face to face." Matt. 5 : 8, "The pure in heart shall see God." Rev. 14 : 13, "Blessed are the dead who die in the Lord."

7. Sanctification once begun is never wholly lost. It fluctuates with the fidelity of the believer, but he never

falls back into the stupor and death of the unregenerate state. L. C., 79. "They whom God hath sanctified by his Spirit shall constantly persevere to the end, and be saved." John 10:28, 29, "My sheep shall never perish, neither shall any pluck them out of my hand." Rom. 11:29, "The gifts and calling of God are without repentance." Phil. 1:6, "He which hath begun a good work in you, will perform it, unto the day of Jesus Christ." 1 Pet. 1:5, Believers are "kept by the power of God through faith unto salvation."

Exhortations to diligence, and warnings against carelessness and failure are consistent with the certain perseverance of the believer, because: (*a*) While the certainty is objective in God, it may not be subjective in man. God knows that a particular man will certainly persevere, because he purposes that he shall, and he will realize his purpose by the operation of his Spirit within him; but the man does not know this unless he has assurance of faith. Many believers do not have this highest degree of faith, and hence are more or less subject to doubts and fears Exhortations to diligence, and warnings against apostasy, suit such an experience as this. But one who is assured of salvation by the witness of the Holy Spirit would not require to be warned against apostasy, while in this state of assurance. (*b*) Exhortations to struggle with sin, and warnings against its insidious and dangerous nature, are one of the means employed by the Holy Spirit to secure perseverance. The decree of election includes the means as well as the end. Now if success in the use of means is certain, there is the strongest motive to employ them; but if success is uncertain, then there is little motive to use them. St. Paul employs the certainty of success as a motive to struggle. "Fight the good fight of faith; lay hold on eternal life, *whereunto thou art called*," 1 Tim. 6:12.

It must be remembered that salvation is certain, not because the person believes that he has once believed in the past, but because he now consciously believes. If from his present experience and daily life he has reason to think that he is truly a believing Christian, then he has reason to expect that he will continue to be one. Cromwell, according to the anecdote, committed an error in inferring his good estate, because he believed that he was once a believer.[1]

That sanctification is never lost, is proved also by its connection with justification. Justification naturally tends to sanctification. Gal. 5: 6, "Faith worketh by love." Trust in Christ's blood of atonement spontaneously impels to the resistance of sin; and if there be no struggle against sin, it is clear proof that there is no true trust in Christ's sacrifice. Justification supplies the only efficient motive to obedience. Hence the obedience of the believer is called "new obedience," because of the new motive from which it springs, viz.: the atoning love of the Redeemer. It is also denominated "the obedience of Christ," 2 Cor. 10:5. Gratitude to Christ, and love of him for the forgiveness that comes through his death, are the springs of this evangelical obedience and sanctification. The strongest inducement for a Christian to obey the divine law, is the fact that he has been graciously pardoned for having broken the law. He follows after sanctification, because he has received justification. He obeys the law not in order to be forgiven, but because he has been forgiven. 2 Cor. 5:4, "The love of Christ constraineth us not to live unto ourselves, but

---

[1] The passage in Heb 6: 4–6 is hypothetical, as is proved by verse 9: "We are persuaded better things of you, and things that accompany salvation, though we thus speak" A supposition which is not an actual or even a possible case is sometimes made, for the sake of illustrating or enforcing truth. In 1 Cor 13: 1–3, Paul supposes the existence of Christian faith without that of Christian charity. In Gal. 1:8, he supposes that an angel from heaven may preach another gospel than the true one. In Matt 13·21, 22, the stony-ground hearer is not a true believer. In 2 Pet 2.20, 21, the "dog who turns to his own vomit," is a false professor His "knowing the way of righteousness" is superficial knowledge, like that of the stony-ground hearer.

unto him which died for us." And the love meant, is Christ's redeeming love. 2 Cor. 7:1, "Having these promises [of forgiveness], let us cleanse ourselves from all filthiness of the flesh and spirit." Because God has blotted out all his past sin, the believer has the most encouraging of all motives to resist all future sin. Had God not pardoned the past, it would be futile to struggle in future. In 2 Pet. 1:4, it is said that the "exceeding great and precious promises are given to us in order that by these we might be partakers of a divine nature, having escaped the corruption of the world through lust." Sanctification does not justify; but justification sanctifies. And there being this close connection between the two, sanctification can no more be wholly lost than justification can be.

The necessary connection between sanctification and justification is taught by both Paul and James; between whose views there is a verbal, but not a logical contradiction. Paul, in Rom. 4:4–13, assumes that saving faith is living faith and produces works, but he says nothing particularly upon this latter point: First, because his object is to *contrast* faith and works; and, secondly, because the opponent with whom he was disputing did not claim to be justified by faith of any kind, true or false, but by works altogether. James, on the other hand, not only assumes that saving faith is living faith and produces works, but speaks particularly and emphatically upon this latter point: First, because he is not contrasting faith and works; and, secondly, because he was contending with hypocrites, who claimed that what they called "faith alone," and "faith only," and what James calls "dead faith," is a faith that would save the soul. Hooker (on Justification) remarks that justification is spoken of by St. Paul in the narrow sense, as exclusive of sanctification; but by St. James in the wide sense, as inclusive of it. Paul means justification without its fruits; James means justification with its fruits. The former speaks of faith simply; the latter of working faith.

Paul describes faith as the antithesis of works; James describes faith as producing works.[1]

---

[1] The seeming contradiction between Paul and James disappears, if James is understood to put, by metonomy, the effect for the cause; the work of faith for faith itself When he says that "Abraham was justified by works" (James 2 21), and "Rachel was justified by works" (James 2 · 25), he means that they were justified by a faith that produced works, or a *working* faith Abraham's "work" proved that his "faith" was genuine, and therefore might well stand for and represent it It was a "work of faith," 1 Thess. 1 3. Shedd Sermons to the Spiritual Man, Sermon XIX.

## CHAPTER VII.

### THE MEANS OF GRACE.

THE Means of Grace are means of sanctification. They suppose the existence of the principle of divine life in the soul. "The outward and ordinary means whereby Christ communicates to his church the benefits of his mediation, are, all his ordinances; especially the word, sacraments, and prayer; all of which are made effectual to the elect for their salvation." L. C. 154. The means of grace are administered within the visible Church, and to its members.[1] Consequently, church membership is requisite to obtaining the benefits of the means of grace and sanctification Some of these benefits cannot be enjoyed at all, outside of the visible Church: those, namely, connected with the administration of the sacraments, and the fellowship and watch of Christians; and none of them can be enjoyed in their fulness, by one who has not separated himself from the world by confessing Christ before men.[2]

---

[1] When the world of unregenerate men are said to have the means of grace, the means of *conviction* under common grace, not of sanctification under special grace, are intended "The Spirit of God maketh the reading, but especially the preaching of the word, an effectual means of enlightening, convincing, and humbling sinners, of driving them out of themselves, and drawing them unto Christ" L C. 155

[2] Respecting the nature of the Church, Calvin (Dedication to the Institutes) presents the Protestant view in two fundamental positions (*a*) That the Church may exist without a visible form, because it is both invisible and visible. The former is composed of all who are really united to Christ; the latter, of all who profess to be united to Christ The former has no false members, the latter has, as the parables of the tares and the net show (*b*) That the visible form of the Church is not distinguished by external splendor, but by the pure preaching of God's word, and the legitimate administration of the sacraments. The Romanist

1. Confession of faith and church fellowship is a means of sanctification This is one of "the ordinances of Christ," *all* of which, according to the Westminster statement, are means of grace. Christ commands his disciples to confess him before men. Matt. 10 : 32, 33, "Whosoever shall confess me before men, him will I confess also before my Father which is in heaven. But whosoever shall deny me before men, him will I also deny before my Father which is in heaven." Compare Matt. 16 : 16–18. The use of this means of spiritual growth is often enjoined in the Epistles. Rom. 10 : 9, 10 ; Heb. 10: 25.

Man is a social being, and his religious like his secular welfare depends upon association with others like-minded. Confession of faith and church membership promote sanctification : (*a*) By personal sympathy. (*b*) By the watch and discipline of fellow-Christians. Those who cherish a hope that they are believers, yet make no public acknowledgment of their faith, omit an important means of grace, and hinder their own sanctification. Moreover, such a neglect of an explicit ordinance of Christ casts doubt upon the reality of the supposed faith. There would be more ground for hope, were this doubt removed by the confession of faith.

2. The Word of God is a means of grace and sanctification, in two aspects of it: (*a*) As law. The purpose of this is, to point out the duty which God requires of man as a subject of his government. The effect of the word in this form upon the believer, is to produce self-knowledge and humility. The believer by the law is made acquainted with indwelling sin. Meekness and lowliness of heart are the effect of the word, in this aspect of it. He is kept "poor in spirit" (*b*) As gospel. The purpose of this is, to dis-

---

**contends that the Church exists only in a visible form, and that this form is in the see of Rome and her order of prelates, alone Rome makes the invisible and visible churches identical and coterminous For a concise and able statement of the prelatical theory of the Church, see Jeremy Taylor's Consecration Sermon.**

close the fulness of Christ to meet this spiritual poverty. Preaching should combine the two in just proportions, in order to the sanctification of believers.

The efficacy of the word is from the Holy Spirit applying it. The Spirit does not operate upon the truth, but upon the soul. John 18 : 43, 47, "Why do ye not understand my speech? even because ye cannot hear my word. He that is of God heareth God's word: ye therefore hear them not because ye are not of God." 1 Cor. 2 : 14, "The natural man cannot know the things of the Spirit because they are spiritually discerned." In using the word, the Divine Spirit works directly upon the soul, and produces two effects: (*a*) The understanding is enlightened, and enabled to perceive the truth spiritually. (*b*) The will is renewed and inclined towards it. The aversion of the heart to truth is overcome. Some Lutheran divines represent the Holy Spirit as operating upon the truth, so that the truth becomes an efficient by means of this superadded quality or power. The Reformed theologians regard the Holy Spirit as the sole efficient, and the truth as only an instrument.

3. The Sacraments are means of grace and sanctification.[1] In the classical meaning, "sacramentum" was the oath of allegiance taken by the soldier. It was also the money pledged by contending parties in a litigated case. It implied obligation of some kind. The classical is not the Biblical, or the ecclesiastical signification. The Latin fathers employed sacramentum as the equivalent of *μυστήριον.* The sacrament was a "mystery." The Vulgate translates *μυστήριον,* in Eph. 1 : 9; 3 : 23; 5 : 32, by sacramentum. But as a mystery is exhibited or explained by a symbol, the "sacramentum" was also a "symbolum." Calvin: Inst., IV. xiv. 2.

In the Biblical and ecclesiastical use, a "sacrament" is a sign or symbol of a Christian mystery: of the mystery of

[1] On this subject, see the thorough discussion of Calvin Institutes, IV. xiv.–xvii.

regeneration, in the case of baptism; of the mystery of vicarious atonement in the case of the Lord's supper. These two sacraments exhibit and certify, by sensible emblems, to the believing recipient, these two mysterious facts in redemption. The Westminster Larger Catechism (Q. 162) so defines. "A sacrament is a holy ordinance instituted to signify, seal, and exhibit to believers the benefits of Christ's mediation, to strengthen their faith, to oblige them to obedience, to cherish their love and communion one with another."

The following are the fundamental positions in the Reformed theory of the sacraments. (*a*) They are means of grace, dependent like the other means upon the accompanying operation of the Holy Spirit and consequent faith in the soul of the recipient. Says Calvin (Inst., IV. xiv. 9), "All the energy of operation belongs to the Spirit, and the sacraments are mere instruments which without his agency are vain and useless, but with it, are fraught with surprising efficacy." "The grace which is exhibited in or by the sacraments is not conferred by any power in them; neither doth the efficacy of a sacrament depend upon the piety or intention of him that doth administer it, but upon the work of the Spirit." Westminster Confession, XXVII. iii Matt. 3:11, "I indeed baptize you with water, but he shall baptize with the Holy Ghost." 1 Cor. 12:13, "By one Spirit we are all baptized into one body." 1 Cor. 11:28, "Let a man examine himself and so let him eat." Rom. 2:28, "Neither is that circumcision which is outward." 1 Pet. 3:21, "The antitype whereunto, namely baptism, doth also now save us (not the putting away of the filth of the flesh, but the answer of a good conscience towards God), by the resurrection of Jesus Christ." (*b*) In the sacrament of the supper, the bread and wine are both symbols, and memorials of Christ's body. They both emblematize, and remind of a particular fact: namely Christ's atoning death. This is founded on Luke 22:19, "This is [i.e.

represents][1] my body; this do in remembrance of me." The first clause describes the sacrament as symbolic; the second as mnemonic. "Our Lord Jesus instituted the sacrament called the Lord's supper, for the perpetual remembrance of the sacrifice of himself in his death, and a commemoration of the one offering of himself upon the cross." Westminster Confession, XXIX. i. ii (*c*) The act of truly partaking of the Lord's Supper is mental and spiritual, not physical and carnal. The Westminster Confession (XXIX. vii.) teaches that the "worthy receiver *spiritually* receives and feeds upon Christ crucified," and denies that he "*carnally* and *corporally* receives or feeds upon Him." It also denies that "the body and blood of Christ are corporally or carnally in, with, or under, the bread and wine," and asserts that they are "really, but spiritually, present to the faith of believers, as the elements themselves are to their outward senses."

The points in this statement of most importance are: (*a*) The believer, in worthily partaking of the Lord's supper, consciously and confidently relies upon Christ's atoning sacrifice for the remission of his sins. This is meant by the phrase, "Feed upon Christ crucified." The allusion is to Christ's words in John 6:53-56, "Except ye eat the flesh of the Son of man, and drink his blood, ye have no life in you." The flesh and blood of Christ signify the expiatory death of Christ. To "drink Christ's blood," is to trust in Christ's atonement in a *vital* manner, and with a *vivid* feeling of its expiatory efficacy. The Lord's Supper can have no meaning, if his vicarious sacrifice is denied.

(*b*) The "presence" of Christ is not in the bread or the wine, but in the soul of the participant. Christ, says the Westminster Confession, is "present to the *faith* of believers," and faith is mental and spiritual. The statement of Hooker (Polity, V. lxvii.) upon this point is explicit and

[1] The substantive verb, in this passage, has the same signification as in Gal 4.24. "These [women] are the two covenants."

excellent. "The real presence of Christ's most blessed body and blood is not to be sought for in the *sacrament*, but in the worthy *receiver* of the sacrament. I see not which way it should be gathered by the words of Christ, when and where the bread is his body, or the cup his blood; but only in the very heart and soul of him which receiveth them. As for the sacraments, they really exhibit, but for aught we can gather out of that which is written of them, they are not really, nor do they really contain in themselves, that grace which with them, or by them, it pleaseth God to bestow." Again he remarks (V. lxvii.), "No side denieth but that the soul of man is the receptacle of Christ's presence. Whereby the question is driven to a narrower issue, nor doth anything rest doubtful but this, whether, when the sacrament is administered, Christ be whole [wholly] within man only, or else his body and blood be also externally seated in the very consecrated elements themselves. Which opinion, they that defend are driven either to *consubstantiate* and incorporate Christ with elements sacramental, or to *transubstantiate* and change their substance into his; and so the one to hold him really, but invisibly, moulded up with the substance of those elements, the other to hide him under the only visible show of bread and wine, the substance whereof, as they imagine, is abolished, and his succeeded in the same room."

With this statement of Hooker, Calvin (Inst., IV. xvii. 31) agrees. "They are exceedingly deceived, who cannot conceive of any presence of the flesh of Christ in the supper, except it be attached to the bread. For on this principle they leave nothing to the secret operation of the Spirit, which unites us to Christ. They suppose Christ not to be present unless he descends to us; as though we cannot equally enjoy his presence, if he elevates us to himself. The only question between us, therefore, respects the manner of this presence; because they place Christ in the bread, and we think it unlawful for us to bring him down from heaven. Let the reader judge on which side the truth lies. Only let us hear no more of that calumny, that Christ is excluded from the sacrament unless he be concealed under the bread. For as this is a heavenly mystery, there is no necessity to bring Christ down to the earth, in order to be united to us."[1]

This view of Hooker and Calvin respecting the solely spiritual presence of Christ in the Supper was that of the founders of the English Church, and entered into their form of worship. In the Office for the Communion of the Sick, in the Episcopal Prayer Book, it is said: "If a man by reason of extremity of sickness, or any other just impediment, do not receive the sacrament of Christ's body and blood, the minister shall instruct him that if he do truly repent him of his sins, and steadfastly believe that Jesus Christ hath suffered death upon the cross for him and shed his blood for his redemption, earnestly remembering the benefits he hath thereby, and giving him hearty thanks therefor, *he doth eat and drink the body and blood of our Saviour Christ* profitably to his soul's health, although he do not receive the sacrament with his mouth."

The Romish theory of the sacraments is, that they convey both regenerating and sanctifying grace by their own nature and efficiency: by the mere external muscular performance (ex opere operato) of the rite of baptism, or of the supper, the effect is produced in the soul. Bellarmine (De Sacramentis, II. i.) defines the theory thus: "The sacraments convey grace by the virtue of the sacramental action itself instituted by God for this end, and not through the merit of either the agent or the receiver."

The Lutheran doctrine of the sacrament of the Supper

---

[1] The presence of Christ in the bread and wine themselves would be a local and extended presence, because bread and wine are local and extended substances But the presence of Christ to "the faith of a believer" is a presence in his soul, which is an illocal and spiritual presence, because the soul is an illocal and spiritual substance.

teaches: (*a*) That its efficacy is conditioned upon faith in the recipient. In this, it agrees with the Reformed doctrine. (*b*) That its efficacy is due to an intrinsic virtue, resulting from the presence of Christ's glorified body in and with the bread and wine. This co-presence of Christ's glorified body in the emblems makes the sacrament efficacious to the believer. In this, the Lutheran differs from the Calvinistic doctrine. The latter finds the efficacy of the sacrament of the Supper solely in the operation of the Holy Spirit in the heart of the believer. "The sacraments become effectual means of salvation, not by any power in themselves, but only by the working of the Holy Ghost." Westminster L. C., 161.

The Lutheran asserts that Christ is "spiritually present in the sacrament of the Supper as to the *manner*, but corporeally present as to the *substance*." That is to say, the substance of Christ's spiritual and glorified body as it now exists in heaven, not of his material and unglorified body as it once existed on earth, is actually present in and with the sacramental emblems. Consequently, the spiritual and glorified body of Christ is present in the bread and wine, wherever and whenever the sacrament is administered. This requires the ubiquity of Christ's glorified body, whereby it can simultaneously be in heaven and on earth. But the glorified body of Christ, like that of his people, though a spiritual body, has form, and is extended in space. The description of Christ's body after his resurrection and at his ascension proves this. But one and the same form cannot occupy two or more spaces at one and the same moment. Christ's glorified body can *pass* from space to space instantaneously, but cannot *fill* two spaces at the same instant. When Christ's body passed through, the "doors being shut" (John 20 : 26), and stood in the midst of the disciples, his body was no longer on the outside of the doors, and could not be.

Hooker (V lxvii.) defines the Lutheran, the Romish, and

the Reformed views of the Supper as follows: "There are but three expositions made of the words, 'This is my body.' The first: 'This is in itself, before participation, really and truly the natural substance of my body, by reason of the co-existence which my omnipotent body hath with the sanctified element of bread'—which is the Lutheran's interpretation. The second: 'This is in itself, and before participation, the true and natural substance of my body, by force of that deity which with the words of consecration abolisheth the substance of bread, and substituteth in the place thereof my body'—which is the Popish construction The third: 'This hallowed food, through concurrence of Divine power, is, in verity and truth, unto faithful receivers, instrumentally a cause of that mystical participation, whereby as I make myself wholly theirs, so I give them in hand an actual possession of all such saving grace as my sacrificed body can yield, and their souls do presently need. This is to them, and in them, my body.'"

According to this statement of Hooker, which agrees with that of the Reformed symbols, there are but three generic theories of the Sacraments: the Reformed, the Lutheran, and the Romish. Some would find a fourth theory represented by Zwingle. This comes from a misapprehension of the views of the Swiss reformer. The difference between Zwingle and Calvin upon sacramentarian points has been exaggerated. Zwingle has been represented as denying that the sacrament of the Supper is a means of grace, and that Christ is present in it. The following positions in his Ratio Fidei disprove this. He asserts that the sacraments are: 1. Res sanctae et venerandae 2 Testimonium rei gestae praebunt. 3. Vice rerum sunt quas significant; since they represent what cannot in itself be directly perceived. 4. Res arduas significant: having value not for what they are materially, but for what they signify; as a bridal ring is not worth merely the gold of which it is made. 5. They *enlighten* and *instruct* through the analogy between the symbol and the thing symbolized. 6. They bring *aid* and *comfort* to faith. 7. They take the place of (vice) an oath. These positions accord entirely with those in the First Helvetic Confession, which contains Calvin's view of the sacraments; and also with those presented in the Articles of Agreement between the churches of Zurich and Geneva. Hagenbach (§ 258) asserts that Zwingle taught that the sacrament is "both a symbol (signum), and a means of strengthening faith." Sigwart and Zeller, in their monographs upon Zwingle, take the same view. The writer of the article, Lord's Supper, in Kitto's Encyclopedia, represents Zwingle as holding that the Lord's Supper, by presenting under sensible emblems the sufferings and death of Christ, and bringing them to vivid remembrance, deepens penitence, stimulates faith, calls out love, and in this way is a means of sanctification equally with hearing the word, or any other means of grace employed by the Holy Spirit.

Zwingle asserted as strongly as Calvin the *spiritual* presence of Christ in the sacrament, denying with him the carnal and corporeal presence, either in the form of transubstantiation or consubstantiation. "Christ," he says, "is spiritually present in the consciousness of the believer (fidei contemplatione). In the recollection of his sufferings and death, and by faith in these, his body is spiritually eaten. We trust in the dying flesh and blood of Christ, and this faith is called the eating of the body and blood of Christ." Expositio Fidei (De Eucharistia). Compare Expositio Fidei, IV. 63, 64; Ed. Niemeyer. The corporeal presence of Christ he denied, appealing to the authority of Augustine, as follows: "Augustinus dixit Christi corpus in aliquo coeli loco esse oportere, propter visi corporis modum. Non est igitur Christi corpus magis in pluribus locis quam nostra corpora." Expositio Fidei, IV. 51. Ed. Niemeyer

Zwingle regarded the sacrament of the Supper as a means of grace and sanctification, because of its *didactic* character; because, by "evidently setting forth before the eyes Jesus

Christ crucified" (Gal. 3 : 1), it *teaches* in a vivid and special manner the great truth of Christ's atonement and redemption, and confirms the soul of the believer in it. It is an object-lesson. In this respect, the function of the sacrament is like that of the word. Gospel truth is taught by both alike. Both alike are employed by the Holy Spirit in enlightening, strengthening, and comforting the mind of the believer. This feature in Zwingle's view is sometimes cited to prove a radical difference between him and Calvin. But Calvin is even more explicit and positive, on this point. "The office of the sacraments," he says (Inst., IV. xiv. 17), "is *precisely the same as that of the word of God*, which is to offer and present Christ to us, and in him the treasures of heavenly grace; but they confer no advantage or profit without being received by faith. It is necessary to guard against being drawn into error, from reading the extravagant language used by the fathers with a view to exalt the dignity of the sacraments; lest we should suppose there is some secret power annexed and attached to the sacraments, so that they communicate the grace of the Holy Spirit, just as wine is given in the cup; whereas the only office assigned to them, is to testify and confirm his benevolence towards us; nor do they impart any benefit, unless they are accompanied by the Holy Spirit to open our minds and hearts, and render us capable of receiving this *testimony*. For the sacraments fulfil to us, on the part of God, the same office as messengers of joyful intelligence, or earnests for the confirmation of covenants, on the part of men." God "nourishes our faith in a spiritual manner by the sacraments, which are instituted for the purpose of placing his *promises* before our eyes for our contemplation, and of serving as pledges of them" (IV. xiv. 12). "For this reason, Augustine calls a sacrament 'a visible word;' because it represents the *promises* of God portrayed as in a *picture*, and places before our eyes an *image* of them" (IV. xiv. 5, 6). "Connected with the preaching of the gospel, another assistance and support of our faith is afforded us in the sacraments" (IV. xiv. 1). "There is no true administration of the sacrament without the *word*. For whatever advantage accrues to us from the sacred supper requires the *word;* whether we are to be confirmed in faith, exercised in confession, or excited to duty, there is need of *preaching*. Nothing more preposterous, therefore, can be done with respect to the supper than to convert it into a mute action, as we have seen done under the tyranny of the pope" (IV. xvii. 39). "The person who supposes that the sacraments confer any more upon him than that which is offered by the *word* of God, and which he receives by a true faith, is greatly deceived. Hence also it may be concluded that confidence of salvation does not depend on the participation of the sacrament, as though that constituted our justification, which we know to be placed in Christ Jesus alone, and is to be communicated to us no less by the preaching of the word than by the sealing of the sacraments, and that it may be completely enjoyed without this participation" (IV. xiv. 14).

This view of the nature of the sacrament of the Supper as didactic, is also confirmed by considering the nature and purpose of a *symbol*. The purpose of a symbol is, to teach a certain truth by a visible sign or token. The ocean is a symbol of God's immensity, and the sun of his glory. The "invisible things," or *truths*, relating to God, are emblematized and impressed by "the things that are made," Rom. 1:20. The heavens are a symbol of God, because they "declare the glory of God," Ps. 19:1. The cross is a symbol in all Christendom of the sacrifice of Christ. It teaches emblematically the truth that the Son of God died for man's sin. The ark, again, is a symbol of the church, and teaches that men are safe within the kingdom of God. In the case of all these natural symbols, there is no efficacy in the *symbol* as such, but only in the *truth* taught by it. The ocean, the sun, the cross, the ark, make no spiritual impression as mere water, light, and wood. It is only the immensity and glory of God, as taught by the symbols of the ocean and the sun, that affect the mind. It is only the mercy of God, as suggested by the symbol of the cross and the ark, that produces the spiritual effect.

The bread and wine of the Lord's Supper are *specially* and *divinely appointed* symbols, differing in this respect from all natural symbols. They are also *seals* as well as symbols; differing in this respect, also, from natural symbols. But as symbols they are didactic, and teach that truth which is the heart of the Christian religion: namely, that the broken and bleeding body of Christ is the oblation for sin.[1] They are "holy signs and seals of the covenant of grace, *immediately instituted* by God, to represent Christ and his benefits, and to confirm our interest in him." Westminster Confession, XXVIII 1. But in this instance, too, as in that of natural symbols, it is the *truth* taught by the symbols, and not the symbols themselves, that strengthens the faith of the participant, deepens his gratitude, enlivens his hope, and sanctifies his heart. As mere bread and wine, the symbols produce no spiritual effect in the soul of the believer. When the Holy Spirit enlightens the mind of the participant to perceive the gospel-truth which these emblems "exhibit, signify, and seal," then, and only then, do they become means of sanctification. It is not because the glorified body of Christ is conjoined with them, as the Lutheran asserts; or because they are converted into the glorified body of Christ, as the Romanist asserts; that they are effectual. It is because of the spiritual presence of Christ in the soul of the participant, and the spiritual perception of the truth signified and sealed by the

[1] The Lord's Supper took the place of the Jewish passover. "Christ our passover is sacrificed for us," 1 Cor 5 7. The passover was a divinely appointed symbol, reminding of and setting forth the deliverance of the first-born by the sprinkling of blood. But the paschal lamb was also typical of the Lamb of God. So that the visible emblem in the instance both of the passover and the supper teaches the expiation of sin by Christ's vicarious sacrifice.

emblems, as Calvin and Hooker say, that they are means of grace.[1]

The sacrament of Baptism is the sign and seal of regeneration. It is emblematic and didactic of this doctrine. Baptism is not a means of regeneration, as the Lord's Supper is of sanctification. It does not confer the Holy Spirit as a regenerating Spirit, but is the authentic token that the Holy Spirit has been, or will be conferred; that regeneration has been, or will be effected. This is taught in Rom. 4:11. Abraham "received the sign of circumcision, a seal of the faith which he had being yet uncircumcised." Baptism is Christian circumcision ("the circumcision of Christ," Col. 2:11), and takes the place of the Jewish circumcision; so that what is true of the latter is of the former. Paul, Cornelius, and the eunuch were regenerated before they were baptized. As circumcision was not absolutely necessary to salvation, neither is baptism. This is shown by the omission of it in Mark 16:16, when damnation is spoken of.

Baptism, being the initiatory sacrament, is administered only once. While symbolical only of regeneration, it yet has a connection with sanctification. Being a divinely appointed sign, seal, and pledge of the new birth, it promotes the believer's growth in holiness by encouragement and stimulus. It is like the official seal on a legal document. The presence of the seal inspires confidence in the genuineness of the title-deed; the absence of the seal awakens doubts and fears. Nevertheless, it is the title-deed, not the seal, that conveys the title.

Baptism is to be administered to believers and their children.[2] Acts 2:38, 39, "The promise [of the gift of the

---

[1] See, upon this point, Calvin · Institutes, IV. xvii 9-12, 33, 36, 39

[2] Proselyte baptism included the whole family, males and females, adults and infants. It was associated also with the circumcision of the males Some time before the Advent, the whole nation of the Idumeans embraced Judaism rather than be expelled from their country. Josephus says that Helena, queen of

Holy Ghost, ver. 38] is unto you and your children." Rom. 11:16, "If the root be holy, so are the branches." 1 Cor. 7:14, "The unbelieving husband is sanctified by the wife, and the unbelieving wife is sanctified by the husband: else were your children unclean: but now are they holy." Matt. 28:19, "Go teach [disciple] all nations, baptizing them." If the command had been, "Go teach all nations, circumcising them," no one would have denied that infants were included in the command. Infants are called disciples, in Acts 15:10. "Why tempt ye God to put a yoke [namely, circumcision] upon the neck of the disciples?" Accordingly, the Westminster Confession (XXVIII. iv.) affirms that "the infants of one or both believing parents are to be baptized."[1]

The baptism of the infant of a believer supposes the actual or prospective operation of the regenerating Spirit, in order to the efficacy of the rite. Infant baptism does not confer the regenerating Spirit, but is a sign that he either has been, or will be conferred, in accordance with the divine promise in the covenant of grace. The actual conferring of the Holy Spirit may be prior to baptism, or in the act itself, or subsequent to it. Hence baptism is the sign and seal of regeneration, either in the past, in the present, or in the future. The Westminster Confession (XXXVIII. vi.) teaches that "the efficacy of baptism is not tied to that moment of time wherein it is administered;" in other words, the regenerating grace of the Spirit, signified and sealed by the rite, may be imparted when the infant is baptized, or previously, or at a future time. The baptism is administered in this reference, and with this expectation. "Baptism is to be administered, to be a sign and seal of regeneration and ingrafting into Christ, and that even to in-

---

Adiatum, and her son, became proselytes. On this subject, See Maimonides. Wall History of Baptism. Lightfoot Hammond On Baptism.

[1] Calvin Institutes, II. 508–510, 516. Jeremy Taylor. Liberty of Prophesying, XVIII.

fants." Larger Catechism, 177. Under the old dispensation, the circumcision of the flesh was a sign and seal of the circumcision of the heart. Deut. 10:16; 30:6. "God," says Calvin (IV. xvi. 5), "did not favor infants with circumcision without making them partakers of all those things which were then signified by circumcision." Similarly, under the new dispensation, the baptism of the body of the infant is the sign and seal of the baptism of the soul by the Holy Ghost.

The infant of the believer receives the Holy Spirit as a regenerating Spirit, by virtue of the covenant between God and his people. Gen 17:7, "I will establish my covenant between me and thee, and thy seed after thee in their generations, for an everlasting covenant, to be a God unto thee, and to thy seed after thee." Acts 2:39, "The promise [of the gift of the Holy Spirit, ver. 38] is unto you and your children." The infant of the believer, consequently, obtains the regenerating grace by virtue of his birth and descent from a believer in covenant with God, and not by virtue of his baptism God has promised the blessing of the Holy Spirit to those who are born of his people. The infant of a believer, by this promise, is born into the church, as the infant of a citizen is born into the state. "Children born within the pale of the visible church, and dedicated to God in baptism, are under the inspection and government of the church." Directory for Worship, IX. They are church members by reason of their birth from believing parents; and it has been truly said, that the question that confronts them at the period of discretion is not, Will you join the visible church, but, will you go out of it." Church membership by birth from believers is an appointment of God under both the old and the new economies; in the Jewish and the Christian church.

Baptism is the *infallible* sign of regeneration, when the infant dies in infancy. All baptized infants dying before the age of self-consciousness, are regenerated without exception. Baptism is the *probable* sign of regeneration, when the infant lives to years of discretion. It is possible that the baptized child of believing parents may prove, in the day of judgment, not to have been regenerated, but not probable. The history of the church and daily observation show it to be the general fact that infant church members become adult church members. Yet exceptions are possible. A baptized infant, on reaching years of discretion, may to human view appear not to have been regenerated, as a baptized convert may. The fact of unregeneracy, however, must be proved, before it can be acted upon. A citizen of the state must be presumed to be such, until the contrary appears by his renunciation of citizenship, and self-expatriation. Until he takes this course, he must be regarded as a citizen. So a baptized child, in adult years, may renounce his baptism and church membership, become an infidel, and join the synagogue of Satan; but until he does this, he must be regarded as a member of the church of Christ. Such instances are exceedingly rare, both in church and state. The possible exceptions to the general fact that baptism is the sign of regeneration are not more numerous in the case of baptized infants, than of baptized converts. Says Hodge (Theology, III. 590), "It is not every baptized child who is saved; nor are all those who are baptized in infancy made partakers of salvation. But baptism signs, seals, and actually conveys its benefits to all its subjects, whether infants or adults, who keep the covenant of which it is a sign. It does not follow that the benefits of redemption may not be conferred on infants at the time of their baptism. That is in the hands of God. What is to hinder the imputation to them of the righteousness of Christ, or their receiving the renewing of the Holy Ghost, so that their whole nature may be developed in a state of reconciliation with God. Doubtless this often occurs; but whether it does or not, their baptism stands good; it assures them of salvation, if they do not renounce their baptismal covenant."

The reason why there is not an *infallible* connection between infant baptism and regeneration, when the infant lives to years of discretion, so that all baptized children of true believers are regenerated without a single exception, is the fact that the covenant is not observed on the human side with absolute perfection. Should the believer keep the promise on his part with entire completeness, God would be bound to fulfil the promise on his part. But the believer's fulfilment of the terms of the covenant, in respect to faith in God's promise, to prayer, to the nurture and education of the child, though filial and spiritual, is yet imperfect. God is, therefore, not absolutely *indebted* to the believer, by reason of the believer's action, in respect to the regeneration of the child. Consequently, he may exercise a sovereignty, if he so please, in the bestowment of regenerating grace, even in the case of a believer's child. We have seen (p. 126) that the regeneration of an unbaptized adult, depending as it does upon election, cannot be made infallibly certain by the use of common grace, though it may be made highly probable by it. In like manner, the regeneration of a baptized child, depending also upon election, may be made highly probable by the imperfect faith and fidelity of the parents, yet not infallibly and necessarily certain.

The *mode* of baptism which is by far the most common in the history of the Christian church is sprinkling or pouring. From the time of Christ to the present, a vastly greater number have been sprinkled than have been immersed At the present day, sprinkling is the rule throughout Christendom, and immersion the exception. The former mode is catholic; the latter is denominational.

Sprinkling was the common mode of baptism in the Old Testament, and this fact furnishes the strongest presumption that it was the mode of Christ and his apostles. As the Apostolic polity confessedly grew out of the Jewish synagogue, it is equally certain that the Apostolic ceremonial and ritual grew out of the Jewish. Polity and ritual are indissolubly associated. Baptizing under the Old economy was an important rite, and would certainly influence the mode under the New. The Old Testament baptism, therefore, is of the utmost consequence in settling the dispute respecting the mode of baptism and its subjects. The following particulars are to be noted:

1. Sacramental baptism by the Levitical priest was always administered by sprinkling, never by immersion. (*a*) The whole congregation at Sinai were baptized by sprinkling. Ex. 24:6–8. Heb 9:19, 20. (*b*) The Levites when consecrated to office were baptized by sprinkling. Numbers 8:7, "Thus shalt thou do unto them to cleanse them: sprinkle water of purifying upon them." (*c*) Lepers and defiled persons when restored to the congregation were baptized by sprinkling. Lev. 14:4–7; 49–53. Numb. 19:18, 19; 31:19, 22, 23. Luke 5:14. (*d*) Gentiles when admitted to the Jewish church were baptized by sprinkling. Num. 31:12, 19. These baptisms could be performed only by a priest, or by some "clean person" appointed to act for him. Num. 19:18, 19, "A clean person shall sprinkle water upon the unclean." The baptism in these instances was sacramental: i.e., had reference to guilt, and expiatory cleansing. Hence the blood of a sacrificial victim was sprinkled upon the congregation at Sinai, and upon the Levites, and restored lepers. No individual could baptize himself, with this sacramental and expiatory baptism. It was a priestly act, and required the priest or his appointed agent.

2. Baptism by Jehovah, in both the Old economy and the New, is by sprinkling or pouring. The Jehovah of the Old Testament is the Christ of the New, and is the Great High Priest. He baptizes with the Holy Spirit. Matt. 3:11, "He shall baptize you with the Holy Ghost and with

fire." This baptism is never by immersion. Isa. 52:15, "He shall sprinkle many nations." Ezek. 36:25, "Then will I sprinkle clean water upon you, and ye shall be clean. A new heart will I give you." Heb. 10:22, "Let us draw near to God, having our hearts sprinkled (ἐῤῥαντισμένοι) from an evil conscience." Heb. 12:24, "The blood of sprinkling (ῥαντισμοῦ) that speaketh better things than the blood of Abel" 1 Pet. 1:2, "Elect unto sprinkling of the blood of Jesus Christ." Isa. 32:15, "Until the Spirit be poured upon us from on high." Joel 2:28. Prov. 1:23 "I will pour out my Spirit unto you."

3. Ceremonial baptisms, or washings, were administered by sprinkling or pouring; not by immersion. These baptisms had reference not to the guilt of sin, but its pollution. Sometimes they were administered by the person himself, and sometimes by the priest. When a man ceremonially washed his hands, this was called a "baptism." Luke 11:38, "When the Pharisee saw it, he marvelled that he had not first washed (ἐβαπτίσθη) before dinner." Mark 7:4, "When they come from the market, except they wash [baptize, βαπτίσωνται, A D F. Rec. Tisch.; are sprinkled, ῥαντίσωνται, ℵ B C. Lachm. Hort], they eat not; and many other things there be which they have received to hold, as the washings (βαπτισμοὺς) of cups, pots, and brazen vessels, and of tables." The ceremonial "baptism" of the hands was performed by having a servant pour water upon them; and the ceremonial "baptism" of cups, pots, vessels, and tables, was by sprinkling or pouring; as in Num. 19:18, "A clean person shall sprinkle water upon the tent, and upon all the vessels, of the unclean person."[1]

---

[1] Whether the "baptism" of Naaman (2 Kings 5 10, 14) was sacramental or ceremonial, is doubtful If it was sacramental, like that of the restored leper under the Levitical economy, it was performed by a priest or his deputy, and was administered by sprinkling. This is the view of Baird Bible History of Baptism, p 157 He explains the command, "Go wash" (2 K 5 10), by Acts 22·16· Ananias said to Saul, "Rise, baptize thyself (βάπτισαι), and wash away thy sins." Here the baptism is described as self-administered, as it is in Naa-

Now, since sprinkling or pouring was the invariable mode of baptism under the Old economy, it is probable in the very highest degree that John the Baptist employed this mode. Baptism was a priestly act, as is implied in the inquiry, "Why baptizest thou, if thou be not the Christ, nor Elijah, nor that prophet?" John 1:25. John was a priest of the family of Aaron (Luke 1:5), and naturally administered the rite by sprinkling, or pouring, as the Jewish priest had administered it from time immemorial. There is not a scintilla of proof that he introduced immersion. And this same mode would naturally be adopted by the Apostles, when our Lord substituted baptism for circumcision, and transferred the rite from the Old dispensation to the New; from the Jewish to the Christian church. Peter associates "preaching peace by Jesus Christ," with "the baptism which John preached." Acts 10:36, 37.[1]

The principal supports of the mode by immersion are: (*a*) The custom in the Patristic church of immersing in the laver of the baptistery; and (*b*) The classical meaning of *βάπτω* and *βαπτίζω*.

Concerning the first argument, it is to be noticed, first, that the baptistery dates from a period when Christianity had become powerful, and able to erect churches with all the appointments of an imposing ritual. The Apostolic church could not do this. The baptistery and laver are as late as the fourth century. Furthermore, the first baptismal fonts were too small for immersing. The fresco in the catacombs of St. Calixtus (200 A.D. according to Rossi) represents the rite administered by pouring from the vessel upon the person standing upright. The "Teaching of the

---

man's case, though really administered by another. If, on the other hand, Naaman's "baptism" was ceremonial, like the ceremonial washing of the blind man in the pool of Siloam (John 9 7), it was by pouring

[1] On the Old Testament baptism, see the valuable treatise of Baird Bible History of Baptism. Mosheim Commentaries, I 89, 90

Apostles" (A.D. 160) says that baptism may be performed by pouring. Secondly, a more profuse application of water than that of sprinkling or pouring belongs to a period in the history of the church when baptism was held to be regeneration itself. If water be efficacious when applied by the officiating minister, then immersion would be deemed more efficacious than sprinkling. Immersion grew with the growth of the sacramentarian theory of baptism, and the doctrine of baptismal regeneration.

Respecting the classical meaning of *βάπτω* and *βαπτίζω*, it is to be observed that these words had no *technical* or *ritual* signification in classical Greek. They were never used to denote a pagan rite. There were purifying rites in the Greek and Roman worship, but they were not called "baptisms." The Greeks denominated their purifying rite *κάθαρσις*, and the Romans theirs, lustratio. Sprinkling was the mode in both. The nouns *βαπτισμος*, *βαπτισμα*, and *βαπτιστης* are not in the classical vocabulary. They were coined by Jews and Christians from *βαπτίζω*, in order to denote the rite of purification in the Jewish and Christian churches. Consequently, it is the secondary technical use in the Jewish and Christian scriptures, not the primary untechnical meaning in the Greek classics, which must be considered in determining the mode of baptism.[1]

The classical meaning of *βάπτω* and *βαπτίζω* is, to dip into water, to sink under water, to dye or tinge in a fluid. The classical meaning would favor baptism by immersion; as the classical meaning of sacramentum would prove that the Christian sacrament is an oath. But in Hebraistic and New Testament Greek, *βάπτω* and *βαπτίζω* are employed in a secondary ceremonial signification, to denote a

---

[1] In the later time of the Roman Empire, when public baths were erected, the bathing-tub, or labrum, was called "baptisterium" The term was probably borrowed from the Christian usage But the labrum was not large enough to immerse the whole body Water was taken from it, and poured upon the head of the person standing in it, or beside it. Anthon's Dictionary of Antiquities, Article Baths, p. 148

Jewish and Christian rite. Consequently, their meaning in the Septuagint and New Testament must be determined by their ritual and historical use, not by their classical The word "pagans" (pagani), etymologically and classically, denoted persons living in the villages (pagi) outside of the large towns and cities. Classically, "pagans" were "villagers." As Christianity spread first among the inhabitants of the cities, the villagers were the unevangelized; and thus "pagan" came to mean "heathen," instead of "villager." Similarly, βάπτω and βαπίτζω, which in heathenism denoted any *unceremonial, non-ritual* immersion into water, when adopted by Judaism and Christianity, came to have the secondary signification of a ceremonial sprinkling or affusion of water. And he who argues that baptism means immersion in the Scriptures, because in the classics the primary meaning of βάπτω and βαπτίζω is to immerse, commits the same error with him who should argue that a pagan is a villager, because this was the original signification of paganus; or that the Christian sacramentum is an oath, and not a symbol, because this is its meaning in Livy and Tacitus.

The word βαπτίζω is employed in the Septuagint, to signify a ritual purification performed by applying water to a person or thing so as to wet it more or less, but not all over and entirely.[1] The passages that have been quoted (pp. 579, 580) prove indisputably, that the mode in which the baptismal water of ritual purification was applied under the Levitical law was sprinkling or pouring. There was no immersion of the body in the sacramental baptism for guilt,

---

[1] An example of the application of the term "baptize" to a wetting of the person that is not immersion, is found in Dan. 4. 33. Nebuchadnezzar's "body was wet (ἐβάφη) with the dew of heaven" Another is found in Judith 12 7 Judith "washed herself (ἐβαπτίζετο) in a fountain of water by the camp" That this was not an immersion is highly certain, because the fountain would be used for drinking, and culinary purposes And though the washing was "in the night," yet in a camp there would be nearly as little privacy by night as by day.

or in the ceremonial baptism for pollution. And the spiritual baptism of the Holy Ghost is pouring, not immersing There is no good reason for supposing that the New Testament use of βαπτίζω is different from that of the Septuagint.

Historically, there is the highest probability that John the Baptist, and Christ's apostles, employed the old mode, and did not invent a new one like immersion, so different from the mode in both Jewish and Gentile lustrations. Furthermore, the circumstances and customs of the Jews necessitated sprinkling or affusion. It is morally certain, that such baptisms as those of Pentecost (Acts 2:41), of the eunuch (Acts 8:36), of Cornelius and his family (Acts 10:47), and of the jailer (Acts 16:33), were not administered by immersion. In the narrative of the baptism of the eunuch, it is said that "the way that goeth down from Jerusalem to Gaza is desert," Acts 8:26. The whole region is sandy and dry, with only here and there a small spring of water. In the account of the baptism of Cornelius and "all his house" (Acts 10:2), the phraseology implies that the baptismal water was brought into the room. "Can any man forbid *the* water (τὸ ὕδωρ), that these should not be baptized?" Acts 10:47. This phraseology would be unnatural, if the water in question were in a river, pond, or reservoir; but natural, if it were in a vessel. No one would "forbid" the Hudson or Connecticut river. It is improbable, that within the precincts of the jail there was either a stream or reservoir of water sufficient for immersing, in the dead of night, "the jailer and all his." The immersion of three thousand in Jerusalem on one day, at Pentecost (Acts 2:41), would have required the use of the public reservoirs of the city, which the Jewish authorities would have been as little likely to have allowed, as the common council of New York city would in a similar case.[1]

---

[1] The preposition εἰς, rendered in the authorized version, "into" (Acts 8 38), and "in" (Mark 1 9), might be rendered "unto," or "at" (comp. Acts 8.

Christ certainly had reference to the Old Testament baptism, and to John's baptism, when he said to Nicodemus, "Except a man be born of water and of the Spirit, he cannot enter into the kingdom of God," John 3 : 5. Christian baptism in the name of the Trinity had not yet been instituted. Nicodemus was a Pharisee, and our Lord wished to rid him of all self-righteousness, by teaching him that he must confess sin with "publicans and sinners," and submit to the old and common Jewish rite that was emblematic of forgiveness and cleansing. Though he was "a ruler of the Jews," and "a master of Israel," he must take the same attitude with the multitude who "were baptized in Jordan, confessing their sins," Matt. 3 : 5. "All the people that heard John, and the publicans, justified God, being baptized with the baptism of John. But the Pharisees and lawyers rejected the counsel of God against themselves, being not baptized of him," Luke 7 : 29, 30. This is our Lord's account of John's baptism, and of the state of mind in those who submitted to it, and those who rejected it. John's baptism was like that of Peter on the day of Pentecost, "a baptism of repentance for the remission of sins," Luke 3 . 3; Acts 2 : 38; 19 : 4. And the remission in both cases alike was through Christ, "the Lamb of God who taketh away the sin of the world," John 1 : 29. John directed his disciples to Christ, exactly as the apostles did theirs. "John looking upon Jesus, as he walked, saith, "Behold the Lamb of God," John 1 : 36. "Then said Paul, John verily baptized with the baptism of repentance, saying unto the people, that they should believe on him which should come after him, that is, on Jesus Christ," Acts 19 : 4. The apostles were baptized with John's baptism, and were not re-baptized by Christ. Apollos "knew

---

40), equally well So, likewise, ἀπὸ and ἐκ may be rendered "from," as well as "out of," in Matt. 3 16, Mark 1 : 10, Acts 8 39 The clause, "were baptized in [the] Jordan" (ἐν τῷ 'Ιορδάνῃ) does not necessarily denote immersion, any more than the phrase, "He lives in the Connecticut," does.

only the baptism of John" (Acts 18 : 25), and was not re-baptized.[1]

Immersion has been supported by the equivocal rendering of the verb συνθάπτω, in Rom. 6 : 4; Col. 2 : 12. In Rom. 6 : 4, the rendering is, "buried by baptism;" in Col. 2 : 12, "buried in baptism." The English word "bury" is applicable either to burial in earth or in water; but the Greek word συνθάπτω is applicable only to burial in earth. No one would render it by "immerse." The English word "bury" can suggest immersion, but the Greek cannot. Consequently, when a person unacquainted with the original reads in the English version of a "burial in baptism," or "by baptism," a burial in water is the only idea that enters his mind; an idea which the Greek positively *excludes*. For when a dead body is "buried" in a tomb as our Lord was, it comes into no contact with water, and is carefully protected from it. Had συνθάπτω been translated literally, by "entombed," instead of "buried," this text never would have been quoted, as it so frequently has been, to prove that Christian baptism is immersion. Christ's entombment, or burial in Joseph's sepulchre, has not the slightest connection with his baptism at the Jordan, and throws no light upon the mode in which he was baptized; and, consequently, it throws no light upon the mode in which his disciples were. Matthew Henry (On Rom. 6. 4) remarks as follows: "Why this 'burying in baptism' should so much as allude to any custom of dipping under water in baptism, any more than our 'baptismal crucifixion' and

---

[1] There is an apparent exception to this, in Acts 19 5 Bengel's explanation is, that these persons, "had not known that they were bound by the baptism of repentance to *faith in Jesus Christ.*" John's baptism had not been administered to them with an intelligent understanding, on their part, of the *meaning* of the rite. Had it been, they would not have been "baptized in the name of the Lord Jesus" Says Bengel (On Acts 19 5), "the baptism which is mentioned in Matt 3 6, and Matt 28 19, was one, otherwise, there would not have been 'the beginning of the gospel' in John the Baptist (Mark 1. 1–3), and the Lord's supper in Matt 26 would be older than baptism in Matt. 28."

death should have any such reference, I confess I cannot see. It is plain, that it is not the *sign*, but the *thing signified* in baptism, that the apostle here calls 'being buried with Christ;' and the expression of 'burying' alludes to Christ's burial [in a tomb]. As Christ was buried [in a tomb] that he might rise again to a new and more heavenly life, so we are, in baptism, buried [in a tomb], that is, cut off from the life of sin that we may rise again to a new life of faith and love."

# ESCHATOLOGY.

# ESCHATOLOGY.

## CHAPTER I.

### THE INTERMEDIATE OR DISEMBODIED STATE.

Augustine: Enarratio in Ps. vi. Cap. 6; Sermo clxxviii Cap 3; City of God, XXI xxv. Aquinas Summa, III. (Supplement), lxix.–lxxii. Calvin: Institutes, III. v Ursinus · Christian Religion, Qu. 57 (§ 2). Usher · Answer to a Jesuit's Challenge. Witsius: Apostles' Creed, Dissertation XVIII. Cudworth: Intellectual System, III 320–331. Turrettin: Institutio, XIII. xv Pearson: Creed, Article V. Howe The Redeemer's Dominion over the Invisible World Jeremy Taylor · Liberty of Prophesying, Section VIII. Newton: Intermediate State. Watts: Souls between Death and Resurrection. Burnet Thirty-nine Articles, Art. III. Heylin. History of Presbyterianism (On Hades) Perowne: On Immortality. Rice. On Immortality Isaac Taylor: Physical Theory of Another Life. Edwards: Sermon on 2 Cor. 5:8. Whateley: The Future State. Delitzsch · Biblical Psychology, VI Kitto: Encyclopedia, (Article Hell). Herder: Spirit of Hebrew Poetry. Stuart. Exegetical Essays (Article Sheol) Alford State of the Blessed Dead. Konig: Christi Hollenfahrt. Huidekoper: Christ's Mission to the Underworld. Schweitzer: Hinabgefahren zur Hölle als Mythus. Plumptree. Intermediate State. Bartlett: Life and Death Eternal Lange On 1 Pet. 3. 18–22, Rev xix xx. West · On 1 Pet. 3:18–22; 4·6. (Presbyterian Quarterly, April, 1875, Presbyterian Rev, March, 1878) Hodge · Theology, III. 724–770. Dabney: Theology, 462, 820–829. Smith: Theology, 601–607.

Eschatology (ἐσχάτων λόγος) is that division in Dogmatics which treats of the Intermediate or Disembodied State, Christ's Second Advent, the Resurrection, the Final Judgment, Heaven, and Hell. Revelation does not give minute details upon these subjects, yet the principal features are strongly drawn, and salient.

The doctrine of the Intermediate State has had considerable variety of construction, owing to the mixing of mythological elements with the Biblical. The representations of Christ in the parable of Dives and Lazarus have furnished the basis of the doctrine. The most general statement is, that the penitent, represented by Lazarus, is happy, and the impenitent, represented by Dives, is miserable.

The doctrine taught in Scripture that the body is not raised until the day of judgment, implies that the condition of all men between death and resurrection is a *disembodied* one. This doctrine has been greatly misconceived, and the misconception has introduced grave errors into eschatology. Inasmuch as the body, though not necessary to personal consciousness, is yet necessary in order to the entire completeness of the person, it came to be supposed in the Patristic church, that the intermediate state is a dubious and unfixed state; that the resurrection adds very considerably both to the holiness and happiness of the redeemed, and to the sinfulness and misery of the lost. This made the intermediate, or disembodied state, to be imperfectly holy and happy for the saved, and imperfectly sinful and miserable for the lost. According to Hagenbach (§ 142), the majority of the fathers between 250 and 730 "believed that men do not receive their full reward till after the resurrection" Jeremy Taylor (Liberty of Prophesying, § 8) asserts that the Latin fathers held that "the saints, though happy, do not enjoy the beatific vision before the resurrection." Even so respectable an authority as Ambrose, the spiritual father of Augustine, taught that the soul "while separated from the body is held in an ambiguous condition" (ambiguo suspenditur).[1]

[1] It is often difficult to say positively, and without qualification, what the opinion of a church father really was upon the subject of Hades, owing to the unsettled state of opinion One and the same writer, like Tertullian, or Augus-

The incompleteness arising from the absence of the body was more and more exaggerated in the Patristic church, until it finally resulted in the doctrine of a purgatory for the redeemed, adopted formally by the Papal church, according to which, the believer, between death and the resurrection, goes through a painful process in Hades which cleanses him from remaining corruption, and fits him for Paradise. The corresponding exaggeration in the other direction, in respect to the condition of the lost in the disembodied state, is found mostly in the Modern church. The modern Restorationist has converted the intermediate state into one of probation, and redemption, for that part of the human family who are not saved in this life.

The Protestant reformers, following closely the Scripture data already cited, which represent the redeemed at death as entirely holy and happy in Paradise, and the lost at death as totally sinful and miserable in Hades, rejected altogether the patristic and mediaeval exaggeration of the corporeal incompleteness of the intermediate state. They affirmed perfect happiness at death for the saved, and utter misery for the lost. The first publication of Calvin was a refutation of the doctrine of the sleep of the soul between death and the resurrection. The limbus and purgatory were energetically combated by all classes of Protestants. "I know not," says Calvin (Institutes, II. xvi. 9), "how it

tine, for example, makes different statements at different times This accounts for the conflicting representations of dogmatic historians One thing, however, is certain, that the nearer we approach the days of the Apostles, the less do we hear about an underworld, and of Christ's descent into it Little is said concerning Hades, by the Apostolical fathers In the longer recension of Ignatius ad Smyrnaeos (Ch ix ), they are exhorted to "repent while yet there is opportunity, for in Hades no one can confess his sins" Justin Martyr (Trypho, Ch v ) simply says that "the souls of the pious remain in a better place, while those of the wicked are in a worse, waiting for the time of judgment" The extracts from the fathers in Huidekoper's volume on Christ's Mission to the Underworld, show the uncertainty that prevailed The same is true of those in Konig's Christi Höllenfahrt, notwithstanding the bias of the author. For proof of the unsettled state of opinion among the fathers on many points of doctrine, see Jeremy Taylor's Liberty of Prophesying, VIII

came to pass that any should imagine a subterraneous cavern, to which they have given the name of limbus. But this fable, although it is maintained by great authors, and even in the present age is by many seriously defended as a truth, is after all nothing but a fable."

The doctrine of the intermediate or disembodied state, as it was generally received in the Reformed (Calvinistic) churches, is contained in the following statements in the Westminster standards. "The souls of believers are, at their *death*, made perfect in holiness, and do immediately pass into glory [The Larger Catechism (86) and Confession (1) say, "into the highest heavens"]; and their bodies, being still united to Christ, do rest in their graves till the resurrection. At the *resurrection*, believers, being raised up in glory, shall be openly acknowledged and acquitted in the day of judgment, and made perfectly blessed in full-enjoying of God to all eternity." Shorter Catechism, 37, 38. According to this statement, there is no essential difference between Paradise and Heaven. The Larger Catechism (86) asserts that "the souls of the wicked are, at *death*, cast into hell, and their bodies kept in their graves till the resurrection and judgment of the great day." The Larger Catechism (89) and Confession (1) say that "at the *day of judgment*, the wicked shall be cast into hell, to be punished forever" According to this, there is no essential difference between Hades and Hell

The substance of the Reformed view, then, is, that the intermediate state for the saved is Heaven without the body, and the final state for the saved is Heaven with the body; that the intermediate state for the lost is Hell without the body, and the final state for the lost is Hell with the body. In the Reformed, or Calvinistic eschatology, there is no intermediate Hades between Heaven and Hell, which the good and evil inhabit in common. When this earthly existence in ended, the only specific places and states are Heaven and Hell. Paradise is a part of Heaven;

Hades is a part of Hell. A pagan underworld containing both Paradise and Hades, both the happy and the miserable, like the pagan idol, is "nothing in the world." There is no such place.

This view of Hades did not continue to prevail universally in the Protestant churches. After the creeds of Protestantism had been constructed, in which the Biblical doctrine of Hades is generally adopted, the mythological view began again to be introduced. Influential writers like Lowth and Herder gave it currency in Great Britain and Germany. "A popular notion," says Lowth (Hebrew Poetry, Lect. VIII.), "prevailed among the Hebrews, as well as among other nations, that the life which succeeded the present was to be passed beneath the earth; and to this notion the sacred prophets were obliged to allude, occasionally, if they wished to be understood by the people, on this subject." Says Herder (Hebrew Poetry, Marsh's Translation, II. 21), "no metaphorical separation of the body and soul was yet known among the Hebrews, as well as among other nations, and the dead were conceived as still living in the grave, but in a shadowy, obscure, and powerless condition." The theory passed to the lexicographers, and many of the lexicons formally defined Hades as the underworld. It then went rapidly into commentaries, and popular expositions of Scripture.

The Pagan conception of Hades is wide and comprehensive; the Biblical is narrow and exclusive. The former includes all men; the latter, only wicked men. The Greeks and Romans meant by Hades, neither the grave in which the dead body is laid, nor the exclusive place of retribution, but a nether world in which all departed souls reside. There was one ᾅδης for all, consisting of two subterranean divisions: Elysium and Tartarus[1] In proportion as the

[1] The Pagan nomenclature is self-consistent, but the Pagan-Christian is not. In the Pagan scheme, Hades is a general term having two special terms under it, namely, Elysium and Tartarus But in the paganized Christian scheme,

Later-Jews came to be influenced by the Greek and Roman mythology, the Septuagint Hades, which is narrow and definite because confined to the evil, became wide and indefinite because it was made to include both the good and evil. In scripture, Hades is descriptive of moral character. Whoever goes to Hades is ipso facto a wicked man, and like Dives goes to punishment and misery. In mythology, Hades is non-descriptive of moral character. He who goes to Hades is not ipso facto a wicked person. He may be either good or evil; may go either to happiness or misery. This mythological *indefiniteness*, when injected into the definiteness of the inspired representation of Hades, takes off the solemn and terrible aspect which it has for the sinner in Scripture, and paves the way for the assertion that when the sinner goes to Hades he does not go to punishment and misery.

This mythological influence upon the eschatology of the Later-Jews is seen in Josephus. He describes Samuel as being called up from Hades. Antiq., VI. xiv. 2. Yet in another place (Wars, III. viii. 5), he says that "the souls of the good at death obtain a most holy place in *heaven*, while the souls of the wicked are received by the darkest place in *hades*." Here is the same vacillation between the Biblical and the mythological view which appears in many of the Christian fathers. The mythological influence increased, until the doctrine of purgatory itself came into the Jewish apocryphal literature. Purgatory is taught in 2 Maccabees, 12:45. Manasses, in his Prayer, asks God not "to condemn him into the lower parts of the earth." The Syna-

---

Hades does double duty, being both a general and a special term When the Pagan is asked, "Of what does Hades consist?" he answers, "Of Elysium and Tartarus" But when the mythological Christian is asked, "Of what does Hades consist?" he must answer, "Of Paradise and Hades" He cannot answer, "Of Paradise and Tartarus," because the latter is Gehenna, which he denies to be in Hades Hence he converts the whole into a part of itself To say that Hades is made up of Paradise and Hades, is like saying that New York City is made up of the Central Park and New York City.

gogue, according to Charnocke (Discourse II.) believed in a purgatory.[1]

That class of commentators, lexicographers, and theologians who contend that Hades denotes an underworld, and deny that it means either hell or the grave, appeal to Pagan and Rabbinical authorities in proof. This assumes that there is no essential difference between the Hades of Scripture and that of the nations; that the inspired mind took the same general view with the uninspired, of the state of souls after death; that Moses, Samuel, David, and Isaiah, together with Christ and his Apostles, agreed in their eschatology with Homer, Plato, Virgil, the Egyptian "Ritual of the Dead," and the Babylonian tablets. A close adherence to the text and context of Scripture shows, we think, that this assumption is unfounded Upon such an unknown subject as the future state, the appeal must be made to Revelation alone. Because the Assyrians, Babylonians, Egyptians, Greeks, and Romans believed that all human spirits at death go to one and the same underworld, it does not follow that it is a fact, or that the circle of inspired men who wrote the Scriptures believed and taught it. And because the Jewish Rabbins came to adopt the mythological eschatology, it does not follow that the Biblical eschatology is to be interpreted by their opinions[2]

---

[1] On the Influence of Hellenism upon the Later-Judaism, see Edersheim. Messianic Prophecy and History Lecture IX.

[2] The strong tendency of the Later-Jews to adopt both the customs and opinions of the heathen nations is noticed by Chemnitz, in his learned and thorough examination of the Tridentine doctrine of Purgatory Examen · De Purgatorio, II "Ex philosophorum ratiocinationibus, et ex superstitiosis gentium sacrificiis, quae ubique usitata erant, cum, quidem, sicut de caris absentibus ita etiam de mortuis naturalis quaedem cura et sollicitudo animis nostris insita est, ad Judaeos etiam hujus opinionis contagium quoddam, inclinato jam Judaismo, serpere coepit Quanquam enim incisio carnis, et evulsio capillorum, in luctu mortuorum, expresse prohibita erant (Lev xix, Deut. xiv), ex conversatione tamen inter gentes, Israelitis etiam prophetarum tempore illa usurpari coepta fuisse, ex Jeremiae, cap xvi, non obscure colligitur Sicut a gentibus etiam tibicines in funerum curatione mutuati sunt (Mat ix), juxta versum poetae 'cantabat moestis tibia funeribus' Eadem ratione tandem post prophetarum

Revealed religion may be properly illustrated by ethnical religion when the latter agrees with the former; not when it conflicts with it. When mythology is an echo, even broken and imperfect, of Scripture, it may be used to explain inspired doctrine; but not when it is a contradiction. The meaning of Hades must therefore be explained by the connection of thought in the Scriptures themselves, and not by the imagination of uninspired man peering into the darkness beyond the grave, and endeavoring to *picture* the abode of departed spirits. The mythological eschatology is a picturesque and fanciful conjecture respecting the unseen world. The Biblical eschatology is the description of it by an eye-witness: namely, God speaking through prophets, apostles, and Jesus Christ.

The Pagan conception passed also into the Christian church. It is found in the writings of many of the fathers, but not in any of the primitive creeds. "The idea of a Hades (שאול), known to both [the Later] Hebrews and Greeks, was transferred to Christianity, and the assumption that the real happiness, or the final misery of the departed, does not begin till after the general judgment and the resurrection of the body, appeared to necessitate the belief in an intermediate state, in which the soul was supposed to remain, from the moment of its separation from the body to the last catastrophe Tertullian, however, held that the martyrs went at once to paradise, the abode of the blessed, and thought that in this they enjoyed an advantage over other Christians, while Cyprian does not seem to know about any intermediate state whatever." Hagenbach: History of Doctrine, § 77.[1]

---

tempora, etiam orationes et sacrificia pro mortuis, Judaei imitari coeperunt circa annum 170 ante natum Christum, cujus exemplum extat 2 Maccabaeorum xii Id quod tum fieri coepit, cum collapsa doctrina, et rebus omnibus, cum in imperio tum in templo, perturbatissimis, Judaei una cum foederibus, etiam lingua, appellationibus, moribus, et ritibus, conformitatem cum gentibus quaererent et affectarent sicut tota historia Maccabaeorum ostendit."

[1] As an example of the degree to which the mythological view of the condition

According to this Hellenized conception of the Intermediate State, at death all souls go *down* to Hades; in inferna loca, or ad inferos homines. This is utterly unbiblical. It is connected with the heathen doctrine of the infernal divinities, and the infernal tribunal of Minos and Rhadamanthus. The God of revelation does not have either his abode, or his judgment-seat, in Hades. From Christ's account of the last judgment, no one would infer that it takes place in an underworld. In both the Old and New Testament, the good dwell with God, and God's dwelling-place is never represented as "below," but "on high." Paradise is the third heaven (2 Cor. 12:1, 4), and none of the heavens are in the underworld. Elijah "went up by a whirlwind into heaven," 2 Kings 2:11. The saints remaining on earth at the Advent go up "to meet the Lord [and the saints that have been with him] in the air," 1 Thess. 4:17. Compare 2 Thess. 4:14; Eph. 4:8; John 17:24; Acts 7:25; Luke 23:42, 43, 46; Prov. 15:24. David expects to be "received to glory." Christ describes the soul of a believer, at death, as ascending to Paradise. "The beggar died, and was carried by the angels to Abraham's bosom. The rich man also died, and was buried. And in Hades he lifted *up* his eyes, being in torments, and seeth Abraham afar off, and Lazarus in his bosom." Luke 16:22, 23. According to this description, Abraham's bosom and Hades are as opposite and disconnected as the zenith and the nadir. To say that Abraham's bosom is a part of Hades, is to say that the heavens are a compartment of the earth. St. Matt. (8:11) teaches that Abraham's bosom is in heaven: "Many shall recline (*ἀνακλιθήσονται*) with Abraham, in the kingdom of heaven." Paradise is separated from Hades by a "great chasm," Luke 16:26. The word *χάσμα* denotes space either lateral

---

of the dead had worked itself into the Christian church in the first part of the third century, see the fanciful description of Hades by Hippolytus in a fragment of his Discourse against the Greeks

[illegible]

tion between a supernal and an infernal paradise The paradise spoken of by Christ, in Luke 24:33, is evidently the same that St. Paul speaks of, in 2 Cor. 12:3, 4, which he calls "the third heaven."

It is sometimes said that there is no "above" or "below" in the spiritual world, and therefore the special representation in the parable of Dives and Lazarus must not be insisted upon. This, certainly, should not be urged by those who contend for an *under*world. Paradise and Hades, like Heaven and Hell, are both in the universe of God. But wherever in this universe they may be, it is the Biblical representation (unlike the mythological), that they do not constitute *one system*, or *one sphere* of being, any more than Heaven and Hell do. They are so contrary and opposite, as to exclude each other, and to constitute two separate places or worlds; so that he who goes to the one does not go to the other.[1] This contrariety and exclusiveness is metaphorically expressed by space vertical, not by space lateral. Things on the same plane are alike. Those on different planes are not. If Paradise is above and Hades is beneath, Hades will be regarded as Hell, and be dreaded. But if Paradise and Hades are both alike beneath, and Paradise is a part of Hades, then Hades will not be regarded as Hell (as some affirm it is not), and will not be dreaded Hades will be merely a temporary resi-

[1] Respecting the entire separation between the good and the evil, see 1 Sam 25 29, Ps 26 9, 28 3

dence of the human soul, where the punishment of sin is imperfect, and its removal possible and probable.

A portion of the fathers, notwithstanding the increasing prevalence of the mythological view, deny that Paradise is a compartment of Hades. In some instances, it must be acknowledged, they are not wholly consistent with themselves, in so doing. According to Archbishop Usher (Works, III. 281), "the first who assigned a resting-place in hell [Hades] to the fathers of the Old Testament was Marcion the Gnostic." This was combated, he says, by Origen, in his second Dialogue against Marcion. In his comment on Ps 9:18, Origen remarks that "as Paradise is the residence of the just, so Hades is the place of punishment (*κολαστήριον*) for sinners." The locating of Paradise in Hades is opposed by Tertullian (Adv. Marcionem, IV. 34), in the following terms: "Hades (inferi) is one thing, in my opinion, and Abraham's bosom is another. Christ, in the parable of Dives, teaches that a great deep is interposed between the two regions. Neither could the rich man have 'lifted up' his eyes, and that too 'afar off,' unless it had been to places above him, and very far above him, by reason of the immense distance between that height and that depth." Similarly, Chrysostom, in his Homilies on Dives and Lazarus, as quoted by Usher, asks and answers: "Why did not Lazarus see the rich man, as well as the rich man is said to see Lazarus? Because he that is in the light does not see him who stands in the dark; but he that is in the dark sees him that is in the light." Augustine, in his exposition of Ps 6, calls attention to the fact that "Dives looked *up*, to see Lazarus." Again, he says, in his Epistle to Euodius, "it is not to be believed that the bosom of Abraham is a part of Hades (aliqua pars inferorum) How Abraham, into whose bosom the beggar was received, could have been in the torments of Hades, I do not understand. Let them explain who can." Again, in De Genesi ad literam, XII. 33, 34, he remarks: "I confess, I have not yet found that the place where the souls of just men rest is Hades (inferos). If a good conscience may figuratively be called paradise, how much more may that bosom of Abraham, where there is no temptation, and great rest after the griefs of this life, be called paradise." To the same effect, says Gregory of Nyssa (In Pascha): "This should be investigated by the studious, namely, how, at one and the same time, Christ could be in these three places: in the heart of the earth, in paradise with the thief, and in the 'hand' of the Father. For no one will say that paradise is in the places under the earth (ἐν ὑποχθονίοις), or the places under the earth in paradise; or that those infernal places (τὰ ὑποχθόνια) are called the 'hand' of the Father." Cyril of Alexandria, in his De Exitu Animi, remarks: "Insontes supra, sontes infra. Insontes in coelo, sontes in profundo. Insontes in manu dei, sontes in manu diaboli." Usher asserts that the following fathers agree with Augustine, in the opinion that Paradise is not in Hades: namely, Chrysostom, Basil, Cyril Alexandrinus, Gregory Nazianzen, Bede, Titus of Bostra, and others.[1]

These patristic statements respecting the supernal locality of Paradise agree with Scripture. "The way of life is *above* to the wise, that he may depart from sheol *beneath*," Prov. 15:24. When Samuel is represented as "coming up from the earth" (1 Sam. 28:7–20), it is because the body reanimated rises from the grave.[2] This does not prove that the soul had been in an underworld, any more than the statement of St. John (12:17) that Christ "called Lazarus out of his grave" proves it. Paradise is unquestionably the abode of the saved; and the saved are with

[1] The Council of Ferrara-Florence (1438–9,), composed of Greek and Latin bishops, which attempted to unite the Latin and Greek churches, decided "that the souls of the saints are received immediately into heaven, and behold God himself as he is, three in one," Taylor: Liberty of Prophesying, VIII.

[2] In the narrative concerning the witch of Endor, the term Sheol is not once used.

Christ. The common residence of both is described as on high. "When he ascended up on high, he led captivity captive," Eph. 4:8. "Father, I will that they also whom thou hast given me be with me where I am, that they may see my glory," John 17:24. "Those which sleep in Jesus, God will bring with him" [down from Paradise, not up from Hades], 2 Thess. 4:14. At the second advent, "we which are alive and remain shall be caught up in the clouds, to meet the Lord in the air," 1 Thess. 4:17. Stephen "looked up into heaven, and saw Jesus standing on the right hand of God," Acts 7.55. Christ said to the Pharisees, "Ye are from beneath, I am from above," John 8:23. Satan and his angels are "cast down to Tartarus," 2 Pet. 2:4. The penitent thief says to Christ: "Lord, remember me when thou comest into thy kingdom." Christ replies: "This day shalt thou be with me in paradise," Luke 23:42, 43. This implies that paradise is the same as Christ's kingdom; and Christ's kingdom is not an infernal one. Christ "cried with a loud voice, Father into thy hands I commend my spirit, and having said this, he gave up the ghost," Luke 23:46. The "hands" of the Father, here meant, are in heaven above, not in "shoel beneath." These teachings of Scripture, and their interpretation by a portion of the fathers, evince that Paradise is a section of Heaven, not of Hades, and are irreconcilable with the doctrine of an underworld containing both the good and the evil

Another stimulant, besides that of mythology, to the growth of the doctrine that the intermediate state for all souls is the underworld of Hades, was the introduction into the Apostles' creed of the spurious clause, "He descended into Hades" Biblical exegesis is inevitably influenced by the great oecumenical creeds. When the doctrine of the descent to Hades was interpolated into the oldest of the Christian symbols, it became necessary to find support for it in Scripture. The texts that can, with any success, be used for this purpose, are few, compared with the large number that prove the undisputed events in the life of Christ. This compelled a strained interpretation of such passages as Matt. 12 : 40 ; Acts 2 : 27 ; Rom. 10 : 7 ; 1 Pet. 3 : 18–20 ; 4 : 6, and largely affected the whole subject of eschatology as presented in the Scriptures.

The Apostles' creed, in its original form, read as follows: "Suffered under Pontius Pilate; was crucified, dead, and buried; the third day he rose again from the dead." This is also the form in the two creeds of Nice (325) and Constantinople (381): a certain proof that these great oecumenical councils did not regard the Descensus as one of the articles of the catholic faith. The first appearance of the clause, "He descended into Hades," is in the latter half of the fourth century, in the creed of the church of Aquileia. Pearson, by citations, shows that the creeds, both ecclesiastical and individual, prior to this time, do not contain it. Burnet (Thirty-nine Articles, Art III ) asserts the same. Rufinus, the presbyter of Aquileia, says that the intention of the Aquileian alteration of the creed was not *to add a new doctrine*, but *to explain an old one;* and therefore the Aquileian creed *omitted* the clause, "was crucified, dead, and buried," and substituted for it the new clause, "descendit in inferna." Rufinus also adds, that "although the preceding Roman and Oriental editions of the creed had not the words, 'He descended into Hades,' yet they had the sense of them in the words, 'He was crucified, dead, and buried.'" Pearson: Creed, Article V. The early history of the clause, therefore, clearly shows that the "Hades" to which Christ was said to have descended was simply the "grave" in which he was buried.[1]

Subsequently, the clause went into other creeds. The

[1] Coleridge (Works, V 278) remarks: "This clause was not inserted into the Apostles' creed till the sixth [fourth] century after Christ. I believe the original intention of the clause was no more than vere mortuus est, in contradiction to the hypothesis of a trance or suspended animation"

Athanasian (600) follows that of Aquileia, in inserting the "descent" and omitting the "burial." It reads: "Who suffered for our salvation, descended into Hades, rose again the third day from the dead." Those of Toledo, in 633 and 693, likewise contain it. It is almost invariably found in the mediaeval and modern forms of the Apostles' creed, but *without the omission*, as at first, of the clause, "was crucified, dead, and buried:" two doctrines thus being constructed, in place of a single one as at first. If, then, the text of the Apostles' creed shall be subjected, like that of the New Testament, to a revision in accordance with the text of the first four centuries, the Descensus ad inferos must be rejected as an interpolation.

While the tenet of Christ's local descent into Hades has no support from Scripture, or any of the first oecumenical creeds, it has support, as has already been observed, from patristic authority.[1] "The ancient fathers," says Pearson (Article V.), "differed much respecting the condition of the dead, and the nature of the place into which the souls, before our Saviour's death, were gathered; some looking on that name which we now translate hell, hades, or infernus, as the common receptacle of the souls of all men, both the just and unjust, while others thought that hades, or infernus, was never taken in the Scriptures for any place of happiness; and therefore they did not conceive the souls of the patriarchs or the prophets did pass into any such infernal place" This difference of opinion appears in Augustine, who wavered in his views upon the subject of Hades, as Bellarmine concedes. Pearson (Art. V.) remarks of him, that "he began to doubt concerning the reason ordinarily given for Christ's descent into hell, namely, to bring up the patriarchs and prophets thence, upon this ground, that he thought the word infernus [ᾅδης] was never taken in Scripture in a good sense, to denote the abode of the right-

[1] See Hagenbach History of Doctrine, §§ 77, 78, 141, 142 Smith's Ed.

eous."[1] Pearson cites, in proof, the passages already quoted from Augustine's Epistle, and Commentary on Genesis. On the other hand, in his City of God (XX. 15), Augustine hesitatingly accepts the doctrine that the Old Testament saints were in limbo, and were delivered by Christ's descent into their abode. "It does not seem absurd to believe, that the ancient saints who believed in Christ, and his future coming, were kept in places far removed, indeed, from the torments of the wicked, but yet in Hades (apud inferos), until Christ's blood and his descent into these places delivered them." Yet in his exposition of the Apostles' creed (De Fide et Symbolo), Augustine makes no allusion to the clause, "He descended into Hades." And the same silence appears in the De Symbolo, attributed to him After expounding the clauses respecting Christ's passion, crucifixion, and burial, he then explains those concerning his resurrection and ascent into heaven. This proves that when he wrote this exposition, the dogma was not an acknowledged part of the catholic faith.[2] Still

---

[1] Notwithstanding the currency which the view of Hades as the abode of the good and evil between death and the resurrection has obtained, it would shock the feelings, should a clergyman say to mourning friends "Dry your tears, the departed saint has gone down to Hades"

[2] The Episcopal Church does not regard the "descent into hell" as a necessary part of the Christian faith In the Order for Evening Prayer, it is said that "any churches may omit the words, 'He descended into hell'" The Forty-two Articles of Edward VI. explain the clause to mean a descent into Hades, and preaching to the Old Testament saints in prison there The Elizabethan Thirty-nine Articles give no explanation, but contain both clauses Hence Pearson concludes that the Episcopalian has some liberty in the interpretation of this article His own method is, first, to explain the Scripture, and then to explain the creed as it now reads in its modern form His explanation of Scripture is, that in the clause, "Thou wilt not leave my soul in hell" soul is metonymically put for body, and hell means the grave· Because (*a*) In the Hebrew, soul is frequently put for body (*b*) Sheol means grave in many places (*c*) The Aquileian creed so intended Still, he says, "though this may be a probable interpretation of the words of David, yet it cannot pretend to be an exposition of the creed as it *now* stands" in the Thirty-nine Articles: that is, as containing *both* clauses Because when both clauses are retained, as in the Thirty-nine Articles, the second must be more than a mere repetition and explanation of the first. For if one merely explains the other, one would

later, Peter Chrysologus, archbishop of Ravenna, and Maximus of Turin, explain the Apostles' creed and make no exposition of the Descent to Hades. The difference of opinion among the fathers of the first four centuries, together with the absence of scriptural support for it, is the reason why the Descensus ad inferos was not earlier inserted into the Apostles' creed. It required the development of the doctrine of purgatory, and of the mediaeval eschatology generally, in order to get it formally into the doctrinal system of both the Eastern and Western churches.[1]

---

be omitted, as Rufinus says was the case in the Aquileian creed, and as is the case in the Athanasian symbol Hence Pearson decides that the form of this article, *as it is adopted in the Thirty-nine Articles*, requires to be explained as the Descensus ad inferos, in order to avoid tautology But the form itself, he shows to be a late addition to the Apostles' creed If both clauses are retained, the explanation proposed by Whitby (On Acts 2 26, 27) is consistent with Scripture. "The scripture doth assure us that the soul of the holy Jesus, being separated from his body, went to Paradise (Luke 23 43), and from thence it must descend into the grave or sepulchre to be united to his body that this might be revived And thus it may be truly said "He was dead and buried, his soul descended afterwards into Hades (the grave), to be united to his body, and his body being thus revived, he rose again the third day'"

[1] Baumgarten-Crusius (Dogmengeschichte, II § 109) finds three stadia in the development of the dogma of the Descent to Hades. 1 The descent was the burial itself put into an imaginative form 2 The descent was a particular condition or status of Christ resulting from his burial. 3 The descent was entirely separate from the burial, being another and wholly distinct thing.

Van Oosterzee's history of the clause, "He descended into hell," is, as follows "As concerns the history of this article, the conviction was expressed even by some of the earliest of the fathers—Justin Martyr, Irenaeus, Tertullian, Clemens Alexandrinus, and others—that Jesus, after his burial, actually tarried in the world of spirits, and by some of them, also, that he there preached the gospel, while the romantic manner in which this mysterious subject is presented in the apocryphal Gospel of Nicodemus is well known Gnosticism, especially, warmly espoused this idea, according to Marcion, this activity of the Lord was directed to delivering the victims of the Demiurge, and leading them upwards with himself From the symbols of the Semi-Arians, this much-debated article appears to have passed over to those of the orthodox church, according to some, with a view to controvert Apollinarism In the Expositio Symboli Aquileiensis of Rufinus, this formula is found, and especially through his influence it appears also to have passed over into other confessions of faith, although it is remarkable that in the Nicene Creed mention is made only of 'was buried,' in the Athanasian Creed, on the other hand, only of 'descended into hell' It is manifest from this, that both expressions were first employed by many interchangeably, though very soon greater stress was laid upon the latter, and its contents

The personal and local descent of Christ into Hades—whether to deliver the Old Testament saints from limbo; or to preach judicially, announcing condemnation to the sinners there; or evangelically, offering salvation to them—if a fact, would have been one of the great cardinal facts connected with the incarnation. It would fall into the same class with the nativity, the baptism, the passion, the crucifixion, the resurrection, and the ascension. Much less important facts than these are recorded. St. Matthew speaks of the descent of Christ into Egypt, but not of his

---

regarded as the indication of a special remedial activity of the Lord. As the doctrine of purgatory became more developed, the conception found wider acceptance that the Lord had descended into the lower world, in order to deliver the souls of the Old Testament believers from their subterranean abode, the limbus patrum Especially under the influence of Thomas Aquinas, was developed the doctrine of the Romish Church, that the whole Christ, both as to his divine and human nature, voluntarily repaired thither, to assure to the abovementioned saints the fruits of his death on the cross, and to raise them out of this prison-house to the full enjoyment of heavenly blessedness According to Luther, on the other hand, who regards the Decensus as the first step in the path of the exaltation, the Lord, after his being made alive according to the spirit, and, immediately upon his return from the grave, descended, body and soul, into hell, there to celebrate his triumph over the devil and his powers (Col. 2 15), and to proclaim to them condemnation and judgment The Reformed theologians either understood the expression in the sense of 'buried,' or explained it of the final anguish and dismay of the suffering Christ This latter is the view of Calvin (Inst, II., xvi ), and of the Heidelberg Catechism (Ans. 44). Some divines, the Lutheran Aepinus, e g , even maintained that the reference is to the sufferings of hell, which Christ endured in his soul, while his body was lying in the grave No wonder that the Formula Concordiae declared this article to be one 'qui neque sensibus, neque ratione nostra comprehendi queat, solo autem fide acceptandus sit,' which, however, did not prevent its being possible to say, on the other side, that 'there are almost as many dissertations concerning the Descensus as there are flies in the height of summer' (Witsius ) Left by the supra-naturalism of the past century entirely in a misty obscurity, it was wholly rejected by the Rationalists, as the fruit of an exploded popular notion, to which, according to Schleiermacher, nothing but a fact wholly unnoticed by the apostles (unbezeugte Thatsache) served as a basis Only in our day has the tide turned, and theologians of different schools have begun to return with increased interest, yea, with manifest preference to this dogma, and to bring it into direct connection not only with soteriology, but also with eschatology" In the face of this historical account, Van Oosterzee proceeds to defend the doctrine of a local descent to Hades, founding upon Ps 16 10, Acts 2 25-31, 13 : 33-37; Eph. 4. 8-10, 1 Pet 3. 19-21, 4. 6. Dogmatics, II 558 sq.

descent into Hades. Such an act of the Redeemer as going down into an infernal world of spirits, would certainly have been mentioned by some one of the inspired biographers of Christ. The total silence of the four Gospels is fatal to the tenet. St. Paul, in his recapitulation of the principal events of our Lord's life, evidently knows nothing of the descent into Hades "I delivered unto you that which I also received, how that Christ died for our sins; and that he was buried, and that he rose again the third day," 1 Cor. 15 : 3, 4. The remark of bishop Burnet (Thirty-nine Articles, Art. III.) is sound. "Many of the fathers thought that Christ's soul went locally into hell, and preached to some of the spirits there in prison; that there he triumphed over Satan, and spoiled him, and carried some souls with him into glory. But the account that the Scripture gives us of the exaltation of Christ begins it always at his *resurrection*. Nor can it be imagined that so memorable a transaction as this would have been passed over by the first three Evangelists, and least of all by St. John, who coming after the rest, and designing to supply what was wanting in them, and intending particularly to magnify the glory of Christ, could not have passed over so wonderful an instance of it. The passage in St. Peter seems to relate to the preaching to the Gentile world, by virtue of that inspiration that was derived from Christ."[1]

---

[1] Augustine, Bede, Aquinas, Erasmus, Beza, Gerhard, Hottinger, Clericus, Leighton, Pearson, Secker, Hammond, Hofmann, and most of the Reformed theologians, explain 1 Pet. 3 18–20 to mean, that Christ preached by Noah to men who were "disobedient" in the days of Noah, and who for this cause were "spirits in prison" at the time of Peter's writing. The participle πότε, qualifying ἀπειθήσασι, shows that the disobedience (or disbelief) occurred "when the ark was a-preparing" But the preaching must have been contemporaneous with the disobedience, or disbelief. What else was there to disobey, or disbelieve? Says Pearson (Creed, Art II), "Christ was really before the flood, for he preached to them that lived before it This is evident from the words of St. Peter (1 Pet. 3 18-20). From which words it appeareth, first, That Christ preached by the same Spirit by the virtue of which he was raised from the dead but that Spirit was not his [human] soul, but something of a greater

The Early-Patristic and Reformed view of the Intermediate State agrees with the Scriptures, as the following particulars prove.

1. Both the Old and New Testaments represent the intermediate state of the soul to be a disembodied state.

---

power; secondly, That those to whom he preached were such as were disobedient, thirdly, That the time when they were disobedient was the time before the flood, when the ark was preparing. The plain interpretation is to be acknowledged for the true, that Christ did preach unto those men which lived before the flood, even while they lived, and consequently that he was before it. For though this was not done by an immediate act of the Son of God, as if he personally had appeared on earth and actually preached to that world, but by the ministry of a prophet, by the sending of Noah 'the eighth preacher of righteousness' yet to do anything by another not able to perform it without him, as much demonstrates the existence of the principal cause, as if he did it himself without any intervening instrument."

Another proof of the correctness of this interpretation is the fact that Christ's preaching to "the spirits in prison" was πνεύματι, only. The total θεάνθρωπος did not preach The σάρξ, or human nature, of Christ had no part in the act. But Christ's *personal* and *local* preaching in Hades would require his whole Divine-human person, as much so as his preaching in Galilee or Jerusalem The Formula Concordiae (IX 2) so understands and teaches "Credimus quod tota persona, deus et homo, post sepulturam, ad inferos descenderit, Satanam devicerit, etc." Christ's preaching through Noah—"a preacher of righteousness" (2 Pet. 2 5), and therefore an "ambassador of Christ" (2 Cor 5·20)—might be done through his divinity alone See Eph 4 20, 21; Acts 26.23; John 10 16, for instances in which Christ's preaching by others is called his preaching. It is objected that the phrase, he, "*went* and preached" (πορευθεὶς ἐκήρυξεν), in 1 Pet 3·19, would not apply to a preaching that was instrumental and spiritual But the same use is found in Eph. 2 17 Christ '*came* and preached (ἐλθὼν εὐαγγελίσατο) to you which were afar off." The reference is to Christ's preaching to the Gentile world by his apostles Christ, in his own person, did not preach to them which were "afar off," and he forbade his disciples to do so until the time appointed by the Father, Matt. 10 5, Acts 1 4 The objection that actually living men upon earth would not be called "spirits" is met by Rom 13.1; 1 John 4.1, 3, and by the fact that at the time of Peter's writing the persons meant are disembodied spirits.

The passage 1 Pet 4 6, sometimes cited in proof of the descensus ad inferos, refers to the preaching of the gospel to the spiritually "dead in trespasses and sins." This is Augustine's interpretation (Ep. ad Euodium, VI 21). In Eph. 4·9, τὰ κατώτερα μέρη τῆς γῆς, to which Christ "descended" from "on high," signifies this lower world of earth St. Paul is speaking here of the incarnation. The incarnate Logos did not descend from heaven to hades, nor ascend from hades to heaven Compare Isa. 44 23, "Shout, ye lower parts of the earth." This is the opposite of the "heavens," which are bidden to "sing." In

Gen. 49 : 33, "Jacob yielded up the ghost, and was gathered unto his people." Job 10 : 18, "Oh that I had given up the ghost." Job 11 : 20 ; 14 : 20. Jer. 15 : 9, "She hath given up the ghost." Eccl. 8 : 8, "There is no man that hath power over the spirit to retain the spirit ; neither hath he power in the day of death" Eccl. 12 : 7, "Then shall the dust return to the earth as it was ; and the spirit shall return to God who gave it." Matt. 27 : 50, "Jesus, when he had cried again with a loud voice, yielded up the spirit." Luke 23 : 46, "When Jesus had cried with a loud voice he said, Father, into thy hands I commend my spirit; and having said this, he gave up the spirit." Acts 7 · 59, "Stephen called upon God, saying, Lord Jesus, receive my spirit." 2 Cor. 5 : 8, "We are willing rather to be absent from the body, and to be present with the Lord." 2 Cor. 12 : 2, "I knew a man in Christ about four years ago, whether in the body or out of the body, I cannot tell." 2 Cor. 5 : 2, 3, "We groan, earnestly desiring to be clothed upon with our house which is from heaven: if so be that being clothed "we shall not be found naked." 2 Pet. 1 : 14, "Knowing that shortly I must put off this my tabernacle, even as our Lord Jesus Christ hath showed me." Rev. 20 : 4, "I saw the souls of them that were beheaded for the witness of Jesus." Rev. 6 : 9, "I saw under the altar the

---

Acts 2 19 this world is called *ἡ γῆ κάτω*. Hades would be *τὰ κατώτατα μέρη τῆς γῆς* In Rom 10 7, Christ's descent "into the deep," (*ἄβυσσον*) is shown by the context to be his descent into the grave

Whatever be the interpretation of 1 Pet. 3 18-20, such a remarkable doctrine as the descent to Hades should have more foundation than a single disputed text. The doctrine itself is so obscure that it has had five different forms of statement. 1 Christ virtually descended into Hades, because his death was efficacious upon the souls there. 2 Christ actually descended into Hades 3 Christ's descent into Hades was his suffering the torments of hell 4 Christ's descent into Hades was his burial in the grave. 5. Christ's descent into Hades was his remaining in the state of the dead, for a season The Westminster Larger Catechism (50) combines the last two "Christ's humiliation after his death consisted in his being buried, and continuing in the state of the dead, and under the power of death, till the third day, which hath been otherwise expressed in these words, 'He descended into hell.'"

souls of them that were slain for the word of God." In accordance with this, the prayer for the burial of the dead in the Episcopal Order begins as follows: "Forasmuch as it hath pleased Almighty God, in his wise providence, to take out of this world the soul of our deceased brother, we therefore commit his body to the ground." And God is addressed as the One "with whom do live the spirits of those who depart hence in the Lord; and with whom the souls of the faithful, after they are delivered from the burden of the flesh, are in joy and felicity."

Belief in the immortality of the soul, and its separate existence from the body after death, was characteristic of the Old economy, as well as the New. It was also a pagan belief. Plato elaborately argues for the difference, as to substance, between the body and the soul, and asserts the independent existence of the latter. He knows nothing of the resurrection of the body, and says that when men are judged, in the next life, "they shall be entirely stripped before they are judged, for they shall be judged when they are dead; and the judge too shall be naked, that is to say, dead; he with his naked soul shall pierce into the other naked soul, as soon as each man dies." Gorgias, 523

That the independent and separate existence of the soul after death was a belief of the Hebrews, is proved by the prohibition of necromancy in Deut. 18:10–12. The "gathering" of the patriarchs "to their fathers" implies the belief. Death did not bring them into association with nonentities. Jehovah calls himself "the God of Abraham, Isaac, and Jacob," and this supposes the immortality and continued existence of their spirits; for, as Christ (Luke 20:28) argues in reference to this very point, "God is not the God of the dead, but of the living;" not of the unconscious, but the conscious. Our Lord affirms that the future existence of the soul is so clearly taught by "Moses and the prophets," that if a man is not convinced by them, neither would he be "though one should rise from the dead," Luke 16 : 29.

Some, like Warburton, have denied that the immortality of the soul is taught in the Old Testament, because there is no direct proposition to this effect, and no proof of the doctrine offered. But this doctrine, like that of the Divine existence, is nowhere formally demonstrated, because it is everywhere assumed. Most of the Old Testament is nonsense, upon the supposition that the soul dies with the body, and that the sacred writers knew nothing of a future life. For illustration, David says, "My soul panteth after thee." He could not possibly have uttered these words, if he had expected death to be the extinction of his consciousness. The human soul cannot long for a spiritual communion with God that is to last only seventy years, and then cease forever. Every spiritual desire and aspiration has in it the element of infinity and endlessness. No human being can say to God, "Thou art my God, the strength of my heart, and my portion, for threescore years and ten, and then my God and portion no more forever." When God promised Abraham that in him should "all the families of the earth be blessed" (Gen. 12 : 3), and Abraham "believed in the Lord, and he counted it to him for righteousness" (Gen. 15 . 6), this promise of a Redeemer, and this faith in it, both alike involve a future existence beyond this transitory one. God never would have made such a promise to a creature who was to die with the body; and such a creature could not have trusted in it. In like manner, Adam could not have believed the protevangelium, knowing that death was to be the extinction of his being. All the Messianic matter of the Old Testament is absurd, on the supposition that the soul is mortal. To redeem from sin a being whose consciousness expires at death, is superfluous. David prays to God, "Take not the word of truth out of my mouth; so shall I keep thy law continually *forever and ever*," Ps. 119 : 43, 44. Every prayer to God in the Old

Testament implies the immortality of the person praying. "My flesh faileth, but God is the strength of my heart *forever*," Ps. 63 : 2. "Trust ye in the Lord *forever*, for in the Lord Jehovah is everlasting strength," Isa. 26 : 4. The nothingness of this life only leads the Psalmist to confide all the more in God, and to expect the next life. "Behold, thou hast made my days as an handbreadth; and mine age is as nothing before thee: verily, every man at his best state is altogether vanity. And now, Lord, what wait I for? my hope is in thee," Ps. 39 : 5, 7. As Sir John Davies says of the soul, in his poem on Immortality:

> "Water in conduit pipes can rise no higher
> Than the well-head from whence it first doth spring:
> Then since to eternal God she doth aspire,
> She cannot be but an eternal thing."

That large class of texts which speak of a "covenant" which God has made with his people, and of a "salvation" which he has provided for them, have no consistency on the supposition that the Old Testament writers had no knowledge and expectation of a future blessed life. The following are examples. Gen. 17 : 7, "I will establish my covenant between me and thee, and thy seed after thee, in their generations, for an everlasting covenant, to be a God unto thee, and to thy seed after thee." Gen. 49 : 18, "I have waited for thy salvation, O Lord." Ex. 6 : 7, "I will take you to me for a people, and I will be to you a God" Deut. 33 : 3, 29, "Yea, he loved the people; all his saints are in thy hand. Happy art thou, O Israel: who is like unto thee, O people saved by the Lord." Job 13 : 15, "Though he slay me, yet will I trust in him." Isa. 33 : 22, "For the Lord is our judge, the Lord is our lawgiver, the Lord is our king; he will save us." Hab. 1 : 12, "Art thou not from everlasting, O Lord, my God, mine Holy One? we shall not die." Ps. 31 : 5, "Into thine hand I commit my spirit; thou hast redeemed me, O Lord God of truth."

It is impossible to confine this "covenant" of God, this "love" of God, this "salvation" of God, this "trust" in God, and this "redemption" of God, to this short life of threescore years and ten. Such a limitation empties them of their meaning, and makes them worthless. The words of St. Paul apply in this case: "If in *this* life only we have hope in Christ, we are of all men most miserable," 1 Cor. 15:19. Calvin (Inst., II., x., 8) remarks that "these expressions, according to the common explanation of the prophets, comprehend life, and salvation, and consummate felicity. For it is not without reason that David frequently pronounces how 'blessed is the nation whose God is the Lord, and the people whom he hath chosen for his own inheritance;' and that, not on account of any *earthly* felicity, but because he delivers from death, perpetually preserves, and attends with everlasting mercy, those whom he hath taken for his people." In the same reference, Augustine (Confessions, VI. xi 19) says: "Never would such and so great things be wrought for us by God, if with the death of the body the life of the soul came to an end." When God said to Abraham, "Thou shalt go to thy fathers in peace" (Gen. 15·15), he meant spiritual and everlasting peace. It was infinitely more than a promise of an easy and quiet physical death. When Jacob, on his death-bed, says: "I have waited for thy salvation, O Lord" (Gen. 49:18), he was not thinking of deliverance from physical and temporal evil. What does a man care for this, in his dying hour.

The religious experience delineated in the Old Testament cannot be constructed or made intelligible, upon the theory that the doctrine of immortality was unknown, or disbelieved. The absolute trust in God, the unquestioning confidence in his goodness and truth, the implicit submission to his will, the fearless obedience of his commands whatever they might be, whether to exterminate the Canaanites or slay the beloved child, and the hopeful serenity with which they met death and the untried future, would have been impossible, had the belief of Enoch, Abraham, Moses, Samuel and the prophets, concerning a future existence, been like that of Hume, Gibbon, Voltaire, and Mirabeau.

Another reason why the Old Testament contains no formal argument in proof of immortality and a spiritual world beyond this, is, because the intercourse with that world on the part of the Old Testament saints and inspired prophets was so immediate and constant. God was not only present to their believing minds and hearts, in his paternal and gracious character, but, in addition to this, he was frequently manifesting himself in theophanies and visions. We should not expect that a person who was continually communing with God would construct arguments to prove his existence; or that one who was brought into contact with the unseen and spiritual world by supernatural phenomena and messages from it, would take pains to demonstrate that there is such a world. The Old Testament saints "endured as *seeing* the invisible."[1]

2. The Scriptures teach that the intermediate state for the believer is one of blessedness. The disembodied spirit of the penitent thief goes with the disembodied Redeemer directly into Paradise. Luke 23:43, "To-day shalt thou be with me in paradise." Paradise has the following marks: (*a*) It is the third heaven. 2 Cor. 12:2, 4, "I knew a man caught up to the third heaven. He was caught up into paradise, and heard unspeakable words which it is not lawful for a man to utter." Rev. 2:7, "To him that overcometh will I give to eat of the tree of life, which is in the midst of the paradise of God." (*b*) It is "Abraham's bosom." Luke 16:22, "The beggar died,

---

[1] Compare Mozley Essay on Job.

and was carried by the angels into Abraham's bosom." Matt. 8 : 11, "Many shall come from the east and west, and shall recline (ἀνακλιθήσονται) with Abraham, and Isaac, and Jacob, in the kingdom of heaven." (*c*) It is a place of reward and happiness. Luke 16 : 25, "Remember that thou in thy lifetime receivedst thy good things, and likewise Lazarus evil things: but now he is comforted." 2 Cor. 5 : 8, "To be absent from the body, is to be present with the Lord" Phil. 1:23, "I am in a strait betwixt two, having a desire to depart and to be with Christ; which is far better." Phil. 1 : 21, "For me, to die is gain." 1 Thess. 5 : 9, 10, "Christ died for us, that whether we wake or sleep, we should live together with him." Acts 7 : 59, "They stoned Stephen, calling upon God, and saying, Lord Jesus, receive my spirit." According to Luke 9: 30, 31, Moses and Elijah coming directly from the intermediate state "appear in glory," at the transfiguration.

The Old Testament, with less of local description, yet with great positiveness and distinctness, teaches the happiness of believers after death. Gen. 5 : 24, "Enoch walked with God: and he was not; for God took him" Num. 23:10, "Let me die the death of the righteous, and let my last end be like his." Gen. 49:18, The dying Jacob confidently says, "I have waited for thy salvation, O Lord." Ps. 16 : 9–11, "My flesh shall rest in hope. For thou wilt not leave my soul in hell; neither wilt thou suffer thine holy one to see corruption. Thou wilt show me the path of life; in thy presence is fulness of joy; at thy right hand there are pleasures forevermore." Ps. 17:15, "As for me, I shall behold thy face in righteousness. I shall be satisfied, when I awake with thy likeness." Ps 49:15, "God will redeem my soul from the power of the grave; for he shall receive me." Ps. 73 : 24–26, "Thou shalt guide me with thy counsel, and afterward receive me to glory. Whom have I in heaven but thee? and there is none upon earth that I desire beside thee. My flesh and my heart faileth; but God is the strength of my heart, and my portion forever" Ps. 116:15, "Precious in the sight of the Lord is the death of his saints." Isa. 25:8, "He will swallow up death in victory." This is quoted by St. Paul, in 1 Cor. 15:54, to prove the resurrection of the body. Hosea 13:14, "I will ransom them from the power of the grave: I will redeem them from death. O death, I will be thy plagues; O grave, I will be thy destruction." This also is cited by St. Paul, in 1 Cor. 15:55. Dan 12:2, 3, "Many of them that sleep in the dust of the earth shall awake to everlasting life. And they that be wise shall shine as the brightness of the firmament; and they that turn many to righteousness as the stars forever and ever" Job 19:25–27, "I know that my Redeemer liveth, and that he shall stand at the latter day upon the earth. And though, after my skin, worms destroy this body, yet in my flesh shall I see God; whom I shall see for myself, and mine eyes shall behold."[1] St. Paul teaches that the Old Testament saints, like those of the New, trusted in the Divine promise of the resurrection "I stand and am judged for the hope of the promise made of God unto our fathers: unto which promise [of the resurrection], our twelve tribes, instantly serving God day and night, hope to come. For which hope's sake, king Agrippa, I am accused of the Jews. Why should it be thought a thing incredible with you that God should raise the dead?" Acts 26:6–8; comp. 23:6. "These all died in faith, not having received the promises, but having seen them afar off, and were persuaded of them, and embraced them, and confessed that they were strangers and pilgrims on the earth. For they that say such things declare plainly that they seek a country. And, truly, if they had been mindful of that

[1] The common opinion of the church, ancient, mediaeval, and modern, is, that this passage teaches both immortality and the resurrection De Wette, Ewald, and even Renan find the doctrine of immortality in it. See Perowne. On Immortality. Note III

country from whence they came out, they might have had opportunity to have returned. But now they desire a better country, that is, an heavenly," Heb. 11:13–16. These bright and hopeful anticipations of the Old Testament saints have nothing in common with the pagan world of shades, the gloomy Orcus, where all departed souls are congregated

3. The Scriptures teach that the intermediate state for the impenitent is one of misery. The disembodied spirit of Dives goes to Hades, which has the following marks: (*a*) Hades is the place of retribution and woe. Luke 16: 23, 25, "In Hades he lifted his eyes, being in torments. And Abraham said, Son, remember that thou in thy lifetime receivedst thy good things, and now thou art tormented" Christ describes Dives as suffering a righteous punishment for his hard-hearted, luxurious, and impenitent life. He had no pity for the suffering poor, and squandered all the "good things" received from his Maker, in a life of sensual enjoyment. The Redeemer of mankind also represents Hades to be inexorably retributive. Dives asks for a slight mitigation of penal suffering, "a drop of water." He is reminded that he is suffering what he justly deserves, and is told that there is a "fixed gulf" between Hades and Paradise. He then knows that his destiny is decided, and his case hopeless, and requests that his brethren may be warned by his example. After such a description of it as this, it is passing strange that Hades should ever have been called an abode of the good.[1]

(*b*) Hades is the contrary of heaven, and the contrary of

[1] Müller regards it as so unquestionable, from the description in the parable of Dives and Lazarus, that Hades is not a place for repentance and salvation, that he places future redemption after the day of judgment. He asserts that "those theories of ἀποκατάστασις which represent it as taking place in the interval between death and the general resurrection directly violate the New Testament eschatology. If, therefore, the idea of an ἀποκατάστασις πάντων is to be maintained, it must be referred to a period lying beyond the general resurrection" Sin, II. 426.

heaven is hell. Matt. 11:23, "Thou Capernaum, which art exalted unto heaven, shalt be brought down to hades." This is explained by our Lord's accompanying remark, that it shall be more tolerable in the day of judgment for the land of Sodom than for Capernaum:" showing that to "be brought down to hades" is the same as to be sentenced to hell.

(*c*) Hades is Satan's kingdom, antagonistic to that of Christ. Matt. 16:18, "The gates of hades shall not prevail against my church." An underworld, containing both the good and the evil, would not be the kingdom of Satan. Satan's kingdom is not so comprehensive as this. Nor would an underworld be the contrary of the church, because it includes Paradise and its inhabitants.

(*d*) Hades is the prison of Satan and the wicked. Christ said to St. John, "I have the keys of hades and of death," Rev. 1:18; and describes himself as "He that openeth, and no man shutteth, and shutteth, and no man openeth," Rev. 3:7. As the supreme judge, Jesus Christ opens and shuts the place of future punishment upon those whom he sentences. "I saw an angel come down from heaven having the key of the bottomless pit, and a great chain in his hand, and he laid hold on the dragon, that old serpent, which is the devil, and Satan, and bound him a thousand years, and cast him into the bottomless pit, and shut him up," Rev. 20:1–3. All modifications of the imprisonment and suffering in Hades are determined by Christ. "I saw the dead, small and great, stand before God; and the books were opened, and the dead were judged out of those things which were written in those books; and death and hades gave up the dead which were in them, and they were judged every man according to their works; and death and hades were cast into the lake of fire," Rev. 20:12–14 This indicates the difference between the intermediate and the final state, for the wicked. On the day of judgment, at the command of incarnate God,

Hades, the intermediate state for the wicked, surrenders its inhabitants that they may be re-embodied and receive the final sentence, and then becomes Gehenna, the final state for them. Hell without the body becomes hell with the body.[1]

(*e*) Hades is inseparably connected with spiritual and eternal death. "I have the keys of hades and of death," Rev. 1:18. "Death and hades gave up the dead which were in them," Rev. 20:13. "I saw a pale horse; and his name that sat upon him was Death, and hades followed him," Rev. 6:6. Hades here stands for its inhabitants, who are under the power of ("follow") the "second death" spoken of in Rev. 2:11; 20:6, 14; 21:8. This is spiritual and eternal death, and must not be confounded with the *first* death, which is that of the body only. This latter, St. Paul (1 Cor. 15: 26) says was "destroyed" by the blessed resurrection of the body, in the case of the saints but not of the wicked. See p. 638. The "second death" is defined as the "being cast into the lake of fire," Rev. 20:14. This "death" is never "destroyed;" because those who are "cast into the lake of fire and brimstone, with the devil that deceived them, shall be tormented day and night forever and ever," Rev. 20:10.

(*f*) Hades is not a state of probation. Dives asks for an alleviation of penal suffering, and is solemnly refused by the Eternal Arbiter. And the reason assigned for the refusal is, that his suffering is required by justice. But a state of existence in which there is not the slightest abatement of punishment cannot be a state of probation. Our Lord, in this parable, represents Hades to be as immutably retributive as the modern Hell. There is no relaxation of penalty in the former, any more than in the latter. Abraham informs Dives that it is absolutely impossible to get from Hades to Paradise. "Between us and you there is a

[1] If Hades in this passage means an underworld, it would include Paradise, and thus Paradise would be cast into the lake of fire.

great gulf fixed, so that they which would pass from hence to you cannot; neither can they pass to us that would come from thence." After this distinct statement of Abraham, Dives knows that the case of a man is hopeless, when he reaches Hades. "Then, said he, I pray thee, therefore, father, that thou wouldst send Lazarus to my father's house: for I have five brethren; that he may testify unto them, lest they also come to this place of torment," Luke 16:27. The implication is, that if they do come to it, there is no salvation possible for them. Abraham corroborates this, by affirming that he who is not converted upon earth, will not be converted in Hades. "If they hear not Moses and the prophets, neither will they be persuaded though one rose from the dead," Luke 16:31.

In the nine places from the New Testament which have been cited in this discussion, the connection shows that Hades denotes the place of retribution and misery. There are three other instances in the received text (two in the uncial) in which the word is employed, and denotes the *grave:* namely, Acts 2:27, 31; 1 Cor. 15:55. In 1 Cor. 15:55, ℵ A B C D, Lachm., Tisch., Hort, Rev. Ver., read ϑάνατε.

In Acts 2:27, it is said: "Thou wilt not leave my soul in hades, neither wilt thou suffer thine Holy One to see corruption." The soul, here, is put for the body, as when we say, "The ship sank with a hundred souls." The same metonymy is found frequently in the Old Testament. Lev. 21:1, "There shall none be defiled for a dead body." Heb. "for a soul" Lev. 19:28, "Ye shall not make any cuttings in your flesh for the dead:" Heb "for a soul" Num. 6:6, "He shall come at no dead body;" Heb. "dead soul." Comp Lev. 5:2; 22:4; Num. 18:11, 13; Hag 2:13. See p. 637, for Pearson's proof of this metonymy.

That soul is put metonymically for body, and that Hades means the grave, in Ps. 16:10, is proved by the following considerations: (*a*) St. Peter says that "David being a prophet spake of the *resurrection* of Christ, that his soul was not left in hades, neither did his flesh see corruption," Acts 2:31. But there is no resurrection of the *soul*, in the ordinary literal use of the word. The use here, therefore, must be metonymical. Soul, as in the Old Testament passages cited above, must therefore stand for body. (*b*) Christ's resurrection could not be a deliverance of *both* soul and body from Hades, because both of them together could not be in Hades. Whichever signification of Hades be adopted, only one of the two could be in Hades, and consequently only one of the two could be delivered from Hades. If Hades be the underworld, then only Christ's soul was in Hades, not his body. If Hades be the grave, then only Christ's body was in Hades, not his soul. Accordingly, if Hades be the underworld, then "not to leave Christ's soul in hades" was, to take his soul out of the underworld. But to call this a resurrection of his body, as St. Peter does in Acts 2.31, is absurd. If Hades be the grave, then "not to leave Christ's soul in hades" was, to take his body out of the grave To call this a resurrection of his body is rational. The choice must be made between the two explanations; because, to take both the soul and body of Christ out of Hades is an impossibility. (*c*) The connection shows that "to leave Christ's soul in hades" is the same thing as "to suffer the Holy One to see corruption." David's reasoning, as stated by St Peter in Acts 2:25–27, implies this. David "foresaw the Lord," that is, the Messiah. Respecting this Messiah, David argues that "his flesh shall rest in hope," *because* his "soul shall not be left in hades, nor he be suffered to see corruption." Now, unless "soul" is here put for "flesh" and Hades means the grave, there is a non-sequitur in David's reasoning. That Christ's soul was not left in an underworld, would be no reason why his body should rest in hope and not see corruption.

Again, St. Peter's own reasoning (Acts 2 : 22–27) proves the same thing. After saying that "God had raised up Jesus of Nazareth, having loosed the pangs of death," he shows that this event of Christ's resurrection was *promised*, by quoting the words of David, "Thou wilt not leave my soul in hades, neither wilt thou suffer thine Holy One to see corruption." That is to say, the promise "not to leave Christ's soul in hades" was fulfilled by "raising up Jesus of Nazareth, and loosing the pains of death." And yet again, St. Paul's quotation, in Acts 13 : 35, of this passage from David, shows that he understood soul to be put for body, and hades to mean the grave. Because he entirely *omits* the clause, "Thou wilt not leave my soul in hades," evidently regarding the clause, "Thou wilt not suffer thine Holy One to see corruption," as stating the whole fact in the case: namely, the resurrection of Christ's body from the grave. In Acts 2 : 31, the uncials, Lachmann, Tischendorf, Hort, and R. V. omit *ἡ ψυχή αὐτοῦ.*

The Old Testament term for the future abode of the wicked, and the place of future punishment, is Sheol (שְׁאוֹל). This word, which is translated by Hades (ᾅδης) in the Septuagint, has two significations: (*a*) The place of future retribution. (*b*) The grave.

Before presenting the proof of this position, we call attention to the fact that it agrees with the explanation of Sheol and Hades common in the Early-Patristic and Reformation churches, and disagrees with that of the Later-Patristic, the Mediaeval, and a part of the Modern Protestant church. It agrees also with the interpretation generally given to these words in the versions of the Scriptures made since the Reformation, in the various languages of the world.[1]

---

[1] In committing themselves, as the authors of the Revised Version of the English Bible do in their Preface to the Old Testament, to the position that Sheol and Hades, in the Scriptures, "signify the abode of departed spirits, and correspond to the Greek Hades or the underworld," and that neither term de-

1. That Sheol in the Old Testament signifies the place of future punishment, is proved by the following considerations:

(*a*) It is denounced against sin and sinners, and not against the righteous. It is a place to which the *wicked* are sent, in distinction from the good. "The wicked in a moment go down to sheol," Job 21:13. "The wicked shall be turned into sheol, and all the nations that forget God," Ps. 9:17. "Her steps take hold on sheol," Prov. 5:5. "Her house is the way to sheol, going down to the chambers of death," Prov. 7:27. "Her guests are in the depths of sheol," Prov. 9:18 "Thou shalt beat thy child with a rod, and shalt deliver his soul from sheol," Prov. 23:14. "A fire is kindled in my anger, and it shall burn to the lowest sheol," Deut. 32:22. "If I ascend up into heaven, thou art there; if I make my bed in sheol [the contrary of heaven], behold thou art there," Ps. 139:8. "The way of life is above to the wise, that he may depart from sheol beneath," Prov. 15:24. "Sheol is naked before him, and destruction [Abaddon, R. V.] hath no covering," Job 26:6. "Sheol and destruction [Abaddon, R. V.] are before the Lord," Prov. 15:11. "Sheol and destruction [Abaddon, R. V.] are never satisfied," Prov. 27:20.

---

notes either the place of punishment, or the grave, they have placed themselves in doctrinal opposition, on a very important subject, to James's translators, to Luther and the authors of the principal European versions, and to the missionary translators generally In all these versions, Sheol and Hades are understood to mean either hell, or the grave, and never an underworld containing all spirits good and bad The view of the Reformers, upon this point, is stated in the following extract from the Schaff-Herzog Encyclopedia (Article Hades): "The Protestant churches rejected, with purgatory and its abuses, the whole idea of a middle state, and taught simply two states and places—heaven for believers, and hell for unbelievers. Hades was identified with Gehenna, and hence both terms were translated alike in the Protestant versions. The English (as also Luther's German) version of the New Testament translates Hades and Gehenna by the same word 'hell,' and thus obliterates the important distinction between the realm of the dead (or nether-world, spirit-world), and the place of torment or eternal punishment, but in the Revision of 1881 the distinction is restored, and the term Hades introduced"

If in these last three passages the revised rendering be adopted, it is still more evident that Sheol denotes Hell; for Abaddon is the Hebrew for Apollyon, who is said to be "the angel and king of the bottomless pit," Rev. 9:11.

There can be no rational doubt, that in this class of Old Testament texts the wicked and sensual are warned of a future *evil* and *danger*. The danger is, that they shall be sent to Sheol. The connection of thought requires, therefore, that Sheol in such passages have the same meaning as the modern Hell, and like this have an *exclusive* reference to the wicked. Otherwise, it is not a warning. To give it a meaning that makes it the common residence of the good and evil, is to destroy its force as a Divine menace. If Sheol be merely a promiscuous underworld for all souls, then to be "turned into sheol" is no more a menace for the sinner than for the saint, and consequently a menace for neither. In order to be of the nature of an alarm for the wicked, Sheol must be something that pertains to them alone. If it is shared with the good, its power to terrify is gone. If the good man goes to Sheol, the wicked man will not be afraid to go with him. It is no answer to this, to say that Sheol contains two divisions, Hades and Paradise, and that the wicked go to the former. This is not in the Biblical text, or in its connection. The sensual and wicked who are threatened with Sheol, as the punishment of their wickedness, are not threatened with a part of Sheol, but with the *whole* of it. Sheol is one, undivided, and homogeneous in the inspired representation. The subdivision of it into heterogeneous compartments is a conception imported into the Bible from the Greek and Roman classics. The Old Testament knows nothing of a Sheol that is partly an evil, and partly a good. The Biblical Sheol is always an evil, and nothing but an evil. When the human body goes down to Sheol in the sense of the "grave," this is an evil. And when the human soul goes down to Sheol in the sense of "hell and retribution," this is an evil. Both are threatened, as the penalty of sin, to the wicked, but never to the righteous.

Consequently, in the class of passages of which we are speaking, "going down to sheol" denotes something more dreadful than going down to the grave, or than entering the so-called underworld of departed spirits. To say that "the wicked shall be turned into sheol," implies that the righteous shall *not* be; just as to say that "they who obey not the gospel of our Lord Jesus Christ shall be punished with everlasting destruction" (2 Thess. 1:8, 9), implies that those who do obey it shall *not* be. To say that the "steps" of the prostitute "take hold on sheol," is the same as to say that "whoremongers shall have their part in the lake which burneth with fire and brimstone," Rev. 21:8. To "deliver the soul of a child from sheol" by parental discipline, is not to deliver him either from the grave, or from a spirit-world, but from the future misery that awaits the morally undisciplined and rebellious. In mentioning Sheol in such a connection, the inspired writer is not mentioning a region that is common alike to the righteous and the wicked. This would defeat his purpose to warn the latter.[1] Sheol, when denounced to the wicked, must be as peculiar to them, and as much confined to them, as when "the lake of fire and brimstone" is denounced to them. All such Old Testament passages teach that those who go to Sheol suffer from the wrath of God, as the eternal judge who punishes iniquity. The words, "The wicked is snared in the work of his own hands. The wicked shall be turned into sheol, and all the nations that forget God," Ps. 9:16, 17, are as much of the nature of a Divine menace against sin, as the words, "In the day thou eatest thereof, thou

---

[1] "The meaning of the Hebrew word Sheol is doubtful, but I have not hesitated to translate it hell. I do not find fault with those who translate it grave, but it is certain that the prophet means something more than common death, otherwise he would say nothing else concerning the wicked, than what would also happen to all the faithful in common with them." Calvin: On Ps. 9 17.

shalt surely die," Gen. 2 : 17. And the interpretation which eliminates the idea of endless punishment from the former, to be consistent, should eliminate it from the latter.

Accordingly, these texts must be read in connection with, and be explained by that large class of texts in the Old Testament which represent God as a *judge*, and assert a *future judgment*, and even a future resurrection for this purpose. "Shall not the judge of all the earth do right?" Gen. 18:25. "To me belongeth vengeance, and recompense; their feet shall slide in due time," Deut. 32:35. "Enoch the seventh from Adam prophesied of these, saying, Behold the Lord cometh with ten thousand of his saints to execute judgment upon all, and to convince all that are ungodly among them of all their ungodly deeds which they have ungodly committed," Jude 14:15. "The wicked is reserved to the day of destruction; they shall be brought forth to the day of wrath," Job 21:30. "The ungodly shall not stand in the judgment; the way of the ungodly shall perish," Ps. 1 : 5, 6. "Verily, he is a God that judgeth in the earth," Ps. 58 : 11. "Who knoweth the power of thine anger? even according to thy fear, so is thy wrath," Ps. 90 : 11. "O Lord God, to whom vengeance belongeth, shew thyself. Lift up thyself, thou judge of the earth: render a reward to the proud," Ps. 94:1, 2. "There is a way that seemeth right unto a man, but the end thereof are the ways of death," Prov. 16 : 25. "God shall judge the righteous and the wicked: for there is a time for every purpose, and every work," Eccl. 3:17. "Walk in the ways of thine heart, and in the sight of thine eyes; but know thou that for all these things God will bring thee into judgment," Eccl. 11 : 9. "God shall bring every work into judgment, with every secret thing, whether it be good, or whether it be evil," Eccl 12 : 14. "The sinners in Zion are afraid; fearfulness hath surprised the hypocrites. Who among us shall dwell with devouring fire? who among us shall dwell with everlasting burnings?" Is. 33:14. Of "the men that have transgressed against God," it is said that their "worm shall not die, neither shall their fire be quenched," Is. 66 : 24. "I beheld till the thrones were cast down, and the Ancient of days did sit. His throne was like the fiery flame, and his wheels like burning fire; thousand thousands ministered unto him, and ten thousand times ten thousand stood before him; the judgment was set, and the books were opened," Dan. 7 : 9, 10. "Many of them that sleep in the dust of the earth shall awake, some to everlasting life, and some to shame and everlasting contempt," Dan. 12 : 2. "The Lord hath sworn by the excellency of Jacob, Surely I never will forget any of their works," Amos 8:7. "They shall be mine, saith the Lord of hosts, in the day when I make up my jewels," Mal. 3 : 17.

A final judgment, unquestionably, supposes a *place* where the sentence is executed. If there is a day of doom, there is a world of doom. Consequently, these Old Testament passages respecting the final judgment throw a strong light upon the meaning of Sheol, and make it certain, in the highest degree, that it denotes the world where the penalty resulting from the verdict of the Supreme Judge is to be experienced by the transgressor. The "wicked," when sentenced at the last judgment, are "turned into sheol," as "idolaters and all liars," when sentenced, "have their part in the lake which burneth with fire and brimstone," Rev. 21:8.

(*b*) A second proof that Sheol signifies the place of future punishment, in the Old Testament, is the fact that there is no other proper name for it in the whole volume: for Tophet is metaphorical, and rarely employed. If Sheol is not the place where the wrath of God falls upon the transgressor, there is no place mentioned where it does. But it is utterly improbable that a final sentence would be announced so clearly as it is under the Old dispensation, and yet the place of its execution be undesignated. In modern theology, Judgment and Hell are correlates; each implying the other, each standing or falling with the other. In the Old Testament theology, Judgment and Sheol sustain the same relations. The proof that Sheol does not signify Hell would, virtually, be the proof that the doctrine of Hell is not contained in the Old Testament; and this would imperil the doctrine of the final judgment. Universalism receives very strong support from all versions and commentaries which take the idea of retribution out of the term Sheol; because no texts that contain the word can be cited to prove either a future sentence, or a future suffering. They only prove that there is a world of disembodied spirits, whose moral character and condition cannot be inferred from anything in the signification of Sheol; because the good are in Sheol, and the wicked are in Sheol. When it is merely said of a deceased person that he is in the world of spirits, it is impossible to decide whether he is holy or sinful, happy or miserable.

(*c*) A third proof that Sheol, in these passages, denotes the dark abode of the wicked, and the state of future suffering, is found in those Old Testament texts which speak of the contrary bright abode of the righteous, and of their state of blessedness. According to the view we are combating, Paradise is in Sheol, and constitutes a part of it. But there is too great a contrast between the two abodes of the good and evil, to allow of their being brought under one and the same gloomy and terrifying term Sheol. When "the Lord put a word in Balaam's mouth," Balaam said, "Let me die the death of the righteous, and let my last end be like his," Num. 23 : 5, 10. The Psalmist describes this "last end of the righteous" in the following terms: "My flesh shall rest in hope. Thou wilt show me the path of life; in thy presence is fulness of joy; at thy right hand, there are pleasures for evermore," Ps 16 : 11. "As for me, I will behold thy face in righteousness; I shall be satisfied when I awake with thy likeness," Ps. 17 :

15. "God will redeem my soul from the power of sheol; for he shall receive me," Ps. 49:15. "Thou shalt guide me with thy counsel, and afterwards receive me to glory Whom have I in heaven but thee?" Ps. 73:24. In like manner, Isaiah (25·8) says respecting the righteous, that "The Lord God will swallow up death in victory, and will wipe away tears from all faces;" and Solomon asserts that "the righteous hath hope in his death," Prov. 14:32. These descriptions of the blessedness of the righteous when they die have nothing in common with the Old Testament conception of Sheol, and cannot possibly be made to agree with it. The "anger" of God "burns to the lowest sheol;" which implies that it burns through the whole of Sheol, from top to bottom. The wicked are "turned" into Sheol, and "in a moment go down," to Sheol; but the good are not "turned" into "glory," nor do they "in a moment go down" to "the right hand of God." The "presence" of God, the "right hand" of God, the "glory" to which the Psalmist is to be received, and the "heaven" which he longs for, are certainly not in the dreadful Sheol. They do not constitute one of its compartments If between death and the resurrection the disembodied spirit of the Psalmist is in "heaven," at the "right hand" of God, in his "presence," and beholding his "glory," it is not in a dismal underworld. There is not a passage in the Old Testament that asserts, or in any way suggests, that the light of the Divine countenance, and the blessedness of communion with God, are enjoyed in Sheol. Sheol, in the Old Testament, is gloom, and only gloom. and gloomy continually. Will any one seriously contend that in the passage, "Enoch walked with God: and he was not; for God took him," it would harmonize with the idea of "walking with God," and with the Old Testament conception of Sheol, to supply the ellipsis by saying that "God took him to Sheol?" Was Sheol that "better country, that is, an *heavenly*," which the Old Testament saints "desired," and

to attain which they "were tortured, not accepting deliverance?" Heb. 11:16, 35.

(*d*) A fourth proof that Sheol is the place of future retribution, is its inseparable connection with spiritual and eternal death. The Old Testament, like the New, designates the punishment of the wicked by the term "death." And spiritual death is implied, as well as physical. Such is the meaning in Gen. 2:17. The death there threatened is the very same *θάνατος* to which St. Paul refers in Rom. 5:12, and which "passed upon all men" by reason of the transgression in Eden. Spiritual death is clearly taught in Deut. 30:15, "I have set before thee this day life and good, and death and evil;" in Jer. 21:8, "I set before you the way of life, and the way of death;" in Ezek. 18:32; 33:11, "I have no pleasure in the death of the wicked; but that the wicked turn from his way and live;" in Prov. 8:36, "All they that hate me love death." Spiritual death is also taught, by implication, in those Old Testament passages which speak of spiritual life as its contrary. "As righteousness tendeth to life, so he that pursueth evil pursueth it to his own death," Prov. 11:19. "Whoso findeth me findeth life," Prov. 8:35. "He is in the way of life that keepeth instruction," Prov. 10:17. "Thou wilt show me the path of life," Ps. 16:11. "With thee is the fountain of life," Ps. 36:9. "There the Lord commanded the blessing, even life for evermore," Ps. 133:3.

Sheol is as inseparably associated with spiritual death and perdition, in the Old Testament, as Hades is in the New Testament, and as Hell is in the common phraseology of the Christian Church. "Sheol is naked before him, and destruction hath no covering," Job 26:6. "Sheol and destruction are before the Lord," Prov. 15:11. "Sheol and destruction are never full," Prov. 27:20. "Her house is the way to sheol, going down to the chambers of death," Prov. 7:27. "Her house inclineth unto death, and her paths unto the dead," Prov. 2:18. "Her feet go down to death; her steps take hold on sheol," Prov. 5:5. The sense of these passages is not exhausted, by saying that licentiousness leads to physical disease and death. The "death" here threatened is the same that St. Paul speaks of, when he says that "they which commit such things are worthy of death," Rom. 1:32; and that "the end of those things is death," Rom. 6.21. Eternal death and Sheol are as inseparably joined in Prov. 5:5, as eternal death and Hades are in Rev. 20:14. But if Sheol be taken in the mythological sense of an underworld, or spirit-world, there is no inseparable connection between it and "death," either physical or spiritual. Physical death has no power in the spirit-world over a disembodied spirit. And spiritual death is separable from Sheol, in the case of the good. If the good go down to Sheol, they do not go down to eternal death.

2. That Sheol, in one class of Old Testament passages, denotes the grave, to which all men, the good and evil alike, go down, is clear from the following citations. Before proceeding, however, to this citation, it is to be remarked that this double signification of hell and the grave, is explained by the connection between physical death and eternal retribution. The death of the body is one of the consequences of sin, and an integral part of the total penalty. To go down to the grave, is to pay the first instalment of the transgressor's debt to justice. It is, therefore, the metonymy of a part for the whole, when the grave is denominated Sheol. As in English, "death" may mean either physical or spiritual death, so in Hebrew, Sheol may mean either the grave or hell.

When Sheol signifies the "grave," it is only the *body* that goes down to Sheol. But as the body is naturally put for the whole person, the *man* is said to go down to the grave, when his body alone is laid in it. Christ "called Lazarus out of his grave," John 12:17. This does not mean that the soul of Lazarus was in that grave. When a sick person says, "I am going down to the grave," no one understands him to mean that his spirit is descending into a place under the earth. And when the aged Jacob says, "I will go down into sheol, unto my [dead] son mourning" (Gen. 37 . 35), no one should understand him to teach the descent of his disembodied spirit into a subterranean world. "The spirit of man goeth upward, and the spirit of the beast goeth downward," Eccl. 3 : 21. The soul of the animal dies with the body; that of the man does not. The statement that "the Son of man shall be three days and three nights in the heart of the earth" (Matt. 12 : 40) refers to the burial of his body, not to the residence of his soul.[1] When Christ said to the penitent thief, "To-day shalt thou be with me in Paradise," he did not mean that his human soul and that of the penitent should be in "the heart of the earth," but in the heavenly paradise. Christ is represented as dwelling in heaven between his ascension and his second advent. "Him must the heavens receive, till the time of the restitution of all things," Acts 3 : 21. "The Lord shall descend from heaven with a shout, with the voice of the archangel, and with the trump of God," 1 Thess 4 : 16. "Our conversation is in heaven, from which we look for our Saviour the Lord Jesus," Phil. 3 : 20. But the souls of the redeemed, during this same intermedi-

---

[1] That "the heart of the earth" means the grave, Witsius (Apostles' Creed, Dissertation XVII ) argues in the following manner "Jonah says, that while he was in the bowels of the fish, he was 'in the belly of hell' or of the grave, and 'in the midst (Heb , heart) of the sea:' and in this respect he was a figure of Christ placed in the heart of the earth. This does not mean the hell of the damned, which, as Jerome says, is commonly said to be 'in the midst of the earth ,' but an earthen receptacle, which has earth above, below, and on every side , or more briefly, which is within the earth As the Scripture places Tyre 'in the heart of the sea,' that is, surrounded by the sea , as 'the way of a ship is in the heart of the sea,' when it is surrounded on all sides by the sea , as Absalom was 'alive in the heart of the oak,' that is, in the oak, within its branches—so the grave is 'the heart of the earth' Chrysostom remarks that 'the sacred writer doth not say in the earth, but in the heart of the earth, that the expression might clearly denote the grave, and that no one might suspect a mere appearance [of death].'"

ate period, are represented as being with Christ. "Father, I will that they whom thou hast given me be with me where I am, that they may behold my glory which thou hast given me," John 17:24. "We desire rather to be absent from the body, and to be present with the Lord," 2 Cor. 5:8. When, therefore, the human body goes down to Sheol, it goes down to the grave, and is unaccompanied with the soul.

The following are a few out of many examples of this signification of Sheol. "The Lord killeth, and maketh alive: he bringeth down to sheol, and bringeth up," 1 Sam. 2:6. "Thy servants shall bring down the gray hairs of thy servant our father with sorrow to sheol," Gen 44:31.[1]

---

[1] This text, and Gen 42 38, are parallel to Gen 37 35, and explain Jacob's words, "I will go down mourning into sheol, unto my son" "Gray hairs" are matter and cannot go into a world of spirits

It is objected that Sheol does not mean the "grave," because there is a word (קֶבֶר) for grave. A grave is bought and sold, and the plural is used, but Sheol is never bought and sold, or used in the plural. The reply is, that "grave" has an abstract and general sense, denoted by שְׁאוֹל, and a concrete and particular, denoted by קֶבֶר. All men go to *the* grave, but not all men have *a* grave When our Lord says that "all that are in their graves (μνημείοις) shall come forth" (John 5 28), he does not mean that only those shall be raised who have been laid in a particular grave with funeral obsequies. A man is "in the grave," in the general sense, when his soul is separated from his body and his body has "returned to the dust," Gen 3 19 To be "in the grave," in the abstract sense, is to have the elements of the body mingled with those of the earth from which it was taken. Eccl 12 7 The particular spot where the mingling occurs is unessential. Moses is in the grave; but "no man knoweth of his sepulchre unto this day" We say of one drowned in the ocean, that he found a watery grave. These remarks apply also to the use of ᾅδης and μνημεῖον According to Pearson (Creed, Art V), the Jerusalem Targum, with that of Jonathan, and the Persian Targum, explain שְׁאוֹל, in Gen 37 35, 42 38, by קֶבֶר. To the objection that Jacob knew, or supposed, that his son had been devoured by wild beasts, and consequently had no grave, and, therefore, meant to say that he should go down to the world of spirits to meet him, Rivetus (Exercitatio CLI, in Gen) replies as follows "Per *sepulchrum* non intelligimus stricte, id de quo apud jurisconsultos disputatur, cum agunt de sepulchro violato, sed id referimus ad rationem humationis in genere, quandocumque modo terra reddatur terrae, juxta sententiam divinam, 'Pulvis es, et in pulverem reverteris.' Sepeliri enim dicuntur quicunque terrae redduntur, etiam qui sepeliuntur 'sepultura asini,' quod de Joachimo pronuntiavit Jeremias (22 19) Igitur verba Jacobi 'Descendam ad filium meum lugens in infernum,'

"O that thou wouldest hide me in sheol," Job 14:13. "Sheol is my house; I have said to corruption, Thou art my father: to the worm, Thou art my mother, and my sister," Job 17:13, 14. "Our bones are scattered at the mouth of sheol," Ps. 141:7. Korah and his company "went down alive into sheol, and they perished from the congregation," Num. 16:33. "In sheol, who shall give thee thanks?" Ps. 6:5. "There is no wisdom in sheol whither thou goest," Eccl. 9:10. "I will ransom them from the power of sheol; O sheol, I will be thy destruction," Hosea 13:14. "My life draweth nigh unto sheol," Ps. 88:3. "What man is he that liveth, and shall not see death? Shall he deliver his soul from the hand of sheol?" Ps. 89:48. "The English version," says Stuart, "renders Sheol by grave in thirty instances out of sixty-four, and might have so rendered it in more."

Sheol in the sense of the grave is invested with gloomy associations for the good, as well as the wicked; and this under the Christian dispensation, as well as under the Jewish. The Old economy and the New are much alike in this respect. The modern Christian believer shrinks from the grave, like the ancient Jewish believer. He needs as much grace in order to die tranquilly as did Moses and David. It is true that "Christ has brought immortality to light in the gospel;" has poured upon the grave the bright light of his own resurrection, a far brighter light than the Patriarchal and Jewish church enjoyed; yet man's *faith* is as weak and wavering as ever, and requires the support of God.

Accordingly, Sheol in the sense of the grave is represented as something out of which the righteous are to be

---

id est, in sepulchrum, non possumus melius explicare quam verbis Albini, qui sic ingemiscentis patris exponit querelam: 'In luctu permanebo, donec me terra suscipiat, ut filium meum sepulchrum jam suscepit' Id ipse Jacobus etiam intellexit, qui per vocem sheol locum denotat 'quo senum *cani* cum dolore deducuntur'"

delivered by a resurrection of the body to glory, but the bodies of the wicked are to be left under its power. "Like sheep, the wicked are laid in sheol; death shall feed on them. But God will redeem my soul [me = my body] from the power of sheol," Ps. 49 : 14, 15. "Thou wilt not leave my soul [me = my body] in sheol; neither wilt thou suffer thine Holy One to see corruption," Ps. 16 : 10.[1] This

[1] In support of this interpretation of these words, we avail ourselves of the unquestioned learning and accuracy of Bishop Pearson After remarking that the explanation which makes the clause, "He descended into hell," to mean "that Christ in his body was laid in the grave," is "ordinarily rejected by denying that 'soul' is ever taken for 'body,' or 'hell' for the 'grave,'" he proceeds to say that "this denial is in vain for it must be acknowledged, that sometimes the Scriptures are rightly so, and cannot otherwise be, understood First, the same word in the Hebrew, which the psalmist used, and in the Greek, which the apostle used, and we translate 'the soul,' is elsewhere used for the body of a dead man, and rendered so in the English version Both נפש and ψυχὴ are used for the body of a dead man in the Hebrew, and Septuagint of Num 6 6, 'He shall come at no dead body' (נֶפֶשׁ מֵת). The same usage is found in Lev 5 2, 19 . 28, 21 : 1, 11; 22 · 4, Num. 18 11, 13; Haggai 2 13. Thus, several times, נפש and ψυχὴ are taken for the body of a dead man, that body which polluted a man under the Law, by the touch thereof And Maimonides hath observed, that there is no pollution from the body till the soul be departed Therefore נפש and ψυχὴ did signify the body after the separation of the soul. And it was anciently observed by St. Augustine, that the soul may be taken for the body only 'Animae nomine corpus solum posse significari, modo quodam locutionis ostenditur, quo significatur per id quod continetur illud quod continet' Epist 157, al 190, ad Optatum, De animarum origine, c 5, § 19. Secondly, the Hebrew word שאול, which the psalmist used, and the Greek word ᾅδης, which the apostle employed, and is translated 'hell' in the English version, doth certainly in some other places signify no more than the 'grave,' and is translated so As when Mr Ainsworth followeth the word, 'For I will go down unto my son, mourning, to hell,' our translation, arriving at the sense, rendereth it, 'For I will go down into the grave, unto my son, mourning,' Gen. 37 · 35. So again he renders, 'Ye shall bring down my gray hairs with sorrow unto hell,' that is 'to the grave,' Gen 42 38. And in this sense we say, 'The Lord killeth and maketh alive · he bringeth down to the grave, and bringeth up,' 1 Sam 2 6. It is observed by Jewish commentators that those Christians are mistaken who interpret those words spoken by Jacob, 'I will go down into sheol,' of hell [in the sense of underworld], declaring that Sheol there is nothing but the grave" Pearson, On the Creed, Article V. The position that נפש is sometimes put for a dead body, and that Sheol in such a connection denotes the grave, was also taken by Usher (as it had been by Beza, on Acts 2 :

passage, while Messianic, has also its reference to David and all believers. "I will ransom them from the power of sheol. O death, I will be thy plagues; O sheol, I will be thy destruction," Hosea 13 : 14. St Paul quotes this (1 Cor. 15 : 55) in proof of the blessed resurrection of the bodies of believers—showing that "sheol" here is the "grave," where the body is laid, and from which it is raised.

The bodies of the wicked, on the contrary, are not delivered from the power of Sheol, or the grave, by a blessed and glorious resurrection, but are still kept under its dominion by a "resurrection to shame and everlasting contempt," Dan. 12 : 2. Though the wicked are raised from the dead, yet this is no triumph for them over death and the grave. Their resurrection bodies are not "celestial" and "glorified," like those of the redeemed, but are suited to the nature of their evil and malignant souls. "Like sheep they are laid in sheol; death shall feed upon them," Ps. 49 : 14. Respecting sinful Judah and the enemies of Jehovah, the prophet says, "Sheol hath enlarged herself, and opened her mouth without measure, and their glory shall descend unto it," Isa 5 : 14. Of the fallen Babylonian monarch, it is said, "Sheol from beneath is moved for thee to meet thee at thy coming. Thy pomp is brought down to sheol· the worm is spread under thee, and the worms cover thee," Isa. 14 : 9, 11. To convert this bold personification of the "grave," and the "worm," which devour the bodies of God's adversaries, into an actual underworld where the spirits of all the dead, the friends as well as the enemies of God, are gathered, is not only to convert rhetoric into logic, but to substitute the mythological for the

27 before him), and is supported with his remarkable philological and patristic learning. See his discussion of the Limbus Patrum and Christ's Descent into Hell, in his Answer to a Challenge of a Jesuit in Ireland Works, Vol III

This metonymy of "soul" for "body" is as natural an idiom in English, as it is in Hebrew and Greek It is more easy for one to say that "the ship sank with a hundred souls," than to say that it "sank with a hundred bodies." And yet the latter is the real fact in the case

Biblical view of the future life. "Some interpreters," says Alexander, on Isaiah 14 : 9, "proceed upon the supposition, that in this passage we have before us not a mere prosopopoeia or poetical creation of the highest order, but a chapter from the popular belief of the Jews, as to the locality, contents, and transactions of the unseen world. Thus Gesenius, in his Lexicon and Commentary, gives a minute topographical description of Sheol as the Hebrews believed it to exist. With equal truth a diligent compiler might construct a map of hell, as conceived by the English Puritans, from the descriptive portions of the Paradise Lost." The clear perception and sound sense of Calvin penetrate more unerringly into the purpose of the sacred writer. "The prophet," he says (Isa. 14 : 9), "makes a fictitious representation, that when this tyrant shall die and go down to the grave, the dead will go forth to meet him and honor him." Theodoret (Isa 14 : 9) explains in the same way. He remarks on the words, "Hell from beneath is moved for thee, to meet thee," etc., that, "it is the custom of Scripture sometimes to employ a figure, in order to state a thing more clearly. In this place the prophet introduces death as endowed with mind and reason, and expostulating with the king of Babylon."

From this examination of texts, it appears that Sheol, in the Old Testament, has the same two significations that Hades has in the New. The only difference is, that in the Old Testament, Sheol less often, in proportion to the whole number of instances, denotes "hell," and more often the "grave," than Hades does in the New Testament And this, for the reason that the doctrine of future retribution was more fully revealed and developed by Christ and his apostles, than it was by Moses and the prophets.

If after this study of the Biblical data, there still be doubt whether Sheol and Hades denote sometimes the place of retribution for the wicked, and sometimes the grave, and not an underworld, or spirit-world, common to both the good and evil, let the reader substitute either spirit-world or underworld in the following passages, and say if the connection of thought, or even common-sense, is preserved: "The wicked in a moment go down to the spirit-world." "The wicked shall be turned into the spirit-world, and all the nations that forget God." "Her steps take hold on the spirit-world." "Her guests are in the depths of the spirit-world." "Thou shalt beat thy child with a rod, and shalt deliver his soul from the spirit-world." "The way of life is above to the wise, that he may depart from the spirit-world beneath." "In the spirit-world, who shall give thee thanks?" "There is no wisdom in the spirit-world, whither thou goest." "I will ransom them from the power of the spirit-world; O spirit-world I will be thy destruction." "Like sheep the wicked are laid in the spirit-world; death shall feed upon them. But God will redeem my soul from the power of the spirit-world" "The gates of the spirit-world shall not prevail against the church." "Thou Capernaum which art exalted unto heaven shalt be brought down to the spirit-world." "Death and the spirit-world were cast into the lake of fire." "I saw a pale horse, and his name that sat upon him was Death, and the spirit-world followed him."

## CHAPTER II.

### CHRIST'S SECOND ADVENT.

Augustine: City of God, XX. Aquinas: Summa, III. (Supplement), xc. Ursinus: Christian Religion, Q 52 Pearson: Creed, Art. VII. Browne: On the Second Advent. Cunningham: Second Advent of Christ Alford: Commentary on Rev. 19 and 20. Wordsworth: Commentary on Rev. 19 and 20 Craven: Lange's Commentary on Rev. 19 and 20. Duffield: Second Coming of Christ: Millenarianism Defended. Crosby The Second Advent Merrill: The Second Coming of Christ. Lee: Scripture Doctrine of the Coming of our Lord. Strong: Theology, 566–574.

The teaching of Scripture is explicit, that Jesus Christ shall come again from heaven to earth, in a visible bodily form. "While the apostles looked steadfastly towards heaven as he went up, behold two men stood by them in white apparel, which also said, Ye men of Galilee, why stand ye gazing up unto heaven? This same Jesus, which is taken from you into heaven, shall so come, in like manner as ye have seen him go into heaven," Acts 1:10, 11. Christ himself, being solemnly adjured by the high priest to say whether he was "the Christ the Son of God," replies "Thou hast said. Hereafter shall ye see the Son of man sitting on the right hand of power, and coming in the clouds of heaven," Matt. 26:63, 64. St. John, seeing the event in ecstatic vision, says, "Behold he cometh with clouds, and every eye shall see him, and they also which pierced him," Rev. 1:7.

The passages of Scripture which must chiefly be relied upon, in constructing the doctrine of the Second Advent, are Matt. 25; Matt. 26:64; 1 Cor. 15; 2 Thess. 2; Rev. 20 and 21.

The doctrine which the Church very early derived from the Scriptures respecting Christ's second coming, is found in the statement of the Apostles' creed: "The third day Christ rose from the dead; he ascended into heaven; and sitteth at the right hand of God the Father Almighty; from thence he shall come to judge the quick and the dead." According to this statement, there is no corporeal advent of Christ upon earth after his resurrection, until he leaves his session with the Father and comes directly "from thence" to the last judgment.

The doctrinal statement in the Apostles' creed, consequently, precludes a premillennial advent of Christ. According to this theory, there are two corporeal resurrections; the first, of the righteous alone, supposed to be taught in Rev. 20:4, 5; the second, that of both the righteous and the wicked at the end of the world, taught in Matt. 25: 31–46. There is an interval of a thousand years between the two, and during this period Christ reigns in corporeal presence upon the renovated earth.

Premillenarianism was the revival of the pseudo-Jewish doctrine of the Messianic kingdom, as this had been formed in the later periods of Jewish history by a materializing exegesis of the Old Testament. See Neander: History, I. 650 sq. Its most flourishing period was between 150 and 250 Its prevalence in the church at that time has been much exaggerated. That it could not have been the catholic and received doctrine, is proved by the fact that it forms no part of the Apostles' creed, which belongs to this period, and hence by implication is rejected by it. "Chiliasm," says Neander (I. 651), "never formed a part of the general creed of the church. It was diffused from one country [Phrygia], and from a single fountain-head." In the preceding period of the Apostolic fathers, 100 to 150, it had scarcely any currency. There are no traces of it in Clement of Rome, Ignatius, and Polycarp. In Barnabas, Hermas, and Papias it is found; but these are much less influential names than the former. The early Apologists, Tatian, Athenagoras, and Theophilus do not advocate it. Alford (On Rev. 20 : 4, 5) is greatly in error, in saying that "the whole church for three hundred years from the apostles understood the two resurrections in the literal premillenarian sense."

Rev. 20 : 4–6, is the chief and nearly the sole support of the doctrine of two corporeal resurrections. In explaining it, reference must be had to other passages of Scripture, especially Matt. 25. Christ himself here gives an account of his own final advent, and he speaks of only one corporeal resurrection.

In order to harmonize Matt. 25, with Rev. 20 : 4–6, the term "resurrection," in the latter passage must have a tropical signification. And this is supported by the phraseology employed by St. John. "I saw the souls (ψύχας) of them that were beheaded for the witness of Jesus, and they lived (ἔζησαν) and reigned with Christ a thousand years. This is the first resurrection" The "living and reigning" is the "resurrection." Had St. John intended a literal resurrection, he would have said, "I saw the bodies of them that were beheaded:" and would have employed the verb ἀνίστημι, as is the case in the New Testament generally, and not the verb ζῶ, or ἀναζῶ. The Revelator, in vision, sees the martyrs and other witnesses for Christ as disembodied spirits dwelling in paradise, and describes them not as *rising*, but as "living and reigning" with Christ for a thousand years. This "living and reigning," he calls "the first resurrection." They lived with Christ by their faith in him, and this spiritual life was a spiritual resurrection from "death in trespasses and sins," Eph. 2 : 1. Having thus "risen with Christ" (Coloss. 3 : 1), they sought "those things which are above where Christ sitteth on the right hand of God," and as the reward of their eminent spirituality and devotion, even to martyrdom, reign in the heavenly paradise with Christ in his spiritual reign, during that remarkable period of the triumph of the gospel upon earth which is denominated the millennium Special honor in heaven, granted to particular persons for extraordinary service and suffering in Christ's cause upon earth, is spoken of elsewhere. To the apostles our Lord says, "When the Son of man shall sit on the throne of his glory, ye also shall sit upon twelve thrones judging the twelve tribes of Israel," Matt. 19 : 28. This certainly is to be interpreted metaphorically, not literally.

The tropical use of "resurrection" to denote regeneration is a characteristic of St. John, as well as of St. Paul. In John 5 : 25–29, our Lord speaks of two resurrections, the first of which is spiritual, and the second is corporeal. "Verily, verily, I say unto you, The hour is coming, and *now is*, when the dead shall hear the voice of the Son of God : and they that hear shall live." The reference, here, is to the regeneration of the human soul, which is often called a resurrection, as the following passages show : John 5 : 24, "He that believeth on me is passed from death unto life" John 11 : 25, 26, "He that believeth in me, though he were dead, yet shall he live, and whosoever liveth and believeth in me shall never die." Rom. 6 : 4, "As Christ was raised from the dead, even so we also should walk in newness of life." Eph. 5 : 14, "Arise from the dead, and Christ shall give thee life." Col. 3 : 1, "If ye be risen with Christ, seek those things that are above." Eph. 2 : 6, "When we were dead in sins, God quickened us, and raised us up, and made us sit together in heavenly places in Christ Jesus." Col. 2 : 12, "Entombed with him in baptism, wherein also ye are risen with him through the faith of the operation of God."

After speaking of regeneration as a spiritual resurrection, our Lord proceeds to speak of another resurrection which he describes as corporeal. "Marvel not at this. for the hour is coming [he does not say, "and now is"], in the which all that are in their graves shall hear his voice, and shall come forth, they that have done good unto the resurrection of life, and they that have done evil unto the resurrection of damnation." This is the literal resurrection of the body; and this is the "second resurrection," in relation to the first tropical resurrection. The regeneration of the soul, according to St. Paul, results in the resurrection of the body. "If the Spirit of him that raised up Jesus from the dead, dwell in you, he that raised up Christ from the dead shall also quicken your mortal bodies by his spirit that dwelleth in you," Rom. 8 : 11. It should be noticed, that while Christ, in John 5 : 25–29, mentions directly both resurrections, St. John, in Rev. 20 : 5, 6, directly mentions only one, namely, the "first resurrection." He leaves the "second resurrection," namely, that of the body, to be inferred. That the "first resurrection," in Rev. 20 : 6, is spiritual, is proved still further by the fact that those who have part in it are "blessed and holy," and not "under the power of the second death," and are "priests of God." The literal resurrection is not necessarily connected with such characteristics, but the tropical is.

In Rev. 20 : 5, it is said that "the rest of the dead lived not again until the thousand years were finished"[1] The remainder of the believing dead do not "live [and reign with Christ]" until the final consummation at the end of the world. The martyrs are honored above the mass of believers, by a co-reign with the Redeemer during the millennium. The church generally does not participate in the triumph of its Head until after the millennium and final judgment.

Augustine (City of God, xx. 6–10) gives this explanation of the two resurrections. The binding of Satan, he says,

---

[1] Tischendorf, Hort, A B, Vulg, read ἔζησαν, instead of ἀνέζησαν, in Receptus. The Revised version omits "again."

is spiritual, and the reign of Christ on earth is also spiritual. The martyrs, as disembodied spirits, reign spiritually with their Lord. Augustine (City, XX. vii.) mentions the opinion of some who believed that the saints will rise on the completion of six thousand years from the creation, and will live upon the earth to celebrate the millennial sabbath. "This opinion," he adds, "would not be objectionable, if it were believed that the joys of the saints in that sabbath shall be spiritual, and consequent on the presence of God, for I myself, too, once held this opinion. But as they assert that those who then rise again shall enjoy the leisure of immoderate carnal banquets, furnished with an amount of meat and drink such as not only to shock the feeling of the temperate, but even to surpass the measure of credulity itself, such assertions can be believed only by the carnal. They who do believe them are called by the spiritual, Chiliasts; which we may literally reproduce by the name of Millenarians." See Wordsworth: On John 5:24–29.

# CHAPTER III.

## THE RESURRECTION.

Athenagoras: On the Resurrection. Justin Martyr: On the Resurrection. Tertullian: On the Resurrection. Augustine City of God, XX. xx. xxi. Aquinas. Summa, III (Supplement) lxxv.–lxxxvii. Calvin: Institutes, III. xxv Pearson On the Creed, Art. XI. Witsius: Apostles' Creed, Dissertation XIX Ursinus: Christian Religion, Qu. 57. Cudworth: System, III 314–319 (Ed. Tegg). Howe: Blessedness of the Righteous, X. Horsley: On the Resurrection. South: On the Resurrection (Sermon LII.). Rawlinson Egypt, X. Speaker's Commentary: On Dan 12 (Excursus). Goulburn: On the Resurrection. Landis: On the Resurrection.

The doctrine of the resurrection of the body was from the first a cardinal and striking tenet of Christianity. The resurrection of Christ made it such. Perhaps no article of the new religion made greater impression, at first view, upon the pagan. When the philosophers of Athens "heard of the resurrection of the dead, some mocked, and others said, We will hear thee again of this matter," Acts 17:32. The immortality of the soul and its disembodied existence were familiar to them. Socrates, in the Phaedrus (245), argues that "the soul is immortal, for that is immortal which is ever in motion; but that which is moved by another, in ceasing to move ceases to live." And in the Phaedo (114), after his description of the underworld, he adds, "I do not mean to affirm that the description which I have given of the soul and her mansions is exactly true—a man of sense ought hardly to say that. But I do say that, inasmuch as the soul is shown to be immortal, he may venture to think, not improperly or unworthily, that something of the kind is true." "As for thy body," says Marcus Aurelius (Meditations, X.), "it is but a vessel or case that compasseth thee about. It is but an instrument, like a carpenter's axe. Without the soul, which has power to use it, the instrument is of itself of no more use to us than the shuttle is of itself to the weaver, or the pen to the writer, or the whip to the coachman."

The doctrine of the transmigration of the soul is wholly different from that of the resurrection. In this case, the soul goes into another body than its own. "The Egyptians believed in the transmigration of souls, so that the soul in a destined cycle wandered through the bodies of every species of animals, till it returned to a human body; not to the one it had formerly occupied, but to a new one." Heeren: Egyptians, II. According to Rawlinson (Egypt, X.), "the good soul, having just been freed from its infirmities by passing through the basin of purgatorial fire, re-entered its former body, rose from the dead, and lived once more a human life upon earth. This process was reiterated, until a certain mystic cycle of years became complete, when finally the good soul attained the crowning joy of union with God, and absorption into the Divine essence." The soul of the evil, according to Lenormant, goes through transmigrations, until it is finally annihilated. "This latter point is not, perhaps, universally allowed," says Rawlinson (I. 318).

The early fathers maintained the doctrine of the resurrection of the body with great earnestness and unanimity against the objections of the skeptics; of whom Celsus was acute and scoffing in his attack. Most of them believed in the resurrection of the very same material body. Justin Martyr, according to Hagenbach, teaches that cripples will rise as cripples, but at the instant of resurrection, if believers, will be made physically perfect. In his tract on the Resurrection (IV.), he argues that the miracles of Christ wrought upon the body prove the fact of its resurrection. "The same power that could say, Arise, take up thy bed and walk, could say to the dead body, Come forth. If on earth Christ healed the sicknesses of the flesh, and made the body whole, much more will he do this in the resurrection, so that the flesh shall rise perfect and entire." The Alexandrine school, alone, adopted a spiritual theory of the resurrection. Origen went so far as to assert that a belief in the resurrection of the body is not absolutely essential to the profession of Christianity, provided the immortality of the soul were maintained.

The Patristic view of the resurrection passed into the Middle Ages with little modification, excepting that in connection with the materialism of the Roman Christianity it naturally became more materialistic. The poetry of Dante, and the painting of Angelo powerfully exhibit it. In the Protestant system, a real body, and one that preserves the personal identity, is affirmed; but the materialism of the Papal, and to some extent of the Patristic church, is avoided by a more careful attention to St. Paul's distinction between the natural body (*σῶμα ψυχικὸν*) and the spiritual body (*σῶμα πνευματικὸν*).

Respecting the probability of a resurrection of the body, it may be remarked that it is no more strange that the human body should exist a second time, than that it has existed the first time. That a full-formed human body should be produced from a microscopic cell, is as difficult to believe, upon the face of it, as that a spiritual resurrection-body should be produced out of the natural earthly body. The marvels of embryology are, a priori, as incredible as those of the resurrection. The difference between the body that is laid in the grave, and the body that is raised from the grave, is not so great as the difference between the minute embryonic ovum and the "human form divine," represented by the Antinous or the Apollo Belvidere. If the generation of the body were, up to this time, as rare an event as the resurrection of the body, it might be denied with equal plausibility. The question of St. Paul, in Acts 26 : 8, applies here: "Why should it be thought a thing incredible that *God* should raise the dead?" The omnipotence that originated the body can of course re-originate it. Even if the extreme view be adopted, that there must be the very same material particles in order to the identity of the body, this is not an impossibility for God. For as Pearson (Article XI.) remarks: "Though the parts of the body of man be dissolved, yet they perish not, they lose not their own entity when they part with their relation to humanity; they are laid up in the secret places, and lodged in the chambers of nature, and it is no more a contradiction that they should become the parts of the same body of man to which they did belong, than that after his death they should become the parts of any other body, as we see they do." Only in this case, a particle of matter that had once been a constituent in two or more *human* bodies, could not be a constituent of two or more resurrection-bodies, because this would involve the simultaneous presence of an atom in two or more places.

The resurrection of the body was taught in the Old Testament, and for this reason it was the common belief of the Jews in the time of Christ. John 11 : 24, Mark 6 : 16; 12 : 23. Passages that teach it are: Isa. 26 : 19, "Thy dead men shall live; together with my dead body shall they arise." Ezekiel 37 : 1–14, where the parable of a spiritual resurrection implies a bodily resurrection. Ps. 16 : 9, "My flesh also shall rest in hope." Dan. 12 : 2, "Many that sleep in the dust of the earth shall awake." The majority of commentators find the resurrection in Job 19 : 23–27. The translation of Elijah, and the reappearance of Samuel at Endor, favor the doctrine of the resurrection of the body. The careful sepulture of the body by Abraham and the Old Testament saints proves the expectation of the resurrection. Gen. 49 : 29.

The apocrypha teaches the resurrection. 2 Maccabees 7 : 9, 23.

The principal points in the Scripture representation are the following:

1. Christ suddenly and unexpectedly descends from heaven accompanied by angels, and reproduces the bodies of all the dead. Matt. 25 : 31, 32. John 5 : 28, 29. Acts 24 : 15. 1 Thess. 4 : 16. The generation living upon earth at the time of the resurrection will instantaneously be re-embodied. 1 Thess. 4 : 17, compared with 1 Cor. 15 : 51. In the Westminster Confession (XXXII. ii) it is said that "such as are found alive shall not die, but be changed." The meaning is, that they will not die gradually like men generally; not that they will altogether escape the penalty of death. All in Adam must die. Says Augustine (City, XX. xx.), "Neither do we suppose that in the case of these saints, the sentence 'Earth thou art, and unto earth shalt thou return,' is null, though their bodies do not on dying fall to the earth, but both die and rise again at once, while caught up into the air. For not even the saints shall be quickened to immortality unless they first die, however briefly."

2. The body thus reproduced is a "spiritual body," for both the good and the evil. 1 Cor. 15 : 44, 53. By *σῶμα πνευματικόν* is meant a spirit-like body: that is, a body adapted to the future spiritual world. It is antithetic to the *σῶμα ψυχικόν*, or the "flesh and blood" spoken of in 1 Cor. 15 : 15, by which is meant the present earthly body suited to the present sensuous world. The body is not converted into spirit; "aliud est corpus fieri spirituale quoad qualitates ratione claritatis, agilitatis, subtilitatis, et similium; aliud vero fieri spiritum, seu mutari in naturam spiritus." Turrettin, Institutio, XIII. xix. 19.

In denominating the present body *ψυχικόν*, and the future body *πνευματικόν*, St. Paul distinguishes between *ψυχή* and *πνεύμα*, in the same way that he does in 1 Thess.

5 : 23, and Heb. 4 : 12. The latter denotes the higher side of the human soul: the "rational soul;" and the former its lower side: the "animal soul." Usually, the two are not distinguished in this way, either by St. Paul, or by the other New Testament writers, since they constitute one soul (ψυχή) in distinction from the body (σῶμα); and are sometimes designated in their unity by πνεύμα, and sometimes by ψυχή. Commonly, the sacred writers speak of man as constituted of "body and soul," or "body and spirit," and not of "body, soul, and spirit." But in 1 Cor. 15 : 44, as in 1 Thess. 5 : 23, and Heb. 4 : 12, St. Paul requires the distinction between the "animal" and the "rational" soul for the purposes of his discussion, and accordingly makes it.[1] Shedd: On Romans 8 : 10.

The *σῶμα ψυχικόν*, or "natural" body, is marked by the qualities of the ψυχή, or "animal" soul: namely, by physical appetites and passions, such as hunger, thirst, and sexual appetite. These are founded in "flesh and blood," or that material substance of which the present human body is composed. The resurrection, or "spiritual" body, on the other hand, will be marked by the qualities of the πνεύμα or "rational soul." It will not be composed of flesh and blood, but of a substance which is more like πνεύμα than like ψυχή; more like the rational than the animal soul.

That the resurrection-body of both the good and the evil will have the common characteristic of being destitute of fleshly appetites and passions, and will be a "spiritual" in distinction from a "natural" body, is proved by Matt. 22 : 30, "They neither marry nor are given in marriage, but are as the angels of God;" 1 Cor. 15 : 50, "Flesh and blood cannot inherit the kingdom of God;" Rev. 7 : 16, "They hunger no more, neither thirst any more."

[1] The trichometry in Heb. 4 : 12 is one of the coincidences with Paul's usage in his undoubted epistles, which go to prove that he is the author, directly or indirectly, of Hebrews.

But while alike in this particular, the spiritual body of the redeemed differs in several important respects from the spiritual body of the lost. Dan. 12 : 2, "Some shall awake to everlasting life, and some to shame and everlasting contempt." John 5 : 28, 29, "All that are in the graves shall come forth, they that have done good, unto the resurrection of life, and they that have done evil, unto the resurrection of damnation." (*a*) The spiritual body of the redeemed is a "celestial" body, 1 Cor. 15 : 40. That of the lost is not. (*b*) It is a "glorified" body, 1 Cor. 15 : 43; Phil. 3 : 21. That of the lost is not. (*c*) It is a "resplendent" body; "the righteous shall shine forth as the sun," Matt. 13 : 43. That of the lost is not. The difference between the blessed and the miserable resurrection is also marked by *ἐξανάστασις*, instead of *ἀνάστασις*, in Phil. 3 : 11; by the phrase *τῆς ἐκ νεκρῶν*, Luke 20 : 35; and by the assertion that there is an order in the resurrection from the dead, "Every man in his own order, they that are Christ's at his coming," 1 Cor. 15 : 23. Cudworth: System, III. 315. Ed. Tegg.

The spiritual body is not wholly a new creation ex nihilo, as the Manichaeans asserted, but is the old body transformed. 1 Cor. 15 : 44, 53, "It is sown a natural body; it is raised a spiritual body. This corruptible must put on incorruption, and this mortal must put on immortality." When Christ raised Lazarus in Bethany, the body raised was identical as to the very particles It was not a spiritual body, because there was no transformation. It had been sown a natural body, and it was raised a natural body. This resurrected body of Lazarus will require to be changed, before it can be the spiritual body of the final resurrection.

The resurrection-body is an identical body. An identical body is one that is recognized by the person himself, and by others. No more than this is required in order to bodily identity. A living man recognizes his present body as the same body that he had ten years ago; yet the material particles are not the same identically. "We shall rise again with the same bodies we have now as to the substance, but the quality will be different." Calvin: Institutes, III. xxv. 8. "The dead shall be raised up with the self-same bodies, and none other, although with different qualities." Westminster Confession, XXXIII. ii. In saying that the substance is the same, but the quality is different, Calvin does not mean that *all* the qualities will be different. This would be incompatible with sameness of substance. But some of the qualities are changed. Calvin explains his statement in the following words: "Just as the very body of Christ which had been offered as a sacrifice was raised again, but with such new and superior qualities as though it had been altogether different." Certain qualities of the "natural" body will still belong to the "spiritual," such as extension, figure, etc. The difference will be in the secondary, rather than in the primary properties of the natural body.

That the spiritual body is recognized, is proved by Luke 9·30–33. Moses and Elijah were recognized by Christ, and pointed out to the disciples. Luke 13:28, "Ye shall see Abraham, and Isaac, and Jacob, and all the prophets in the kingdom of God." John 14:3; 20:16, 17, 20. Christ prepares a place for his people and receives them individually. 2 Sam. 12:23, "I shall go to him, but he shall not return to me" Gen. 49:33, "Jacob was gathered unto his people." Gen. 25.8, "Abraham died and was gathered to his people."

That the spiritual body does not consist of the very same particles of matter with the natural body, no more, no less, and no different, is proved by St. Paul's illustration in 1 Cor. 15:35–40. "Thou sowest not that body that shall be; but God giveth it a body as it hath pleased him. All flesh is not the same flesh, but there is one flesh of men, another of fishes, and another of birds. There are also celestial bodies, and bodies terrestrial." The ten or more grains of wheat that are produced by germination and growth from the single grain sown, are not composed of exactly the same atoms of matter that constituted the seed-kernel. There are many more atoms in them, which have been collected from the soil and the atmosphere. And yet there is the perpetuity, in each of these ten or more new grains, of something that existed in the single seed-grain The vegetable life in this latter has passed into the former, and become the constructive principle in each of the ten or more grains. When Paul says that "that which thou sowest is not quickened except it die," he does not mean the death of *everything* in the seed-kernel. Should the germ in the kernel die, there would be no quickening and no new individual grains. That which dies, is the integument, or covering of the germ. This dies and rots; but some part even of this reappears in the new grains of wheat. The growing plant is nourished by the decaying integument, similarly as the ovum is nourished by the yolk. Yet the particles of the decaying integument do not make up the total sum of the particles in the new grain. Still other particles have to be gathered, by the transmitted vital principle, from the soil and atmosphere, in order to make out the whole amount required for the new individuals.

It should be carefully observed, that St. Paul does not mean that the resurrection of the body is the same in every particular with the reproduction of grain by germination. It is only an illustration, and not an explanation In the case of germination, one grain becomes ten or twenty grains. But in the case of resurrection, one body becomes only one body. The transformation in the first instance, is of one individual into many individuals; in the latter instance, of one individual into one individual. The special point in the illustration is, that the transformation in the instance of the seed-grain does not entirely destroy the old substance; so that there is some sameness of substance between the old and the new. But the sameness between the spiritual body and the natural body is much closer than that between the ten grains of new wheat, and the one grain from which they were produced. It is evident that the apostle intended, by the illustration, to teach that while the resurrection of the body is a supernatural and creative act, it is not such in the sense of originating *all* the materials from nothing The resurrection-body is founded upon, and constructed out of, the previously existing earthly body.

Employing St. Paul's threefold distinction in 1 Thess. 5 : 23, man is a synthesis of *πνεῦμα*, *ψυχή*, and *σῶμα*. The brute is a synthesis of only *ψυχή* and *σῶμα* Man is composed of a rational soul, an animal soul, and a body; the brute is composed of an animal soul, and a body. An animal soul has intelligence in its lower forms, but not reason, or the power of intuitive perception in mathematics, morals, and religion. The difference between the rational soul and the animal soul is marked in Gen. 2 : 7, and Gen. 1 : 20, 21, 24. In the first passage, a living soul (נֶפֶשׁ חַיָּה) is attributed to Adam, but it is inbreathed by God. In the latter passages, a living soul is attributed to the lower animals, but it is merely created, not inbreathed by God. The death of an animal, is the death of both the body and the incomplex animal soul, not the separation of the latter from the former, and the continued life of the latter. The death of a man, is the separation of the complex rational-animal soul from the body, or the departure of the *πνεῦμα-ψυχή* from the *σῶμα*, the continued conscious existence of the former, and the decomposition of the latter. The substance of the *σῶμα* is mortal, and dissolves and "returns to dust as it was." The substance of the *πνεῦμα-ψυχή* is immortal, and is not changed in the least by being separated from the *σῶμα*. In this *πνεῦμα-ψυχή*, or rational soul, is the nucleus, or, to use St. Paul's illustration from the grain of wheat, the germ of the resurrection-body. The ψυχή, which is united with the πνεύμα and constitutes one indivisible principle with it, is the inner reality of the body, the σῶμα; standing for, and representing it in the interval between death and the resurrection.[1] Though the σῶμα is scattered to the four winds, and like Wyckliffe's ashes, has been cast into the Avon, and floated into the Sevein, and finally into the sea, yet the ψυχή, the organific and constructing principle of the σῶμα, is still united with the πνεύμα. And in the instance of the believer, the πνεῦμα-ψυχή is united with Christ; so that thus it may be said (Westminster L. C., 86) that the believer's "*body* is still united to Christ" between death and the resurrection, although the material particles that composed it are "scattered at the grave's mouth, as when one cutteth and cleaveth wood upon the earth," Ps. 141 : 7. Says Poor (Lange, On 1 Cor. 15 : 35–40), "The rational soul, the πνεύμα-ψυχή, is the true substance of the body: that which *stands under* the outward visibility of a corporeal form, and imparts to it its reality. If this be so, it is easy to see that when by death the materials of our present bodily structure are all dissolved and scattered abroad, this vital organic principle, through the supernatural agency of God at the sounding of the last trump, may gather to itself and assimilate new materials of a different nature from 'flesh and blood,' and build up a spiritual body suited to the new condition of things." Compare a similar statement in Hodge: Theology, III. 779.

In the instance of the unbeliever, the πνεύμα-ψυχή is not united to Christ by faith, and therefore it is not said that his "body is still united to Christ" between death and the resurrection. The rational soul of the unbeliever is preserved for "the resurrection of damnation" (John 5 : 29),

---

[1] Howe (Vanity of Man, as mortal) denominates the soul, "the statique individuating principle" of the body.

by the omnipotence of God in the exercise of his providence merely, not of his redeeming grace.[1]

---

[1] In 1 Cor 2:14, fallen man is denominated ἀνθρώπος ψυχικός, because he is ruled by the animal rather than the rational soul In saying that "that was not first which was spiritual, but that which is natural" (1 Cor. 15 46), the order as it *now* exists after apostasy, and not the original order, is given Sin is prior to salvation, and is presupposed by redemption But by creation, man is first "spiritual" and holy, and afterward becomes "natural," and sinful.

## CHAPTER IV.

### THE FINAL JUDGMENT.

Augustine: City of God, XX. xxi.–xxx. Aquinas: Summa, III. (Supplement) lxxxix. xc. Calvin: Institutes, III. xxxv. 7 Ursinus: Christian Religion, Qu 52. Bates: On Eternal Judgment. Newton: On the General Judgment. Jeremy Taylor: Christ's Advent to Judgment (Sermons).

THE doctrine of the Final Judgment was, from the first, immediately connected with the resurrection of the body. Mankind "must all appear before the judgment-seat of Christ, that every one may receive the things done in his *body*," 2 Cor. 5 : 10. The fathers founded their views of the day of doom, upon the representations and imagery of Scripture. They believed that a general conflagration will immediately follow the last judgment, which some said will destroy the world; while others ascribed only a purifying agency to it. Augustine (City, XX. xvi. xxiv.) holds that this world is to be changed, not destroyed, and is to be the "new earth" spoken of in the apocalypse Some, like Tertullian and the more rhetorical of the Greek fathers, enter into minute details; while others, like Augustine, endeavor to define dogmatically the facts couched in the figurative language of the Bible. In the Middle Ages, representations varied with the bent of the individual theologian. One popular opinion was, that the judgment will be held in the valley of Jehoshaphat. Aquinas maintained that the last judgment will be mental, because the oral trial of each individual would require too much time. In the Modern church, the course of thinking has been similar to that in the Ancient and Mediaeval. The symbols of the different Protestant denominations explicitly affirm a day of judgment, at the end of the world. Individual speculations, as of old, vibrate between the extremes of materialism and idealism.

According to Scripture, there is a *private* judgment at death, and a *public* judgment at the last day 1. The private judgment is proved by the following particulars: (*a*) The Bible teaches that the human soul when it leaves the body meets God directly, as it never has before. Eccl. 12: 7, "The dust shall return to the earth as it was; and the spirit shall return unto God who gave it." This implies self-consciousness in the immediate presence of God; and this implies self-knowledge in that presence. 1 Cor. 13: 12, "Now I know in part, but then shall I know even as also I am known." Compare Ps. 139: 1–6. But this self-consciousness and self-knowledge at death is a private individual judgment. Every man when he dies knows his own moral character; and knows it accurately. Consequently, at death every man either acquits or condemns *himself*. What St. Paul says is done in the public judgment of the last day, is also done in the private judgment on the day of death: "The conscience bears witness, and the thoughts accuse or else excuse one another," Rom. 2:15. Consequently, the private judgment at death indicates the moral state of the soul. "It is appointed unto men once to die, but after this, judgment," Heb. 9:27.[1] (*b*) The private judgment at death and the public judgment at the last day coincide, because in the intermediate state there is no alteration of moral character, and consequently no alteration of the sentence passed at death. We have presented the proof from Scripture, that Sheol or

---

[1] In this passage, κρίσις is anarthrous The writer does not say that *the* judgment immediately succeeds the death of the body, but that *a* judgment does.

Hades is a state of retribution and misery, and Paradise a state of reward and blessedness. The parable of Dives and Lazarus teaches that the impenitent spirit goes to Hades at death, and that Hades is Hell without the body. Consequently, the destiny of the impenitent is known and determined at death. The same parable teaches that the penitent spirit goes to Paradise at death, and that Paradise is Heaven without the body Consequently, the destiny of the penitent is also known and determined at death. Penitence or impenitence at death is therefore the state of mind that settles the everlasting condition of the individual. Christ teaches that "to die in sin," is to be hopelessly lost. John 8:21, 24. Every man who has the publican's feeling when he dies, and cries, "God be merciful to me a sinner," is forgiven through the blood of Christ. "To this man, saith the Lord, will I look, even to him that is poor and of a contrite spirit," Isa 66:2. "Blessed are the poor in spirit, for theirs is the kingdom of heaven," Matt. 5:3. Every man who at death is destitute of the publican's feeling, is unforgiven. Ps. 138·6, "The proud he knoweth afar off." Isa. 2:12, "The day of the Lord of hosts shall be upon every one that is proud and lofty." Every penitent pagan is saved; every impenitent nominal Christian is lost.

2. That there is, secondly, a day of judgment and a public judgment, is distinctly and often asserted by our Lord. Matt. 11:22, 24, "It shall be more tolerable for Tyre and Sidon in the day of judgment." Matt. 12:41, "The men of Nineveh shall rise in the judgment with this generation." Matt. 25:34–41, contains a detailed account of the day of judgment. Matt. 5:22, "Whosoever shall say, Thou fool, shall be in danger of hell fire." John 6:39, 40, 44, "I will raise him up at the last day." Acts 17:31, "He hath appointed a day, in the which he will judge the world in righteousness" Rom. 2:16, "The day when God shall judge the secrets of men by Jesus Christ" Mal-

achi 3 : 17, "That day when I make up my jewels." Eccl. 11 : 9, "For all these things God will bring thee into judgment." Eccl. 12 : 14, "God shall bring every work into judgment, with every secret thing." Gen. 18 : 25 ; Deut. 32 : 35 ; Job 21 : 30 ; Ps. 1 : 5, 6 ; 58 : 11 ; 90 : 11 ; 94 : 1, 2 ; Prov. 16 : 25 ; Eccl. 3 : 17 ; Is. 34 : 14 ; 66 : 24 ; Dan. 7 : 9, 10 ; 12 : 2 ; Jude 14, 15.

The Biblical representations of the Last Judgment are as follows: (*a*) The preparation. Christ with the angelic host unexpectedly descends in bodily presence, and the throne of judgment is set Matt. 25 : 31 ; Rev. 21 : 11. Acts 1 : 11, "This same Jesus that is taken up from you into heaven shall come in like manner as ye have seen him go into heaven." His human nature is one reason why the Son of God is the judge John 5 : 27. (*b*) The congregation of all men before the throne of judgment. Matt. 25 : 32; Rom. 14 : 10; Rev. 21 : 12. (*c*) The separation of the evil from the good Matt. 25 : 32, 33. Plato (Republic, X 614) represents the judges as bidding "the just to ascend by the heavenly way on the right hand, and the unjust to descend by the lower way on the left hand." (*d*) The disclosure of character and conduct, so that the grounds of the judgment to be passed upon both classes may be clearly known. Matt. 25 : 34–46 Rom. 2 : 16, "God shall judge the secrets of men, by Jesus Christ." Heb. 4 : 13, "All things are naked, and opened (τετραχηλισμένα) unto the eyes of him with whom we have to do." 1 Cor. 4 : 5, "The Lord will bring to light the hidden things of darkness, and will make manifest the counsels of the hearts." In particular, the temporal good which the evil have enjoyed in this life, and the temporal evil which the good have experienced, will be explained. See Augustine : City of God, XX. ii.

Respecting the last judgment, Augustine (City of God, XX. xiv.) says that there will not be an angel for each man to recite to him the deeds he has done, but we must understand by the phrase, "another book was opened," that by divine power "every one shall recall to memory all his own works, whether good or evil, and shall mentally survey them with a marvellous rapidity, so that this knowledge will either accuse or excuse, and thus all and each shall be simultaneously judged."

## CHAPTER V.

### HEAVEN.

Augustine: City of God, XI. xii. Aquinas: Summa III. (Supplement) xcii.–xcvi. Calvin: Institutes, III. xxv. 11. Ursinus: Christian Religion, Qu. 58. Dante. Paradise, xxx.–xxxiii. Baxter: Saints' Everlasting Rest. Howe: Blessedness of the Righteous. Bates: On Heaven Owen. Person of Christ, XIX.

THAT the blessedness of the redeemed is endless, has been the uniform faith of the Church. Representations concerning the nature of this happiness vary with the education and intellectual spirit of the age or individual. Justin Martyr regarded the blessedness of heaven as consisting, mainly, in the continuation and increase of the happiness of the millennial reign. Origen held that the blessed dwell in the aerial regions, and pass from one heaven to another as they advance in holiness. At the same time, he condemns those who expect any sensuous enjoyment. The Greek theologians Gregory Nazianzen, and Gregory of Nyssa, follow Origen. Augustine believed that the heavenly happiness consists in the enjoyment of peace which passes knowledge, and the beatific vision of God. One important element in it consists in indefectibility: the deliverance from all hazard of apostasy; the non posse peccare et mori. The schoolmen held the patristic views, but with an endeavor to systematize. They divided heaven into three parts: the visible heavens or the firmament; the spiritual heaven, where saints and angels dwell; and the intellectual heaven, where the beatific vision of the Trinity is enjoyed. See Dante: Paradise, xxx.–xxxiii. The

Modern church maintains the doctrine of the everlasting blessedness, but in a more spiritual form than prevailed in either the Ancient or the Mediaeval church. The more common opinion is, that this world is not to be either annihilated or destroyed, but renovated for the abode of the redeemed. Turrettin defends this view. Institutio, XX. v. Anselm (Cur deus homo, I. 18) says: "We believe that the material substance of the world must be renewed, and that this will not take place until the number of the elect is completed, and that happy kingdom be made perfect, and that after its completion there will be no change."

The Scripture representation of the heavenly state is as follows:

1. It is marked by sinless perfection. Eph 5:27, "A glorious church, without spot or wrinkle." Rev. 19:14, The "armies" of heaven are "clothed in fine linen, white and clean" Rev. 19:8, "The Lamb's wife is arrayed in fine linen, which is the righteousness of saints." Rom. 8:21, "The creature shall be delivered from the bondage of corruption into the glorious liberty of the children of God." Heb. 12:23, "The spirits of just men made perfect" are in the "heavenly Jerusalem." 2. It is marked by impeccability, or indefectibility. Rom. 8:35–39. 1 Thess. 4:17, "We shall ever be with the Lord." Heb. 4:9, "A rest remaineth to the people of God" 1 John 3:2, "We shall be like him." Indefectibility, or the absence of that possibility of apostasy which was connected with man as created, renders his state as redeemed more blessed because of the sense of security Eden was uncertain; heaven is certain. This is the absolute *rest* into which he enters. There is to be no probation, nor temptation, internal or external. "Every man who not merely supposes but certainly knows that he shall eternally enjoy the most high God, in the company of angels and beyond the reach of ill—this man, no matter what bodily torments afflict him, is more blessed than was he who, even in that great felicity of paradise,

was uncertain of his fate." Augustine: City of God, XI. xii. Compare De Dono Perseverantiae. 3. It is chiefly mental happiness; the vision of the Divine perfections and delight in them. 1 Cor. 13:12, "Then shall we see face to face." 1 John 3:2, "We shall see him as he is." Job 19:27, "Whom I shall see for myself." Rev. 4:10, 11; 5 passim; 7:9 sq.; 21:3 sq.; 22:4. Ps. 17:15, "I shall behold thy face in righteousness." Ps. 16:11, "In thy presence is fulness of joy" 4. It is the personal presence of the Mediator with his redeemed people. Rev. 14:4, "They follow the Lamb whithersoever he goeth." John 17:24, "Father, I will that they whom thou hast given me be with me where I am; that they may behold my glory." This is an element in the heaven of redeemed man that does not enter into that of the angels. See Owen: Person of Christ, XIX.

# CHAPTER VI.

## HELL.

Augustine: City of God, XXI. Aquinas: Summa III. (Supplement) xcvii.–xcix. Dante: Inferno. Calvin: Institutes, III. xxv 12. Howe Redeemer's Tears over Lost Souls. Bates · On Hell. Pearson. Creed, Art VII Newton: The Final State. Bunyan. Sighs from Hell. Edwards: Eternity of Hell Torments; Sinners in the Hands of God. Edwards: Against Chauncy Hopkins: Future State. Stuart: Exegetical Essays (Sheol and Aion). Alexander: On Universalism. Muller: Sin, II. 191, 418–431. Bartlett: Life and Death Eternal. Goulburn Everlasting Punishment. Farrar: Eternal Hope. Pusey: Everlasting Punishment (Historical). Fisher · Discussions (History of the Doctrine of Future Punishment). Edersheim: Life of Jesus, II, Appendix xix. (Jewish views). Riemensnyder: Doom Eternal. Mead: The Soul Here and Hereafter. Rice: On Immortality Davidson: Doctrine of Last Things. Hovey: State of the Impenitent Dead. Hudson: Debt and Grace. Lewis: Ground and Nature of Punishment. Cheever: Capital Punishment. Woolsey: Political Science, II. viii. Morris: Is there Salvation after Death?

### § 1. THE HISTORY OF THE DOCTRINE.

The common opinion in the Ancient church was, that the Future Punishment of the impenitent wicked is endless. This was the catholic faith; as much so as belief in the Trinity. But as there were some church fathers who deviated from the creed of the church respecting the doctrine of the Trinity, so there were some who dissented from it in respect to that of eternal retribution. The deviation in eschatology, however, was far less extensive than in trinitarianism. The Semi-Arian and Arian heresies involved and troubled the Ancient church much more seriously than did the Universalism of that period. Long controversies, ending in oecumenical councils and formulated statements, were the consequence of the trinitarian errors, but no oecumenical council, and no authoritative counter-statement, was required to prevent the spread of the tenet of Restoration. Having so little even seeming support in Scripture and reason, it gradually died out of the Ancient church by its own intrinsic mortality. Neander (History, II. 737), speaking of the second period in his arrangement (312–590), when there was more Restorationism than in the first, says: "The doctrine of eternal punishment continued, as in the preceding period, to be dominant in the creed of the church. Yet, in the Oriental church, in which, with the exception of those subjects immediately connected with the doctrinal controversies, there was greater freedom and latitude of development, many respectable church teachers still stood forth, without injuring their reputation for orthodoxy, as advocates of the opposite doctrine, until the time when the Origenistic disputes caused the agreement with Origen in respect to this point also [viz. Restorationism] to be considered as something decidedly heretical." Hagenbach (History of Doctrine, § 78) says of the period down to A.D. 250: "Notions more or less gross prevailed concerning the punishment of the wicked, which most of the fathers regarded as eternal."

The principal deviation from the catholic doctrine of endless retribution was in the Alexandrine school, founded by Clement and Origen. The position taken by them was, that "the punishments of the condemned are not eternal, but only remedial, the devil himself being capable of amelioration." Gieseler, I. 214. Thus early was the question raised, whether the suffering to which Christ sentences the wicked is for the purpose of correcting and educating the transgressor, or of vindicating and satisfying the law he has broken: a question which is the key to the whole controversy. For if the individual criminal is of greater consequence than the universal law, then the suffering must refer principally to him and his interests. But if the law is of more importance than any individual, then the suffering must refer principally to it.

Origen's Restorationism grew naturally out of his view of human liberty. He held that the liberty of indifference and the power of contrary choice, instead of simple self-determination, are the substance of freedom. These belong inalienably and forever to the nature of the finite will. They cannot be destroyed, even by apostasy and sin Consequently, there is forever a possibility of a self-conversion of the will in either direction. Free will may fall into sin at any time; and free will may turn to God any time. This led to Origen's theory of an endless alternation of falls and recoveries, of hells and heavens; so that practically he taught nothing but a hell. For, as Augustine (City of God, XXI. xvii) remarks, in his refutation of Origen, heaven with the prospect of losing it is misery."[1] "Origen's theory," says Neander (I. 656), "concerning the necessary mutability of will in created beings led him to infer that evil, ever germinating afresh, would still continue to render necessary new processes of purification, and new worlds destined for the restoration of fallen beings, until all should again be brought back from manifoldness to unity, so that there was to be a constant interchange between fall and redemption, between unity and manifoldness."

Traces, more or less distinct, of a belief in the future restoration of the wicked are found in Didymus of Alexandria, the two Gregories, and also in Diodore of Tarsus and Theodore of Mopsuestia: the leaders of the Antiochian school. All of these were more or less under the influence of Origen Origen's opinions, however, both in trinitari-

[1] "Qui existimabat posse se miserum esse, beatus non erit." Cicero: De Finibus, II. 27.

anism and eschatology, were strongly combated in his own time by the great body of contemporary fathers, and subsequently by the church, under the lead of Epiphanius, Jerome, and Augustine.

The Mediaeval church was virtually a unit in holding the doctrine of Endless Punishment. The Reformation churches, both Lutheran and Calvinistic, adopted the historical and catholic opinion.

Since the Reformation, Universalism, Restorationism, and Annihilation, have been asserted by some sects, and many individuals. But these tenets have never been adopted by those ecclesiastical denominations which hold, in their integrity, the cardinal doctrines of the trinity and incarnation, the apostasy and redemption, although they have exerted some influence within these denominations. None of the evangelical churches have introduced the doctrine of Universalism, in any form of it, into their symbolical books The denial of endless punishment is usually associated with the denial of those tenets which are logically and closely connected with it: such as original sin, vicarious atonement, and regeneration. Of these, vicarious atonement is the most incompatible of any with universal salvation; because the latter doctrine, as has been observed, implies that suffering for sin is remedial only, while the former implies that it is retributive. Suffering that is merely educational does not require a vicarious atonement in order to release from it. But suffering that is judicial and punitive can be released from the transgressor, only by being inflicted upon a substitute. He, therefore, who denies personal penalty must, logically, deny vicarious penalty. If the sinner himself is not obliged by justice to suffer in order to satisfy the law he has violated, then, certainly, no one needs suffer for him for this purpose.

Within the present century, Universalism has obtained a stronger hold upon German theology than upon any other, and has considerably vitiated it. It grew up in connection with the rationalism and pantheism which have been more powerful in Germany than elsewhere. Rationalism has many of the characteristics of deism, and is vehemently polemic toward evangelical truth. That it should combat the doctrines of sin and atonement, is natural. Pantheism, on the other hand, has to some extent been mingled with evangelical elements. A class of anti-rationalistic theologians, in Germany, whose opinions are influenced more or less by Spinoza and Schelling, accept the doctrines of the trinity, incarnation, apostasy, and redemption, and assert the ultimate salvation of all mankind. Schleiermacher, the founder of this school, whose system is a remarkable blending of the gospel and pantheism, has done much toward the spread of Restorationism. The following are the objections which this theologian (Glaubenslehre, § 163, Anhang) makes to eternal damnation: "(*a*) Christ's words in Matt. 25:46; Mark 9:44; John 5:29, are figurative. (*b*) The passage 1 Cor. 15:25, 26, teaches that all evil shall be overcome. (*c*) Misery cannot increase, but must decrease. If it is bodily misery, custom habituates to endurance, and there is less and less suffering instead of more and more.[1] If, on the other hand, it is mental suffering, this is remorse The damned suffer more remorse in hell than they do upon earth. This proves that they are better men in hell than upon earth. They cannot, therefore, grow more wretched in hell, but grow less so as they grow more remorseful. (*d*) The sympathy which the saved have with their former companions, who are in hell,

---

[1] Satan, in Milton's Paradise Lost (II. 274-278), suggests that custom may mitigate the pains of hell.

> "Our torments also may, in length of time,
> Become our elements, these piercing fires
> As soft as now severe, our temper changed
> Into their temper, which must needs remove
> The sensible of pain."

will prevent the happiness of the saved. The world of mankind, and also the whole universe, is so connected that the endless misery of a part will destroy the happiness of the remainder."[1] These objections appeal mainly to reason. But the two assumptions, that hell is abolished by becoming used to it, and that remorse is of the nature of virtue, do not commend themselves to the intuitive convictions.

Besides the disciples of Schleiermacher, there are trinitarian theologians standing upon the position of theism, who adopt some form of Universalism Nitzsch (Dogmatics, § 219) teaches Restorationism. He cites in support of it only two passages out of the entire scriptures: namely, 1 Pet. 3:19, which speaks of the "preaching to the spirits in prison;" and Heb. 11:39, 40, "These received not the promises." These two passages Nitzsch explains as teaching that "there are traces of a capacity in another state of existence for comprehending salvation, and for a change and purification of mind;" and upon them, solely, he founds the sweeping assertion that "it is the Apostolical view, that for those who were unable in this world to know Christ in his truth and grace, there is a knowledge of the Redeemer in the other state of existence which is never inoperative, but is either judicial or quickening."

Rothe (Dogmatics, II. ii. 46–49, 124–131) contends for the annihilation of the impenitent wicked, in the sense of

---

[1] Respecting this very common objection, Müller (Sin, I. 239) makes the following remark "The primary meaning of κρίσις is discrimination and separation, and implies that the main contrast between man and man in relation to the future state is made manifest by the *cessation of intercourse* between those who obey God, and those who resist him Beings whose relations to God are diametrically opposite, and persistently so, differ so greatly from each other that other ties of relationship become as nothing in comparison Bonds of union among men arising out of the relationships of natural life must give way of themselves, if the tie which binds man's spiritual consciousness and will to his Creator be on either side wholly severed. For those bonds have not in themselves an eternal significance, save so far as they are included in that relation to God which is of everlasting importance"

the extinction of self-consciousness. Yet he asserts that the aim of penalty is requital, and the satisfaction of justice: an aim that would be defeated by the extinction of remorse. Julius Muller (Sin, II. 418–425) maintains that the sin against the Holy Ghost is never forgiven, because it implies such a hardness in sin as is incapable of penitence. But he holds that the offer of forgiveness through Christ will be made to every human being, here or hereafter. "Those who have never in this life had an opportunity of knowing the way of salvation will certainly be placed in a position to accept and enter upon this way of return, if they will, after their life on earth is ended. We may venture to hope that in the interval between death and the judgment many serious misconceptions, which have hindered men from appropriating truth in this life, will be removed."[1] The use of the term "misconception" would seem to imply that some who had the offer of salvation in this life, but had rejected it, will have the opportunity in the next life to correct their error in this. Dorner (Christian Doctrine, IV. 416–428), after giving the arguments for and against endless punishment, concludes with the remark, that "we must be content with saying that the ultimate fate of individuals, namely, whether all will attain the blessed goal or not, remains veiled in mystery." His further remark that "there may be those eternally damned, so far as the abuse

---

[1] In placing the time of repentance "between death and the judgment" (II 425), Müller appears to contradict what he says in II 426, 429: "It is clear that those theories of an ἀποκατάστασις which represent it as taking place in the interval between death and the general resurrection, directly violate the New Testament eschatology If the idea, therefore, is to be maintained, it must be referred to a period lying beyond the general resurrection The αἰών μελλων ['world to come'] does not mean the time and state immediately ensuing upon death, but the period when the kingdom of the Messiah shall be fully realized and revealed the period which follows the resurrection and the judgment. Christ's words [Matt 12·32], therefore, inspire the glorious hope that in 'the world to come,' in far distant aeons, they who here harden their hearts against God's revelation, and can expect only a verdict of condemnation in the day of judgment, shall find forgiveness and salvation."

of freedom continues eternally, but in this case man has passed into *another class* of beings," looks in the direction of annihilation: suggesting that sin may finally destroy the humanity of man, and leave him a mere brute. Respecting the future offer of mercy, Dorner asserts that "the final judgment can take place for none before the gospel has been so addressed to him that free appropriation of the same was possible." Christian Doctrine, III. 77.

Universalism has a slender exegetical basis. The Biblical data are found to be unmanageable, and resort is had to human sentiment and self-interest. Its advocates quote sparingly from scripture. In particular, the words of Christ relating to eschatology are left with little citation or interpretation. Actual attempts by the Restorationist to explain what the words, "Depart from me, ye cursed, into everlasting fire prepared for the devil and his angels," *really mean*, are rare. The most common device is to dismiss them, as Schleiermacher does, with the remark that they are figurative. Some words of St. Paul, on the other hand, whose views upon sin, election, and predestination, however, are not especially attractive to this class, are made to do yeoman's service. Texts like Rom. 5 : 18, "As judgment came upon all men unto condemnation, so the free gift came upon all men unto justification;" and 1 Cor. 15 : 22, "As in Adam all die, so in Christ shall all be made alive," are explained wholly apart from their context, and by emphasizing the word "all." When St. Paul asserts that "the free gift came upon all men unto justification," this is severed from the preceding verse, in which the "all" are described as "those which receive abundance of grace, and of the gift of righteousness." And when the same apostle affirms that "in Christ shall all be made alive," no notice is taken of the fact mentioned in the succeeding verse, that not all men are "in Christ"—the clause, "they that are Christ's at his coming," implying that there are some who are *not* "Christ's at his coming."

## § 2. THE BIBLICAL ARGUMENT.

The strongest support of the doctrine of Endless Punishment is the teaching of Christ, the Redeemer of man. Though the doctrine is plainly taught in the Pauline Epistles, and other parts of Scripture, yet without the explicit and reiterated statements of God incarnate, it is doubtful whether so awful a truth would have had such a conspicuous place as it always has had in the creed of Christendom. If, in spite of that large mass of positive and solemn threatening of everlasting punishment from the lips of Jesus Christ which is recorded in the four Gospels, the attempt has nevertheless been made to prove that the tenet is not an integral part of the Christian system, we may be certain that had this portion of Revelation been wanting, this attempt would have been much more frequent, and much more successful. The Apostles enter far less into detailed description, and are far less emphatic upon this solemn theme, than their divine Lord and Master. And well they might be. For as none but God has the right, and would dare, to sentence a soul to eternal misery for sin; and as none but God has the right, and would dare, to execute the sentence; so none but God has the right, and should presume, to delineate the nature and consequences of this sentence. This is the reason why most of the awful imagery in which the sufferings of the lost are described is found in the discourses of our Lord and Saviour. He took it upon himself to sound the note of warning. He, the judge of quick and dead, assumed the responsibility of teaching the doctrine of Endless Retribution "I will forewarn you whom ye shall fear: Fear him who after he hath killed hath power to cast into hell; yea, I say unto you, Fear him." "Nothing," says Dr. Arnold, "is more striking to me, than our Lord's own description of the judgment. It is so inexpressibly forcible, coming from his very own lips, as descriptive of what he himself would do." Stanley: Life of Arnold, I. 176.

Christ could not have warned men so frequently and earnestly as he did against "the fire that never shall be quenched," and "the worm that dieth not," had he known that there is no future peril fully corresponding to them. That omniscient Being who made the statements respecting the day of judgment, and the final sentence, that are recorded in Matt 25: 31–46, could neither have believed nor expected that all men without exception will eventually be holy and happy. To threaten with "everlasting punishment" a class of persons described as "goats upon the left hand" of the Eternal Judge, while knowing at the same time that this class would ultimately have the same holiness and happiness with those described as "sheep upon the right hand" of the judge, would have been both falsehood and folly. The threatening would have been false. For even a long punishment in the future world would not have justified Christ in teaching that this class of mankind are to experience the same retribution with "the devil and his angels;" for these were understood by the Jews, to whom he spoke, to be hopelessly and eternally lost spirits.[1] And the threatening would have been foolish, because it would have been a brutum fulmen, an exaggerated danger, certainly in the mind of its author. And for the persons threatened, it would have been a terror only because they took a different view of it from what its author did—

[1] Edersheim (Life of Jesus, II 789) asserts that the schools of Shammai and Hillel both taught the doctrine of eternal punishment "These schools represented the theological teaching in the time of Christ and his Apostles, showing that the doctrine of Eternal Punishment was held in the days of our Lord, however it may have been afterwards modified" Edersheim adds, that "the doctrine of the eternity of punishment seems to have been held by the Synagogue throughout the whole first century. In the second century, there is a decided difference in Rabbinic opinion, some denying the doctrine of endless retribution In the third century, there is a reaction and a return to former views."

they believing it to be true, and he knowing it to be false!

The mere perusal of Christ's words when he was upon earth, without note or comment upon them, will convince the unprejudiced that the Redeemer of sinners knew and believed, that for impenitent men and devils there is an endless punishment. We solicit a careful reading and pondering of the following well-known passages. "When the Son of man shall come in his glory, and all the holy angels with him, then shall he sit upon the throne of his glory; and before him shall be gathered all nations, and he shall separate them one from another, as a shepherd divideth his sheep from the goats. And he shall set the sheep on his right hand, but the goats on the left Then shall he say unto them on the left hand, Depart from me, ye cursed, into everlasting fire, prepared for the devil and his angels. And these shall go away into everlasting punishment," Matt. 25:31–33, 41, 46. "If thy right hand offend thee cut it off: it is better for thee to enter into life maimed than having two hands to go into hell, into the fire that never shall be quenched; where their worm dieth not, and the fire is not quenched. And if thy foot offend thee, cut it off: it is better for thee to enter halt into life, than having two feet to be cast into hell, into the fire that never shall be quenched; where their worm dieth not, and the fire is not quenched. And if thine eye offend thee, pluck it out: it is better for thee to enter into the kingdom of God with one eye, than having two eyes to be cast into hell fire; where their worm dieth not, and the fire is not quenched," Mark 9:43–48. "What shall it profit a man, if he shall gain the whole world, and lose his own soul? What is a man advantaged, if he gain the whole world, and be cast away?" Mark 8:36; Luke 9:25. "The rich man died and was buried, and in hell he lifted up his eyes being in torments," Luke 16:22, 23. "Fear not them which kill the body, but are not able to kill the soul: but rather fear him which is able to destroy both soul and body in hell," Matt. 10 : 28. "The Son of man shall send forth his angels, and they shall gather out of his kingdom all things that offend, and them which do iniquity, and shall cast them into a furnace of fire: there shall be wailing and gnashing of teeth," Matt. 13 : 41, 42. "Many will say to me in that day, Lord, Lord, have we not prophesied in thy name? Then will I profess unto them, I never knew you: depart from me, ye that work iniquity," Matt. 7: 22, 23. "He that denieth me before men shall be denied before the angels of God. Unto him that blasphemeth against the Holy Ghost, it shall never be forgiven," Luke 12 : 9, 10. "Woe unto you, ye blind guides. Ye serpents, ye generation of vipers, how can ye escape the damnation of hell?" Matt. 23 : 16, 33. "Woe unto that man by whom the Son of man is betrayed! it had been good for that man if he had not been born," Matt. 26 : 24. "The Lord of that servant will come in a day when he looketh not for him, and at an hour when he is not aware, and will cut him in sunder, and appoint him his portion with unbelievers," Luke 12 : 46. "He that believeth not shall be damned," Mark 16 : 16. "Thou Capernaum, which art exalted unto heaven, shalt be brought down to hell," Matt. 11 : 23. "At the end of the world, the angels shall come forth and sever the wicked from among the just, and shall cast them into the furnace of fire," Matt. 13 : 49, 50. "Then said Jesus again to them, I go my way, and ye shall seek me, and shall die in your sins: whither I go ye cannot come," John 8 : 21. "The hour is coming in which all that are in their graves shall hear my voice, and shall come forth; they that have done good, unto the resurrection of life; and they that have done evil, unto the resurrection of damnation," John 5 : 28, 29.

To all this, add the description of the manner in which Christ will discharge the office of the Eternal Judge. John the Baptist represents him as one "whose fan is in his hand, and he will throughly purge his floor, and gather his wheat into the garner, but will burn up the chaff with unquenchable fire," Matt. 3 : 12. And Christ describes himself as a householder who will say to the reapers, "Gather ye together first the tares, and bind them in bundles to burn them," Matt. 13 : 30 ; as a fisherman "casting a net into the sea, and gathering of every kind, which when it was full he drew to the shore, and sat down and gathered the good into vessels, but cast the bad away," Matt. 13 · 47, 48; as the bridegroom who took the wise virgins "with him to the marriage," and shut the door upon the foolish, Matt 25 : 10; and as the man travelling into a far country who delivered talents to his servants, and afterwards reckons with them, rewarding the "good and faithful," and "casting the unprofitable servant into outer darkness, where there shall be weeping and gnashing of teeth," Matt. 25 : 19–20.

Let the reader now ask himself the question: Do these representations, and this phraseology, make the impression that the future punishment of sin is to be *remedial*, and *temporary?* Are they adapted to make this impression? Were they intended to make this impression? Is it possible to believe that that Holy and Divine Person who uttered these fearful and unqualified warnings, eighteen hundred years ago, respecting the destiny of wicked men and devils, knew that a time is coming when there will be no wicked men and devils in the universe of God, and no place of retributive torment? Did Jesus of Nazareth hold an esoteric doctrine of hell: a different view of the final state of the wicked, from that which the common and natural understanding of his language would convey to his hearers, and has conveyed to the great majority of his readers in all time? Did he know that in the far-off future, a day will come when those tremendous scenes which he described—the gathering of all mankind, the separation of the evil from the good, the curse pronounced upon the former and the blessing upon the latter—will be looked back upon by all mankind as "an unsubstantial pageant faded," as a dream that is passed, and a watch in the night?

Jesus Christ is the Person who is responsible for the doctrine of Eternal Perdition. He is the Being with whom all opponents of this theological tenet are in conflict. Neither the Christian church, nor the Christian ministry are the authors of it. The Christian ministry never would have invented the dogma; neither would they have preached it in all the Christian centuries, like Jeremiah, with shrinking and in tears, except at the command of that same Lord God who said to the weeping prophet, "Whatsoever I command thee, thou shalt speak," Jer. 1 : 7.

Having given, in the discussion of the Intermediate State, the proof from Scripture that Sheol and Hades signify the place of punishment for the wicked, we proceed to consider the nature and duration of the suffering inflicted in it[1]

The Old Testament is comparatively silent upon these particulars. Sheol is represented vaguely, as an evil to be dreaded and avoided, and little description of its fearfulness is given by the "holy men of old who spake as they were moved by the Holy Ghost." The New Testament makes a fuller revelation and disclosure; and it is principally the Redeemer of the world who widens the outlook into the tremendous future. The suffering in Hades and

---

[1] There is no dispute that Gehenna denotes the place of retributive suffering. It is employed seven times in Matthew's Gospel, thrice in Mark's, and once in Luke's In every one of these instances, it is Christ who uses the term The only other person who has used it is James (3 : 6) It is derived from גי הנם, valley of Hinnom, Chaldee, גהנם = Γέεννα, Sept Ἐννομ. It was a valley southeast of Jerusalem, in which the Moloch worship was practised 2 Kings 23. 10, Ezek 23 37, 39 It was called Tophet, "abomination." Jer 31 32 King Josiah caused the filth of Jerusalem to be carried thither and burned 2 Kings 23. 10. Robinson asserts that there is no evidence that the place was used in Christ's day for the deposit and burning of offal "Gehenna," at the time of the Advent, had become a technical term for endless torment, as "Paradise" and "Abraham's bosom" had for endless blessedness.

Gehenna is described as "everlasting (*αἰώνιος*) punishment," Matt. 25 : 46; "everlasting (*αἰώνιος*) fire," Matt. 18 : 8; "the fire that never shall be quenched," Mark 9 : 45; "the worm that dieth not," Mark 9 : 46; "flaming fire," 2 Thess 1 : 8; "everlasting (*ἀΐδιος*) chains," Jude 6; "eternal (*αἰώνιος*) fire," Jude 7; "the blackness of darkness forever," Jude 13; "the smoke of torment ascending up forever and ever," Rev. 14 : 11; 19 : 3; "the lake of fire and brimstone," in which the devil, the beast, and the false prophet "shall be tormented day and night, forever and ever," Rev. 20 : 10.

Sensible figures are employed to describe the misery of hell, as they are to describe the blessedness of heaven. It cannot be inferred from the mere use of metaphors, that the duration of either is temporary. Figures are employed to describe both temporal and eternal realities. The Psalmist describes God as a "rock," a "fortress," a "shield," etc.; and man as a "vapor," a "flower," etc. A figure by its "form," as the rhetoricians call it, indicates the intention of the writer. No one would employ the figure of a rock to denote transiency, or of a cloud to denote permanence. Had Christ intended to teach that future punishment is remedial and temporary, he would have compared it to a dying worm, and not to an undying worm; to a fire that is quenched, and not to an unquenchable fire. The ghost in Hamlet (I v) describes the "glow-worm's fire" as "ineffectual," that is, harmless. None of the figures employed in Scripture to describe the misery of the wicked are of the same rhetorical "form" with those of the "morning-cloud," the "early dew," etc. They are invariably of the contrary "form," and imply fixedness and immutability. The "smoke of torment" ascends forever and ever. The "worm" of conscience does not die. The "fire" is unquenchable. The "chains" are eternal. The "blackness of darkness" overhangs forever Had the sacred writers wished to teach that future punishment is for a time only, even a very long time, it would have been easy to have chosen a different species and form of metaphor that would have conveyed their meaning And if the future punishment of the wicked is not endless, they were morally bound to have avoided conveying the impression they actually have conveyed by the kind of figures they have selected. "It is the wilful deceit," says Paley, "that makes the lie; and we wilfully deceive, when our expressions are not true in the sense in which we believe the hearer to apprehend them."

The epithet *αἰώνιος* ("everlasting") is of prime importance. In order to determine its meaning when applied to the punishment of the wicked, it is necessary, first, to determine that of the substantive from which the adjective is derived. *Αἰών* signifies an "age" It is a time-word. It denotes "duration," more or less. Of itself, the word "duration," or "age," does not determine the length of the duration, or age. God has duration, and angels have duration. The Creator has an *αἰών*, and the creature has an *αἰών*; but that of the latter is as nothing compared with that of the former. "Behold thou hast made my days as an handbreadth; and mine age is as nothing before thee," Ps. 39:5

In reference to man and his existence, the Scriptures speak of two, and only two *αἰῶνες*, or ages; one finite, and one infinite; one limited, and one endless; the latter succeeding the former.[1] An indefinite series of limited aeons

[1] The common phrase, "Here, and hereafter," denotes that human existence divides into only two sections When Faust sells his soul to Mephistopheles, both parties understand that there are only two worlds the temporal and the eternal The latter covenants with the former as follows

> "I to thy service *here* agree to bind me,
> To run and never rest at call of thee,
> When over *yonder* thou shalt find me,
> Then thou shalt do as much for me"

The same tremendous truth, that after the temporal the endless follows, is taught in the "mighty line" of Marlowe, in which he describes the emotions of Faustus as "the clock strikes eleven."

with no final endless aeon is a Pagan, and Gnostic, not a Biblical conception. The importation of the notion of an endless series of finite cycles, each of which is without finality and immutability, into the Christian system, has introduced error, similarly as the importation of the Pagan conception of Hades has. The misconceiving of a rhetorical figure, in the Scripture use of the plural for the singular, namely, *τοὺς αἰῶνας τῶν αἰώνων* for *τόν αἰῶνα*, has also contributed to this error.

The two aeons, or ages, known in Scripture, are mentioned together in Matt 12.32, "It shall not be forgiven him, neither in this world (*αἰών*), nor in the world (*αἰών*) to come;" in Mark 10.30, "He shall receive an hundredfold now in this time (*καιρός*), and in the world (*αἰών*) to come, eternal life;" in Luke 18·30, "He shall receive manifold more in this present time (*καιρός*), and in the world (*αἰών*) to come, life everlasting;" in Eph. 1:21, "Above every name that is named, not only in this world (*αἰών*), but also in that which is to come." The "things present" and the "things to come," mentioned in Rom. 8:38; 1 Cor 3:22, refer to the same two ages. These two aeons, or ages, correspond to the two durations of "time" and "eternity," in the common use of these terms. The present age, or aeon, is "time;" the future age, or aeon, is "eternity"[1]

---

"Ah, Faustus,
Now hast thou but one bare hour to live,
And then thou must be damn'd perpetually!
Stand still, you ever-moving spheres of heaven,
That time may cease, and midnight never come;
Fair Nature's eye, rise, rise again, and make
Perpetual day, or let this hour be but
A year, a month, a week, a natural day,
That Faustus may repent and save his soul!
O lente, lente currite, noctis equi'
The stars move still, time runs, the clock will strike,
The devil will come, and Faustus must be damned."

[1] It is relative, not absolute eternity, eternity a parte post, not a parte ante The future aeon, or age, has a beginning, but no ending This is the meaning,

1. The present finite and limited age, or aeon, is denominated in Scripture, "this world" (ὁ αἰών οὗτος, עוֹלָם הַזֶּה), Matt. 12:32; 13:22; Luke 16:8; 20:34; Rom 12:2; 1 Cor. 1:20; 2:6, et alia. Another designation is, "this present world" (ὁ νῦν αἰών, or ὁ ἐνεστώς αἰών), 1 Tim. 6:17; 2 Tim. 4:10; Titus 2:12; Gal. 1:4. Sometimes the present limited age, or aeon, is denoted by αἰών without the article: Luke 1:70, "Which he spake by the mouth of his holy prophets, which have been since the world began" (ἀπ' αἰῶνος); John 9:39, "It was not heard since the world began" (ἀπ' αἰῶνος).

For rhetorical effect, the present limited age, or aeon, is sometimes represented as composed of a number of lesser ages or cycles, as in modern phrase the sum total of finite earthly time is denominated "the centuries," or "the ages." The following are examples: 1 Cor. 2:7, "The hidden wisdom which God ordained before the ages" (πρό τῶν αἰώνων). Compare Eph. 3:9; Col. 1:26. In 1 Tim. 1:17, God is denominated βασιλεύς τῶν αἰώνων, king of the ages of time, and therefore "the king eternal" (A. V.). In Rom. 16:25, a "mystery" is said to have been kept secret χρόνοις αἰωνίοις, "during aeonian times" ("since the world began," A. V.) The ages of the limited aeon are meant. The secret was withheld from all the past cycles of time. In Titus 1:2, "eternal life" is said to have been promised πρό χρόνων αἰωνίων, "before aeonian times," ("before the world began," A. V.). The ages of the limited aeon are meant. God promised eternal life prior to all the periods of time; i.e., eternally promised. In these pas-

---

when in common phrase it is said that "a man has gone into eternity," and that his happiness, or misery, is "eternal" The absolutely eternal has no beginning, as well as no ending, it is the eternity of God The relatively eternal has a beginning but no end, it is the immortality of man and angel. The schoolmen called the former, eternitas, the latter, sempiternitas. Scripture designates the absolute eternity of God, by the phrase, "from everlasting to everlasting," Ps. 90.2. The punishment of the wicked is more properly endless, than eternal.

sages, "aeonian times" is equivalent to "the centuries," or the "long ages"[1] This rhetorical plural does not destroy the unity of the limited age, or aeon. To conceal a mystery from the past "aeonian ages," or the past centuries and cycles of finite time, is the same as to conceal it from past finite time as a whole.[2]

2. The future infinite and endless age, or aeon, is denominated, in Scripture, "the future world," A. V. and R. V. "the world to come" (αἰών ὁ μέλλων, עוֹלָם הַבָּא), Matt. 12:32; Heb. 2:5; 6:5. Another designation is, "the world to come" (αἰών ὁ ἐρχόνενος), Mark 10:30; Luke 18:30. Still another designation is, "*that* world" (αἰών ἐκεῖνος), Luke 20:35. Frequently, the endless age is denoted by αἰών simply, but with the article for emphasis (ὁ αἰών), Mark 3:29, "Hath never forgiveness" (εἰς τὸν αἰῶνα); Matt. 51:29; John 4:14; 6:51, 58; 8:35, 51, 52; 10:28; 11:26; 12:34; 13:8; 14:16; 2 Cor. 9:9; Heb. 5:6; 6:20; 7:17; 2 Pet. 2:17; 1 John 2:17; Jude 13.

The same use of the plural for rhetorical effect, employed in the case of the limited aeon, is also employed in that of the unlimited. The future infinite αἰών is represented as made up of lesser αἰώνες, or cycles, as, in English, "infinity" is sometimes denominated "the infinities," "eternity," "the eternities," and "immensity," "the immensities." The rhetorical plural, in this instance as in the other, does not conflict with the unity of the infinite age, or aeon. The following are examples of this use: Rom. 1:

[1] The Revisers make the reference to be to the unlimited aeon, or to eternity. Their rendering of Titus 1 2, by, "before times *eternal*," involves the absurdity that a Divine promise is made prior to eternity, and of Rom 16 25, by, "through times *eternal*," represents the mystery as concealed during eternity. that is to say, as forever concealed.

[2] The phrases, "end of the ages" (τέλη τῶν αἰώνων), 1 Cor. 10:11; "fulness of the time," Gal 4 4, "fulness of times," Eph 1:10; "these last days" (ἐσχάτος τῶν ἡμερων τούτων), Heb. 1 1, denote the time of the Messiah's first advent: that epoch in the temporal αἰών when the incarnation occurred. Hodge On Eph. 1:10

25, "the creator is blessed forever" (*εἰς τοὺς αἰῶνας*); Rom. 9:5; 11:36; 16:27; 2 Cor. 11:31; Phil. 4:20; Gal. 1:5 (*εἰς τοὺς αἰῶνας τῶν αἰώνων*); 1 Tim 1:17; Rev. 1:6, 18; 4:9, 10; 5:13; 7:12, et alia. The phrases, *εἰς τοὺς αἰῶνας*, and *εἰς τοὺς αἰῶνας τῶν αἰώνων*, are equivalent to *εἰς τὸν αἰῶνα*. All alike denote the one infinite and endless aeon, or age.

Since the word aeon (*αἰών*), or age, in Scripture, may denote either the present finite age, or the future endless age, in order to determine the meaning of "aeonian" (*αἰώνιος*). it is necessary first to determine *in which of the two aeons*, the limited or the endless, the thing exists to which the epithet is applied; because anything in either aeon may be denominated "aeonian." The adjective follows its substantive, in meaning. Onesimus, as a slave, existed in this world (*αἰών*) of "time," and when he is called an aeonian, or "everlasting" (*αἰώνιος*) servant (Philemon 15), it is meant that his servitude continues as long as the finite aeon in which he is a servant; and this is practically at an end for him, when he dies and leaves it. The mountains are denominated aeonian, or "everlasting" (*αἰώνια*), in the sense that they endure as long as the finite world (*αἰών*) of which they are a part endures. God, on the other hand, is a being that exists in the infinite *αἰών*, and is therefore *αἰώνιος* in the endless signification of the word. The same is true of the spirits of angels and men, because they exist in the future aeon, as well as in the present one. If anything belongs solely to the present age, or aeon, it is aeonian in the limited signification; if it belongs to the future age, or aeon, it is aeonian in the unlimited signification. If, therefore, the punishment of the wicked occurs in the *present* aeon, it is aeonian in the sense of temporal; but if it occurs in the *future* aeon, it is aeonian in the sense of endless. The adjective takes its meaning from its noun.[1]

---

[1] "Αἰών de quocunque temporis spatio ita dicitur, ut, quale sit, judicari debeat in singulis locis ex orationis serie et mente scriptoris, rebus adeo et personis de quibus sermo est" Schleusner, in voce

The English word "forever" has the same twofold meaning, both in Scripture and in common use. Sometimes it means as long as a man lives upon earth. The Hebrew servant that had his ear bored with an awl to the door of his master, was to be his servant "forever," Exod. 21:6 Sometimes it means as long as the Jewish state should last. The ceremonial laws were to be statutes "forever," Lev. 16:34. Sometimes it means, as long as the world stands. "One generation passeth away, and another generation cometh; but the earth abideth forever," Eccl. 1.4. In all such instances, "forever" refers to the temporal aeon, and denotes finite duration. But in other instances, and they are the great majority in Scripture, "forever" refers to the endless aeon; as when it is said that "God is over all blessed forever." The limited signification of "forever" in the former cases, does not disprove its unlimited signification in the latter That Onesimus was an "everlasting" (*αἰώνιος*) servant, and that the hills are "everlasting" (*αἰώνια*), no more disproves the everlastingness of God, and the soul; of heaven, and of hell; than the term "forever" in a title-deed disproves it. To hold land "forever" is to hold it "as long as grass grows and water runs;" that is, as long as this world, or aeon, endures.

The objection that because *αἰώνιος*, or "aeonian," denotes "that which belongs to an age," it cannot mean endless, rests upon the assumption that there is no endless *αἰών*, or age It postulates an indefinite series of limited aeons, or ages, no one of which is final and everlasting. But the texts that have been cited disprove this. Scripture speaks of but two aeons, which cover and include the whole existence of man, and his whole duration. If, therefore, he is an immortal being, one of these must be endless. The phrase "ages of ages," applied to the future endless age, does not prove that there is more than one future age, any more than the phrase "the eternities" proves that there is more than one eternity; or the phrase "the infinities" proves that there is more than one infinity. The plural in these cases is rhetorical and intensive, not arithmetical, in its force.

This examination of the Scripture use of the word *αἰώνιος* refutes the assertion, that "aeonian" means "spiritual" in distinction from "material" or "sensuous," and has no reference at all to time or duration; that when applied to "death," it merely denotes that the death is mental and spiritual in its nature, without saying whether it is long or short, temporary or endless. Beyond dispute, some objects are denominated "aeonian," in Scripture, which have nothing mental or spiritual in them. The mountains are "aeonian." The truth is, that *αἰών* is a term that denotes time *only*, and never denotes the nature and quality of an object. All the passages that have been quoted show that duration, either limited or endless, is intended by the word. Whenever this visible world in the sense of the *matter* constituting it is meant, the word employed is *κοσμός*, not *αἰών*. It is only when this world in the sense of the *time* of its continuance is intended, that *αἰών* is employed. St. Paul, in Eph 2:2, combines both meanings. The heathen, he says, "walk *κατὰ τὸν αἰῶνα τοῦ κόσμου τούτου*—according to the course [duration] of this world [of matter]." In Heb. 1:2; 11:3, where *αἰῶνες* denotes the "worlds" created by God, it is, as Lewis (Lange's Ecclesiastes, p. 47) remarks in opposition to Winer and Robinson, "the time sense, of worlds *after* worlds," not "the space sense, of worlds *beyond* or *above* worlds," that is intended.

In by far the greater number of instances, *αἰών* and *αἰώνιος* refer to the future infinite age, and not to the present finite age; to eternity, and not to time. Says Stuart (Exegetical Essays, 13, 16), "*αἰώνιος* is employed 66 times in the New Testament. Of these, 51 relate to the future happiness of the righteous; 7 relate to future punishment: namely, Matt. 18:8; 25:41; 46; Mark 3:29; 1 Thess 1:9; Heb. 6:2; Jude 6; 2 relate to God; 6 are of a miscellaneous nature (5 relating to confessedly endless things, as covenant, invisibilities; and one, in Philemon 15, to a perpetual service). In all the instances in which *αἰώνιος* refers to future duration, it denotes endless duration; saying nothing of the instances in which it refers to future punishment. The Hebrew עוֹלָם is translated in the Septuagint by *αἰών*, 308 times. In almost the whole of these instances, the meaning is, time unlimited; a period without end. In the other instances, it means *αἰών* in the secondary, limited sense; it is applied to the mountains, the Levitical statutes, priesthood, etc." The younger Edwards (Reply to Chauncy, XIV.) says that "*αἰών*, reckoning the reduplications of it, as *αἰώνες τῶν αἰώνων*, to be single instances of its use, occurs in the New Testament in 104 instances; in 32 of which it means a limited duration. In 7 instances, it may be taken in either the limited or the endless sense In 65 instances, including 6 instances in which it is applied to future punishment, it plainly signifies an endless duration."

An incidental proof that the adjective *αἰώνιος* has the unlimited signification when applied to future punishment, is the fact that the destiny of lost men is bound up with that of Satan and his angels. "Then shall he say unto them on the left hand, Depart from me, ye cursed, into everlasting fire, prepared for the devil and his angels," Matt. 25 : 41. These are represented in Scripture as hopelessly lost. "The devil that deceived them shall be tormented day and night forever and ever," Rev. 20 : 10. The Jews, to whom Christ spoke, understood the perdition of the lost angels to be absolute. If the positions of the Restorationist are true in reference to man, they are also in reference to devils. But Scripture teaches that there is no redemption for the lost angels. "Christ took not on him the nature of angels," Heb. 2 : 16.

Respecting the nature of the "everlasting punishment," it is clear from the Biblical representations that it is accompanied with *consciousness*. Dives is "in torments,"

Luke 16 : 23. "The smoke of their torment ascendeth up forever and ever," Rev. 14 : 11. "Fear hath torment," 1 John 4 : 18 ; and the lost fear "the wrath of the Lamb," Rev. 6 : 16. The figures of the "fire," and the "worm" are intended to denote conscious pain. An attempt has been made to prove that the punishment of the wicked is the extinction of consciousness. This doctrine is sometimes denominated Annihilation. Few of its advocates, however, have contended for the strict annihilation of the substance of the soul and body. The more recent defenders maintain the doctrine of Conditional Immortality. According to this view, the soul is not naturally immortal. Some of this class contend that it is material. It gains immortality only through its redemption by Christ[1] All who are not redeemed lose all consciousness at the death of the body, and this is the "spiritual death" threatened in Scripture. As the death of the body is the extinction of sensation, so the death of the soul is the extinction of consciousness. The falsity of the theory of Annihilation, in both of its forms, is proved by the following considerations:

(*a*) Death is the opposite of birth, and birth does not mean the creation of substance. The conception and birth of an individual man is the uniting of a soul and a body, not the creation ex nihilo of either ; and the physical death of an individual man is the separation of a soul and body, not the annihilation of either. Death is a change of the mode in which a substance exists, and supposes that the substance itself continues in being.

> "Ne, when the life decays and forme does fade,
> Doth it consume and into nothing goe,
> But chaunged is and often altered to and froe.
> The substaunce is not chaunged nor altered,
> But th' only forme and outward fashion."
>
> FAIRY QUEEN, III. vi.

---

[1] This theory was presented by Dodwell · Epistolary Discourse, that the Soul is a principle naturally mortal Immortalized by the pleasure of God. London, 1706.

The death of an animal substance makes an alteration in the relations of certain material atoms, but does not put them out of existence. Dead matter is as far from nonentity as living matter. That physical death is not the annihilation of substance, is proved by 1 Cor. 15:36, "That which thou sowest is not quickened except it die." Compare John 12:24. In like manner, the death of the soul, or spiritual death, is only a change in the relations of the soul, and its mode of existence, and not the annihilation of its substance. In spiritual death, the soul is separated from God; as in physical death, the soul is separated from the body. The union of the soul with God is spiritual life; its separation from God is spiritual death. "He that hath the Son hath [spiritual] life, and he that hath not the Son hath not [spiritual] life," 1 John 5:12. (*b*) The spiritually dead are described in Scripture as conscious. Gen. 2:7 compared with Gen. 3:8. "In the day thou eatest thereof, thou shalt surely die;" Adam and Eve "hid themselves." After their fall they were spiritually dead, and filled with shame and terror before God. The "dead in trespasses and sins walk according to the course of this world," Eph. 2:1, 2. "She that liveth in pleasure is dead while she liveth," 1 Tim. 5:6. "You being dead in your sins hath he forgiven," Coloss. 2:13. "Thou livest, and art dead," Rev. 3:1. Spiritual death is the same as the "second death," and the second death "hurts," Rev. 2:11; and its smoke of torment "ascends forever and ever," Rev. 19:3. (*c*) The extinction of consciousness is not of the nature of punishment. The essence of punishment is suffering, and suffering is consciousness. In order to be punished, the person must be conscious of a certain pain, must feel that he deserves it, and know that it is inflicted because he does. All three of these elements are required in a case of punishment. To reduce a man to unconsciousness would make his punishment an impossibility. If God by a positive act extinguishes, at death, the remorse of a hardened villain, by extinguishing his self-consciousness, it is a strange use of language to denominate this a punishment. Still another proof that the extinction of consciousness is not of the nature of punishment is the fact that a holy and innocent being might be deprived of consciousness by his Creator, but could not be punished by him. God is not obliged, by his justice, to perpetuate a conscious existence which he originated ex nihilo. For wise ends, he might suffer an unfallen angel not only to lose consciousness, but to lapse into his original nonentity. But he could not, in justice, inflict retributive suffering upon him. (*d*) The extinction either of being, or of consciousness, admits of no degrees of punishment. All transgressors are "punished" exactly alike. This contradicts Luke 12:47, 48; Rom. 2:12. (*e*) According to this theory, brutes are punished. In losing consciousness at death, the animal like the man incurs an everlasting loss. The Annihilationist contends that the substance of punishment is in the result, and not in its being felt or experienced. If a transgressor is put out of conscious existence, the result is an everlasting loss to him, though he does not know it. But the same thing is true of a brute. And if the former is punished, the latter is also. (*f*) The advocate of Conditional Immortality, in teaching that the extinction of consciousness is the "eternal death" of Scripture, implies that the continuance of consciousness is the "eternal life." But mere consciousness is not happiness. Judas was conscious, certainly, when he hung himself, even if he is not now. But he was not happy. (*g*) The extinction of consciousness is not regarded by sinful men as an evil, but a good. They substitute the doctrine of the eternal sleep of the soul, for that of its eternal punishment. This shows that the two things are not equivalents. When Mirabeau lay dying, he cried passionately for opium, that he might never awake. The guilty and remorseful have, in all ages, deemed the extinction of consciousness after death to be a blessing; but the advocate of Conditional Immortality explains it to be a curse. "Sight, and hearing, and all earthly good, without justice and virtue," says Plato (Laws, II. 661), "are the greatest of evils, *if life be immortal;* but not so great, if the bad man lives a very short time." (*h*) The fact that the soul depends for its immortality and consciousness upon the upholding power of its Maker does not prove either that it is to be annihilated, or to lose consciousness. Matter also depends for its existence and operations upon the Creator. Both matter and mind can be annihilated by the same Being who created them from nothing. Whether he will cease to uphold any particular work of his hand, can be known only by revelation. In the material world, we see no evidence of such an intention. We are told that "the elements shall melt with fervent heat," but not that they shall be annihilated. And, certainly, all that God has said in revelation respecting creation, redemption, and perdition, implies and teaches that he intends to uphold, not to annihilate the human spirit; to perpetuate, not extinguish its self-consciousness.

The form of Universalism which is the most respectable, and therefore the most dangerous, is that which concedes the force of the Biblical and rational arguments respecting the guilt of sin, and its intrinsic desert of everlasting punishment, but contends that redemption from it through the vicarious atonement of Christ is extended into the next world. The advocates of this view assert that between death and the final judgment the application of Christ's work is going on; that the Holy Spirit is regenerating sinners in the intermediate state, and they are believing and repenting as in this life. This makes the day of judgment, instead of the day of death, the dividing line between "time" and "eternity;" between *ὁ αἰών οὗτος*, and *αἰών ὁ μέλλων*. And this makes the intermediate state a third aeon by itself, lying between "time" and "eternity;" between "this world" and "the world to come."

That the "intermediate state" is not a third aeon, but a

part of the second endless aeon, is proved by the following considerations:

1. First, by the fact that in Scripture the disembodied state is not called "intermediate." This is an ecclesiastical term which came in with the doctrine of purgatory, and along with the exaggeration of the difference between Paradise and Heaven, and between Hades and Gehenna. 2. Secondly, by the fact that in Scripture death is represented as the deciding epoch in a man's existence. It is the boundary between the two Biblical aeons, or worlds. Until a man dies, he is in "this world" (ὁ νῦν αἰών); after death, he is in "the future world" (αἰών ὁ μέλλων) The common understanding of the teaching of Scripture is, that men are in "time," so long as they live, but when they die, they enter "eternity." "It is appointed unto men once to die, but after that judgment," Heb 9 : 27. This teaches that prior to death man's destiny is not decided, he being not yet sentenced; but after death his destiny is settled. When he dies, the "private judgment," that is, the immediate personal consciousness either of penitence or impenitence, occurs. Every human spirit, in that supreme moment when it "returns to God who gave it," knows by direct self-consciousness whether it is a child or an enemy of God, in temper and disposition; whether it is humble and contrite, or proud, hard, and impenitent; whether it welcomes or rejects the Divine mercy in Christ. The article of death is an event in human existence which strips off all disguises, and shows the person what he really is in moral character. He "knows as he is known," and in this flashing light passes a sentence upon himself that is accurate. This "private judgment" at death, is reaffirmed in the "general judgment" of the last day.

Accordingly, our Lord teaches distinctly that death is a finality for the impenitent sinner. Twice in succession, he says with awful emphasis to the Pharisees, "If ye believe not that I am he, ye shall die in your sins," John 8 : 21,

24. This implies, that to "die in sin," is to be hopelessly lost. Again, he says, "Yet a little while is the light with you. Walk while ye have the light, lest darkness come upon you: for he that walketh in darkness knoweth not whither he goeth. While ye have light, believe in the light, that ye may be the children of light," John 12:35, 36. According to these words of the Redeemer, the light of the gospel is not accessible in the darkness of death. "The night cometh, wherein no man can work," John 9: 4. The night of death puts a stop to the work of salvation that is appointed to be done in the daytime of this life. St. Paul teaches the same truth, in 1 Thess. 5:5–7, "Ye are all the children of light, and the children of the day: we are not of the night, nor of darkness. Therefore let us not sleep, as do others; but let us watch and be sober. For they that sleep, sleep in the night; and they that be drunken, are drunken in the night." "God said unto him, Thou fool, this night thy soul shall be required of thee: then whose shall those things be which thou hast provided? So is he that layeth up treasure for himself, and is not rich towards God," Luke 12:20, 21. The end of a man's life on earth is often represented as the decisive moment in his existence. "He that endureth to the end, shall be saved," Matt. 10:22; 24:13. "Jesus Christ shall confirm you unto the end," 1 Cor. 1:8. "Whose house are we, if we hold fast the confidence, and the rejoicing of the hope firm unto the end," Heb. 3:6. "We are made partakers of Christ, if we hold the beginning of our confidence steadfast unto the end," Heb. 3:14. "We desire that every one of you do shew the same diligence to the full assurance of hope unto the end," Heb. 6:11. "He that overcometh, and keepeth my works unto the end, to him will I give power over the nations," Rev. 2:26. In these passages, the end of life, or of this world is meant. No one would think of the end of the intermediate state, or of eternity, as the *τέλος*, or *τέλους*, in the mind of the writer.

With these New Testament teachings agrees the frequent affirmation of the Old Testament, that after death nothing can be done towards securing salvation. "The wicked is driven away in his wickedness [at death]; but the righteous hath hope in his death," Prov. 14:32. "When a wicked man dieth, his expectation shall perish," Prov. 11:7. "In death there is no remembrance of thee: in the grave who shall give thee thanks?" Ps. 6:5. "Wilt thou show wonders to the dead? Shall the dead arise and praise thee? Shall thy loving-kindness be declared in the grave?" Ps. 88:10, 11. "The dead praise not the Lord, nor any that go down into silence," Ps. 115:17. "To him that is joined to all the living, there is hope: for the living know that they shall die; but the dead know not anything, neither have they any more a reward," Eccl. 9:4–6. These passages do not teach the utter unconsciousness of the soul after death, in flat contradiction to that long list already cited (p. 613 sq.) which asserts the contrary, but that there is no alteration of character in the next life. "In death, there is no [happy] remembrance of God" [if there has been none in life]. "The dead shall not arise, and praise God" [in the next world, if they have not done so in this world]. "Shall God declare his loving-kindness [to one] in the grave" [if he has not declared it to him when upon earth]?

The parable of Dives proves that death is the turning-point in human existence, and fixes the everlasting state of the person. Dives asks that his brethren may be warned *before* they die and enter Hades; because after death and the entrance into Hades, there is an impassable gulf between misery and happiness, sin and holiness. This shows that the so-called "intermediate" state is not intermediate in respect to the essential elements of heaven and hell, but is a part of the final and endless state of the soul. It is "intermediate," only in reference to the secondary matter of the presence or absence of the body.

The asserted extension of redemption into the endless aeon, or age, is contradicted by Scripture. Salvation from sin is represented as confined to the limited aeon, by the covenant between the Father and the Son. The most important and explicit passage bearing upon this point is 1 Cor. 15 : 24–28, "Then cometh the end, when Christ shall have delivered up the kingdom to God, even the Father, when he shall have put down all [opposing] rule, and all [opposing] authority and power. For he must reign, till he hath put all *enemies* under his feet." St. Paul here states the fact, disclosed to him by revelation from God, that the redemption of sinners will not go on forever, but will cease at a certain point of time. The Mediator will carry on his work of saving sinful men, until he has gathered in his church, and completed the work according to the original plan and covenant between himself and his Father, and then will surrender his mediatorial commission and office (βασιλείαν). There will then no longer be any mediation going on between sinners and God. The redeemed will be forever united to their Divine Head in heaven, and the wicked will be shut up in the "outer darkness." That Christ's mediatorial work does not secure the salvation of all men during the appointed period in which it is carried on, is proved by the fact that when "the end cometh," some men are described as the "enemies" of Christ, and as being "put under his feet," 1 Cor. 15 : 24, 25 All of Christ's redeemed "stand before his throne," Rev. 14 : 3; 19 : 4–7; 21 : 3. They are in the "mansions" which he has "prepared" for them, John 14 : 2, 3.

The reason assigned for Christ's surrender of his mediatorial commission is, "that *God* may be all in all," 1 Cor. 15 : 28; not, that "God even the *Father* may be all in all," 1 Cor. 15 : 24. It is the Trinity that is to be supreme. To Christ, as an incarnate trinitarian person, and an anointed mediator, "all power is [temporarily] given in heaven and upon earth" (Matt. 28 : 29), for the purpose of saving sinners. As such, he accepts and holds a secondary position of condescension and humiliation, when compared with his original unincarnate position. See p. 354 sq. In this reference, he receives a "commandment" (John 10 : 18), and a "kingdom" (1 Cor. 15 : 24). In this reference, as believers "are Christ's," so "Christ is God's," 1 Cor. 3 : 23 ; and as "the head of the woman is the man," so "the head of Christ is God," 1 Cor. 11 : 3. But when Christ has finished his work of mediating between the triune God and sinful men, and of saving sinners, this condition of subjection to an office and a commission ceases. The dominion (*βασιλείαν*) over heaven and earth, temporarily delegated to a single trinitarian person incarnate, for purposes of redemption and salvation, now returns to the Eternal Three whence it came, and to whom it originally belongs. The Son of God, his humanity exalted and glorified, and his Divine-human person united forever to his church as their head, no longer prosecutes that work of redemption which he carried forward through certain ages of time, but, with the Father and Spirit, Three in One, reigns over the entire universe: over the holy "who stand before the throne," and over the wicked who are "under his feet," and "in the bottomless pit."

The confinement of the work of redemption to the limited aeon, which terminates practically for each individual at the death of the body, is taught in many other passages of Scripture. "My spirit shall not always ["for ever," R. V.] strive with man, for that he also is [sinful] flesh ; yet his days shall be an hundred and twenty years," Gen. 6 : 3. This teaches that the regenerating agency of the Divine Spirit in the sinner's heart was to be restricted to the hundred and twenty years which for a time was the average length of human life. "O that they were wise, that they would consider their latter end," Deut. 32 : 29 "Teach us so to number our days, that we may apply our hearts unto wisdom," Ps. 90 : 12. "Every one that is godly shall pray unto thee in a time when thou mayest be found," Ps. 32:6. "Because I have called, and ye refused; I have stretched out my hand, and no man regarded; but ye have set at naught all my counsel, and would none of my reproof; I also will laugh at your calamity; I will mock when your fear cometh. Then shall they call upon me, but I will not answer; they shall seek me early, but they shall not find me," Prov. 1:24–28. "Whatsoever thy hand findeth to do, do it with thy might; for there is no work, nor device, nor knowledge, nor wisdom, in the grave whither thou goest," Eccl. 9:10 "Seek ye the Lord while he may be found; call ye upon him while he is near," Isa. 55:6. "Take heed to yourselves lest at any time your hearts be overcharged with surfeiting, and drunkenness, and cares of this life, and so that day come upon you unawares: for as a snare shall it come on all them that dwell on the face of the earth," Luke 21:34, 35. "Watch, therefore, for ye know not what hour your Lord cometh. The Lord of that servant shall come in a day when he looketh not for him, and shall cut him asunder, and appoint him his portion with unbelievers: there shall be weeping and gnashing of teeth," Matt. 24:42, 50. "If thou hadst known, even thou, at least in this thy day, the things which belong unto thy peace! but now they are hid from thine eyes," Luke 19:42. "Strive to enter in at the strait gate: for many, I say unto you, will seek to enter in, and shall not be able When once the master of the house is risen up, and hath shut to the door, and ye begin to stand without, and to knock at the door, saying, Lord, Lord, open unto us, he shall answer, and say unto you, I know you not whence ye are," Luke 13:24, 25. "We beseech you that ye receive not the grace of God in vain. For he saith, I have heard thee in a time accepted, and in the day of salvation have I succored thee: behold now is the accepted time; behold now is the day of salvation," 2 Cor 6·2. "To-day if ye will hear his voice, harden not your hearts," Heb. 3:7. The argument in Heb. 3:7–19 is to the effect, that as God swore that those Israelites who did not believe and obey his servant Moses during the forty years of wandering in the desert should not enter the earthly Canaan, so those who do not "while it is called, To-day"—that is, while they are here in time—believe and obey his Son Jesus Christ, shall not enter the heavenly Canaan. "Take heed lest there be in any of you an evil heart of unbelief. But exhort one another daily, while it is called, To-day," Heb. 3:12, 13. "God limiteth a certain day, saying in David, To-day, after so long a time [of impenitence], To-day, if ye will hear his voice, harden not your hearts," Heb. 4:7. Hebrews 10:26 speaks of a time when "there remaineth no more sacrifice for sins, but a fearful looking-for of judgment and fiery indignation which shall devour the adversaries of God." "Behold I come quickly; and my reward is with me, to give to every man according as his work shall be. He that is unjust, let him be unjust still; and he which is filthy, let him be filthy still; and he that is righteous, let him be righteous still; and he that is holy, let him be holy still," Rev. 22:11, 12.

If sinners are redeemed beyond the grave, man must be informed of the fact by God himself. There is no other way of finding it out. He has not been so informed, but, if language has any meaning, has been informed of the contrary. Bishop Butler (Analogy, I. ii.) states the case with his usual conciseness and clearness. "Reason did, as it well might, conclude that it should finally be well with the righteous, and ill with the wicked; but it could not be determined upon any principles of reason whether human creatures might not have been appointed to pass through other states of life and being, before that distributive justice should finally and effectually take place. Revelation teaches us that the next state of things after the present is appointed for the execution of this justice; that it shall no longer be delayed, but the mystery of God, the great mystery of his *suffering vice and confusion to prevail*, shall then be finished; and he will take to him his great power, and will reign, by rendering to every one according to his works."

The asserted extension of redemption into the period between death and the resurrection cannot be placed upon the ground of obligation and justice; and the only other ground possible, that of the Divine promise so to extend it, is wanting. Our Lord teaches that men prior to his coming into the world are "condemned already," John 3:16. His advent to save them supposes that they are already lost; and they are lost by sin; and sin is man's free self-determination.[1] Consequently, man the sinner has no claim

[1] The strange position has recently been taken, that the rejection of Christ is the only sin that brings eternal death. "No one," says Dorner (Christian Doctrine, IV., 167), "will be damned merely on account of the common sin and guilt. But every one is definitely brought to [guilty] personal decision only through the gospel." Says a writer in the Andover Review (Dec., 1885, p. 574) "No one can be lost without the knowledge of Christ." This implies that man's sin against the moral law is not sufficient to condemn him to eternal death. He must sin against the gospel, before he can be so condemned. Neither original sin nor actual transgression, neither evil inclination nor outward disobedience, both of which are sins against the law, expose a man to hell.

This is an entirely new position, not to be found in the past history of eschatology, and invented, apparently, to furnish a basis for the doctrine of a future offer of redemption. The objections to it are the following. (*a*) It contradicts the whole tenor of scripture. Christ teaches that he came to call actual and guilty sinners to repentance (Luke 5:32); that he came to seek and save that which was really and truly lost (Luke 19:10); that he did not come into the world to condemn the world, because it was already condemned, but to save the world (John 3:17, 18). St. Paul affirms that the whole world, prior to redemption, and irrespective of it, are guilty before God (Rom. 3:19). St. John asserts that the whole world, Gentile and Jewish, unevangelized and evangelized, lieth in wickedness (1 John 5:19). To quote all the passages in which the Bible teaches that men are exposed to eternal death on account of their transgression of the law of God, would be to quote a large part of the Bible. The rejection of the gospel adds a new sin, and a very aggravating one, to the already existing sin against the divine law (John 15:22), but it is not the primary and original ground of condemnation. Men are punished, first of all, because they "have sinned, and come short of the glory of God," Rom. 3:23. (*b*) Unless man has first sinned against the law, he cannot sin against the gospel. If he has not previously committed a damning sin for which Christ has atoned, he cannot reject Christ's atonement any more than an innocent angel can. The rejection of salvation is meaningless, if no damnation has been incurred. If there is no disease, there can be no cure, nor rejection of a cure. (*c*) If no human soul is in

upon God for redemption. Forgiveness is undeserved, whether offered here or hereafter. The exercise of mercy is optional with God. "I will have mercy on whom I will have mercy," Rom. 9:15. It follows from this, that the

---

danger of perdition until it has rejected Christ, then if Christ had never been offered to man no man would be lost. For it he were not offered, he could not be rejected. In this case, it would have been infinitely better for mankind had Christ never come into the world on an errand of salvation Had he remained unincarnate, as he had been from eternity, no one could have refused belief in him, and as unbelief is the only damning sin no one could have been damned (*d*) If "no man can be lost without the knowledge of Christ," then none of the past heathen world who died without this knowledge incurred perdition for the "deeds done in the body," and none of the existing heathen world who are destitute of this knowledge are liable to perdition from this cause. In this case, it is matter of rejoicing that the past generations of pagans never heard of the Redeemer, and it should be an earnest endeavor of the Church to prevent all of the present generation of pagans from hearing of him

Dorner's theory, that "no one will be damned merely on account of the common sin and guilt," is full of inconsistency and self-contradiction. First, he holds that man is in a state of "common sin and guilt," but it is a species of sin and guilt that does not deserve endless punishment, and is not in danger of it. Secondly, he holds that man needs "salvation" from such an unendangered state Thirdly, he holds that God is bound in justice to provide "salvation" from such an unendangered state "The gospel," he says (IV 167), "repentance, and forgiveness of sins, is to be preached to all nations This cannot refer merely to nations as unities, but must refer also to every individual; for otherwise the universality of the gracious purpose would not be sincerely meant; and *if God refused what is indispensable to salvation to the individual, condemnation would be impossible*" Fourthly, he holds that God exhibits mercy, when he does what he is obligated to do

To all this self-stultifying soteriology, the principle enunciated by St Paul (Rom 11 6) is a conclusive reply "If by grace, then it is no more of works; otherwise grace is no more grace But if it be of works, then it is no more grace, otherwise work is no more work." If man's "common sin and guilt" is not damning, then it is no more sin and guilt, otherwise sin and guilt are no more sin and guilt. If Christ's salvation is not from death and hell, then it is no more salvation, otherwise salvation is no more salvation And if God's mercy is justly due to man, then it is no more mercy; otherwise mercy is no more mercy

Julius Müller, though holding (upon the ground of Matt 12 32) "the glorious hope that in the world to come, in far distant aeons, some who here harden their hearts against God's revelation, and can expect only a verdict of condemnation in the day of judgment, shall find forgiveness and salvation" (Sin, II. 429), denies and combats Dorner's position that sin against the gospel is the only damning sin (Sin, II 400) For a very able argument in proof that both evil inclination and outward transgression are damning, see Sin, I. 198–214.

length of time during which the offer of mercy is made to transgressors is likewise optional with God. It may be long or short, according to the Divine will. Should God say to a sinner: "I will pardon your sin to-day, if you will penitently confess it, but not to-morrow," this sinner could not complain of injustice, but would owe gratitude for the mercy thus extended for a limited time. It cannot be said, that unless God offers to pardon man forever and ever, he he is not a merciful Being. Neither can this be said, if he confines redemption to this life, and does not redeem sinners in the intermediate state.[1]

It is here that the logical inconsistency of such theologians as Muller and Dorner appears. Lessing, the first of German critics, makes the following remark respecting the German mind: "We Germans suffer from no lack of systematic books. No nation in the world surpasses us in the faculty of deducing from a couple of definitions whatever conclusions we please, in most fair and logical order" (Preface to the Laocoon). The truth of this remark is illustrated by some of the systems of theology and philosophy constructed in Germany. The reasoning is close, consecutive, and true, in some sections; but loose, inconsequent, and false, as a whole. The mind of the thinker when moving in the limited sphere, moves logically; but moving in the universe, and attempting to construct a philosophy or theology of the Infinite, fails utterly. Many of the trains of reasoning in Schleiermacher's Glaubenslehre are profound, closely reasoned, and correct, but the system as a whole has fatal defects. No one will deny the rigor of Hegel's logical processes in segments, but the total circle of his thinking is pantheistic, and full of inconsistency.

Lessing's remark applies to that type of Universalism of which Muller and Dorner are the best representatives, and the ablest advocates. In the first place, upon "a couple" of

---

[1] Shedd. Sermons to the Natural Man. (Sermon XVIII.)

obscure and dubious scripture texts, they rear the whole great fabric of a future redemption, in direct contradiction to some scores of perfectly plain texts that teach the confinement of redemption to this life. And, secondly, after laying down a theory of sin which represents it as pure self-determination and guilt, sin is then discussed as an evil that is entitled to the offer of a pardon, and a remedy. Muller and Dorner, both alike, explain sin as originating in the free and guilty agency of the finite will, and as requiring an atonement in order to its remission.[1] And yet both alike, when they come to eschatology, assume tacitly, but do not formally assert, that the Divine Perfection requires that the offer of forgiveness be made, sooner or later, to every sinner; that there will be a defect in the benevolence, and a blemish in the character, of the Supreme Being, if he does not tender a pardon to every transgressor of his law. Their eschatology thus contradicts their hamartiology.

The extension of the work of redemption into the future world is made to rest very much, for its support, upon the cases of the heathen and of infants. Respecting the former, it is certain that the heathen are voluntary transgressors of the moral law, and therefore have no claim upon the Divine mercy. Scripture teaches that they perish because of their sin, and impenitence in sin. It is wicked to sin, and still more wicked not to repent of it. The heathen are chargeable with both. St. Paul describes them as those "who knowing the judgment of God, that they which commit such things are worthy of death, not only do the same, but have pleasure in them that do them," Rom. 1:32. "There is no respect of persons with God For as many as have sinned without [written] law shall also perish without [written] law," Rom. 2:11. "The Gentiles show the

[1] The merit of Muller, in particular, in respect to a profound and true view of sin is very great. No theological treatise of this century has more value upon this subject, than his.

work of the law written in their hearts, their conscience bearing witness, and their thoughts accusing, in the day when God shall judge the secrets of men by Jesus Christ," Rom. 2:14, 15. "The Gentiles walk in the vanity of their mind, having the understanding darkened, being alienated from the life of God through the ignorance that is in them, because of the blindness of their heart, who being past feeling have given themselves over unto lasciviousness to work all uncleanness with greediness," Eph. 4:17. "Remember that ye being in time past Gentiles, were at that time without hope, and without God in the world," Eph. 2:11, 12. "Murderers, whoremongers, and idolaters, shall have their part in the lake of fire and brimstone: which is the second death," Rev. 21:8. Jesus Christ said from heaven to Saul of Tarsus, that he had appointed him to be "a minister and witness to the Gentiles, to open their eyes, to turn them from darkness to light, and from the power of Satan unto God, that they may receive forgiveness of sins and inheritance among them that are sanctified by faith," Acts 26:16–18. There is, consequently, no ground for asserting that justice and obligation require that the pardon of sins be tendered to the heathen in the next life.[1]

[1] "The distinction," says Müller (Sin, I 207), "between superable and insuperable ignorance will affect our calculation of the degree of guilt A man cannot be reproached on account of ignorance regarding things accidental and changeable, but to be ignorant of those fundamental truths whereof conscience informs him, and of their bearing upon conduct, is the sign of a sinful perversion of the inner life. If, from the moment when he first heard the voice of conscience, his aim always had been simply and solely to know what that voice tells him, and unconditionally to obey, there would be no sins of ignorance to be laid to his charge. But the sinfulness of human nature, in this respect, prevents our exculpating him thus from the guilt of particular sins. It is the unrighteousness of man that hinders the development of truth in his consciousness. Rom 1·18. And hence we find that savages, when they have been converted from the abominations of idolatry—from lust and murder, and unbridled selfish impulse—to the faith of Christ, never excuse themselves on the ground of ignorance, but in deep humiliation feel the reproaches of an awakened conscience St. Paul recognizes the mitigation of guilt in the case of the heathen, when he says regarding the χρόνοι τῆς ἀγνοίας (Acts 17 30), 'God over-

It does not follow, however, that because God is not obliged to offer pardon to the unevangelized heathen, either here or hereafter, therefore no unevangelized heathen are pardoned. The electing mercy of God reaches to the heathen. It is not the doctrine of the Church, that the entire mass of pagans, without exception, have gone down to endless impenitence and death. That some unevangelized men are saved, in the present life, by an extraordinary exercise of redeeming grace in Christ, has been the hope and belief of Christendom. It was the hope and belief of the elder Calvinists, as it is of the later.[1] The

looked them' But he by no means considers the sinful heathen to be free from guilt" For a powerful description of heathen depravity, see Thucydides History, II. 53, III. 82 And for a powerful specimen of human depravity, see the "Plebeian's Speech," in Machiavelli History of Florence, III iii

[1] The following extract from Witsius (Apostles' Creed, Dissertation II) exhibits the hopeful view which the elder Calvinism took of the possible extent to which God's decree of election reaches "Doctrines may be said to be necessary, either to salvation, or to religion, or to the church. A doctrine, without the knowledge and belief of which God does not save persons who have come to years of moral consciousness, is necessary to salvation; a doctrine, without the profession and practice of which no one can be considered religious, is necessary to religion, and a doctrine, without which no one is admitted to the communion of the visible church, is necessary to the church There may be articles without which persons ought not to be admitted to the fellowship of the church, that should not, for that reason, be regarded as absolutely essential either to religion or to salvation Although we might not dare to pronounce a sentence of condemnation against a particular man, we ought not, in defiance of order and discretion, to receive him forthwith into the bosom of our church, whatever sentiments he might hold, and to whatever sect he might belong And with respect to religion, what falls within the sphere of duty is manifest. But how far it may please a gracious God, or how far it may be possible for him in consistency with his perfections and character, to extend his forbearance to anyone, and *save his soul*, notwithstanding his errors and sins, or, in short, what are the lowest attainments without which no man is saved—who can tell? For this distinction in doctrines, I am indebted to the celebrated Hornbeck (Socinianismi Confutatio, tom I. p 209)

"Again, the *knowledge* of those doctrines which are necessary to salvation admits of various degrees. It is in different measures of clearness, abundance, and efficacy, that divine revelation, the means of grace, and the communications of the Spirit are enjoyed; and a corresponding diversity takes place in the degrees of knowledge which the saints attain In some it is clear, distinct, steady, and accompanied with a very firm and decided assent, in others it is more confused, more implicit and latent, subject to occasional wavering, and attended with an

Second Helvetic Confession (I. 7), after the remark that the ordinary mode of salvation is by the instrumentality of the written words, adds: "Agnoscimus, interim, deum illuminare posse homines etiam sine externo ministerio, quo et quando velit: id quod ejus potentiae est" The Westminster Confession (X. 3), after saying that "elect infants dying in infancy are regenerated and saved by Christ through the Spirit, who worketh when and where and how he pleaseth," adds, "so also are all other elect persons [regenerated and saved by Christ through the Spirit] who are incapable of being outwardly called by the ministry of the word." This is commonly understood to refer not merely,

---

assent that is yielded with difficulty. The command of God indeed lays an indispensable obligation upon all men to make every possible effort to attain a most clear, distinct, and assured knowledge of divine truth. It cannot, however, be questioned, that the Deity, in his unbounded goodness, receives many to the abodes of bliss whose knowledge even of the principal articles is very indistinct, and such as they are hardly capable of expressing in their own words. The smallest measure of the requisite knowledge appears to be this, namely that when an article of faith is *explained*, the mind so far at least apprehends it, as to recognize and *embrace* it as true

"Furthermore, *times* must be distinguished It admits of no doubt that under the bright dispensation of the Gospel, a more extensive and explicit knowledge is necessary to salvation than was required under the Old Testament economy, for it is reasonable that both knowledge, and the necessity of knowledge, should increase in proportion to the measure of revelation afforded Under the Old dispensation, nay, during the time of our Saviour's abode on the earth, *it was possible for a man to be a true believer, and in a state of grace, who was ignorant of the sufferings, the death, and the resurrection of Christ*, and who even presumed to object to the testimony of Christ himself respecting these momentous topics, as is clear from the instance of Peter (Matt 16. 21-23); or, who, though he believed in general in the Messiah, yet knew not that Jesus is the Christ, as appears from the history of Cornelius the centurion (Acts 10 2-4). No one, however, I suppose, would now acknowledge any person [in Christendom] as a true believer, who should discover ignorance of these truths respecting the Lord Jesus; and still less a person who should contradict them when represented to him On this subject, the remark of Thomas Aquinas (Secunda Secundae, I. 7) deserves to be quoted · 'The articles of faith,' says he, 'have increased with the lapse of time, not indeed with respect to the faith itself, but with respect to explicit and express profession. The same things which are believed explicitly, and under a greater number of articles by the saints in latter days, were all believed implicitly, and under a smaller number by the fathers in ancient times.'"

or mainly, to idiots and insane persons, but to such of the pagan world as God pleases to regenerate without the use of the written revelation. One of the strictest Calvinists of the sixteenth century, Zanchius, whose treatise on predestination was translated by Toplady, after remarking that many nations have never had the privilege of hearing the word, says (Ch. IV.) that "it is not indeed improbable that some individuals in these unenlightened countries may belong to the secret election of grace, and the habit of faith may be wrought in them." By the term "habit" (habitus), the elder theologians meant an inward disposition of the heart. The "habit of faith" involves penitence for sin, and the longing for its forgiveness and removal. The "habit of faith" is the broken and contrite heart, which expresses itself in the prayer, "God be merciful to me a sinner." It is certain that the Holy Ghost can produce, if he please, such a disposition and frame of mind in a pagan, without employing, as he commonly does, the written word. The case of the blind man, in John 9 : 36–38, is an example of the "habit of faith," though produced in this instance through the instrumentality of the written law. "Jesus saith unto him, Dost thou believe on the Son of God? He answered and said, *Who is he*, Lord, that I might believe on him? And Jesus said unto him, Thou hast both seen him, and it is he that talketh with thee. And he said, Lord, I believe And he worshipped him." Here was sorrow for sin, and a desire for redemption from it, wrought in the heart by the Divine Spirit, prior to the actual knowledge of Christ as the Saviour of sinners. The cases of the centurion Cornelius, and the Ethiopian eunuch, are also examples of the "habit of faith." These men, under the teaching of the Spirit, were conscious of sin, and were anxiously inquiring if, and how, it could be forgiven. That there is a class of persons in unevangelized heathendom who are the subjects of gracious influences of this kind, is implied in St. Paul's affirmation, that "they are not all Israel, which are of Israel," Rom. 9 : 6 ; and that "they which are of faith, the same are the children of Abraham," Gal. 3 : 7. It is taught also in Matt. 8 : 11 ; Luke 13 : 30 : "Many shall come from the east and west, and shall sit down with Abraham, and Isaac, and Jacob, in the kingdom of heaven, but the children of the kingdom [those who have had the written word] shall be cast out. And, behold, there are last which shall be first, and there are first which shall be last." This affirmation of Christ, was called out by the "habit of faith, or disposition to believe, in that Gentile centurion, respecting whom he said, "I have not found so great faith, no, not in Israel," Matt. 8 : 5–10.[1]

The true reason for hoping that an unevangelized heathen is saved is not that he was virtuous, but that he was *penitent.* A penitent man is necessarily virtuous; but a virtuous man is not necessarily penitent. Sorrow for sin produces morality; but morality does not produce sorrow for sin. A great error is committed at this point. The Senecas, the Antonines, the Plutarchs, and such like, have been singled out as the hopeful examples in paganism. It is not for man to decide what was the real state of the heart; but the *writings* of these men do not reveal the sense of sin; do not express penitence; do not show a craving for redemption There is too much egotism, self-consciousness, and self-righteousness in them. The man,

---

[1] "It is a very significant fact that the subject of the book of Ruth is a *heathen* woman, she is, indeed, the *third* heathen woman in the genealogy of David and Christ, being preceded by the Canaanitess Tamar (Gen 38) and the Canaanitess Rahab Ruth is the most noble of all, a consecrated flower of paganism turning with a longing desire to the light and salvation of Israel The fact that these three females are brought forward and ingrafted on the chosen line or family, conveys a very expressive lesson to the Israelites, abases their national pride, and bears testimony (by being both a fulfilment and a type) to all that had been promised to Abraham respecting his seed, namely, that in him should '*all* families of the earth be blessed,' Gen 12 . 3. Of those who are blessed in the seed of Abraham, Naomi represents the people of God who are to proceed from the ancient people of the covenant, and Ruth represents those proceeding from the heathen world" Kurtz Sacred History, § 66

judged by his books, is moral, but proud. He is virtuous, but plumes himself upon it. This is not a hopeful characteristic, when we are asking what are the prospects of a human soul, before the bar of God. "To this man will I look, saith the Lord, even to him that is poor, and of a contrite spirit, and trembleth at my word," Isa. 66:2. "Blessed are the poor in spirit; for theirs is the kingdom of heaven," Mat. 5:3.

This line of remark holds good in Christendom, as well as in Heathendom. There is a class of men in modern society marked by morality, and lofty self-respect, but by no consciousness of sin, and no confession of it. And judged by New Testament principles, no class of mankind is farther off from the kingdom of heaven. There is no class that scorns the publican's cry, and spurns the atoning blood, with such decision and energy as they. To them, the words of Christ, in a similar case, apply: "The publicans and the harlots go into the kingdom of heaven before you," Mark 21.31. The Magdalen is nearer the Divine Pity than the Pharisee. And upon the same principle, those benighted children of ignorance and barbarism who feel their sin and degradation, and are ready to listen with docility to the missionary when he comes with the tidings of the Infinite Compassion, are nearer to heaven, than the children of a gilded and heartless civilization, who have no moral unrest, and turn a deaf ear to all the overtures of mercy.[1]

This extraordinary work of the Holy Spirit is mentioned by the Redeemer, to illustrate the sovereignty of God in the exercise of mercy, not to guide his church in their evangelistic labor. His command is, to "preach the gospel to every creature." The extraordinary work of God is

---

[1] The passage, "In every nation, he that feareth God and worketh righteousness is accepted with him," Acts 10 35, is often explained as teaching that there are in every nation some who live virtuous and exemplary lives, and upon this ground obtain the rewards and blessedness of the future. This would be

not a thing for man to expect and rely upon, either in the kingdom of nature or of grace. It is his ordinary and established method which is to direct him. The law of missionary effort is, that "faith cometh by hearing, and hearing by the word of God," Rom. 11:17.

---

salvation by works, which is impossible, according to St. Paul. This is the error in the question put by Dante to the "eagle" (Paradise, xix. 66 sq ):

"A man
Is born on Indus' banks, and none is there
Who speaks of Christ, nor who doth read nor write;
And *all his inclinations and his acts,*
*As far as human reason sees, are good;*
And *he offendeth not in word or deed:*
But unbaptized he dies, and void of faith
Where is the justice that condemns him?"

This is an imaginary case of perfect obedience There is no such man.

It is with reference to such an interpretation of this text, that the Westminster Confession (X 4) asserts, that "men not professing the Christian religion cannot be saved in any other way whatever, be they never so diligent to frame their lives according to the light of nature and the law of that religion which they do profess," because their "diligence" is a *failure* The Thirty-nine Articles assert that no man, either in Christendom or Heathendom, can be saved by his morality and virtue "They also are to be had accursed that presume to say, that every man shall be saved by the law or sect which he professeth, so that he be diligent to frame his life according to the law, and the light of nature For Holy Scripture doth set out unto us only the name of Jesus Christ, whereby men must be saved" Article XVIII In the passage above cited, the phrase "fearer of God," and "worker of righteousness," is employed *technically*, by St. Peter, to denote *a man inquiring after the way of salvation*: somewhat as it was among the Jews, to signify a proselyte of the gate Guericke Church History, p 29. This is evident from the fact, that to this "devout" Cornelius who "feared God with all his house," Acts 10 2, the apostle preached Christ as the *Saviour of sinners*, "through whose name, whosoever believeth in him shall receive remission of sins," and that Cornelius believed, and was baptized. Acts 10 36–48 He would not have done this, had he expected that his "fearing God" and "working righteousness," in other words his own morality and virtue, would save him. In Acts 13 26, the "fearers of God" (οἱ φοβούμενοι τὸν θεὸν) are distinguished from "the stock of Abraham," or native-born Jews They were the proselytes of the gate Into this class of "fearers of God," fall the "devout Greeks" (οἱ σεβόμενοι Ἑλλῆνες), Acts 17 4, the "devout persons" (οἱ σεβόμενοι), Acts 17 17, and Lydia, "a worshipper of God" (σεβομένη τὸν θεὸν), Acts 16 14. Lydia went to the Jewish oratory (προσεύχη), in which the audience was divided into Jews and proselytes, each class occupying seats by themselves As examples of inquirers after salvation, take Augustine, and his friends Alypius and Nebridius. Confessions, VI. x.

Two errors, therefore, are to be avoided: First, that all men are saved; secondly, that only a few men are saved. Some fifty years ago, Schleiermacher surprised all Lutheran Germany with a defence of the Calvinistic doctrine of election; but the surprise was diminished, when it appeared that he held that God has elected, and will save, every human creature without exception. This cannot be squared with Scripture. On the other hand, some Calvinists have represented the number of the reprobated as greater than that of the elect, or equal to it.[1] They found this upon the words of Christ, "Many are called, but few are chosen." But this describes the situation at the time when our Lord spake, and not the final result of his redemptive work. Christ himself, in the days of his flesh, called many, but few responded to the call from his gracious lips. Our Lord's own preaching was not as successful as that of his apostles, and of many of his ministers. This was a part of his humiliation, and sorrow. But when Christ shall have "seen of the travail of his soul," and been "satisfied" with what he has seen; when the whole course of the gospel shall be complete, and shall be surveyed from beginning to end; it will be found that God's elect, or church, is "a great multitude which no man can number, out of *all* nations, and kindreds, and peoples, and tongues," and that their voice is as the voice of many waters, and as the voice of mighty thunderings, saying, "Hallelujah, for the Lord God omnipotent reigneth," Rev. 7:9; 19:6. The circle of God's election is a great circle of the heavens, and not that of a treadmill.

Respecting the more difficult case of infants: the Scriptures do not discriminate and except them as a class from the mass of mankind, but involve them in the common sin and condemnation. "Suffer little children to come unto me [their Redeemer]," Luke 18:16. "The promise [of salva-

[1] Compare Augustine: City of God, XXI xii.

tion] is unto you, and to your children," Acts 2 : 39. The fall in Adam explains their case. Adopting the Augustino-Calvinistic statement of this fall, it can then be said that infants, like all others of the human family, freely and responsibly "sinned in Adam, and fell with him in his first transgression." Westminster Shorter Catechism, 16. This is no more impossible, and no more of a mystery, in the case of infants than of adults. If it be conceded that the whole race apostatized in Adam, infants are righteously exposed to the punishment of sin, and have no claim upon the Divine mercy. The sin which brings condemnation upon them is original sin, and not actual transgressions. But original sin is the sinful inclination of the will. An infant has a rational soul; this soul has a will; this will is wrongly inclined; and wrong inclination is self-determined and punishable.[1] If sinful inclination in an adult needs to be expiated by the atoning blood of Christ, so does sinful inclination in an infant. Infants, consequently, sustain the very same relation to the mercy of God in Christ that the remainder of the human race do. They need the Divine clemency, like the rest of mankind. The "salvation" of infants supposes their prior damnation. Whoever asserts that an infant is "saved," by implication concedes that it is "lost." The salvation of an infant, like that of an adult, involves the remission and removal of sin, and depends upon the unmerited and optional grace of God. This being so, it cannot be said, that God would treat an infant unjustly, if he did not offer him salvation in the intermediate state. And upon the supposition, now common in the evangelical churches, that all infants dying in infancy, being elect, are "regenerated and saved by Christ through the Spirit, who worketh when, and where, and how he pleaseth" (West-

[1] "Quamvis infantes non sint legis capaces quoad actum, sunt tamen quoad habitum, utpote creaturae rationales, quibus lex praescribit omnimodam sanctitatem, tam habitualem quam actualem." Turrettin. Institutio, IX. i 9.

minster Confession, X. 3), there is no need of any such offer.[1]

## § 3. THE RATIONAL ARGUMENT.

The chief objections to the doctrine of Endless Punishment are not Biblical, but speculative. The great majority of students and exegetes find the tenet in the Hebrew and Greek Scriptures. Davidson, the most learned of English rationalistic critics, explicitly acknowledges that "if a specific sense be attached to words, never-ending misery is enunciated in the Bible. On the presumption that one doctrine is taught, it is the eternity of hell torments. Bad exegesis may attempt to banish it from the New Testament Scriptures, but it is still there, and expositors who wish to get rid of it, as Canon Farrar does, injure the cause they have in view by misrepresentation. It must be allowed that the New Testament record not only makes Christ assert everlasting punishment, but Paul and John. But the question should be looked at from a larger platform than single texts: in the light of God's attributes, and the nature of the soul. The destination of man, and the Creator's infinite goodness, conflicting as they do with everlasting punishment, remove it from the sphere of rational belief. If provision be not made in revelation for a change of moral character after death, it is made in reason. Philosophical considerations must not be set aside even by Scripture." Last Things, 133, 136, 151.

---

[1] Toplady, one of the highest Calvinists of the Church of England, remarks as follows, respecting the salvation of all infants dying in infancy: "The rubric of the Church of England declares that 'it is certain by God's word that children which are baptized, dying before they commit actual sin, are undoubtedly saved.' I believe firmly the same. Nay, I believe more. I am convinced that the souls of all departed infants whatever, whether baptized or unbaptized, are with God in glory. And I think my belief warranted by an authority which cannot err: Matt. 18:14." Church of England Vindicated. The elder Alexander remarks on this point: "As the Holy Scriptures have not informed us that any of the human family departing in infancy will be lost, we are permitted to hope that all such will be saved." Life, 585.

Consequently, after presenting the Biblical argument, for Endless Punishment, it becomes necessary to present the rational argument for it. So long as the controversy is carried on by an appeal to the Bible, the defender of endless retribution has comparatively an easy task. But when the appeal is made to human self-love and sentiment, or to ratiocination, the demonstration requires more effort. And yet the doctrine is not only Biblical, but rational. It is defensible on the basis of sound ethics and pure reason Nothing is requisite for its maintenance but the admission of three cardinal truths of theism: namely, that there is a just God; that man has free will; and that sin is voluntary action. If these are denied, there can be no defence of endless punishment—or of any other doctrine, except atheism and its corollaries.

The Bible and all the creeds of Christendom affirm man's free agency in sinning against God. The transgression which is to receive the endless punishment is *voluntary*. Sin, whether it be inward inclination or outward act, is unforced human agency. This is the uniform premise of Christian theologians of all schools. Endless punishment supposes the freedom of the human will, and is impossible without it. Could a man prove that he is necessitated in his murderous hate, and his murderous act, he would prove, in this very proof, that he ought not to be punished for it, either in time or eternity. Could Satan really convince himself that his moral character is not his own work, but that of God, or of nature, his remorse would cease, and his punishment would end. Self-determination runs parallel with hell.[1]

---

[1] Many of the arguments constructed against the doctrine of endless punishment proceed upon the supposition that original sin, or man's evil inclination, is the work of God that because man is *born* in sin (Ps 51 : 5), he was *created* in sin All the strength and plausibility of John Foster's celebrated letter lies in the assumption that the moral corruption and impotence of the sinner, whereby it is impossible for him to save himself from eternal death, is not self-originated and self-determined, but infused by his Maker "If," says he,

Guilt, then, is what is punished, and not misfortune. Free and not forced agency is what feels the stroke of justice. What, now, is this stroke? What do law and justice do when they *punish?* Everything depends upon the right answer to this question. The fallacies and errors of Universalism find their nest and hiding-place at this point. The true definition of punishment detects and excludes them.[1]

Punishment is neither chastisement nor calamity. Men suffer calamity, says Christ, not because they or their parents have sinned, "but that the works of God should be made manifest in them," John 9 : 3. Chastisement is inflicted in order to develop a good, but imperfect character already formed. "The Lord loveth whom he chasteneth," and "what son is he whom the earthly father chasteneth not?" Heb. 11 : 6, 7. Punishment, on the other hand, is retribution, and is not intended to do the work of either calamity or chastisement, but a work of its own. And this work is to vindicate law; to satisfy justice. Punishment, therefore, as distinguished from chastisement, is wholly *retrospective* in its primary aim. It looks back at what has been done in the past. Its first and great object is *requital.* A man is hung for murder, principally and before all other reasons, because he has voluntarily transgressed the law forbidding murder. He is not hung from a prospective aim, such as his own moral improvement, or for the purpose of deterring others from committing murder. The remark of the English judge to the horse-thief, in the days

"the very nature of man, as *created* by the Sovereign Power, be in such desperate disorder that there is no possibility of conversion and salvation except in instances where that Power interposes with a special and redeeming efficacy, how can we conceive that the main portion of the race, thus morally impotent (that is, really and absolutely impotent), will be eternally punished for the inevitable result of this moral impotence?" If this assumption of concreated depravity and impotence is correct, Foster's objection to eternal retribution is conclusive and fatal.

[1] For a discriminating and thorough statement of the aim of punishment, and its distinction from chastisement, see Muller. Sin, I. 244-251

when such theft was capitally punished, "You are not hung because you have stolen a horse, but that horses may not be stolen," has never been regarded as eminently judicial. It is true that personal improvement may be one consequence of the infliction of penalty. But the consequence must not be confounded with the purpose. Cum hoc non ergo propter hoc. The criminal may come to see and confess that his crime deserves its punishment, and in genuine unselfish penitence may take sides with the law, approve its retribution, and go into the presence of the Final Judge, relying upon that great atonement which satisfies eternal justice for sin; but even this, the greatest personal benefit of all, is not what is aimed at in man's punishment of the crime of murder. For should there be no such personal benefit as this attending the infliction of the human penalty, the one sufficient reason for inflicting it still holds good, namely, the fact that the law has been violated, and demands the death of the offender for this reason simply and only. "The notion of ill-desert and punishableness," says Kant (Praktische Vernunft, 151. Ed Rosenkranz), "is necessarily implied in the idea of voluntary transgression; and the idea of punishment excludes that of happiness in all its forms. For though he who inflicts punishment may, it is true, also have a benevolent purpose to produce by the punishment some good effect upon the criminal, yet the punishment must be justified, first of all, as pure and simple requital and retribution: that is, as a kind of suffering that is demanded by the law without any reference to its prospective beneficial consequences; so that even if no moral improvement and no personal advantage should subsequently accrue to the criminal, he must acknowledge that justice has been done to him, and that his experience is exactly conformed to his conduct. In every instance of punishment, properly so called, justice is the very first thing, and constitutes the essence of it. A benevolent purpose and a happy effect, it is true, may be conjoined with punishment; but the criminal cannot claim this as his due, and he has no right to reckon upon it All that he deserves is punishment, and this is all that he can expect from the law which he has transgressed." These are the words of as penetrating and ethical a thinker as ever lived.[1]

Neither is it true that the first and principal aim of punishment, in distinction from chastisement, is the protection of society, and the public good. This, like the personal benefit in the preceding case, is only secondary and incidental. The public good is not a sufficient reason for putting a man to death;[2] but the satisfaction of law is. This view of penalty is most disastrous in its influence, as well as false in its ethics. For if the good of the public is the true reason and object of punishment, the amount of it may be fixed by the end in view. The criminal may be made to suffer more than his crime deserves, if the public welfare, in suppressing this particular kind of crime, requires it. His personal desert and responsibility not being the one sufficient reason for his suffering, he may be made

---

[1] Beccaria and Bentham are the principal modern advocates of the contrary theory, viz that punishment is founded on utility and expediency. Beccaria's position is, that the standard of crime is the injury which it does to society He refers exclusively to the public good, and never appeals to the moral sentiment. Penny Cyclopaedia, Art Beccaria Bentham takes the same view, connecting it with the utilitarian ethics From these writers, this theory has passed considerably into modern jurisprudence Austin, a popular writer on law, follows Bentham

The theory which founds morality upon righteousness, and punishment upon justice, is historical Plato (Laws, X 904, 905) held that punishment is righteous and retributive Cicero (De Legibus, I 14 sq ) contends that true virtue has regard to essential justice, not to utility Grotius defines penalty as "the evil of suffering which is inflicted on account of the evil of doing" The great English jurists, Coke, Bacon, Selden, and Blackstone, explain punishment by crime, not by expediency Kant, Herbart, Stahl, Hartenstein, Rothe, and Woolsey, define punishment as requital for the satisfaction of law and justice Woolsey's Political Science, II viii Compare Coleridge Works, V 447

[2] Hence, those who found punishment upon utility, and deny that it is retributive, endeavor to abolish capital punishment. And if their theory of penalty is true, they are right in their endeavor.

to suffer as much as the public safety requires. It was this theory of penalty that led to the multiplication of capital offences. The prevention of forgery, it was once claimed in England, required that the forger should forfeit his life, and upon the principle that punishment is for the public protection, and not for strict and exact justice, an offence against human property was expiated by human life. Contrary to the Noachic statute, which punishes only murder with death, this statute weighed out man's life-blood against pounds, shillings, and pence. On this theory, the number of capital offences become very numerous, and the criminal code very bloody. So that, in the long run, nothing is kinder than exact justice. It prevents extremes in either direction: either that of indulgence or that of cruelty.[1]

This theory breaks down, from whatever point it be looked at. Suppose that there were but one person in the universe. If he should transgress the law of God, then, upon the principle of expediency as the ground of penalty, this solitary subject of moral government could not be punished: that is, visited with a suffering that is purely retributive, and not exemplary or corrective. His act has not injured the public, for there is no public. There is no need of his suffering as an example to deter others, for there are no others. But upon the principle of justice, in distinction from expediency, this solitary subject of moral government could be punished.

The vicious ethics of this theory of penalty expresses itself in the demoralizing maxim, "It is better that ten guilty men should escape than that one innocent man should suffer." But this is no more true than the converse, "It is better that ten innocent men should suffer than that one guilty man should escape." It is a choice of equal evil and equal injustice. In either case alike, justice is tram-

[1] See the remarks of Graves (Pentateuch, II. ii.), upon the excellence of the Mosaic code in this particular.

pled down In the first supposed case there are eleven instances of injustice and wrong; and in the last supposed case there are likewise eleven instances of injustice and wrong. Unpunished guilt is precisely the same species of evil with punished innocence. To say, therefore, that it is better that ten guilty persons should escape than that one innocent man should suffer, is to say that it is better that there should be ten wrongs than one wrong against justice. The maxim assumes that the punishment of the guilty is not of so much consequence as the immunity of the innocent. But the truth is, that both are equally required by justice.

The theory that punishment is retributive, honors human nature, but the theory that it is merely expedient and useful degrades it. If justice be the true ground of penalty, man is treated as a person; but if the public good is the ground, he is treated as a chattel or a thing. When suffering is judicially inflicted because of the intrinsic gravity and real demerit of crime, man's free will and responsibility are recognized and put in the foreground; and these are his highest and distinguishing attributes. The sufficient reason for his suffering is found wholly within his own person, in the exercise of self-determination. He is not seized by the magistrate and made to suffer for a reason extraneous to his own agency, and for the sake of something lying wholly outside of himself—namely, the safety and happiness of others—but because of his own act. He is not handled like a brute or an inanimate thing that may be put to good use; but he is recognized as a free and voluntary person, who is not punished because punishment is expedient and useful, but because it is just and right; not because the public safety requires it, but because he owes it. The dignity of the man himself, founded in his lofty but hazardous endowment of free will, is acknowledged.

Supposing it, now, to be conceded, that future punishment is retributive in its essential nature, it follows that it must be endless from the nature of the case. For, suffering must continue as long as the reason for it continues. In this respect, it is like law, which lasts as long as its reason lasts: ratione cessante, cessat ipsa lex. Suffering that is educational and corrective may come to an end, because moral infirmity, and not guilt, is the reason for its infliction; and moral infirmity may cease to exist. But suffering that is penal can never come to an end, because guilt is the reason for its infliction, and guilt once incurred never ceases to be. The lapse of time does not convert guilt into innocence, as it converts moral infirmity into moral strength; and therefore no time can ever arrive when the guilt of the criminal will cease to deserve and demand its retribution. The reason for retribution to-day is a reason forever. Hence, when God disciplines and educates his children, he causes only a temporary suffering In this case, "He will not keep his anger forever," Ps 103:9. But when, as the Supreme Judge, he punishes rebellious and guilty subjects of his government, he causes an endless suffering. In this case, "their worm dieth not, and the fire is not quenched," Mark 9:48.

The real question, therefore, is, whether God ever *punishes.* That he chastises, is not disputed. But does he ever inflict a suffering that is not intended to reform the transgressor, and does not reform him, but is intended simply and only to vindicate law, and satisfy justice, by requiting him for his transgression? Revelation teaches that he does. "Vengeance is mine; I will repay, saith the Lord," Rom. 12:19 "Vengeance belongeth unto me, I will recompense, saith the Lord," Heb. 10:30. Retribution is here asserted to be a function of the Supreme Being, and his alone. The creature has no right to punish, except as he is authorized by the Infinite Ruler. "The powers that be are ordained of God. The ruler is the minister of God, an avenger to execute wrath upon him that doeth evil," Rom. 13:1, 4. The power which civil government has to punish crime—the private person having no such power—is only a delegated right from the Source of retribution. Natural religion, as well as revealed, teaches that God inflicts upon the voluntary transgressor of law a suffering that is purely vindicative of law. The pagan sages enunciate the doctrine, and it is mortised into the moral constitution of man, as is proved by his universal fear of retribution. The objection, that a suffering not intended to reform, but to satisfy justice, is cruel and unworthy of God, is refuted by the question of St. Paul: "Is God unrighteous who taketh vengeance? God forbid: for how then shall God *judge* the world?" Rom. 3: 5, 6. It is impossible either to found or administer a government, in heaven or upon earth, unless the power to punish crime is conceded.

The endlessness of future punishment, then, is implied in the endlessness of guilt and condemnation. When a crime is condemned, it is absurd to ask, "How long is it condemned?" The verdict "Guilty for ten days" was Hibernian Damnation means absolute and everlasting damnation. All suffering in the next life, therefore, of which the sufficient and justifying reason is guilt, must continue as long as the reason continues; and the reason is everlasting If it be righteous to-day, in God's retributive justice, to smite the transgressor because he violated the law yesterday, it is righteous to do the same thing to-morrow, and the next day, and so on ad infinitum; because the state of the case ad infinitum remains unaltered. The guilt incurred yesterday is a standing and endless fact. What, therefore, guilt legitimates this instant, it legitimates every instant, and forever.

The demand that penal suffering shall stop when it has once begun, is as irrational as the demand that guilt shall stop when it has once begun. The *continuous* nature of guilt necessitates the endlessness of retribution. A man, for illustration, is guilty of profanity to-day. God, we will suppose, immediately begins to cause him to suffer in his mind, as the righteous requital for his transgression of the third commandment. The transgressor immediately begins to feel remorse for his sin. Why, upon principles of justice, should he feel remorse for his profanity to-day, and not feel it to-morrow? Why should he feel it to-morrow, and not feel it a million years hence? Why should he feel it a million years hence, and not feel it forever? At what point should remorse stop? If we suppose the state of the case to be unchanged; if we suppose no penitence for the profanity, and no appropriation of the only atonement that cancels guilt; then the mental suffering which the profanity deserves and experiences now, it always must deserve and experience. The same reasoning will apply to whatever suffering besides remorse enters into the sum-total of future punishment.[1]

Again, the endlessness of punishment follows from the *indivisibility* of guilt. The nature of guilt is such that it cannot be divided up and distributed in parts along a length of time, and be expiated in parts, but is concentrated whole and entire at each and every point of time. The guilt of the sin of profanity does not rest upon the transgressor, one part of it at twelve o'clock, and another part of it at half-past twelve, and another part of it at one o'clock, and so on. The *whole* infinite guilt of this act of sin against

---

[1] The intrinsic endlessness of guilt is vividly described by Carlyle. "From the purpose of crime to the act of crime there is an abyss, wonderful to think of. The finger lies on the pistol, but the man is not yet a murderer nay, his whole nature staggering at such a consummation, is there not a confused pause rather—one last instant of possibility for him? Not yet a murderer, it is at the mercy of light trifles whether the most fixed idea may not yet become unfixed. One slight twitch of a muscle, the death-flash bursts, and he is *it*, and will for Eternity be it, and Earth has become a penal Tartarus for him; his horizon girdled now not with golden hope, but with red flames of remorse, voices from the depths of Nature sounding, Woe, woe on him! Of such stuff are we all made, on such powder-mines of bottomless guilt and criminality—'if God restrained not,' as is well said—does the purest of us walk? There are depths in man that go to the length of lowest Hell, as there are heights that reach highest Heaven—for are not both Heaven and Hell made out of him, made by him, everlasting miracle and mystery as he is?" French Revolution, III. i. 4.

God lies upon the sinner at each and every instant of time. He is no more guilty of the supposed act, at half-past twelve, than at twelve, and equally guilty at both these instants. Consequently, the *whole* infinite penalty can justly be required at any and every moment of time. Yet the whole penalty cannot be paid at any and every moment by the suffering of that single moment. The transgressor at any and every point in his endless existence is infinitely guilty, and yet cannot cancel his guilt by what he endures at a particular point. Too long a punishment of guilt is thus an impossibility The suffering of the criminal can never overtake the crime. And the only way in which justice can approximately obtain its dues, is by a never-ceasing infliction. We say approximately, because, tested strictly, the endless suffering of a finite being is not strictly infinite suffering; while the guilt of sin against God is strictly infinite. There is, therefore, no over-punishment in endless punishment.[1]

It will be objected that though the guilt and damnation of a crime be endless, it does not follow that the suffering inflicted on account of it must be endless also, even though it be retributive and not reformatory in its intent. A human judge pronounces a theft to be endlessly a theft, and a thief to be endlessly a thief, but he does not sentence the thief to an endless suffering, though he sentences him to a penal suffering. But this objection overlooks the fact

[1] It must be remembered, that it is the *degree*, together with the endlessness of suffering, that constitutes the justice of it. We can conceive of an endless suffering that is marked by little intensity in the degree of it Such, according to Augustine, is the suffering of unbaptized infants (mitissima omnium) It is negative banishment, not positive infliction. An evil that is inflicted in a few hours may be greater than one inflicted in endless time One day of such torment as that of Satan would be a greater distress, than a slight physical pain lasting forever. The infinite incarnate God suffered more agony in Gethsemane, than the whole finite human race could suffer in endless duration Consequently the uniformity in the endlessness must be combined with a variety in the intensity of suffering, in order to adjust the future punishment to the different grades of sin. See Soteriology, pp 461, 462.

that human punishment is only approximate and imperfect, not absolute and perfect like the Divine. It is not adjusted exactly and precisely to the *whole* guilt of the offence, but is more or less modified, first, by not considering its relation to God's honor and majesty; secondly, by human ignorance of the inward motives; and, thirdly, by social expediency. Earthly courts and judges look at the transgression of law with reference only to man's temporal relations, not his eternal. They punish an offence as a crime against the State, not as a sin against God. Neither do they look into the human heart, and estimate crime in its absolute and intrinsic nature, as does the Searcher of hearts and the Omniscient Judge.[1] A human tribunal punishes mayhem, we will say, with six months' imprisonment, because it does not take into consideration either the malicious and wicked anger that prompted the maiming, or the dishonor done to the Supreme Being by the transgression of his commandment. But Christ, in the final assize, punishes this offence endlessly, because his all-seeing view includes the sum-total of guilt in the case: namely, the inward wrath, the outward act, and the relation of both to the infinite perfection and adorable majesty of God. The human tribunal does not punish the inward anger at all; the Divine tribunal punishes it with hell fire: "For whosoever shall say to his brother, Thou fool, is in danger of hell fire," Matt. 5:22. The human tribunal punishes seduction with a pecuniary fine, because it does not take cognizance of the selfish and heartless lust that prompted it, or of the affront offered to that Immaculate Holiness which from Sinai proclaimed, "Thou shalt not commit adultery." But the Divine tribunal punishes se-

[1] "Human laws," says Paley (Moral Philosophy, I. iii.), "omit many duties, such as piety to God, bounty to the poor, forgiveness of injuries, education of children, gratitude to benefactors. And they permit, or, which is the same thing, suffer to go unpunished, many crimes, such as luxury, prodigality, caprice in the disposition of property by will, disrespect to parents, and a multitude of similar examples."

duction with an infinite suffering, because of its more comprehensive and truthful view of the whole transaction. And, in addition to all this imperfection in human punishment, the human tribunal may be influenced by prejudice and sefishness.

> "In the corrupted currents of this world,
> Offence's gilded hand may shove by justice;
> And oft 'tis seen, the wicked prize itself
> Buys out the law. But 'tis not so above.
> There is no shuffling, there the action lies
> In his true nature; and we ourselves compelled
> Even to the teeth and forehead of our faults,
> To give in evidence"—HAMLET, III. iv.

Again, human punishment, unlike the Divine, is variable and inexact, because it is to a considerable extent *reformatory* and *protective*. Human government is not intended to do the work of the Supreme Ruler. The sentence of an earthly judge is not a substitute for that of the last day. Consequently, human punishment need not be marked, even if this were possible, with all that absoluteness and exactness of justice which characterizes the Divine. Justice in the human sphere may be relaxed by expediency. Human punishment may sometimes be more severe, and sometimes less severe, than exact requital demands, but Divine punishment may not be. The retributive element must, indeed, enter into human punishment; for no man may be punished by a human tribunal unless he deserves punishment: unless he is a criminal. But retribution is not the *sole* element when man punishes. Man, while not overlooking the guilt in the case, has some reference to the reformation of the offender, and still more to the protection of society. Here, in time, the transgressor is capable of reformation, and society needs protection. Hence civil expediency and social utility modify exact and strict retribution.

For the sake of reforming the criminal, the judge sometimes inflicts a penalty that is less than the real guilt of the offence. For the sake of shielding society, the court sometimes sentences the criminal to a suffering greater than his crime deserves. Human tribunals, also, vary the punishment for the same offence: sometimes punishing forgery capitally, and sometimes not; sometimes sentencing those guilty of the same kind of theft to one year's imprisonment, and sometimes to two.

But the Divine tribunal, in the last great day, is invariably and exactly just, because it is *neither reformatory nor protective.* In eternity, the sinner is so hardened as to be incorrigible, and heaven is impregnable. Hell, therefore, is not a penitentiary. It is righteous retribution, pure and simple, unmodified by considerations either of utility to the criminal, or of safety to the universe. In the day of final account, penalty will not be unjustly mild for the sake of the transgressor, nor unjustly severe for the sake of society. Christ will not punish incorrigible men and devils (for the two receive the same sentence, and go to the same place, Matt. 25 : 41), for the purpose of reforming them, or of screening the righteous from the wicked, but of satisfying the broken law. His punishment at that time will be nothing but just requital. The Redeemer of men is also the Eternal Judge; the Lamb of God is also the Lion of the tribe of Judah; and his righteous word to wicked and hardened Satan, to wicked and hardened Judas, to wicked and hardened pope Alexander VI., will be: "Vengeance is mine; I will repay. Depart from me, ye cursed, that work iniquity," Rom. 12 : 19; Matt. 25 : 41; 7 : 23. "The Lord Jesus shall be revealed from heaven, with his mighty angels, in flaming fire, taking vengeance on them that know not God, and that obey not the gospel," 2 Thess. 1 : 7, 8. The wicked will receive their desert, and reap according as they have sown. The suffering will be unerringly adjusted to the intrinsic guilt: no greater and no less than the sin deserves. "That servant which knew his lord's will [clearly], and did not according to his will, shall be beaten with many stripes; but he that knew not [clearly], and did commit things worthy of stripes, shall be beaten with few stripes. As many as have sinned without [written] law, shall also perish without [written] law; and as many as have sinned under [written] law, shall be judged by the [written] law," Luke 12:47, 48; Rom. 2:12.

It is because the human court, by reason of its ignorance both of the human heart and the true nature of sin against a spiritual law and a holy God, cannot do the perfect work of the Divine tribunal, that human laws and penalties are only provisional, and not final. Earthly magistrates are permitted to modify and relax penalty, and pass a sentence which, though adapted to man's earthly circumstances, is not absolute and perfect, and is finally to be revised and made right by the omniscient accuracy of God. The human penalty that approaches nearest to the Divine, is capital punishment. There is more of the purely retributive element in this than in any other. The reformatory element is wanting. And this punishment has a kind of endlessness. Death is a finality. It forever separates the murderer from earthly society, even as future punishment separates forever from the society of God and heaven.

The difference between human and divine punishment is well stated by Paley (Moral Philosophy, VI. ix): "The proper end of human punishment is not the [exact] satisfaction of justice, but the prevention of crimes. By the satisfaction of justice, I mean the retribution of so much pain for so much guilt; which is the dispensation we expect at the hand of God, and which we are accustomed to consider as the order of things that perfect justice requires. Crimes are not by any government punished in proportion to their [exact] guilt, nor in all cases ought to be so, but in proportion to the difficulty and the necessity of preventing them The crime must be prevented by some means or other; and consequently whatever means appear necessary to this end, whether they be proportionable to the [exact] guilt of the criminal or not, are adopted rightly. It is in pursuance of this principle, which pervades indeed the whole system of penal jurisprudence, that the facility with which any species of crime is perpetrated has been generally deemed a reason for aggravating the punishment. This severity would be absurd and unjust, if the [exact] guilt of the offender was the immediate cause and measure of the punishment.

On the other hand, from the justice of God we are taught to look for a gradation of punishment exactly proportioned to the guilt of the offender. When, therefore, in assigning the degrees of human punishment we introduce considerations distinct from that of guilt, and a proportion so varied by external circumstances that equal crimes frequently undergo unequal punishments, or the less crime the greater, it is natural to demand the reason why a different measure of punishment should be expected from God: why that rule which befits the absolute and perfect justice of the deity should not be the rule which ought to be preserved and imitated by human laws. The solution of this difficulty must be sought for, in those peculiar attributes of the Divine nature which distinguish the dispensations of Supreme wisdom from the proceedings of human judicature. A Being whose knowledge penetrates every concealment; from the operation of whose will no act or flight can escape; and in whose hands punishment is sure: such a Being may conduct the moral government of his creation in the best and wisest manner, by pronouncing a law that every crime shall finally receive a punishment proportioned to the guilt which it contains, *abstracted from any foreign consideration whatever*, and may testify his veracity to the spectators of his judgments, by carrying this law into strict execution. But when the care of the public safety is intrusted to men whose authority over their fellow-creatures is limited by defects of power and knowledge; from whose utmost vigilance and sagacity the greatest offenders often lie hid; whose wisest precautions and speediest pursuit may be eluded by artifice or concealment; a different necessity, a new rule of proceeding results from the very imperfection of their faculties. In their hands, the uncertainty of punishment must be compensated by the severity. The ease with which crimes are committed or concealed, must be counteracted by additional penalties and increased terrors. The very end for which human government is established requires that its regulations be adapted to the suppression of crimes. This end, whatever it may do in the plans of Infinite Wisdom, does not, in the designation of temporal penalties, always coincide with the proportionate punishment of guilt." Blackstone, also (Com. IV. i.), alludes to the same difference in the following words: "The end, or final cause of human punishments, is not atonement or expiation for the crime committed; for that must be left to the just determination of the Supreme Being."

The argument thus far goes to prove that retribution in distinction from correction, or punishment in distinction from chastisement, is endless from the nature of the case: that is, from the nature of guilt. We pass, now, to prove that it is also rational and right.

1. Endless punishment is rational, in the first place, because it is supported by the human conscience. The sinner's own conscience will "bear witness" and approve of the condemning sentence, "in the day when God shall judge the secrets of men by Jesus Christ," Rom. 2 · 16. Dives, in the parable, when reminded of the justice of his suffering, is silent. Accordingly, all the evangelical creeds say with the Westminster Larger Catechism (89), that "the wicked, upon clear evidence and full conviction of their own consciences, shall have the just sentence of condemnation pronounced against them." If in the great day there are any innocent men who have no accusing con-

sciences, they will escape hell. We may accommodate St. Paul's words (Rom. 13:3, 4), and say: "The final judgment is not a terror to good works, but to evil. Wilt thou, then, not be afraid of the final judgment? Keep the law of God perfectly, without a single slip or failure, inwardly or outwardly, and thou shalt have praise of the same. But if thou do that which is evil, be afraid." But a sentence that is justified by the highest and best part of the human constitution must be founded in reason, justice, and truth. It is absurd to object to a judicial decision that is confirmed by the man's own immediate consciousness of its righteousness.

> "For what, my small philosopher, is hell?
> 'Tis nothing but full knowledge of the truth,
> When truth, resisted long, is sworn our foe:
> And calls eternity to do her right."—YOUNG.

The opponent of endless retribution does not draw his arguments from the impartial conscience, but from the bias of self-love and desire for happiness. His objections are not ethical, but sentimental. They are not seen in the dry light of pure truth and reason, but through the colored medium of self-indulgence and love of ease and sin.

Again, a guilty conscience expects endless punishment. There is in it what the Scripture denominates "the fearful looking-for of judgment, and fiery indignation, which shall devour the adversaries" of God, Heb. 10:27. This is the awful apprehension of an evil that is to last forever; otherwise, it would not be so "fearful." The knowledge that future suffering will one day cease would immediately relieve the apprehension of the sinner. A guilty conscience is in its very nature hopeless. Impenitent men, in their remorse, "sorrow as those who have no hope," 1 Thess. 4:13. Unconverted Gentiles "have no hope, and are without God in the world," Eph. 2:12. "The hope of the wicked shall be as the giving up of the ghost," Job 11:20.

"The hypocrite's hope shall perish," Job 8:13. Consequently, the great and distinguishing element in hell-torment is despair, a feeling that is impossible in any man or fallen angel who knows that he is finally to be happy forever. Despair results from the endlessness of retribution. No endlessness, no despair.[1] Natural religion, as well as revealed, teaches the despair of some men in the future life. Plato (Gorgias, 525), Pindar (Olympia, II.), Plutarch (De sera vindicta), describe the punishment of the incorrigibly wicked as eternal and hopeless.

In Scripture, there is no such thing as *eternal* hope. Hope is a characteristic of earth and time only. Here in this life, all men may hope for forgiveness. "Turn, ye prisoners of hope," Zech. 9:2. "Now is the accepted time; now is the day of salvation," 2 Cor. 6:2. But in the next world, there is no hope of any kind, because there is either fruition or despair. The Christian's hope is converted into its realization: "For what a man seeth, why doth he yet hope for it?" Rom. 8:24.

"Soon shall close thine earthly mission,
Soon shall pass thy pilgrim days;
Hope shall change to glad fruition,
Faith to sight, and prayer to praise."

---

[1] "If," says Pearson (Creed, Art V), "we should imagine any damned soul to have received an express promise of God, that after ten thousand years he would release him from those torments and make him everlastingly happy, and to have a true faith in that promise and a firm hope of receiving eternal life, we could not say that that man was in the same condition with the rest of the damned, or that he felt all that hell which they were sensible of, or all that pain which was due unto his sins; because hope, and confidence, and relying upon God, would not only mitigate all other pains, but wholly take away the bitter anguish of despair." It is obvious, that if God makes any such promise in his word, either expressly, or by implication, despair is not only impossible to the believer of Scripture, but is a *sin*. No man should despair And if God does not make any such promise, but man makes it to his fellow-sinner, in saying, as Satan did to Eve, "Thou shalt not surely die," and the human promise is believed, the effect will be the same There will be no despair, until the reckless human falsehood is corrected by the awful demonstration at death.

And the impenitent sinner's hope of heaven is converted into despair. Canon Farrar's phrase "eternal hope" is derived from Pandora's box, not from the Bible. Dante's legend over the portal of hell is the truth: "All hope abandon, ye who enter here."[1]

That the conscience supports endless retribution, is also evinced by the universality and steadiness of the dread of it. Mankind believe in hell, as they believe in the Divine Existence, by reason of their moral sense Notwithstanding all the attack made upon the tenet in every generation, by a fraction of every generation, men do not get rid of their fear of future punishment. Skeptics themselves are sometimes distressed by it. But a permanent and general fear among mankind cannot be produced by a mere chimera, or a pure figment of the imagination. Men have no fear of Rhadamanthus, nor can they be made to fear him, because they know that there is no such being. "An idol is nothing in the world," 1 Cor. 8:4. But men have "the fearful looking-for of judgment" from the lips of God, ever and always. If the Biblical hell were as much a nonenity as the heathen Atlantis, no one would waste his time in endeavoring to prove its non-existence. What man would seriously construct an argument to demonstrate that there is no such being as Jupiter Ammon, or such an animal as the centaur? The very denial of endless retribution evinces by its spasmodic eagerness and effort to disprove the tenet, the firmness with which it is entrenched in man's moral constitution. If there really were no hell, absolute indifference toward the notion would long since have been the

[1] The words of Paul, in 1 Cor. 13·13, are sometimes cited to prove the eternity of hope, because it "abides" But in this passage, "faith, hope, and charity" are contrasted with the supernatural charismata of chapter 12 These latter are transitory, but the former "abide," because they are essential to the Christian life here upon earth. But in respect to the eternity of "faith," St Paul teaches that it is converted into "sight," 2 Cor 5·7, and that "hope" is converted into "fruition," Rom 8·24 Charity is "greater" than faith and hope, because it is not changed into something else, but is eternal

mood of all mankind, and no arguments, either for or against it, would be constructed.

And finally, the demand, even here upon earth, for the punishment of the intensely and incorrigibly wicked, proves that retribution is grounded in the human conscience. When abominable and satanic sin is temporarily triumphant, as it sometimes has been in the history of the world, men cry out to God for his vengeance to come down. "If there were no God, we should be compelled to invent one," is now a familiar sentiment. "If there were no hell, we should be compelled to invent one," is equally true. When examples of depravity occur, man cries: "How long, O Lord, how long?" The non-infliction of retribution upon hardened villany and successful cruelty causes anguish in the moral sense. For the expression of it, read the imprecatory psalms and Milton's sonnet on the Massacre in Piedmont.

2. In the second place, endless punishment is rational, because of the endlessness of sin. If the preceding view of the relation of penalty to guilt be correct, endless punishment is just, without bringing the sin of the future world into the account. Man incurs everlasting punishment for "the things done in his body," 2 Cor 5:10. Christ sentences men to perdition, not for what they are going to do in eternity, but for what they have already done in time. It is not necessary that a man should commit all kinds of sin, or that he should sin a very long time, in order to be a sinner "Whosoever shall keep the whole law, and yet offend in one point, he is guilty of all," Jas. 2:10. One sin makes guilt, and guilt makes hell.[1]

But while this is so, it is a fact to be observed that sin is

---

[1] "O fearful thought! one act of sin  
Within itself contains  
The power of endless hate of God,  
And everlasting pains."  
FABER Hymn on Predestination.

actually being added to sin, in the future life, and the amount of guilt is accumulating. The lost spirit is "treasuring up wrath," Rom. 2:5. Hence, there are degrees in the intensity of endless suffering. The difference in the grade arises from the greater resoluteness of the wicked self-determination, and the greater degree of light that was enjoyed upon earth. He who sins against the moral law as it is drawn out in the Sermon on the Mount, sins more determinedly and desperately than the pagan who sins against the light of nature. There are probably no men in paganism who sin so wilfully and devilishly as some men in Christendom. Profanity, or the blaspheming of God, is a Christian and not a Heathen characteristic.[1] They are Christian peoples who force opium and rum on helpless pagans. These degrees of sin call for degrees of suffering. And there are degrees in future suffering, because it is infinite in duration only. In intensity, it is finite. Consequently, the lost do not all suffer precisely alike, though all suffer the same length of time. A thing may be infinite in one respect and finite in others. A line may be infinite in length, and not in breadth and depth. A surface may be infinite in length and breadth, and not in depth. And two persons may suffer infinitely in the sense of endlessly, and yet one experience more pain than the other.

The endlessness of sin results, first, from the nature and energy of sinful self-determination. Sin is the creature's act solely God does not work in the human will when it wills antagonistically to him. Consequently, self-determination to evil is an extremely vehement activity of the will. There is no will so wilful as a wicked will. Sin is stubborn and obstinate in its nature, because it is enmity and re-

[1] It is related of Dr Scudder, that on his return from his mission in India, after a long absence, he was standing on the deck of a steamer, with his son, a youth, when he heard a person using loud and profane language "See, friend," said the doctor, accosting the swearer, "this boy, my son, was born and brought up in a heathen country, and a land of pagan idolatry, but in all his life he never heard a man blaspheme his Maker until now."

bellion. Hence, wicked will intensifies itself perpetually. Pride, left to itself, increases and never diminishes. Enmity and hatred become more and more satanic. "Sin," says South, "is the only perpetual motion which has yet been found out, and needs nothing but a beginning to keep it incessantly going on." Upon this important point, Aristotle, in the seventh book of his Ethics, reasons with great truth and impressiveness. He distinguishes between *ἀκολασία* and *ἀκρασία*; between strong will to wickedness, and weak self-indulgence. The former is viciousness from deliberation and preference, and implies an intense determination to evil in the man. He goes wrong, not so much from the pull of appetite and passion, as purposely, knowingly, and energetically. He has great strength of will, and he puts it all forth in resolute wickedness. The latter quality is more the absence than the presence of will; it is the weakness and irresolution of a man who has no powerful self-determination of any kind. The condition of the former of these two men, Aristotle regarded as worse than that of the latter. He considered it to be desperate and hopeless. The evil is incurable. Repentance and reformation are impossible to this man; for the wickedness in this instance is not mere appetite; it is a principle; it is cold-blooded and total depravity.

Another reason for the endlessness of sin is the bondage of the sinful will. In the very act of transgressing the law of God, there is a reflex action of the human will upon itself, whereby it becomes unable to perfectly keep that law. Sin is the suicidal action of the human will. A man is not forced to kill himself; but if he does, he cannot bring himself to life again. And a man is not forced to sin, but if he does, he cannot of himself get back where he was before sinning. He cannot get back to innocency, nor can he get back to holiness of heart. The effect of vicious habit in diminishing a man's ability to resist temptation is proverbial. An old and hardened debauchee, like Tiberius or

Louis Fifteenth, just going into the presence of Infinite Purity, has not so much power of active resistance against the sin that has now ruined him, as the youth has who is just beginning to run that awful career. The truth and fact is, that sin, in and by its own nature and operation, tends to destroy all virtuous force, all holy energy, in any moral being. The excess of will to sin is the same thing as defect of will to holiness. The human will cannot be forced and ruined from without. But if we watch the influence of the will upon itself; the influence of its own wrong decisions, and its own yielding to temptations; we shall find that the voluntary faculty may be ruined from within; may surrender itself with such an absorbing vehemence and totality to appetite, passion, and selfishness, that it becomes unable to reverse itself and overcome its own inclination and self-determination. And yet, from beginning to end, there is no compulsion in this process. The transgressor follows himself alone. He has his own way, and does as he likes. Neither God, nor the world, nor Satan, forces him either to be, or to do, evil. Sin is the most spontaneous of self-motion. But self-motion has consequences as much as any other motion. And moral bondage is one of them. "Whosoever committeth sin is the slave of sin," says Christ, John 8:35.

The culmination of this bondage is seen in the next life. The sinful propensity, being allowed to develop unresisted and unchecked, slowly but surely eats out all virtuous force as rust eats out a steel spring, until in the awful end the will becomes all habit, all lust, and all sin. "Sin, when it is finished, bringeth forth death," Jas. 1:15. In the final stage of this process, which commonly is not reached until death, when "the spirit returns unto God who gave it," the guilty free agent reaches that dreadful condition where resistance to evil ceases altogether, and surrender to evil becomes demoniacal The cravings and hankerings of long-indulged and unresisted sin become organic, and drag the man; and "he goeth after them as an ox goeth to the slaughter, or as a fool to the correction of the stocks, till a dart strike through his liver," Prov. 7:22, 23. For though the will to resist sin may die out of a man, the conscience to condemn it never can. This remains eternally. And when the process is complete; when the responsible creature, in the abuse of free agency, has perfected his moral ruin, and his will to good is all gone; there remain these two in his immortal spirit: sin and conscience, "brimstone and fire," Rev. 21:8.

Still another reason for the endlessness of sin, is the fact that rebellious enmity toward law and its Source is not diminished, but increased, by the righteous punishment experienced by the impenitent transgressor. Penal suffering is beneficial only when it is humbly accepted, is acknowledged to be deserved, and is penitently submitted to; when the transgressor says, "Father, I have sinned, and am no more worthy to be called thy son; make me as one of thy hired servants," Luke 15:18, 19; when, with the penitent thief, he says, "We are in this condemnation justly; for we receive the due reward of our deeds," Luke 23:41. But when in this life retribution is denied and jeered at; and when in the next life it is complained of and resisted, and the arm of hate and defiance is raised against the tribunal; penalty hardens and exasperates. This is impenitence. Such is the temper of Satan; and such is the temper of all who finally become his associates. This explains why there is no repentance in hell, and no meek submission to the Supreme Judge. This is the reason why Dives, the impenitent sensualist, on discovering that there is no reformation in Hades, asks that Lazarus may be sent to warn his five brethren, "lest they also come into this place of torment."[1]

---

[1] Müller (Sin, I 240) exposes the error of supposing that punishment is remedial in its nature, and adapted to produce penitence and reformation, in the following terms: "The distinctive purpose of divine punishment cannot be the

3. In the third place, endless punishment is rational, because sin is an infinite evil: infinite, not because committed by an infinite being, but against one. We reason invari-

---

improvement of the person punished, because this is the object of *redemption* If punishment were the means appropriate to this end, there would be no need for redemption, or rather, if this object is attained by redemption, of what use is the severity of punishment? Are we to suppose that when redemption proves ineffectual for the improvement of man, punishment must be resorted to, to attain the object? It would then follow that punishment is more effectual for man's regeneration than redemption The conflict between the sphere of punishment and that of redemption becomes all the more perplexing, when we recollect that the main feature of redemption is the doing away with punishment by the forgiveness of sins If punishment be remedial, is it a kindness to free man from it before it has accomplished its work? And how is it possible that redemption, which is the removal of punishment, should renovate, if punishment itself does so also? And yet the influence of punishment in preserving, and re-establishing the power of moral goodness in the sufferer, must not be wholly denied. Punishment, on the one hand, acts as a barrier against the desolating inroads of sin by reasserting the fixed ordainments of the law; and, on the other hand, it bears witness to the sinner of the crushing power wherewith evil recoils upon himself, and makes him tremble when he surrenders himself to it In these two ways, it *prepares* man for the work of redemption. But in its own distinctive nature, it is not adapted or calculated to produce a true improvement, an inward renovation of the sinner. On the contrary, the two spheres, that of redemption, which alone can accomplish a true renewal, and that of punishment, mutually exclude one another Whenever a living participation in the blessings of redemption begins, punishment, properly so called—*δίκη*, *ἐκδίκησις*, *τιμωρία*—ceases, but, so long as man continues to be the subject of God's righteous punishment, he is excluded from those blessings, John 3 36."

Twesten (Dogmatik, Th II. § 39) argues in the same manner. "Punishment is not a proper means of reformation, for true reformation can issue only from free self-determination It is voluntary in its nature. But a self-determination that is brought about by the fear of pain would not be moral, and of the nature of virtue Any reformation effected from a selfish motive is not genuine reformation. Furthermore if true reformation could be produced by punishment, why should not the legal and punitive method of the Old Testament have been the only one? The old economy was full of threatenings and penalties, and of fearful examples of their actual execution. Why did God send his Son, and make a new covenant and economy of mercy? Of what use is redemption, or the *remission* of punishment, if punishment is in itself healing and remedial? The Scriptures never represent punishment as reformatory The proper punishment of sin is death Rom 6 23 As temporal death, which is the extreme penalty in human legislation, is not intended to reform the criminal, and reinstate him in human society, but forever cuts him off from it, so eternal death, in the Biblical representation, is not intended to be a means of educating the sinner and fitting him for the kingdom of heaven, but forever banishes and excludes him from it."

ably upon this principle. To torture a dumb beast is a crime; to torture a man is a greater crime. To steal from one's own mother is more heinous than to steal from a fellow-citizen. The person who transgresses is the same in each instance; but the different worth and dignity of the objects upon whom his action terminates makes the difference in the gravity of the two offences. David's adultery was a finite evil in reference to Uriah, but an infinite evil in reference to God. "Against thee only have I sinned," was the feeling of the sinner in this case. Had the patriarch Joseph yielded, he would have sinned against Pharaoh. But the greatness of the sin as related to the fellow-creature is lost in its enormity as related to the Creator, and his only question is: "How can I do this great wickedness and sin against God."[1]

[1] Those who deny the position that sin is an infinite evil forget that the principle upon which it rests is one of the commonplaces of jurisprudence: the principle, namely, that crime depends upon the object against whom it is committed as well as upon the subject who commits it. The merely *subjective* reference of an act is not sufficient to determine whether it is a crime. The act may have been the voluntary act of a person, but unless it is also an offence against another *person*, it is no crime. To strike is a voluntary act, but to strike a post or a stone is not a culpable act. Furthermore, not only crime, but *degrees* of crime depend upon the objective reference of a personal act. Estimated only by the subjective reference, there can be not only no culpability, but no difference in culpability. Killing a dog is no worse than killing a man, if merely the subject who kills, and not the object killed, is considered. Both alike are voluntary acts, and of one and the same person. If, therefore, the gravity of the act is to be measured solely by the nature of the person committing it, and not by that of the thing against whom it is committed, killing a dog is as heinous as killing a man.

Now this principle of jurisprudence is carried into theology by the theologian. The violation of the moral law is *sin* and *guilt*, only when viewed objectively in reference to God primarily, and to man secondarily. Viewed merely and wholly in reference to the trangressor himself, it is not sin and guilt at all. It is sin only as committed against God, or man. Again, it is only the objective reference that will yield *degrees* of sin. One and the same act may be simultaneously an offence against an individual, a family, a state, and God. Measured by the nature and qualities of the offender himself, it has no degrees. But measured by the nature and qualities of these moral objects against whom it is committed, it has degrees of turpitude. As the first three are only finite in worth and dignity, the culpability is only certain degrees of the finite. As the last is infinite in worth and dignity, the culpability is infinite also. Compare Edwards: Justice of God, Works, IV. 228.

The incarnation and vicarious satisfaction for sin by one of the persons of the Godhead, demonstrates the infinity of the evil. It is incredible that the Eternal Trinity should have submitted to such a stupendous self-sacrifice, to remove a merely finite and temporal evil The doctrine of Christ's vicarious atonement, logically, stands or falls with that of endless punishment. Historically, it has stood or fallen with it. The incarnation of Almighty God, in order to make the remission of sin possible, is one of the strongest arguments for the eternity and infinity of penal suffering.

The objection that an offence committed in a finite time cannot be an infinite evil, and deserve an infinite suffering, implies that crime must be measured by the time that was consumed in its perpetration. But even in human punishment, no reference is had to the length of time occupied in the commission of the offence. Murder is committed in an instant, and theft sometimes requires hours. But the former is the greater crime, and receives the greater punishment.

4. In the fourth place, that endless punishment is reasonable, is proved by the preference of the wicked themselves. The unsubmissive, rebellious, defiant, and impenitent spirit prefers hell to heaven. Milton correctly represents Satan as saying: "All good to me becomes bane, and in heaven much worse would be my state;" and, also, as declaring that "it is better to reign in hell than to serve in heaven." This agrees with the Scripture representation, that Judas went "to his own place," Acts 1 : 25.

The lost spirits are not forced into a sphere that is unsuited to them. There is no other abode in the universe which they would prefer to that to which they are assigned, because the only other abode is heaven. The meekness, lowliness, sweet submission to God, and love of him, that characterize heaven, are more hateful to Lucifer and his angels, than even the sufferings of hell. The wicked would be no happier in heaven than in hell. The burden and anguish of a guilty conscience, says South, is so insupportable, that some "have done violence to their own lives, and so fled to hell as a sanctuary, and chose damnation as a release." This is illustrated by facts in human life. The thoroughly vicious and ungodly man prefers the license and freedom to sin which he finds in the haunts of vice, to the restraints and purity of Christian society. There is hunger, disease, and wretchedness, in one circle; and there is plenty, health, and happiness, in the other. But he prefers the former. He would rather be in the gambling-house and brothel than in the Christian home. "Those that, notwithstanding all gracious means, live continually in rebellion against God; those that impenitently die in their sins; those that desire to live here forever, that they might enjoy their sweet sins; those that are so hardened and naturalized in their vices, that if they were revived and brought again into this world of temptations, would certainly return to the pleasures of sin; is it not right that their incorrigible obstinacy should be punished forever?" Bates, On Eternal Judgment, III.

The finally lost are not to be conceived of as having faint desires and aspirations for a holy and heavenly state, and as feebly but really inclined to sorrow for their sin, but are kept in hell contrary to their yearning and petition They are sometimes so described by the opponent of the doctrine, or at least so thought of. There is not a single throb of godly sorrow, or a single pulsation of holy desire, in the lost spirit. The temper toward God in the lost is angry and defiant. "They hate both me and my father," says the Son of God, "without a cause," John 15:24, 25. Satan and his followers "love darkness rather than light," hell rather than heaven, "because their deeds are evil," John 3:19. Sin ultimately assumes a fiendish form, and degree. It is pure wickedness without regret or sorrow, and with a delight in evil for evil's sake. There are some men who reach this state of depravity even before they die. "Some men's sins are evident (R. V ) beforehand, going before to judgment," 1 Tim. 5 : 24. They are seen in the callous and cruel voluptuaries portrayed by Tacitus, and the heaven-defying atheists described by St. Simon. They are also depicted in Shakespeare's Iago. The reader knows that Iago is past saving, and deserves everlasting damnation. Impulsively, he cries out with Lodovico: "Where is that viper? bring the villain forth." And then Othello's calmer but deeper feeling becomes his own: "I look down towards his feet—but that's a fable : If that thou be'st a devil, *I* cannot kill thee." The punishment is remitted to the retribution of God.[1]

---

[1] It ought to be noticed, that the "hatred" of Himself, and of his Father, which Christ attributes to "the world," John 15 · 18, 19, and which is a distinguishing element in impenitence, does not necessarily imply sensuality and vice. Sin may be wholly intellectual: what St. Paul denominates "spiritual wickedness," Eph 6 12. The most profound of Shakespearean critics calls attention to "the passionless character of Iago It is all will in *intellect*." Coleridge Works, IV. 180. The "carnal mind" manifests itself in two ways The proud spirit of the moralist is one phase of it, the self-indulgent spirit of the voluptuary is the other The Pharisee represents the first; Dives the last Both alike confess no sin, and implore no forgiveness. In illustration of the former, consider the temper of a certain class of intellectual men toward the cross of Christ They are perhaps austerely moral By temperament, taste, study, and occupation, they have even an antipathy to sensuality They "scorn delights, and live laborious days." But present for their acceptance those truths of the New Testament which involve the broken and contrite heart, and their whole inward being rises in vehement recoil Of the effect of the doctrine of election, Calvin remarks that "when the human mind hears of it, its irritation breaks all restraint, and it discovers as serious and violent agitation as if alarmed by the sound of a martial trumpet" Inst, III xxii 1 So, too, when the authoritative demand of Jesus Christ, to confess sin, and beg remission through atoning blood, is made to David Hume, or David Strauss, or John Stuart Mill, none of whom were sensualists, it wakens intense mental hostility Now without asserting which theory in religion is true, that of the New Testament, or that of the skeptic, is it not clear, that *if* there be another life, and *if* the teaching of the New Testament shall prove to be the absolute truth, the latter person must be classed with the "haters of God?" Will not the temper of this unsensual and intellectual man towards what is found, in the end, to be eternal verity, be as thoroughly of the nature of enmity, as that of the most immoral and hardened debauchee?

Muller alludes to unsensual and intellectual sin in the following terms:

5. In the fifth place, that endless punishment is rational, is proved by the history of morals. In the records of human civilization and morality, it is found that that age which is most reckless of law, and most vicious in practice, is the age that has the loosest conception of penalty, and is the most inimical to the doctrine of endless retribution. A virtuous and religious generation adopts sound ethics, and reverently believes that "the Judge of all the earth will do right," Gen. 18:25; that God will not "call evil good, and good evil, nor put darkness for light and light for darkness," Isa. 5:20; and that it is a deadly error to assert with the sated and worn-out sensualist: "All things come alike to all; there is one event to the righteous and the wicked," Eccl. 9:2.

---

"That which makes sin to be sin, and which is the evil of evil, is the *selfish isolation* of the man which it involves There are cases, with some it is the rule of life, where a man keeps himself free from wild ungovernable passions, and only seldom is guilty of overt acts which conscience recognizes as sins, yet in his inmost heart 'the *I*, that gloomy despot,' rules supreme, he stands alone in the world, shut up within himself, and in a chaos of selfish endeavors, preferences, antipathies, without any true participation in the joys and sorrows of mankind, estranged from God. In such a state, the principle of sin, though shut up within, rules with no less real power than where its dominion is manifest in glaring wickedness and vice, and a wild disorder of the outward life." Sin, I. 136 He also notices that mere intellectuality is no certain preservative against sensuality and vice. "A superficial observation of life has led to the conclusion that immorality decreases in proportion as the growth of the intellectual nature increases, and the 'children of this generation' pride themselves in no small degree upon the discovery that culture and not Christianity is the means of true freedom, and the panacea for all the disorders of the world. But a single unbiassed and penetrating glance at life will suffice to dissipate these illusions. We oftentimes find the deepest moral degradation and disorder in the very highest stages of culture, a frivolity of mind resolving all the relations of life into rotteness, and utter insensibility to every impulse of holy love, and a cold, calculating, self-conscious egotism, which puts from it the call to sacrifice any one of its own interests as something altogether absurd—the men with whom it comes in contact being regarded merely as ciphers, by whose help its own aggrandizement may be attained. Mental culture does not eradicate a single tendency of moral depravity, it only veils and refines them all; and so far from redeeming the man, if it be not sanctified by a higher principle, it really confirms within him the dominion of sin" Sin, I 306, 307 In corroboration of this, see the discriminating remarks of Thomas Arnold on the character of Sylla. Encyclopædia Metropolitana Roman Republic, Ch XXI

The French people, at the close of the last century, were a very demoralized and vicious generation, and there was a very general disbelief and denial of the doctrines of the Divine existence, the immortality of the soul, the freedom of the will, and future retribution. And upon a smaller scale, the same fact is continually repeating itself. Any little circle of business men who are known to deny future rewards and punishments are shunned by those who desire safe investments. The recent uncommon energy of opposition to endless punishment, which started about ten years ago in this country, synchronized with great defalcations and breaches of trust, uncommon corruption in mercantile and political life, and great distrust between man and man. Luxury deadens the moral sense, and luxurious populations do not have the fear of God before their eyes. Hence luxurious ages, and luxurious men, recalcitrate at hell, and "kick against the goads." No theological tenet is more important than eternal retribution to those modern nations which, like England, Germany, and the United States, are growing rapidly in riches, luxury, and earthly power. Without it, they will infallibly go down in that vortex of sensuality and wickedness that swallowed up Babylon and Rome The bestial and shameless vice of the dissolute rich, that has recently been uncovered in the commercial metropolis of the world, is a powerful argument for the necessity and reality of "the lake which burneth with fire and brimstone."

A single remark remains to be made respecting the extent and scope of hell. It is only a spot in the universe of God. Compared with heaven, hell is narrow and limited. The kingdom of Satan is insignificant in contrast with the kingdom of Christ. In the immense range of God's dominion, good is the rule, and evil is the exception. Sin is a speck upon the infinite azure of eternity; a spot on the sun Hell is only a corner of the universe. The Gothic etymon (Hohle, Holle) denotes a covered-up hole. In

Scripture, hell is a "pit," a "lake;" not an ocean. It is "bottomless," but not boundless. The Gnostic and Dualistic theories, which make God, and Satan, or the Demiurge, nearly equal in power and dominion, find no support in Revelation. The Bible teaches that there will always be some sin, and some death, in the universe. Some angels and men will forever be the enemies of God.[1] But their number, compared with that of unfallen angels and redeemed men, is small. They are not described in the glowing language and metaphors by which the immensity of the holy and blessed is delineated. "The chariots of God are twenty thousand, and thousands of angels," Ps 68:17. "The Lord came from Sinai, and shined forth from mount Paran, and he came with ten thousands of his saints," Deut. 22:2 "The Lord hath prepared his throne in the

---

[1] "There is this certainty," says Hooker (Polity, V xlix), "that life and death divide between them the whole body of mankind What portion either of the two hath, God himself knoweth, for us he hath left no sufficient means to comprehend, and for that cause hath not given any leave to search in particular who are infallibly the heirs of the kingdom of God, and who are castaways Howbeit, concerning the state of all men with whom we live, we may till the world's end always presume that as far as in us there is power to discern what others are, and as far as any duty of ours dependeth upon the notice of their condition in respect to God, the safest axioms for charity to rest itself upon are these 'He which believeth, already is the child of God, and he which believeth not as yet, may become the child of God' It becometh not us, during life, altogether to condemn any man, seeing that for anything we know there is hope of every man's forgiveness, the possibility of whose repentance is not cut off by death And therefore charity, which 'hopeth all things,' prayeth also for all men"

To the same effect says Zanchius (Predestination, III) "I grant that there are some particular persons mentioned in the Divine word, of whose reprobation no doubt can be made, such as Esau and Judas. But now the canon of scripture is completed, we dare not, we must not pronounce any man living to be non-elect, be he at present ever so wicked The vilest sinner may, for aught we can tell, appertain to the election of grace, and be one day wrought upon by the Spirit of God This we know, that those who die in unbelief, and are finally unsanctified, cannot be saved because God in his word tells us so, and has represented these as marks of reprobation But to say that such and such individuals, whom perhaps we now see dead in sins, shall never be converted to Christ, would be a most presumptuous assertion, as well as an inexcusable breach of the charity which hopeth all things"

heavens, and his kingdom ruleth over all," Ps. 103:21. "Thine is the kingdom, and the power, and the glory," Matt. 6:13. The Lord Christ "must reign till he hath put all enemies under his feet," 1 Cor. 15:25. St. John "heard a voice from heaven as the voice of many waters, and as the voice of a great thunder," Rev. 14:1. The New Jerusalem "lieth four-square, the length is as large as the breadth; the gates of it shall not be shut at all by day; the kings of the earth do bring their honor into it," Rev. 21 16, 24, 25. The number of the lost spirits is never thus emphasized, and enlarged upon. The brief, stern statement is, that "the fearful and unbelieving shall have their part in the lake that burneth with fire and brimstone," Rev. 21:8. No metaphors and amplification are added, to make the impression of an immense "multitude which no man can number." [1]

We have thus presented the rational argument for the most severe and unwelcome of all the tenets of the Christian religion. It must have a foothold in the human reason, or it could not have maintained itself against all the recoil and opposition which it elicits from the human heart. Founded in ethics, in law, and in judicial reason, as well as unquestionably taught by the Author of Christianity, it is no wonder that the doctrine of Eternal Retribution, in spite of selfish prejudices and appeals to human sentiment, has always been a belief of Christendom. From theology

---

[1] Calvin, explaining the elect "seven thousand," in Rom 11·4, remarks that "though this stands for an indefinite number, it was the Lord's design to specify a great multitude Since, then, the grace of God prevails so much in an extreme state of things, let us not lightly give over to the devil all those whose piety does not openly appear to us" Zwingle thought that all who died in early childhood are regenerated and saved Edwards (Against Chauncy, XIV) denies that it is an article of his faith, that "only a small part of the human race will finally be saved" Hopkins (Future State, V) asserts that "there is reason to believe that many more of mankind will be saved than lost, yea, it may be many thousands to one" Hodge (Theology, III 879) says that "we have reason to believe that the number of the finally lost, in comparison with the whole number of the saved, will be very inconsiderable."

and philosophy it has passed into human literature, and is wrought into its finest structures. It makes the solemn substance of the Iliad and the Greek Drama. It pours a sombre light into the brightness and grace of the Æneid. It is the theme of the Inferno, and is presupposed by both of the other parts of the Divine Comedy. The epic of Milton derives from it its awful grandeur. And the greatest of the Shakespearean tragedies sound and stir the depths of the human soul, by their delineation of guilt intrinsic and eternal.

In this discussion, we have purposely brought into view only the righteousness of Almighty God, as related to the voluntary and responsible action of man We have set holy justice and disobedient free-will face to face, and drawn the conclusions. This is all that the defender of the doctrine of retribution is strictly concerned with. If he can demonstrate that the principles of eternal rectitude are not in the least degree infringed upon, but are fully maintained, when sin is endlessly punished, he has done all that his problem requires. Whatever is just is beyond all rational attack.[1]

But with the Christian Gospel in his hands, the defender of the Divine justice finds it difficult to be entirely reticent, and say not a word concerning the Divine mercy. Over against God's infinite antagonism and righteous severity toward moral evil, there stands God's infinite pity and desire to forgive. This is realized, not by the high-handed and unprincipled method of pardoning without legal satisfaction of any kind, but by the strange and stupendous method of putting the Eternal Judge in the place of the human criminal; of substituting God's own satisfaction for that due from man. In this vicarious atonement

[1] Said one of the deepest and most profoundly penitent of human spirits "I have had more than a glimpse of what is meant by death and outer darkness, and the worm that dieth not—and that all the hell of the reprobate is no more inconsistent with the love [benevolence] of God, than the blindness of one who has occasioned loathsome and guilty diseases to eat out his eyes, is inconsistent with the light of the sun"—Cottle: Reminiscences of Coleridge, 282.

for sin, the Triune God relinquishes no claims of law, and waives no rights of justice. The sinner's Divine Substitute, in his hour of voluntary agony and death, drinks the cup of punitive and inexorable justice to the dregs. Any man who, in penitent faith, avails himself of this *vicarious* method of setting himself right with the Eternal Nemesis, will find that it succeeds; but he who rejects it, must through endless cycles grapple with the dread problem of human guilt in his own person, and alone.

The Christian Gospel—the universal offer of pardon through the self-sacrifice of one of the Divine Persons—should silence every objection to the doctrine of Endless Punishment. For as the case now stands, there is no necessity, so far as the action of *God* is concerned, that a single human being should ever be the subject of future punishment. The necessity of hell is founded in the action of the *creature*, not of the Creator. Had there been no sin, there would have been no hell; and sin is the product of man's free will. And after the entrance of sin and the provision of redemption from it, had there been universal repentance in this life, there would have been no hell for man in the next life. The only necessitating reason, therefore, for endless retribution that now exists, is the sinner's *impenitence* Should every human individual, before he dies, sorrow for sin, and humbly confess it, Hades and Gehenna would disappear.

For the Scriptures everywhere describe God as naturally and spontaneously merciful, and declare that all the legal obstacles to the exercise of this great attribute have been removed by the death of the Son of God "for the sins of the whole world," 1 John 2:2. In the very midst of the holy revelations of Sinai, Jehovah proclaimed it to be his inherent and intrinsic disposition to be "merciful and gracious, long-suffering, forgiving iniquity and trangression," Ex. 34:6, 7. Nehemiah, after the exile, repeats the doctrine of the Pentateuch: "Thou art a God ready to pardon, gracious and merciful, and of great kindness," Nehem. 9:17. The Psalmist declares that "the Lord is ready to forgive, and plenteous in mercy unto all that call upon him," Ps. 86:5. "The Lord taketh pleasure in them that fear him, in those that hope in his mercy," Ps. 147:11. From the twilight of the land of Uz, Elihu, feeling after the promised Redeemer if haply he might find him (Job 33:23), declares that "God looketh upon men, and if any say, I have sinned, and perverted that which was right, and it profited me not; he will deliver his soul from going down to the pit, and his life shall see the light," Job 33: 27, 28. The Bible, throughout, teaches that the Supreme Being is sensitive to penitence, and is moved with compassion and paternal yearning whenever he perceives any sincere spiritual grief. He notices and welcomes the slightest indication of repentance. "The eye of the Lord is upon them that fear him, upon them that hope in his mercy," Ps. 33:18. "Whoso confesseth and forsaketh his sins shall have mercy," Prov. 28:13. The Heavenly Father sees the prodigal when he is "yet a great way off." He never "breaks the bruised reed," nor "quenches the smoking flax." If there be in any human creature the broken and contrite heart, the Divine Pity speaks the word of forgiveness and absolution. The humble confession of unworthiness operates almost magically upon the Eternal. Incarnate Mercy said to the heathen "woman of Canaan" who asked for only the dogs' crumbs, "O woman, great is thy faith; be it unto thee even as thou wilt," Matt. 15:28. The Omnipotent is overcome, whenever he sees lowly penitential sorrow. As "the foolishness of God is wiser than man," so the self-despairing helplessness of man is stronger than God. When Jacob says to the Infinite One, "I am not worthy of the least of all thy mercies," yet wrestles with him "until the breaking of the day," he becomes Israel, and "as a prince has power with God," Gen. 32:10, 24, 28. When Jehovah hears Ephraim "bemoaning himself," and saying, "Turn thou me, and I shall be turned," he answers, "Ephraim is my dear son. I will surely have mercy upon him," Jer 31 : 18, 20.[1]

Now the only obstruction, and it is a *fatal* one, to the exercise of this natural and spontaneous mercy of God, is the sinner's hardness of heart The existing necessity for hell-punishment is not chargeable upon God. It is the proud and obstinate man who makes hell. It is his impenitence that feeds its perpetual fires. For so long as the transgressor does not grieve for sin, and does not even acknowledge it, it *cannot* be pardoned. Almightiness itself cannot forgive impenitence, any more than it can make a square circle. Impenitence after sinning is a more determined and worse form of sin, than sinning is in and of itself. For it is a tacit *defence* and *justification* of sin. If after trangression the person acknowledges that he has transgressed, and asks forgiveness for so doing, he evinces that he does not excuse his act, or defend it. On the contrary, he renounces his act, condemns it, and mourns over it. But if after trangression the person makes no acknowledgment, and asks no forgiveness, he is repeating and intensifying his sin. He justifies himself in his act of rebellion against authority, and thus aggravates the original fault. It is for this reason, that impenitence for sin is more dreadful than sin itself. A penitent sinner can be forgiven ; but an impenitent sinner cannot be. The former God pities, and extends the offer of mercy to him To the latter God holds out no hope, because he cannot.

This is what gives to human existence here upon earth its dark outlook. All the gloom, discontent, and anxiety of

---

[1] Beatrice expresses the same truth to Dante, in the words

"Whene'er the sinner's cheek
Breaks forth into the precious-streaming tears
Of self-accusing, in our court the wheel
Of justice doth run counter to the edge"

PURGATORY, xxxi 36.

human life grow out of this. This is what makes "all the uses of this world so weary, stale, flat, and unprofitable." Men are *impenitent.* They give no heed to the voice of conscience; know little of remorse, nothing of genuine sorrow. They are stolid and lethargic in sin; or else angrily deny the fact. They bend no knee in self-abasement before the All-Holy; they do not cry, "O Lamb of God that takest away the sins of the world, grant me thy peace." Human life is wretched and despairing, not because there is no mercy in the sweet heavens, but because there is no relenting, no softening, in the human heart. One is weary of hearing the incessant wail of the agnostic and the cynic over the "mystery" of this existence; the monotonous moan of the pessimist that life is not worth living. A sincere confession of what the consciousness of every man will tell him is the absolute truth respecting his character and conduct, when tried by a spiritual and perfect standard, would drive away this false view of earthly existence as the miasmatic fog is blown by the winds. But instead of confessing sin, and imploring its forgiveness, men stand complaining of its punishment, or employing their ingenuity in endeavoring to prove that there is none; and then wonder that the heavens are black and thunderous over their heads. Not by this method, will the sky be made clear and sunny. Whoever will cast himself upon the Divine Compassion will find life to be worth living; but he who quarrels with the Divine Justice will discover that he had better not have been born.

What the human race needs is—*to go to the Divine Confessional.* The utterance of the Prodigal should be that of every man, "Father, I have sinned." The utterance of the Psalmist should be that of every man: "O thou that hearest prayer, unto thee shall all flesh come. Iniquities prevail against me: as for our transgressions, thou shalt purge them away." "God commandeth all men everywhere to repent," Acts 17 : 30. But so long as man glosses over, or conceals, the cardinal fact in his history, he must live under a cloud, and look with anxiety and fear into the deep darkness beyond. It is useless to contend with the stubborn fact of moral evil by the ostrich-method of ignoring, and denying. The sin is here, in self-consciousness, terrible and real, the lancinating sting of pain and the deadly sting of death, in this generation and in all generations. Kant, the ethical and the metaphysical, is right when he affirms that the noumenon of sin is the dark ground under the phenomenon of life. *Confession*, therefore, is the only way to light and mental peace. The suppression of any fundamental form of human consciousness necessarily results in unrest Man's words about himself must agree with his true character and condition; otherwise he becomes insincere, miserable, and false. The denial of moral evil is the secret of the murmuring and melancholy with which so much of modern letters is filled. Rousseau made a confession, but not truthful, not humble; and hence it brought him no repose. Augustine made a confession, genuine, simple, thoroughly accordant with the facts of human nature; and the outpouring of his confidences into the ear of Eternal Purity and Mercy brought the peace that passes all understanding, and the immortal life that knows no melancholy, and no dissatisfaction. These historic persons are types of the two classes into which all men fall: the penitent and the impenitent.

The king in Shakespeare's Hamlet, writhing with selfish remorse but destitute of unselfish sorrow, in his soliloquy exclaims:

> "Try what repentance can: what can it not?
> Yet what can it, when one *cannot* repent?
> O wretched state! O bosom black as death!
> O limèd soul; that struggling to be free
> Art more engaged!"

Bunyan's man of Despair, in the iron cage, when assured by Christian that "the Son of the Blessed is very pitiful," replies: "I have so hardened my heart, that I *cannot* repent"

In these powerful delineations, these profound psychologists of sin bring to view a peril that environs free will Pardon may be proffered by God, but *penitence may become impossible through the action of man.* "There are some sins," says Augustine, "that follow of necessity, from foregoing sins that occurred without necessity." The adoption of atheism is a sin without necessity. It is the voluntary action of man. But the hardness of heart that results from it, results of necessity. No man is forced to be an infidel; but if he is one, he *must* be an impenitent man A luxurious and skeptical age should remember this. That man *cannot* repent, who drowns himself in pleasure, and never seriously reflects upon his accountability to his Maker. That man *cannot* repent, who expends the energy of his mind in the endeavor to prove that all human action is irresponsible, and the threatenings of Revelation an idle tale. They who have "eyes full of adultery *cannot* cease from sin," 2 Pet. 2:14. Absorption in worldliness, and adoption of infidel opinions, make repentance an impossibility. Sensuality and atheism harden the human heart, and render it impervious to the Christian Religion.

# INDEX.

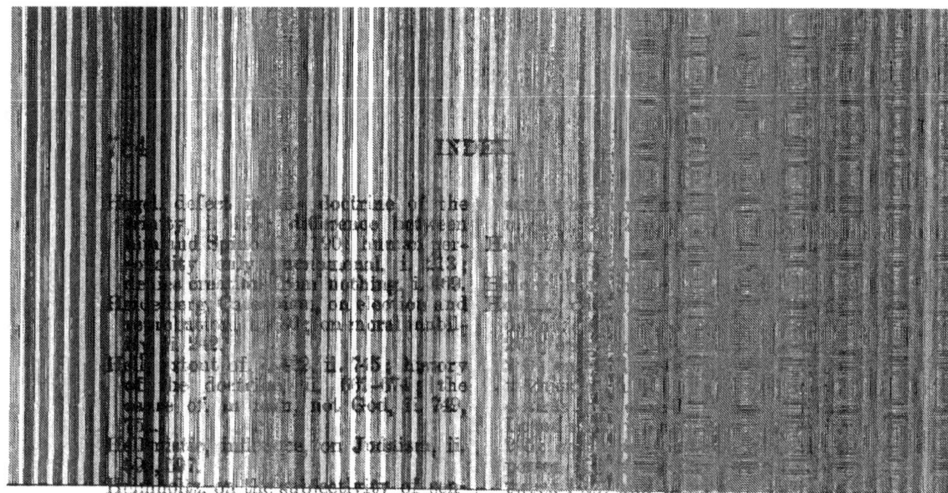

# QUESTIONS.

## INTRODUCTION.

Topics in theological introduction? Characteristics of a true method? Most common method in theology? Objections to the christological method? Principal objects of theological science? Divisions of theological science? Proper mode of investigating theological topics? Source of theological science? Meanings of "dogma?" Difference between dogmatic and biblical theology? Relations of each to the other? Aim of polemic theology? Of systematic theology? Comparative extent of theological science? Distinction between theology and ethics?

Wide and restricted significations of the term theology? Two definitions of theology in the wide signification? Etymology of "religion?" Augustine's, Turrettin's, and Westminster definition of theology? Objection made to this definition? Aquinas's reply? Definition of "science?" Scientific value of the skeptical estimate of Christian theology? Illustrations of it? Illustrate the self-consistence of theological science by the trinity and decrees? Distinction between scientific and perfect knowledge?

First characteristic of theological science? Meaning of this? Illustrations? The materialistic estimate of physical and moral science? Refutation of it by reference to the laws of matter and motion? Newton's, Leibnitz's, and Whewell's statement respecting physical laws? Kind of necessity in moral laws? Illustrations of this? Kant's view upon this point? Reasons why physical science is relative knowledge?

Second characteristic of theological science? Distinction between positive and perfect knowledge? Proper use of negatives in definitions? Nature of the position that the knowledge of God is negative? Show the positive nature of the idea of eternity? Of the idea of spirit.

## BIBLIOLOGY.

Definition of Bibliology? Objection to making it a division in theological science? Answer? Two significations of "revelation?" Biblical texts referring to each? Relation of unwritten revelation to consciousness? Biblical view of intuitive knowledge? Use of the term "revelation" in the Patristic church? Subsequent modification? General characteristic of the unwritten revelation? Reason for this?

Technical signification of "revelation?" Contents of the written revelation? Difference between natural religion in Paganism and in Scripture? Difference between history in Scripture and ordinary history? What is the strictly supernatural element in revelation?

Distinction between inspiration and revelation? Define plenary inspiration? Turrettin's and Westminster definition? Biblical texts in proof? Prevalency of the doctrine of plenary inspiration? Middle theory of inspiration? Objections to it? Examples of revelation in distinction from inspiration? How is revelation generally indicated in Scripture? Difference between education and revelation? Between literature and revelation? Negative definitions of inspiration? Positive definition? Elements in inspiration? Psychological relations of inspiration? Meaning of verbal inspiration? Proofs that thought suggests language? First objection to plenary inspiration? Reply? Second objection? Reply? How far does the Bible teach science? Points of difference between the science of the Bible and the contemporary science? Modes in which the Divine communication in revelation is made?

Definition of authenticity? Of credibility? Proofs of the authenticity of the New Testament? Proofs of its credibility?

Nature of the evidence for miracles? Comparative strength of the evidence for historical and miraculous events? Force of monumental testimony?

First theory antagonistic to the credibility of the New Testament? Reply? Second theory antagonistic? Difference between a myth and a legend? Objections to the mythical theory? Difference between historical and saving faith? Why cannot saving faith be produced by the historical argument? Biblical proof of this? Westminster statement? Reasons for this?

New Testament proof of the credibility of the Old Testament? Proofs of the authenticity of the old Testament? Definition of canonicity? Evidence for the canonicity of the Old Testament? Evidence for the canonicity of the Gospels? First conciliar action respecting the canon of the New Testament?

## THEOLOGY (DOCTRINE OF GOD).

Christ's definition of God? Explain the omission of the article with πνεῦμα? Difference between the spirituality of God and that of the finite spirit? Three characteristics of the spirituality of the infinite spirit? Errors resulting from exaggerating the difference between the infinite and the finite spirit? From exaggerating the resemblance?

First predicate of God as a spirit? Biblical proof that God is an essence? Meaning of term of essence, or substance, as applied to God? Plato's definition of substance? How is spiritual substance known? Gnostic error on this point? Tertullian's meaning in ascribing "body" to God?

Westminster definition of God? How far does invisibility distinguish spiritual substance from material? Describe the two modes of matter? Meaning of invisibility in some Biblical texts? Biblical proof that spirit is without body and parts? Etymological signification of "substance?" Objection to the view that spirit is not substance, but a series of exercises or activities? Historical proof of the validity of the idea of spiritual substance? Spinoza's view of mind and matter? Plato's view? Comparative amount of unextended and extended substance?

Meaning of the term "passion" in the Westminster definition of God? Why is "passion" inapplicable to God? Erroneous interpretation of the term "passion?" Consequence of this error? Biblical statements respecting feeling in God? Criterion for determining what is literal and what is metaphorical in the Biblical representation? Two fundamental forms of feeling in God? Are these opposites or contraries? Distinction between these terms? How is moral wrath in God compatible with blessedness in God? Aristotle's definition of happiness?

Second predicate of God as a spirit? Define personality? Distinction between consciousness and self-consciousness? Peculiarity of the object, in self-consciousness? Illustrate by the brute and man? Has God consciousness as separate from self-consciousness? Why is consciousness dual and self-consciousness trinal? Consequent bearing of the doctrine of the trinity upon the doctrine of the divine personality? Error of pantheism respecting the divine personality? Refutation? Spinoza's objection to an infinite personality? Reply? Difference between the Infinite and the All? Distinction between the personality of the Godhead and the personality of a divine Person? Patristic term for the latter?

Distinction between "being" and "existence"? Why is there no syllogistical argument for the divine existence in the Scriptures? Nature of the Biblical evidence for the existence of God? Biblical texts? What attributes of God does the pagan know, according to Rom 1·19, 20? Sins charged upon the pagan in Rom 1:20, 21, 22? Westminster statement respecting the light of nature and responsibility? Proof of an innate knowledge of God in Rom 1.18, 19? Meaning of the terms ἀποκαλύπτω and φανερόω? Definition of an "innate" idea? Position of Plato and Cicero concerning man's natural knowledge of a deity? Position of the early Christian apologists? Evidences for monotheism in paganism, from scripture? From literature? Effect of apostacy upon the innate idea of God? Objection to innate knowledge drawn from the imbruted condition of some tribes of men? Reply? Proof that the doctrine of innate knowledge of God does not conflict with that of total depravity? Proof that the idea of God does not come from education? Proof of the divine existence from the God-consciousness and the self-consciousness? What inference follows respecting the strength of the evidence for a deity? Reason why the denial of personal existence is less common than the denial of a deity? Relative historical order of monotheism, pantheism, and polytheism? Erroneous view of the order in which these occur? Twofold source of the relics of monotheism in paganism? Why is not natural religion sufficient for man?

Uses of a syllogistical argument for the divine existence? Anselm's statement of the ontological argument? Two points upon which it hinges? First objection to the argument? Reply? Connection between essence and existence in the Infinite? In the Finite? Fallacy in Kant's objection? Second objection to the ontological argument? Reply? Third objection? Reply? Fourth objection? Reply? Des Cartes's statement of the ontological argument? Variation in it? Clarke's statement of it? Criticism upon it? Scripture use of the ontological argument? Value of the ontological argument in relation to materialism? Nature of the cosmological argument? Aquinas's statement of it? Kant's objection to it? Reply? Clarke's objection to it? Reply? Hume's objection? Reply? Nature of the teleological argument? Biblical form of it? Popular value of this argument? Sciences that furnish excellent materials for it? Objection to the teleological argument? Reply? Nature of the moral argument? Two forms of it? Nature of the historical argument?

Characteristic of the earlier Trinitarianism? Relation of triunity to personality? Defect in the deistic and Socinian idea of the divine unity? Defect in the Sabellian and Pythagorean trinity? Biblical idea of unity as applied to God? Difference between the unity of God and that of a creature? Difference between unity and singleness? Implication contained in the "plenitude" mentioned in Eph 3. 19, and Col. 1:19; 2:9? Proof of the trinality of God from the Christian experience? Biblical proof of the divine unity? Evidence from reason?

Source of the doctrine of the trinity? Two general classes of texts proving the trinity? Texts of the first class in the New Testament? Opinions respecting Old Testament trinitarianism? General manner in which the trinity appears in the Old Testament? Five lists of trinitarian texts in the Old Testament? Views of the Jews at the time of the advent respecting the Holy Spirit?

Earliest use of the term trinity? Distinction between "trinal" and "triple"? What distinction is the key to the construction of the doctrine of the trinity? In what sense is the doctrine scientific or rational? First proposition in the statement of the doctrine? Terms denoting the essence? Why did the Schoolmen and elder Protestant theologians prefer the term "essence" to the term "substance"? Etymology of each? Meaning of "substance," taken by itself? Error resulting from contemplating the divine substance abstractly and apart from interior distinctions? Particular incommunicable characteristics of the divine essence?

Second proposition in the statement of the doctrine? Why is this side of the doctrine the most difficult? Terms denoting the personal distinction? St. Paul's definition of a trinitarian person? Hooker's definition? Elder Protestant definition? Fisher's definition? Definition of the hypostatical character? Illustrate its incommunicability? Turrettin's statement respecting the difference between person and person, and person and essence? Biblical proof that the three persons are objective to each other? Difference between a trinitarian person and the Godhead? Error of tritheism? Use of the term "modal" in this reference? Sabellian use of the term "modal"? Different meanings of the term "God" in scripture? Two classes of hypostatical characteristics? Mention the opera ad intra. Three characteristics of these immanent activities? Biblical proof of them? Westminster statement of them? Definition of generation and spiration? Meaning of the term "communicate"? Authorities for the use of the term "emanation" in this connection? Distinction between "communication" and "derivation" of essence? Recapitulation of the internal characteristics in reference to the several persons? Difference between a divine and a human person? Why is the divine unity numerical, not specific? Meaning of circumincession? Scripture texts? Meaning of the terms "first," "second," and "third," applied to the persons? Scripture proof of this? Illustrate the equality of Father and Son by the human relationship? Meaning of the term "subordination"? Distinction between the filial, and the Arian and theanthropic subordinations? Mention the opera ad extra. Scripture evidence for them? Why is the external characteristic of one person sometimes attributed to another? Is the internal characteristic so attributed?

Scripture proof that the term Father denotes an eternal relation? Distinction between the hypostatical and the providential paternity? Passages in which the latter is mentioned? Trinitarian characteristic of the first person? Patristic term for it? Waterland's distinction between self-existence and necessary existence? Is the Father fons deitatis, or fons trinitatis?

Proof that the term Son denotes an eternal relation? Socinian distinction between deity and divinity? Crucial term to denote the deity of the Son? First class of texts proving the deity of the Son? Second class? Third class? Socinus's explanation of creation and miracles as attributed to Christ? Answer? Fourth class of texts? Proof of the deity of the Son from his trinitarian relations? From his mediatorial office? Scripture proof of eternal generation? Augustine's classification of texts referring to the Son?

Why is the third person called the "Spirit?" Why called the "Holy" Spirit? Socinian view of the Holy Spirit? Proof from scripture of the personality of the Holy Spirit? Of the deity of the Holy Spirit? Two fundamental characteristics of the procession of the Spirit? Scholastic explanation of the difference between generation and procession? Turrettin's explanation? Dispute between the Latin and Greek churches? Turrettin's remark upon it?

Definition of the attributes? Two divisions of them? Importance of the attributes in reference to the knowledge of God? Several classifications of the attributes? Westminster classification? Definition of each? Define the divine self-existence? Define the divine simplicity. Its relation to trinity? Definition of the divine infinity? Biblical texts? Immensity? Texts? Omnipresence? Texts? Negative definition of omnipresence? Positive definition? Meaning of the "special presence" of God? Socinian and deistical theory of omnipresence? Definition of eternity? Texts? Defect in the definition of eternity as "time without beginning and end?" Scholastic explanation of eternity? Principal characteristics of eternal as distinguished from temporal existence? Is evolution applicable to God? Difficulties in supposing that God's consciousness is successive? Can a creature have a successionless consciousness? Has God memory? Definition of immutability? Texts? Reasons why God is immutable? Explanation of texts which ascribe repentance to God? Definition of omnipresence? Texts? Three characteristics of the Divine omniscience? Meaning of foreknowledge as applied to God? Definition of scientia simplicis intelligentiae? Of scientia media? Definition of the divine wisdom? Final end prescribed by wisdom? Why is not the happiness of the creature the final end? Definition of the divine power? Distinction between the divine energy ad intra and ad extra? Which is intended when omnipotence is spoken of? Biblical proof of omnipotence? What limitation to divine power? Is it really a limitation? Scholastic distinction between absolute and relative omnipotence? Error involved in it? Three modes in which the divine power is manifested? Texts? Definition of the divine holiness? Texts? Difference between holiness in God and in a creature? Two general modes in which the divine holiness is manifested? Four special modes in which holiness is manifested in law? Two modes in which it is manifested in emotion? Texts? Position of holiness among the attributes? Definition of justice? Its relation to holiness? General definition of justice? Definition of rectoral justice? Of distributive justice? Texts? Two forms of distributive justice? Characteristic of remunerative justice? Biblical proof?

Westminster statement? Two reasons why remuneration is gracious? Two kinds of reward for obedience? Texts? Definition of retributive justice? Texts? Other terms besides "retributive?" Two modes in which retributive justice is expressed? Nature of the demerit of sin? Reason for this? Consequent difference between the merit of reward and the merit of punishment? Defect in the explanation of sin by the divine "concursus?" Explain the sovereignty of God in reference to the exercise of retributive justice? Scholastic dictum? Explain Gen. 2 17, and Ezek. 18 . 4, in reference to the substitution of penalty? Relation of the divine displeasure to the person of the sinner as distinct from his sin? Necessary conditions required by retributive justice in case of substitution of penalty? Socinian conception of justice? Scholastic distinction between the absolute and relative necessity of justice? Error in which it is founded? Four proofs of the fundamental position of retributive justice? Primary aim of retributive justice? Define commutative justice De-fine public or general justice. Criticism upon it? Definition of the divine goodness? Texts? Definition of benevolence? Illustration from Aristotle? Ways in which the divine benevolence is shown? Texts? Definition of mercy? Why does the fact of the exercise of this attribute require a revelation? How early was it revealed? Definition of grace as distinguished from mercy? Is there a general manifestation of mercy and grace? Biblical proof? What are the modes? Definition of special mercy and grace? Texts? Definition of the divine veracity? Texts? Three ways in which it is manifested?

Natural place in a theological system, of the doctrine of decrees? Westminster definition of the divine decree? What activities of the divine essence are not included in the divine decree? Why? Distinction between the formation and the execution of the divine decree? For the divine mind are there many decrees? Relation of the decree to foreknowledge? Socinian and Arminian views on this point? Relation of the divine decree to a plan or system of the universe? First characteristic of the divine decree? Texts? Meaning of "council" in this reference? Second characteristic? Texts? Third characteristic? Texts? Fourth characteristic? Texts? Westminster statement of the relation of the decree to human freedom? Texts? Proof that there is no contradiction between them? Fifth characteristic? Texts? Definition of the efficacious decree? Modes in which it is executed? Texts? Definition of the permissive decree? Texts? Comparative scope of this decree? Two parts of the permissive decree? Relation of the permissive decree to the divine sovereignty? Principal use of the permissive decree? Error in the Tridentine statement respecting the permission of sin? Westminster statement in opposition? Calvin's view? Defective explanations of the permissive decree? Difference between the divine decree and fate? Distinction between certainty and compulsion?

Distinction between decree and predestination? Greek words employed in New Testament to denote the latter? Hebraistic use of "foreknow" in connection with "predestinate?" Biblical proof? Relation of "foreknowledge" to predestination? Biblical proof? Relation of foreknowledge in the classical use to decree? Westminster statement respecting the number of the predestinated? Texts?

Subdivisions of the decree of predestination? Biblical proof that election respects angels? Nature of election in this instance? Three things implied in angelic election? Possibility of explaining the certainty of sin? Preventability of sin as illustrated by the Christian experience? Relation of the finite will to the First Cause? To second causes? Reason for the permission of sin? Proportion of sin in the universe? Biblical proof that election respects men? What is presupposed in election? Characteristics of the love in which the decree of election originates? Relation of it to the non-elect? Proof that the decree of election is not partial? Biblical proof that the decree of election is immutable? Rational argument for this? Relation of sanctification to election? Texts? Biblical proof that the decree of election is irresistible? Meaning of "irresistible?" Biblical proof that election is unconditional? Rational proof?

Westminster definition of reprobation? Its relation to election? Distinction between preterition and damnation? Relation of preterition to the divine efficiency? Biblical proof of preterition? Definition of national and individual preterition? Texts? Is individual preterition compatible with national election? Texts? Westminster statement? Is individual election compatible with national preterition? Texts? Westminster statement? Zanchius's? Relation of the decree of reprobation to apostasy? Order of decrees in sublapsarianism? Supralapsarian order? Objections to this latter order? Proof that reprobation does not make perdition compulsory? Illustrations of this? Why does reprobation make perdition certain? Reason for the decree of reprobation? Biblical proof? Meaning of "hated" in Rom 9.11? Does reprobation rest upon a foresight of continuance in unbelief? The final end of election and reprobation? Texts? Difference between the Calvinistic and the Arminian predestination? Objection to the doctrine of reprobation? Reply? Distinction between God's desire and his decree, as marked in scripture? Distinction between the revealed and the secret will of God? Twofold meaning of the term "will?" Texts illustrating it? Theological terms for the distinction? Reasons for the universal offer of the gospel? Westminster statement of the relation of election to redemption? Reason for this order? Saumur order of the decrees of election and redemption? Objections to this order? Arminian order of these decrees? Range of truths to which election and reprobation belong? Texts that imply this? Use to be made of these doctrines? Statement in the Thirty-nine articles?

Westminster statement of the ways in which the divine decree is executed? Place of redemption? Biblical proof that creation is the first of the opera ad extra? Twofold meaning of "create" in scripture? The meaning in Gen. 1.1? Value of the clause ex nihilo? Spinoza's definition of "substance?" Its relation to that of Des Cartes? Attitude of pantheism towards the doctrine of creation from nothing? Sense in which the maxim ex nihilo nihil fit is true? Is false? Origen's view of creation? Creation as distinguished from emanation, generation, and development? Tendency of anti-trinitarian theories of God? Source of emanation theories?

What is included in Gen 1:1? Augustine's interpretation? What is described in Gen. 1 2 sq? What interval of time between Gen 1·1 and Gen. 1:2 sq.? Patristic and mediaeval explanation of the term "day" in Gen. 1? Points of agreement between the order of creation as given in Genesis, and as given in geology? Conflict between the Mosaic fiats, and the theory of pseudo-evolution? Objections to the doctrine of the eternity of matter? Conflict between Newton's doctrine of vis inertiae and the theory of molecular motion, in respect to change of motion? In respect to perpetual motion? Why do not the doctrines of the correlation of forces and of the conservation of energy meet the difficulty? Theory of pseudo-evolution? Objections to it? True theory of evolution? Biblical teaching respecting the antiquity of man? Septuagint chronology in the patristic church? Possibility of bringing all human history within the Biblical limits? Proof from Egyptian and Assyrian records? From languages and population? Uncertainty of the conclusions drawn from palaeontology? Opinions of Cuvier and Quatrefages?

Westminster definition of providence? Texts that prove "preservation?" Relation of preservation to creation? Deistic view of providence? Criticism upon it? Pantheistic view of providence? Criticism upon it? First part of God's operation in providence? Biblical proof? Particulars to which providence extends? Texts? Second part of providence? Its relation to "preservation?" Mode of the divine government in the physical universe? Two characteristics of physical laws? Opinions of Galileo and Whewell respecting the second characteristic?

Relation of miracles to government? How does the miracle differ from the ordinary course of nature? Occasion for miracles? Probability of the miracle? Relation of the miracle to the divine personality? Connection between the denial of miracles and materialism? Definition of a miracle? Hume's definition? Objection to it? View of the miracle as resulting from a higher natural law? Objection to it? Hume's argument against miracles? Fallacies in it? Relation of the miracle to redemption?

## ANTHROPOLOGY.

Definition of anthropology? Why is man as redeemed excluded from anthropology? Topics in anthropology?

Westminster statement concerning man's creation? Texts? Two principal points in the statement? Three theories of man's creation? Definition of pre-existence? Its prevalence? Definition of creationism? Its prevalence? Question between traducianism and creationism? Degree of agreement between them? Meaning of the term "substance" in the definition of traducianism? Value of the explanation of traducianism by atoms and corpuscles? Five ways of handling the doctrine of original sin? Three supports of traducianism? Biblical argument for traducianism? Texts cited in favor of creationism? Four particulars in the theological argument for traducianism? Partial adoption of traducianism by creationists? Turrettin's theory of imputation? Logical inconsistency in it? Relation of natural to representative union? To "federal" union? Is the term "represent" found in the Reformation symbols? Terms employed? Westminster terms? Difficulty of explaining the temptation, and the universality of sin, upon the creationist theory? Objections to the Later-Calvinistic separation of punishment from culpability? Difference between union with Adam and with Christ? Physiological argument for traducianism? Definition of "species?" Texts teaching creation by species? True realism and nominalism distinguished from false? Erroneous definition of "human nature?" Universalia ante rem and in re? Physiological reasons for not limiting traducianism to the body? Meaning of the term "nature" in anthropology? Definition of "person" in anthropology? Objection to traducianism drawn from the human nature of Christ? Reply? Objection that traducianism implies division of substance? Reply? Objection drawn from the diversity of matter and mind? Reply? Objection relating to the imputation of Adam's individual sins? Reply? Difference between inherited sin and inherited appetites? Compatibility of inherited sin with responsibility?

Westminster definition of man's primitive state? Texts? Pelagian and Semi-Pelagian views of man's created condition? Tridentine view? Biblical proof that man was created positively holy? Definition of positive holiness, in respect to understanding and will? Argument for concreated holiness from the perfection of man at creation? From the idea of the will? From the nature of spiritual substance? From the nature of a creative act? From the nature of finite holiness? From the facts of regeneration and sanctification? Definition of freedom of will? Difference between infinite and finite freedom? Proof that self-determination is compatible with inability to the contrary? Proof that self-determination excludes indifference? Objection to the definition of freedom as indifference or indetermination? Difference between holy and sinful self-determination?

Elder division of the faculties of the soul? Later division? Founder of it? Definition of the understanding? Its fundamental characteristic? Effect of apostasy upon it? Definition of the will? What is comprehended in it? Relation of the moral affections to the inclination? Augustine's view? Elder-Calvinistic view? Kant's view? Edwards's view? Distinction between the instinctive and the moral affections? Advantage in the twofold division of the faculties? Objections to the threefold division? What is the Biblical division? Meaning of καρδία and its equivalents? Texts? Meaning of πνεῦμα and its equivalents? Texts? Reason for the occasional interchange of the two terms? Twofold distinction in the activity of the will? Des Cartes' discrimination? Points of difference between inclination and volition? Epochs at which inclination begins? Points at which volitions begin? In which is freedom to be found? Kant's view? Edwards's use of the term "choice?" His view of the relation of the outward act, the volition, and the inclination, to each other?

Distinction between voluntary and volitionary action as marked in the Latin and German languages? Confusion arising from not recognizing the distinction? Difference between inclination and instinct? Leibnitz's definition of spontaneity in man and in the brute? Relation of inclination to the moral law? Biblical proof of this?

Westminster statement respecting probation and apostasy? Texts? Ground for the possibility of apostasy? Difference between Adam's perfection and that of God, angels, and the redeemed? Reason for probation? Nature of the merit under the covenant of works? What is the "life" spoken of in Gen 2 : 17? Biblical references to the covenant of works? Nature of the assent to it? Nature of the probationary statute? Why was the first sin wilful? Inexplicableness of sin? First characteristic of the death threatened? Scripture proof? Difference between man's body before and after apostasy? Difference between a possibility and a tendency? Second characteristic of the death threatened? Texts? Third characteristic? Texts?

Westminster statement respecting the voluntariness of the fall? Advantage of Adam's position for standing the trial? Consequent character of the first sin? Disadvantageous position of Adam, upon the Pelagian and Semi-Pelagian theories of creation? Westminster definition of sin? Texts? The primary source and seat of sin? Effect of sin upon the understanding? Resemblance between the origination of sin and creation? Difference between the two?

Westminster definition of the sinful estate of man? First part of it? The particular law transgressed? Its relation to the moral law? The two elements in the first sin? Describe the internal element? Was this element volitionary or voluntary? Account in Genesis of the internal element of the first sin? Comparison between Christ's treatment of the tempter and Eve's? What clause in Gen. 3 : 6 describes the beginning of sin in Eve? Biblical proof that the lust of Eve for the forbidden knowledge was sinful? The external element in Adam's first sin? Are both elements of the first sin imputed to the posterity? Proof texts? Meaning of ἥμαρτον in Rom. 5:12? Biblical proof that ἥμαρτον does not denote the actual sin of each individual? Objections to a passive signification of ἥμαρτον? Two kinds of imputation? General ground of imputation? Traducian ground for the imputation of the first sin? Points of difference between the union of the species with Adam, and the union of the church with Christ? Objection to the sin in Adam drawn from the absence of consciousness? Reply? Second part of the sinful estate of man? Its relation to the first part? Definition of mediate imputation? Illogical nature of the theory? Placaeus's disclaimer? Turrettin's criticism upon it? Wide meaning of the phrase "original sin?" Restricted meaning? Scripture equivalents? Theological equivalents? Meaning of the term "nature" when applied to sin? Augustine's statement in this reference? Definition of original sin with respect to the understanding? Texts? Chief reason why sin blinds? Effect of sin upon the conscience? Texts? Definition of original sin with respect to the will? Texts? Westminster statement respecting the guilt of original sin? Semi-Pelagian, Papal, and Arminian view? Scripture proof that original sin is guilt? Rational arguments for this? Edwards's meaning in saying that the virtue or vice of a disposition does not lie in its origin, but in its nature? His view of the relation of a disposition to a volition? Of the origin of a holy disposition? Of the origin of a sinful disposition? Misapplication of Edwards's position? Distinction between original sin and indwelling sin?

Westminster statement respecting the bondage of sin? Scripture proof? Meaning of the phrase "spiritually good?" Negative definition of inability? Varieties of the instinctive affections? Proof that they are involuntary?

Relation of man's inability to the will, according to the Westminster statement? In what sense is inability moral, not natural? In what sense natural, not moral? Use of these terms in the symbols and by the elder Protestant theologians? Use in the Westminster Confession? Biblical use of the term "natural?" Edwards's divergence from the elder Calvinists?

His definition of "natural ability" with reference to the mental faculties? With reference to inclination? Criticism upon the latter? Does Edwards directly attribute "natural ability" to the fallen will? Explain his denial of "natural ability" in his treatise upon original sin? The real question respecting "ability?" Distinction between capability and actual power? Difference between natural and moral power? Confusion in attributing natural ability to a moral faculty? Edwards's definition of "moral inability?" Is this inability metaphorical in his view? Edwards's definition of "moral necessity?" Does it involve fatalism? Inconsistency in Edwards's doctrine of ability?

Fallen man's inability to holiness defined with reference to inclination? Reason of this inability, from the nature of the finite will? From the nature of finite holiness? From the adorableness of underived holiness? From the reflex action of the will upon itself? Reason of man's ability to originate sin, from the nature of finite self-determination? From the nature of sin? What is the original foundation of moral obligation to obey law? Ratio of ability to obligation at the creation of a moral being? First objection to the doctrine of inability? Reply? Second objection? Negative definition of freedom? Positive definition? Other objections? Replies? Objections to the doctrine of ability?

Definition of actual transgression? Twofold form of actual transgression? Meaning of the phrase "total depravity"?

## CHRISTOLOGY.

Definition of Christology? Old Testament names for the Redeemer? Points of resemblance between the Old Testament and New Testament descriptions of the Redeemer? Westminster definition of Christ's complex person? Biblical texts? Which mode of the Divine essence constitutes the divine nature in Christ's person? Biblical proof? Is the incarnation a transubstantiation of the divine nature? Distinctive characteristic in incarnation? Illustrate the constitution of a theanthropic person by that of a human person? Root and base of Christ's person? Six proofs that the divinity is controlling in Christ's person? Date of the beginning of the theanthropic personality? Texts? Duration of the theanthropic personality? Texts? Effect of the incarnation upon the trinity? Relation of the incarnation to the trinitarian position of the Logos? Illustrate this by the third person of the trinity as related to inspiration, regeneration, and sanctification. Did the Logos unite with a human nature or a human person? Scripture proof? Westminster statement upon this point? Hooker's, Turrettin's, and Owen's? Points of difference between a nature and a person? Which is the more impersonal term? Illustrate by the divine nature and a divine person? Did the Logos unite with human nature as an entire species? Twofold signification of the term "nature"? Effect of incarnation upon the portion of human nature that was assumed into union? Scripture proof? Westminster statement upon this point? Augustine's, Athanasius's, Turrettin's, Pearson's, and Owen's? Scripture proof that the human nature derived from Mary needed sanctification? Statement of the Formula Concordiæ, and of Calvin? Relation of the miraculous conception to the sanctification of Christ's human nature? Difference between traducianism and creationism, in respect to the agency of the Holy Spirit in the miraculous conception? Inference respecting the transmission of original sin, from the miraculous nature of Christ's conception? Does the miraculousness of Christ's conception conflict with the reality of his human sonship? Use of the distinction between nature and person in explaining Christ's single self-consciousness, and twofold consciousness?

Four divine characteristics ascribed in scripture to the Redeemer which prove his deity? Arian misinterpretation of texts descriptive of his mediatorial position? Texts that prove Christ's humanity? First characteristic in Christ's humanity? Biblical proof? Contrary heresy? Second characteristic? Proof texts? Contrary heresy? Objections to Apollinarism? Third characteristic? Contrary heresy? Explain the inconceivability of a divine-human nature. Biblical proof that the two natures constitute but one person? Two classes of texts? Inference from these texts respecting the predication of qualities and acts? Inference respecting the two natures as constituting only one person from Christ's own language? Illustrate the fluctuations in Christ's theanthropic consciousness from human self-consciousness? Effect of Christ's exaltation upon his humanity? May the qualities and acts of one nature be attributed to the other nature? Error of the Later-Lutherans? Technical term for the union of the two natures? Has Christ two wills? Why? Monothelite objection? Reply?

Is the God-man impeccable? Three proofs? Explanation of Christ's impeccability by the union of the natures? Why may not both peccability and impeccability be attributed to Christ, as both impotence and omnipotence may be? Argument for Christ's impeccability from the relation of the two wills to each other? Objection to the doctrine of Christ's impeccability? Reply? Instances of impeccability with temptability? Difference between Christ's temptability and that of fallen man? Proof that temptability and peccability may be in inverse proportion? Scripture statements respecting the greatness of Christ's temptations? Reasons for Christ's temptations? The true test of sympathy with those who are tempted? Degree of Christ's sympathy tried by this test?

## SOTERIOLOGY

Definition of Soteriology? Biblical designations of the God-man? Reason for adopting that of mediator? First characteristic of a mediator? Texts? Second characteristic? Five reasons for this? Texts? Of what is Christ the mediator? Definition of the covenant of grace? Texts? Definition of the covenant of redemption? Texts? Nature of the distinction between the covenant of grace and of redemption? Difference between the covenant of grace under the Old Testament and the New Testament? How marked in the English version?

Three mediatorial offices of Christ? Texts? Westminster statement? Were these offices exercised before the advent?

Texts? Nature of the religious experience under the old dispensation? Westminster definition of Christ's prophetic office? Texts? Two modes in which Christ discharges his prophetic office? Texts? Relation of the Christian ministry to the apostles?

Westminster definition of Christ's priestly office? Biblical definition of a priest? Evidence for the patriarchal priest? Evidence for the antediluvian priest? Is Christ's priestly office administered mediately under the New Testament? Texts? Inference from this respecting the Papal view? Two parts of Christ's priestly work? Texts? Relation of Christ's intercessory work to his atonement? Biblical proof? Relation of the gift of the Spirit to Christ's intercession? Nature of Christ's atonement? Texts? The meanings of ὑπέρ? Why used more than ἀντί? Meaning of vicariousness? Distinction between personal and vicarious atonement? Relation of vicarious atonement to mercy? Fallacy in the Socinian objection to vicarious atonement? Reasons why vicarious atonement cannot be made by a created being? Biblical idea of an atonement? Texts? Meaning of the Hebrew words for atonement and forgiveness? How rendered in the Septuagint, and N. T.? The connection of ideas in this representation? Connection in Scripture between forgiveness and atonement? Texts? In which of the two is the mercy most apparent? Texts? Proof that "reconciliation" and "propitiation" are objective in their signification? Patristic error in the interpretation of λύτρον? True view? Texts that prove that God is both active and passive in respect to the atonement? Proof from the litanies? Scripture doctrine respecting the coexistence of love and wrath in God? Authorities cited? Difference between the wrath of God and that of man? Resemblance between the wrath of God and that of conscience? Relation of the doctrine of vicarious atonement to that of the trinity? Relation of vicarious atonement to the human conscience? Texts? Relation of the acceptance of vicarious atonement to penitence? Difference between penitence and remorse in this respect?

Three kinds of suffering? Definition of "calamity"? Scripture illustrations? Definition of "chastisement"? Circle in which it is administered? Fallacy in the argument drawn from this circle against vicarious atonement? What determines the degree of chastisement? Nature of all suffering for a believer? For the unbeliever? Distinction between providential and redemptive fatherhood? Nature of the divine paternity for the unbeliever? Definition of punishment? Christ's explanation of the lex talionis? St. Paul's view of retribution? Nature of Christ's sufferings? Texts? Source of Christ's ordinary sufferings? Of Christ's extraordinary sufferings? Biblical proof? Was the Father emotionally displacent towards Christ? In what sense did Christ experience the wrath of God? Light thrown upon this point by the covenant between Father and Son? Biblical proof that the Son is voluntary in his sufferings? Definition of Christ's passive obedience? How much does it include? Definition of Christ's active obedience? Why does this constitute a part of the atonement? What is the principal reference of the active obedience? Biblical proof that the active obedience acquires a title to life? Need of this? Distinction between "satisfaction" and "atonement?" Between "satisfaction" and "merit"? Turrettin's remark upon it?

To what divine attribute is atonement correlative? Relation of the divine attributes to each other? Centre of unity for the attributes? Is atonement optional or necessary? Necessary effect of atonement? Universalist inference? Reply? In what sense is the remission of penalty through Christ's atonement an act of justice? Biblical texts? Statement of Anselm and Edwards? Reason why the vicarious satisfaction of justice is the highest form of mercy? Westminster statement in this reference? Distinction between mercy and indulgence? Biblical passages in which it appears? What is the necessary condition of the exercise of mercy? Two grounds of the possibility of substituted penalty? Relation of vicarious substitution to divine sovereignty? First condition in the substitution of penalty? Defect in the illustration from Zaleucus? Difference between an identical and a substituted penalty? Difference between an identical and an equivalent penalty? The cancelling effect of an equivalent penalty?

Second condition in the substitution of penalty? First mode in which these conditions are met by Christ's sufferings? Propriety of the term "penal"? Second mode? Explain the infinity of Christ's sufferings. The infinitude of Christ's suffering compared with the infinitude of man's suffering? Third mode? How is Christ's active obedience supererogatory?

Two significations of the word "extent" as applied to Christ's atonement? Senses in which the atonement is unlimited and limited? Ambiguity in the preposition "for"? Statement respecting "sufficiency" and "efficiency"? Distinction between atonement and redemption? Which is unlimited and which is limited? Westminster statement respecting the purchase of redemption? Biblical texts? Upon what other tenet does the tenet of limited redemption depend? Difference between the Calvinist and the Arminian respecting faith? Objection to the doctrine of a partial ability as applied to the doctrine of redemption? The meaning of "limited" as applied to redemption? Is Christ's atonement separable from the intention to apply it in the mind and decree of God? Five reasons for this? Texts? Texts apparently contrary to limited redemption? Explanation of them? Nine reasons for the universal offer of the atonement that refer to God's relation to the atonement? Three reasons for the universal offer that refer to man's relation to the atonement? Difference between saving faith and assurance of faith? To which species of faith is the atonement offered?

Westminster definition of effectual calling? Effects of it? Consequent relation of regeneration to effectual calling? Romish and Lutheran use of the term regeneration? Reformed use? Use in the seventeenth-century divines? Biblical texts that suggest the wider signification? True meaning of these texts? Turrettin's restricted use of the term regeneration? Distinction between regeneration and conversion? The author of regeneration? Texts? Effect of regeneration upon the understanding? Texts? Characteristic of spiritual knowledge? Effect of regeneration upon the will? Texts? Regeneration defined with reference to inclination? Texts? Characteristics of the operation of the Spirit? Biblical proof that this operation is immediate? Proof from infant regeneration? Meaning of the term "physical" when applied to regeneration? Is man passive in regeneration? How long is he passive? Is the co-operation of man possible in regeneration? Difference between the Augustinian and the Semi-Pelagian theory upon this point? Tridentine view and phraseology? Westminster statement respecting passivity in regeneration? Relation of regeneration to consciousness? Biblical proof of infant regeneration? How is it symbolically taught? Are there "means" of regeneration? Reason for this? What does a means imply? Illustrate by "means" of conviction, conversion, and sanctification? Relation of conversion to regeneration? Man's relation to regeneration? The "preparatives" to regeneration? May man pray for regenerating grace? Biblical proof? Authorities cited? Objections? Answers? Is the connection between the "preparatives" to regeneration and regeneration infallible, or probable?

Definition of conversion? Two converting acts? Westminster definition of saving faith? Distinction between faith and belief? Relation of faith to regeneration? Texts? Two elements in faith? Texts? Peculiarity in the act of faith? Westminster statement? Nature of the believer's union with Christ? Texts? Relation of the legal to the mystical union? Points of difference between the union with Adam and the union with Christ? Four particulars in the Westminster definition of repentance? Texts? Meaning of μετανοέω? Which a prior in the order of nature, faith or repentance? Proof?

Westminster definition of justification? Texts? Connection of justification with faith and regeneration? Texts? Difference between the justification of a sinner and of a righteous person? Meaning of δικαιόω in the New Testament? Texts? Distinction between legal and evangelical righteousness? Definition of "the righteousness of God"? Two parts of justification? Relation of faith to justification? Sense in which faith justifies? Sole ground of justification? Romish view? Is justification gradual? Are future sins included in justification? Distinction between actual and declarative justification? Function of Christ's active obedience in justification? Texts? Piscator's view? Objections to it? Is justification a means or an end? Proof that justification by faith is not contradicted by the final reward for works? Error of the perfectionist?

Two meanings of ἁγιάζειν in New Testament? Westminster definition of sanctification? Texts? Relation of sanctification to regeneration? Scope of sanctification? Texts? Is sanctification gradual? The means of sanctification? Does the believer co-operate in sanctification? Is sanctification completed in this life? Texts? Westminster statement? Is sanctification ever entirely lost? Westminster statement? Biblical texts? Objections to the doctrine of the saints' perseverance? Answers? Relation of sanctification to justification? Motives to obedience furnished by justification? Texts? Agreement of Paul and James?

Westminster statement of the means of grace? Why is confession of faith a means of grace? Texts? Two modes in which the word is a means of sanctification? Westminster definition of a sacrament? Classical meaning of the term? Ecclesiastical meaning? How is the sacrament of the Supper efficacious? Texts? Calvin's statement? Westminster statement respecting the presence of Christ in the supper? Hooker's statement? English Episcopal statement? Romish view of Christ's presence? Lutheran view? Objections to it? Reformed view? Misconception of Zwingle's view? Principal points in it? Explain Calvin's view of the sacrament of the supper as didactic? Corroboration of this, from the nature of a symbol? Difference between natural symbols, and those of the sacraments?

Relation of baptism to regeneration? Biblical proof? Relation to sanctification? Subjects of baptism? What does infant baptism suppose? Upon what does this supposition rest? Texts? Reply to the objection that all persons baptized in infancy are not regenerate? Mode of baptism in the Old Testament? Bearing of this upon the mode in the New? Distinction between sacramental and ceremonial baptism?

How was each administered? Difference between the classical and the ecclesiastical meaning of βαπτίζω? Error of the Baptist on this point?

## ESCHATOLOGY.

Definition of eschatology? Subdivisions? Representation in scripture of the condition of the soul between death and the resurrection? What exaggeration of this in the patristic church? Heresy to which this finally led? Protestant view? Two errors particularly rejected? Westminster statement? Points of difference between the Pagan and the Biblical conception of Hades? Jewish writers in whom the mythological influence is apparent? State of opinion respecting Hades in the patristic church? Influence of the clause regarding the Descensus? History of this clause? Reformed explanation of it? Lutheran explanation? Hooker's explanation? First point in the scripture teaching concerning the intermediate state? Texts? Proof for the doctrine of immortality in the Old Testament? Second point in the scripture teaching concerning the intermediate state? Texts? Third point? Six proofs that Hades is hell without the body? Four proofs that Sheol is hell without the body? Proof that Sheol also means the grave?

Scripture statement concerning Christ's second advent? Statement in the Apostles' creed? What theory precluded by this? Definition of pre-milleniarianism? Its prevalence? Meaning of "first resurrection" in Rev. 20 4–6? Texts? Augustine's interpretation?

Position of the doctrine of the resurrection in the primitive creed? Difference between it and that of transmigration? Probability of the resurrection? Old Testament texts that teach it? Two points in the scripture representation?

Difference between a "natural" and a "spiritual" body? Texts? Between a "spiritual" and a "celestial" body? Texts? Proof that the resurrection-body is an identical body? Meaning of "identical?" Relation of the body raised to the body buried? Difference between the animal's soul and that of man?

Scripture proof of a final judgment? Definition of the private judgment? Texts? Proof of a public judgment? Four particulars in the Biblical description of it? Varieties in the conception of heaven? Four particulars in the Biblical description of it? Difference between Eden and heaven?

Position of the patristic church respecting the doctrine of hell? Of the mediaeval? Of the modern? Principal support for the doctrine? Texts? Is the Christian church and ministry responsible for it? Nature of the objection that figures are employed in describing hell punishment? Gnostic and Origenistic meaning of *αἰών*? Two meanings of *αἰών* in scripture? Texts? Two consequent meanings of *αἰώνιος*? Texts? Rule for determining which of the two senses is intended in a scripture passage? Definition of "conditional immortality"? Eight objections to it? Proof that the "intermediate" state is a part of the endless aeon? Biblical proof that death fixes the endless state of the soul? Objections to Dorner's denial of the damnability of the "common sin" of man? Two principal supports of the doctrine of redemption after death? Inadequacy of them? In what way is an infant saved? In what way is a heathen saved? Westminster statement? View of the elder and later Calvinism?

Three postulates of theism that evince the rationality of endless punishment? Definition of punishment? Aim of it? Scripture proof of its retributive nature? Rational proof? Objections to the view that punishment is reformatory and protective, not retributive? Authorities on both sides? Inference respecting the duration of punishment, from the intrinsic nature, continuity, and indivisibility of guilt? Difference between human and divine punishment? Proof of the rationality of endless punishment from conscience? From the endless cumulation of sin? Reasons for this endless cumulation? From the infinite evil of sin? Proof of this infinity? From the atonement of Christ? From the preference of the wicked? From the history of morals? The relative proportion of hell to heaven? Texts? Authorities?

Who is the cause and author of hell—the Creator or the creature? In what action of man did hell originate? By what action of man is hell perpetuated? The feeling of God towards penitence? Connection between impenitence and hell? Between impenitence and pessimism? How may penitence be made impossible?

CPSIA information can be obtained
at www.ICGtesting.com
Printed in the USA
BVHW020018160323
660508BV00002B/34